FUNNY, PECULIAR

The True Story of Benny Hill

FUNNY, PECULIAR

The True Story of Benny Hill

MARK LEWISOHN

SIDGWICK & JACKSON

First published 2002 by Sidgwick & Jackson
an imprint of Pan Macmillan Ltd
Pan Macmillan, 20 New Wharf Road, London N1 9RR
Basingstoke and Oxford
Associated companies throughout the world
www.panmacmillan.com

ISBN 0 283 06369 6

A CIP catalogue record for this book is available from
the British Library.

Typeset by SetSystems Ltd, SaffronWalden, Essex
Printed and bound in Great Britain by
Mackays of Chatham plc, Chatham, Kent

to GC

with love and thanks

Contents

Contents

Introduction

Summon up an image of Benny Hill and chances are it will be of a moony, schoolboyish face with comfy-cushion cheeks, piercing, naughty blue eyes and a mischievous smile, leering at an under-dressed 'Hill's Angel' and speaking in a country bumpkin's voice.

This is the man who became the world's most popular comedian in the television era. And indeed Benny Hill was a great comedian. His strength lay in comedy architecture, characterization, mime, delightfully light vulgarity and a facility to redeploy jokes of all vintages. He could, at times, be inspired and brilliant; had some of his sketches not been simply crude, or reduced to comic-book level by lame cutaways, he might have been hailed as a successor to Charlie Chaplin or Jacques Tati, not their follower.

Even as comedians go, however, and they can be an odd lot, Benny Hill was unusual. He was not a witty man, rarely cracked jokes, mined a narrow seam of humour and was deeply ill-at-ease working an audience. He was also remarkably ecological, constantly recycling not only his own material but the work of countless others; though he was open about his stealing it is astonishing just how much he pilfered.

His career spanned more than fifty years and he was a star for almost forty of them, a rare longevity. Uniquely for a modern British comedian, he also found universal fame, his TV show being screened in more than a hundred countries. Yet while researching and writing this book, some people would recoil when I mentioned his name. In his home country at least, in these supposedly enlightened and broad-minded times, Benny Hill is taboo.

How did he come to upset people this much? He was by all accounts a gentle and kindly soul who rarely uttered a bad word or caused anyone harm. Intrigued by the dichotomy, I have tried to find out. My objectivity towards Benny Hill as a subject – I like much of his work but a good deal of it I find distinctly unfunny – has, I believe, aided my task. I have no axe to grind one way or the other.

Benny Hill dreamed of being a comedian from the age of twelve, when his grandfather – affiliated to circuses and the stage all his life – took him to a Variety show, a proletarian entertainment of formulaic yet versatile vulgarity. Benny (or Alfie as he was then) hugely admired the saucy comics and their innuendo-strewn jokes; and he also loved the pert young 'maids' in stockings and suspenders, flashing just a hint of knickers, who fussed around the stage. By seventeen he was touring the country in limp Variety revues, as stagehand-cum-extra. It could be a grim business, dirty work for scant pay, but he adored every moment, especially the proximity it afforded to showgirls in various states of undress.

This love for Variety never wavered. Benny Hill modelled himself on the comedians, mostly unknowns, who 'starred' in the shows that came to the local Palace and Hippodrome theatres. Though so much of this humour was about sex, it was always juvenile in approach. So, too, he would suggestively leer at women and make jokes about 'dumplings'. Add to this Variety schooling his passion for clowns and for early silent-film comedians, the influence of BBC radio heroes of the 1930s, the work of wisecracking American comics of the 1930s and 40s, and, in later years, the inventiveness of some French mime artistes, and you have the complete Benny Hill package.

He especially admired the sheer longevity of Variety's comedians. Speaking when aged forty-seven (in David Nathan's excellent book *The Laughtermakers*), Benny Hill remarked, 'One of the joys about them was that they would go on sometimes until they were seventy, and they could still play sketches with girls of nineteen, dancing around the bedsprings with the oil-can, and, when the maid came in, growling, 'I'll 'ave 'er too.' When John Osborne's play *The Entertainer* was in London in 1957, depicting an ageing music-hall comedian who refused to move with the times, Benny Hill went to see it and thought, with rare vehemence, 'You got it all wrong, mate! That's not what it's about.' True to his heroes, Benny kept the ball in the air until dying just two years short of seventy.

Several of my interviewees were certain that a biography of Benny Hill could not extend to more than a couple of dozen pages, so little did he reveal of himself.

Jeremy Hawk, Benny's first regular 'straightman', believes that he was 'semi-detached'. 'He was part this, part that, a bit of this, a bit of that,' Hawk told me. 'He wasn't a whole, and he was never attached to any one thing. I never heard him say, "Oh I'm looking forward to this." He had no sense of elation about his life. It's a pity he didn't get married, it could have changed things, and he might have left behind an interesting child.'

Benny Hill was a lifelong bachelor. Those who didn't know him wonder if he was homosexual; he certainly had a tendency towards camp theatricality, a trait shared by several comedians of his generation. He was, though, simply a man with unrealistic and unrealized adolescent romantic illusions who spent virtually his entire adult life pursuing the unattainable (while looking down on other women who could have made willing partners). He would say that he came close to marriage at least twice, if not three or four times. In truth, he never really came close to it at all and had perhaps just two mature relationships. Benny always used 'pat' lines to explain aspects of his life that puzzled, yet there was generally an element of truth in them – one was that he had 'a mental age of seventeen'.

While he spent most of his life alone, it would be wrong to say that Benny Hill was lonely. He was a *loner*, content to swan around the Continent with only his own company. Apart from pursuing a career in a precarious profession, he spent a lifetime assiduously avoiding risk. His friends and associates speculate still about whether or not he was happy. He certainly wasn't miserable, and he rarely complained about his lot, but, as Jeremy Hawk noted, he never exuded delight either. He just bumbled along the middle ground – and in his own peculiar way brought pleasure, if not so much to himself then to millions of people.

Mark Lewisohn
Hertfordshire, England

Prologue

The premise of Benny Hill's *Eddie in August*, 1969

fade in

ENGLAND IN THE 1960S. SUMMERTIME. A TOWN PARK. MANICURED
FLOWERBEDS, TIDY LAWNS, LOW FENCES, WOODEN BENCHES, A
UNIFORMED PARK-KEEPER. A QUIET SCENE UNDER A BLUE SUBURBAN
SKY – VIEWED OVER THE SOUND OF WISTFUL MUSIC.

A soberly dressed middle-aged MAN, tidy and together, sits eating a
sandwich, homemade and wrapped, with motherly care, in greaseproof
paper.

A pretty NURSE walks by, flashes a beatific smile and waves her hand.
The man believes she has waved at him; romance soars within his heart.
She's the ideal of his dreams, the one he's been yearning for!

Hastily putting away his sandwich, he fashions a chase through the
park, his pace quickening to make up the yards, his heartbeat racing to
make up the years.

She's the one. He knows it. She's beautiful, she's cultured, she's
sophisticated. He trails ten yards behind yet he's more than halfway to the
altar.

Just as he is set to pounce, to declare his undying love, the nurse meets
the object of her wave. Her LOVER. A more manly man, a more dashing
man.

The chaser, now chastened, switches direction. Head down, crushed,
his arms rigid to his body, his legs tight together. It's that familiar
rejection shuffle.

fade out

1

fade in

The man fixes a double-date with the nurse's friend, a PLAIN WOMAN of no appeal to him. They picnic. The man sees his nurse run off into the trees with her lover. The man's face is wretched, haunted. He stuffs a cream cake in his mouth, hard. He ignores the coy glances of the plain woman, whom he despises as cheap.

fade out

fade in

The man's chase ends at the church – but not in the way he has fantasized. He's a bystander, watching the nurse marry Mr Eligible.

While he watches, another PRETTY YOUNG THING happens to give him a sideways glance. Possibly even an encouraging smile.

In an instant, the nurse is forgotten and the man sets off in pursuit once more – his heart soaring, his dreams in the clouds . . .

1. Before Benny: The Alfie Years

PERFORMER

THE OFFICIAL ORGAN OF THE VARIETY ARTISTES' FEDERATION

NEVILLE KENNARD
ENQUIRIES INVITED
P.A.: 21, Chancery Close, Kenton, Mddx., 'Phone: Wordsworth 3950

Vol. LXXIV. No. 1875   THURSDAY, MARCH 5, 1942.   [Registered at the G.P.O. as a Newspaper]   Price 3d.

HARRY BENET
PRODUCTIONS

Telephone: GERRARD 4494   51, BEAK STREET, LONDON, W.1   Telephone: GERRARD 4494

A Brilliant New Revue

SEND HIM VICTORIOUS

By George Hirste and Harry Benet   Original Music by Cyril Dawson

THE CAST INCLUDES:

The New Star **ARCHIE WALLEN** Almost Sane

DOROTHY DEE *The Vital Spark*

PATRICIA, COLIN and VICKI *The Dancing Trio De Luxe*

FRANK CARIELLO *Grave and Gay*

The Greatest Pony Act in Vaudeville
COOKE'S WONDERFUL PONY REVUE

ALF HILL *The Warrior*

Twelve Delightful Scenes, including : Maison Marie's Beauty Parlour
Revolving to The Barrack Square • The Slave Market • North of the Tweed • Town on Parade

The 10 CHARMON GIRLS 10

DOROTHY DALE *Melody and Song*   **JAMES LEA** *The Officers' Mess*

AND (IN NEGOTIATION) ANOTHER POPULAR COMEDIAN

DATES VACANT: APRIL 6 and 13 (North), **MAY 11, 18 and 25, JUNE 22, and JULY ON, with exceptions**

All Coms. Direct to Harry Benet, 51, Beak Street, W.1

1. A Remarkable Ancestry

'The minute Alfie was born he was a sunny, beautiful, happy little boy. A darling.'

Nearly eighty years after the event, the birth of Alfred Hawthorn Hill – later in his lifetime, as Benny Hill, to become The World's Most Popular Comedian – is remembered still by a living witness, aged nineteen at the time.

Alfie was born on January 21 1924, in Southampton. Violet Stevens is his aunt and godmother, one of a score of immediate relatives in a large family; she is the sole surviving member of his parents' generation, sister to his father. Approaching 100, Violet clearly recalls Alfie's entry into the world. 'I came into the room a minute or two after he was born,' she says, 'and I watched the nurse weigh him. He was nearly eleven pounds, a huge baby.'

Size was to be a lifelong problem for him.

Southampton is seventy-seven miles south-west of London in the county of Hampshire – a peninsula at the meeting point of the rivers Test and Itchen, at the top of Southampton Water, into which flows the English Channel. Island nations place special emphasis on their commercial ports, and Great Britain, with its once dominant Empire, has four principal shipping gateways: London, Liverpool, Newcastle and Southampton. All have long histories, have witnessed events happy and tragic and bear pride and scars to tell the tales. As recently as the Falklands and Gulf wars, Southampton watched fleets of fighting-ships depart amid much flag-waving, and their victorious return to even greater celebration.

Viewed today, Southampton's broad streets, twelfth- to eighteenth-century architecture and generous provision of green spaces reflect such glories. But, like most places in Britain, its greatness is now largely in the past, the present is jaded and its future prosperity is even less certain. British history books are full of honour for Southampton, however. From her port, Richard I embarked on his crusade in 1190 and King Henry V marshalled his army in 1414 before victory at Agincourt. The *Mayflower* set sail from here on the first stage of its journey to America in 1620 with the Pilgrim Fathers. The Romans were stationed here, and it was an important Norman town. In 1016 – in a story familiar to all British schoolchildren – King Canute commanded the Southampton tidal waves to recede, and got his feet wet.

In more recent centuries Southampton has been a fashionable resort, the point of embarkation in the Napoleonic wars, an important trading place and, before the advent of commercial air travel, the principal port for ships travelling to and from America.

It was shipping, indeed, and the prospect of American horizons, that brought the Hill family to Southampton.

Alfie's father – also named Alfred Hawthorn Hill – was one of eight children born in different parts of the country to parents who, owing to a succession of difficult circumstances, were living a nomadic existence. Alf Hill himself had become a roamer. In 1912, his nineteenth year, newspapers were full of pictures and stories of a great new ocean liner, RMS *Titanic*, a sumptuously appointed addition to the White Star shipping line that would soon be making her maiden voyage out of Southampton, bound for New York. Desperate for a fresh start, the young and headstrong Alf Hill – 'tall, dark and slim, with lovely dreamy eyes and dark curly hair,' according to his devoted young sister Violet – made his way south in the hope of securing a position as ship's steward.

What happened next is lost in the mists of memory – either he was turned down for a job, or he was distracted once in Southampton and never applied. Either way, when on April 10 1912 the *Titanic* eased out of Southampton Water, carrying more than two 2,000 passengers and crew, Alf Hill was not among them. Five days later, some 350 miles south-east of Newfoundland, she sank and more than 1,500 lives were lost.

News of the tragedy shook the world, and it devastated Southampton. Among the dead crew were 549 local people. But Alf Hill, who'd had his own hard knocks to deal with, was busy pursuing a new goal. He had met a man called Jack Stanley, about the same age, who was opening a small shop to sell surgical appliances, bedpans and douches. This was quite literally a front though, for the major part of Stanley & Co.'s business would be the retailing of condoms, or 'French letters' as they were better known. Some would be sold over the counter to any customer prepared to risk being seen entering Stanley's emporium, but most would sell by mail-order from a room upstairs, the result of discreet press advertisements.

Jack Stanley's store, described in the 1914–15 *Kelly's Directory of Southampton* as 'medical herbalists', began operations from premises at 15a Canal Walk, in an area close to the Town Quay. Known locally as The Ditches, Canal Walk was not a particularly salubrious area. It was tucked away 'back of the walls', the seedy, seamy side of a seafaring centre. Canal Walk reeked of danger – and, indeed, of unidentifiable smells – a darkened, bumpy, narrow street packed with tiny tumbledown stores: butchers, drapers, twine-sellers, a homemade-sweets shop, a stewed-eel-and-pie shop, a primitive amusement arcade. Many of the places were run by immigrants, especially European Jews. It was a subculture straight out of a Dickens novel, the kind of street that mothers forbade their children to visit. If you did go there, the word about town was that you had better make sure the fingers on your wallet were your own.

Contraception was becoming a big – if hushed – business at the beginning of the twentieth century, and most of the major towns and cities in Britain had a store like Stanley & Co., usually found in their equivalent backstreet areas. But it was not welcomed by the police, courts or churches. At the 1920 Lambeth Conference, the Bishop of London called for the sale of such 'unnatural' products to end. Even Marie Stopes, who advocated contraception in general, was against 'French letters' in particular because she felt that men's 'highly stimulating secretions' were beneficial to women who absorbed them.[1]

As ever, though, the forces of free trade overcame resistance. Families advertising in the 'births' column of London newspapers were likely to receive unsolicited offers from resourceful traders of what the law enforcement authorities called 'Malthusian devices'.[2] Primitive sheaths made from animal membranes had been used discreetly by the upper classes in the late eighteenth century; now the advent of rubber technologies made them cheaper to manufacture and so more accessible to the greater public. The men of Southampton were no different from men anywhere else – they saw contraception not just as a means of family planning but as an aid to promiscuity. Being a seafaring town, Southampton also had a burgeoning red-light district; if they were anything like as active as their London counterparts, whose usage of condoms at this time has been documented, then Southampton prostitutes are likely to have been buying Stanley's product by the boxful. Moreover, the Horse & Groom, a pub much used as a whores' pickup, was just yards away on East Street.

Stanley's boomed. Jack moved his enterprise to slightly larger premises at 16 Canal Walk and invited Alf Hill to take a stake in the expansion. Though a street-smart young man, Alf did not have the necessary capital and had to decline his new friend's invitation. Instead, he was appointed manager, on a decent salary, minding the shop and running the mail-order operation while Jack went out and dealt with manufacturers.

In 1914, though, the First World War intervened. That Christmas, both men received their call-up papers and had to decide what to do with the business. Having hatched a plan, they hastened to visit Alf's parents, then living in the latest of innumerable locations, in Boston, Lincolnshire. The scheme called for Alf's folks to relocate yet again, this time down to Southampton. They could take care of Stanley's until the lads got back from the war.

The Hill family history is an extraordinary one.

Alf's father – that is, the paternal grandfather of Alfie ('Benny') – was Henry Hawthorn Hill, born in 1870. His father, Joseph Henry Hill, had become (like his father before him) a surgeon. Aged eighteen, Joseph had married Lydia Charlotte Hawthorn, after whom the middle name Hawthorn was bestowed upon succeeding male generations – until the tradition ended with the childless 'Benny'.

Henry was born at Joseph and Lydia's temporary home in East Retford, a Nottinghamshire market town. Then, after they had moved back to the Hills' native Yorkshire, Joseph died, aged just nineteen, when Henry was only fourteen months. Already recovering from tuberculosis, Joseph had been summoned to help a woman about to give birth; venturing out in his pony-and-trap in the depth of a Huddersfield winter, he caught pneumonia and was dead forty-eight hours later.

At the age of seven Henry was orphaned, after Lydia died of a chest infection, and he was then raised by two uncles. One was Alfred Hill, a physician and surgeon, Irish Trinity-trained. Uncle had a skeleton in the cupboard – literally – and the young Henry got to learn the name of every bone in the body, in Latin. The other uncle was Henry Hawthorn, a piano teacher. The Hawthorns had an artistic bent – Benjamin Hawthorn, Lydia's father, ran an academy of music with his wife, which was at one time staffed by their ten children; some of the children also painted – canvases by two of them hung at the Royal Academy in London.

The two uncles bore the expense of sending Henry to school and taking care of him during holidays. During one vacation Alfred Hill had to attend to the pregnant wife of the renowned circus promoter Bob Fossett. Along with the theatre, circuses were the principal form of entertainment in Victorian Britain and Fossett was one of the leading promoters. Telling an oft-told story from her childhood, Violet Stevens recalls, 'The uncle said to my father, "I can't leave you alone, so you'll have to come with me. While I'm attending to Mrs Fossett you can have a look around and see all the animals." Uncle Alfred was detained quite some time and young Henry was shown around the "living wagons", absolutely loving it. In those days, it was a ten-day confinement when you had a baby and the uncle and my father went along every day for ten days. The circus people got to call him "the doctor's boy".'

From this point on, the circus entranced Henry . . . and thence his offspring, and a direct connection can be traced to the career of Alfie 'Benny' Hill. 'He wanted to be, and should have been, a doctor,' affirms Violet of her father, 'but he got the circus in his blood.' Whenever Fossett's was in town Henry would be given tickets and permitted to play with the chimpanzees. He had developed a deep affinity and understanding for them. Like the fictional Doctor Dolittle, Henry fancied that he could 'talk to the animals'. One of his children was to do the same.

Henry did not go to university. Up to the age of sixteen he was set to follow in his father's footsteps, working in medicine, but then there was a quarrel over his education, and, seemingly overnight, the trust fund dried up. Henry's schooling in Leeds ended abruptly and he was put to an apprenticeship with a chemist in London. He was never to inherit his parents' estate and instead was found employment as an assistant in a chemist's shop in the St Bride's district, working among the journalists on nearby Fleet Street and the frock-coated City bankers.

When Henry was eighteen he married Sophia Mandrell.[3] Herself an orphan, she too had been robbed of a father at a tender age. (Henry and Sophia were also related to one another, as non-blood cousins, by way of a complicated arrangement of marriages and re-marriages, half-sisters and half-brothers.) Moreover, her father, William, had died a harrowing death. Though Sophia was born in the family home in Stow-on-the-Wold, Gloucestershire, William Mandrell's job as a dairyman took the family to a cattle farm in Enfield Highway, Middlesex, just north of London, and from here also to the City – Shoe Lane, just off Fleet Street – where he founded the business that became the ABC chain of bakeries and restaurants. The Mandrells lived comfortably, with their Enfield cottage and a flat over the Shoe Lane premises, and were so financially secure that Sophia was sent away to boarding-school. One day, though, in 1878, when Sophia was six, William Mandrell saw some thugs beating up a policeman. He rushed to the rescue and received a brutal kick in the testicles, rendering him unconscious. He suffered a heart attack, never regained consciousness and died four hours later.

Henry and Sophia's marriage, in September 1889, took place in St Bride's parish church, witnessed by friends and Sophia's sister. At the time of the wedding Sophia, just seventeen, was seven months' pregnant. On her wedding night, emotional over the events of the day, her probably unsought pregnancy, her dead parents and the loss of domestic comforts, Sophia cried uncontrollably. Family legend has it that, doing his best to comfort her, Henry responded, 'But now you have me!'

When they became grandparents – to Alfie and a good many others – Henry and Sophia Hill asked to be called 'GP' and 'Nana'. GP, Henry explained, stood for Grandpa. One wonders, too, whether it also stood for General Practitioner, his father's and grandfather's profession, and his too – rightfully – though one that would elude him all his life. Henry and Sophia brought eight children into the world. Yet despite his wedding night promise to his bride, Henry wasn't around very much over the next twenty years.

Their first child, Marian, born in Brixton, south London, died at the age of three after her nightdress caught fire. Their second, Rose, was taken away from the couple and raised in Aylesbury, Buckinghamshire, by Sophia's sister, after whom she had been named; she was not to figure in the rest of their lives. Then two boys were born, Leonard and Alfred, both in Leytonstone, east London, the latter on December 12 1893.

By this point, Henry was making heavy weather of finding a steady job. Rebelling against his chemist's apprenticeship, he became a tram conductor. Then he hit the road, travelling from town to town as an itinerant entertainer. For a while, he worked a circus-like performing-dogs act in the doorways of public houses, hoping that benevolent passers-by would throw a copper or two in his hat.

'It was always said that GP was "travelling",' says Tony House, one of his many nephews. 'We were told that all eight Hill children were born in a different town. It was all rent-avoiding moonlight flits, sleeping on straw in attics, the children being sent to school without shoes or socks. They were very poor. Occasionally, though, Henry would send the family a five-shilling postal order or suddenly return home, at which point all would be forgiven, he'd make Nana pregnant and disappear again. And she would never hear a word said against him and loved him totally. She had all eight children by the time she was thirty-two.'

Henry and Sophia had their final four progeny in a six-year burst from 1899 to 1905, all in the east of England. William (Billy) first saw the light of day in Fleet, just outside Holbeach, Ernest (Ernie) in Cambridge, Cecilia (Cissie) in Ipswich and Violet in Steeple Bumpstead, and every one was born at 'home'. Their birth certificates betray Henry's long-term abandonment of his chemist's training. Twice he is described as a 'circus performer'. At the time of William's birth he was classified as a *comedian*, no less.

All the children suffered real privation during their childhood, and, though they inherited a natural brightness and intelligence, their education was affected from having to change schools so frequently. But Sophia and Henry, when he was around, ensured that their family understood the ways of the world and were imbued with total self-respect. As Alfie later remembered, 'GP and Nana subtly suggested that, as a Hill, you were a member of a natural élite.'

Obviously, these events greatly shaped their lives. Leonard, tragically, was to contract jaundice and die in his early twenties. Of the other boys, Alfie's cousin Chris, one of two children born to Ernie Hill, would remember this homily from childhood: 'If all three brothers were waiting for a train, and the train came in but was too crowded to board, Ernie would sit down calmly and wait for the next one, Alf would face up to the stationmaster, complaining bitterly that there wasn't enough room, while Billy would be chatting up a woman and be on the train, the woman on his lap, waving goodbye.' Billy's way with women was so effective that after fathering a couple of children in the Southampton area, he kept one step ahead of two angry fathers and married three times in Wales, where it is known that he fathered seven more. Though these children were first-cousins of 'Benny' Hill, little link was maintained, but when a few of them showed up at his funeral in 1992 the family resemblance was outstanding.

Despite his long absences, the force of Henry Hill's character also left other marks on his children – who, encouraged always by their mother, shared a deep affection for their father. His love of the circus soon transferred to them – impacting upon his sons in particular. Before his early death, Leonard was often to be found in full clown costume, performing his spectacular act of walking upstairs on his hands. And Alf was similarly smitten. He greatly admired his older brother and emulated his act. Then, he went and did what so many children of the time dreamed of: he joined the circus.

At the age of just ten, life was anything but easy on the road with Bob Fossett's travelling troupe, but Alf Hill had been experiencing hard – indeed, lean – times since birth, and the business of upping sticks and moving on was the familiar pattern of his few years. His pay was minuscule but he was fed and given board, admittedly in rough conditions, and was a tireless worker, involved in every aspect of circus life – setting up the Big Top, taking entrance money from punters, cooking, and mucking out the animal cages.

Like his father before him, Alf developed a remarkable affinity with animals; his seeming ability to 'talk' to them, to becalm them when they were agitated, would amaze everyone who witnessed it for the remainder of his life. In later years, at Southampton Zoo, Alf would stand speaking to the creatures in a language that he himself had invented. Violet Stevens' son Hugh recalls, 'He could train dogs to do things that were beyond description – I saw it happen on several occasions. And he wasn't only good with animals but birds, too. He had a parrot and he was the only person who could go anywhere near it. It would lie, purring in the palm of his hand, waiting for its stomach to be stroked.'

Bill Jaques, another cousin but on Alfie's mother's side of the family, remembers, 'As we stood there with him, Uncle Alf would tell us that the monkeys were explaining to him how sad they were. None of us was quite sure if they understood what he was saying back to them, but one thing was for certain: Alf always made sure that everything he did, not just talking to animals, was Special, with a capital S.'

Alf also enjoyed spending time with the clowns, learning how to ride a punch and take a tumble, and to support the weight of other men in a human pyramid. But in 1910, at the age of sixteen, he quit the circus and took a succession of jobs typifying a young waif whose life has been emotionally troubled: working funfairs, dabbling on the fringe of the light-fingered pick-pocketing at racecourses, buying and selling goods strictly for cash, keeping on the move. He later said of himself in this period that he was 'the little bird that flew from spike to spike', spike here meaning doss-house. Only occasionally did he return home – wherever home happened to be at that moment.

Alf was learning that, above all else, he must 'look after number one', for no one else could be relied upon to provide his nurturing.

It was at this point, and in this mood, that he heard about the *Titanic* and made his way to Southampton in the hope of securing a job as steward.

Alf Hill had a bad time in the First World War. A very bad time. Jack Stanley, too. They had placed their Canal Walk contraceptive enterprise in the hands of Henry and Sophia thinking, like everyone else, that the war would soon be over. Instead, it lasted four long, awful years and resulted in the death of 22 million people.

When Alf was posted to the Western Front he was probably aware of the fate that awaited him, for his brother Billy had patriotically, almost unthinkingly, volunteered himself for action at fifteen, claiming to be eighteen; his experience of the war in France was then so utterly horrifying that when he actually turned eighteen he had to be dragged kicking and screaming back to the trenches.

Alf's childhood years in the circus and on the road stood him in good stead, though: he knew how to take care of himself. While he witnessed dozens of comrades falling at his side – shot, stabbed, blown up or gassed – he kept himself alive through sheer resourcefulness and physical fitness, on one occasion leaping out of a line of gunfire, on another somehow avoiding a surprise, direct attack from bayonet-wielding Germans who had dropped into the enemy trench and were wantonly slaughtering. Also, his prowess with a rifle, learned from endless hours firing at hollow tin cans in circus and funfair tents, accorded him status as a regimental marksman, a sergeant. In later years, all who went to fairs with Alf would be impressed by his unerring ability to hit bullseye at the rifle range.

Eventually, though, Alf was captured and he spent the remaining years of the war in a Belgian prisoner-of-war camp. Not that his family back in Southampton knew much about it. His sister Violet remembers: 'We had a message from the authorities to say that he'd gone missing and they didn't know what had happened.' The family, of course, assumed that Alf was dead, and it was many months before word filtered back that he had been taken prisoner. The level of deprivation in the POW camps was considerable, and food was in acutely short supply (as indeed it was outside the camp). Down the generations, the Hills had been large people who loved their grub with a zest bordering on gluttony; true to his genetic inheritance, Alf had become a sizeable lad, a strapping six-footer, big-boned and heavy-set. Abating his hunger, by whatever means, became Alf's number one aim until Armistice. By stealing, bribing, illicit trading and fearless devouring of anything even remotely edible, Alf just managed to keep himself alive. His resourcefulness was so remarkable that his fellow POWs called him 'Gilbert the Filbert', a man noted for his obsessive foraging for nuts. Some of these other men would die of starvation or malnutrition.

On one such occasion, Alf's rudimentary knowledge of Yiddish enabled him to scrounge a meal. Through his friendships with the immigrant Jewish shopkeepers back in Canal Walk, Alf could make out the instructions given by a German officer. The German was ordering prisoners returning from a day out lifting potatoes to empty their pockets; just before it came to his turn Alf enquired of a sergeant, 'Pissen?' and was fortunate in being permitted to visit the latrine, where he hastily divested himself of enough spuds – hiding them in a safe place for later retrieval – to guarantee two or three half-decent, if unbalanced, feasts. On another occasion Alf stole a loaf of bread so soon after it had been baked that, upon stuffing it under his shirt, it burned his skin. His nephew Bill Jaques has clear memories of childhood visits to the Hills in the ensuing years – 'Mainly, evenings were taken up with Alf's exploits of the First World War, when he was captured by the Germans. I particularly remember him telling me how he hid some dried peas in his boots, and had to endure much pain during a march, before, eventually, he was able to unlace his boots and pour out the peas prior to eating them.'

Despite such resilience, Alf Hill only just survived to peacetime, and Violet was shocked by his appearance when he finally came home. 'He was like a skeleton, and his flesh had a greeny hue. He'd been starved of real food for so long that he couldn't eat anything without it turning his stomach. It made me cry because I loved him so much.'

Alf had returned to Southampton weighing under 100 pounds. He was also phenomenally angry at the sheer futility of the four-year war, and shared the common view that British soldiers had been thrown into battle like 'lions led by donkeys', with awesome loss of life and, for the survivors, a tragic array of physical ailments and mental scars. Already marked by an extraordinary childhood, Alf's pain ran deep indeed.

While Alf and Jack were away at war, Henry Hill was ensuring that Stanley & Co. remained a going concern, and all the elements of the business remained in good shape for their return. The responsibility was the making of the man. For the first time in his adult life, Henry had stability, a decent income and a solid reason for finding a permanent place to live. Approaching the age of fifty, he finally ceased his wayfaring ways and settled into the role of father and ('call me GP') grandfather; scraping together all he could, Henry bought himself a chemist's shop in Southampton, which comprised a pharmacy at the front and a dentist's chair in the rear.

Although he was unrecognized by the Royal College of Surgeons, one could practise dentistry without formal qualification at this time, and Henry set to work on the local cavities initially from three premises. When a change in the law forced him to choose between the professions, he ditched pharmacy and settled into a sole dental practice at 59 St Mary Street, above a corn and egg merchant.

Henry was finally a medical man, and he revelled in both it and his new-found status, calling himself, fully, Henry Hawthorn Hill, signing himself 'H. Hawthorn Hill', and striding along St Mary Street in patent-leather shoes, cigar in mouth, suit-jacket open to reveal a gold watch-chain on his waistcoat, spats, a cravat, Homburg hat and carrying a black cane with a silver knob. The local shopkeepers touched their forelocks and called him 'Mr Hawthorn Hill'. His overawed grandchildren were a little embarrassed by GP's public loftiness, however, and one of them, Ernie's daughter Kathleen, still smiles as she remembers his local nickname – 'The Lord Mayor of St Mary Street'.

Henry's grandchildren, Alfie included, had their teeth pulled or filled in GP's chair on the top floor of his premises, and the spectre of hearing the Yorkshire-toned command 'Right! You, you and you come up to the surgery and get your teeth checked!' hung over family occasions. But there were compensations. Living once more over something akin to a dairy, reminiscent of her happy childhood, Sophia threw grand tea parties. Here, the unquenchable desire for chocolate éclairs that – like the éclairs themselves – ran thick in the Hill blood was regularly, if temporarily, sated, amid the art deco furniture or in the lino-covered kitchen.

Back at Stanley & Co., business was doing very nicely, too. Alf's knowledge as a street-sharp youngster blended perfectly with Jack Stanley's own talents as a smart operator. Of Irish stock, Jack's father had been a travelling cheapjack in America in the late nineteenth century, hawking dubious goods around the South, and perpetrating scams designed to part unsuspecting folk, usually Negroes, from their hard-earned cash. Now,

Jack and Alf bought condoms in quantity, direct from suppliers or manufacturers, packaged them with quality-bestowing silver and gold labels, gave the products reassuring names (one of them was Safex) and sold them at a handsome profit.

Alf also lived with Jack Stanley and his parents, in their house at 6 Terminus Terrace, and everything was going remarkably smoothly for the hitherto troubled young man.

It was the greatest irony, then, that Alf Hill, successful condom sales-man, should come to accidentally impregnate his girlfriend.

Helen Florence Cave – a bonny-faced twenty-six-year-old – lived with her parents at 48 Newcombe Road, behind the Polygon Hotel, and worked as a clerk at the great Toogood & Sons flour and seed mills, a factory in Woolston, on the western shore of the River Itchen. During the First World War the mill was staffed mostly by women, working twelve-hour shifts and earning £3 a week; after the war, though, the men returned to reclaim their old jobs.

Alf had been courting Helen since 1919, soon after his return from the war. They met at a dance, and Helen was smitten by Alf's physical presence and dashing looks. 'I remember Alf bringing Helen home for the first time,' says his sister Violet. 'I was fifteen so she was ten years older than me, but I fell in love with her instantly. She was beautiful. I said to her, "I can't wait for you to become my sister!" I was always taking care of people – my mother and my sister especially – and Helen seemed to me to be one of those people who needed somebody to take care of her.'

Mercifully perhaps, Helen's history was nowhere near as tempestuous as Alf's. And whereas the Hills had been connected to Southampton for only seven years, Helen had been born there, in her grandparents' home in St Andrews Road, a street of narrow semi-detached houses situated close by East Park, where one day the town's principal *Titanic* memorial would be erected.

Her father, William Frederick Cave, was a carpenter and joiner, as was his father before him. William's additional description of himself as a 'journeyman' indicates his nature: his earnings were meagre but he was a kindly and carefree soul who seemed not to care for the trappings of life.

He and Helen's mother, Alice Augusta Sims, had been living 'in sin' in a tiny terraced house in Threefield Lane, in the south end of town, when Alice fell pregnant. They married in April 1894 – the event at St James church was witnessed by neither set of parents – and Helen arrived on June 21. Less than two years later Helen was presented with a sister, Alice Louise, known to one and all as Louie, but to Alfie as Lulu. 'Benny' and his Auntie Lulu would become extraordinarily attached in later years; observers suggest he was closer to Louie than to his mother.

Born in the Channel Islands, Helen's mother, Alice – Alfie would grow to love her as 'Grandma Cave' – had no profession but was a dutiful daughter. A stern Victorian woman with a strong sense of responsibility, she was dedicated to taking care of people, in particular her ageing parents, whom Helen (and later her own offspring) called 'Grandpa and Grandma Sims'. Grandpa was a policeman, and while on a posting to London in the late 1880s he was involved in the manhunt for Jack the Ripper, the notorious murderer of prostitutes in the city's East End. To the dismay of his enthralled great-grandchildren, Grandpa's gripping tale of the account had no happy ending, for no conclusive arrest was ever made.

When, in May 1921, Helen Cave discovered that she had fallen pregnant, there was only one course of action. Alf Hill 'did the decent thing', proposed marriage and the pair tied the knot with some speed, before the bulge became apparent. This is not to say that they may not have married anyway, but there seems little doubt that the impending arrival of an infant hastened the day. The wedding took place at Southampton Register Office on Helen's twenty-seventh birthday, June 21 1921, with 'H. Hawthorn Hill' and Alice Cave as witnesses. There was little accord between the families, however – Helen had been far from impressed by the nonconformist lifestyle of her groom's clan, and her parents took an especially dim view of their daughter's chosen partner and his bohemian background. Such was their disregard for the Hills that when Alfie and his older brother were children, Grandma Cave would quickly stow away some of the more valuable items in her modest collection of bric-à-brac and *objets d'art*, fearing that, in one way or another, they would be lost to her. When her other grandchildren visited, the items were left out.

Hearing Alf's spellbinding tales of his twenty-six eventful years, Helen determined to 'do better' for him, to be a good and supportive partner and mother to their children; unsaid, perhaps, but not unrealized, was another resolution – she would try to provide a stability hitherto absent from his life. Alf, in turn, was in a position to promise his bride loyalty and, thanks to the brisk condom-selling business, a steady income.

The start, though, was unsteady. Alf and Helen had nowhere to live. It was obvious that he would have to move out of the Stanleys' residence in Terminus Terrace and she her parents' Victorian villa in Newcombe Road. According to paperwork, for the first few months of their marriage Alf and Helen lodged with a couple, William and Maud Beard, in their council house at 218 Portswood Road. Certainly, seven months later, in January 1922, it was here that Helen gave birth to her first child, a boy, Leonard Ernest. His forename was a tribute to Alf's dead brother, his middle name a tip of the trilby to another of Alf's siblings.

Leonard was a troubled baby, and suffered from acute digestive problems. According to Violet, 'Helen told me that he screamed all day and all night and they couldn't stop it. He became so skeletal that my brother Alf had to carry him around on a cushion. Helen said, "I had to run out of the house or I would have killed him." He drove them mad. That he survived was because his father looked after him for twenty-four hours a day. After all that, he was walking about like a skeleton himself.'

There seems little doubt that the shotgun marriage was immediately strained by this turn of events. And Helen's post-natal depression put the relationship to an even greater test. To help improve their situation, Alf promised to find them better accommodation, and shortly afterwards the three moved out of Portswood Road, Southampton's principal north-east thoroughfare, and back to the centre of town, to a busy main street within easy distance of the Stanleys' house and Canal Walk.

Alf found them rooms at 30 Bridge Road, above and behind a shop, E. D. Wishart & Company, electrical engineers who undertook everything from household work to fulfilling a contract with the Red Funnel Steamers. Edward Wishart himself lived elsewhere, so his three-storey accommodation was available for rent. It was while living here that in April 1923 Helen conceived a second time, and nine months later Alfie – later 'Benny' – Hill made his big entrance.

19

2. Alfie

Arriving on January 21 1924, the new baby was named Alfred Hawthorn Hill, identical to his father. Confusion was avoided by the adoption of informal nicknames, Big Alf and Little Alf.[1]

Little Alf then came to be called Alfie. Big Alf, in turn, let the children know that he wanted to be called The Captain. This was not of course his First World War rank, but he wasn't about to deter the youngsters from thinking that it was, and some say he certainly acted as if it had been.

Economically, Britain in the 1920s, like the rest of the world, was having a very rough time indeed. Alfie Hill was born at a time of genuine deprivation, with hardship and poverty all around and a paucity of social programmes in place to aid the sick and needy. Scarcely any houses had heating beyond a single coal- or wood-fire in the grate, most were draughty, few had adequate plumbing and virtually all had outside lavatories. The nation's workers, especially the hugely exploited coal-miners, felt oppressed by the establishment, culminating in the 1926 General Strike which temporarily crippled the country. Three years later, in October 1929, a miserable decade was rounded off with the recession-led Wall Street crash, which impacted dramatically on most, if not all, of the world; suicide and unemployment rates soared in tandem.

As it happened, the Hills managed to survive all this quite nicely. Whatever the prevailing economic circumstances, condoms were still catching on, in Southampton, in Britain, in much of the world, and The Captain would rue not taking a stake in Stanley & Co. when it had been offered to him. Though Alf was well paid, and earned a commission on sales in addition to his salary, Jack Stanley's ownership of the concern, and his opening of a second shop along the coast in Bournemouth, was reaping him a personal fortune, sufficient to buy a mansion set in a couple of acres out at Bassett, the best part of Southampton. Jack Stanley – of Irish ancestry, and fond of quoting from the Bible – would die a million-aire from selling contraceptives.

The Captain never amassed such a fortune, but within weeks of Alfie's birth, the Hills, now a foursome, were at least able to move away from Bridge Road – leaving its pubs, shops, omnipresent horse manure, double-decker omnibuses, cattle market-cum-slaughterhouse and steam railway line – and settle into their first house, a rented detached property in Shirley, a couple of miles north of the bustle. They took possession of a new red-brick villa, named St Helen's, in Wilton Road, and here Alfie would spend his first seven years, enjoying the little patch of grass at the front and the more generous garden behind the house, and safely venturing out to play on to what was then a quiet residential street with more trees than houses. The suburbanite in 'Benny' Hill was shaped here, amid Shirley's clean air and rural greenery.

In contrast to his brother, Alfie was a happy and healthy baby, and, inevitably, prompted a sibling rivalry with Leonard, two years his elder. Len had been 'an accident' but Alfie was planned, and in the subtle and even unintended way of these things, the difference may have been apparent. Hugh Stevens, their cousin, puts it plainly: 'It always struck me that there was a degree of jealousy, and there was never any love lost between them. As a small boy Alfie was really quite afraid of Len. He was very much on his guard that Len would take every opportunity to give him a bump if he wasn't being watched.' Both boys shared common goals, though: they craved the affection of their mother and they feared their father. Len, in particular, acutely felt The Captain's wrath and developed a strong dislike for him that was never to dissipate.

Ever aware of how Len was being treated, Helen – known by some of the family as Nellie – protected him zealously, taking his side in the many father-child disputes that arose. This prompted Big Alf to bemoan, 'She thinks the sun shines out of Len's jacksie!' and to believe that his wife loved her children more than she loved him.

Florence Jaques, who frequently observed the family at close quarters, states quite bluntly, 'Nowadays a man and wife wouldn't tolerate such a marriage, but back in those days people just put up with it. Big Alf could be a nice man on the surface but not at all nice underneath. He was a braggart, a bully, what people nowadays would call a control-freak – he ran the house and expected everybody to do as they were told. Nellie fought him in the only way she knew how, by agreeing with him.'

Alfie's cousin Tony House adds, 'Big Alf was very domineering where Auntie Helen was concerned. He thought a lot of her, but when we went there she hardly got a word in. He had to hold the floor all the time, telling all those tales about being in the trenches in the First World War, real boys' stuff. And he could certainly put his foot down when he wanted to. But I never heard him raise his voice to her, not in front of me anyway. I think it might have been more subtle, more psychological, than that. She seemed to love him, though, and always seemed happy.'

For all of Big Alf's bluster, much of it well-meaning, it was Helen who mainly reared the infant boys. Alf was in the shop for five, sometimes six, days of the week, and Helen was the dutiful housewife. Every day she would prepare breakfast for her husband and then, after he had left for Canal Walk – ready for another day selling condoms, and perhaps fitting a truss or corset on to customers in the Stanley & Co. back room – settle easily into a domestic routine. As her boys were served their breakfast she would read them stories, many of which Alfie would remember for the rest of his life. Then it might be wash-time, Helen carrying the family's dirty laundry into the garden, scrubbing it clean and running it through an iron mangle before pegging the heavy, wet clothes on to the washing-line to dry. Her children were welcome company, and she shared their happiness at play. As it was for so many families at the time, a general atmosphere of austerity pervaded the calendar, thrown into temporary relief at birthdays and Christmas, the latter being the only time that the staple diet of meat-and-two-veg might give way to turkey or ham, a bowl of fruit and a box of dates on the sideboard. Alfie later developed a gag about it.

Helen advocated open affection in her children, with kisses available and enjoyed at all times, and a free-spirited attitude about bodily functions, permitting Len and Alfie to urinate whenever and wherever the need arose – even in the street outside the house, a habit not altogether appreciated by neighbours and passers-by. She also told her children that, if necessary, they should feel able to seek shelter from rain in the doorways of other houses, and that the occupants of those houses 'would understand'. The boys did, but the occupants sometimes did not. Often, when Len was at nursery, Helen would walk Alfie down Wilton Road, up Radway Road and out on to the broad green space of Southampton Common, with its paddling pool, lakes, cricket and football pitches and all manner of animals. Alfie would hold her hand very tightly, brush his rosy cheek against the soft fur trim of her coat and exclaim, 'Lovely mummy!' Such was the strength of his affection that he would take care of Helen as if she was his date, solicitously ensuring that she crossed roads safely and that no thorns would snag her stockings. For the rest of his life, Alfie would return to Southampton Common and allow his mind to run barefoot through the blissful memories.

Big Alf had an altogether different method of parenting. Though he aimed always to be a good father, as indeed he tried to be a good husband, his own formative years had been so tempestuous that he was never going to be the sort of chap to hide his personality under a bushel; out of sheer necessity, though, those in his closest proximity – his wife and children especially – were forced to react against it, one way or another. Len's adult view of his father, jaundiced by the forces at play in his early years, was that Big Alf had a greater affinity for animals than for his children. In bed at night, the first-born would hear his father coming up the stairs and hide under the bedclothes, making out that he was asleep.

With a more generous disposition and less anger than his brother, Alfie was not so openly critical and was certainly more forgiving about The Captain. Nonetheless, he too experienced many unpleasant events that would be seared into his memory. At times The Captain was a willing playmate for his two sons, and loved to spin them engaging yarns about his adventures with the circus and as a street spiv, varying his accent as he described the different parts of England he had visited as a waif. Mostly, though, his patience was brittle thin, his phraseology indignant and his voice loud and imperious.

Visitors to the Hills at this time still carry memories of what they witnessed. 'I lived in fear of Big Alf,' says his nephew Bill Jaques, son of Alfie's Auntie Lulu. 'I didn't hate the man, I just speak as I see, and I thought he was cruel. We used to exchange holidays – Alfie and Len would come to my house and my brothers Don and Fran and I would go to theirs. I remember Uncle Alf saying to me once, "I just spent 1s 6d this afternoon. Who'll give me tuppence for the 1s 6d worth of goods I've just bought?" Tuppence was a lot of money in 1930. And of course, being an innocent child, I said I would do it. After taking my two pennies he gave me 1s 6d worth of used bus tickets, and kept the tuppence. I never got it back. Then he said, "Who wants dinner tonight? It costs sixpence." I didn't have the money and he actually made me go without dinner; in the morning, though, when I was very hungry, he charged me for breakfast.'

Whether showing the children how to play cards (as a well-practised 'sharpie' from his pre-war and army days, The Captain usually won handsomely) or playing word games ('We once played "A for Apple," recalls Bill Jaques, 'and Uncle Alf got *most* upset when I said "L for Leather" because he would have wanted to have thought of it'), The Captain loved to be the ringleader of family activities. He frequently organized mass family outings, perhaps to Shawford Down or across Southampton Water at Hythe, where sport – usually cricket or rounders – would be on the unspoken agenda. Big Alf would take it upon himself to whip everybody into order, commanding, 'Stand there!' or 'Don't move!', demanding that people were 'out' when they perhaps were not, and aggressively chastising the children for dropping 'an easy catch' or not returning the ball at a speed he felt appropriate.

When it was The Captain's own turn to take the bat, however, his attitude would change. Suddenly he was demanding an easy delivery so that he could smite the ball far and wide, lofting it into distant bushes for the children and adults to retrieve. Every so often, though, a deft ball would penetrate his staunch guard, bringing about his genuine dismissal from the field of play. But The Captain would 'refuse to walk', indignantly protesting that he was not out and steadfastly maintaining his position at the crease. Only when he was fed up would he indicate that he'd had enough, at which point the game would be over. 'He'd say, "Please your-self now, I've finished!"' recalls Bill Jaques. Bill's wife Florence observes, 'Benny's later TV comedy sketch in which he played cricket was straight from his childhood. Running away from the action – that was Alfie as a child; being bowled out but refusing to walk – that was his father. He even managed to look like him.'

Big Alf was also terribly keen on boxing, holding that it was a dignified sport, and useful for self-defence. He himself had learned boxing in his years with the circus, a period when, undoubtedly, self-protection was one of the essential mainstays for his survival. Big Alf was renowned in his family for talking confidently with anyone in his vicinity, usually hoping that he would glean some nugget of information to add to his fund of life-knowledge. One of the many traders in Canal Walk whom he talked to in this way was Tommy White, an 1897 challenger for the feather-weight boxing championship of Great Britain, who, retired from the ring, ran a restaurant. Big Alf often buttonholed the former pugilist, trying to pick up tips and hoping to be considered a friend. Tommy gave him some boxing gloves, and soon The Captain was initiating his two sons in the finer points of the sport. He would referee as they squared up to one another; Len, being older and more developed, usually gave Alfie something of a beating.

Occasionally, The Captain himself would pull on the heavy red gloves, and male visitors to the house – children as well as adults – would be expected to square up for a scrap. Bill Jaques recalls, 'He used to make us all box with him and then used to hit us with quite a force, knocking us around something rotten, all over the garden. Len was the biggest boy and on one occasion he managed to get through his father's guard and hit him squarely in the stomach. Big Alf gasped, "Never do that again, son! That punch landed right on my ulcer, from when I was a starving prisoner-of-war." My own father strongly disliked Big Alf for that sort of thing.'

Such was The Captain's insistence on teaching Len and Alfie to box that he took them to a local arena, the Coliseum, where an evening's entertainment comprised a succession of three-round bouts, which he expected his sons to watch and study. Alfie, especially, was entranced – not only by the boxing, so artfully enacted, but by the sheer theatre of it all, with the 'seconds' administering the magic sponge to their young boxer in between the rounds, and the referee, smaller than the boxers and without protection, imperiously commanding their respect and counting down a knockout in the sport's very own curious vocal manner, 'One-ah, two-ah, three-ah . . .' Boxing was to remain a passion for the rest of Alfie's life, and as much as his worldwide travelling in later years was designed to take in cabaret clubs, night-clubs and circuses, where he would define comedy material for his act, he also made sure to attend as many boxing bouts as possible. People who were to find conversation with 'Benny' Hill difficult – which was more or less everyone – had only to steer the subject towards boxing and he would spill over with career statistics and ringside anecdotes for many a happy hour.

The Captain had another major influence on his children. His passion for the circus had never waned, and his big booming voice would regularly be heard entertaining family and visitors with great tales from the Big Top, some his own, others passed down from his father and late, lamented brother Leonard, the man who could effect astonishing gymnastic feats. On special family occasions, virtually from their births, Len and Alfie would be dressed head to toe in colourful clown costumes, homemade as well as purchased, and expected to perform. Len was diffident about this but Alfie found it hugely appealing. He glowed to the sound of laughter and applause, and coveted the hugs and kisses that inevitably followed a good performance. Alfie liked to sing a popular tune of the day, 'Just a Little Love, a Little Kiss', while Big Alf played a one-string fiddle; but impressions and recitations were his favourites, and he further developed an ability to mimic friends and relations, enjoying the generosity of their reaction to being lampooned by such a charmingly innocent young boy. His Aunt Violet remembers visiting Wilton Road at Christmas 1928: 'Alfie was only four but already a gorgeous little boy, very bright, and he brought the house down with a little poem that he could recite:

> When I was three
> And I was only small,
> I planted a twig in my garden,
> And it grew, and it grew, and it grew.
> And now I am four
> And it is even bigger than me!

Another favourite was:

> I'll tell you a story
> If you don't make a noise,

Mustapha and Hassan
Are two little boys.
They both live in Egypt,
The sun there is hot,
Mustapha's a good boy
But Hassan is not.

Alfie was clearly Mustapha.

The cue to entertain didn't only come from The Captain. Alfie's mother was always ready for a laugh, and her sister Louie was especially amusing, forever singing, telling jokes, and besotted with the entertainment scene. 'While Big Alf's humour was cruel, Nellie and Louie both had a very droll, dry sense of humour,' remarks Florence Jaques. 'Louie was especially quick-witted, which is another reason why she and Alfie got on so well. They bounced off one another. Nellie was more droll and, actually, didn't really care for her son's sense of humour as Louie did.'

'I liked Alfie enormously as a child,' says his cousin Hugh Stevens. 'He was always trying to see the funny side of every situation. I looked up to him very much. He was a hero. And he didn't change much over the years – he looked older and heavier but he still had the same attitude.' Bill Jaques saw it slightly differently, though: 'As a child I found Alfie most pleasant, but I preferred Len, being a quieter person. Alfie was an extrovert and always on the go, tapping and fidgeting. I'm sure he was a big challenge to his father.'

Alfie, it seems, got the worst of Big Alf. Len was intelligent and bookish, and had learned to keep out of his father's way, whereas Alfie was active and brash, and so clashes were inevitable.

Alfie developed a system to cope with his father – he pretended he couldn't understand basic instructions or undertake simple tasks. He and Len were often given household chores by The Captain, having to sweep the driveway or weed the garden, and they were expected to pull their weight with full commitment.

Alfie's tactics invariably succeeded. Big Alf's impatience would soon get the better of him, causing him to explode: 'Give it to me, you bloody idiot! Let me do it, I'll show you how it's done!' A favoured expression of Big Alf's was 'You're not in it!' – meaning 'You're out of it!', incapable of performing the required task. Surprisingly perhaps, a flood of child tears would then follow, to be wiped away by Helen while she told her son that his father didn't mean the things he said. 'It's just his way,' she would soothe.

One aspect of life in which Alfie's parents saw eye-to-eye, though, was the necessity for frugality – a trait that, deeply instilled in him as a child, was to remain steadfast for the rest of his life, irrespective of personal wealth.

Accustomed to severe shortages at home in his childhood and from his Artful Dodger lifestyle as a youngster on the road, Big Alf felt a compelling need to exercise extreme caution with his income, and every penny was watched with care. He and Helen were not selfish, but they were certainly parsimonious: they would never own a car and didn't install a telephone until long after it became a general utility. Even when times became a little easier, Helen never had an electric iron: as women had done since time immemorial, she would simply place a flat-iron on top of the kitchen boiler and, to determine when it was hot enough for the job, hold it up to her cheek.

Grandma Cave – Helen and Louie's mother – was herself a thrifty, upright person, always conscious of worth, so Helen did not need persuading that frugality was the key to long-term security. 'Nellie was a very thrifty housewife,' recalls Florence Jaques. 'I think she had to be. Louie, ironically, was the total opposite, a spendthrift. But I think the difference was the husbands they married. I certainly remember when Nellie bought half a dozen eggs too many and Big Alf made her take them back to the shop. He had clearly discovered that whoever controls the purse-strings exercises power in a household.'

Alf and Helen's determination to exercise strict control over their spending outlasted the recession by decades; indeed, they were destined never to change their attitude to money. When their clothes gave out, or their shoes were either too small or beyond repair, the family would cram the items into paper bags and take them down to Canal Walk, where a shop close to Stanley & Co. would take them off their hands in exchange for a few pennies. Gladys Green, who became the Hills' house-cleaner, remembers, 'Mrs Hill was always so very careful with money. She used to save every little thing. One day I threw away a toothpaste tube that had run right down and she was very cross about it because she always used things to the bitter end.'

Just how much the young Alfie was inculcated with his parents' frugality – and also the Hills' typically prodigious appetite – is demonstrated by an account of a family picnic held in the beautiful grounds of Netley Abbey, close to Southampton Water. Bill Jaques recalls, 'There were quite a few hornets about, really nasty ones, and they descended on Alfie who was in the middle of eating a jam sandwich. He got up and started running. People were shouting "Throw it away! Chuck the stupid sandwich away!" but he wouldn't let go of it – he just kept running and eating until the sandwich was consumed and the wasps retired, defeated.'

At the age of five, in January 1929, Alfie went to school for the first time, following his older brother into the infants section at Shirley School, an imposing red-brick three-storey Victorian pile at the northern end of Wilton Road, where the trees stopped and the houses were built in a straight terrace. Although there was one overall headmaster, a Mr Hoare, the school was segregated by age and sex – boys, girls and mixed infants. A naturally bright child, Alfie found lessons easy, albeit scratching on to a slate less so. Morning, lunchtime and afternoon playtimes rendered an education of a different and altogether more invigorating kind, however: girls. The infants, already mixed, shared a playground with the older girls; Alfie Hill had never been in the company of so many females, not just those of his own age, but up to eleven. His eyes widened.

In a way that children can find so natural – albeit in the unspoken knowledge that such acts may be 'naughty' – Alfie showed a great keenness to conduct primitive sexual experiments with girls, and indeed his interest was matched by theirs in him. Having mothered her children with considerable openness, encouraging them to readily express themselves, Helen saw no cause for concern that her youngest was showing a greater interest in girls than in mucking around with the other boys and participating in their endless tests of physical prowess. He already knew how to box and could more than adequately 'take care of himself' if the need arose – as, inevitably, it did from time to time. Now Alfie had a chance to express another side of his personality, and his mother was not going to stop him. Such was the strength of his interest in girls that it wasn't long before they would gather around him in the playground, chanting:

Alfie Hill took a pill,
On the top of Shirley Hill,
Shirley Hill began to shake,
And gave poor Alf the belly-ache!

As he explained to his brother in later years, among the emboldened entries in young Alfie's playground CV was a liaison with an older girl, Molly. Relations between the two were candid, and an 'I'll show you mine if you show me yours' situation quickly developed. On one occasion Alfie was demonstrating to Molly the male art of creative peeing when the feared infants' headmistress, Mrs Vane, caught him mid-signature; he was summoned to her study to receive several hand-thwacks of the cane. Such was Molly's affection for young Alfie that she fought over him with another girl; Alfie was caught in the midst of the encounter and knocked cold when his head had an unexpected conference with the concrete playground.

All this was happening with some speed, because Alfie was destined to stay at Shirley School for only two years. Instead of remaining there until the age of eleven he was removed at seven, just as he was advancing out of the infants', when the Hills left Wilton Road and set up in a brand new property in the Banister Court district of Southampton. A small semi-detached house they could call their own, 22 Westrow Gardens was bought by Alf and Helen for cash – so good was Stanley's business, and, perhaps, so mistrusting were Alfie's parents of banks. The Hills became its first owner-occupiers in 1931, and it would be more than sixty years before the house was owned by anyone else.

Alfie settled quickly into his new school, Western District, situated close by Shirley Road, a relentless ribbon of suburban shops. (One of them, a haberdashery, was run by the mother of Tommy Cooper, a young man whose career as a comic would blossom at the same time as Benny Hill's. Tommy was a tall boy and a giant man; it has been said that his mother 'looked like a miniaturized Cooper in drag'.) Western was closer to the new house, though still a good walk away, and had a reputation for hothousing bright young pupils, achieving annually the greatest number of scholarships to Southampton's grammar schools.

Having been brought up in rented accommodation, the chance, at the age of seven, to live in a house of one's own was hugely attractive for Alfie, as indeed it was for the rest of the family. Much work needed to be done first, and Alfie did his bit, trotting after school each day to the newly created Westrow Gardens – a tiny cul-de-sac – and preparing the small front garden by collecting up bricks and builders' rubble and taking them around to the back of the house where they would be used as hard-core foundation for a shed.

The Captain, too, was busy preparing for the new abode. One of his proudest moments came when he saw a group of council workmen putting in the street lights along Westrow Gardens. As was his way, Big Alf went out and fell into a chat with the men, during which he learned that the nearest lamp to number 22 was being positioned a few yards along the road. So he slipped the men a ten-shilling note and they brought it up and put it plum outside. 'He was thrilled about that,' recalls his nephew Tony House. 'His idea was that he and Helen, who had the front bedroom, could get undressed and into bed without having to put on their light, which would save on the electricity bill. He used to tell that story often, and very proudly, and when he later visited my brother at Bishopstoke, who happened to have a streetlight outside his house, he said to him, "Did you negotiate to get that light put there?"'

Another of The Captain's innovative money-saving ideas was to declare that the garage adjacent to the house was an unfinished construction unfit for its intended use. The effect of this, as shown in the 1930s rates ledger still kept in Southampton Archives, was that he paid to the council £1 12s per annum less than the other homeowners in Westrow Gardens; they had to pay for a 'house, garden and garage' whereas he only had a 'house, garden and outbuilding'. Not buying a car enabled Big Alf to keep this ruse going for decades.

To Alfie and his brother, Westrow Gardens was a hugely exciting place to live, for Banister Court was the fulcrum of Southampton's sporting activities. Literally around the corner was the home ground of Hampshire County Cricket Club, and opposite this was one of several local bowling greens. (It soon counted Big Alf among its members.) In the other direction, only a couple of hundred yards from Westrow Gardens, was The Dell, the home of Southampton Football Club, in those days a long-term fixture of Division Two in the English Football League. Alfie and Len, in common with most local boys, eagerly pursued signatures of the home and visiting players before and after matches, and Alfie became a keen, indeed lifelong, supporter of 'The Saints' – to the point where he would happily cite the name of the team's star goalscorer, Mike Channon, in a 1970s TV sketch. Back along the road from The Dell was South-ampton Ice Rink, where the good burghers could skate and watch ice-hockey matches.

Best of all, though, at the very end of Westrow Gardens – no more than a hundred yards from number 22 – was Banister Court Stadium, which staged greyhound-racing and was home to the Southampton Saints speedway team. Alfie became besotted with the motorcycle sport, newly imported to Britain by an Australian promoter and particularly popular with the working-class public; he spent many childhood years on his pushbike, happily imitating his leather-clad 'dirt-track' heroes, speeding around bends with his left foot trailing behind, producing sparks from the Blakey studs he had carefully nailed to the tips and heels of his shoes. The Captain helped: he brought home bowler-hats and oil-cloth for his two sons from a shop in Canal Walk, and with Helen's assistance fashioned imitations of crash helmets and speedway riders' tabards, complete with numbers on the back. Many an evening Alfie would stand peeping through the fence to see the action; occasionally, he would nip through the turnstiles and inside the stadium, where, cheerfully, he would be sprinkled with cinders as the riders slid their brakeless bikes around the bends of the oval track, and where he would fill his lungs with the heavy aroma of engine fuel. Usually, however, Alfie would lie in his bed, listening to the roar of the machines and the cheering crowds seeping in through the window. Like his passion for boxing, Alfie was to follow speedway for the rest of his life.

The house at 22 Westrow Gardens was a typically English suburban 'semi', slightly on the small side yet tolerably comfortable for a family of four. It had three bedrooms, the third of which, Alfie's, was a 'box room' – situated in the rear, next to the bathroom – with no space to swing the proverbial cat. Len had only a slightly larger room, while The Captain and Helen shared the largest room at the front, with its bay window and convenient outside light. Net curtains hung in every window, behind the leaded glass; there was a driveway to the side, behind a wrought-iron double gate, and the 'outbuilding'. A path around the back led to an outside lavatory that butted up to the kitchen; in the winter months wind would blow sharply up the passage.

With Big Alf's special affinity for animals, the house was also home to a succession of pets, over whom young Alfie became particularly attached. When he was still toddling, his father brought home a marmoset. The tiny monkey was an interesting fellow, but his constant eagerness and appetites soon returned him to the pet shop. As he exited, in came a nanny-goat, which The Captain thought might enable them to save on buying milk. Though the milk was indeed plentiful enough to fill many a bottle, the chore of pulling at the throttles soon palled and Daisy, too, was taken back whence she had come. Dogs and cats followed, as did Laura, an Amazon Green parrot whose calls of 'Is that the milkman?' were soon echoed with the same, if not an even greater frequency, by the precocious impersonator Alfie. 'They had a dog called Spot,' recalls Alfie's cousin Hugh Stevens, 'and one time I was there Auntie Helen wanted the dog out of the kitchen while she was getting the tea ready. Alfie pointed at the dog and shouted "Out, damned Spot!", which I thought was pretty clever.'

Apart from domestic disputes, notably those with his father, it is fair to say that Alfie was probably content at this time in his life. He was bright and doing well at school; he was confident among his peers, both male and female, and in adult company; he was well-mannered and, when appropriate, dutiful and respectful of his 'elders and betters'; he could take care of himself in the company of school bullies and other urban dangers; he had plentiful hobbies and interests; his ample cheeks, good bone structure and winning smile lent him a sunny and open disposition; and he had developed a sense of humour. Crucially, he also seemed to be aware of his place in the family – one with its fair share of quirky ideas and emotional legacies. But though his mother gave him sustenance, she was becoming less interested in his daily development, preferring to leave him to his own devices; and The Captain provided a contradictory blend of paternal affection and stern discipline – both, of course, confusingly, couched in the same sharpened tones. Among those who witnessed Alfie's childhood years, the consensus holds that, for all his apparent confidence, he had to hone his independence and accept that parental love was sometimes short on the ground.

On summer holidays, usually to Bournemouth or the Isle of Wight, Alfie's fooling and comedy impressions alleviated many a dreary afternoon or the prospect of being stuck in a drab guest-house with rain lashing against the window. On one occasion, in Ryde, Alfie took part in a newspaper-sponsored competition for the best kiddies' sand-castle. At The Captain's absolute insistence he created a whale, his father hoping that it would wittily illustrate the paper's slogan 'a whale of a paper'. Working a few feet away from Alfie was a young girl whose creation was enlivened by numerous coloured shells and a variety of seaweed; Alfie determined to persuade the girl to give him some of her surplus materials. 'I flattered her, I gave her sweets, I made her laugh, but she wouldn't give me even a single shell,' he recalled decades later. 'I got nothing – the story of my life!' The girl won the competition, but Alfie's whale gained him a creditable second place (though this was probably not good enough for The Captain). Fully twenty years on, when he was a star, he remarked upon the event in an interview with *TV Mirror*, only this time he claimed to have been the winner; several years later still, in 1962, he made a surprise guest appearance on the BBC's children's TV programme *Blue Peter* . . . judging a children's sand-castle competition.

During another family holiday, in Bournemouth (where Big Alf could pop along and take a look at Jack Stanley's newest and biggest shop), Alfie was much taken with a beach comedy show mounted by a white-faced Pierrot, Willie Cave. The youngster knew of few other comedians at this time and reckoned that Cave was the funniest man in the world. He was most impressed with some of slick Willie's antics, such as professing alarm when he backed himself, posterior first, into a piano. The Pierrot's face also registered concern that someone – a woman, even – had dared to touch him up; Alfie was delighted at such sauce and years later worked much of Cave's act into his own. And he also fell headlong for the charms of Cave's accomplice, even though she was fully clad in the typical Pierrette costume: baggy pyjamas with pom-poms in all the right places.

There were also good times to be had back in Southampton. Going to 'the pictures' was definitely one, Alfie's formative years spanning the silent and 'talkie' eras. Comedy was always his principal attraction, and Alfie adored Charlie Chaplin, Buster Keaton, Harold Lloyd, Chester Conklin, the Keystone Cops and the quintessential double-act Laurel and Hardy. Impressions of all these were added to his repertoire without hesitation. Good times were also had on Southampton Pier, where the Hills would spend occasional summer Saturday nights eating ice-cream. Alfie remembered these times with great clarity decades later:

> I used to work the fruit-machines, the old penny-in-the-slot, and turn the handle. And I used to watch the Charlie Chaplin films. I could never understand why other people wanted to see *What the Butler Saw*. But I was only seven – if I'd have been eight, more than likely I'd have been interested in that, but at seven I wasn't. And there used to be dancing outdoors. You could watch it for nothing, but it was threepence if you wanted to dance. And every time we went there, at some time during the evening, one of the band would put down his instrument, pick up a megaphone, hold it to his mouth and sing 'Lullaby of the Leaves'.[2]

The Captain frequently took his sons fishing across the water at Hythe, and though he was typically hostile about their efforts with the rod, Alfie still enjoyed the trips, riding on the tiny electric railway that ran down the long pier, at the end of which they fished. Visiting temporary funfairs were a part of growing up, too, though Bill Jaques remembers how The Captain would make advance preparations – 'Before leaving for the fair Big Alf would instruct Len and Alfie how to take a wooden ball and spin it into a bucket so that it wouldn't bounce out, so they would win the prize. He also had them practising darts so that they could accurately hit the chosen area of a playing-card. Then he took them to the fairs himself, to make sure they did it right, and if they didn't he would tell them off. They had to win. All through their lives they had to win to please their father.'

Such endeavours, allied to some entrepreneurial skills he had picked up, mostly from The Captain, formed the basis of Alfie's principal hobby in his formative years: trading. The currency was not contraband goods, however, nor anything in his father's line of business, but boys' stuff:

sportsmen's autographs, foreign coins, badges, marbles, bicycle accessories, empty bottles, football boots, cricket bats and the ubiquitous collectable item of the period, the cigarette card. Alfie was an astute and admired wheeler-dealer, holding court in the playground at Western District School, always trading 'up'. One memorable series of transactions involved the successive acquisition and disposal of a cigarette card, a matchbox-size model car, a wooden model yacht on wheels, a magic lantern and a cricket bat, the last of which he then took to a man running a used-goods shop in Canal Walk. Some of the profits were spent on a bag of chips for the walk home – once he had determined, by dint of painstaking observation, which of the local fish-fryers provided the biggest portion for a penny.

In a 1966 interview with John Ellison for the BBC radio programme *Turning Points* 'Benny' Hill recalled this period of his life:

What sort of a little boy would you say you were?

Lovely! [Laughs.] No, I was cocky, and full of guile, and full of confidence, and full of . . . everything. And [I had] what I haven't got now: a great business sense. I used to know the value of every foreign coin there was. Where other kids used to collect stamps I collected foreign coins, and they were really tradable. I'd have a couple of old French francs and swap them for an American half-dollar, saying [to the owner] 'These [French francs] are much nicer than that.' Then I'd be down the bank with it. I'd find a couple of fourteen-carat gold pen nibs and an old ring without the stone and I'd flog them. The second-hand shops in Southampton used to know me very well. I was always in there with cricket bats and little motor-cars and yachts and film projectors and lantern slides and things that you would swap. I was quite a trader.

A year after the family moved into Westrow Gardens, Helen Hill fell pregnant for a third and final time, and in January 1933, in the comparatively opulent surroundings of Ordnance Road Nursing Home, she produced a girl, Diana Helen. All three of Alf and Helen's babies had been born within nine calendar days – Diana came along four days after Alfie's ninth birthday and five days before Len's eleventh; all must have been conceived during or soon after the previous year's Easter holiday.

The arrival of a baby sister was a great thrill for Alfie, and indeed the whole family doted on her. Although he was always being ridiculed by

The Captain for having too many 'seven-day wonder' hobbies, Alfie's big-brotherly affection for Diana was to prove lifelong, even though his dethronement as the youngest child was something for which he may have been unprepared. In later life, when he was a star, he was to give Diana generous financial gifts; in 1933, when he was nine, he launched a baby-fund, placing a piggy-bank in the hall and tapping it in front of visitors to encourage donations. 'Alfie cared a lot for Diana,' declares Bill Jaques, 'and I honestly don't think he was threatened by her arrival because I don't think he felt loved very much himself. He didn't feel rejected because by this time he already was.'

As for The Captain, he too doted on his daughter. 'Oh yes, Big Alf idolized her,' Bill affirms. 'She grew up to have everything – horse-riding, ballet lessons, whatever – the kind of affection that Len and Alfie never had. He lavished on Diana everything he hadn't spent on his sons . . . or his wife.'

Goodwill towards his baby sister was one thing; being turfed out of his own domain, his bedroom, was quite another. To create space for the new arrival Alfie was made to share a room – a bed, too, for a time – with his brother. Though the boys had enjoyed many a common experience together in their first decade, the *entente* had rarely been *cordiale* and primary jealousies were never eradicated. Bringing the two boys together at this time was asking for trouble – both were grappling with the concept of a new and needy sibling in the house, and the first pangs of adolescence were beginning to affect Len. Their cousin Chris, now deceased, used to talk about how, when he visited Westrow Gardens for a holiday, he'd have to sleep in between the two warring boys, and would awake to find them raining punches on one another across him.

Len was also mindful of the ease with which Alfie was passing through his years at Western District. Both boys were intelligent but Len had to knuckle down to achieve good results – which he did, gaining a scholarship to a local grammar school, Taunton's, in the summer of 1933. But Alfie was coming up fast on the rails. At this time in Britain, as it was for decades to come, the crucial test of a child's scholarly ability was the Eleven-Plus examination. The result would dictate whether the child would progress to a 'grammar school', which comprised only these successful children and was therefore more academically inclined, or to a 'secondary modern', where an inferior education would be offered. The standard practice at Western was for children to take the Eleven-Plus twice, first at ten, as a dry run for the following year; if any child passed the exam at ten, however, they could proceed without waiting another twelve months.

Preserved to this day in Southampton Archives is a heavy, olive-green ledger first used more than 100 years ago: the Western District School 'Honours Book'. In keeping with its instigator's insistence that 'the entries made in the book should be written in Indian Ink in clear bold handwriting', the 1934 section lists 'A. H. Hill' as a graduate, bound – like his brother before him – for Taunton's. At the age of ten Alfie had sailed through the Eleven-Plus, gaining a year on Len.

It would mean being a year younger than his classmates at the big new school. A terrifying thought, but a thrilling triumph too. He raced home to Westrow Gardens with the good news, but was crushed to find his mother out, pushing Diana in the pram. Without a house-key, Alfie sat down on the step and wept as his great grand moment ebbed away.

3. 'That's for me!'

Ten years of age, bright enough to be elevated to senior school twelve months early, Alfie Hill arrived at Taunton's with every prospect of leaving there, some seven years hence, bound for university or a profession. Instead, he sank, suffering the ignominy of being held back a year owing to poor results; he quit, certainly not empty-headed but emphatically empty-handed, ahead of his crucial fifth-year School Certificate examinations.

Such was Alfie Hill's failure to stamp his presence here that the 1968 book *A History of Taunton's School 1760–1967* does not mention him in its 484 pages. He brought the proud educational establishment no honour, at least not in a way it saw fit to recognize. Even his success as an entertainer – well set by 1968 – was sufficiently beneath the school's somewhat sniffy line of sight to merit a passing mention. Taunton's boys were not educated to become saucy comedians.

If Alfie Hill's first ten years were essentially happy ones, his next decade was marked by upheaval and the onset of adolescent difficulties from which he was never fully to recover.

In September 1934, Alfie Hill was one of scores of new boys filing in to the imposing Taunton's edifice in the Highfield area of Southampton. It was, according to the school prospectus, 'One of the healthiest districts in the borough, and faces one of the most picturesque portions of Southampton's famous Common. The beauty of the approach and surroundings gives to the School an environment which is certain to exert a most beneficial influence on a boy's character during his most impressionable years.' Clearly, this was a school that took itself a mite seriously.

Whether top or bottom of the class, boys were referred to only by their surnames; in print, by initials and surnames. Taunton's lofty aims – to secure 'sound moral, mental, and physical development, thus ensuring the best preparation for after school days' – made zero impact on A. H. Hill.

Dressed in school colours – blue, white and black – short trousers, grey socks, black shoes, tie and compulsory cap, and with a satchel slung over his shoulder, Alfie would walk each morning to Taunton's, sent on his way with a kiss from his mother. He grumbled that the school set too much homework, which he resisted all he could. He strongly disliked the sciences and mathematics, and though he was to build a sound career on comedy writing, his inability to master the techniques of English grammar held him back in examinations. On the credit side, Alfie showed a high degree of promise in art – especially in drawing, painting and sculpture – and he exhibited a skill in speaking foreign dialects, notably the obligatory French.

The clear, stated aim of Taunton's was to prepare students for university education. (The school motto was *respice finem* – 'keep your goal always in mind'.) Membership of the Debating Society was strongly encouraged, even junior boys ardently discussing such motions as 'That the Progress of Science is Detrimental to Civilization', 'That the Englishman is Conceited', 'That Cyclists Should be Taxed' and, in the wake of cricket's 'bodyline' bowling scandal, 'That Test Matches Should be Abolished'. *Taunton's School Journal* was hyper-critical of the quality of such debates. Alfie did not participate.

The school held mock elections simultaneous with real General Elections. There was the Musical Society, the Natural History Society and the annual Speech Night at Central Hall, Southampton; there were New Forest camps and school holidays; and the Chess Club ambitiously mounted a 'Living Chess Match'. Boys, clad as playing pieces in white and black outfits, stood on a huge chequered cloth. But instead of taking advantage of these opportunities, Alfie Hill saw to it that he slipped through the net, filling his leisure time with matters of more personal import.

Taunton's also held great store by sport, especially cross-country running, cricket, hockey and 'soccer', and participation here was unavoidable. But Alfie's antics as a football goalkeeper were purposely comedic, and while one of the period's most exciting school days came in 1936, when a film was shown in the hall of Taunton's old boy Donald Finlay claiming a silver medal for Great Britain in the 110 metres hurdles at the Berlin Olympics, Alfie himself was no runner or jumper. The first mention of A. H. Hill in the *School Journal*, already some three years after his arrival at Taunton's, was in the 1937 sports day results, where he was listed as a competitor in the 100 Yards (Juniors) sprint. He did not trouble the medallists; his red and black sash probably cut more of a dash than his physical effort. He also showed as a participant in the four-boy relay race, but glory, alas, was not theirs either. L. E. Hill – Leonard – did manage to win the Half-Mile (Colts) though, probably one of the few occasions when the boy could boast a personal success to please his father.

Remarkably, A. H. Hill also does not show in any of the *Journal* articles about Taunton's copious stage productions, neither as performer nor backstage crew. Had he stayed on into the Sixth Form then it is conceivable that he might have featured, but the opportunity to participate at a younger age was there for the taking and Alfie spurned it, time after time after time. Only once did he dare to take part, being cast as Guinea Pig in *Alice in Wonderland*. He appeared in the trial scene, without a costume but holding a card signifying his role, and his sole contribution was to waggle his ears and declare ''Ere, 'Ere.' But Alfie fluffed the part. A fit of shyness overwhelmed him – the prospect of looking out over the footlights into the audience was simply too terrifying for the boy whose self-confidence had somehow haemorrhaged. It was a problem he never fully overcame.

It may even have been with Alfie in mind that a *Journal* correspondent later wrote, 'Nothing spoils the general effect of a production more than poor work in the minor parts.' As a stern taskmaster to the support actors and dancers in his later TV shows, Alfie surely would have echoed this sentiment with a resounding ''Ere, 'Ere.'

Alfie had few friends. Kenneth Ball, who was in the same form for four years and often walked to school with him, recalls, 'He didn't associate with anyone in particular and I don't remember him having any close friends. It's not that he was a loner, he just never did anything of note one way or the other. Sometimes he might sidle up to you and tell you something he had come across or knew to be funny, just in the way that he did on television in later years, and occasionally we'd talk about girls, but I never knew him to chase after one. And he certainly wasn't a comedian. People laughed neither with him nor at him – he was just very ordinary.'

One of the few good memories of Taunton's that Alfie carried into adult life was of Dr Horace King, head of the English department. King was inspirational, that rarity among teachers – one who makes a genuine connection with his pupils. Throughout his five years at Taunton's, Alfie felt misunderstood by the masters, who breezed the corridors with their black gowns billowing out back, donned mortar-boards for assembly and strictly maintained the boys' place, demanding respect whether or not they had earned it. Their adherence to the curriculum was bound to leave behind the boy whose talents were not scholastic but leaping off in a different direction. King alone showed Alfie a more human side and was wont to be amusing among the pupils, reaching out to establish a mutual respect. Alfie even felt confident enough to 'cheek' the good doctor, and the master, to his credit, did not reach for the cane but encouraged him all he could. Kenneth Ball believes that King may have had quite an influence over the future comedy star. 'Dr King was always sympathetic and helpful,' he says. 'He would do anything to encourage people to write. I can well imagine how this would have helped Alfie.'

Alfie was in fact becoming cheekier by the day. 'I was a king-size show-off,' he later said of himself in this period, although his Taunton's masters, marking consistently under-achieving homework and tests, might well have wondered what he had to boast about. But the young boy had fallen under the spell of the radio – 'wireless' as it was then known – and was enamoured of everything he heard: the myriad types of programmes – serious music, light music, talks, religion, drama, children's stories, sport, comedy and more. He was fascinated even by programme titles and by the names of some of the broadcasters – people like the announcer D. W. Grinnell-Milne, *Children's Hour* author H. Mortimer Batten, the actor Moultrie Kelsall, the historical playwright L. du Garde Peach, and some of the names that T. Alvar Liddell read in the news, like the British naval commander Admiral Sir Reginald Ranfurly-Plunkett-Ernle-Erle-Drax. This miracle electronic box with its warm, glowing valves and resonating bass, parked in the corner of the lounge at 22 Westrow Gardens, opened up new horizons and influenced Alfie Hill's life beyond measure.

Apart from English-language foreign stations Radio Luxembourg and Radio Normandy, both receivable across the English Channel, domestic radio at this time was in the monopolistic hands of the British Broadcasting Corporation.[1] This was, then, resolutely 'a BBC world', wherein the King's English was enunciated with great precision and clarity; where broadcasters, though unseen by their audience, wore full evening dress; and where the sworn efforts of Sir John (later Lord) Reith, the stern Scots-born BBC director-general, fastidiously ensured politeness, decorum and the absence of any questionable material. Reith's BBC set out to 'educate and inform'; blessedly, it also deigned to entertain.

Alfie was a devoted listener from the moment he returned home from school each day, when Taunton's masters were requiring that homework be his priority. At this time of the afternoon there were children's programmes, principally *The Children's Hour*, which, though it rarely ran the full sixty minutes, was required listening for all young people. With the careful nurturing of trustworthy announcer/listener relationships it typified broadcasting of its era – the presenters called themselves 'Uncle' this or 'Auntie' that, and their weekly column in the BBC's listings magazine *Radio Times*, like the programmes themselves, actually opened with the cheery yet archaic 'Hullo'.

'Uncle Mac' – Derek McCulloch – was the quintessential *Children's Hour* presenter, coming across as a kindly old soul on whose knees children could be safely seated while being entertained with, perhaps, a *Toytown* story (the character Larry the Lamb – 'Baa, I'm only a little lamb, sir' – was much-loved) or an extract from *Winnie the Pooh* or a reading from Norman Hunter's story about a dotty inventor, *The Incredible Adventures of Professor Branestawm*. *Children's Hour* could also be educational, with piano pieces, talks about Scott of the Antarctic and visits to the Crystal Palace poultry show or Cruft's dog show. Alfie lapped it all up, his ear pressed close to the speaker, scrutinizing every syllable and embedding them in his psyche. Passive listening was not Alfie's style – he proverbially glued himself to the set.

He was hugely impressed, too, by *adventure*. The era of *Dick Barton* –

Special Agent, a serial that gripped boys all over the nation, was still some time away, but there was actor-writer Arnold Ridley's *The Ghost Train*,[2] and Edgar Wallace's detective thrillers, real edge-of-the-chair radio. Alfie was enthralled by the dash and dare, the triumph of good over adversity, and later set some of his TV comedy in this sphere. In 1953, just as his career as a TV comedian was beginning to take off, he took the starring role in a BBC radio adventure serial, *Danger is Our Business*, playing it straight but hamming it up in what his keen-eared experience told him were all the right places.

The 1930s was also the era of the dance-band, a craze originating in America but sweeping Britain. All over the country, men and women were doing the Charleston, the foxtrot and the tango, and bandleaders, the best ones leading resident light orchestras in the major London hotels and restaurants, were becoming superstars. The BBC would broadcast 'relays' featuring Ambrose from the Mayfair Hotel, Carroll Gibbons at the Savoy, Sydney Lipton at the Grosvenor House, Lew Stone at the Monseigneur restaurant, and, indeed, embraced the proletariat too, with broadcasts from the hundreds of *palais de danse* all over the country. Britain was simply dance-band crazy. Musicians Sid Phillips, Nat Gonella, Lou Preager and Harry Roy were heroes, and crooners like Sam Browne and, especially, Al Bowlly (of 'Goodnight Sweetheart' fame) were mobbed by adoring fans. Though too young to do any mobbing himself, Alfie Hill developed an interest bordering on the fanatical, scrupulously memorizing the names of the bandleaders, their leading musicians and their songs, even the obscure.

The BBC had its own resident bandleader, Henry Hall, a bespectacled hero who jauntily donned his double-breasted tuxedo and slipped a carnation through his button-hole before launching into his signature tune, 'Here's to the Next Time'. In 1934 the BBC gave Hall his own show, *Henry Hall's Guest Night*, and listeners hearing his hesitantly spoken introduction, 'This *is* Henry Hall speaking and tonight *is* my Guest Night', would be reassured that they were in for a cosy time. Alfie was hooked too, so when, in 1950, the BBC asked him to perform the comedy spot on *Henry Hall's Guest Night*, the boy was *made*.

Above all else, though, Alfie adored the Variety shows, within which, after sitting through the often eccentric array of miscellaneous acts, he could hear the comedians. The BBC had created a dedicated Variety department in 1933, headed by former *Radio Times* editor Eric Maschwitz. Married to actress Hermione Gingold, Maschwitz was a talented individual, composer of popular songs including 'These Foolish Things' and 'A Nightingale Sang in Berkeley Square', writer of the stage musical (and later film) *Goodnight Vienna,* and creator of *In Town Tonight,* the BBC's flagship pot-pourri of music and star interviews. He was soon at the helm of scores of tip-top radio entertainment shows with comedy to the fore.

Before Maschwitz's appointment, radio comedy was limited both in terms of scope and space in the Reithian schedule. Typical fare was the White Coons concert party, a perfectly acceptable name in 1930s Britain. Adapted from a seaside troupe, the White Coons comprised a succession of acts such as one might see in a Variety theatre or music-hall, usually headed by sisters Elsie and Doris Waters in their comedy *alter egos* Gert and Daisy, or by Tommy Handley or the monologist Stanley Holloway, followed down the bill by a soubrette, a soprano, another comedy double-act, a banjo player and pianists. This is a typical extract:

Daisy Do you like me new lino?
Gert Ooh, yerse!
Daisy Bert got it from one of them men who always have a bit over from a job.
Gert Pattern's a bit bright, ain't it?
Daisy Yerse. Still, it'll soon wash orf.

As radio comedy became Variety-accented so the young Alfie Hill, at home in semi-detached suburban Southampton, fell in love with a number of comic luminaries. Stainless Stephen was one. His name betrayed Sheffield roots, where stainless steel goods were made, and his style was 'punctuation comedy', as in 'This is Stainless Stephen comma comedian question-mark' and 'This is Stainless aimless brainless Stephen semi-colon broadcasting semi-conscious at the microphone semi-frantic.' Alfie adored such wordplay and added it to his burgeoning pantheon of impressions.

Another early hero was Gillie Potter, an erudite comic self-described as 'that sham Harrovian who bears upon his blazer the broad arrows of a blameful life'. Potter's comedy often involved the village of Hogsnorton, and he effected mock 'talks' about its goings-on, usually beginning with

'Good evening, England. This is Gillie Potter talking to you in English!' Much of 'Benny' Hill's TV comedy would be set in a fictitious town, Dimpton.

Catchphrases such as these were the essence of new radio comedy, just as they were on the Variety stage and in the music-halls, and most radio comics aimed to get one away which, with any luck, they would be able to employ for years, perhaps even for the rest of their careers. Most seem ridiculous taken out of context, especially several decades later, but that they played a major role in a comic's persona at this time is beyond doubt. Will Hay had his 'Good morning, boys', Harry Tate used to howl 'How's yer father!', Fred Kitchen yelled 'Meredith, we're in!', Sandy Powell ubiquitously harked 'Can you 'ear me, mother?', the Western Brothers' greeting was 'Good evening, cads!' and Alfie's all-time radio hero, the Liverpool-born Arthur Askey, had several catchphrases in his armoury: 'Hello playmates!', 'Ay-thang-yew' ('I thank you'), 'Doesn't it make you want to spit?' and 'Before your very eyes'.

All these, and more, were heard frequently within the walls at 22 Westrow Gardens, first, through the radio loudspeaker and then, *ad infinitum*, uttered by Alfie Hill, the teenage boy who didn't know how or when to stop and who seemed to be compensating for a severe loss of confidence with a non-stop barrage of vocal impressions and silly chit-chat, as if in very fear of silence. Quietened at school, Alfie had become noisy at home to a deafening degree; although walking upstairs on his hands was way beyond him, he was fast developing into the best Hill clown yet. Even The Captain found Alfie funny, although he would leave the room rather than let the boy see that he had cracked his defences.

Radio listening could be enhanced by a fertile imagination, of course, but apart from the occasional star photograph in *Radio Times* or by collecting *Radio Celebrities* cigarette cards there was little chance of Alfie getting to see the acts that were making such an impression on him. For physical comedy he therefore relied upon close observations of film stars, continuing his impersonations of Chaplin's lopsided shuffle, W. C. Fields' sly-mouthed Southern drawl and Oliver Hardy's delicate tie-twiddle and beseeching look to the camera. He added to this roster the gangster swagger of Jimmy Cagney, the suave urbanity of Claude Rains, the gruffness of cigar-chomping Canadian Ned Sparks, the jut-lipped expos-

tulations of cockney Gordon Harker, the country-yokel characterizations
of Claude Dampier, the chinless wonder enacted by Jack Hulbert, and the
Gallic crooning of Maurice Chevalier. In his 1966 BBC *Turning Points*
interview 'Benny' Hill recalled: 'My dad was always saying "If you could
remember your history lessons the way you remember who was in what
film . . ."'

To impersonate Mae West, merely affecting her vulgar innuendo was
not enough – Alfie had to don the garb, too, as he also did to affect a
startling impression of the British film and stage comedienne Cicely
Courtneidge. His cousin Bill Jaques recalls, 'As a child, Alfie was always
dressing-up. Cross-dressing, really – I'd go up to his room and he'd have
lipstick on, and his mother's clothes.'

Anything to get a laugh.

Puberty hit Alfie Hill at about twelve and as his voice dropped and
body developed, his confidence went out of the window. If he became
nervous or anxious he would chew at his fingernails. This was a trend that
his parents considered the thin end of the wedge; Helen daubed a bitter
solution on them to discourage the habit but Alfie bit them all the same.
He also began to blush at unexpected moments. And, more than anything,
Alfie was confused by the sudden onset of sexual maturity. Always a boy
for the girls, he felt certain of his desires but became tongue-tied at the
prospect of actually talking to any of them. Going to an all-boys school
did not help – he was unfamiliar with the maturing female, how they
thought, how they worked.

At this time, an incident occurred that would, over the coming decades,
be played out time and again in the life of Alfie Hill – he fell in love with
someone who had no interest in him, and he was too uncertain, too
inhibited, too terrified of rejection, to do anything concrete about it.

Twenty-three years later, the story was related by 'Benny' Hill in
conversation with BBC radio broadcaster Roy Plomley, when he was the
subject of *Desert Island Discs*:

Record number four? Oh. Oh dear. This is 'I Think of You with Every
Breath I Take' by Bing Crosby. There's quite a story to this one. This
is my very first romance, the biggest I think I've ever had. I don't think
I could ever love anybody the way I loved this girl.

I was twelve and she was fourteen and I went to an Eastleigh fairground during the September Carnival week, when I was staying with my uncle and aunt. And I saw this girl, this beautiful girl, in a green coat, with long brown hair, riding on a merry-go-round. I never spoke to her but I fell like mad for this girl.

I asked my cousin Chris all about her and he explained where she lived and everything, and said that every lunchtime she took her father's lunch into his shop in Market Street. And for the rest of the term, back at school, between September and Christmas, [I was] waiting for the Christmas holiday. I couldn't think of anything but this beautiful girl in a green coat.

So, comes the first day of the Christmas holiday, I said, 'Well mum, I think I'll go out for a walk today, a nice long walk to keep me fit. Can I have some sandwiches and that?' So mother packed me up some sandwiches and said, 'You'll be all right, wrap up warm!' I walked six miles into Eastleigh, stood at the end of Market Street until this beautiful girl came down the other end of the street, watched her go into the shop with her father's lunch, waited about three-quarters of an hour while he ate it and then watched her come out again with the empties and go home. I finished my sandwiches and thought my day was made.

I used to do this every day, day after day, right through the holidays, six miles there, six miles back, in rain, shine, hailstorms, snow, the lot.

You never spoke to her?

Never. Never, ever spoke to her. I wouldn't do that. At the end of the holiday I went back to school.

And this is your song?

This is our tune, yes.[3]

Oddly, this very practice – taking lunch to father in the shop – was one that Alfie himself had to do, on Saturdays during termtime, more frequently during school holidays and during his early adulthood when he was in town. Big Alf was loath to close Stanley's doors at lunchtime for fear of losing passing trade; also, eating out meant spending money. So Helen cooked him a hot lunch, served it on a plate, with a second plate covering, and the meal would be rushed down to Canal

Walk from Westrow Gardens, as fast as the carrier could manage the two-mile walk.

The sights that greeted Alfie at Stanley & Co. must have made quite an impression on the pubescent boy. Customers who dared enter the shop faced a glass-topped counter across its width, at which stood The Captain, wearing a brown overall on top of his suit. Behind the counter was his office, imbued with the stench of the fat cigars that the increasingly wealthy Jack Stanley smoked on his now infrequent visits. On the office wall was an eighteenth-century erotic print that had come into Alf's possession after he became accepted as a member of the local Freemasonry. A male-fantasy piece, it depicted a busty young chambermaid who had attempted to eavesdrop on a secret Masonic meeting taking place in the floor below. The rotten attic floorboards from where she was listening had given way and the wench was stuck fast, her top half in the attic, her lower regions protruding through the ceiling of the floor below, where the Masons were at liberty to have their way with the poor girl, or at least take a long, lingering, lustful look.

Upstairs from the office was the packing-room, frequently visited by Alfie. Stanley's mail-order business had itself gone through the ceiling; orders were pouring in from all over the world. Customers who visited the Canal Walk shop still talk about Big Alf's fascinating collection of foreign stamps, torn from envelopes sent from countries near and far, their enclosed cash and money-orders perpetually adding to Jack Stanley's wealth.

But condoms were not then packaged as they are today, ready-rolled, shrink-wrapped and tucked inside in a cardboard slipcase. In the 1930s, and later, Stanley & Co. took possession of boxes of loose latex sheaths direct from suppliers and had to check each and every one for holes. Standing solid and erect on an upstairs workbench was a giant wooden penis, and it was the job of a Stanley's packer to carefully roll each condom down over the cockstand. If no bubble came to the top – if the condom went flat – there was obviously a hole somewhere.

Condoms also came in different thicknesses and lengths – Stanley's customers would stipulate the size they wanted: large, small, medium, thick, thin – so the wooden penis had to be long enough and wide enough to test the different kinds. Could the sheer girth of such a phallus and its unyielding rigidity have panicked a sexually immature and insecure teenager into believing that he did not – could not possibly – 'measure up'?

Doris Lamb, a Stanley's packer in the late 1940s, remembers the routine well. 'After my three-month training period I could check 500 condoms a day,' she says. 'I wore rubber gloves, and if I found one with a hole I'd peel it off and throw it on one side. Mr Hill would count these rejects at the end of each day and send them back to the suppliers. The good ones I'd roll up again, very gently, so that they didn't crease, I'd flatten the tops over, sprinkle them with French chalk, and lay them in a box ready for sending out. I could fit one hundred condoms into the largest box, and all our mail-orders were sent wrapped in brown paper, destined for New Zealand, Australia, Canada, India and other places. Mr Hill used to take them down to the Post Office every day.'

Although it constituted the core business, Stanley's didn't only sell 'French letters', diaphragms and pessaries. In his office Big Alf personally fitted out customers with artificial limbs, hernia trusses and surgical corsets to overcome ruptures. For incontinence sufferers the shop sold tubes that ran down the leg into a container, the same appliance that fighter-aircraft pilots would use during the coming Second World War. Impotence 'cures' were also sold.

Like all other surgical-appliance shops of the period, Stanley & Co. also dabbled in dubious 'marriage-guidance' literature. Though light years away from the explicit books and periodicals available today on every High Street, these publications were the closest thing to soft-porn then being sold over the counter. Volumes like *The Mystery of Sex, What Every Wife Should Know* and, for any passing masochists or sadists, *Pleasures of the Torture-Chamber* were among the stock. One such book, *Life-Long Sex Harmony*, written by William Elliott and published in 1939, typifies the theories being spouted at this time by earnest (and often quasi-religious) quacks. The cover drawing depicts a man and woman, lithe and naked, ascending steps into a sun-filled Garden of Eden, and Elliott's text rhapsodizes so mellifluously about marital intercourse that all else is decried as harmful. Male teenage masturbation is 'almost indefensible ... with dangers of future misery such as impotence and sterility', and 'night-emissions' are 'an even more serious matter'. With such literature, in the absence of any other more obviously erotic material, being read for titillation by teenagers, it is a miracle that Britain did not breed generations of sexual misfits. (Or maybe it did.)

Alfie coped with all this in his usual manner – by twisting potential trauma into laughter. The stigma of being seen entering Stanley's emporium – or being recognized once inside – caused most personal customers to act in a decidedly furtive manner. The front door at 16 Canal Walk had a musical-chime bell and it was often ringing; if he was paying The Captain a visit, Alfie would quietly observe these customers, studying their mannerisms and the clandestine way in which they made their purchases. Back at Westrow Gardens he would enact his impressions to hilarious effect, wearing a long raincoat, pulling a hat down over his eyes, pussyfooting around the point about what he wanted to buy, finally mumbling his needs under his breath, glancing everywhere to avoid direct eye-contact, fumbling for the right change and then quickly shoving a brown-paper bag into his pocket. Still not much more than a child, Alfie Hill was learning about adult sexual embarrassment far earlier than most.

To some, Big Alf's association with Stanley & Co. was beyond the pale. His nephew Tony House remembers: 'Stanley's was looked down on by a lot of people because it sold condoms. A strict Methodist woman over the road in Westrow Gardens would have nothing to do with the Hills because "Mr Hill ran that sex shop."'

But while such opinions could be easily repelled by a family, it was not so easy for Alfie to avoid embarrassment individually, especially at school, where the verbal cruelty of children knows no restraint. From an early age he grew to recognize the signs – a gang of schoolkids would gather on one side of the playground and then the rhythmic sing-song taunting would begin:

'Al-fie's dad sells French-ies!'

Whatever it was that his father was selling, and perhaps in his earliest years he didn't yet understand, it was clearly worthy of others' disgust. In time, the boy developed a retort, usually, 'That's right, and he can do you some cheap!', but the fact that he was being singled out for an association with something soiled and grubby, of which he himself was innocent, must have left some sort of mark.

Meanwhile, life at home was becoming more interesting. Len had joined the Woodcraft Folk, similar in scope to the Boy Scouts but born of the burgeoning co-operative movement and founded on socialist ideals. Having quietly rebelled against his parents – his father especially – for many years, Len was becoming more brave, and he found sustenance in the company of these like-minded, independent youngsters, girls as well as boys. 'They were a nature-loving crowd,' recalls Tony House, 'dressed all in green. Len soon became very left-wing with his views, and got involved in the communist movement.' Though a Labour voter, Big Alf was damning about his eldest son's choice of friends, but wise enough to refrain from denying his involvement. Alfie, meanwhile, disinterested in politics but desperate to socialize with girls, begged his brother to let him join the crowd. Len adamantly refused. Having found something of his own, a means of having fun beyond what he saw as the narrow confines of the Hill family, he was not about to let his brother in on the act.

Alfie became a choirboy instead. Though nominally Church of England, the Hills were not in the least religious, and Alfie had been in a church only once before, when he was christened. Typically, though, the wheeler-dealer was not interested in singing hymns – he had discovered that the Reverend Brummitt at St Mark's C. of E., adjacent to The Dell football ground, paid choirboys sixpence to sing on Sundays, and Alfie was keen on the money. He also relished the prospect of an imminent choirboys' outing to the Isle of Wight. Helen was made to buy him a surplice but, having been on the trip, Alfie immediately resigned his position. It wasn't even a good day out – he threw up on both the outward and return ferry journeys.

Though The Captain was deeply suspicious of organized religion, and espoused no particular belief, he was forthright in his respect for Jewish people, whom he saw as survivors, and usually winners. Bill Jaques recalls, 'Big Alf was always going on about how Jewish people were rich, and that it was good to get in with them. He admired Jews greatly, always wanted to be Jewish, claimed to speak Yiddish, and said he knew a lot of Jewish people – a butcher, for example, who could get kosher meat for them at a reduced price.' Violet Stevens confirms this – 'My brother and Helen had many Jewish friends, in fact their best friends were Jews.' Ever a keen card player, Big Alf loved Jewish card-games, *clubyos* and *kalooki* in particular, and Alfie learned to play them too. Across Westrow Gardens, the Hills were especially close to Mimi and Philip Levy. Mimi would regularly send across a plate of homemade delicacies, which all five Hills would grab at, Big Alf sputtering through sticky lips, 'Only the Jews make food as good as this!' Ever on the lookout for a bargain, he used Jewish friends and Masonic contacts to negotiate discounts for everything the Hills needed, including school clothing, rarely paying more than the wholesale price. 'Make friends with Jewish people,' The Captain instructed his children, 'and you won't go wrong.'

Through the 1920s and 30s, Henry Hawthorn Hill, Alfie's beloved 'GP', had been a benevolent figure to his many grandchildren, giving them free dental treatment from his surgery on St Mary Street and taking them on local outings. His love of the circus and comedians had never wavered, and he stayed in close touch with show folk, maintaining many friendships with clowns, acrobats and comedians in particular. Cultivated in the 1870s, Henry's connections with Fossett's circus remained strong, and through Bob Fossett he had been introduced to another great Big Top promoter, Bertram Mills. GP derived great pleasure from taking his grandchildren to the circus whenever it came to Southampton, gaining credibility in their young eyes by personally introducing them to its leading participants. Conveniently, the Big Top would be set up in Archers Road, just around the corner from Westrow Gardens.

As an evening sideline to dentistry, Henry had latterly taken up free-lance writing, penning an occasional 'Southampton Notes' column for *The World's Fair*, the weekly journal for circus, carnival and funfair folk, market traders, magicians and Variety performers. Henry wrote under the byline 'Aitch Aitch', and the family would all benefit from the free 'press' tickets.

Last week for four days we had the great Mills Circus . . . Mr Bertram Mills having kindly sent me some tickets for self and party, you may be sure I was there, had a splendid seat, and saw a lovely show. I was greatly interested in Miss Priscilla Kayes [who] as becomes the daughter of the redoubtable 'Buff Bill' gave a most fearless and pleasing show.

The lions were splendid specimens. I had the pleasure of being introduced to Miss Kayes. I was enabled to amuse her by telling her of incidents that happened before her time, for instance about her dad having the shop in Briggate and the defence he put up when they tried to evict him.[4]

Though it boasted far fewer entertainment venues than London and the major English cities, Southampton was nonetheless sufficiently thriving in this respect to have merited the publication of *What's On in Southampton*, published every Friday from 1909 to 1934, price one penny. In addition to listings for the town's myriad cinemas, its pages featured showbill advertisements for the Empire Theatre (the last-built of the great Moss group of theatres), the Grand, the Palace and the Hippodrome. The Palace featured films as well as Variety stage-shows fronted by top London comics such as Jimmy Jewel; the Hippodrome (situated, fantastically, on Ogle Road) was the real McCoy for Variety, featuring touring radio comics like Stanelli in his *Stag Party*, and regularly staging a 'gigantic spectacular revue' such as *The Spice of Paris*, which promised '34 stupendous scenes, 100 people, 1,000 costumes, with comedy sensation Angus Watson'. Way down the bill would be acts like the Original Can-Can Girls and the not-yet-famous striptease act Phyllis Dixey.

Variety had grown directly out of music-hall, which itself emerged out of the tavern tap-rooms, sing-song saloons, supper-rooms and 'free and easies' that proliferated in Britain in the early nineteenth century. The twin British male passions of drinking and singing led to riotous evenings in such venues, where men could eat, drink and listen to songs of breathtaking obscenity, delivered by performers both professional and amateur. The singers and comedians would be introduced on stage by a chairman who would just about manage to maintain order by banging a gavel. In such a heady atmosphere, the saloons fast spiralled out of control – by the early 1840s some could accommodate as many as 800 rowdy drinkers and the song material was excessively ribald. Women were banned from such places or, at most, allowed to stand at the back, watching the proceedings through a grille.

The music-hall gained prominence with the passing of the Theatres Registry Act in 1843, when the Lord Chamberlain informed saloon proprietors that they had the choice of turning their venues into legitimate theatres with dramatic entertainments, but without being able to sell drinks in the auditorium, or music-halls with a drinking licence. One enterprising theatre manager, Charles Morton ('the father of the halls'), used this change in the law to popularize the music-hall, opening it up to women and staging more reputable acts. Such music-halls quickly opened up around Britain, becoming hugely popular with the middle and lower classes. Thousands of entertainers packed bills up and down the country, the best known being George Robey, a comedian who specialized in a sophisticated form of vulgarity; the one-time child star turned caricature comedian Dan Leno; and the sensational Marie Lloyd, a vulgar genius of the stage whose Cockney humour and suggestive songs endeared her to millions, especially Londoners, to whom she was known as 'Our Marie'.

'Variety', a name used to describe an entertainment selection as early as 1841, then took over as music-hall declined, when such fare began to move into more conventional auditoria, either existing or newly built theatres with tiered seating. A new style, revue, arrived in Britain from Paris, accenting the disconnected structure of Variety so that each and every show comprised not one or two acts but perhaps a dozen, with comedians, singers and dancers drawing the crowds and an extraordinary array of 'speciality' acts padding out the bill. Many of these revealed a clear line back to the circus – acrobats, illusionists, feats of physical endurance, performing animals and so on. Unrelated to the circus, nudity was also becoming increasingly commonplace in Variety, although with one strict and ludicrous proviso enforced by law – that the woman must remain motionless.

The comedians usually fell into two camps – the standup and the sketch comic. The latter usually worked with what was known as a 'feed' or 'foil' or 'straightman', who allowed the main comic to have all the funny lines. Sometimes he starred within an ensemble. More often than not the material was that classic British fudge – 'good honest vulgarity', jokes about escaping wind and 'nudge-nudge' hints and glances about the sexual act.

In America a similar revolution was taking place. Men-only gambling dens and honky-tonks in frontierland before the Civil War led to the founding of vaudeville. Twentieth-century comedians such as W. C. Fields and the Marx Brothers began in vaudeville, while an English music-hall impresario, Fred Karno, took a troupe of British performers across to America to perform in vaudeville theatres in 1913, two of whom – Charlie Chaplin and Stan Laurel – went on to enormous success in the rapidly developing film industry. The more ribald element of American entertainment then found a natural home in burlesque, where standup comedians – Phil Silvers, to name but one – would hone their skills playing to audiences who really had not come to see them at all, but were waiting, usually impatiently, to see the next striptease act. The best-known British example of an American burlesque house with home-grown Variety overtones (or maybe undertones) was the tiny Windmill Theatre in Soho, London, which combined comedy and motionless nudes and staged some 60,000 performances from 1932 until its closure in 1964, most of them tortuously titled *Revudeville*.

One night in 1936, when Alfie Hill was twelve, GP took him, and Len, to Southampton's Hippodrome for the first time. The star attraction was Horace Goldin, 'The Royal Illusionist And Master Of Magic', whose 'Lady Sawn In Half' act was so convincing that audiences would gasp at the crucial moments. As well as Goldin there were the usual array of acts completing the bill. Alfie was enraptured by what he saw, and paid many return visits to 'the Hip' as well as venturing into the Palace Theatre. He was fascinated not only by the shows themselves but by the posters outside, where the name of the bill-topping performer would be ranged in large black type across the top, with lower-order acts appearing from left to right down the poster, with the bottom-of-the-bill performers in small typesize, but still in elongated upper-case, just above the printer's name. Most of the acts – and certainly all of the comedians – also had what was known as 'bill matter' under their name, either their catchphrase or an upbeat, abbreviated description of their act.

Alfie especially loved the Variety comics. Sam Mayo (bill matter: 'The Immobile One') made a strong early impression. A droll, lugubrious comic, he worked on stage in a yellow wig and tatty brown dressing-robe, standing stock still at the piano while singing archaic songs. Others who entertained in front of the impressionable Alfie at this time included Scott Sanders ('The Old Philosopher') and the act Noni & Horace ('Musical Absurdity'). The multi-lingual and musical Noni, a bald-wigged clown in extended shoes, had tearfully told the audience at the 1928 Royal Variety Show, 'No one ever sends me flowers.' Queen Mary was said to be so moved that she sent backstage a stem from her bouquet. Henceforth, Noni's bill matter would also state, space permitting, 'The Clown To Whom The Queen Gave A Flower'.

And not only were the comics funny, they were often aided in their sketches by glamorous girls – busty French maids in low-cut short dresses, who would bend over to flick a feather-duster, raising their rear-ends to the audience to reveal a generous glimpse of stocking-top, suspenders and frilly underwear. For the sexually precocious Alfie, riddled with paranoia and insecurity around women, this was nirvana.

Nearly sixty years later, still with a gleam in his eye, he remembered these early visits to Southampton's Variety shows in a BBC TV *Omnibus* tribute, *Clown Imperial*:

> My grandfather, my father's father, loved the music-hall, loved the theatre, and, if we were very good children, about once a month he would take us to the Palace Theatre. There'd be the principal comedian, who was always billed as the 'star comedian'. He never was a star but he had top billing. It was–

FRED FOSDYKE

in

Don't Be Cheeky!

with

....

and there was always a troupe of girls, anything between about six and sixteen [in number]. There was a straightman who usually doubled baritone. There was a soubrette who played the French maid. And there was an older comedienne, and so on.

> But the comedian used to come on and get more applause than anybody else. He was always surrounded by pretty dancing ladies and the audience loved him. The fat women in the audience would go [affecting sound of belly-laughter] 'Ooh, what he said! Ooh, isn't it awful!' and applaud.

> And I thought, 'Hey, he must get more money than anybody else

because he's got top billing. He's surrounded by beautiful girls. Every-body loves him. *That's for me!'*

Until now, Alfie had never expressed any desire to follow a particular career. But the combination of his adolescent uncertainty with the female sex, and his envy at watching, not only comedians, but comedians sur-rounded by nubile semi-clad women, struck a powerful chord. He had always been able to make people laugh, and his ability to entertain friends and family was unquestioned. If he could do so while working with beautiful girls, being able to glimpse them backstage in the dressing-rooms as well as on stage, he would be in heaven. It would, in essence, provide him with a risk-free intimacy.

From this point, Alfie Hill had but a single goal in mind – to become a professional comedian. How, he knew not. When, he knew not. But something would work out. In the meantime, he ate and drank comedy with a single-minded determination to find out 'how it worked', studying gramophone records and the wireless and getting along to Southampton's Variety theatres as frequently as possible, seeing such shows as *Cheeky Days, Don't be Saucy!, Naughty but Nice, Toujours les Femmes, The Naughty Girls of 1937* and *Ooh La La, l'Amour!*

In particular, Alfie studied Max Miller ('The Cheekie Chappie'), probably the greatest British standup comedian of all time. The consum-mate 'patter' or 'front-cloth' comic, Maxie was the king of Variety, possessed of a sublime sense of timing and a remarkable ability to mix in heaps of sexual innuendo without actually saying anything offensive – a crucial ability at this deeply conservative time. Miller's trademark was the tailed-off punchline, where he would leave the last word or two unspoken, or perhaps end only with an ''ere!' as he cascaded into the next joke. This would allow the audience to work out where the joke was heading and laugh just as if he had completed it. Then he'd reproach them for their filthy minds:

'Ooh, you *wicked* lot! You're the kind of people who get me a bad name!'

Audiences adored Max with a passion, recognizing his uniqueness. 'Miller's the name, lady,' he'd exclaim to a woman in the audience, 'and there'll never be another!' Dressed with great flamboyance in a white trilby hat, white shoes, white kipper-tie and garish silk plus-fours, he commanded rapt attention and repaid it many times over with an uproarious stage act, usually drawn from his fabled 'Blue Book'. Moments after walking on stage Miller would flash two books to the audience, one white and the other blue, and ask them which they would rather he used. Predictably enough, the answer would be 'blue', but the responsibility for the decision was the audience's, not Miller's, thereby 'exonerating' him from what would follow.

> I like the girls who do,
> I like the girls who don't,
> I hate the girl who says she will,
> And then she says she won't.
> But the girl I like the best of all,
> And I think you'll say I'm right,
> Is the girl who says she never does,
> But she looks as though she m . . .'ere!

Showing the same tenacity with which he had pursued his Eastleigh belle, Alfie now turned his attention stagewards. Instantly, his schooling was doomed. 'If he'd had the will to do schoolwork then he'd have achieved good results,' considers his cousin Tony House. 'He had a good brain, whereas Len had to burn the midnight oil, swotting hard. Len got there in the end, passing all his exams, but it was a slog. Alfie could have done it easily if he'd have put his mind to it. But he just gave up.'

So recklessly did he abandon his education, indeed, that Taunton's headmaster F. J. Hemmings took the drastic step, used only on rare occasions, of holding the pupil back a year in the hope that he would make up lost ground. Alfie was in the 'fourth form' for two years, 1937–8 and again in 1938–9, although because he had commenced his secondary schooling a year early, at ten instead of eleven, no real difference was made to his leaving age. But Alfie must have been distressed at the prospect of wasting another unproductive year in class when he wanted to be out there 'treading the boards'.

This wanton rejection of his schooling brought Alfie into direct conflict with his father, who, in the time-honoured tradition, carried the 'don't do as I did, do as I say' argument. But it was no use. Just as grandfather Henry Hawthorn Hill had determinedly pursued his unconventional goals as a young man, and just as his son Alfred Hawthorn Hill had left to join the circus at the age of ten, so now the younger Alfred Hawthorn Hill was set on pursuing his goal. He was as hell-bent on rebellion as they had been, and took no more advice and heeded no more warnings than they had done, in earlier decades.

4. Milk-O!

Alfie Hill's first problem as a fledgling comedian was that he didn't have any material. He already recognized the paucity of some other comics' acts, on the bills at the Palace and the Hippodrome, watching them sweat to win over the audiences with scarcely a good joke or an idea of wit in their head.

Like all fledgling funny-men, Alfie's earliest performances relied totally on other people's material, gleaned mostly from radio: a soupçon of Ted Ray, a dash of Max Miller, a sprinkling of Jimmy Jewel. His mother bought him a bowler-hat – a comedy prop since the days of Robey, Laurel and Hardy – and after daubing makeup on his face, the teenager would perform to himself in front of the mirror, adopting the persona of a variety of characters and affecting a steadily increasing range of voices.

The boy was getting along to the Palace at every opportunity now; waiting for GP to provide a free ticket once a month was no longer enough, so he used The Captain's technique of pressing a coin or two into an expectant palm – in this case, the tunicked commissionaire's – in the hope of gaining illegal admission. A friend from Taunton's, Tex Southgate, would sometimes accompany Alfie; on one occasion, after Alfie had quietly pushed a few coins into the usher's closed hand, the two boys sprinted up the stairs towards the circle when a stern voice called after them, 'What? Two of you for thruppence?'

Throughout this period, although firmly backing a loser for once, Big Alf maintained his strict disapproval of his youngest son's ambitions. He warned Alfie that show-business was not all splendour, as he himself knew well from his carefree circus youth. 'Big Alf had a passion for security which became an obsession and was reflected in his attitude towards spending money,' considers Alfie's cousin Hugh Stevens. 'He didn't like Alfie's theatrical aspirations because they were too insecure.' Believing that the boy was dazzled by the prospect of seeing his name in lights, but blinded to the harsher realities of the profession, Alf persuaded his own father to make clear the pitfalls. Henry also knew all too well the grime behind the glamour.

A contact was made with a friendly Variety juggler visiting South-ampton and Alfie was escorted backstage by his father and grandfather to see the cold dressing-room, with its cracked vanity mirror, inadequate lighting and dirty sink. But the adults' efforts were in vain. As they passed down a backstage corridor Alfie glimpsed a group of half-dressed showgirls. From that moment on, he was impervious to any counter-arguments.

But if Alfie was going to become a performer he needed practice. One of his earliest comedy spots was with his brother, entertaining Woodcraft Folk around a campfire. For this occasion, Len invited Alfie to form a temporary double-act, and they worked up a sketch satirizing the differ-ences between BBC radio, known to all, and the less-received Radio Luxembourg. The brothers' act went well, up to the climax in which Len was meant to thwack his younger brother over the head with a gong. In his determination to get it right, Len used too much force and Alfie was sent staggering, just maintaining consciousness, effecting a jelly-legged totter reminiscent of Stan Laurel. Assuming it was part of the act, the Woodcraft audience laughed hard; Alfie milked the applause dry.

Alfie's desire to stake his independence – especially from The Captain – can be gauged from his reaction when his Auntie Louie's two eldest sons, Don and Fran, cycled all the way to Westrow Gardens from their home in Bexleyheath, Kent, a distance of one hundred miles. Alfie, aged fourteen, expressed his intent to do the same in the other direction, visiting his favourite aunt without spending money on public transport. This meant upgrading his childhood bicycle into a full-size model. To achieve this he effected a particularly successful series of trades that earned him several pounds, and by dodging and saving in equal measure was able to scrape together the full £13 required for a deluxe Raleigh racer. Admiring his son's determination, and perhaps keen to build bridges with him, Big Alf offered to loan Alfie some of the money if he was prepared to find the rest, but Alfie wanted to own the bike outright from the outset

– in particular, he didn't want his father, in a position of part-ownership, to begin lecturing and hectoring over its use.

'It took about seven hours for my brothers Don and Fran to make the journey,' remembers Bill Jaques. 'Alfie left at five o'clock in the morning but had failed to arrive by afternoon tea-time. My mother was becoming worried and sent a telegram down to Southampton saying "Where is he?" He finally arrived at eleven that night, with everyone worried out of their wits that he'd had an accident or been abducted. When asked where he had been all this time he said that he'd had his lunch on the way and fallen asleep at the verge-side.' (Another, probably more fanciful, ending of this story has Alfie claiming that he took shelter from rain 'under some woman's umbrella'. It was, at least, a logical extension of his mother's suggestion to the infant Alfie that seeking shelter in private doorways was perfectly proper.) The journey over, Alfie had a delightful time with the Jaques family, ecstatic in the company of his beloved Auntie Louie most of all. Citing this very trip, one of his eight chosen records on *Desert Island Discs* in 1959 was 'Would You', by Frank Chacksfield and his Orchestra, because 'Auntie Louie would be in the kitchen singing her head off, and this is usually what she sang.'

Having been held back a year, Alfie was finally set to enter the fifth-form at school, at the end of which he would take the decisive School Certificate exams and then leave. But at this very time, on September 3 1939, Britain declared war on Germany. In anticipation, a mass child-evacuation programme began in the preceding days: tens of thousands living in areas of potential danger were swept from their families to be deposited in safer havens, away from where the Luftwaffe would be dropping its bombs. Taunton's had already made plans to evacuate *en masse* thirty miles along the south coast to Bournemouth. Because it had no harbour or shipping, bombing here was distinctly unlikely. Southampton, however, was an obvious target.

While Len was considered old enough to stay in Southampton, plans also had to be made for Diana's evacuation – she was now six and a pupil at St Mark's primary school. Alf and Helen's solution was that she must accompany Alfie and the other Taunton's pupils to Bournemouth. Hoping for 'action' in his new environment, away from his parents and big brother, the teenager was dismayed at the prospect of having his kid sister tugging at his waist every evening.

Taunton's evacuation files are still in Southampton Archives. Early morning on September 2, staff, children and assorted helpers assembled at the school and walked in formation down to Central Station. The Hill siblings were in Party C, comprising three Taunton's masters, the chemistry master's wife, three mothers and forty-three children, of whom four were infants and thirty-nine were fifteen-year-old boys. The children walked two abreast in full uniform – blazers, ties and caps – some in short trousers, others in long, each with a satchel containing the accoutrements of wartime evacuation, as stated in a list sent to all parents: gas mask, identity card, ration book, food for the day, change of underclothing, night clothes, handkerchiefs, spare stockings or socks, house shoes or plimsolls, warm coat or mackintosh, toothbrush, comb and towel. Alfie and Diana were waved goodbye at Central Station, his parents' anxious entreaty – 'You will look after her, won't you!' – ringing in Alfie's ears as the train chuffed out.

The billeting of all these Southampton children in Bournemouth was a chaotic affair, undertaken in a series of heavy showers, with many boys sleeping at desks, awaiting their instructions. Alfie and Diana were taken to lodge with an elderly working-class couple whose 'parenting' of the Hill children was much more restrictive than even Alf and Helen's. Alfie's hopes of being footloose and fancy-free nosedived still further.

As he later recounted, the so-called 'Taunton's School at Bournemouth School' was a tiresome bore for Alfie, who had already made up his mind to leave at the earliest opportunity, perhaps even before taking the vital exams. He did scant work here, but had at least a little fun. Tex Southgate taught him how to play guitar, and Alfie, Tex and another boy performed at one of several entertainments designed to galvanize the children's spirits, many of the young being profoundly disturbed at having left the bosom of their family. The trio called themselves the Hills Brothers, not because Alfie was the leader but because they parodied the Mills Brothers, the popular black American crooners whose songs, along with those of the Inkspots, they performed. At other school events, Alfie tried out his standup comedy routine but 'died' every time, his nerve failing him when he stepped in front of an audience.

Many of these Taunton's entertainments owed to the man-management qualities of Alfie's favourite schoolmaster, Dr Horace King. Alfie and King had definitely connected, and Alfie was delighted to follow his former master's successful post-Taunton's career in later years – after leaving in 1947 to become headmaster at a London secondary school King entered politics, representing two Southampton constituencies as a Labour MP before becoming Speaker of the House of Commons in 1965 and, as life peer Lord Maybray-King in 1971, Speaker of the House of Lords. King alone – more so, certainly, than Alfie's father – encouraged the young boy to pursue his goal; in return, when, as Benny Hill, the former boy had well and truly 'made it', he was delighted to compère an evening honouring Dr King's political successes.

In this first year of the war, Horace King's principal morale-raising effort was a staging of *A Midsummer Night's Dream*, performed in a Bournemouth hall in May 1940. Some part or other, possibly a major one, could have been Alfie's for the asking . . . but Alfie was no longer around to ask. He had quit. He turned sixteen at the beginning of 1940, and with the expected German bombing of Southampton – indeed, all of England – not forthcoming, he had returned, with Diana, to Westrow Gardens. Alfie's school days were over, and for his five years at grammar school he had – on paper at least – nothing to show. The 'qualifications' section of any future job application form would have to be left blank.

Predictably, The Captain was furious – unlike his own father, he had provided the means for his son to gain a steady education from which to profit for the rest of his life. And now the boy was throwing it all away . . . and for what? Alfie's decision caused problems in the family for a while. 'There was a big argument about it,' recalls Alfie's cousin Tilly Underwood. 'GP and Uncle Alf had a "set-to". Uncle Alf liked to be the boss, whereas GP wasn't the bossy sort. Alf liked to tell people what to do.'

Says Tony House, 'Uncle Alf really wanted Alfie to stay on and get his university matriculation, and go down that route. But Alfie felt that he didn't need it: he was going to make it on his own. And so he did, but for a long time he was out of favour with his father. It was only when he became successful that Uncle Alf let the relationship improve, when his "fatherly pride" kicked in.'

In Britain, this initial period of the Second World War had become known as the 'phoney war'. The country was committed to armed combat with Germany and yet the first months after September 1939 were virtually without incident, save for the imposition of rationing, and the nightly 'blackout' designed to deprive the expected German bombers of navigational aid. Like so many others, Big Alf had feared an air attack on the first day; in London and other parts of the south-east, the warning sirens were indeed sounded, by accident, within minutes of Prime Minister Neville Chamberlain's radio address to the nation, announcing that the country was at war; millions spent the first hours of the war underground while, above them, the blue skies were untroubled. From bitter experience, though, Big Alf sensed that this was the calm before the storm. He'd fought in the First World War and knew how events would deteriorate far beyond minor inconveniences – especially now that wars were fought in the air.

The BBC, certainly, was taking its role desperately seriously. In a special emergency issue, *Radio Times* declared 'Broadcasting Carries On!' and explained to wireless listeners how 'you can expect to get your news at every hour "*on* the hour" as the Americans say. In other words,' the magazine laboured, clearly recognizing that both phrase and concept were unfamiliar, 'every time the hands of the clock reach the hour, between 7am and midnight, there will be a news broadcast.'

The stations too were reorganized: the BBC's National and Regional channels were merged into one all-encompassing Home Service. Programmes in the first week of war included a number of talks: 'Making the Most of Dried Food', 'Making the Most of a Wartime Larder' and 'The Amateur Handyman in Wartime'. Depicting many BBC Variety Department stars, including Tommy Handley, Sam Costa and Leonard Henry, *Radio Times* insisted, 'Laughter is never more needed than in war-time.'

British radio comedy was about to enter a pivotal phase in its development, from which all post-war comics, 'Benny' Hill included, would benefit.

Laughter was something the sixteen-year-old Alfie Hill was indeed hoping to generate, although not yet on the BBC. In fact, he didn't know where to go. Gloriously free of school, he began to put the word about: 'boy seeks stage opportunities'. He entered a local talent contest where, despite the poor quality of the acts, he could only finish second, the winner, he was fond of recalling in later years, being 'a bloke who ate broken glass and razor blades, and sewed buttons on his face.' Ah, the joys of British talent contests.

He also auditioned for Bobbie's Concert Party, a semi-pro outfit that performed in municipal halls and private parties in the Southampton area, as far out as Eastleigh. Details about their engagements are scarce, indeed little is known today about 'Bobbie', him(or her)self. Alfie's comedy act was somewhat on the thin side anyway, and, of course, entirely 'borrowed' from others, a trait he would forever find hard to resist. Appearing on stage in a shabby knee-length raincoat and flat-cap, with a muffler scarf wound around his head, he complained about the poor weather, chucking a fistful of torn-up white paper into the air and emerging from the blizzard exclaiming, 'Oh God, what a night!'

Alfie's second spot hinted more at his future material. Repeating a gag he had heard a comedian perform at the Hippodrome, he appeared as a vicar, dressed in a dog-collar and flat black hat made by his mother, and addressed his congregation:

> Will all ladies bringing eggs for the harvest festival please lay them in the vestry . . .

> I am sorry to have to report that this year very few ladies have become young mothers, despite the strenuous efforts of the Bishop and myself.

This latter joke drew a laugh from the sparse audience, but Alfie was swimming in dangerous waters. As Max Miller was wont to point out to any young comedians asking the great man's advice, 'blue' material is unseemly in the hands of the very young. Older – though not *old* – men might be able to get away with it, in the right circumstances, but virginal young boys won't get far with smut.

It was at this time that Alfie Hill took his first proper job, that of weighbridge clerk at the Phœnix Wharf & Coal Company, situated on

Marine Parade. His job was to weigh the lorries as they arrived empty, and to weigh them again when they departed with a full load. 'Then you take one from the other and, believe it or not, you get the amount of coal that's on the lorry,' he carefully explained in a later BBC radio interview, before adding the expected punchline 'unless they put in a fat driver the second time.' Even for a lad of sixteen, this was tedious stuff, well below the potential of a boy who, only six years earlier, had been deemed bright enough to be awarded a grammar school scholarship a year in advance of most others.

Here, in his ramshackle Phœnix office overlooking the River Itchen, Alfie lost his heart for a second time . . . and with the same sad result as the first. 'She worked in the office and I fell madly in love with her,' he remembered years later. 'After trying to pluck up courage I finally asked if I could take her home. She said yes, but had come to work on a bicycle and pedalled off. I trotted alongside, chatting away. She rode all four miles back to where she lived and I didn't even get a kiss for my trouble.'

The pay was poor, too: Phœnix offered the school-leaver fifteen shillings a week. 'I'll have to ask my mum,' he replied. Helen said that as Len was being paid £1 a week in his first job surely he should earn 17s 6d. Phœnix agreed, but it didn't matter much, anyway: Alfie quit after three weeks. His parents were relieved – the Germans had not yet begun to bomb Southampton but the time was growing ever closer, and Marine Parade was just about the most dangerous place to be.

The first thing the Luftwaffe's planes dropped on Southampton was not a bomb. They dropped propaganda leaflets. Then they dropped bombs. Nearly 500 tons of high explosive rained down on the Hampshire port, mostly in a horrifying thirteen-month period from June 1940 to July 1941. The statistics make grim reading, their very exactness emphasizing the catastrophe. First the docks, shipyards and aircraft factories were targeted, and then Southampton as a whole; 630 people were killed, 898 seriously hurt and 979 slightly injured; 936 homes were destroyed, 2,563 damaged so badly they had to be demolished, 8,927 seriously damaged but saved, and 32,019 slightly damaged. Everyone was affected, and several of the important places in Alfie's young life were wiped off the map.

His cherished Hippodrome was destroyed, as was the Palace. Neither was rebuilt. Canal Walk was all but wiped off the map – although, ironically, Stanley's was the only erection to remain upstanding. Taunton's was extensively damaged, and many of its former pupils would be killed in the armed forces before the war was over. The speedway stadium was reduced to rubble. Even 22 Westrow Gardens was hit, falling into the 'slightly damaged' category.

Situated close to Marine Parade and the river, St Mary Street was a particularly dangerous area. GP and Nana moved out to their daughter Cissie's house in Eastleigh, but GP commuted every day back to the dental surgery. One day a mine exploded at the rear of St Mary Street and the blast swept through, blowing him from one end of a passage to the other. 'He never recovered,' says Cissie's son Tony House. 'He went slowly off his mind from that day onwards.'

Henry Hawthorn Hill – 'The Lord Mayor of St Mary Street' – died in December 1942, aged seventy-two; Alfie was away and so missed the funeral.[1]

The blast that hit Westrow Gardens did not injure the Hill family. Len was now living away from home and Alf, Helen and Diana had already moved out. The Captain had found them a safe house, just across the River Test at Hounsdown, in a farming community on the edge of the New Forest. It was not an area that Hitler would bother to bomb. For the rest of the war the three of them cosseted up in Halderford, an asbestos-clad timber-frame bungalow situated in an unfinished road reassuringly named The Retreat.

As for Alfie, he had left home good and proper. No way, he huffed and puffed, was he going to live out in the sticks.

Big Alf recognized the signs when a boy has to get away, and made one last attempt to 'manage' his wilful son's departure. Hugh Stevens remembers, 'One of his fellow Freemasons was a manager for Woolworth's in Southampton. Big Alf asked the man if he thought there would be an opening for his son to go into Woolworth's as a trainee manager. The answer was yes, and it was arranged that Alfie would do this at the Eastleigh branch, six miles to the north.'

Located on Leigh Road, in the centre of Eastleigh, this was a typical branch of F. W. Woolworth & Co. – double-fronted, swing-doors, parquet floor, everything selling for threepence and sixpence, which was the nearest equivalent to American founder Frank Winfield Woolworth's brilliant marketing concept of the 'five and dime' store, where everything sold for five or ten cents. (In Germany, the company had '25 ja 50 pfennigs' stores.) If selling items that had a greater value than sixpence, Woolworth's would separate them out, so that a saucepan would cost sixpence, as would its lid, and socks were sold individually at sixpence each, a shilling the pair.

Alfie did not serve the public, though. He was a stockroom clerk, based one floor above the shop, and clear demarcation of staffing ensured that he did not come into direct contact with customers. The work was exhausting – there was a lift for transporting the goods, but there was also an attic which could only be reached by stairs. Wearing a khaki overall just like his father's at Stanley & Co., Alfie unloaded delivery lorries, shifted crates, lugged rolls of lino and, after daily closing, swept the parquet floor, oiling it on Saturday afternoons when the shop closed half-day. Another chore was humping around great sacks of peanuts. 'I didn't mind working for peanuts,' he later reflected, 'but it was working *with* peanuts that began to get me down.' Says Hugh Stevens, 'Alfie didn't care at all for the way in which things were done by Woolworth's, where people who were going to end up as managers had to start by sweeping the floor. He got sick of it very quickly.'

Still, he was popular with the other staff. Apart from Alfie and the manager, Mr Dean, everyone else at the branch was female. 'There were twenty to thirty girls, a manager and *me*. It was bee-yoo-tee-ful!' Benny recalled in an interview fully forty years later. He remembered, too, how some of those girls crept up on him one day and poured Californian Poppy perfume over him. 'No matter how many baths I had, I smelled of Californian Poppy for months,' he said.

'We called him Sunny Boy because he was always smiling and joking,' remembers Hilda Kite, a contemporary in the stockroom. 'I must say, though, he was exasperating at times, because whenever we asked him a question, about the work or anything, we could never get a serious answer out of him. He usually turned the question around to something funny.'

Another colleague confirms this view. 'He was quite pleasant,' remembers Doreen Jannaway. 'He called me "Miss", and if I asked him to do something, he'd do it, but he didn't hold a great conversation. And he was a bit slapdash with his work. His mind was elsewhere. He wasn't cut out for the job, really.'

True to form, Alfie fell in love again here at Woolworth's, his third 'romance' to date. The object of his desires was Jean, a blonde, two years his senior, who worked on the perfume counter. 'Her attitude towards me was one of amused tolerance,' he reflected decades later. ' "You make me laugh, Sunny Boy," was about the only reaction I ever got out of her.' Reminiscing in a 1969 interview with the British popular weekly *Reveille*, he further recalled, 'They say humility is good for the soul. If it is, mine improved every time a dog made a mess near the perfume counter. I would have to clean it up, blushing like a beetroot, under the eyes of the blonde assistant whom I adored.'

The 'romance' went no further. Alfie was of course only sixteen, an age when everyone has ludicrous relationships, if indeed they have any at all. Nonetheless, a pattern was emerging, wherein Alfie was falling head over heels for women who simply were not interested in him. This 'rejection' – it was really nothing of the sort – he found crushing, and the dreaded feeling would be forged into his consciousness, never to be forgotten but often to be repeated.

Alfie did derive some benefit from his six-month employment at Woolworth's though: he watched the faces and mannerisms of the shop customers, adding them to his store of impressions. Another keen observation was of Mr Dean. Alfie noticed how, though paid well enough, the manager 'looked harassed and rather old'. 'I wanted my luck *earlier* in life,' he would reflect in these later interviews.

So, once again, Alfie resigned.

His departure from Woolworth's was met with much more than resignation from his father. Big Alf was simply furious that Alfie was chucking in this God-given opportunity at 'making something of himself'. He had arranged the position though Masonic contacts and felt personally thwarted, and perhaps even humiliated. Alfie, it seems, knew this would be the result. 'Alfie's leaving Woolworth's so soon was really a payback to his father,' reflects Hugh Stevens. 'It was a slap in the face to Big Alf for having arranged this job on his behalf, when he himself was more inclined to pursue a theatrical future.' The relationship between father and son had never been at such a low ebb.

It is perhaps no coincidence, then, that young Alfie found himself a substitute father at this time. Through contacts made by friends of friends of friends, he was taken in as a lodger by an Eastleigh family, the Browns, who lived in a semi-detached council-house at 8 The Nook, a cul-de-sac even smaller than Westrow Gardens back in Southampton. Albert Nelson Brown, known as Nelson, was a shift worker on the railways, one of the town's principal sources of employment. His wife, Constance Irene, known as Irene, was a housewife and mother of two children, Dennis, six, and Pauline, two. For just over a year, from July 1940 to August 1941, Alfie became Nelson and Irene's surrogate third child, and also 'uncle' to their two little 'uns – to Pauline, especially. 'We used to play out in the road,' she says. 'He made a big fuss of me.'

'Though I knew him as "Uncle Alf" my dad looked upon him as a son,' says Pauline. 'He was really very fond of him. My mum didn't get attached to people as much as my dad, who was an easy-going placid chap, with a good sense of humour, quite different from what I know of Alf's own father. I think this is why they got on so well, and he was the same with Alf as he was with me and my brother – totally supportive, totally behind us.'

Nelson Brown's support of Alfie's stage aspirations was indeed in marked contrast to The Captain's acid viewpoint, and the boy revelled in the 'paternal' enthusiasm. In the latter stages of his stint at Woolworth's, Alfie had learned about a local concert party outfit organized by a Mrs Ivy Lillywhite, and he had charmed his way in. Nelson Brown did all he could to help the young boy. 'They used to sit up quite late,' remembers Pauline. 'My dad was Alf's try-out for all the jokes he was planning to perform at his next show.'

A music teacher by day, Ivy Lillywhite was one of those solid citizens upon whom local entertainments have always depended. She ran a dance-band – drums, violin, trumpet and guitar, with Ivy herself on piano – that played at clubs, dances, parties and civic events, and she also took over the running of Eastleigh's annual pantomime. While still at Woolworth's, Alfie had heard on the grapevine that one of Ivy's band had been drafted into the armed forces, and he had gone around to her house and presented himself.

Mrs Lillywhite, now deceased, later hand-wrote an account of the meeting on a few sheets of Basildon Bond notepaper seen by the author:

> I went to the door and a tall, pleasant, nicely spoken young man was there. He said, 'I hear one of the men in your band has been called up, and I wondered if you could use me.' Of course, I asked him what he could do, so he performed on his guitar and sang a song. Neither were exceptionally good but I sensed there was some unusual talent hidden there. He had a good rhythm, which helped, and his singing sometimes went over quite well.

Alfie also performed some funny turns for Ivy Lillywhite – a vicar, a farmer, a Max Miller-like cockney, and different accents of Britain. 'I had had quite a lot of experience in this sort of thing,' she wrote. And she evidently felt the boy needed encouragement: 'I took him to as many performances as possible. His efforts weren't always appreciated but that all adds up to experience. He improved very much and was a very likeable young man.'

Initially, Alfie was merely a member of the band, and his contributions were almost silent: without amplification, his guitar was drowned out by the other musicians. But Alfie himself was far from quiet. His nervous, fidgety, incessant chitter-chatter, so endearing to Ivy Lillywhite, was not so well received by the drummer, Sid Dumper, who exclaimed to Alfie, 'If you could play your guitar as well as you can talk you'd go a long way.'

Showing a strong desire to push himself, Alfie was soon suggesting to Ivy that the band could use a singer, and that they need look no further than he to be the man on the mike. Thus the Eastleigh townsfolk began to find a sixteen-year-old crooner in their midst at Saturday-night dances, a robust, rosy-cheeked lad who, dipping into his BBC radio memory-bag, pulled out Louis Armstrong's 'Careless Love', and also gave a passable rendition of a new show-song, 'Who's Taking You Home Tonight?' His voice, young but pleasant, could hold a tune.

But what Alfie Hill really craved were opportunities to perform as a comedian. Most engagements called only for the band. Local amateur Variety shows were more promising, though, and it so happened that a special Sunday concert, organized by none other than Dr Horace King, was being held at Eastleigh Town Hall to raise funds for the production of Spitfire fighter planes, one of the great British hopes for air supremacy in the war.

IN AID OF THE

Eastleigh Spitfire Fund

A MATINEE VARIETY

CONCERT

under the patronage of His Worship
the Mayor, will be held at

The Town Hall, Eastleigh,

on **Sunday, October 27th, 1940**

Doors open 2 p.m. Commence 2.15 p.m.

Admission 1/- and 6d.

Your patronage is earnestly solicited
in this effort to provide the town's first
Spitfire

Ivy Lillywhite and her band were an integral part of the show, and Alfie pressed Ivy into letting him do a comedy spot. It was his biggest test yet, and all the family came up from Southampton to be in the audience, even GP and Nana. Everyone, that is, except The Captain, who would have nothing to do with it. This was Alfie's Biggest Moment in all his sixteen years. He played a little drums, which went well. Then he suffered a setback when, playing along on guitar to 'Begin the Beguine', he broke a string. 'I shall never forget his face,' Ivy Lillywhite later recalled. 'He was heart-broken, as if it was the end of the world.'

But things improved when Alfie took his comedy spot. A younger lad, Jack Jones, friends with Ivy's son John, recalls, 'I was on the curtain, opening and closing it. To the accompaniment of Mrs Lillywhite's band he opened with a performance of Al Jolson's "Mammy", down on one knee, halfway through singing "Why don't you look where you're going? Then you wouldn't be crying!" Then later on in his act he said, "I can tap-dance with this foot," turned around and said, "and I can also tap-dance with this foot" and of course it was the same foot. I got his act off to a T, and often used to do it afterwards.'

The show was a success, and for the first time Alfie had been able to conquer his stage-fright. GP, the dentist and savvy *World's Fair* reviewer, commended his grandson afterwards, advising him to 'Smile, boy, smile! Show those good teeth!' A week later, page three of the *Eastleigh Weekly News* carried a glowing review, which, in passing, declared:

Mr Alfred Hill was very clever as a comedian, keeping the audience in fits of laughter.

It was Alfie's first press notice.

A regular pattern of rehearsals with Ivy Lillywhite at her house at 45 Dutton Lane, and performances at such venues as the Town Hall, the Unity Club, the Working Men's Club & Institute, and the Central Working Men's Club, was how Alfie spent most evenings during his time in Eastleigh.

Having left Woolworth's, he also needed a day job. Work wasn't hard to come by because many local men were serving King and Country, so Alfie found himself a new position in no time: he became a milkman. 'He got the job in a huff, really,' declares Alfie's cousin Hugh Stevens, 'to show his dad that he could find work for himself, any work he wanted.'

As with his Woolworth's position, Alfie's tenure as a milkman, riding his horse and cart through the Hampshire countryside, has become the stuff of legend – not least because one of the comedian's greatest successes in later years was his song 'Ernie (the Fastest Milkman in the West)', a number one single in Britain in 1971, full of references to these distant pounding hoofbeats and the rattling of the crates.

James Hann & Son were desperate for staff. As early as March 1940 they had placed an advertisement in the *Eastleigh Weekly News*:

DORSET DAIRIES

We are deeply concerned that many of our customers have found their milk arriving late just recently, the reason for this being we are fast losing so many of our valued staff.

New staff is *[sic]* being trained as quickly as possible and you can depend that every endeavour is made to speed up delivery with our usual clock-like regularity.

You doubtless know of our many difficulties: severe winter weather, 'flu epidemic and serious staff disloca-tion, and we are confident that you will give us your kind co-operation and continued support under the restricted conditions now prevailing.

25 per cent of our staff is actually serving and
25 per cent is standing on call for H.M. Forces.
We are proud of them.

JAMES HANN & SON

So Alfie was now a milkman, his third job inside a year. It was December 1940, just in time to receive a share of the 'Christmas box', a useful supplement to his wage of just under £1 a week.

At first, to learn the ropes – or perhaps the reins – Alfie was merely a milk-boy, out on the roads assisting an old chap named Bill, working the Campbell Road–Southampton Road–Dutton Lane–Barton Road round. Ivy Lillywhite's son John, who formed a good friendship with Alfie at this time, would sometimes tag along and remembers the period well. 'I used to meet them in Southampton Road on a Saturday and sit on top of the horse-drawn float,' he says. 'One time I was sitting on the cart when Bill got his whip out to give the horse a tickle, and it bolted. And we were hanging on for grim death. The horse went straight down Dutton Lane, left into Bishopstoke Road, right into Barton Road and then stopped. The rattling sound was *tremendous.*'

On this occasion, Alfie had managed to save the day, if not some of the bottles, by remembering the words of The Captain, who, as a child working in the circus, had learned how a sawing motion with reins can stop a runaway horse. Some of the special Hill 'way with animals' was trickling down the generations.

The wartime reduction in manpower meant that Alfie, though only just turning seventeen, was soon given his own round. Leaving The Nook at 5.30 every morning, he'd trot down to Hann's in the centre of town, get the horse ready, load up the cart with milk and other dairy products and perhaps a few vegetables, and cluck the horse into motion at seven. Speaking on BBC radio in 1966, he remembered the period with enormous fondness:

> I really enjoyed being a milkman. I had a country round, from Eastleigh to Fair Oak, and I used to go nearly a mile before my first customer. The rest of the boys had town rounds. So if there was a horse which wasn't experienced in the shaft, which was a bit edgy, they gave it to me because if he wants to run it's a country road. So I used to get the fresh ones, the bolters. And then I used to come back into Eastleigh over Station Hill, down into Market Street at a gallop, with the bottles a-jingling, pretending that I was on the stagecoach riding into Dodge City, the wheels skidding around the corners.

It was a glorious time for the teenager, out on his cart in a smart green overall, enacting scenes from the cowboy films he had admired in the cinema and in all those Wild West children's books and on the wireless. His imagination could and did run riot. On more than one occasion Harry Hann, the 'Son' in James Hann & Son, had to reprimand Alfie for over-exuberance, bawling him out across Factory Road, where the depot was situated, rather than in his office inside.

But Alfie was carefree. Eastleigh was very much a country town (it has since been ravaged by developers), and he adored seeing the trees and fields at dawn as he headed out towards Bishopstoke and Fair Oak, alone on the roads with Daisy the mare, tipping his green peaked-cap to the occasional farmer as he trotted smartly by the fields. As he approached houses he would call out with great gusto 'Milk-O!' or 'Whoop-di-wayee!' or 'Ya-ho! Milk for the babies, cream for the mums!' And when the cowboy mood returned he would clutch the reins tighter, sit back and call into the clear Hampshire morning:

It's your misfortune – and none of my own
Yip-a-hi! Yip-a-ho! Git along, little dogies!
Ya know that Wyoming will be your new home!

Naturally, Alfie also enjoyed cheeking the other staff back at the dairy. Hann's employed many women, who (irrespective of their looks) were called Hann's Beauties. One of them, Hazel Wigg, remembers Alfie as if it was yesterday and not sixty years ago. 'What we later saw on the telly is exactly how Alfie was then,' she says. 'He was a *rascal*. He used to come in, pick off my cap and race around the floor with it, or hide. Or if I was writing out my list for the next day he'd take my pad. And it wasn't just me: he'd torment all of us. In the end I walloped him good and proper. I didn't mean to hit him so hard but he had been irritating me. "My word, Hazel," he said, "I didn't expect that." I said, "Well, if you will torment people when they're busy!"'

Out on the milk-round Alfie learned too about *life*. Food-rationing had been introduced in Britain early in 1940 and Alfie's order-book, which denoted the requirements for each house, had to be qualified by the increasingly severe restrictions on milk, butter and eggs. 'I was becoming an amateur psychologist,' he recalled in a 1955 interview. 'The little tricks those housewives would play to get eggs, or extra milk, the countless little dramas they would enact to prove that their husbands were serious invalids, simply dying because they couldn't get an egg . . .'

Unless men lived alone, seeing the milkman was deemed to be a woman's work. One of them on Alfie's round would come to the front door without her false teeth, covering her mouth with a dish-towel. The result was that she was incoherent, and Alfie would stand on her doorstep scratching his head, trying to figure out what she was saying. Several of the women, distressed at having to feed their families on so little, ranted at Alfie for failing to deliver their full requirements, as if rationing was somehow his personal fault. Mostly, though, the housewives liked the young lad, and many a time he would be invited in for a cup of tea and slice of toast.

In later years, as Benny Hill, he helped give publicity to the milk cause, working with the National Milk Publicity Council; in a late 1960s press release he recalled another aspect from these Eastleigh days. 'There was one odd little thing I noticed about the average customer. She was governed, regulated or intimidated – or fancied she was – by a mysterious collection of people she would describe as "them". These people would minister to her needs and make life comfortable for her. "They" would provide ration books and egg allocation cards. "They" had to come and repair broken pipes. "They" would do something about the smell on the landing . . .'

The ever-observant Alfie was making mental notes, just as he had done watching the embarrassed customers in his father's shop, steadily develop-ing a fund of characters who would underpin a comedy career to span the next fifty years.

'He was popular at Hann's, and he was popular on the rounds,' recalls Hazel Wigg of the boy whose relentless cheeriness and love of popular music caused him to become known as 'Eastleigh's singing milkman'. 'He used to come in dressed up with a scarf around his hat, with a few curlers sticking out and a pinny on, and he'd act out what he'd seen at one of the houses. "Yes milkman, I'll have three pints today!" in a high-pitched woman's voice. Picture him on TV and you have him as a lad. He used to have us in stitches. I don't think he'd had much of a life as a youngster and all us women felt motherly towards him.'

John Lillywhite confirms this view. 'I remember walking with him up Dutton Lane – he had a slightly effeminate walk even then – and all the old ladies used to laugh and chuckle at him. He used to have everybody laughing when he knocked on the doors. Not by telling jokes but by character, by personality.'

Throughout this period, Alfie was burning the candle at both ends, attending or performing at dances and clubs until 2am, and up with the cart again at 5.30, living with the Browns and socializing with the Lillywhites. To the Browns, Alfie was a good source of humour. 'He kept a drum kit and a guitar in the house and used to hammer away at them,' says Pauline. 'And he used to sing to us the kind of funny songs he later had in his TV shows. My dad later told me that Alf would have him, my mum and my brother in absolute hysterics.'

To Ivy Lillywhite's son John, Alfie was a pal. 'We had a cupboard under the stairs, and in wartime kept a reserve of tinned food there. Being young, hungry lads, he and I would bring out tins of stewing-steak and open them up. Then we'd sit and listen to music together on the radio.

He had a tremendous knowledge of big bands – he could name all the players. "That's so-and-so on drums, that's so-and-so on sax . . ." He had a very clever brain and seemed a confident person. He was certainly happy, at least in our company.'

To Ivy herself, though, this young protégé was a little too raw to be living away from home. He wasn't really earning enough to look after himself properly, walking around Eastleigh in shabby clothes, the holes in his shoes letting in water. Her husband Leslie, who worked with the Southern Railway fire brigade, gave Alfie a pair of fireman's black boots, which the teenager cheerfully stomped around in for a while. But Ivy felt that the impasse between Alfie and his father had gone on long enough. One day she told the boy that he must visit his parents and mend the relationship; Ivy went too, to make sure he didn't chicken out, and also took son John along for the ride. The three of them descended on Halderford, the bungalow abutting the New Forest, and, as Ivy had hoped, managed to thaw the ice a little. Though initially suspicious of Ivy's interest in his young son, The Captain was relatively mollified: the boy was safe under her wing, and would probably be back home soon, his ludicrous adventure done and dusted.

Alfie was enjoying Eastleigh, though. Except when he had to stay and groom the horse, polish the brasses and apply dubbin to the leather harness, he finished his milk-round by 1.30 most days. Then he might amble over to Ivy Lillywhite's to try out new ideas for his occasional comedy spot while she did her best to get on with the housework. 'He looked upon her as a bit of mother-figure,' reflects John Lillywhite. 'She told me years later that he had discussed his troubles with her.'

If he wasn't at Ivy's, Alfie would pop into either of the two Eastleigh cinemas, the Regal (which had matinées on Mondays, Wednesdays and Thursdays) or the Picture House (Tuesday, Fridays and Saturdays). Sitting in the darkened stalls, watching a continuous programme comprising a main feature, a B-movie and sometimes a 'coloured travelogue', Alfie scoffed a lunch that would have had makers of acne cream rubbing their hands – cakes, ice-creams and sweets. Best of all, the Regal featured an organist in between pictures, Derek Ronald, whom Alfie recognized as the resident pre-war player at the Plaza in Southampton. To Alfie, seeing the organist rising up out of the orchestra pit, and listening to its pipey music, was one of the great thrills of going to the pictures. When, in 1969, he made his own cinema film, *The Waiters*, the opening and closing scenes depicted him in best Derek Ronald guise, hands dancing on the mighty, illuminated Wurlitzer, body half-turned, a fixed grin on his lips.

Southampton was now in the midst of a Luftwaffe bombing blitz, and Eastleigh was having its share of troubles, too. Under the headline 'What to do – Should Invasion Come', the local newspaper carried some stern advice, cautioning 'Should parachutists come down near one's home the best guidance is: Don't give any German anything. Don't tell him anything. Hide your food and your bicycles. Hide your maps. See that the enemy gets no petrol. If you have a car or motor-cycle, put it out of action when not in use.' Eastleigh formed its own regiment of Home Guard defence volunteers, who – in true *Dad's Army* style – made their HQ at a Drill Hall and publicly appealed for chairs, tables 'and any other articles that would make the men feel comfortable'. A temporary coal shortage led to people burning shelves, fences and clothes-posts; one desperate woman, it was reported, burned the rollers from her mangle.

When the air-raid sirens sounded everyone had to dash for cover. Hann's milkmen and Beauties were under clear instructions from Harry Hann to 'stay with the horse', to try to keep them calm. In the evenings, people gathered in garden shelters or in communal refuges. One night, out together at an evening performance, Alfie – ever a woman's protector – was escorting Ivy Lillywhite back to Dutton Lane when German planes flew overhead and began to drop their load. Seeking haven in a public shelter, Alfie did his best to keep spirits up by telling a few jokes, but his cockiness was abruptly halted when, after the all-clear siren had been sounded, news spread that a young girl had been killed in the raid.

There was some uplifting news, though. In February 1941 Prime Minister Winston Churchill passed through Eastleigh *en route* to Southampton, waving to crowds and, as the *Weekly News* staunchly reported, 'wearing a yachting cap and a navy blue great-coat and smoking a freshly-lit cigar'. And there was still entertainment to be found. Another matinée concert for the Spitfire Fund was held on December 1 1940 at the Southern Railway Institute, in the presence of the mayor and mayoress. A review in the following *Weekly News* read:

Alf Heel *[sic]* (comedian) was again up to his usual high form and did some very clever impersonations.

Presciently, though with the exaggeration typical of local newspapers, it continued:

This young man is destined to have a very successful future in the entertainment world.

'We went to several of the Sunday-afternoon concerts,' remembers Nelson Brown's daughter Pauline. 'My dad remarked in later years that some of the things Alf said were quite near the mark, especially for a Sunday, though everybody laughed. Alf would say to my dad that on the Monday he'd be out on his milk-round and people, having had time to think things over, would say to him, "That really wasn't very nice, to say things like that on a Sunday!"'

Alfie was now performing more and more, turning up at working-men's clubs, the Comrades Club and in the occasional 'smoking concert' at the Unity Club, improving all the while and standing on stage in a cheap 'n' loud check-jacket, bright red tie ('Thank God it's a tie! I thought it was me tongue hanging out!' – a line he would include in his act for at least another fifteen years) and grey pork-pie hat with a little orange feather in the band.

As a 'guest of the week' on the BBC radio programme *Woman's Hour* in 1955, he laughed as he told interviewer Jean Metcalfe how he knew the times were getting better:

One night at a working-men's club the fee was five shillings. The show went rather well and the chap came up to me and, quite sincerely, he said, 'You was worth every penny of 7s 6d.'

A year after arriving in Eastleigh, Alfie Hill was clearly beginning to carve out a reputation – and, finally, a decent income, some weeks as much as thirty shillings. But the combination of late nights and early starts was exhausting, and his successes as a comedian, though modest, were serving only to fuel a desire to pursue higher goals. An idea began to take shape in the boy's mind that he really could 'make it' as a professional comic. He became anxious to catch as many top shows as possible, and to seek advice from professionals. With the Hippodrome and Palace theatres in Southampton bombed, Alfie had to look elsewhere, and one afternoon in the second week of July 1941 he took the train into northern Hampshire, to Basingstoke, and trotted along to the Grand Theatre to see what was going on.

What was going on was *Blue Pencil*, a touring Variety show featuring 'Radio's Wittiest Wise-Crackers', Jimmy and Arthur Smeddle. The brothers Smeddle were one of literally hundreds of ordinary acts working the halls all over the country, playing twice-nightly shows. The phrase 'blue pencil' was not theirs – it was chiefly the domain of Jack Warner (comic, actor and brother of Elsie and Doris Waters), who used it to denote material allegedly questioned by the censor, thereby hinting that, although passed fit for use, the jokes could well be on the cusp of what passed in 1941 for decency. (Which, to be sure, wasn't exactly daring.)

Alfie watched the first house wide-eyed. Then, in the interlude before everyone came out to do it all again, he presented himself at the stage door and asked to see the Smeddles. Gaining admission, he entered their dressing-room and did his damnedest to impress the professional troupers, rattling off a succession of quickfire jokes reminiscent of Max Miller (although nowhere near as good).

The Smeddles responded in a way Alfie could scarcely have dared to imagine. 'All right son, we'll give you a start in show-business!' The brothers then explained how they were booked to play in Chesterfield, Crewe and Workington in the next three weeks, but after that they would be in London. 'Leave us your address and we'll write to you shortly,' they assured. 'Then you can start in the act.'

Alfie returned to Eastleigh fleet of foot; the next morning he handed in a week's notice at Hann's, then dashed around to Dutton Lane bursting to tell Ivy Lillywhite the good news. Then he went back to The Nook and informed Nelson Brown that he would soon be moving out. The information was received coolly at Halderford, however. 'There was complete apathy from his parents,' says Alfie's cousin Bill Jaques. 'Even his mother was indifferent. "Get a *proper* job, Alfie, one with a pension. You could be a postman . . ."' Disappointingly for the boy, his beloved Auntie Louie felt the same, too. But no, he was going to do it his way.

The Smeddles never did get back in touch with Alfie. 'Perhaps they had lost my address. Perhaps they had found somebody better. Or cheaper.

Well, no hard feelings,' he wrote of this period – from the comfort of 1955.

At the time, though, Alfie felt let down, and perhaps sensed he had been naïve. Having burned his bridges in Eastleigh, however, it was time to move on. But not back to Southampton and certainly not to Hounsdown, where the end of his great adventure would be too embarrassing to face.

Four weeks after meeting the Smeddles, Alfie travelled to Hounsdown only to pack a small cardboard suitcase. Selling his guitar and drum kit for £15, and drawing on his savings, he had a little under £20 tucked into the pocket of his garish checked jacket as he arrived at Southampton station and bought a ticket for London.

5. The Dogsbody's Dogsbody – with Small Parts

Alfie had been in London only once before, on a trip with his father and brother in 1938, visiting Regent's Park Zoo and catching a show at the Palladium. But the London of 1938 was entirely different to the London of 1941. The capital had been blitzed by German bombers and the damage was severe. Ugly was the sight that greeted Alfie Hill, a boy on the run at seventeen years of age, as – tatty suitcase in hand – he stepped out of Waterloo Station the seventh day of August. But he had not come as a tourist. He had come in pursuit of fame and fortune. Of experience, he was bereft; bravura and innocent determination he had in spades.

On the bookstall at Waterloo, Alfie bought the current issue of *The Stage*, the weekly newspaper *de rigueur* for all who work in the business of entertainment in Britain. Scarcity of paper had reduced the publication to just eight pages, and production cutbacks curtailed the use of photographs, but the thin read was still perhaps the best fourpence the young lad had spent. Until now, his knowledge of London's show-business scene was on a par with his familiarity of the city – virtually non-existent. Now he could turn the pages and see before him the names of all the halls and theatres. Most pages contained advertisements placed by Variety acts looking for work, like North Country comedienne Hylda Baker, who was touring a show, *All Girls Together*. Another ad indicated that striptease act Phyllis Dixey (known to her fans as a natural blonde) had smashed the box-office record in Aldershot. The big-name comedians – Arthur Askey, Robb Wilton, Tommy Handley, Dave Morris, Tommy Trinder and George Formby – all had advertisements of their own, and there were listings for touring Variety revues – none, clearly, steeped in the highbrow – including *Glamorous Desires, Nights of Gladness, Une Nuit Excitante, Silk Stocking Scandals, Fun and Dames, We Can Shake It, Naughty but Nice,*

Naughty Girls and *Naughty, Naughty*. For the price of a train fare, Alfie had pulled into paradise.

The boy strode across Waterloo Bridge and up the Strand, and his spirits soared again at the sight of so many theatres. These were 'legit' venues, no place for a green, saucy comedian, but encouraging nonetheless. Then he found himself a café and sat devouring every word of *The Stage*. The most interesting page was the inside front cover, which, by tradition, listed the Variety 'Calls' for the coming week – detailing the venues, which shows were playing where and who was in them. (Jimmy and Arthur Smeddle, finally back south again, were playing in Camden Town, but Alfie certainly wasn't going there.)

As he was fond of recalling in later years, Alfie drew a ring around the London theatres and set out to visit them. This was in itself tricky – he couldn't head for the Chelsea Palace without first finding out where Chelsea was, nor the Kilburn Empire, the Chiswick Empire and the Metropolitan in Edgware Road. Remembering the maxim 'If in doubt, ask a policeman', Alfie sought the advice of a London bobby. The policeman cheerfully obliged – he studied Alfie's copy of *The Stage*, told the lad which theatres were within reach and pointed him in the direction of a bus-stop. It was a good omen.

After threading its way through the ravaged streets, Alfie's double-decker finally delivered him to the Chiswick Empire. The current show here was *Mad Hatters of 1941*, starring Syd Seymour and his Mad Hatters, a British copy of the American musical comedy act Spike Jones and his City Slickers. Alfie came here first because he had seen Syd's show in Southampton before the war; his merry pranksters were sure to require a youngster who was keen, comedic and musical. 'I expected a big North Countryman full of confidence,' he recalled in a 1969 interview. 'I was surprised when Syd came to the door. He looked much smaller and older, besides having a twitch.'

The comic disappointed . . . 'Sorry, son, there's nothing for you.'

Beaten but unbowed, Alfie headed for the Brixton Empress. The current show here was *Sailors Don't Care*, starring Ernie Lotinga, a past-his-prime northern comedian renowned for being lewd. But again there was nothing for Alfie. At the Streatham Hill Theatre *Rhapsodies of 1941* was playing; his stage-door ministrations came to naught here, too. And it was getting late. Alfie bought himself some fish and chips and, without anywhere to sleep, and keen to preserve his scant savings, dossed down for the night in a crude concrete air-raid shelter on Streatham Common. Bombing had more or less ended by now, and Alfie had little company. He awoke the next morning to find a rat staring him in the face.

Though it was summer, 1941 had a particularly wet August, and it was a damp Alfie who trudged to a Lyons Corner House café for breakfast. Pushing aside his cup and saucer, he wrote a couple of letters: one to his mother, telling her not to worry, that he was doing fine; the other, curiously perhaps, was a missive to Jean, his beloved from the Woolworth's perfume counter in Eastleigh, no doubt telling her that he was about to become a big star on the London stage.

Then the big-star-to-be ducked into the Lyons lav for a wash and brush-up.

Another bus took Alfie back across the Thames, to the Chelsea Palace. A revue, *Follow the Fun*, was in residence for the week, and Alfie's stage-door knocking brought out the tour manager, Harry Flockton Foster. His response to Alfie's cheeky pitch – truly 'I'm better than Max Miller, and I don't want so much money!' – was more encouraging. Because of the war, capable young backstage crew were in short supply, and the company could probably use this keen, strapping lad. *Follow the Fun* was a Harry Benet (pronounced 'Bennett') show, part-financed by a young Jewish immigrant, Bernard Delfont, who had just given up performing and turned to promotion. Foster jotted down Benet's Soho office address and suggested a Monday morning visit. 'Tell him I sent you!' Foster called out as Alfie's head soared into the clouds.

That weekend, walking the daytime streets and sleeping rough in the Streatham shelter, Alfie prepared for what might be the biggest meeting of his life. How would he introduce himself, what would he say and how would he say it? Was he, a seventeen-year-old Hampshire boy, confident enough to stride into the West End office of one of Britain's top impresarios and pitch himself? Er . . . no, he wasn't. But James Cagney could do it! Calling up Cagney's confident celluloid swagger from his fund of Westrow Gardens impressions, Alfie practised and practised his spiel (which grew less, not more, convincing as the weekend trickled by).

Monday morning. Benet's office was at 51 Beak Street, and Alfie had to ask the way before he found it, situated close by a nondescript thorough-fare, Carnaby Street. Wearing his pork-pie hat with the little orange feather tucked into the side band, Alfie burst in on the big boss.

As he later recalled, 'To my shame, instead of going into Harry Benet's office with my hat in hand, I pushed it back on my head and sat on his desk. I said:

I'm a comic. If you want your audiences rolling in the aisles, I'm your man!

Harry Benet was a pleasant-looking cove, a circus and Variety promoter already well into his sixties, with short-cut grey hair and kindly eyes. 'Sit down, son,' Alfie heard the impresario say. '*In that chair*. Now listen. It can take a long time to become a principal comedian, and no one is going to accept a comic who doesn't look as though he's started shaving.

'But if you stick with me you can learn your trade properly. Like George Lacy. He started with me as a property boy and look at him now, lad, he's topping the bill in my revue *Let the Band Play!*'

Alfie's encyclopedic knowledge of comedians had already accessed the data: Lacy ('The Ace Of Jokers') was one of Britain's most revered pantomime dames, although the veteran had a reputation for salacious material.

'I'll tell you what, lad,' Benet continued, mindful of a vacancy in his touring company, 'I'll take you on as ASM on *Follow the Fun*.'

Alfie didn't know what an ASM was or did, but it didn't exactly sound like a stage role. 'Does that mean I can play parts?' he queried, his auda-city, not quite extinguished, betraying his anxiety to perform.

Benet laughed. 'Yes, there may be small parts, too.'

'And how much?'

'Well, many years ago I started Lacy on £2 a week. I'll start you on £3. You begin tonight, at East Ham Palace. You'd better buy yourself a set of overalls.'

ASM, Alfie soon found out, stood for Assistant Stage Manager, a post that encompassed being property-boy. The SM's job was an inglorious one. The closest he got to being on stage was setting it up, erecting and arranging scenery; the biggest part of the job, however, was taking the scenery down after the week's final show, stowing it away, arranging transportation to the next town and ensuring it was all put back together in the next theatre for another week's run.

And Alfie was ASM – the dogsbody's dogsbody.

Still, three days after arriving in London, Alfie Hill had his first job in show-business. There was no contract – Alfie wasn't looking for one, and Benet had a reputation in the business for being true to his word, operating on a handshake.

East Ham, over in east London, was in a hell of a mess. It was near the docks, hit time and again by German bombing raids, but the 1,600-capacity Palace had survived, just. At the outbreak of war, the British government had banned all forms of public entertainment, but it took only days for the prohibition to crumble. Now with official blessing once more, the dance-halls, cinemas and theatres were back in business.

In its fifth week on tour around Britain, *Follow the Fun* – 'a new revue in 14 scenes' – opened in East Ham on Monday, August 11 1941; as was Variety custom, it played two separate 'houses' nightly for six days, ending on the Saturday. Sunday was when shows moved on, ready to open in another town for a further six nights.

No star names peopled the cast, which was headed by comedian Hal Bryan ('A Fellow Of Infinite Jest') with Teddy Brogden, leading lady Ivy Luck, Daly & Lea, 10 Gordon Ray Girls, 10 Cilla's Dogs and a 'strong supporting company' – a euphemism for the weaker, lower-order acts whose names are unlikely to bring in any business.

Yes sir, dogs. Animals still played their part in providing Variety entertainment, hoofers every last one of them. Cilla's Dogs, a circus act run by Priscilla Kayes (whom, coincidentally, Henry Hawthorn Hill had praised in his *World's Fair* article quoted in Chapter 3 – 'GP' had been friends with her father fully forty years earlier) had been trained to play football on the stage. It wasn't all they did on there, and the ASM had to clear up afterwards. Shades of his Woolworth's work all over again. Later on in the tour, Pepino's Wonder Circus – elaborately trained ponies and monkeys – joined the fray, with similar results.

But there were compensations, not least in the attractive frames of the Gordon Ray Girls, high-kicking away on stage and changing in and out of skimpy costumes backstage, where Alfie's position gave him every reason to loiter. From drooling over such shows at the Southampton

Hippodrome, Alfie Hill was now actively involved in their production, smelling the greasepaint and, more compellingly for the seventeen-year-old, savouring the suspenders. Thirty years later, in an interview for the 1971 book *The Laughtermakers*[1] he declared with absolute relish:

> Can you imagine a lad of that age suddenly flung in with twelve chorus girls? It was 'Can I carry this for you, love?' all the time. Oh, it was my initiation. It was lovely. Oh, those days'll never come back.

It didn't take long for Alfie to make his stage debut. After the show's opening number, in which the cast sang 'Make It a Party!' and arrived on stage in a 'boat' ('Hello, folks! How splendid to be back again in Venice upon Thames!'), Alfie would close the 'tabs' (stage curtaining) and open them again for the first comedy skit, featuring Hal Bryan and his straight-man. The opening line – spoken by the 'foil' in a pastiche of the current wartime catchphrase 'Go to it!' – was 'Hallo, Hal, going to it?', at which point the fellow of infinite jest would respond 'No, coming from it!' Cue (hopefully) the first laugh and three further fun-packed minutes about how being *extra* friendly with a barmaid can earn you a bigger glass of beer.

But first house on Wednesday night, while Alfie was behind the tabs laying a kitchen table ready for the next scene, he could hear only one voice out front. Hal Bryan's. 'Oh, it's ever so LONELY here in East Ham. All on me tod and NOT A SOUL IN SIGHT.'

Something was wrong.

Realizing that the straightman had gone missing, Alfie dashed around looking for the stage manager and had no luck. ('He was in the pub next door, having a drink,' he later recalled.) So with shaking knees and trembling hands, and still wearing his ASM's overalls, Alfie ventured meekly on to the big stage.

Interviewed in February 1966 for the BBC radio programme *Turning Points*, he recounted the incident:

> I was so nervous, and my ears started going – the blood going through your head so fast, thumping at your ear-holes, and you're slightly deaf. And in a quavering voice, it must have been a very high-pitched one, I said, 'Hello, Hal, going to it?' And he said 'No, I'm just coming from it. Thanks. Well, you've turned up! ... Do you know where you can get any beer around here?'

Alfie didn't yet know any of the lines, and for the next few minutes the principal comedian whispered them to his novice straightman – beginning with ''Round the corner, at the pub' – who then repeated them as loud as he could. ''ROUND THE CORNER, AT THE PUB!'

> I went right through the sketch. We went off all right, and what was so nice was that for the rest of that house, and the rest of the next house, all the girls were saying, 'Oh, you were great! To go on so quick!' I remember I couldn't stop smiling. My face was almost aching with this smile, it wouldn't go. I was feeling so pleased it was ridiculous. I must have looked like a Cheshire cat.
>
> Hal Bryan said nothing, though, and I thought, 'I wonder if he was upset at me doing it? Perhaps he'd rather have been left on his own?' But at the end of the night, after everybody had gone, I'm packing up the props, all the bits and pieces, putting them back in the old tea-chest, and he's hanging about purposely. He came down by himself, put a ten-bob note in my hand, gripped me by the arm and said, 'You're going to be a trouper, son!' It was a big moment in my life.

After six nights in East Ham, *Follow the Fun* moved on. Ironically, the next week was at the Empress, Brixton, where only ten days earlier Alfie had been turned away empty-handed. Then, after three more weeks in London – at the Bedford, Camden Town; the Palace, Walthamstow; and the Alexandra, Stoke Newington – the tour hit the road, venturing up to Norwich. Though the cast altered slightly – snooker champion Joe Davis joined for some weeks, performing trick shots that were seen by the audience from a mirror positioned at forty-five degrees over the table – Alfie was not given any grand stage roles. But with his 'small parts' he was at least treading the boards a little. In a comedy court sketch he had to wear a policeman's uniform:

Judge Next case, please.
Clerk of the Court Call Mrs Worthington!
Policeman CALL MRS WORTHINGTON!

And in the twice-nightly finale, Alfie would don a Union Jack waistcoat and go on stage as John Bull, joining the rest of the cast dressed up as service-men and -women. Like most (if not all) wartime Variety shows, *Follow the Fun* felt obliged to maintain a staunchly patriotic stance in at least one of the sketches, usually the close, to send audiences back to their own personal battlefronts in determined mood.

The irony, of course, was not lost even on a naïve seventeen-year-old. Except for those genuinely too old for call-up, the stage performers and backstage crew included a fair few shirkers, people who pleaded poor health or were homosexual or objected conscientiously. 'You had to laugh at the hypocrisy,' Hill later reflected. 'When we faced the audience and sang "Land of Hope and Glory" I would have hysterics.'

He could laugh. Being seventeen, too young yet for conscription, he had nothing to worry about.

Moving on around the country – Salford, Wood Green (north London), Grimsby, Lincoln, Bath, Cardiff and finally Hanley – Alfie began to learn about professional show-business. The Captain and GP were right, it was a very long way from glamorous. But the young lad was having a ball. In each town or city he'd board with a local landlady, usually one recommended by performers in previous shows that had passed through. Stage artists down the decades have enjoyed swapping their often hair-raising anecdotes of showbiz landladies, and Alfie soon had a fund of his own, women who would have *none of that*. 'Not in my house, oh no, I keeps a *respectable* house, and if you don't like it you can *clear orf aht of it!*'

Such establishments were pretty bleak at the best of times – cold, threadbare and restrictive; in wartime, with rationing, shortages and black-outs in force, they were especially so. What a life!

Alfie observed, too, the *chutzpah* of show-business promoters. When a couple of holes appeared in the touring schedules for *Let the Band Play* and *Follow the Fun*, perhaps because of bomb-damaged theatres, Harry Benet took out an advertisement in *The Stage*, proclaiming:

> £1,000,000 has been taken by these revues, the sale of War Bonds, and the Income Tax collector, during the last four weeks. Managers who wish to be in on the second million should write direct to Harry Benet or Bernard Delfont.

Follow the Fun closed in the first week of December 1941. As was tradition, virtually everyone in the profession gave up their year-round endeavours to busy themselves in a Christmas pantomime. None more so than Benet, who presented pantos this season in Bournemouth, Bristol, Wolverhampton, Dudley and Plymouth. Within days of *Follow the Fun* ending, Alfie found himself at the Bournemouth Pavilion, setting up scenery for the Boxing Day opening of *Robinson Crusoe*. Again, his participation remained more behind-the-scenes than on-stage, and his name didn't figure in any of the advertising, which must have disappointed the youth. Two years earlier he had been evacuated here as a failing schoolboy. How satisfying it would have been to have 'had his name in lights'.

Harry Benet's production was a ripping success, seen by more than 25,000 local citizens in a record-breaking run that ended on the last day of January 1942. Sixteen hundred children of men serving the Crown were treated to a free show that was resolutely upbeat. A preview piece in the *Bournemouth Daily Echo* had noted that Benet would be 'excluding all references to the war, for he feels that the public want to get right away from the troubles of the outside world and remember there is still a fairyland of fantasy.'

Alfie was once again 'ASM and small parts', and none of the latter was sufficient to gain him a mention in lengthy reviews published in both *The Stage* and the *Bournemouth Daily Echo*. Alfie later labelled these roles 'a spit and a cough'. Most memorably, he joined in a cannibal dance, blacking-up his hands and face, wearing a fake nose-bone, frizzy black wig, black body-stocking and grass skirt, and carrying a spear, hopping on stage to a jungle-drum beat from the orchestra pit. It was a performance the heavily set youth ensured was weightier than required. But the reviewers overlooked his contribution, noting instead the versatile performance of the principal comedian, the quaintly named Walter Niblo, 'nimble of foot and glib of tongue'.

Also mentioned were the ballet sequences, the acrobatic tumblers, and the 'equestrian eccentricities of Lulu the almost human horse'. (In a later Hill TV skit, the rear end of a pantomime horse breaks the act, complaining bitterly of being farted at in the face by the man in front.) One review also cited the 'Man Friday who can play the xylophone with his toes' and the comic Dudley Dale, 'who wears arresting costumes with coy femininity. As Mrs Crusoe he can kick a high toe and is very funny as a ballerina.'

Pantomime tradition has always dictated that the leading male roles are played by women, and vice versa, thus the idea is considered 'normal'. But it is also, of course, bizarre.

Telling men from women in the theatrical world can anyway be problematic. As a member of a professional touring company, Alfie was now encountering homosexuality for the first time, something for which performing as the Boy Wonder of Eastleigh's working-men's clubs had not prepared him. With his slightly effeminate gait, he was already assumed to 'bat for the other side'. So when Alfie was asked outright if he was 'queer', his innocent response – 'No, I'm feeling fine!' – caused much amusement. And during the run of *Follow the Fun*, when one of the lithe young performers had peered out into the audience and beheld the abundance of 'trade', Alfie had no idea what the fellow was talking about.

Leonard Hill cycled over to Bournemouth to see his brother and *Robinson Crusoe* and was amazed at the gay antics of the svelte young chorus boys with whom Alfie had to share local accommodation: elegant young men who performed a pirouette before they farted and who sat around gossiping bitchily about the other cast members. Hitherto unaware of even the notion of homosexuality, Alfie was taking it all in, and warily keeping his distance. Simultaneously, however, he was finding the women dancers aloof. Experienced hands at backstage relationships, they considered Alfie too callow, too green, to get involved with.

A man had thought otherwise, however. In September 1941, just after he had joined the tour, *Follow the Fun* had played at the Palace, Walthamstow, in east London. Preparing the show backstage, Alfie realized that he had left behind the company's ironing-board at the previous week's venue, across London in Camden Town. Having returned there on the bus, Alfie was accosted backstage by Toni, of the novelty dance act Toni and Tim. While Toni was a mainstay, the 'Tim' changed quite frequently, depending on who was available. Looking over the strapping young Alfie Hill, sizing him up and down, imagining him in white tie and tails – and out of them, too, no doubt – Toni offered Alfie the chance to become the next Tim. 'Come up to my Maida Vale flat tomorrow and we'll discuss it,' the dancer suggested.

When Alfie, innocence personified, made the visit, his lemonade was laced with gin and Toni was patting the 'casting-couch', inviting the youngster to take a seat next to him. Promising his new friend stardom, Toni began unbuttoning the boy's shirt and leaned over for a kiss, reasoning, 'We've got to be friends if we're going to work together!'

The boy jumped up. 'I don't kiss men, that'd be silly. If you want me in this act, you'll have to take me for my talent alone!'

This grand response was giddy stuff. Alfie's gin-soaked head was giddy, too. As he swept out of the flat he stumbled over the doormat.

After *Robinson Crusoe*, Alfie was at a loose end. But with a new revue in preparation, due to begin touring in March, Harry Benet assured Alfie of a place in the company and, in the meantime – to dissuade him from running off elsewhere – found him work at a London scenery workshop, in Penrose Street, just south of the Elephant and Castle district. Dressed in a new boiler-suit, which he never took off, Alfie helped paint huge stage backcloths, drawing upon his natural artistic talent to depict trees and clouds. He also performed some basic carpentry, nailing and screwing together scenic sets. During his twenty-year run of shows at Thames Television decades later, Benny Hill often supplied set-design drawings to the production team, indicating construction and showing precise measurements. He was utilizing the knowledge picked up here, in a cold warehouse by a railway bridge in the blackout winter of wartime London 1942.

In return for agreeing to act as fire-watcher, standing on the roof every night and looking out for German incendiary bombs, Alfie was also permitted to sleep in the warehouse, making his bed on a pile of hessian sacks. This meant he could save his wages. To save more, he lived through the next month on a diet of bread and tea. He bathed, only occasionally, at a local public 'slipper baths'. To mark his eighteenth birthday, the other men in the workshop encouraged him to get out one night. He nipped across the Thames to see a show at the Hippodrome, *Get a Load of This*, a musical starring the Viennese-born comedian/musician Vic Oliver, Winston Churchill's son-in-law.

But dressed, still, in his boiler-suit, Alfie's appearance drew disapproving glances from the well-heeled London theatre crowd.

Alfie's loyalty to Benet was paying off, though. Grandly touted by the promoter (and co-author) as 'the Revue Of Revues', *Send Him Victorious* hit the road in March 1942, opening – with more of a whimper than a bang one suspects – with a week at the Tivoli, Grimsby. Though still ASM, Hill was among the cast named in a whole-page advertisement placed by Benet on the front cover of *The Performer*, 'the official organ of the Variety Artistes' Federation', dated March 5 1942:

ALF HILL *The Warrior*

Why he was 'The Warrior' has proven impossible to uncover. Nor is it known what being 'The Warrior' entailed. All that's certain is that, irrespective of his billing, the lad from Southampton was considered too raw a comedian to be allowed anything remotely close to his own standup spot.

But 'The Warrior' he was, and it was his first-ever bill matter. At least he could be thankful he wasn't 'Grave And Gay' like Frank Cariello, or 'The Officers' Mess' (James Lea) or 'Almost Sane' (comedian Archie Wallen), the more experienced members of the cast whose names he propped up.

And professionally, note, he was Alf Hill, no longer Alfie. Alf was more mature-sounding, reasoned the aspiring star, now fully grown at five foot ten inches. The boy was becoming a man.

Titled after the lyric of the National Anthem, *Send Him Victorious* was another drawn-out revue, the blurb promising 'Twelve Delightful Scenes, including Maison Marie's Beauty Parlour, Revolving To The Barrack Square, The Slave Market, North Of The Tweed and Town On Parade'. The dance act Patricia, Colin and Vicki ('The Dancing Trio De Luxe') did various displays, the final one being a mixture of adagio, acrobatic and Russian dancing. 'For a man of such spare figure, it is remarkable how Colin manages to lift the girls about,' one reviewer noted. Headlining comedians Archie Wallen and Dave Jackley (son of George 'The Indignant Comedian' Jackley and brother of Nat 'Rubberneck' Jackley) performed the barrack square sketch, and another in which they played a couple of soldiers returning home after a long absence. Old 'Grave And Gay' delivered a character study of an ageing army pensioner in the monologue 'I Forget', and the Ten Charmon Girls drilled about the stage in smart uniforms – bringing the usual incongruous dash of glamour to the horrifying war currently unfolding across much of the globe.

As ASM, Alfie was having to pay rapt attention backstage, forever setting up the next scene – twelve scenes a show, two shows an evening, 144 scenes a week, sometimes a matinée too, before everything was dismantled and packed away, ready for putting on the train to the next week's destination, where it would all be reassembled for the next gross.[2] In August, when the show played at the Victoria Theatre in Burnley, the SM had to rush off to London to be with his sick wife. Alfie was temporarily promoted in his stead. At the age of eighteen, to be stage manager of a touring revue – and, as The Warrior, part-time performer – was no mean achievement, wartime or otherwise. It can only have been to his dismay that he still had to clean up after animals. For in addition to the comics and dancers, *Send Him Victorious* featured Cooke's Pony Revue, a circus and Variety attraction for already well in excess of 100 years. Four pure white Shetland ponies came on stage to dance, play percussion and engage in boxing, accompanied by Adelaide Cooke and her mother, both dressed in stylish gowns, furs and jewellery. Those today who mourn the death of Variety have a good point – nothing remotely like it has come along since.

The tour ran and ran, from spring to summer to autumn, from Grimsby to Scunthorpe to Scarborough, York, Manchester, Chester, Harrogate, Doncaster, Weston-super-Mare, Aldershot, Wood Green, Shepherd's Bush, Leeds, Hackney, Hull, Kettering, Harrow, Burnley, Rochdale, Chatham, Bath, Kilburn, Woolwich, Walthamstow, Clapham, Derby, West Hartlepool, Newcastle and Blackpool. In the *Grimsby Evening Telegraph* Teddy Glanvill proclaimed, 'It is only the National Anthem which enables the final curtain to fall on this 100% show. It's marvellous.' (He didn't say anything about The Warrior, though.) And the *Manchester Guardian* declared, 'It is a good deal more intelligent than most revues, and the freshness of the production alone is a recompense for some frowsy memories.' (Again, no mention of The Warrior.)

But The Warrior on stage was not at all keen at being one off stage. In July 1942 Alfie had turned eighteen-and-a-half, at which point he became eligible for conscription into military service. Soon afterwards, a manila envelope bearing the unmistakable legend OHMS arrived at the bungalow on the edge of the New Forest. It was Alfie's call-up. The Captain shuddered once more, remembering all too clearly his appalling experiences in the First World War.

A law-abiding citizen all his young life, Alfie Hill was in a quandary. Avoiding call-up was a criminal offence, but he was finally out there having fun. He hadn't run away from home at sixteen only to go into battle at eighteen. He had longed to break into show-business, and had; was he going to chuck it in so soon? Then he realized. With *Send Him Victorious* on tour, shifting around the country from week to week, he could always ignore the letters, and claim, if and when the authorities caught up with him, that he hadn't received anything.

The ruse worked only until mid-November. After a week in Rhyl, north Wales, *Send Him Victorious* switched to the New Theatre, Cardiff, for its final engagement before the pantomime season kicked in once again. On the Friday night, Alfie was standing side-stage when he felt a tap on his shoulder. He turned to face two military policemen and the query, 'Are you Alfred Hawthorn Hill?' Answering in the affirmative, he was escorted to Cardiff police station and thrown into the cells.

Though he never admitted publicly to his avoidance scam, Alfie revealed it to Norman Crisp – a contemporary at both Western and Taunton's schools, and in later years the writer of several prominent BBC television drama series. Crisp bumped into Hill in Southampton later in the winter of 1942–3. 'He was in army private's uniform,' Crisp says. 'He told me that after leaving Taunton's he had gone on to the stage, and was touring. And he had thought to himself that when he came across notification in writing to report for military service, he would keep quiet. "I won't bother about it because they'll never find me," he said. So he kept on doing the tour. But of course they did find him – the police descended on him, and he served his time in jankers.'

Alfie was forced to admit to having 'given himself up'. The alternative, being formally charged with avoidance of call-up, would have led to criminal court proceedings. Compelled to surrender his shoelaces, lest he consider hanging himself, he spent three nights behind bars in Cardiff before being whisked off to a nearby camp. Here he was locked away a second time, in the detention room. He was also instructed to scrub it clean, down on his hands and knees, with a mangy sponge and cold water. This was no way to treat an ASM with small parts.

Three further days later he was taken off to a camp at Lincoln, the town where, a little over a year earlier, he had been *Following the Fun* at the Theatre Royal. No chance of such levity now. To get to Lincoln, over in the east of England, he was escorted by a pair of military policemen, by train from Cardiff to Paddington, across London by tube and up again on the mainline from King's Cross. He was all but route-marched the entire journey. Alfie's biggest fear was that someone 'in the business' would recognize him.

Alfie's military 'career' began here at Lincoln at Christmas 1942. The bawling regimental sergeant-major, brutish at the best of times, made Hill's life especially miserable because he felt sure the new soldier had tried to dodge call-up. Alfie began a hectic six-week training period, saluting everything in sight, endlessly marching and enduring dawn gymnasium exercises. The hapless gym antics of many of the conscripts, Alfie surely included, inspired the budding comedian with one of his most enduring TV sketches for later years, performed several times for the cameras.

Though Britain (with her allies) went on to win the war, there is little doubt that much of her military machine's might was backed by an archaic leadership of men that was arrogant, foolish and demeaning. In common with most conscripts, Alfie discovered a class-ridden army full of pointless exercises designed to keep the men mindful of 'their place'. Only at the very end of hostilities, in 1945, did his army service have any significance. Until then, as he later admitted, it was awful. 'I loathed it,' he complained. 'Route marches, manoeuvres, oh how I resented it. Half the sergeants were power-mad, calling us privates up from the ranks and yelling, "You're a dozy little man! What are you?" And we had to reply, "I'm a dozy little man, sergeant."'

After his basic training, Alfie was subjected to a raft of tests, the outcome of which would determine his placement for the duration of the war. He passed the clerk's test. But such was the army's organizational ineptitude that he was considered most suited to the Royal Electrical and Mechanical Engineers, REME (pronounced 'Reemy') for short, as a driver-mechanic. What a joke – if there was anyone on Earth less mechanically minded, Alfie had yet to meet him. And he had never driven a car. Moreover, because The Captain had never owned one, he had only been a passenger on the rarest of occasions. Now he was destined to spend his remaining years in uniform – an open-ended period – fixing engines and driving trucks.

Re-posted from Lincoln to Staines, west of London, Alfie was taught to drive in a London taxi-cab *sans* roof and with a wooden bench added in the front, leaving just space enough for an instructing sergeant and a couple of learner drivers. From here it was on to Brighton and a fitter's course. In a test, Alfie came in forty-first out of forty-two conscripts. Finally, in July 1943, some seven months after being thrown into jail in Cardiff, he was posted to a REME unit supporting an anti-aircraft searchlight battery stationed in Arnold, the Nottingham suburb.

But while his electrical and mechanical skills were next to useless, Alfie contributed in another way – by improving morale.

Though useless with a wrench – he would labour for hours over the simplest of mechanical tasks – he would work with a laugh, a song and a shout. He was never short of company. For the most part his fellow privates were a willing audience – even if few of them could work out what was driving the young man on; none of them had any desire to scribble down on a scrap of paper their thoughts and observations about army life and read it out as if he were a BBC comedian.

Alfie's (albeit limited) experience as an entertainer enabled him to reach out to his comrades on a humour level, blending impudence with innuendo and now adding the occasional lampoon of a commanding officer. The chaps in Alfie's platoon were 'regular guys', your average cigarette-smoking, beer-drinking, *Daily Mirror*-reading Britisher with few pretensions of grandeur. They (and their wives) would always be his favourite audience.

Alfie was never anything better than a disastrously bad driver. At the wheel on a night manoeuvre in Anglesey, north-east Wales, his road weaving prompted a sergeant to bark, 'Look! That idiot Hill's taken over now!' Sure enough, his lorry ended up in a ditch, earning Craftsman Hill 14332308 a very severe dressing-down.

Tony House saw his cousin Alfie for the first time in more than two years in this period: 'I don't know if he was on leave or stationed locally but he was driving an army lorry and it was parked outside my house in Kipling Road, Eastleigh. He was a big man by now, in army uniform, and he had a dark leather body-warmer worn over the top of his serge battledress. Unfortunately, I didn't see him actually driving the vehicle, because I subsequently heard how comical it was.'

Alfie spent the best part of two years safe on British soil. In May–June 1940, before he was enlisted, the British had retreated from mainland Europe at Dunkerque. But in June 1944 the Allies secured a landing at Normandy, beginning the liberation of Western Europe and the front that would see Germany pushed back to the point of obliteration, and Hitler's suicide, within a year. Alfie did not participate in the bloody Normandy landings, nor their immediate aftermath, although his and the other REME outfits were responsible for waterproofing vehicles before and after D-Day so that they could be driven off boats, safely resist a short period in the sea and then drive on to the beach.

Three months later Alfie's REME battery also made the journey over to France, waved off from Southampton by Helen and Big Alf. It was Alfie's first sight of foreign soil, one that the intrepid globetrotter of future years would never forget.

His outfit set up base at Gravelines, between Calais and Dunkerque, where a pocket of German soldiers had been trapped by the encircling Allied troops. Having broken out of the German siege at the Normandy beachhead, the Allies had ensnared their besiegers, after which the two sides lobbed a few incendiaries at one another. Always some distance behind the surging Allied front, the pocket was the closest that Craftsman Hill came to being in a life-threatening position during the Second World War.

But most of this period in northern France was spent relatively quietly. Alfie extended his basic command of French and enjoyed the kind of rural café idyll that he would return to endlessly for the rest of his life. In these later years, Alfie revealed too that he had enjoyed the odd *liaison* during this Gallic period. Details are sketchy, but the young man lost his virginity on French soil in the early weeks of 1945, around his twenty-first birthday, bedding the attractive younger wife of a blackmarketeer café owner.

From Gravelines the battery drove across liberated Belgium and into

Germany, the war nearly over, setting up base at Melle, near Osnabrück. Seeing the pitiful, half-starved German children, Alfie was instrumental in staging a Christmas party. He persuaded fellow soldiers to sell their cigarette rations to raise money for presents, he encouraged the American allies to hand over a few Hershey bars, and he walked the Melle streets dressed as Santa Claus, with a table-tennis ball, painted red, stuck on the end of his nose. The local children followed him yelling '*Zirkus clown!*'

Germany was overrun by the Allies and the war sped to a close in the spring of 1945. For Alfie, military service had not been dissimilar to his time at Taunton's. Just as he could have been an academic achiever had he applied his mind, or – perhaps more accurately – overcome certain crises of confidence, so he had endeavoured to 'drop out' of REME as much as he could. When volunteers had been required Alfie had always been conspicuously absent. When a job had needed to be done, typically, he had done it slowly and not very well, blaming his lassitude on the army for posting him to a branch of the services inappropriate to his talents.

Just after he was conscripted, a fortune-teller had predicted to Alfie that he would become 'a leader of men'. On this occasion, at least, the sooth-sayer was laughably wrong. He made absolutely sure that he never came within a whiff of promotion. Rather, like a British version of Ernie Bilko, he reserved his cunning to dodging guard-duty.

What Alfie ought to have done was not to wait until his call-up avoidance was detected but to *volunteer* for the services. He could have cited his ASM experience and asked to be posted to the British army's Entertainments National Service Association, ENSA, which mounted morale-boosting shows all over the world. In this way he could have 'done his bit' for King and Country while aiding his show-business training and aspirations.

Instead, as he told BBC radio interviewer John Ellison in 1966, his years aged nineteen to twenty-one had amounted to little more than a waste of time:

> For the first three years [I was in the army] I was what was laughingly called a normal soldier, a sort of driver-mechanic. But not a very good one. I've driven everything from Scammells and those big Leylands and

the Jeeps and motor-bikes. This is why I don't run a car now. I've driven miles and miles, starting at ten at night, all through the night, all through the day, all through the next night, and no lights at night, with a little tin of water to keep putting over your face to keep yourself awake.

Though the war was over, demobilization of soldiers didn't happen overnight. The extraordinary task of mopping up, rebuilding bridges and roads, dealing with refugees and re-establishing civil order takes time. Few British soldiers were reprieved of their duties until late into 1946, many much later. It wasn't until summer 1947 that Alfie Hill was demobilized. But, undoubtedly, life became a sight easier for everyone now that the conflict was over. Soon, a poster was pinned on the Melle camp notice-board to tempt any talented servicemen hitherto unattached to the entertainments divisions to apply for transfer to the Central Pool of Artists (CPA).

Alfie applied but heard nothing. Under-used, and bored to the back teeth with REME, he visited CPA's headquarters in London during his next home leave.

And in this interim period, Alfie had obviously been doing some serious thinking. He didn't want to go back on the Variety circuit as 'ASM and small parts', and he didn't have the self-belief to step on stage and face an audience alone. Especially in the barn-like Variety theatres capable of seating more than 1,000. Projection beyond the first few rows would forever be a problem for him. So he had arrived at a momentous decision. Performing would have to take a back-seat, relegated by a new strand to his career – comedy writing.

To build a fund of material, he declined to spend these early post-war months whooping it up with his REME buddies, who were making up for lost years by attending dances and fraternizing with women. Instead, Alfie elected to stay in the barracks, pen in hand.

But it was to be the first of numerous occasions in the next twenty-five years when he attempted to change the direction of his career, only to be thwarted.

At the Upper Grosvenor Street HQ Alfie met Charlie Chester, the famous radio and stage comedian presently attached to the CPA in a talent-finding mission. When Alfie offered himself as scriptwriter Chester replied, 'Pity! We're not taking scriptwriters at present. But there's always room for somebody with a good act. We're holding auditions tomorrow – why don't you come along?'

So Alfie put his new career on hold for the time being.

But, an act? Alfie had never worked *an act* before, at least not one that he hadn't filched from Max Miller. Where the heck was he going to get an act in the next twenty-four hours?

Walking into the heart of London from Westminster, Alfie was in desperate need of comedic inspiration. And about the only place to see comedy in the daytime was at the Windmill Theatre in Soho, owned by the impresario Vivian Van Damm – VD to his friends – and home of the *Revudeville* nude shows. The Windmill was an invaluable training ground for scores of hopeful comedians too.

Performing at the Windmill was tough for comics because they were merely providing the 'filler' material in between the fan-dancing acts and nude tableaux. 'Any additional artificial aid to vision is NOT Permitted' the programme stoutly declared; the demand for a front-row view here was such that as soon as a seat became available men would clamber over the stalls. This became known as the 'Windmill Steeplechase'. And there were always one or two men in long raincoats who masturbated while the dancers were doing their stuff. For a long time a venue of ill-repute, the Windmill had gained perhaps its greatest notoriety as the one entertainment venue in London that carried on during the Blitz. 'We Never Closed' became its proud slogan. One wagster remodelled this to 'We Never Clothed'.

This day, however, Alfie was more interested in the comedians than the crumpet. And there was one Windmill comic who made a particular impact, Peter Waring, who was using material scripted for him by a young writer still attached to the RAF, Frank Muir.

Hill remembered the moment in the book *The Laughtermakers*:

Waring was the biggest influence on my life. He was delicate, highly strung and sensitive. He always worked in tails and smoked a cigarette. He did throwaway stuff like 'A bachelor is a man who's got no children . . . to speak of.' When I saw him I thought, 'My God, it's so easy. You don't have to come on shouting, "'Ere, 'ere, missus! Got the music, 'Arry? Now missus, don't get your knickers in a twist!" You can come on like Waring and say, "Not many in tonight. There's enough room at the back to play rugby. My God, they *are* playing rugby."'

When I saw him that day at the Windmill I didn't pinch his material but I went back to my Auntie's house in Bexleyheath and worked out an act which involved telling a shaggy-dog story about an Irishman, a Scotsman, a Welshman, a West Countryman and a Cockney. This gave me the chance to do all my accents. The next morning I did it for the audition.[3]

Alfie's performance before Colonel Lazbury and his crusty cohorts on the CPA audition panel went down a storm and he left with assurances of a position in a show. Returning to Germany, he was disappointed that the transfer from REME took three interminable weeks to come through, but then it did, and Alfie became a member of the so-called Stars in Battledress troupe, set to spend the remainder of his army life as an entertainer.

Returning to London he was billeted in Grosvenor Square, in ritzy Mayfair, and rehearsed hard for his first role. But his Waring-like performance had given the producers quite the wrong impression – they saw Hill as ideal material for an awfully-awfully middle-class 1930s musical play, *Happy Week-end!*, not at all 'Alfie'. The part required him to act, sing and dance. A fish out of water, he struggled through the rehearsals while the director, a Major McGregor, tore his hair out.[4]

Whatever fate held in store for him, Alfie knew he was about to take an important step in his career, prompting him finally to adopt a stage name. He had already dabbled with Alf Hill during the run of *Send Him Victorious*. But even that wasn't right – he knew it would often be reduced to 'Alf 'ill', which, to use his own words, would make him seem like a 'coster comic'.

He had, for a year or two in REME, been toying with the idea of calling himself Benny Hill, partly in tribute to the great American comic Jack Benny, whose work he hugely admired, and partly because it would make him sound Jewish, and Jewish comedians – like Jack Benny – numbered among the best in the business. It would do him no harm to be thought of as Jewish. It might even help get him some work, considering how many show-business agents and managers were also Jews.

Perhaps, too, Alfie was being mindful of The Captain's paternal diktat all those years ago in Westrow Gardens – 'Make friends with Jewish people and you won't go wrong.'

Happy Week-end! opened at the opera house in Calais and then set off on a tour of British army camps, by which point the scenery, carted around Europe for a couple of years, was looking distinctly shabby. Seeing the production, the bandleader Jack Payne is reputed to have commented, 'Why does the play take place in a public lavatory?' It was also way too twee and gentrified for its audiences, the British 'Tommy' whose attention span was prone to wander at anything long. 'Benny' realized the problems and set to work on the dialogue, adding a number of common, contemporary touches that went down well. When the tour of *Happy Week-end!* finished he was despatched back to Germany, to the army's entertainment headquarters near Lüneburg, just south of Hamburg, where his next posting was to be compère-comedian of an army Variety show. This was more like it.

The final dress-rehearsal for the new show took place before an audience of two – a major and his sergeant. Benny had scribbled off a raft of new material, designed to effect an untroubled transition from act to act. He was really rather proud of himself – it was suddenly all coming along nicely. But then disaster struck. After the rehearsal the major commended all of the acts and then turned to the compère and declared that he wasn't up to the task. 'Some people are comedians, some are not, and you're not,' the officer offered. 'The audience won't stand for you – they'll give you the bird.'

For the first time, but not the last, Benny Hill was being told what a rotten comedian he was. Worse still, he was ordered to leave the company and to return to his old REME unit. It was a double-whammy that sent him reeling.

But he was lucky. Another man had stood watching the dress-rehearsal, a Jewish Yorkshireman sergeant, Harry Segal, who was in charge of an army revue called *It's All in Fun*, in which he also performed as comedian. A veteran trouper of pre-war Variety shows, though without having made a breakthrough into broadcasting and so national fame, Segal's opinion of

Benny's compèring and comedic qualities was in marked contrast to the major's.

Now deceased, Harry Segal recorded an account of what occurred:

In my opinion the major was wrong – I could see that Benny's comedy was far ahead of its time. And when I saw the look on his face! He was so upset, so depressed, so heartbroken at being dropped from the show and being sent back to his unit. He went back to his room and started to pack his kit-bag. I went up to him, put my hand on his shoulder, and said, 'Now listen. I will try and get you out on tour with my troupe, as props and stagehand, and once we get away from here I promise you that you will be in the show.' I went to see the major, who agreed that, provided Benny would not step foot on to the stage as an entertainer [I could do this]. So out we went on tour.

Benny was back to being a stage manager, resigned to spending the rest of his days in uniform 'lumping huge wicker-baskets and crates of stage props'. But he and Harry had become friends. 'We toured everywhere,' Segal later remembered, 'bomb sites, church halls, towns, villages, fields, travelling miles and miles to the small, isolated places no one had heard of. One date we played was to an audience of Polish troops who couldn't speak a word of English.

'We always got a meal after the show, some good, some terrible, and we would beg, borrow or scrounge wherever we could. On one trip we stopped the truck by a farm and Benny and I went to the farmhouse and asked the farmer's wife, a big fat German lady, if she had any eggs. She gave us a large bag full in exchange for cigarettes, chocolate and soap. She then said to us, "Would you like some chickens?" "Not half!" We hadn't had chicken for ages. She picked up a chicken and was just going to wring its neck when Benny and I looked at each other, turned and ran. She shouted, in English, "What kind of soldiers are you?"'

One night *It's All in Fun* played to servicemen in a tiny theatre in the castle in Celle, a few kilometres north of Hanover. Harry Segal was short of performers this evening because two of them had gone down with the flu. Disobeying the major's order and risking all this entailed, he set to work on his insecure young pal.

'I said to Benjy, "Get on that stage!" He said, "I'm sorry, Harry, no, not tonight." I said, *"Benjy, get on that stage!"* but still he wouldn't go on. I made it an *order* and *pushed* him in front of the audience.'

When the reluctant, vulnerable comedian heard his first laugh, his confidence came back, and then there was no stopping him. As 'second comic' Benny was straightman to Harry Segal in a double-act and also performed his own solo spot. He ditched (temporarily) the Waring-like shaggy-dog story and instead gave an early airing to a newly written piece that he would use for decades to come, a cod-German character named Toto, shuffling on stage with a bowler-hat pulled down over his eyebrows, splaying his ears, talking about places in London 'Edgvare Strasse, Gilders Groin, Marble Arse', wishing people 'a good body every evening' and remarking about a woman's figure as having 'kleine Sitzen und grossen Titzen'. His innate ability to pick up the cadences of foreign languages was paying dividends.

Among the audience was one Richard Stone, recently demobilized from the army but given the honorary rank of colonel in a part-time position as head of a new, peacetime organization, Combined Services Entertainment. Stone was investing the rest of his energies in establishing a talent agency partnership back in London. He was probably scouting for likely clients. Afterwards, Stone said to Hill, 'If you ever need an agent, I shall be one after all this is over. When you're in London come and talk to me.'

In his professional life, and on numerous occasions in his private life, Benny Hill had an unconquerable Achilles' heel. He was deeply wounded by rejection, and retired into a shell to lick his wounds.

'I'm a rather funny sort of chap, easily hurt,' he wrote of this period in 1955, 'and the brush-off I had been given by the officer in charge gave me such an inferiority complex that I was really scared to face an audience again. But the sergeant had given me an order, so somehow I got up on that little stage and began cracking a few gags. Luckily, the audience laughed and I went off after about eight minutes to good applause. If that audience had given me the bird there would be no Benny Hill today. I'd probably have chucked the whole thing.'

Though frail of confidence and uncertain of his direction, Benny had been set back on the road to eventual success thanks to the timely intervention of a kindly stranger.

Typically, being an agreeable man himself, Benny Hill never forgot it, and repaid the debt time and again in the ensuing decades . . . as he grew to become The World's Most Popular Comedian.

2. Benny Hill:
Comedy Specialist

NEXT Week—September 1st - FIRST LONDON APPEARANCE at the
Palace, Camberwell of

BENNY HILL

The Comedian with "a Personality Like Sunshine"

BROADCASTING WED. SEPT. 3rd 9.15-10 p.m. in CARROLL LEVIS' "VARIETY ROUNDABOUT"

Available Immediately for Variety, Cabaret or Revue
(With exceptions, Concerts booked)

also FREE FOR PANTOMIME . . Entirely Original Material . . Scripts written for Revues.

No Sole Agent   Inquiries : Frank Woolf, "Show World"

Lyceum (Howard and Wyndham) (7, Mat. Sat., 2.30). Festival Season. Old Vic Co. in "The Taming of the Shrew" and "Richard II".

EASTBOURNE

Hippodrome (U.V.A.) Douglas Byng, 6 Zio Angels, Douglas Francis, De Lampe and Dodge, Bashful Boys, Chic Elliott, Mayer and Kitson.

FOLKESTONE

Pleasure Gardens (U.V.A.). James Shirwell presents "Message for Margaret".

FELIXSTOWE

Ranelagh (Hands). "Ranelagh Revels," Kenneth Blain, Ernie Moss, Helen Jaye, Marlie Caird, Murray Brown and Michael Blair, Val Duval, Donald Hatton and "Cabaret Calling" Girls.

GATESHEAD

Empire 3 Spallas, Birb and Ninette, Moja and Myna, Billy Maxam, Mignon Jarrold, Arlette Noel, Brooklyn Three.

GLASGOW

King's (Howard and Wyndham) (8, Sat., 6 and 8.30). "Half Past Eight," Harry Gordon, Beryl Reid, Jack Holden, Helen Crerar, etc.

Royal (Howard and Wyndham) (7.30, Mat., Sat., 2). Cecliw Productions present "Gardenia Lady".

Alhambra (Moss) (11) (7.15 Mat., Sat., 2.30). Wilson Barrett Co. presents "Arsenic and Old Lace".

Empire (Moss) (11) (6.10 and 6.25). Hamilton and Vassi, Gaston Palmer, Foster and Clarke, Jack Durant, Two Cromwells, Hutch, Fred Emney and Co., Henry Piat and Nandy.

Pavilion (Collins) (11). Tommy Morgan presents "Clairty's Cavalcade," Tommy Morgan, Tommy Yorke, Margaret Milne, Jimmy Dunn, Arthur Boynan, Morganettes, Rita Maher, Billy Leslie, Billy Cameron, Nicky Kidd, Five Smith Bros., Betty Melville, devised and produced by Pete Davis.

GRIMSBY

Palace (Pope) (11.30). Cecil Buckingham presents "Strike a New Note," with Freddie Frinton, Desmond and Marko, Mars Cranford and Nena, Charles Byrne, Doreen Raworthy, Sherman Fisher Girls, etc.

HANLEY

Theatre Royal. Robb Wilton, Lauri & Morgan, Rex Roper and Maisie, Anita, Joan Janssen, Dinks & Trixie Patson, Jack Muldoon Four, Stothard, Bobs and Rita Rema.

HOLLAND-ON-SEA

Queen's (Hands) "Holland Highlights," Ron Swayne, Eric Wilson, George Ford, Winnie Holman, Ivy Esta, Russell Sisters, etc.

HALIFAX

Palace (MacNaghten) (12). "Give It To Joe."

HUDDERSFIELD

Palace (MacNaghten) (12). Frank E. Franks, The Marellys, Charlie Higgins, Marco and Max, Freddie Harrison, Rose Marie, O'Reilly, Tom Robinson, Bunty St. Clair, George and Lydia, Gene Boyne, Huntley MacDonald.

HULL

New (Delfont). "Meet Mr. Manhattan."

Tivoli (Wade Rose). George Elrick, Jones and Thomas, Sylvestri, Velda and Vann, Moore and Hatton, Trixie and Anton, Ravel, Tiki and Dot, Dennis Gilbert.

IPSWICH

Hippodrome (Regis) (6 and 8.10, Mat. Sat., 2.30) Afrique, Victor Barna and Alec Brook, Cleel and Moreny, Kardomo, Mary Priestman, Joe King, Eve Milton, Mills Sisters and Michael.

LEEDS

City Varieties (Delfont). "Tin Pan Alley," with Billy Thorburn, Heath and Deane, Les Morgan, Leslie Lewis, 6 Melody Girls, Harry Pringle and Co.

Grand (Howard and Wyndham) (6.30, Mat. Tues., Sat., 2). Jack Boyer presents "Just William".

Empire (Moss) (11) (6 and 8.15). George and Lita Calienta, Turner Layton, Three Admires, Ethel Reynell, Dave and Joe O'Gorman, Stainless Stephen, Musical Derricks and Tony.

Theatre Royal (Moss) (6 and 8.15). Harry Hanson presents The Court Players.

LEICESTER

Opera House (Stoll) (6.30, Mat. Wed. Sat., 2.15). "Charley's Aunt.

Palace (Stoll) (11) (6 and 8.15). Felix Mendelssohn and his Hawaiian Serenaders, 3 Atlantas, Joan Winters and Guy Fielding, Charles Hague, Valmar Trio, Woods and Jarrett, Johnny Lockwood.

LINCOLN

Theatre Royal (Pope) (11.30). Harry Hanson presents The Court Players.

LITTLEHAMPTON

Pavilion (Hands). "Holiday Highlights," Bunny Baron, Freddie Hills, Brenda Hollandy, Sid Rodge, Peggy Ann Tyler, Terry Waterman and Babs, June and Odette, Barbara Francis, Marie Anthie.

LIVERPOOL

Empire (Moss) (11) (6.45, Mat. Sat., 2) The Covent Garden Opera Company.

Court (Howard and Wyndham) (6.30, Mats., Wed., Sat., 2.30). Bramba present "School for Spinsters"

Shakespeare (Collins) (11). Charles Shadwell and his Orchestra, Jack Crisp and Jill, Bob Kerns and Mary Lou, Frank Marx and Iris, Earle and Lewis, Sereno and Joy.

LLANDUDNO

Grand (Delfont). "Rebecca."

LUTON

Grand (Dennis). Ernie Lotinga's "Barnacle Bill"

MANCHESTER

Hippodrome (Stoll) (11) (6.15 and 8.30). Elsie and Doris Waters, Ivor Moreton and Dave Kaye, Swiss Stars, Albert Whelan, Pharos and Marina, Fred Hearne and Co., George Mansfield and Bernie Harris, Pop White and Stagger.

Opera House (Howard and Wyndham) (7, Mats. Wed. Sat., 2). Emile Littler presents "Song of Norway," with John Hargreaves, Janet Hamilton-Smith, etc.

6. The Sunshine Personality

The Second World War was won, but at home the battle was merely entering a new phase. Britain after the war – not just in the short term but for virtually a decade – struggled severely: rationing of essential foodstuffs was in place until 1953, there were fuel shortages, hundreds of thousands of homeless and sick, far too many orphaned children, and millions of bereaved. This had been a war to defeat Hitler, not a mission to conquer, so there were no 'spoils' for the victor, just a prolonged battle to rebuild lives, infrastructure and, hopefully, a more just society.

In May 1947, fully two years after VE night, when all of Britain had celebrated wildly the end of a grim six-year war in Europe, Benny Hill was demobilized from the services, a free man once more, given £52 and a pin-striped grey suit by His Majesty's grateful government.

It was make or break time for the aspiring young comedian . . . or comedy writer. He wasn't sure which. But he deposited the cash in a Post Office savings account, tucked the passbook into his inside breast-pocket and set off to find accommodation.

Representations from his parents – if indeed there were any – would have been brushed aside. Benny had no school qualifications or skilled apprenticeship to his name and there was considerable competition for employment. He was determined to forge ahead in his only chosen line of business – show-business.

That meant staying in London, and within hours of arriving back in the capital he had found himself his first permanent abode, centrally situated – a flat above a café at 14a Queensway, a hop and a skip from Bayswater Road and, beyond that, Kensington Gardens. It was also opposite Queensway tube station; Benny would be catching plenty of trains and buses over the next few years. He didn't know it, but he was about to launch into easily the most hectic period of his life, one that would see him working, mostly flat out, for some thirteen years.

He occupied the apartment along with three women – Molly, Dorothy and Hilda, a hairdresser, secretary and dancer – but there was still *none of that*. Bill Jaques visited his cousin 'Benny' at this time. 'The three girls were across the corridor. He didn't actually share, they were in the next room. He said to me "They're nice, aren't they?" But he wasn't at ease in their company.' Typically, Benny harboured hopes of entanglement; equally typically, he was to be disappointed. The women weren't interested in their man about the flat except when something needed *un*screwing.

Benny had a tough baptism in these early Queensway days. If there was work around he wasn't sure how to find it. He spent his first evening in London at a Combined Services Entertainment party, looking for familiar faces and some useful advice. He found neither.

About the only employment he could obtain was in ciné-Variety, a sphere of stage entertainment that many Variety comedians wouldn't touch with even their worst enemy's bargepole. It entailed clambering up on stage in a cinema and performing during the short 'intermission', while patrons were slurping Kia-Ora orange squash and wrestling to divest ice-cream spatulas from their paper encasings. It was soulless work, almost devoid of audience interest.

Bill Jaques was walking with his cousin one evening in Hyde Park when someone advised Benny that there was a chance of such work this very night. Benny literally ran back to his flat to pick up the bits and pieces necessary for his act. 'He was on stage in the interval between films at a Bayswater cinema,' says Jaques. 'Henry Fonda in *The Long Night*, that kind of thing. And he went on stage with a banjo in his hand. He told me later, "I can't play it, but they often think I might." Afterwards, when we went back to his flat, he took off his coat and just had on his stiff collar, dickey and cuffs. No shirt – he said he couldn't be bothered to wash it.'

Benny was familiar with living on a tight budget. Since leaving home at sixteen he had scarcely earned more than £3 a week. But all the same, his £52 'demob' grant was dwindling rapidly, given that he needed props, day clothes, the complete evening-dress kit (tuxedo, trousers, frilly shirt and bow-tie) for cabaret or after-dinner engagements, plus £2 5s a week for his room and enough to fund the customary Hill-sized diet. In a letter back home he told his mother of his problems. His Aunt Violet recalls, 'He also told Helen that he was finding it a bit difficult to get rations. So I wrote to him – I always wrote to him – and said, "You can get porridge oats, which are very good for you and off the ration. Make yourself some porridge." And I sent him half a dozen of my eggs. I had to wrap them in lots of paper. He wrote and told me he'd received them and was very grateful.

'He was still making up his mind whether he should stick it out in London or go back home. He was hoping to get on, and was thankful for my encouragement because he hadn't received any from his father, and his mother was worried about him being in London on his own. But I said to him "Stick it out, you'll make it."'

Benny very nearly didn't 'stick it out', however, and his fate hinged – as these things so often do – on a single improbable moment. In a later BBC radio interview he recalled the circumstances:

I had high hopes of being a great comic. But it wasn't easy. Nothing was happening. I was getting the odd working-men's club and the occasional dinner, and I had my £52 gratuity from the army. But soon I was down to just fourteen shillings in the Post Office [account] and owed about three weeks' rent.

I thought, 'This is being silly. I'd better pack this up and go home to mum and dad. Perhaps I could get a job in Southampton and maybe go out at night doing a bit of semi-pro dance-band work around the clubs, and settle for that.' It didn't worry me unduly.

So I went to Victoria Coach Station, thinking, 'Well, it's cheaper than the train, I'll get a bus down to Southampton.' And as I was wandering around there – waiting, or looking up the times of the buses or something – I passed the Biograph cinema and Danny Kaye was showing there in *Wonder Man*. I thought I'd go and have a look and then catch a later bus.[1]

When I came out I had changed my mind. I didn't say to myself, 'Well if he can do it, anybody can,' it wasn't like that, but I kept on thinking, 'Well, he did it, and I'm sure there were times *he* was about to get on a bus and go home.'

So I thought, 'I'll have another go,' and came back.

That I'd say, was the main turning point.

Back in his Queensway flat (propitiously for Benny, the three women had not yet let it to anyone else) the poverty-stricken comedian surveyed his options, and in need of inspiration he went to the news-stand to splash a few more pennies on the weeklies. There was *The Stage*, as reliable as ever, with its news and views about all aspects of theatrical entertainment. There was *The Performer*, which had given The Warrior his first professional name-check some five years earlier. And there was a newcomer, the slimmer, less authoritative but more reader-friendly *Show World*, launched just after the war. The managing editor – he probably washed the tea-cups, too – was Frank Woolf. Benny paid a visit to *Show World*'s attic office just off Leicester Square.

A relentless trader of goods in his childhood, Benny suggested a barter to Frank Woolf. He would write a regular, humorous column for *Show World*, free-of-charge, if Woolf would permit him the occasional free advertisement. Woolf liked the boy and went further, agreeing to act as his 'personal adviser' and take phone messages on his behalf, which Benny would collect by phoning in or visiting in person, climbing the hundred steps from street level.

The issue of July 30 1947 bore the first fruits of the relationship. Page eight carried a block advert.

A *New Comedy personality* . . .

BENNY HILL

Available **NOW** for . . . **Variety** . . . and . . . **Concerts**

NO SOLE AGENTS

Coms: c/o 'SHOW WORLD' or Phone WHI 7161

Four pages further on, a couple of columns were given over to an 800-word essay, 'My Uncle Silas', 'by Benny Hill, a new comedy discovery who also writes material'. Benny's reasoning was that he stood a better chance of making the grade if he was known as both a writer and performer. All being well, he could write his way to personal success.

Top, left to right: Benny's mother, Helen Cave, at the time she met . . . Alf Hill, back from a gruelling experience in the First World War. Sophia Hill – Alf's mother, Benny's steadfast Nana. The resemblance is unmistakable.

Middle: The Hills, newly settled in Southampton. *Standing, left to right*: Billy, Leonard (already suffering from the jaundice that would kill him), Alf (Benny's father), Ernie and Violet. *Seated*: Cissie, Nana and the manicured Henry Hawthorn Hill, Benny's grandfather, whose circus background and sideline as an entertainments journalist fuelled Benny's desire to become a comedian.

Right: Circus had been in the family for fifty years before Benny's birth. His Uncle Leonard displays typical prowess.

Left: Alfie – Benny – Hill as a babe in arms, with mother Helen and elder brother Leonard. **Right**: Benny Hill's birthplace: 30 Bridge Road (later 111 Bernard Street), Southampton – the central house, with the shop front. This photograph was taken in 1941, the terrace having somehow survived German bombing. The house is still there today, although no one realizes its significance.

Left: Canal Walk, Southampton, 1922 – a murky backstreet of arresting sights and smells. The photograph was taken outside Stanley & Co., where Benny's father, The Captain, discreetly sold condoms to prostitutes and sailors on shore leave.

Right: The Captain with his sons, wife and infant daughter Diana, circa 1937. Benny (standing, left) is now thirteen.

Top and middle left: The grammar school boy. Chirpy and keen at twelve, adolescent and unsettled at fourteen.

Top right: Craftsman Hill (front, right) with his fellow REME conscripts. The photo was taken in Wetteren, Belgium, as the war approached its end.

Left: The unwilling soldier. **Right**: Benny with his good friend and wartime comedy mentor Harry Segal. (Photo taken 1956.)

The Sunshine Personality takes his first faltering steps to stardom.

Left, top to bottom: Three handout publicity photos: the BBC radio novice of 1947; the self-conscious summer show 'feed' of 1949; early 1950s, nearly a star.

Above: The only known photograph of double-act Reg Varney and Benny Hill in action, taken during the four month run of *Gaytime* at the Cliftonville Lido, 1948.

Facing page: The young comedian, twenty-five, relaxing on a Cornish beach during another *Gaytime* summer season; Newquay, 1949. He had made his TV debut that spring.

Top left: Happy with Mum, but is The Captain about to blast?

Top right: The support comic, with main star Ron Clark; *Gaytime*, 1949.

Above: Perpetually nervous on the Variety stage, but Benny makes a fight of it; Leeds Empire, August 1954.

Top: With ventriloquist Peter Brough and pesky Archie Andrews, unlikely radio stars of the 1950s. Benny was a big catch for their BBC show *Archie's the Boy!*

Above left: Benny with his close friend – and broadcasting 'foe' – Bob Monkhouse.

Above right: Benny with his great mentor Kenneth Carter, the producer who ironed out the cruder aspects of his Variety act for 1950s television audiences.

August 25, 1954—The Sketch—147

A MAN OF MANY PARTS

*

A RANDOM SELECTION OF SOME OF
POPULAR COMEDIAN BENNY HILL'S
TV PERSONALITY IMPERSONATIONS

Screen "Tele-Snaps" by John Cura.

PHILIP HARBEN.

"WHAT'S MY LINE?" PANEL.

THE FILM ADDICT.

MUFFIN, THE MULISH MESSENGER.

BARBARA KELLY.

THE MODEST MANNEQUIN.

THE INDIAN LOVER.

GILBERT HARDING.

THE TEDDY BOY.

THE DRUMMER.

LADY BARNETT.

MR. SCUTTLE, THE FOREMAN.

HERBERT FUDGE (The Singer of Madrigals).

DAVID NIXON.

MISS PRIMROSE HILL.

Benny Hill's quick-changing versatility in the live *Showcase* so astonished TV viewers that the voguish *Sketch* magazine treated its well-heeled readers to a page of action 'Tele-Snaps'. The *What's My Line?* 'guy' was the inevitable central attraction.

Failing that, he could write somebody else's way to success. There were plenty of comics around. They all needed material.

'My Uncle Silas' was essentially a collection of gags, some old, some new, many borrowed, one or two light-bluish. Each piece of wit was unrelated to the one before but they held together on the loose frame of the fictitious uncle's life:

> Now, my Uncle Silas was never a very important man. His only claim to fame is that he originated the gag about the two 'cellos: where one 'cello says to the other 'cello, 'Who was that piccolo I saw you with last night?' and other 'cello replies, 'That was no piccolo that was my fife!' To most people, Uncle Silas was just a man, pure and simple – well, simple anyway!

Here and there, too, were hints at autobiography:

> Now Uncle Silas first started on a series of adventurous careers, when, at the age of 16, he was kicked out of the house by his parents. Well, they didn't exactly kick him out, they just took him to the city boundary and pointed. Uncle Silas was not afraid of life (he'd seen too much of it on [*sic*] the movies) and he soon found where his talents lay, so he took to the theatre. Unfortunately, the theatre didn't take to him.

And it ended with a dash of sauce:

> What's he doing now? Well, at 85 years of age he's working on a farm raising rabbits. Well, I mean at 85 he can't raise much else. Well, you wouldn't expect him to raise horses, would you?

And self-promotion:

> But sometimes, on a cold winter's night he sits around his old fire, sips his coca [*sic*] and just thinks. What does he think about? Well, he thinks what a success he'd have been if he had the charm, talent and personality of his young nephew. See what I mean?

It wasn't exactly Stephen Leacock, S. J. Perelman or P. G. Wodehouse, and there's no telling if any Variety or broadcasting comics used the material. No fee would have been due to the writer, who was not necessarily the *creator* of the gag anyway. Benny had begun to buy the gag book compendiums originating out of America, such as *1000 Jokes*, which featured a photo of Groucho Marx on its cover and, inside, jokes helpfully arranged by subject matter. With five of these he had 5,000 gags to peruse, and purloin, and if he added *Ten Thousand Jokes, Toasts And Stories*, a New York publication by Lewis and Fay Copland, he had three times as many. Comedians on both sides of the Atlantic had been quietly plundering these books for years. But in Britain Benny was the only one to regurgitate them for his own comedy column.

With the exception of three issues, a 'by Benny Hill' piece appeared in *Show World* every week through to April 1948, after which they became occasional. When his last column was published, in June 1949, it was the fifty-third, representing perhaps half a book's worth of gags. Most of them continued the 'Family Portraits' series begun with 'My Uncle Silas', and some implied a Jewish background: 'My Brother Yasha', 'My Uncle Vanya', 'My Uncle Emanuel', 'My Cousin Nickevo'. Other articles included spoof star-interviews and hoax advertisements, areas that would prove fertile ground for Benny Hill comedy ideas in the ensuing decades.

Underneath that first column, back in July 1947, was an editorial notice announcing that Carroll Levis, the Canadian-born but London-based impresario famed for his amateur talent-spotting show *Discoveries*, would be mounting a new series of weekly Variety shows for 'up-and-coming professionals' at the Camberwell Palace, south London. This alone was enough to catch Benny Hill's eye; moreover, each Wednesday night, forty-five minutes of the second 'house' was to be relayed live by the BBC Light Programme in the series *Variety Roundabout*.[2]

Though most would know him in later years as an unassuming individual, Benny Hill's determination at this point in his life, when he was desperate to become established in the comedy sphere, was considerable. With Frank Woolf advising him, he frequently pushed himself forward without invitation or hesitation. Week commencing Monday September 1 1947 he was indeed among the acts at the Camberwell Palace, paid £10 for six twice-nightly shows, including the broadcast. It was his first decent wage. When two rival agents claimed they had helped him secure the job, and sought 10 per cent commission, he was perfectly happy to proffer both men their £1.

Frank Woolf, who sought no fee, went to town for his protégé, giving Benny his first *Show World* editorial (which oddly misspelled his first name):

> Bennie Hill, the new young comedian with 'a personality like sunshine' has been immediately booked by the astute Will Collins for Camberwell Palace next week. He will be broadcasting on the Wednesday evening. Bennie is contributing a distinctly humorous story each week in *Show World* which puts him in the front rank of humorous writers. His Variety is just as good, and he is already busy with concerts. His stage style will easily put him in the front rank of comedians within the next six months.

The future front-rank comedian himself also went for the big push, designing one of the most desperate advertisements ever placed by a struggling artiste:

DEAR MISTER AGENT

If you have not yet seen me
this week at the
CAMBERWELL PALACE
please do so before SUNDAY

yours (I hope!)

BENNY HILL

All around the border of the ad, printed ten times, were the words 'Calling all Agents'.

Though in contact with a former BBC producer turned agent, Philip Brown, whose Wigmore Street base was handily close to the BBC's Broadcasting House head office and studios, and also with Joe (father of Joan and Jackie) Collins, Benny had made no pact with any 'sole agent', and seems to have been resisting, for the time being, the temptation to contact Richard Stone.

At 9.15pm on September 3 1947, immediately after *Gracie's Working Party*, which starred the northern 'songstress' Gracie Fields, *Variety Roundabout* took to the airwaves. It was typical post-war BBC fare.

The orchestra struck up a signature tune ('An Actor's Life for Me') and then a relentlessly cheery announcer, Bob Andrews, addressed the microphone:

> Thank you and a good evening, Ladies and Gentlemen. All's well at Camberwell, the audience is in a merry mood and the Artists are in tip-top form. So come on Listeners and join in the fun – the *Variety Roundabout* has got everything. Our roundabout revolves, round and round it goes, and where it stops nobody knows!

Later in the show, Carroll Levis also spoke. 'In this programme you will have the opportunity of picking Stars of Tomorrow from professional artistes who are climbing the Stairway to Stardom. I know that you join me in wishing all the young people taking part in these broadcasts every success in their chosen profession.'

It wasn't all comedy. But after Les Lee had been on to perform the monologue made famous by Stanley Holloway, 'With 'Er 'Ead Tucked Underneath 'Er Arm', and June Adair had crooned 'Dear Old Donegal', the orchestra played in Benny Hill with thirty seconds of 'Stars and Stripes', the Sousa march he had chosen as his 'signature', playing him on and off Variety and radio stages for many years to come. The appeal of starting and finishing his act with a march was one that would stay with Benny for ever.[3]

Benny rendered a five-minute 'patter', then the standard word for a standup act. Remarkably, considering his well-set nervousness at performing in front of theatre audiences, let alone the prospect of being beamed into several million British hearths, he went on without a script. Interviewed in January 1955 for the Light Programme show *These Radio Times*, he recalled:

> I learnt it all the night before, and just had a bash. It was pretty terrible, I dare say – just a string of gags. I remember my pay-off was 'And now, Ladies and Gentlemen, finally I would like to do something serious for you. I would like to give you Lincoln's famous Gettysburg address.
> Number 10, Castle Street, Gettysburg.

After this, Benny was fast out of the blocks. When the week at Camberwell was over he went to the BBC Light Entertainment offices at

Aeolian Hall in New Bond Street and presented himself to the *Variety Roundabout* producer, Eric Spear.[4] 'How was it?' Hill asked. 'Was it really good?' Spear was put on the spot: 'Yes – er – very good.'

'Well, if it was very good there must be another one, mustn't there? I can't leave it at this!'

Spear eyed the pushy young comic. 'Aren't you keen!'

'Yes, I am,' came the prompt reply.

So Spear called a colleague, Joy Russell-Smith. 'What do you do?' she asked of Benny – and without skipping a beat he broke into his act.

The two producers were impressed. More than fifty years later, their brief report is still on file at the BBC:

Comedian. Original fresh style. English calypso – delightful. Groom for Seeded.

'Groom for Seeded' indicates that, with a little nurturing, they thought him likely to be a good broadcaster. Russell-Smith set about making arrangements for a formal audition before a review panel of producers, though – mindful of a vacant spot in an imminent programme – she also wasn't going to wait for their response. 'What are you doing Sunday week?' she enquired of the comedian. It was an offer of work, not a proposition, and Benny knew it. 'I hope I'm working for you!'

'Yes, you are,' the producer replied, 'you're on first on *Variety Bandbox*.'

WE TOLD YOU SO!

You can hear

Benny Hill

in '*VARIETY BANDBOX*'

next Sunday, October 5th

DON'T MISS THIS

THEN RING – FRANK WOOLF

NO SOLE AGENT

Launched in 1942 primarily as a services entertainment, and still simultaneously broadcast around the globe by the BBC's General Overseas Service, *Variety Bandbox* had a reputation for developing comedians, although Frankie Howerd, who was to be its biggest find, had yet to make his breakthrough. This was An Important Broadcast. Benny went all out to make the biggest of impressions.

Transmitted live from the People's Palace, a theatre in the Mile End Road, east London, this edition of the show also featured Michael Howard and Peter Brough. Howard was a former Shakespearean actor who, uniquely, had ditched his profession and turned to Variety, performing the kind of shaggy-dog jokes that Benny Hill liked so much. (It was a disastrous career move for Howard – he was declared bankrupt by the early 1950s.) Even more ridiculously, Brough was a ventriloquist, every bit as much a star on radio as he was on stage. More so, in fact, and his series *Educating Archie*, featuring the witty dummy Archie Andrews, was about to take Britain by storm.

Benny opened with five unconnected and tepid gags, the first three of which were strung together by means of 'relating' the characters. The first was about a man, 'my pal Charlie'. The second, which could have been about any woman, was linked by making her Charlie's wife. The third, which could have been about any bloke, followed as 'Now her brother Harry . . .'

The fourth and fifth gags brought welcome relief, but the jokes were equally lame. It was all second-hand, third-rate material, plundered from gag books. After a barman has hit a customer with a wet dish-towel, the barman says, 'There's nothing like a good fright to cure hiccups. I bet you haven't got hiccups now.'

The man replies, 'I never did have any – it's for my wife. She's outside in the car.'

This tenuous linking of single – often unfunny – gags, drawn from clapped-out gag books and clipped-out cartoons or newspaper 'funnies', was one that Benny Hill would continue to exploit for the rest of his career. The idea was his, the material was not, nor was it in any way distinctive.

But then, at last, listeners to this *Variety Bandbox* also heard something else from Benny Hill, something new, different and original. Plucking a guitar, he launched into a calypso:

The Sunshine Personality

Down in Havana or about that locality
They sing a song of great topicality,
This type of song, as you probably know,
Is commonly called a calypso.

Well I thought tonight by way of a change
I'd sing this type of song to you and try to arrange
It so the lyrics are up to date
And in a form you will appreciate.

Happy, happy, happy are we,
We live in the land of the brave and the free.

The government have to make import cuts
On films and food and coconuts.
So a shipload of beef is now the equivalent
Of a film starring Olivia de Havilland.

Happy, happy, happy are we,
We live in the land of the brave and the free.

A sick producer saw his doctor one day
And said 'What makes me feel this way?'
Said the doctor, who was very wise,
'You're seeing Inkspots before your eyes.'

Happy, happy, happy are we,
We live in the land of the brave and the free.

We have two Bev'ns in our Cabinet.
Aneurin is the one with the gift of the gab in it.
Although the other Bev'n is the taciturnist
He knows the importance of being Ernest.

Happy, happy, happy are we,
We live in the land of the brave and the free.

Housewives approve the farmer's plan
To eliminate the middle man.
I therefore hope you'll like my humour,
It's straight from produce to consumer.

Happy, happy, happy are we,
We live in the land of the brave and the free.

As a form of music, the West Indian calypso was still largely unknown in Britain in 1947, although the post-war immigration programme that was just beginning led to a surge in its popularity within the next decade. Benny, who must have heard a calypso somewhere along the way, was possibly the first British comedian to perform one in this period. Moreover, he could pen a good lyric, expressing himself concisely and with good humour. A few other comics were trying to create comedy songs at this time, but none could match his facility.

Benny thought that the act went well. The BBC was not minded to agree. Its staff-eyes-only Listener Research Report canvassed public opinion and computed 'appreciation' percentages for each of the acts. Benny rated easily the worst, with a mere nineteen. Peter Brough notched forty-nine and Michael Howard fifty-two.

Not only was his appearance on *Variety Bandbox* a disappointment, but when Benny formally auditioned for BBC radio, on October 10, his comedy style was summarily dismissed. 'I'll be doing patter, with a couple of accent gags included; & finishing with an original topical number,' he wrote to Joy Russell-Smith, with obvious confidence, from Queensway. (Again, the letter is still on file.)

The report states:

Ronald Waldman 'The only trouble with him was that he didn't make me laugh *at all* – and for a comedian that's not very good. It's a mixture of lack of comedy personality and lack of comedy material.'

Harry Pepper 'Joy Russell-Smith gave him a good send off as he has done a good show on *Bandbox*. I find him without personality and very dully unfunny.'

Vernon Harris 'Passable material, but he has a quite unfunny personality and so just doesn't come over.'

The panel was a distinguished one. Waldman was a senior producer in the Variety department; Harris, a producer, had worked as scriptwriter on the hugely popular Arthur Askey and Richard 'Stinker' Murdoch pre-war radio comedy *Band Waggon*, and was also now writing movies on the side; and Pepper had produced the White Coons concert party, the one young Alfie had heard so frequently on the radio.

The conclusion of these esteemed gents was that Hill was 'Grade 4', and so decidedly *not* suited to radio. It was only because he had already broadcast that this judgement was not implemented; he was permitted to continue, should any producers wish to engage him.[5]

Having come through some early traumas, Benny was beginning to think that he had a future in the business. He already had some basic business cards; now he returned to the stationers and ordered headed paper. The name Benny Hill was set in red script, centred along the top line. Slightly to the right, one line down, in black, was the legend COMEDY SPECIALIST. And below this, common to the stationery of all Variety acts, were three lines for addresses. The second and third would always be completed in pen, and were as good an indication as any that the performer had plenty of work. Benny had the printer typeset the first line with what, although he hadn't lived there for seven years, remained the only situation guaranteed to find him:

Permanent address: 22 Westrow Gardens, Southampton
This week: ....
Next week: ....

This became a hectic period for Benny, as he strove, first flush, for stardom. At the end of September he secured a Variety booking, a week at the Playhouse in Weston-super-Mare, a seaside resort in the south-west of England, out of season and now quite desperately dreary. He was plumb bottom of the bill, behind Burton Seeley ('America's Romantic Singing Troubadour'), Jimmy Fenton & Corinne ('The Spiv And His Girl Friend'), Eve Milton ('Glamorous Contortioniste'), Helena ('Anglo-Russian Cartooniste'), Dom & Josie ('International Accordionists') and Eric Wood ('Violinist Versatile'). Benny's bill matter, almost certainly self-chosen, was 'The Sunshine Personality', one that would stick for a couple of years.

Maureen Riscoe, a soubrette/comedienne later to work a summer season with Benny, remembers the lifestyle of a Variety performer at this time. 'It was very hard work. Often deserted theatres. You always had to remember to rush to put your band-parts down, centre-stage, for the house-orchestra. If you didn't, the other acts would beat you to a song and you might get left out. You had to have a lighting-plot. And if you didn't know people on the circuit it was such a lonely life. You went to the theatre, you did your act and then you were finished, wondering where to go and what to do in some town you didn't know, where everything had closed early.'

Another unusual engagement occurred in mid-November, when Benny was among a score of acts taking part in *Spotlight*, an 'intimate revue' for young talent being staged at the Twentieth Century Theatre in Westbourne Grove, west London. (Far from suggesting a sexual connotation, the word 'intimate' implied a middle- or upper-class entertainment, polite acts, as distinct from the more raucous kinds of revue populating the Variety halls.)

Managed by the Rudolf Steiner educational organization, the Twentieth Century claimed to have staged the professional debut of Laurence Olivier in 1917, and other luminaries to have trodden its boards included Margaret Rutherford, Rex Harrison, Henry Irving and, surprisingly perhaps, the original music-hall idol, Marie Lloyd. Benny Hill might have been distinctly out of place here but for the fact that *Spotlight* featured no fewer than twenty-five acts – singers, dancers, musicians and several comedians – and each only had a few minutes to get on, work and get off. One of them was Bob Monkhouse, an RAF corporal still completing his National Service, whose destiny was also to become a star comedian. As yet, though, he was more green than Benny.

'Benny and I immediately got on very well,' says Monkhouse. 'He was very, very generous with other comedians. He knew what he was doing and what he wanted to do and had no resentment of anyone else. None at all.'

Benny had re-tooled his act for these two evenings before the Twentieth Century Theatre's more plummy crowd:

> I did a silly thing the other day. I got engaged. I got engaged to a girl called Cleopatra. Of course, that's not her real name. I call her Cleopatra because I'm always trying to seize 'er.
>
> I took her to the pictures the other night. We missed the big film but we caught next week's trailer. It went something like this: *Fanny* – the stirring drama of a woman who killed for love, and of a man who loved to kill. And don't forget to bring the kiddies . . .

He then enacted several scenes of ludicrous high drama, ending with impressions of two Hollywood actors, Peter Lorre and Sydney Greenstreet.

The inscrutable Lorre was one of Benny's favourite impressions – he also cropped up in the German 'Toto' skit.

A committed student of comedy since the age of four, Bob Monkhouse was in a unique position to study Benny Hill's style in this period.

'Benny, as somebody else, was sensational,' he says. 'Benny as a smooth, sharply-dressed compère, rubbing his hands together and leaning to one side and then the other, never clicked. And his way of continuing without getting laughs was to conduct conversations with himself as if he *hadn't meant* to get a laugh. So he'd say "She was a robust girl, all 'row' and no . . . no wonder they liked her, *as a matter of fact . . .*" and he'd start mumbling to himself to cover the fact that there was no laughter.

'No one else did that. The comedian's normal thing was self-interruption. You'd do your tag-line and then say ". . . *and then again you know*" and the audience would laugh. Bob Hope would bolt "*I wanna tell ya*" on the end of his tag-lines, as if to say, "I am continuing and not expecting you to laugh, and there you go and interrupt me." This technique was fairly common among Variety comics in the 1930s and 40s. Billy Maxam would say something like, "He's the man who asked the foreman what to do with the extra pole, *and you know ladies and gentlemen it's a funny thing . . .*" Relentless it was, at the end of every story "*and you know ladies and gentlemen it's a funny thing . . .*" But Benny's version of it was unique, this strange *talking to himself*.'

Monkhouse was doing all he could to get his comedy career off the ground, and Benny helped him. And they were only two among scores of young comics and writers freshly 'demobbed' and teeming in the capital. It was the older comedians, the stay-at-homes, who were killed off by the war. The young men who returned from battle were determined to make up for lost time; several had formed comedy alliances with army buddies; many – like Benny – had performed for Stars in Battledress. A comedy revolution was taking place, one that would see a youthful stranglehold on the scene, especially on radio, within a few short years.

In the late 1940s, though, the group had little money and shared a remarkable 'all for one and one for all' comradeship. 'Everybody knew each other,' recalls Denis Norden, whose post-war partnership with Frank Muir made them, quite quickly, the top comedy writers in the business. 'There was so much going on. Everybody had shared the common experience of being in the services, and we spoke a language and a shorthand together. We hadn't had any youth, as it were – we'd spent those years in the various forces. It makes a kind of bond that is impossible to imagine. Pre-war and post-war was a great divide. And Benny was part of this penniless group who used to share their tips for getting by. All of us took whatever work was on offer.'

In addition to Benny Hill and Bob Monkhouse these young Turks included Peter Sellers, Michael Bentine, Spike Milligan, Harry Secombe, Tony Hancock, Alfred Marks, Dick Emery, Norman Wisdom, Frankie Howerd, Bill Kerr, Dave Allen, Max Bygraves, Jimmy Edwards, Jon Pertwee, Tommy Cooper and a double-act, Morecambe and Wise. When this 'new wave' crashed on to the shores of British comedy they swept all before them. It was a *coup d'état*, one that held firm until 1980, at which point the next insurrection – in the form of 'alternative comedy' – broke through and, again, blew away the oldies. Though the young men of the 1940s were never bestowed with the epithet 'alternative', this is very much what they were . . . albeit some less so than others.

The young hopefuls decamped in the West End. Several worked at the Windmill, others – including Benny – auditioned there but failed. 'It's impossible to explain the power of the Windmill,' declares Denis Norden. 'First of all, there were naked girls who appeared six times a day, and secondly you ate with them, because there wasn't time for anybody to go out and eat. In that time and at that place, this was Broadway and Hollywood rolled into one.'

Another popular meeting place was Charing Cross Road, where many of the agents had offices. A 1948 issue of *The Performer* published a poem by one Jack Herbert, *Round Charing Cross Road*, which, in part, read:

The comics were talking in groups here and there,
As though in this old world they hadn't a care,
And amidst the loud laughter the gags quickly flowed;
You can bet it was somewhere round Charing Cross Road.

There were dozens of pros, some young and some old,
And I wonder what kind of stories were told,
Were they tales of approval their audience showed?
'Cos you hear lots of laughter round Charing Cross Road.

The man-in-the-street is at times apt to stare:
'Who are all these groups standing here, standing there?
They talk a strange language, they do, I'll be blowed,'
He can't get the 'Palary'[6] – round Charing Cross Road.

One particular rendezvous was an alleyway beside Wyndham's Theatre, again on Charing Cross Road. On a Monday morning, agents who booked entertainment for pubs and clubs would gather here to fill the slots. These gigs usually paid the comedian all of £1, possibly an extra ten shillings for a second spot. Benny went on to work them all. 'I played the larger pubs,' he recalled in a 1969 interview with *Reveille*, 'like the White Swan at Walthamstow or the Tithe Farm near Harrow, with the till ringing up bar sales right through the act. Then I began to get the odd Masonic dinner at three guineas, and the odd Ladies' Night at the Connaught Rooms at seven guineas.'

Again looking back in later years, Benny reckoned to have performed in venues at virtually every stop on the London Underground tube map. Working-men's clubs were the most frequent booking, as far afield as Uxbridge, Edmonton, Tilbury, Tottenham and Harlesden.

He recalled, too, an example of his act in these places, where there was a greater degree of freedom, for the censor supreme, the Lord Chamberlain, had no jurisdiction over clubs:

Often there would be women in the front row, breast-feeding their babies. I would look down at the baby and say 'After you, Georgie!'

'You'll be lucky,' from the mother, like as not.

'Oh, I hope so, darlin',' I would come back cheekily.

Almost invariably a man would get up to go to the gents in the middle of your act.

'Could you hear me?' I would ask as he came back.

'No.'

'Well I could hear you!'

These were difficult venues but Benny took it upon himself to counsel the less experienced Bob Monkhouse in working them. 'He would advise me how far I could go with material at particular clubs, saying, "At *x* you can be a bit bluer than you can at *y*." One club he sent me to was the

Ridgeway in Hammersmith, but I got beer thrown over me. I was singing a parody of "A You're Adorable" – "A, I'm adorable, B, I'm so beautiful" and someone shouted out "C, you're a cunt!" and threw his beer over me, after which everyone else threw their beer over me. Beer was cheap at this time. In another place I got hit in the chest with a box of nails. The nails went everywhere, which I meant I couldn't get down on my knee and do my Jolson act.'

Benny always made his seniority quite clear, as Monkhouse recalls. 'He used to show off because he was more experienced than me. But he was also being very generous and very kind. Other comics weren't. "You'll have to get your knees brown, Bob," he'd say. I think it was an army expression, meaning that you weren't really a seasoned soldier until you'd got brown knees – from the sun, presumably. Another expression was "You'll be sorry!" as you walked in through the stage door. That was also from the services days. Stupid stuff. But he gave me lots of advice. Benny introduced me to a Mr Kent, who looked after Petula Clark. Benny said, "You'll love this. He books big bands into big cinemas on a Sunday and they always use a young comedian as a compère." So I started doing those, thanks to Benny. And he also told me what fees to ask. "If you've got to go as far as Yarmouth, it's got to be £15!"'

It never seemed to concern Benny that a fellow pro might take away a booking that had been coming to him. 'He seemed quite sanguine about that,' reflects Monkhouse. 'There was something utterly, utterly innocent about Benny and it was never subverted by anything in his life. It remained right there until the day he died, a kind of peaceful self-sufficiency that I had never encountered in anyone else – particularly the neurotic lot who call themselves comedians.'

Benny was Mr Ever-Ready. He never went out without a suede pouch containing his 'five and nine' makeup, as worn by all old stagers. He also carried around a tube of Gordon Moore's Cosmetic Toothpaste, long used by music-hall artistes to tint their gums red, giving the appearance of whiter, brighter teeth all the way to the back of the stalls. Benny used it to redden his tongue, and with the red tie he had bought in Eastleigh in 1941 he now had an extension to his old shock joke. As Bob Monkhouse remembers, 'Every time a gag died Benny would say, "Thank God it's a tie, I thought it was me tongue hanging out!" Sometimes you'd hear it three or four times in the same act.'

But of course there was a low for every high at this time. One rather pathetic story has Benny booked for a musical cabaret evening at a south London club. Wearing his dinner-jacket and carrying his guitar, he journeyed south of the river mostly on foot, only to find on his arrival at the club that he was not expected. 'You can go on last,' the entertainments secretary (a position referred to by all as 'The Insect', a corruption of 'ensec') told Benny. But then the other acts overran and time ran out. When Benny arrived on stage the chairs were being stacked, the bar was closing and the last few customers were milling around by the door. Not having performed, Benny received no fee, and without the fee he had no money for transport home. So he walked, perhaps ten miles, and as he crossed Waterloo Bridge it rained cats and dogs.

Back at the BBC, Benny was slowly progressing. Radio producer Brian Johnston – later to become the country's best loved cricket commentator – booked him to compère and introduce *Works Wonders* early in 1948, his first appearance on the Home Service, a more august station than the Light Programme. The show was designed to spotlight amateur talent working in factories around Britain, running cheek by jowl with *Workers' Playtime*, which featured professional artistes visiting the factories. Maximum production was vital in this post-war rebuilding period and the BBC played a full part in maintaining morale.

Benny's fee was the standard ten guineas,[7] which was decent enough, and the programme took him to a factory in Slough where the headache tablet Aspro was made:

> Well, here we are in the canteen of this very modern factory. In front of me hundreds of happy, smiling faces, and behind me the works band ready to get us off to a grand start with 'The Savoy American Medley'! [music is played]
> Well now, that was really fine, wasn't it? You could almost hear the dollars jingling!

Arcane, corny . . . it never got much better. As compère, Benny's task was to introduce each act, using jokes as linking material:

Ah, how I love women. They're so feminine, aren't they? I met a lovely girl this morning in Slough. She told me she was a nurse. I said, 'Oh, I wish I was ill.' She said, 'Why?' I said, 'Well, it would be wonderful to be nursed by you.' She said, 'It would be more than wonderful, it would be a miracle. I'm in the maternity ward.'

Radio was far and away the dominant broadcasting medium at this time, some shows attracting audiences of 20 million and beyond. Television was only toddling and there were few TV sets ('receivers') in existence. The BBC had launched the world's first regular TV service in 1936, but then suspended transmissions at the outset of the Second World War, fearing that the Germans could use the signals as a navigational aid. The service closed down on September 1 1939, at the end of a Mickey Mouse cartoon film. When broadcasts resumed in June 1946 the BBC ran the same Mickey Mouse film and announcer Leslie Mitchell declared, with prime British understatement-cum-hauteur, 'As I was saying, before we were so rudely interrupted . . .'

Still, TV remained available only to Londoners, and it wasn't until 1949 that the service extended beyond the capital. That wasn't going to stop Benny Hill. In December 1947, the agent Philip Brown applied for and secured a preliminary audition for the 'compère comedian', to take place in a quiet hall in Rodmarton Mews, just off Baker Street. 'Your performance should not exceed ten minutes in length. COSTUME IS ESSENTIAL,' were the instructions. It evidently went well because Benny was invited to perform a second test, before cameras, out at Alexandra Palace, the elevated point in north London that served as television's first studio and transmitter. The BBC auditioned ten hopefuls at a time and provided a free bus from Broadcasting House, provided that applicants were there 'sharp on time at 2.15'.

This wintry afternoon in February 1948, Benny Hill stepped in front of television cameras for the first time, acquainting himself with a medium with which he was unfamiliar, but which would catapult him to an unlikely global fame.

The camera might not lie, but it does suit some performers better than others. Judging from even this rudimentary audition at Alexandra Palace, it suited Benny Hill right away. The audition report card tells that Hill was perceived as 'A young man of very pleasant appearance in dinner jacket' who gave an 'Impression of complete Concert Party, arranged in cameo form'.

The conclusion was 'Has talent & a good personality. Should prove suitable Tele Variety with this material. Is also an efficient compère.' But such talent and good personality would not be seen by the viewing public for another year.

In earlier decades, the Variety Artistes' Federation, the performers' trade union, had had cause to fear the onset of radio, and had attempted to implement rules about the amount of Variety broadcasting, to protect its members' interests. But VAF had even greater reason to fear television. It knew that people would prefer to stay at home for their entertainment instead of going out to a local theatre, and it recognized too that TV would give little airtime to such valiant Variety veterans as Jack Joyce, 'The World-Famous One-Legged Dancing Comedian', whose job-seeking advertisements appeared in *The Stage* at this time. These concerns quickly proved justified. Television – or 'video', as *The Performer* disdainfully called it – hammered the last nails into Variety's coffin, spelling the end for clog dancers, footballing dogs, tap-dancing xylophonists and humorous unidexters.

Benny played his third week in Variety at one of London's foremost venues, Collins' Music Hall, in Islington, in November 1947. The show was reviewed in *The Stage* (which, as an actors' newspaper, has a reputation for effusive critiques):

> Benny Hill is a promising new comedian. He already has a mastery of the casual conversational technique, his material glitters with wit – if not always tasteful – and he instinctively knows when to keep his pleasant-looking features grave or smiling.

The question-mark over the tastefulness of Benny's stage material is apposite. Working comedians in this period had to be ever mindful of their place of performance, as there were differences in what was acceptable. Single-week Variety shows, like this one at Collins', permitted the comic some latitude since it was impractical for a show to be closed when it was due to end anyway within a few days. But Variety tours – *Follow the Fun*, *Send Him Victorious* and the literally hundreds of others – were different. Places of entertainment in London (and, for the duration of his visit, any other place where the King was temporarily residing) were subject to the scrutiny of the Lord Chamberlain, who wielded the dreaded 'blue pencil', exercising an unbridled and often ludicrous degree of censorship over the content of all stage shows. And once his office had approved a script it could not be altered.

Around the country, major towns and cities had a Watch Committee, run by the local council, whose task was to scrutinize the visiting entertainments and report any transgressions. These committees were famously inconsistent, and what was acceptable to one could easily rouse the ire of another. A travelling Variety show featuring nudes, *This is the Show*, was acceptable all over the country, but when it arrived in York the title – though not the show itself – was banned because of the way the wording was set out on posters, with emphasis on the initial capital letters. The episode was not lost on Benny Hill – in a 1970 TV show he depicted a poster in which, covered partially by a door, only the initial letters in a Variety poster were visible. It read Theatre Ifield Tarbuck Shaw. (Unable to leave an idea alone, he did it again in 1972 with KNICKERS, and returned to TITS once more seven years later.)

The strictest censorship dictum in post-war Variety was saved for nudity, where the regulation still permitted naked women on stage only if they remained motionless. Even the tours mounted by Phyllis Dixey, the foremost stage nude, and the *Revudeville* shows at the famous Windmill had to toe the line: the scantily clad dancers were choreographed, but the nudes formed a static tableau.

Another censor was Miss Cissie Williams, the bane of every Variety comedian's life for decades. She was the bookings manager for the Moss Empires, the leading circuit in the country, a redoubtable woman, respected and feared in equal measure. She zealously shouldered the responsibility of booking acts into Moss theatres, a job she carried out with *élan*. But if anyone transgressed acceptability there would be ructions. A comic using the word 'bloody' would be reprimanded. If he uttered it a second time he'd be kicked off the show.

The less censorious working-men's clubs permitted a comedian to say 'ruddy' but they still ran a risk if saying 'bloody'. As Bob Monkhouse recalls, 'I used to say "Sex is a wonderful thing between two people.

Between six, bloody fantastic." And there might be a complaint about the fact that I had said "bloody", but not about the fact that sex with six people was better than between two. There could also be no fanny jokes, and anything about giving birth was right out. You could do jokes about "fairies" and "pansies", though – they were very big. When you think of the agony this must have put some homosexuals through . . .'

Like all comedians, Benny Hill had to temper his act for the radio, where he was, at best (or worst), only mildly saucy. The jokes would remain the same but some of the words were changed. Women's breasts would become cows' udders. Chickens laying eggs could be used in place of women giving birth. The word 'pregnant' was banned – you had to say 'expecting'. In 1948 the BBC produced a *Variety Programmes Policy Guide*, a pocket-sized green hardback marked 'private and confidential' and 'for writers and producers', which set out the guidelines of acceptability. It was an anachronism even then; it is ludicrously outmoded now:

There is an absolute ban upon the following:–

Jokes about –
    Lavatories
    Effeminacy in men
    Immorality of any kind

Suggestive references to –
    Honeymoon couples
    Chambermaids
    Fig leaves
    Prostitution
    Ladies' underwear, e.g. winter draws on
    Animal habits, e.g. rabbits
    Lodgers
    Commercial travellers

Extreme care should be taken in dealing with references to or jokes about –
    Pre-natal influences (e.g. 'His mother was frightened by a donkey')
    Marital infidelity
Good taste and decency are the obvious governing considerations.

The vulgar use of such words as 'basket' must also be avoided.

135

The 'green book' also set out clear guidelines about the usage of 'American Material' and 'Americanisms', Libel and Slander, Biblical References, Religious References, Political References, Physical and Mental Infirmities, Drink, Expletives, Impersonations, and Mentions of Charitable Organizations.

Considering all this, it's a miracle that there was anything left to be funny about, but the plethora of radio comedy as the 1940s tumbled into the 1950s proved otherwise. Still, the restrictions did tie the writers' hands. With religion, royalty, physical disability, colour and homosexuality the principal taboos, Frank Muir and Denis Norden jokingly suggested a script that began ' "C-C-C-Christ!" said the King, "that one-legged nigger's a poof!" ' Unable to employ his trademark suggestiveness, the great Max Miller had particular trouble broadcasting. One tale, possibly apocryphal, has the BBC crying 'foul' after he tried to get away with an optician's eye-test joke – 'Every time I see F you see K'. If this is true, Miller must have known it would land him in the hottest of water. (This story has also been attributed to the northern comic Frank Randle.)

In his occasional early broadcasts, Benny Hill too fell victim to censorship. A script he submitted for *First House – Look Who's Here!* in January 1950 bore numerous blue pencil marks before the live broadcast. A conversation between two pigeons – 'I haven't really been shopping though I did leave a small deposit on a new hat' – was crossed through by the producer. Also deleted was Benny's suggestion that he'd found a suitable room in his house to place a statue of *The Thinker*. The censor also didn't care for violence. Sections of a conversation between two men who owned a hopeless greyhound (a limp joke much used by Benny in his BBC broadcasts), one saying to the other, 'Let's drown the little perisher' and 'Let's wring its neck', were also excised.

Beyond working-men's clubs, there wasn't a great deal of work around for Benny in the spring of 1948. So when his brother suggested a short holiday to Paris, he jumped at the chance. Having enjoyed – or, perhaps more accurately, endured – a bumpy relationship thus far, Len and Ben had found some common ground in the early post-war years, and Len occasionally travelled up from Southampton to spend weekends with his kid brother in the capital. Although the war had robbed Len of the opportunity to attend university, his exam results at Taunton's had encouraged him to seek a professional career, and it wasn't long before he became a teacher at Shirley School, the same establishment that he and Alfie had attended twenty years earlier. Len was studying English and enjoyed literary verse. He also wrote a little, and contributed some lines to his brother's work, although he was never credited. He later claimed to have written the penultimate verse in Benny's *Variety Bandbox* calypso, the one citing the 'two Bev'ns in our Cabinet'. It was undoubtedly the best verse in the piece.

Benny hadn't got as far south as Paris during the Second World War, and the keen Francophile couldn't wait to savour the atmosphere of the great city. Len booked them into a tiny hotel on the Quai de la Mégisserie, where they were taken aback, as all British tourists have been in France, at the design and condition of the *pissoirs*. Though the brothers made sure to see the Eiffel Tower and the other principal sights, Benny was keenest to visit Montmartre, to tramp its streets, to idle away time in the clubs and cafés, to be among the artists, dancers and bohemians. He also had to visit the celebrated saucy night-time revues. At Le Concert Mayol, Benny became a huge admirer of the artiste Magda while Len enjoyed the rare delight of an amply endowed nude dancer tripping off the stage and falling almost into his lap. Plenty that evening for the Hills to laugh about as they larked their way back to their hotel.

The brothers also went to see Edith Piaf in concert. Dressed all in black, the diminutive 'sparrow' with the husky, throbbing voice sang all her songs of heartbreak and despair, her anguished and defiant ballads, leaving the Southampton lads emotionally wrung out. It was, Benny later accepted, one of the great nights of his life.

Although his sibling relationship was on better terms, Benny seems not to have enjoyed any female alliances at this time; indeed it would appear that he was sublimating any need for meaningful attachment while trying to build his career. As he would often point out in later interviews, what kind of a partner could he have been for a woman when he was hoping to be working seven nights a week and travelling from town to town?

But this wasn't the whole truth. In reality, the insecurities that had drained his confidence since puberty had not deserted him. Recognizing his crucial uncertainties, and inability to find love and commit to a relationship, Benny had already developed the rejoinder he would use for the rest of his life when asked why he remained a bachelor:

Why buy a book when you can join a lending library?
(*from Benny Hill's script for* Beginners, Please! – *BBC radio, October 25 1947*)

Through his liaison with the French café owner's wife towards the end of the war, Benny was no longer a virgin, but he seems to have established a firm distaste for sexual intercourse.

Benny shared these intimate thoughts and feelings with very few people, but did so with good friend Bob Monkhouse. 'He must have decided that I was a bit of a Lothario and perhaps knew some things that he didn't,' Monkhouse considers. 'It was a reversal of roles, in that he had always been the guy who knew more about show-business than I did, and to whom I asked questions. But in this particular case, we were sitting in an after-show coffee joint in Shaftesbury Avenue, drinking coffee and eating buns, and he said, "What really turns you on, Bob? Do you like girls tied up and that?"

'I explained to him that basically I just loved women, and didn't require gym-slips or anything to turn me on.

'"Oh," he said, "I only love factory girls. I love taking them out and being their knight in shining armour, and showing them a good time that they couldn't otherwise have." He said he didn't like sophisticated women, or women as old or older than him – he wanted his women to be more naïve than he was, women who would look up to him. He also said that it was fellatio he wanted, or masturbation. He had a slight distaste about women's pudenda and explained about an experience he'd had, when he was in the army I think, with a dirty woman, and he didn't like the smell. "But Bob, I get a thrill when they're kneeling there, between my knees, and they're looking up at me. And I want them to call me Mr Hill, not Benny. 'Is that all right for you, Mr Hill?' That's lovely, that is, I really like that." I asked him why and he said, "Well, it's respectful."'

Whatever he planned on doing with women, there was still the problem of finding them. And, indeed, of finding work. In his weekly column in *Show World* Benny took the liberty of addressing the issues head-on:

Artistes wanted
Girl wanted for nude posing act. Beginners might suit if ambitious.
Auditions in my flat any time after midnight. Phone: BAY 2719.

Engagements required
Vacant immediately, Benny Hill, talent and good looks. Plays three
instruments, comedy, feed, compère, impressionist, sings, dances, writes
straight and comedy dialogue, music, lyrics, stage manager, publicity,
etc., etc., and very smart – well, smart enough to get a free advert,
anyway!! BAY 2719.

The overused exclamation-marks were typical. And BAYswater 2719
was, of course, Benny's phone number at 14a Queensway.

Work was still thin on the ground. It was now April 1948 and Benny
hadn't appeared on radio since January; and, save for another bottom-of-
the-bill week in Weston-super-Mare, he was having precious little joy
wangling his way on to Variety bills too. Becoming desperate once again,
Benny even went to the bizarre extreme of posing for a body-building
magazine, just to earn a few shillings.

The caption read:

He's no Mr Britain, either. But at 5'10' and 13st 10lb, Benny is tough
and fit with no excess fat.

Pulling in his stomach and pushing out his chest, he finally looked
every inch the boxer The Captain would have wished him to be.

Relief arrived in May, when Benny was invited to participate in an
eight-week BBC Home Service radio series, *Listen, My Children*. The
producer, Pat Dixon, was a maverick – bald head, beaky nose, prone to
turning up at BBC departmental meetings carrying a Confederate flag. He
had spotted Benny early on, writing to him in late 1947 with this series
in mind, and inviting him to participate in a couple of untransmitted trial
recordings in which, he wrote in correspondence, Benny was 'exceptionally
good'. But he only wanted Benny for his voices; he asked Frank Muir and
Denis Norden to write the script. This was a drawback for Benny, who
was rarely comfortable performing work that he himself hadn't delivered.
But he was in no position to refuse.

Listen, My Children was a clear antecedent of another programme

Dixon went on to produce, *The Goon Show*. It was an attempt at creating a 'radio' rather than a 'stage' comedy, to move away from character-driven humour epitomized by *Band Waggon* and Tommy Handley's wonder series *It's That Man Again*, loved by one and all as *ITMA*. Dixon's series had no regular characters, no catchphrases, not even a studio audience, and there was a satirical edge to the humour, some avant-garde jazz in between the items and a clutch of young, unknown performers who would soon be among the upper echelons of broadcasting, including Benny, Harry Secombe, Jon Pertwee and the comic-actress Patricia Hayes.

With an opportunity to show off his wide range of dialects, and throw a good dollop of ham and corn on top, Benny found the work easy. In one sketch he played a cowboy, using the Wild West voice he had flexed on his morning milk-rounds back in Eastleigh:

> Careful with that thar Winchester, Zeke! Pointin' right at this hyar stranger, it is. Now, pardner, I guess you'll be wantin' to hear us sing?

In the fifth programme in the series, Benny and Harry Secombe played a couple of young men in a restaurant about to spend a double-date with two women, played by Carole Carr and Pat Hayes. Harry's gal is obviously a scorcher but Pat is plainly plain. Benny would replicate the style and dialogue of this Muir–Norden piece on many occasions in his later TV shows – continuing, too, to cast Hayes as the unlikely vamp and himself as the reluctant Romeo.

> **Jessie (Pat)** Oh, I'm just certain we're going to be ever such good
> friends – really I am. Aren't we, Charlie?
> **Charlie (Benny)** Uh-huh.
> **Jessie** I bet we'll get along just like a house on fire, won't we? Come
> on, Charlie – move a little closer to me!
> **Charlie** Oh, all right.
> **Jessie** No . . . closer, closer.
> **Charlie** All right.
> **Jessie** Come on . . . a little closer.
> **Charlie** All right.
> **Jessie** Charlie! You just passed me.

Later, Benny's character begins to get caustic:

Jessie Can I have a cocktail? I mean, that is if they know how to make
them properly here. Of course, in most places they're not put
together right.
Charlie Look who's talking!

All seemed promising, and the programmes went out twice, a swift
repeat following the first airing, but the BBC's Listener Research Report
was damning. *Listen, My Children* rated the worst 'appreciation' percentage
for any comedy series in years, the consensus being that 'the programme
was dull, disjointed and completely lacking in any entertainment value
whatsoever'.

Once again, Benny was running on almost empty. With no further
radio broadcasts on the horizon, no TV and no Variety tours, he had just
one last booking in his diary. At the end of May 1948 he had got himself
on to the bill for a week's Variety at the Kilburn Empire, north London –
an ignominious single spot in the second half of the show. The engagement marked the Southampton lad's first anniversary as a professional
comic in the big city, and the numerous avenues down which he had
travelled, with a blend of hope and bluster, had mostly amounted to dead-
ends. Where would he go from here?

The answer was Margate.

In the Kilburn audience one evening was Richard Stone, the agent and
part-time CSE colonel who had seen Benny perform at Celle on the night
Harry Segal had pushed the frantically insecure comedian back on stage.
Stone hadn't heard from Benny Hill in the past twelve months, and he
probably hadn't given him a thought either, but he was looking for a
double-act 'feed' for his client Reg Varney, another former REME soldier
and Stars in Battledress performer who was trying his luck post-war.
Under Stone's wing, Varney indeed was beginning to go places – he had
already played in a 'legit' London revue, and he was to be the headlining
act in a summer season at Margate promoted by a man named Hedley
Claxton. Stone and Claxton watched Benny at work at the Kilburn
Empire and judged that he would fit the bill. Claxton also had another
comedian he was considering, however, the as yet scarcely known Peter
Sellers.

Unable to decide, Claxton arranged a face-to-face audition for Benny

Hill and Peter Sellers. No audio or film exists of this unique showdown of two of Britain's primary comedy stars to be, but Benny Hill's photographic memory was still in focus more than forty years later when he recalled the exact details in a letter to Sellers' biographer, Roger Lewis:

> Two of us turned up for an audition at Mac's Rehearsal Rooms in Great Windmill Street. Peter, who I'd not heard of, did George Formby, played the uke and told a few gags. I did some impressions and a shaggy-dog story. I got the job – which paid £14 a week.

Once again, Benny Hill's career had teetered on the edge of oblivion, and been rescued. So having previously said farewell to the Browns and Lillywhites and Eastleigh, and his friend Harry Segal and Stars in Battledress, now it was time to bid a fond *adieu* to Molly, Dorothy, Hilda and Queensway.

This time the suitcase was packed for the Kent coast.

This time, however, Benny was to be another comedian's 'feed'. His straightman, foil, stooge. The Abbott not the Costello, the Wise not the Morecambe. That it was 'better than nothing' Benny Hill would have been the first to agree. But was this what he wanted?

7. Doubled Up

It is more than forty years since Variety breathed its last, and music-hall went long before. But even now, with the majority of people in Britain taking their holidays abroad, the seaside show survives.

Its endurance can be explained by a number of factors, one being that the shows play to a captive audience – people who have arrived in a resort, settle for a week or two and look to be entertained when they're not bathing, boozing, snoozing or promenading. Another factor, especially true of decades past, was that the seaside show generally provided slightly more genteel entertainment than could be found on other stages, enabling it to break beyond an essentially working-class audience and appeal also to the middle-classes. In the right place and at the right time, a seaside show was socially acceptable even to those who might look disdainfully upon 'coarse' Variety during the other months of the year. Poet John Betjeman mused nostalgically on the ' "Co-Optimists" down by the pier' in his piece *Margate, 1940*.

It was Margate, indeed, where Benny Hill was bound in the summer of 1948, set for a long season at the Cliftonville Lido. Cliftonville is situated in the east end of Margate. It *is* Margate – the two are separated merely by a short esplanade – but Cliftonville likes to consider itself distinct, and more refined. Whatever the presumptions, by 1948 Margate was well established as the 'Blackpool of the south', a pleasure resort within easy reach of London. It was here, in the late eighteenth century, that the bathing-machine had first been used, upon which George III became a convert to the cause. Train-loads of Londoners now descended on the town daily, festooned with all the accoutrements of a British seaside holiday – buckets and spades, a beach-ball, a Thermos flask, a windbreak and pockets full of copper coins to drop into slot-machines in the vast Dreamland amusement arcade.

Benny was booked to appear in *Gaytime*, a show named with all the innocence of the era when 'gay' meant nothing more than to be bright and merry. The 1,200-seat Lido Theatre was part of an unwieldy entertainment complex that also included two cafés (each with its own dance band), a cinema, several bars with live entertainment, a bathing pool, a bandstand terrace, a 'tea lawn', a putting green, tennis courts, hairdressing salons and the Tropical Aquarium and Snake House. It was a package designed to keep customers on the premises, satisfying all their holiday needs and taking all their holiday money. There were rival attractions, however – Margate also had several theatres, and in the same week that *Gaytime* opened, a garage in Cliftonville had a 'one week only' display of Hermann Goering's bullet-proof car. So Britain did have its 'spoils of war' after all.

Gaytime required Benny to perform as 'second comic', with his own solo spot, 'feed' in the double-act sketches with Reg Varney, and be company manager, in charge of keeping the troupe ship-shape and ready for the stage. All for £14 a week, out of which he had to pay for his meals, and lodge in a local guest-house.

Varney was unquestionably the star. He was the one for whom the autograph hunters waited at the stage door, he was the one invited to open local bazaars and church fêtes, kiss babies and judge bathing-beauty contests on the beach. He was the one for whom agent Richard Stone had secured a whopping £75 a week and percentage of the box-office. Reg Varney had the prized block-capitals at the top of the posters. Benny Hill's name was 'down where the bicycles were kept'.

Varney had already been in the business a long time. On file at the BBC is a letter he wrote in 1935 applying for a radio audition. 'I can see by my own eyes that it's cheek you want to get on in this world,' the eighteen-year-old had declared. Reg had bags of it. A hard-working lad from Canning Town, in the impoverished East End of London, he had slogged his way around the country playing piano, singing and performing comic turns. Now, under Richard Stone, he was starting to be noticed in London, impressing with a range of facial expressions and athleticism around the stage. There were few better than Varney at performing 'bits of business' – mime, movements and a miscellany of physical antics. 'I'm working on my face all the time,' he said in a 1949 *Daily Mail* interview.

'Other comedians can borrow your gags but they can't pinch your phizog.' As it transpired, Varney's big-time breakthrough would occur after that of his Margate 'feed' – he had to wait until the 1960s before attaining celebrity, first in the BBC TV situation comedy *The Rag Trade*, and then in his own comedy vehicle *On the Buses*, a remarkably successful, resolutely 'blue-collar' sitcom on British commercial television in the 1970s.

Varney's fate this summer of '48 rested to an extent on his supporting partner, Benny Hill. Though hitherto a stranger, his was soon a friendly face. Varney recalls, 'Hedley Claxton came to see me and said, "Your new feed is not very experienced and I'm hoping you can show him a few pointers. Be patient with him." And then I met Benny for the first time. He had a nice smile and was a bit taller than me, and from the very first go I could see that he had potential. We became a great team. He did the verbal stuff on stage and I did all the "business". Once we got used to one another we were good together, and we knew it.' Benny understood the science of the comedy double-act.

A Yorkshireman, and formerly a comedian, Hedley Claxton ran a number of summer shows at different resorts, travelling around by train, working on scripts on a portable typewriter as he went. He had a pronounced lisp, and people in the business called him 'Hedley Claxxthton' behind his back.

'Hedley was a very nice person, a gentle man, and he never asked for the moon,' says Varney. 'But he did give us his old stage material to perform, really old-fashioned stuff, and we had to throw it out because it was so dreadful.' Benny strove to fill the place of Claxton's antiquities. 'Even then, he was a brilliant writer,' reflects the admiring Varney. 'He wrote us a beautiful "Art of Flirting" gag, about how to get off with a girl':

Benny When you say 'I love you' you've got to say it with feeling!
Reg [does comedy 'business', shaping up to feel a girl by whatever parts protrude]
Benny No, no! Not with your hands! She's a titled lady. You've got to address her correctly.
Reg [after some more facial 'business'] Pardon?
Benny You must say 'Your grace . . .'
Reg For what we are about to receive, may the Lord . . .

A good deal of writing was required for *Gaytime* because, although the season ran for close on four months, the programme changed five times within every fortnight, the idea being that Claxton might tempt the same punters through the door more than once, and even, for the nutters, all five times. To generate this many comedy ideas Benny needed all his American gag books, and he also sought inspiration from the cinema. Varney remembers, 'We'd meet in the mornings to pick up mail, then I'd go off to have a game of golf and he'd have lunch at the digs. Then while I went back to bed off he'd go to the pictures, taking his little notebook with him. He went every single afternoon, and when I came to the theatre in the evenings he'd give me an ear-bashing about what film he'd seen. I used to say to him, "But did you get it all down?" and he'd say, "You bet!" He had bits of paper *everywhere*.'

Benny also had another source for his comedy 'ideas'. In 1943, when America had joined the Second World War, a new Europe-based radio station had been launched to cater for the entertainment of her troops. The American Forces Network, AFN, took all the top name big-band and comedy shows from the major US radio networks, stripped them of their sponsorship plugs and commercials and broadcast them continuously in Europe. And when the war finished, AFN continued. By straining over the fading night-time medium- and short-waves, comedy students could not only hear their idols – Jack Benny, Bob Hope, Fred Allen, Henny Youngman, Jimmy Durante, Edgar Bergen and others – but also purloin their material. These American comics had the best scriptwriters in the world – how simple it was to cherry-pick their gags for British consumption, with virtually no danger of being caught. Benny was an enthusiastic devotee of AFN.

'People who really wanted to filch would still be listening at four o'clock in the morning,' says Denis Norden, 'straining to listen through very poor reception, with a pencil and paper standing by. The great thing then was to get the gags into your script as soon as possible. There were a few comedians who did this, and a couple of writers. Some of those ideas and lines that Benny "imported" did service for many years, well up to his 1980s TV shows.'

The Margate cinema visits were solo outings, and Benny remained steadfastly unattached the entire summer. 'Everybody liked him,' says Varney. 'He was a mum's boy, and women loved him like a mum loves a son. My wife Lil certainly thought of him this way, and he loved Lil like a mother. But he was a loner outside of work. We never went anywhere together.'

Gaytime was a slick show, with comedians on stage every alternate item – sketch, blackout, music, sketch, blackout, dance. The Gaytime Dancers, usually choreographed by a ballerina no less, added the requisite glamour, and Claxton's stage sets and costumes were impressive. But the audiences saw two distinctly different aspects of Benny Hill. As a 'feed', a role with which he was forever dissatisfied, he was quite brilliant. As a solo 'patter' comedian, which was where he was desperate to succeed, he was nervous, hesitant and uncomfortable.

'When Benny and I were together we were fantastic,' reflects Varney. 'We had such a rapport. For example, one night the backcloth roller got stuck, so Benny said to me, "Quick, Reg, get down there!" I was still in my dressing-gown. Benny said he just had to get some trousers on. As I went down the steps on to the stage I heard him telling the audience that a planned waterfall scene couldn't be used because the effect had packed up. I went on stage and said the same. And he said, "What are you doing? I've just told them what's going on. I'm the compère, you shut up!" And we did ten minutes of brilliant material, verbal and with lots of looks and expressions, until the roller was fixed. The timing was fantastic.

'But when Benny did his own act it was like watching someone else. I could see he was all tensed up, unable to relate to the audience. One time we were working together he said to me, "It's got to the point where I dread doing the act. My lips get so dry I can't spit a tanner." I said, "The trouble is, Ben, you are a completely different person when you're working with me and when you go out there on your own." I felt that he needed to find a *style*.'

Keen to promote the best in his partner, Reg sensed that Benny, ever the restless fidget, needed to relax a little more. 'I'd suffered myself in the past, but had gone to see a diet reformist, who also showed me how to relax. I decided to teach Benny to relax, explaining how to concentrate on each part of the body, from head to toe, letting go of the muscles one by one. He said he'd have a shot at it, but the next morning he came back saying, "I started doing it but I got so tired I turned over and went to sleep." '

It was 'a good line', *très amusant*, but typical Benny. He was never prepared to take a serious look inside, to seek explanations or answers to aspects of his personality.

Gaytime played from mid-June to the beginning of October, and was a decent hit for Hedley Claxton. The working-class London holidaymakers took to Varney as one of their own, and Claxton shrewdly put him under summer-season contract for a further two years. He was less certain about Benny Hill, however, keeping him on the summer payroll but relegating him to a lesser show, in Newquay, for 1949. Here he would be 'feed' to Ron Clark ('The Modern Funatic'); Benny went to see his next comedy partner at the first opportunity, anxious to set off this new relationship on a good footing. Clark spent a week at the end of the 1948 summer season at the Margate Theatre Royal and recalls, 'One matinée performance, very sparsely attended, drew hearty laughter from a solitary bloke in the fifth row. And there was Benny.'

Another meeting that occurred at this time was between Reg Varney and Benny's parents. *Gaytime* played in Bournemouth as a warm-up for Margate. *En route*, Benny and Reg dropped in to Westrow Gardens. 'I met all the family,' says Varney. 'His mum was "a real mum", a darling. And I liked Len, although he and Benny were chalk and cheese. You never saw two brothers so different.

'At first, Benny's dad was very friendly, full of bonhomie, but then I realized there was more to him. He offered me a drop of scotch and told Len to fetch the bottle of VAT 69 from the other room. Len couldn't believe it.

'When Len came back with the bottle he was about to pour me a drink when his dad piped up, "Don't mess about! Give the bloke a bloody drink, will you? Give it to me!" and he poured me the tiniest measure I've ever seen. It hardly dampened the bottom of the glass.'

Benny may have had reason to believe that The Captain's cold war against his stage leanings was beginning to thaw. A couple of articles about 'Southampton's new star comedian' had appeared in the *Southern*

Daily Echo at the time of the BBC radio series *Listen, My Children*, giving him cause for a smidgen of pride. Now, some eight years after the boy had made his stage debut, The Captain announced he would come to Bournemouth to see *Gaytime*. It would be the first time he had seen his son perform. But Benny could have predicted the outcome. Backstage after the show, Big Alf raved on and on about the splendours of another act, the Radio Revellers ('four men, one song, it's the way the voices blee-eend that helps the tune along'). With no one else able to get a word in, the gathered company shifted from foot to foot and cast glances at one another as Big Alf's enthusiasm flowed unchecked, until Helen seized upon a pause to make their excuses and depart. He hadn't said a word to, or about, his son.

Reg Varney's style of comedy suited the deployment of a 'feed', and as he and Benny Hill had knitted together effectively, Varney made clear to his agent his desire to see the partnership continue. This being so, it made sense for Richard Stone to sign Hill to his agency also, so that he could arrange for the 'feed' to be available when Varney needed him.[1] Accordingly, effective from November 1948, Benny Hill tied himself to an agency for the first time, becoming a client of Felix de Wolfe & Richard Stone.[2] Little did Stone realize the extraordinary good fortune this purely expedient arrangement would bring. In the long term, Varney's contract earned him no special reward, and the comedian moved on to another agency in 1956; Hill's quiet loyalty reaped Stone's business 10 per cent of an eventual multi-million pound income.

Richard Stone, who died while this book was being written, was not your archetypal agent. Not for him the omnipresent fat cigar, nor that hallmark of a shady deal, the wad of used notes stuffed in an old envelope and shiftily delivered. Tall, with a rod-straight back, Stone carried stature and possessed a sense of importance. When he signed his name on a letter the single word 'Richard' would sweep from within an inch of the left edge of the paper to within an inch of the right. He had, too, a distinctive wandering eye, so people could never be certain if he was looking at them or someone else. His nickname among comics was 'old wall-eye'; Dave

Allen, the inspired Irish comedian who, like Benny Hill, became a loyal, long-term client, said at Stone's memorial service, 'He was the only man who, playing golf, could address the ball and the hole at the same time.'

Born in 1920 and raised in Surrey, Richard Stone had taken up a stage career strictly against the wishes of his father. Jack Stone worked on the London Stock Exchange and expected his son to follow suit, funding a Charterhouse School education in preparation. Instead, his school years behind him, the young man enrolled at the Royal Academy of Dramatic Art (RADA) and from there went into repertory theatre and performed in concert-parties. He was treading the boards in the north of England at the same time that a young Alfie Hill was having his first dabble in Eastleigh.

Before serving in the Second World War, in the Royal Horse Artillery Regiment, Stone took some initial steps towards becoming an impresario, and when the war was over – as well as being the colonel in charge of Combined Services Entertainment – he moved to London, going into partnership with Felix de Wolfe. Funded by (a now mollified) Jack Stone, they opened their first office in Wardour Street, in a curtained-off area at the back of Felix's father's music business, before switching to William IV Street, between Covent Garden and Charing Cross station. Each partner had his own distinct client-list; Benny Hill was Stone's and his contact with de Wolfe was minimal. Stone was at home with comedians, de Wolfe with actors. It was a productive mix, lasting until the partnership ended twenty years later, after which the two men opened separate agencies and scarcely spoke to one another again.

Back in London himself, Benny Hill was without a place to live. Leaving for Margate four months earlier, he had let the Queensway apartment go without making other plans. So began a tricky period of short-term lets. His first stop was Cricklewood, north London, where he lodged with a show-business couple, Bill and June. The husband and wife spent most nights apart, but when together there was scant harmony. Benny, the gooseberry, quickly moved on. He relocated nearby but here again he was caught in domestic crossfire. He left once more. He was beginning to echo his father's description of himself as a young man, 'the little bird that flew from spike to spike'. It had been a situation familiar, too, to the late 'Aitch Aitch'.

Benny finally found lodging at 62 Ambler Road, Finsbury Park, in a three-storey villa literally within sight of the North Bank stand at Arsenal Football Club, and just a short walk from the Empire, Finsbury Park, a hallowed Variety theatre. He stayed here for around a year. It was a crowded house, with eleven – predominantly Irish – occupants sharing at one time. Competition for the bathroom was intense. Ada Buckle, the landlady, provided a simple diet for her boarders but was wont to cater rather better for herself, being particularly partial to strawberries. If anyone cast covetous eyes on her plate she would place a protective arm around it and screech, '*You're not 'avin' any, you're not 'avin' any!*'

Benny had some more radio work this autumn. *Listen, My Children* had been fatally wounded but the premise breathed a last gasp in a new guise, *Third Division*. It had the same producer, writers Frank Muir and Denis Norden were joined by Paul Dehn, and the large cast now included three of the four men who would soon revolutionize radio comedy with *The Goon Show* – Harry Secombe, Peter Sellers and Michael Bentine (the mad genius, of Peruvian stock out of Watford, who would quickly strike up a mutual appreciation society with Benny Hill).

Despite all this, perhaps the most remarkable aspect of *Third Division* is that it was the first comedy to air on the BBC's Third Programme. The Third catered for those who sought a diet of highbrow classical music, experimentation, and earnest food for thought, and its dedicated if minority audience seldom tuned their dial elsewhere. Your average 'Brit', eternally scared of 'culture', kept *well* away. A theatre poster for those arch funsters the Crazy Gang declared with curious pride, 'Nervo and Knox – Never Heard On The Third'.

Third Division was another interesting experiment, but the cerebral audience took to it no more than those Home Service listeners who had pronounced *Listen, My Children* such a disappointment. And Benny's contribution was again minor, just character voices, although, appropriately, he was invited to speak the subtitle at the start of the programme:

Robert Beatty For no particular reason it is called
Bruce Belfrage *Third Division.*
Robert Beatty With the added subtitle . . .
Benny Hill *Some Vulgar Fractions* [sniggers vulgarly]

Obviously, few could snigger as vulgarly as Benny Hill.

Third Division never returned after its six-week run. If the series is remembered at all today, it is because it gave the first airing to a Muir–Norden piece that, issued on an album a decade later, would become one of Peter Sellers' best loved recordings, the mock travelogue 'Balham – Gateway to the South'. In the original radio version, though Sellers was to the fore, Benny Hill contributed a significant character part.

Muir and Norden, with Sid Colin, also wrote another radio show at this time, *Starlight Hour*, in which Benny again worked as 'feed', though not with Reg Varney. Now he was teamed with the genial Jewish comic-actor Alfred Marks. They, and also Peter Sellers, were resident comedians on this weekly show, which ran throughout the autumn of 1948. Denis Norden was therefore in a good position to observe Benny. 'If you were to ask me if Benny stood out from the crowd in any way,' he says, 'the short answer is no. He felt himself very much in the shadow of people like Peter and Alfred. Especially Alfred, who was a much more command-ing figure in every way. Benny wasn't exactly shy but there was always a sense that he was holding back, that there was always a reserve about him. And he always shot off straight away when we finished, he didn't stay around to socialize.' (This might also have been because Hill had duped the BBC into believing that he was taking the train up from Southampton for each of the Monday-night live broadcasts. For this, in addition to his ten guineas fee, he was reimbursed £1 1s 7d for the fare and given a £1 7s 6d subsistence allowance. He was, in fact, getting the bus down from Finsbury Park. Benny was no money-grabber, but the ruse was so easy to pull and so commonly done that it was probably hard to resist.)

'Benny usually played a moronic character – the one who said "Duh?"' Denis Norden recalls of his scripts. 'And he and Alfred were absolute masters of dialect and could talk to each other in what appeared to be Russian or French or whatever we asked of them. They made a very good team. Benny always got *the idea* – he knew straight away what we were driving at. Like most of our generation, he was very clued up on the Hollywood trends and dialogue clichés. And he had a way of setting a scene for a character, physically as well as vocally. He told me that to be a Nazi officer you keep your hand on an imaginary holster, with the thumb tucked inside the belt. And as soon as you say "*Zo, Inglisman!*"

you're immediately *it*. In those days, immediately post-war, one wrote a lot of that kind of material. So he was obviously talented, Benny. Just *how* talented we never twigged.'

One of Richard Stone's first coups as agent for Reg Varney had been to arrange his participation in *The Boltons Revue*, a Christmas-season intimate revue at the tiny art-deco Boltons Theatre, situated amid the grand houses of Drayton Gardens, Kensington. Formerly a bijou cinema (in later years it became so once again, the arty Paris-Pullman), the Boltons Theatre Club was every inch a part of London's 'royal borough' – Princess Margaret was a member, and it was occasionally favoured by a visit from Queen Mary, wife of the late King George V. Varney had performed in the 1947 *Revue* which had then transferred into the West End. Now, as he was booked to appear (without Benny Hill) in a Christmas pantomime, Stone persuaded the management to take his new client instead.

Frank Woolf was predictably delighted for his ward. *Show World* declared, 'Benny Hill finds his métier in the new smart *Boltons Revue* in Kensington.' Anything *less* like Benny's métier would be hard to imagine. But he dug out of mothballs his mock-German Toto piece, he played a character named the Lion Heart's Queen in a three-hander sketch called Three Queens, and he gave a London airing to a new piece titled 'Ribbing the Hips', which was a pastiche of a Variety show. 'Ribbing': to poke fun at, 'the Hips': the Hippodromes.

Bob Monkhouse came to see his friend at the Boltons. 'I thought he was very good. Benny always had difficulty projecting in large venues but this was a very intimate theatre. I don't think there *was* anything after Row G, just 250 people sitting there in a rather large living room. By calling his spot "Ribbing the Hips" he was able to do exactly what he normally did in Variety except that, because it was an intimate revue, he could label it "satire".'

The *Stage* reviewer fell hook, line and sinker. 'The impression of present-day Variety, contributed by Benny Hill, is almost true to life. [And] in "Toto" he breaks into Anglo-German in a vivid study of a Berlin music-hall comic.'

A case of revue misleading the review – Toto was nothing but a straightforward comedy spot in which Hill hugged his shoulders up so that he had no neck, and pulled his bowler-hat down so that his ears stuck out, upon which he was mildly rude in mock German. It was scarcely 'a vivid study'.

The Boltons Revue 1948–49 opened four days before Christmas, and a second edition was launched a month later, with a substantially different programme. The *West London and Chelsea Gazette* commented that Benny Hill and fellow cast member Stanley Beard's new items 'Corn in Cornwall' and 'Bad Form at St Dominic's' – nothing is known about the content of either – were 'particularly witty and cleverly exploited'.

This may, too, have been the opinion of Queen Mary, who, 'hatless and wearing a wine-coloured coat', attended the Saturday matinée on February 5, accompanied by a couple of ladies-in-waiting, the Marquis of Cambridge and Lady Helena Gibbs. Benny had to tailor his act for the royal ears, Toto's saucy 'kleine Sitzen und grossen Titzen' giving way to 'kleine Kürzen und grossen Burzem'. The *Kensington News and West London Times* reported, 'Her Majesty received the entire cast after the show and said how much she had enjoyed the revue.' Now here was a cutting to send to The Captain. (And what it didn't say is that the Queen even spoke to Benny, declaring, 'Young man, I thought you were most amusing.' Benny bowed and mumbled a 'Thank you, ma'am.')

This *Boltons Revue* did not transfer to the West End, but it travelled to Brighton for a short run at the Theatre Royal. *Evening Argus* reviewer 'P.B.' was most gratified with the royally approved company, citing 'high spirits, enthusiasm, a disarming and infectious will to please, and an abundance of talent'.

He reserved his highest praise for Benny Hill, 'a nimble and accomplished young comedian, equally at ease as a one-man Variety show, as a Calypso singer, as a corrupted schoolboy in a maliciously witty echo of the Lynskey tribunal,[3] or as Toto, who tells long, inscrutable and very funny stories in low German'.

All this time, television was slowly developing. Post-war expansion was afoot and there was increasing public demand for TV sets, even though they were priced at almost £100. (British households at this time were existing on an average £375 a year.) For the time being, though, supply restrictions were causing production delays. More material than silicon chips and a circuitry board went into the manufacture of television sets in this period. They were pieces of *furniture*, with a tiny monochrome screen set into a huge wooden console, and perhaps four battleship knobs underneath to control the picture. The knobs were, however, powerless to prevent the problems that frequently blighted programmes mid-broadcast. The sight of a card reading 'Technical Fault – Do Not Adjust Your Set' was part and parcel of television viewing at this time and would remain so for at least another decade.

Viewing was also restricted by hours of broadcast. It would be another five decades before twenty-four-hour television was standard in Britain. In this very early period a typical day's schedule would comprise an hour's demonstration film in the morning – designed to help shops sell sets – then the day's first programme would air from three until four in the afternoon. After this, the service closed again until 8.30. One or two evening programmes would then be shown, followed by the news, with closedown at 10.15 or 10.30. In total, there were three hours of TV a day, and only the one BBC channel to watch.

Benny Hill made his debut television appearance on March 23 1949, in the programme *Music-Hall*, broadcast live on a Wednesday evening from Alexandra Palace. In a role he had previously fulfilled in the radio show *Works Wonders*, he was the compère, using gags to link the items and fill a short solo spot all to himself. This time the cast were not amateurs, though – there was Benny's radio pal Alfred Marks, the comedy vocalist Leslie Sarony, the Austrian singer Joe Ortnes, The Seven Volants – a remarkable tumbling troupe led by one Johnny Hutch,[4] a fifteen-piece orchestra under the leadership of Eric Robinson, and, top of the bill, the singer Vera Lynn, the forces' sweetheart and a national heroine. (Some cynical show-business folk had already started complaining that the Second World War had been planned by Lynn's agent.) Naturally, during the show, she sang 'We'll Meet Again'.

The BBC was not to commence TV audience research until 1950, but a *Music-Hall* production file exists, showing that the budget for the forty-five-minute programme was £400, out of which Benny was paid thirteen guineas. There was a studio audience of sixty, and four (virtually fixed) cameras were used, one solely for the credit caption-cards at the end. In an internal memo about Marks, Ortnes and Hill's dressing-room requirements, it was written: 'if necessary all in one D.R. but preferably separate ones. Joe Ortnes is an Austrian!'

For once, the BBC files then disappoint – there is no surviving script. However, Benny's material certainly would have been tamed. There was considerable censorship of scripts for television, as indicated in a couple of memos in the same file, referring to other editions of *Music-Hall*. One, preceding an April broadcast, was a reminder to the producer that 'the Variety show on this night should not have any particularly exaggerated forms of dancing, since it is still just in Holy Week.'

Another referred to an appearance the same month by the great northern comic Norman Evans.[5] The man whose job title was Controller, Television, Norman Collins, berated his producer for allowing the comedian to air risqué material:

> We have to give the *appearance* of the complete freedom of the Music Hall while observing the standards (higher ones) that are normal in the home. For this reason we seek to avoid medical jokes, particularly sexual medical jokes, and though Norman Evans may be able to fling a Music Hall audience into fits of laughter every time he dresses up as a rednosed harridan and includes references to 'hot flushes', it is our job to tell him that he has to forego that particular streak of humour when he appears on Television.

Down in Southampton, Alf and Helen Hill were unable to see their son's first TV appearance. Television reception remained confined to the London area and it wasn't until November 1954 that the south of England could receive pictures.[6] Still, there must have been a modicum of pride in the modest Westrow Gardens household that their Alfie had got his picture in *Radio Times*, albeit only the London-area edition.

And so we see him, on page thirty-one. A fresh-faced young man in jacket and tie, a towering quiff building up to the left, those 'sunshine personality' eyes fixed keenly to the right. Though twenty-five, he looks not much more than a boy, aged somewhere between fourteen and eighteen.

After a couple of further broadcasts on *Variety Bandbox*,[7] and in monthly Muir–Norden programmes *The April Revue* and *The May Revue* ('some oblique observations in the margin of the month'), it was summer season once again, and Benny headed down to Newquay, on the Atlantic coast in Cornwall, for another of Hedley Claxton's *Gaytime* shows. The deal was much as before, with Benny now working as 'feed' to Ron Clark, but his bill matter was no longer 'The Sunshine Personality'. Now he was 'As Modern As Tomorrow'. And if the *Radio Times* photograph of Benny had been almost disconcertingly boyish, his image in the *Gaytime* souvenir programme was simply awful. Shot in London by leading show-business photographers Landseer, it must contest for the worst 'handout' photo of all time. Benny's bow-tie looks plastic, he wears a rigid, over-toothy grin and his eyes are fixed far up and left, betraying clear signs of panic. It is the photograph of an acutely self-conscious young man.

Gaytime ran for eighteen weeks at the tiny Cosy Nook Theatre in Newquay. ('Patrons are respectfully asked not to drop Ice Cream wrappers, etc. on the carpet.') Claxton visited on the show's opening, handing out gifts for his artistes – an orange and a hairbrush – then it was *to work*: five separate programmes over two weeks, Mondays to Saturdays, one show every night and matinées on wet afternoons. This latter arrangement meant that the cast couldn't stray far in case it rained. Fortunately, it was one of Britain's better summers. Donald Scott ('The Popular Baritone') had a two-seater MG, and he and Benny, sometimes with a girl from the show wedged into the back, would occasionally take off for an afternoon, finding isolated beaches on the north Cornwall coast. A keen photographer, Scott took many shots of Benny this summer. Here he is on a beach, relaxing with Peggy Batchelor ('The Sophisticated Entertainer'), cracking walnuts in the dunes, and sporting a confident smirk as he leans on a cricket-bat, shirt removed but clad still in white woolly vest, well-worn pin-striped grey trousers, socks and black shoes.

Benny spent most mornings in his simple digs, writing scripts for a concurrent radio show for which he had just been engaged, *Petticoat Lane*.[8] The recordings took place in London every Sunday evening and the BBC was paying Hill's return train fare from Newquay. Late every Saturday night Donald Scott would run him to Plymouth, where he'd catch the sleeper train to the capital, arriving the next morning. First thing Monday he would dash back to Cornwall.

After writing, Benny would sometimes socialize. 'We got on extremely well,' says Ron Clark. 'We used to play on the putting-green, and we went to the pub where we'd test each other on gags. One of us would say "restaurant" or "railways" or whatever, and the other would have to tell a joke on that subject. We used to score points – add a point for a joke, subtract a point if you couldn't think of one.'

Benny wrote himself and Ron a footballing sketch. Clark recalls, 'I'd come on stage as a dopey twit in football gear, with bulging socks and cap side-twisted, a Simple Simon attitude. Benny said, "Then Matthews came along..." "Jessie Matthews?" I'd ask. "No, Stanley, you twit!"' Not everything was original, though. Another favoured joke was 'I saw a fork in the road', with its oh-so-creaky punchline, 'Well why didn't you pick it up?' 'I always thought that Benny patterned himself on Max Miller,' says Clark. 'A lot of the jokes weren't original but Benny wove the old stories into new methods of presentation.' Newquay audiences also got to see the ubiquitous Toto.

Donald Scott, meanwhile, observed contradictions in Benny's character. 'He was very quiet. Even when we were out he was never cracking jokes or happy or bright. If the occasion occurred he could tune into it and become jolly, but left alone he would be rather rapt in thought. I believe he was thinking about jokes and things. On the other hand, when I used to take him out in the car he used to embarrass me. I kept the hood down in the good weather and if there were any girls on the street he'd wolf-whistle. I'd think, "I wish he wouldn't do that. It's so awfully rude." But I never actually saw him *with* any women.'

Ron Clark shares this last observation, and found it equally curious. 'He was a good-looking bloke, very charming and lovely to everybody. But he never seemed to latch on to any girl. At least two of the girls in the show loved him, and the mother of one of them was very keen in pressing her daughter on to Benny, though he seemed to just laugh it off. But my wife

Gay was staying with us in Newquay and Benny thought the world of her. She used to darn his socks for him, and sewed his trousers after he bent down one day and put a big split in the behind. He used to pull her leg and say, "If you weren't married to Ron I'd marry you myself!"'

As it happens, Benny could have married shortly after the Newquay summer came to an end. Having returned to London, he went out as 'feed' to Reg Varney in a touring revue, *Montmartre*. One of the show's soubrettes was Joy St Edmund, nineteen, with whom Benny went on to have his first meaningful relationship.

A young dancing-school teacher and performer from Leeds, Joy fitted Benny's image of an ideal woman – wavy blonde hair and a fine, pretty face. Contrary to later public perception, he seems never to have been 'a breast man', but Joy was well built all the same.

'In *Montmartre* we opened with 'La Vie en Rose' and then did a few sketches together,' she recalls. 'We found that we got along well, and after a while just the two of us started working together in Sunday concerts that Benny would fix up. I was the typical feed for him – the busty blonde in a grass skirt who was chased across the stage with a lawnmower. But the act never went well and we cried on each other's shoulders. The relationship led from there.

'He was very handsome, with lovely fair hair, and we cared for each other very deeply. I called him "Bennissimo" and he called me "Podge". We were also trying to get an act together, and work always came first for Benny. He was always talking about the business, about why he didn't get laughs in the right places, and he was forever listening to AFN, getting ideas from Jack Benny and people like that. It was out of season and we stayed in some dreadful digs. The food was often meagre, and if you wanted heat you had to put a shilling in the meter.'

A full relationship developed. 'We had to have single rooms and then sneak about in the night. "Quick, the landlady's coming, get under the bed!" – that kind of thing. You'd sneak around, and get back to your own room in the morning before the landlady came up with a cup of tea.[9]

'We made love, but I'm sure it wasn't the highlight of his life – or mine, although he was "my first". He was a caring lover, very gentle, but not at all exciting in bed, not a bit "Wham, bam, thank you mam." He was simply working so hard trying to get his act together, always listening to AFN, that sex wasn't his main interest in life. He was capable, and he enjoyed it, but he wasn't very sexual. He wasn't a dirty old man, and he wasn't a dirty young man either.'

One could surmise that the prospect of marriage would have still been anathema to Benny at this time in his life, as he continued to struggle for fame. Being married and having a family, which he told Joy he wanted, would have meant compromising his career. And yet, it was marriage that he sought: 'He said to me, "When things work out, we could get married. I think we'd make a good team." I said, "OK then, I'll think about it." He said, "So are we engaged?" And I said, "Well if you say we are, we are." We were going to buy engagement rings but never got around to it, though he bought me a cheap, everyday ring. I felt that we ought to be waiting until we'd made some money before deciding anything. Really, though, I just didn't want to get tied up. I was too young.'

The relationship lasted at most only a few months and was in many ways out of character for Benny. Nonetheless, it was still sufficient for Joy to gain some vivid impressions of him – accurate ones, too, in so far as they are echoed by scores of his associates and acquaintances.

'He was shy and not very confident. He didn't find it easy to relax, but when he did he laughed a lot and fooled around. He had a temperament but not a temper, and was mostly gentle and caring. He didn't have close friends and was never "one of the guys", going out for a drink with the boys.

'He wasn't mean, but he was quite happy to have a cup of tea and a bun as opposed to a slap-up meal. He wouldn't have stayed in a swish hotel even if he had the money. He preferred to be with "the man in the street" and would observe and talk to the dustman. He said to me once, "That's where I get my comedy from."'

The relationship dwindled when Joy, short of money, secured work in a West End show. 'We drifted apart,' she says. 'The relationship was more likely to have developed into a brother-sister one than husband-wife. I had been a pleasant interlude for him. And then I met somebody else. Benny got a bit funny about it but a few months later he rang and asked if I was OK. He said that things were starting to work out for him too.'

Joy later became an air-hostess, and continues to teach dancing all these decades later. She giggles still, more than fifty years on, as she recollects her relationship with Benny Hill. Her abiding memory is one of great affection: 'Killing ourselves laughing over ideas that we then realized wouldn't get a laugh on stage.'

Joy St Edmund's observations about Benny's attitude to money ring true. As a child, Alfie Hill had seemed intent on scrimping as much cash as he could. The adult Benny Hill seemed completely unconcerned by it. Even in this early period, where money was hard to come by and easy to spend, Benny possessed an extraordinarily laissez-faire attitude. In May 1949, the BBC's Programme Accountant – showing, it must be said, admirable qualities – sent Benny a letter about some money the Corporation was trying to pay him.

> On 9th July 1948 we sent you our cheque H28665 for £5.5.0 in payment of the fee due to you for the reproduction on 1st July of 'Listen My Children' originally recorded on 29th May (broadcast on 29th June).
>
> We have been notified by our bank that you have not presented this cheque for payment and consequently it has now become out of date.
>
> Would you please return the cheque to us, or if you have no trace of it, inform us so we can arrange for a new cheque to be sent.

The letter drew a handwritten reply on the COMEDY SPECIALIST notepaper, dated May 11 1949.

> I have no trace of the cheque.
> As this is probably due to carelessness on my part, I offer my apologies for any inconvenience this may cause you.
> Yours faithfully,
> Benny Hill

Another incidence of type occurred around the same time. The army major who had been so brutally frank about Benny's planned Stars in Battledress act in Lüneburg, Germany, was running a pub somewhere in Kent and was evidently being troubled by his conscience. 'He was holding a New Year's Eve party,' says Richard Stone, 'and rang to ask me if he could book Benny for £30. Benny was reluctant to have anything to do with it, but I persuaded him because the money was so good. But the party was cancelled, or something happened, anyway he was given a £30 cheque without having to do the work. But he never cashed cheques. And one day soon afterwards he was walking down Charing Cross Road when he bumped into Harry Segal. Harry said to him, "I've got a booking but I can't afford the costume and the props, so I'm going to have to turn it down." Benny asked how much he needed and Harry replied "£30". Benny fished in his pocket and gave him the cheque.'[10]

Benny's days of performing in army shows were not yet behind him, incidentally, and he would remain active in this area for another dozen years. Fulfilling his duties with Combined Services Entertainment, Richard Stone was still putting together shows for the boys in serge, sending performers all over the world. In early 1950 Benny found himself on a tour of European army bases; in the audience at a show in Graz, Austria, was his cousin, Hugh Stevens, serving in the Intelligence Corps. 'It was a sort of concert party, small scale and low key, and Benny was the comic,' Stevens recalls. 'I had no idea he was in it but just decided to go along and there he was, on stage. He did some mock-German and some mild "seaside-postcard" humour, and was good-*ish*. His reception was on the cool side. It wasn't what you would call a particularly sophisticated show, and most of the people I was with had already been to university and considered themselves rather superior to that level of entertainment.'

Benny was more at home back on British stages. *Montmartre* had reunited him with Reg Varney and it was an enjoyable venture, a short eight-week tour in the run up to Christmas 1949. With Alfred Marks heading the cast, *Montmartre* had already broken box-office records during a long Brighton residency, and it was standard Variety business that the show would then travel, trading on its good name but featuring a different cast – in this case, the star being Varney. The production remained impressive, as Joy St Edmund recalls. 'French musicians were playing outside the theatre, and as the audience came in the tabs were already open and there was a Montmartre street scene on stage. Then a trio of musicians walked through the stalls and up on to the stage to begin the show.'

After this came the Can-Can Girls and a range of what was called 'Continental Specialities' – two Hungarian classical dancers, a comedienne turned contortionist cum acrobatic dancer, 'a West Indian torch singer' (Mona Baptiste) and the Eight Parisian Lovelies, balletic art students who danced while painting portraits of four topless models. When he had visited Paris the previous year, Montmartre had been Benny Hill's kind of place. *Montmartre* was his kind of show.

Once again, Benny served as straightman to Varney, their skits taking place before a backdrop of Parisian café, night-club and street scenes. A review in *The Stage* read, 'Benny Hill capably feeds in comic scenes, and makes a successful solo appearance with a fund of appreciated stories'; during a week at the Theatre Royal in Bath, the *Bath & Wilts Chronicle & Herald* praised the pair as 'humorists-in-chief'.

The tour opened in October 1949 in Ramsgate, Kent; during the second week, at Chatham, Varney's father died. But a 'show must go on' spirit prevailed. 'I adored my dad, but I had to stand on stage and try to be funny,' Varney says. 'One of my lines in a sketch was "You'll find the body upstairs." It was very difficult, but if anybody carried me through a show it was Benny, that night. He put his arm around my shoulder and said "Don't worry, Reg, we'll do it."'

After moving on to Weymouth, Walthamstow, Bath and then ending with three weeks in London, at the Metropolitan (Edgware Road) and a couple of venues dear to Benny's heart, the Palaces in East Ham and Chelsea, *Montmartre* came to an end. Benny then went straight into rehearsals for the pantomime *Aladdin* at the Richmond Theatre, south-west of London.

Benny Hill, with his fresh, open countenance, is an ideal Wishee-Washee. He is put through the mangle but had some trouble with Henry, the donkey, at the opening performance on Boxing Day afternoon. Henry, we regret to say, let his two scenes down badly. When we saw him at rehearsal he was pushing Benny all over the stage, but when he had to do it before an audience he just would not answer to his cue. He seemed to prefer to be chased by Benny rather than do the chasing himself. No wonder Benny suggested he had too much Christmas pudding![11]

It would be wrong to say that the 1950s dawned brightly for Benny Hill. Being chased around a stage by two men in a donkey-suit can pall after a day or two, let alone some thirty-four performances, and it's hardly Danny Kaye. And after this, as he moved up to and beyond his twenty-sixth birthday, his diary mostly comprised midweek cabaret bookings and

Sunday concerts. He was on the move again, too – leaving Arsenal's shadow, he spent some four months back in his first London abode, above the café at 14a Queensway, and then headed back to north-west London, to 62 Brondesbury Villas, Kilburn, where he lodged with several Irish navvies in a large, double-fronted Victorian house. It seemed to Benny that landlady Miss Kathleen Birkett was accommodating one of the men sexually, too. When a lodger broke the toilet cistern, but no one owned up, she threatened to eject them all . . . except for her one handy Paddy. In a 1971 TV show, Benny cited the incident in a monologue – 'Ted' – performed fully in the style of a 1940s Variety act:

> Ted's in these here digs, and the landlady treats 'em like pigs,
> Well you can't blame her 'cause they ain't exactly élite.
> One day she goes round the bend,
> She says 'All right, pack your things, that's the end,
> Clear out – you ain't even having a bite to eat!'

> The others all goes white but Ted, he says 'All right,
> I know there's plenty of landladies could use some extra lovin'.
> I'll not be homeless long 'cause I'm virile and I'm strong . . .'
> She said, 'I'm not talking to you, your dinner's in the oven.'

Soon afterwards, unable to buck the Birkett cistern, Benny moved on once more, back up to Cricklewood, taking lodgings at 6 Thorverton Road – a plain, family-sized semi-detached within easy reach, as Benny's accommodation always had to be, of bus routes and a station. He stayed here for eighteen months. Cricklewood had a mixed population, predominantly Irish and Jewish. A good twenty or more buses would pass hourly down the main street and anti-Semitic conductors were prone to call out 'Crickelevitch' as their vehicles trundled through.

Another summer season for Hedley Claxton beckoned, this year back at the Cliftonville Lido with Reg Varney. It was Varney's third consecutive summer here and his stature had grown considerably. Residents and visitors loved him – on posters and handbills he was now 'Margate's favourite star comedian', and Richard Stone had negotiated a £100 a week fee, with a 10 per cent share of box-office takings in excess of £1,000. Benny's straight fee would have been not much more than £25. A review of *Gaytime* in *The Stage* stated: 'Seldom in theatrical history has such a welcome been given to any artist as that which the audience gave to Reg Varney, the principal comedian, on his entrance in the opening scene.'

The marathon nineteen-week season, from May to October, began with a warm-up week in Weymouth. Among Reg and Benny's new sketches, co-written, was 'On the Centre Court' (also known as 'What the Deuce'). Reg reckoned he could extract maximum 'business' from an impression of the great French tennis player Suzanne Lenglen; she had won the Wimbledon singles title five years in succession, but the British, typically, chose to remember her as the first player to wear a short dress, under which could be snatched a glimpse of frilly knickers.

'We wrote it together,' says Varney. 'We were sitting in the back garden of my house in St Lawrence and he was scribbling it down on the back of a Players cigarette packet. Dialogue like "I'm going to serve!" "Well, I'll have a gin-and-tonic." I was a girl who joined a tennis club to find a man. Benny was the good-looking tennis coach. My sister, a dressmaker, made the dress and big frilly underwear for me, and when I ran on stage a scream would go up. It was magic, and it built from there. It became a classic.'

As usual, Benny Hill's biggest role was not so much to be funny himself but to give Varney the time and space in which to shine, improvising his 'bits of business'. Benny knew what to do. If anyone suggests that all it entailed was to stand around while the star got on with it, Varney dismisses such criticisms with a wave of a hand. 'Benny did nothing *superbly*,' he says. 'He would wait and wait while I pranced around doing my thing, giving me every chance to get the laughs.'

As usual, the *Gaytime* company was a large one. Working as soubrette and character comic on the show was Maureen Riscoe, a popular broad-caster in the BBC radio comedy *Much-Binding-in-the-Marsh* and the daughter of Arthur Riscoe, a well-known North Country comedian. Warm, and disarmingly frank, she struck up a good-natured friendship with Benny. 'I thought he was a lovely performer at this time,' she remarks. 'He was very relaxed and had lots of personality. He lived for the gags and the applause.

'Once you got over the initial shock of work in these summer seasons you had some free time, and I quickly realized that Benny never left the theatre. He was always in there, sitting in the corner of the dressing-room for hours on end with his gag books. He had every American gag book going and he was always at it – a besotted worker.

'Having found the gags in these books Benny would turn them around slightly. Then he tried them out on my mother, a sweet, wonderful lady with a great sense of humour and very big laugh. She came along when we did the trial week in Weymouth and we all stayed in the digs. Benny said to me, "Your mother's wonderful! I know that if she really belts out laughing then it's a good gag, and I'll have it in the show by tomorrow. But if she only sniggers then I won't put it in." And of course my mother *adored* Benny. He was such a polite and nice man.'

Again, *Gaytime* was a roaring success. *The Stage* remarked along the way:

> The return of Benny Hill was popular, his portrayal of a German comedian being punctuated by loud laughter. In addition, he is an admirable foil to Reg Varney in their many appearances together.

And:

> Reg Varney makes the humour bubble. Mr Varney, of the rubber face, comes across with topical fare for every member of the family, and this year he is well aided and abetted by Benny Hill. In all their programmes the pair could not wish for a better reception as single turns or in their dual efforts.

A note of caution was sounded, however, by Margate's local paper, the *Isle of Thanet Gazette*:

> In their dual efforts Benny makes an excellent foil. These two boys should 'go places' when they have had more experience, although I thought some of the lines were a little too broad for the family audience.

For Benny Hill, however, 'Margate, 1950' would carry one overriding memory. He had another of his pitiable 'relationships', and was spurned once more. This time it was worse. He went so far as to propose marriage to a woman who scarcely even felt she knew him, and who seemed to be blissfully unaware of his growing intent. He was shattered when she rejected his premature offer, and thirty, even forty, years later he would still speak about it to acquaintances and in interviews, evoking sympathy and comfort for his allegedly still bruised heart.

The woman's name was Elizabeth, and she was a soubrette in another show being staged in the town. The performers in the various entertainments would get to know one another and Benny got to know Elizabeth: they went out once or twice and Benny wooed her with flowers and a box of chocolates. Elizabeth was of 'good stock' – a doctor's daughter with a wealthy background, well-spoken, clear-headed and pretty. His desire to marry and 'settle down' unfulfilled after his uncharacteristic relationship with Joy St Edmund, Benny decided to grasp the nettle. Benny got stung.

His method of proposing marriage was unusual, to say the least. Lacking the nerve to ask Elizabeth in person, he popped out of the Cliftonville Lido one evening during a *Gaytime* interval, tripped to a phone box on the sea-front and dialled the backstage number at her theatre. After they had exchanged pleasantries for a while Benny blurted his proposal. Elizabeth was evidently too taken aback to respond immediately, but she promised to think it over and call him the next morning at his digs. She did, and the answer, inevitably, was no. Perhaps hoping to soften the blow, she told Benny she was in love with someone else. Benny was incredulous – so courteously and solicitously he had charmed her, he found it hard to accept she would want anyone but him.

Benny handled the 'rejection' in his customary manner, retreating deep inside himself. On his own, he would stomp about, kicking and throwing objects around at his digs and also in his *Gaytime* dressing-room. In company, though, he put a lid on it. It is entirely consistent with Benny's behavioural pattern that Reg Varney saw next to nothing of his comedy partner's distress. 'I know now that he was a bit heartbroken, a bit knocked back, but he never showed it. He never showed anything. I remember us having a lot of laughs that summer.' Reg never knew that (according to interviews he gave in later years) Benny felt suicidal and had to call the doctor to have sleeping-pills prescribed.

Benny did confess his despair to Maureen Riscoe. 'I realized that Benny wasn't getting any sex during the show,' she says. 'He certainly wasn't the kind to go around picking up young holidaymakers. I kept pushing him, saying, "You're queer!" He roared with laughter and then told me the story. He said he was madly in love with this woman in another show and that she had just turned him down. He told me on the quiet. I got the impression it was his first tragedy. He was absolutely stricken.'[12]

Benny did what Benny always did in such situations – buried himself in work.

Richard Stone was becoming particularly active in bringing top London impresarios down to Margate. The only trouble was, he was bringing them down to see Reg Varney. 'I honestly was favouring Reg at the time, not Benny,' says Stone. 'I used to drive down to Margate in my little pre-war Morris 8 with people like Tom Arnold and Alfred Black, and say, "This is my star . . . oh, and I represent the other feller as well." I was not that clever.'[13]

Among the VIPs Stone enticed to Margate was a BBC television producer, Michael Mills. Stone had been trying all summer to get the BBC interested in putting Varney in a regular TV series. As Varney was best seen within a double-act, that meant Mills taking a look at him with Benny Hill. Stone conveyed Mills to Margate to meet the comedians and audition material.

Messrs Reg Varney & Benny Hill
The Lido Theatre, Margate

Dear Reg and Benny
To sum up last night. Michael Mills was most impressed with you both as performers and as potential television serial artistes. He did however feel that most of the material and your very obvious, and indeed correct, stage technique would have to be completely cleared from your mind before embarking on a venture of this sort.

He felt that one of the best ideas was the one which Reg expounded just before we left about 'Exercising the Eyes'. He was not so keen on 'Comedy Band'. I would say therefore that your two acts, 'Tale of a Tail' and 'Exercising the Eyes' with several alternative ideas written into a form of television presentation bearing in mind all that Michael Mills said could form a basis of this trial programme in October. Michael is not prepared to make this a booking until he has seen further evidence of the way your minds are working on this subject and suggests that the sooner Benny can come to town and meet him at lunch time at the Holborn Restaurant, bringing with him your various ideas, the sooner the decision as to whether or not the programme goes on can be made.

I am sending a copy of this letter to Michael.

With best wishes,

Yours sincerely,

Richard Stone

The agent's wish did not prevail, as no series developed. But Benny had fished in his grab-bag of ideas and on a Saturday night in October, the 21st, the one-off 'trial' TV show resulted, *Mud in Your Eye*. It was an intimate revue, blending music and comedy, the latter substantially written by Benny (who was making only his second TV appearance).

During the sixty-five-minute broadcast, Reg mugged his way through 'The Galloping Major' and 'Tea for Two' and Benny did his Toto act yet again. Together they performed 'The Tale of a Tail' (written by Neville Kennard) and a sketch Benny wrote expressly for Varney's phizog antics, 'The Eyes Have It'. Benny and composer-choreographer Johnny Brandon co-wrote a further piece, 'Schmoville Hilly-Billy', in which Reg and Benny sang the old standard 'Feudin' and Fightin'' and Benny wheeled out the old sauce:

Girl Oh Elmer, you're cute.

Boy Gosh, Emmylou, I loves ya! Love ya eyes, love ya lips, love ya neck . . .

Girl What 'bout my *hair*?

Boy I ain't goin' that a way.

'It was a very good show,' says Varney, 'a one-off for TV, never performed on stage, and done live from Alexandra Palace. It was all quick-change, and half the time we were working in our underpants, with the tops on. That was the only way to make the changes. We were told "just look at the top of the camera", but in those days, if the director went in for a close up, the camera would come right up to your face. It was like putting a finger to your nose – Benny went cross-eyed.'

The TV show was well done but viewers of the medium were rare. Varney drew the most praise from the small sample audience canvassed by BBC Viewer Research, but the general consensus was one of disappointment. Benny was still learning his television craft, and the raw edges were showing. There was one moment of innovation, however, and it was the producer's idea. Donald Scott – Benny's friend from the 1949 summer season in Newquay – was a singer on *Mud in Your Eye*, and recalls its unusual climax. 'At the end of the show Michael Mills said that we should throw fake mud – flour and water, probably – at a piece of plate glass positioned in front of the camera lens. It stuck and gradually filled it in, so that the picture went black piece by piece.'

When Reg Varney and Benny Hill were first paired in the summer of 1948, they had continued to work separately outside the double-act. Now they seemed to be becoming a team, Varney and Hill. Like Morecambe and Wise. But in such partnerships the 'feed' has to concede that his cohort will draw most of the laughs and be considered 'the funny one'. Not every comic is able to accept this. As someone who had toiled for almost a decade in the lower echelons of the business, Benny was certainly facing a dilemma. With Varney, he was finally getting noticed, but not in the way he wanted. And without Varney . . . what?

During the Margate summer season, Varney and Hill, partners unequal, had made their radio debut. Benny was by far the more experienced broadcaster of the two. He had been on radio many times, Varney – his humour being mostly visual – scarcely at all. Inspired by 'Gert and Daisy', and a piece Varney had written while in the army, 'Bill and Harry – On Behalf of the Working Class' (the subtitle was pinched off the comedian Billy Russell), Benny wrote a two-hander for their joint July appearance on *Summer Showtime*. Soon after *Mud in Your Eye* came a second radio spot, on the prestigious *Henry Hall's Guest Night*, broadcast live to the nation from the BBC's 'Paris' studio on Regent Street, London.

Bill 'n' 'Arry – the characters were cockneys – sat in a pub, knocking back pints of beer and chatting ignorantly about their lives and the world about them:

Harry (Reg) I see Fred's getting married next week.
Bill (Benny) Who to?
Harry That girl from the Post Office.
Bill Yes, but I thought he was only flirting with her.
Harry So did he.
Bill Isn't that the girl who goes in for his boat racing lark?

Harry Mmm. Just think of it. Eight girls all in the same boat.

Bill Wouldn't mind stroking a crew like that meself.

Harry Mind you, rowing takes it out of you, you know.

Bill I suppose it does.

Harry Well, take 'er. She used to be a robust girl. Now she's all row and no . . . wonder, really. It's strenuous work all right.

Bill 'Ave another one, 'Arry?

Harry Ta. I'll 'ave a bitter.

The piece ended with Harry and Bill, and the BBC Variety Orchestra, singing 'Cockney Ragtime Band'.

Richard Stone was enthused – he saw big prospects for a double-act, 100 per cent on his books. BBC radio producer Bryan Sears did not like what he heard, however. Stone had urged him to listen to the *Henry Hall* broadcast and then book the pair for *Variety Bandbox*. But Sears responded to the agent:

> I did not honestly feel that the act was successful. My impression listening was not of a partnership but of two separate personalities going in opposite directions. I am sorry to disappoint you over this but feel it would be absurd to pretend that I thought it was suitable if I did not sincerely feel so.

It is clear from the scripts that while Benny was stretching himself to write in dialogue form for the first time, the resulting material was, in itself, hardly challenging – just the usual litany of simple, tenuously connected, recycled gags but placed in a two-handed situation. In their next broadcast, back on *Henry Hall's Guest Night* in February 1951, it wasn't much better:

> **Bill (Benny)** 'Ere, you know that Austrian piece who came to live next door? I showed 'er all over the garden yesterday. I showed 'er all me 'ollyocks and chrysanths. Then she says, ''Ave you got an Edelweiss?' I says, 'Yes, but let's 'ave a look at the garden first.'
>
> **Harry (Reg)** Does she speak English?
>
> **Bill** Didn't at first. But I taught her a few words. Taught her to say 'Yes', of course. Certainly. Never taught her to say 'No'.
>
> **Harry** I 'ear George is getting married.

Bill Who to?

Harry Rita, of course.

Bill What, that fat piece?

Harry In the best places they say plump.

Bill But she ain't plump in all the best places. Cor, what a size she is, though. The minute I laid eyes on 'er I says to meself, 'All that meat and no potatoes.'

Benny – one cannot help noticing – was having trouble giving away the 'best' lines like a 'feed' should.

Bill and 'Arry were heading the wrong way, and fast. When they made their fourth radio appearance, on *Music-Hall*, the audience reaction was disastrous – a mere 8 per cent considered their performance 'exceptionally enjoyable'. The family act Ted and Barbara Andrews, with their talented infant daughter Julie, scored 34 . . .

. . . But it was all of no import anyway, for the Varney and Hill double-act was about to break up, and in the most shattering manner.

8. After Sunderland, Anything Goes

'And now meet the man who was born with the theatre in his blood –
and since then has left a lot of blood in the theatre – BENNY HILL!'
(from Anything Goes, *BBC Light Programme, March 27 1952)*

Some 270 miles from London, give or take a yard, Sunderland could be
another country. Away up on the bracing north-east coast, overlooking
the North Sea, life has been tough for its inhabitants. The Industrial
Revolution had a marked impact on the local area, shipbuilding (when
Britain still had such an industry) and coal-mining (until it too was
dismantled) being the principal sources of employment, but the workers,
undertaking labour of national importance, have been treated shabbily and
poor housing has been endemic.

Sunderland people have learned to be resolute and resilient; their broad
north-east accent is often impenetrable to outsiders – which is how they
like it – and they have a long and understandable tradition of despising
'soft southerners'. In 1951, the Sunderland Empire patrons certainly
didn't care very much for one particularly soft southerner, a diffident
Southamptonian named Benny Hill, and they let him know it in their
customary fashion. The effect was devastating.

Even Max Miller, the cockney-like 'Cheeky Chappie' who was king of
standup in these decades, knew enough to venture north no more
frequently than the great northern comedians strayed south – which was
hardly at all. Miller once explained to Arthur Askey why he didn't play
Glasgow by saying, 'I'm a comedian, not a missionary.' He could equally
have been speaking of the Sunderland Empire.

Today's term 'global village' underlines how much has changed in the
past fifty years – the media, in all its manifest forms, permits instantaneous

173

access to places the world over. But half a century ago, before the homogenization brought about by television, there was no such unity – not even among the different counties of England. More revolutionary even than radio, TV became the great leveller, bringing familiarity with disparate dialects and regional points of view. 'Before television,' says Reg Varney, 'if you went up north and they suspected you were a cockney they did *not* want to know.'

Bill Lyon-Shaw, a television producer shortly to enter Benny's story, reflects: 'Before the war I ran my own revues, two of them, one in the north and one in the south, and I learned very early on about the north-south divide. The southern comics would never go well in the north and vice versa. And *every* southerner died at Sunderland.

'A lot of the Sunderland audience worked at the shipyards, and they used to throw washers on to the stage, which could cut you. One Variety performer, a third-rate magician called Chung Lung Foo, dressed as a Chinaman with the hat and the pigtail, did the "lady in a box" disappearing trick at the Sunderland Empire. And he did it all in pidgin English – "*Plitty lady go into box.*" And when it came to the end of the act he said, "*Where plitty lady gone?*" and a man in the audience shouted out "*She's flucked off, you silly clunt!*"'

The Sunderland Empire had such a daunting reputation among southern comedians that when Jimmy Edwards – whose comic persona was that of a bluff, roistering country squire – placed an advertisement in *The Performer* at Christmas 1949, reflecting on his past twelve months, he remarked, with obvious amazement, 'NB: I got laughs at Sunderland!!'

Benny, who was performing there in a touring revue, did not.

Growing tired of being in a double-act as 'feed' to Reg Varney, Benny had balked at the suggestion of the *Sky High* tour management, the brothers George and Alfred Black, that he not perform his own solo spot. This was the highest profile tour of his career to date, so despite his egg-shell confidence he insisted otherwise. It was to be his undoing.

Sky High was a successful London Palladium revue with a good name. So good that it could be traded upon – *Sky High* tours ran for several years at the start of the 1950s but only the title remained constant; the performers, the scenes, changed from promotion to promotion, although there was always the usual mix of comedy, scantily clad girls, dance acts and a novelty piece or two, in this case an operatic duo, and a pair of xylophonists rendering 'Danny Boy'. Richard Stone remembers, 'It was what we called a number-two revue. Reg Varney was a big name for Hedley Claxton but he wasn't yet a big name for George and Alfred Black, who were national promoters. To them, he was just a comic. So this production of *Sky High* didn't play the number-one theatres, the biggest venues, it played the number-twos, slightly smaller.'

The tour opened in February 1951 at the New Cross Empire, in south London. Benny's solo spot was split into two parts: a Peter Waring-style 'shaggy-dog' story (about a man who knocks on another's hotel room door every night and asks for the use of soap and a towel) and a mildly suggestive, slightly effeminate one-man portrayal of the balcony scene from *Romeo and Juliet* which necessitated the kind of ludicrous quick-change performance that would later become a Hill trademark.

In addition to their tennis sketch, Reg Varney had written a new double-act piece for them, 'Out for the Count', set in a boxing ring. Based on a Hedley Claxton idea, it was entirely 'business', giving Reg – as Albert the Avalanche – endless opportunities to mug and indulge in physical antics. 'I used to come on and affect working-out and warming-up for a bout,' he says, 'and Benny knew when I was going to do something different and fell in with everything I did.'[1]

The Stage liked what it saw. Reviewing the opening week at New Cross it declared:

> [Varney's] lady tennis champion and his display of boxing are character-
> izations with every gesture and line constructed to enhance their
> comedy. Benny Hill is closely associated with Mr Varney, proves an
> admirable foil, and is successful, too, in his own particular offering, with
> its burlesques and stories.

That was south London. After New Cross, *Sky High* hit the road, playing Luton and Cambridge. When it got to Peterborough, in the Midlands, the *Northamptonshire Evening Telegraph* reviewer was also enthusiastic:

> Bright is the word that can be applied to the costumes, the setting, and
> the humour, the latter entirely in the hands of Reg Varney and Benny
> Hill. Their turns include two hilarious sporting sequences, 'Out for the
> Count' and 'On the Centre Court', and Reg, as a tennis belle of the

175

twenties, needs little script to get his laughs. Benny Hill's excerpts from 'Romeo and Juliet' imply that there is plenty of unsuspected humour in Shakespeare that has escaped Bowdler.

From here *Sky High* played Easter week in Northampton (where Benny, usually the essence of rude health, temporarily contracted fibrositis) and then finally swung north, settling for a week at the Tivoli theatre in Hull. This is where things started to go badly wrong for Benny boy. The audience at Hull, the North Sea port, certainly didn't care to listen to a southerner's drawn out shaggy-dog story, or his crude Shakespeare lampoon. They became restive and Benny could scent danger. 'Benny's act was always the weak bit,' says Varney. 'The show dipped there, but he got away with it because the rest of the show was good enough. Until we got to Sunderland, that is.'

At the Sunderland Empire, Benny's act – and Benny – came off the rails.

'I'll never forget it,' Varney continues. 'It was a Monday night [April 9 1951] and a packed house. With Benny feeding me, we did "The Art of Flirting" gag right at the beginning because we knew it was a strong start. Then there was a *scena* – a musical story with dancing – and then Benny went on to do his act.

'We used to share a dressing-room because we could bounce off one another while we were getting ready. I was in the dressing-room and could hear clapping. I thought, "Great! Benny's going big tonight," but then I listened more closely and the clapping was all together and in singles. That was the first time in my life I'd ever heard "the slow handclap".

'Benny came off stage, staggered back to the dressing-room and was sick in the sink. I could have cried for him.'

Within a minute the theatre manager burst in, shouting.

'Benny Hill?'

'Yes, sir?'

'You've got a bloody rotten act, haven't you?'

'I'm sorry about that. What shall I do?'

'Get off the show – as quick as you can.'

George and Alfred Black heard about the rumpus right away and despatched a representative to the scene. The manager was still shouting. The Blacks were on the phone, Richard Stone likewise. Career-changing decisions were being taken inside a few hot-headed minutes.

The upshot was that the Blacks were prepared to let Benny stay in *Sky High* but only as 'feed' to Varney – his solo spot would have to be axed.

'If my act comes out I will have to come out, too,' Benny defiantly replied, anxious not to lose the last part of himself to a permanently passive role.

'In that case,' he was told, 'we'll be sorry to lose you.'

Benny didn't leave *Sky High* straight away. Though his confidence was shot, he kindly stayed for the following week, Salford, only as 'feed', in order to train his replacement, Roy Jefferies. Another comic, Peter Dulay, was drafted in to fill his solo spot. And then it was all over – the double-act Varney and Hill was no more. 'He gave me a cigarette case as a token of thanks,' says Varney with a note of sadness still. 'Benny had been "my other half" – we had rapport and could do everything together. I was heartbroken. I couldn't even go and see him off, because I was rehearsing his replacement. I never had a feed as good as Benny again. Show-business is like that: it can be the loveliest job and it can be the world's worst job.'

Benny's career had been in crises before, but this was a humdinger. And he had been rejected before, but never so publicly. Moreover, Richard Stone was furious with his client. As far as the agent was concerned, Varney was on his way to becoming a major success, and Benny's breaking of the double-act would hamper that progress.

Benny recalled in his 1969 *Reveille* interview:

Richard Stone was not pleased. He told me I had been a fool.

'You were on a good, steady wicket, getting £35 a week. Reg Varney is going to be a big star at the Palladium, and there was a future for you in being his straightman. Look at Jerry Desmonde.'

Jerry had been straightman to Sid Field and was by then famous in his own right, always in demand.

'But I don't want to be a straightman, I want to be a comedian,'
I said.

'Well, I can't book you as such and I don't know anyone who can.'

Benny's relationship with Richard Stone could well have ended here.
Reg Varney remembers that Stone was willing to let Benny leave his
agency if he wished – 'He said to Benny, "Now you're out of the show I
don't want to take your few coppers. You go off and sort something out"
and Benny replied, "No, you might as well have it as somebody else" –
and with that one move he eventually made Richard Stone a millionaire.'
All the same, what was Benny going to do now? Had he taken stock – as
indeed he might have done – he would have realized that his prospects of
earning anything greater than small-change were far from rosy. It was four
years since he had come out of the army. After a rocky start he had
wangled his way on to radio but then suffered the ignominy of failing the
audition. After this, his broadcasts had been few and mostly given to
voicing other writers' character parts, or working an uninspired cockney
dialogue routine. He was, in short, no great radio performer.

He had played working-men's clubs and cabaret without ever feeling
comfortable. Summer shows were easier, but these had turned him into
being a mere 'feed', standing by while his fellow comedians stole all the
laughs.

More than anything, Benny had come to loathe 'live' work. If he never
went on stage again it would be too soon. Consistently unable to project
beyond the first few rows of stalls, engulfed by the big stages, his nerves
frazzled, his mouth dry, his heart thudding, his legs shaking, it was an
awful way to earn a living. But who ever heard of a comedian who didn't
work the stage? Benny hadn't.

There was only one step left. He decided to relegate, and possibly
abandon, the Variety stage, and to make further broadcasts only if invited.
And once again, as he had attempted towards the end of his army years,
he would concentrate on becoming a comedy *writer*. He had his pile of
American gag books and war-chest of clipped-out newspaper 'funnies', the
tried and tested jokes, the young acorns and old chestnuts, scribbled on
hundreds of pieces of paper and carted around in old paper bags and
cardboard shoe-boxes – perhaps these could be his career ticket.

As doggedly determined as ever, Benny returned to London, to his bedroom in the simple semi-detached house in Thorverton Road, Cricklewood.

For someone aiming to become a full-time writer there was plenty of inspiration in London this summer of 1951. Though some rationing was still in force, the wartime gloom that had blanketed England since the end of hostilities was finally beginning to lift. The Labour Government launched the great Festival of Britain, which looked cheerfully towards a happier, brighter future. Battersea Pleasure Gardens opened, quickly attracting more than 2 million people, with more than 120,000 piling in on a single day.[2] And on the stage there was Buster Keaton, the great American comedian of the early film era, adored by Benny, who was headlining a national Variety tour.

A product of a later generation of American comedians was also in town, Red Skelton playing a season at the London Palladium. When, thirty years from this point, Benny Hill himself became a huge star in America, many seasoned observers drew comparisons between him and Skelton (who, despite this and later visits, remains largely unknown in Britain). Certainly the similarities between the two are considerable. An article published in *The Stage* during Skelton's Palladium run is also strangely true of Benny's life, and his attitudes as a comic:

> His act includes a wide range of comedy characters ... Says Red Skelton, 'When I am portraying a certain type of person I try always to keep within the bounds of real life, so far as basic characterization is concerned. As long as the essentials of the character are credible it does not matter how far you stray in terms of jokes or actions. In preparing my characters I study people in everyday life and then adapt what I've noticed to my own interpretation of the character.'
>
> For years Red Skelton has written his own material. 'I guess that's because no one knows what suits me better than I do myself.' He is proud of his talents as a writer of verse, as a composer and a painter. He started in showbiz at ten. His father was a clown. Now he combines vaudeville with his film and television work.

The piece ended by noting that Skelton had been struck by the receptiveness of his London Palladium audiences.

One young man was being especially receptive. He had his notebook out and was scribbling as fast as he could.

Benny's habit as a comedy magpie, was also – to his credit – one to which he was happy to admit. Speaking only four years later, on the 1955 BBC Light Programme show *These Radio Times*, he told interviewer Rex Palmer:

> The demand is always greater than the supply. That's something we [comedians] all have to face. Let's say there's nothing really new, only a new angle to it, that's all. There's only a certain number of gags and comic situations to go round. It's up to the comics to make the most of them in their own particular way.
>
> These days you're always hearing artistes talking about 'my' material, or saying that somebody pinched 'my' gags. But, if you go into it, you'll find it's not theirs any more than it's anybody else's. Personally, I say live and let live. I never mind if people do my material . . .

Back in 1951, looking over the past year, Benny acknowledged that his most satisfying venture had been the television revue *Mud in Your Eye*. His scripts had suited the small screen and it was a medium in which he felt his work could shine. One look at the crowds milling around the windows of the Cricklewood shops that sold televisions was enough to convince Benny that TV was the future. He explained in 1966:[3]

> I knew that television was the coming thing, and I thought, 'What they're going to need is material.' I was living up in Cricklewood at the time and it was summer and so for nine weeks I was sitting in the garden in the sunshine, with just my shorts on, and my glass of lemonade, writing television material.

Despite the after-effects of the Sunderland quake, Benny had remained Richard Stone's client, and in late May the agent wrote identical letters to three BBC TV light entertainment producers, Bill Ward, Bill Lyon-Shaw and Walton Anderson:

> Benny Hill, who was so successful in 'Mud in Your Eye' with Reg Varney, is now available. In addition to a number of single acts, which

he has prepared especially for TV, he has also written a number of TV comedy scripts, and should you be interested in meeting him to discuss these, I am sure it would not waste your time.

Lyon-Shaw responded a few weeks later. He contacted Stone and the agent persuaded the producer to see Benny at work. Despite his loathing of the stage, Benny was having to play the occasional concert to keep the money coming in. 'I went to see him somewhere out in the sticks and he was bloody dreadful,' recalls Lyon-Shaw, fully five decades later. 'He wasn't a good standup comic at all. He was just telling jokes, really, and I think he finished with a funny song. Very, very, second-rate theatre-type material. I felt he had tremendous personality, though, and when I talked to him afterwards he was terribly keen – to do anything, really.'

Shaw felt strongly that television needed to discover its own talent, and he was actively searching for comic-actors – rather than stage comedians – to turn into TV comics. 'We used to do fifteen-minute programmes from Alexandra Palace and we tried everybody,' he says. 'Standup comics just didn't work, they didn't come "through the screen". The only one who did was "Mr Pastry", Richard Hearne. He was a comic-actor, a young man playing an old man, and he created comedy situations. I felt that we needed more of that.'

Benny packed a sheaf of papers into a carrier-bag and walked from Cricklewood down to Lime Grove, to the BBC's new studios in Shepherd's Bush, west London. Here in itself was a sign of the changing times: Lime Grove had been a film studio, now television was beginning to boom and the cinema was finding life difficult.

Benny had told Lyon-Shaw that he had some original material to present, and here it was, an unsteady mountain of scrappy paper. The producer had long sensed that TV required not only a new generation of comedians but also dedicated material, and, though his sense of presentation was somewhat lacking, Benny Hill seemed to be just the ticket.

What happened next became one of the most told tales of Benny Hill's career. Lyon-Shaw sent the comic along the corridor to see the Head of Light Entertainment, Ronald Waldman. Benny seemed (or feigned) not to recognize the executive, nor did Waldman recognize him – which is just as well on both counts. Back in 1947, before he moved to TV, Waldman had been one of the senior radio producers who had failed Benny Hill at his audition, the one who said, 'The only trouble with him was that he didn't make me laugh *at all*. It's a mixture of lack of comedy personality and lack of comedy material.'

Benny plonked a swaying pile of papers in front of Waldman and said, 'Pick any of those forty sketches, any one you like, and read it. I've not put them in any particular order. Tell me if you think I've got any promise as a scriptwriter.' Waldman pulled out a sheet from the pile and doubtless blanched – as others had done and would continue to do over the decades – over the scrawly, almost indecipherable handwriting. 'You read it,' he responded, 'work it for me.'

Benny worked one of the scripts, then another, and Waldman was soon wiping away tears of laughter. If he had cried back in 1947 the tears would have been those of pain.

The punchline to this episode has been contradicted over the years. According to most sources, including Benny, Waldman remarked, 'Who would suit this material best?' to which the writer replied, 'Terry-Thomas? Arthur Askey?' 'No,' said the TV executive, 'I think it would suit you – would you like your own show?'

The alternate version, also given by Benny, has him as an eager beaver, answering 'Me' to Waldman's first question.

Either way, on such a flimsy scenario, Benny Hill – only twice before on TV – was given his own show at the age of twenty-seven. It was called *Hi There!* and went out on the BBC for forty-five minutes on Monday August 20 1951.

'Up to this point television had been restricted to a tiny studio at Alexandra Palace,' says Bill Lyon-Shaw. 'Now we were going into a big studio for the first time, Studio G at Lime Grove, with lots of scope, and Benny came crashing through the screen. He was funny, he was young, he was new, he wasn't known, he wasn't a stage name that we were putting on. Out of the blue, there he was. Ronnie had said, "Give him a show," and we did, and it was a great success.'

As this was before the era of tele-recording and video, *Hi There!* disappeared into the ether on transmission, never to be seen again. But the script still exists:

(opening caption: *Hi There!*)

Benny Hill Hi there!

(Muriel Cooke seated on couch. Camera left.)

Muriel Why, hello Benny. Come and sit down.

(He enters and sits next to Muriel.)

Benny Oh, I've brought you some flowers. (Gives them to her.)

(Muriel places flowers in vase.)

Benny Muriel – I – I – I – [He turns] Muriel darling, I want to ask
you something. I have been meaning to ask you for some time, but
this is the first time we have been alone together. Oh Muriel, can I
– I mean may I – may I . . . watch your television set?

(switches on TV set)

The rest of the programme was much like any other edition of *The
Benny Hill Show* made over the next forty years – old radio, stage and
simple gag book jokes delivered with a unique twist, plus Benny giving
exaggerated 'looks' to the camera, Benny as a succession of restaurant
waiters, Benny doing foreign dialects, including French and German. Even
his acrobatic friend Johnny Hutch was featured.

One sketch was the tried and trusted 'Ribbing the Hips', Benny's
supposed Variety satire which was really just some limp jokes strapped
together. But it did include this tellingly autobiographical piece:

And finally here is an English Variety comic. The 'second spot' comic.
For this they use what is known as a 'bash bash' comic. He is usually a
cockney with a loud check suit, a white felt hat with the brim turned
up in front, and a red tie. Now this red tie is very important because
whenever he is stuck for a line or whenever a pet gag falls with a
sickening thud, he looks down at this red tie and says 'Cor-bli, I
thought my tongue was hanging out!'

The best sketch was the opener, 'The Torch', set in 'an ultra smart
cycle shop'. It was one of Benny's newest pieces (the script was marked
'The property of <u>BENNY HILL</u>') and the former 'feed', having become
the star, now had his own straightman, the broadcaster David Jacobs.
Benny was the salesman, selling Jacobs, the customer, a pocket-sized torch
brand-named Sparko. The punchline was that after Jacobs had bought the

Sparko and was walking off, Hill called him back – 'Just a moment, sir, you forgot the battery' and produced a car battery, placing it with a thump on the counter.

As Benny's first TV straightman, Jacobs was, by his own admission, a flop. 'What a failure I was,' he smiles. 'I couldn't help laughing. It's very difficult if someone makes you giggle. Henry McGee [Benny's straightman from 1968 to 1991] is an actor, so come what may he can keep a straight face. I couldn't do it.'

As with his first *Show World* article, Benny also couldn't resist plugging himself. In the middle of the show the scene reverted to him and Muriel Cooke watching this very show on TV:

Benny Well, it hasn't been too bad up to now, has it?
Muriel It's been rather good.
Benny I like that young fellow who played all those waiters. He is very
  good. You know, they should give him a series.

Bill Lyon-Shaw was inclined to agree. During rehearsals at the Jewish Lads Club in Hanway Place, just behind Oxford Street – a good portent for Benny – he found the comic keen and resourceful. 'The great thing about him was that he was one of the few people who wrote his own material. He would come up and say, "I see a situation where I can do so-and-so" and it usually worked. He was creating situations for himself, which was bloody useful because writers were very thin on the ground.'

The producer also noted Benny's interest in the TV *medium*. 'He wasn't the first to think of comedy in televisual form but he was one of two, Eric Sykes being the other. But Benny was the first to be interested in the *techniques* of television, asking the cameramen, "How can I get so-and-so effect?" He was always seeking information from the technicians, vision and sound. He wanted to learn.'

Lyon-Shaw ran into difficulties after the broadcast. Cecil McGivern, the BBC's Controller of Television Programmes, and a stickler for decency, called him in over one of Benny's lines:

1st man What's French for 'the other'?
2nd man L'amour.

184

'I thought it was very funny,' says Lyon-Shaw, 'but McGivern said it was a double-entendre and "We don't want any more of that." I was told to *watch it* and he sent a memo to Ronald Waldman saying, "Would you please vet all of Benny Hill's scripts in the future." But of course as times became more permissive Benny was allowed to say such things. In the very end, of course, when he was at Thames, he went right over the top.'

McGivern may not have enjoyed the humour but his assistant did. Unaware as yet of his boss's misgivings, Cecil Madden, Assistant to Controller, Television, wrote him a note:

I thought the comedian Benny Hill last night was good, and worth encouraging.

And there was an excellent review in the *News Chronicle*:

Mark down Benny Hill among the future TV favourites. Age 26, fair-haired and more than a mere idea of what makes visual fun.[4]

The BBC's Viewer Research Report, while not ecstatic, was also encouraging. 'Benny Hill was considered an entertaining new TV person-ality,' it stated. Less positively, it noted that some viewers 'complained that the material was weak and laboured' but then it found a brighter vein once more – 'most viewers welcomed this show as a move towards "brighter week-night entertainment" . . . it was felt that, given time, this could develop into a really popular programme . . .'

Despite his high hopes, Benny did not get his own TV series at this time, though a couple of further opportunities quickly presented themselves – two weeks after *Hi There!* Lyon-Shaw had him compère *Starlight Symphony*, an outside broadcast from the 1951 Radio Show at Earls Court. Then, along with the great comic 'drunk' Jimmy James, Benny was a guest comedian on a Joe Loss Band show, *In the Mood*, in December.

By this point, Benny had moved home again, leaving Cricklewood and heading a mile or so down the Edgware Road to Kilburn, to 40 Mapesbury Road. Here he took a large furnished room in a guest-house belonging to a northerner, Constance 'Connie' Rhodes – another surrogate mother for the boy who left home at sixteen. Among several others living in the substantial, detached house, which was grandly named The Studios for a while, were Connie's son Billy and his wife, Chika Lane. He was dashing with a twiddly moustache, she was his glamorously blonde partner in a comedy-adagio Variety act (bill matter: 'It's All Right For You!'), which they toured with their pet duck, Doolie. The web-footed creature would waddle unscathed from the wreckage of a capsized piano at Empires and Hippodromes countrywide, twice-nightly but never on Sundays.

Television executives were not the only converts to the Benny Hill cause. Earlier in 1951 a Bristol-based radio producer, Duncan Wood, had booked Benny for a couple of editions of *Western Music-Hall* and followed up by putting him into *Variety Ahoy!* (recorded before an audience of Royal Navy sailors) and a couple of *Workers' Playtime* broadcasts from the Channel Islands. Wood and Hill had struck up a good understanding, so when, in October 1951, the producer was planning a new comedy series, which it was hoped might rival the great Frank Muir and Denis Norden show *Take It from Here*, he persuaded Benny to be the principal comedian.

Anything Goes ('half-an-hour in which anything can happen – and probably will!') was similar in structure to its illustrious BBC team-mate. *Take It from Here* starred Jimmy Edwards; Benny Hill was the main man here, and singer Cherry Lind took the Joy Nichols role, joining in with certain comedy sketches. The Muir and Norden show also had a stalwart 'feed', the Australian actor Dick Bentley, and *Anything Goes* had a chap especially good at 'voices', Johnny Morris. This young unknown from the West Country was destined to become a great broadcaster in his own right, particularly as the presenter of the children's BBC TV show *Animal Magic*. His work there and in other series earned him an OBE; Benny, though he became The World's Most Popular Comedian, was never so honoured.

Anything Goes had one key additional element – it was recorded at service camps in the south-west. The first run, eleven shows broadcast only by the BBC's West of England Home Service, were taped at Army, RAF and Navy bases, the fourth before an audience of REME conscripts at Blandford, Dorset. Benny, sad to say, made virtually no capital of this link with his past – not so much unwilling, it would seem, as unable to get behind the jokes and reveal something of himself. After the quickest of passing references he was soon slipping into his usual related/unrelated gags routine:

(play-on music, Sousa's 'Stars and Stripes')
My, it's cold tonight, isn't it? I've just been talking to a brass monkey. Asked me if I was a spot welder!

But it's nice to be back with the REME. Yes, I was in the REME. I spent five years with the Royal Electrical and Mechanical Engineers . . . I was a cook!

Oh, I was very popular with the men. I remember one Christmas Eve two soldiers came into the cookhouse. They said, 'Are you the cook?' I said, 'Yes.' They said, 'Well, we want you to know that you're number one on our hit parade.' Then they hit me! But I had lunch today in the canteen, and I was glad to see that the soldiers are still getting the same fine food I was cooking five years ago. Mind you, it was fresher then!

Anything Goes failed to get anywhere near the same league as the consistently excellent *Take It from Here* and lasted only six months. The writers, never before paired, were a *Bristol Evening Post* sports journalist, Bill Ottewill, and a Weston-super-Mare civil servant, Bill Clout. Benny wrote his own solo pieces and each week ventured down to Bristol to add and delete lines from the two Bills' main ensemble sketch, usually a pastiche of a famous book or film.

Bill Clout remembers, 'He'd come from London by train to Bill Ottewill's flat in Pembroke Road, Bristol, arriving in a taxi. There were no niceties – he was straight into the work. "Let's get down to it!" he'd say. Bill and I had already written the closing sketch and he'd come in and critique it. Whenever he was thinking or writing he'd take out a brown-paper bag full of walnuts and start cracking them. It seemed to help him concentrate.'

Despite having become 'a television star' there was little new from Benny in these scripts – out they all came, jokes from *Variety Bandbox* in 1947 and *Works Wonders* in 1948, veterans of a hundred working-men's clubs and scores of Sunday concerts. 'I remember him saying "I'd rather have a good old tried joke than a brand new untried joke,"' recalls Bill Clout. 'He used to change old jokes into different formats to get fresh laughs from them, and he had also found the formula that any joke sung is twice funnier than when it is spoken. If you analyse his songs they're all just jokes put to music. Having said this, he was always looking for new material. The influence of the American Forces Network on young British comedians has never been explored, but it was strong, and Benny also read all the joke books, especially the American ones. I think they came out monthly and Benny always used to get them. They were the bible for some comedians.

'Benny was quite fascinated with humour and would often know the source of a joke. I used to say "If I've heard a joke twice it's not original, it must be someone else's," but he knew that whoever had the material had probably lifted it from someone else anyway.'

Clout observed, too, Benny's retiring nature. 'On the radio he came over very friendly, a likeable young lad, a bit cheeky, but a chap you could relate to. In person, when we worked with him, he looked and behaved like an Ordinary Chap. There was no side to him and he wasn't egotistical. He just liked humour. But you never really got to know Benny. He'd arrive, rewrite, perform, and off he'd go. To me, though, he was a genius. I loved the way he worked.'

After the initial programmes *Anything Goes* was considered good enough for a national audience, and in February 1952 it transferred to the BBC Light Programme, losing *en route* its services skew – the shows were now recorded in the BBC's Bristol studios. Wherever its home, though, Benny never managed the great radio breakthrough he had long desired. Six editions across both series were subjected to BBC audience research reports and yet on only one occasion did Benny – billed as the star attraction throughout – come out on top as the listeners' favourite performer among the ensemble. One report also noted that many 'complained of old or crude jokes'. Unlike the walnuts, radio was proving very hard to crack.

When *Anything Goes* was recorded at service bases, after-show drinkies and a spot of dinner would be laid on for the cast and crew in the officers' mess. The officers would make a bee-line for Cherry Lind, the show's attractive young singer. Benny, too, was more than a little interested in his supporting player, and wrote a comedy piece staking his claim as a confident man about town. Typically, before anyone else could do so, he also made sure to prick the balloon.

Benny Ah, but I love women. They're so feminine, aren't they? And
I'm so popular with the ladies, too. Why, only tonight when I
arrived here there were dozens of them waiting outside the studio.
I went up to one of them and said, 'And what are you girls waiting
for?' (As if I didn't know!) So she said, 'Well, we heard there was a
tall, good-looking young man coming here tonight and – well – we
thought we'd wait and meet him . . . like to wait with us?' Ah, what
it is to be a ladies' man . . .

Cherry You? A ladies' man? Oh Benny, don't make me laugh!

Cherry already had a boyfriend, so Benny also kept his eyes elsewhere.
'Wyndham, later to become my husband, sometimes came to the *Anything
Goes* recordings,' she recalls. 'One time, as we were eating in the officers'
mess, he said to Benny, "I've just heard a thing about you from the
commanding officer. He says that you're making too much fuss of the
Wrens,[5] and that you've really got to stop it." And Benny said, "My God,
really?" "Yes, you've got to stop all the flirting, all this 'Hello, darling'
stuff." But then Wyndham let slip that he was pulling his leg. Benny
believed the complaint was true because this is what he *had* been doing.

'But Benny was a very lovely man and a lovely performer, and it came
over, I think. He was never gay, not in a month of Sundays, he was too
fond of ladies for that. He liked *femininity*. And whatever Benny did you
could never dislike him. Even in his later television shows, with all the
girls, he never became nasty – he always did his comedy with a twinkle.
You felt that he was very naïve about everything, and so you never took
offence. Watching the TV shows, you knew perfectly well that if he
caught a girl he'd only make them a cup of tea. This is how he was off-
stage, off-screen, too.'

When Benny had been involved in *Montmartre* he and the soubrette
Joy St Edmund had branched out as a twosome for some separate
performances; when these had backfired, they had sought solace in one
another's company and a relationship had formed. There were definite
echoes again now as Benny and Cherry (with a couple of other players
from the show, Harry 'Carruthers' Carter and pianist Freddie Carlé)
decided to hit the road with an *Anything Goes* Variety tour. It was
common practice for successful BBC radio shows to go on stage – there

was a *Take It from Here* revue, and even *The Goon Show* and, later, the soap-opera *The Archers* found their way on to the touring Variety circuit. *Anything Goes* was unusual in one key respect, though – the main artistes, Benny and Cherry, were also the impresarios. Ever the keen observer, Benny had watched and learned from everyone in the game, Harry Benet onwards, about the business of promotion. If the television lark was suddenly to fall flat again, he felt it would be useful not only to write material but also to know about management. *Anything Goes* was his learning curve.

Sadly, it was one that drooped.

The opening week was at the Ritz Theatre, Weymouth, in March 1952. Cherry Lind remembers, 'Richard Stone, who represented us both, suggested we pay off all the acts and have a 60/40 agreement with the management. We thought it was a good idea, but lost a lot of money that first week. The following week we were going to Plymouth, my birthplace. I promised Benny it would be packed, but it wasn't at all. I then hoped it would be full on Friday and Saturday because the Navy would be in town, but they were sent out on manoeuvres and so it was empty again, twice-nightly. It was costing us a fortune. We had one more disastrous week somewhere else and decided to pack it in.'

Once again, the pair sought mutual solace. 'Benny didn't drink at all in those days, and I scarcely did, but we went back to this small hotel and were very despondent. So I sent Benny around to an off-licence and he came back with a bottle of scotch. I asked him, "How much is this tour going to cost us?" and he said "Thousands! But we have *just* that much money." Anyway, we demolished most of this bottle of scotch and nothing seemed to matter for the rest of the evening.'

Benny was falling in love, and intimated that if it wasn't for Wyndham he'd make a move. Certainly, some degree of affection was mutual. 'We were very fond of each other,' Cherry says. 'We had a deep, underlying bond. We never had an affair or anything like that. You didn't in those days and we were very young. But we had a good rapport and were very, very close. Benny really needed someone to look after him, and I loved him – but as a brother.'

So there it is once more. Mothers loved Benny and treated him like a son, but the women Benny pursued looked upon him as a friend or brother.

Benny, in the meantime, fell, and fell hard, for Cherry. In later decades he admitted to having been hopeful of marriage. His affection comes through in a letter he wrote to her a year later, at the end of February 1953.

My dear Cherry

I was going to say 'Where the hell is the Rex, Wilmslow?' But I've just this minute been booked for the Playhouse, Tonbridge, next week. So we're both on the number ones now. I was at Harrow last week with Vic Oliver. Tomorrow I'm doing the Savoy job for Bill Randall. Wish you were there too! On second thoughts, you'd bring Wyndham along too, so no matter.

The series in the west finished last week. I enjoyed doing it. Nice friendly little show. I start a series in the north quite soon. It's a straight show. Just call me Gielgud Hill! It'll take me up north once a week so I'll watch 'The Stage' to see where you're playing and if poss I'll slip over to see you! – excuse me, I'm dribbling.

I have a few Variety dates in the book – May 4 Birmingham, May 11 Boscombe, May 18 Bristol. Playing anywhere near?

After a broadcast at Bristol, Dunc and I went to a speedway ball. We meet a Goon-girl there. She said, ''Ere, you're Benny Lee, aren't you?' So just for fun I said yes. She said, 'Aaah, I seen you in that Anything Goes lot. Proper fool you are. 'Ere, that your sister what sung? 'Er with that skirt too tight for her?' I said, 'No, why' and she said, 'I thought 't was, 'er being Jenny Lee like.' Bumped into Harry Carter. Will you ever forget him at Weymouth trying to be a broad-shouldered spiv? I can still laugh at it now. The happiest week I've had in the biz.

Well my dear I do hope we'll be playing near each other soon.

Till I see or hear from you soon, my love to you,

Benny

(By way of explanation: Benny's reference 'we're both on the number ones now' was an ironic one: such venues were well down the scale in Variety terms. Bill Randall was a pianist. 'The series in the west' was *Debut*, introducing new Variety artists from the West Country, broadcast over eight weeks in January/February 1953 in the BBC's West of England Home Service – Benny was the compère. The 'series in the north' and joke about 'Gielgud Hill' refer to the radio adventure serial *Danger is Our Business* detailed in Chapter 9. 'Dunc' was radio producer Duncan Wood. Benny Lee was a singer, comedian and contemporary of Benny Hill – they were often mistaken for one another and worked in the same radio shows on occasion. Finally, it is interesting that, although Cherry Lind remembers Benny losing 'a lot of money' on the Weymouth promotion, he still felt the week was 'the happiest'. Here was a man who cared more for 'love' than money.)

The year 1952 passed by quietly for Benny Hill. Despite the giddy achievements of 1951 he made only one further television appearance, in February in the magazine show *Kaleidoscope*. But he was clearer in his sense of direction – in October 1951 the double-act Varney and Hill, though defunct for six months, had the chance of a TV series with the famed *Gang Show* producer Ralph Reader. Richard Stone assured the BBC that he would encourage Benny to get back with Reg. Politely, but firmly, Benny said no. He would make it on his own, or not at all.

Strangely, considering his bad experiences on northern stages, Benny Hill was making frequent appearances on the acclaimed radio comedy *Variety Fanfare*, a show with a pronounced northern bias, recorded at Hulme Hippodrome just outside Manchester. *Variety Fanfare* had good exposure, with an evening broadcast in the Light Programme, a lunchtime repeat on the Home Service, further airings on the General Overseas Service and distribution by the BBC's 'Transcription Service', which pressed certain shows on to disc and shipped them to radio stations around the world, from Australia to Zanzibar. Goodness knows what the overseas audiences made of it all.

The eighth appearance that Benny made on the show, broadcast on November 14 1952, still exists in BBC archive.[6] Listening to it today, the first curiosity is that after the opening thirty seconds, when he set the scene for what would follow, and in which he stuttered, Benny Hill's 'own' voice was never heard, just a succession of character pieces. Gone –

lost to the vagaries of a shattered confidence – were the shaggy-dog stories or anything that might in any way be self-revealing.

Using a device he would employ countless times in his TV programmes over the next forty years, the entire act, nine minutes, was bundled together as a pastiche of another show, in this instance (being radio) the Home Service's *Programme Parade*, in which excerpts from the coming day's most interesting broadcasts were featured. Thus Benny lampooned Wilfred Pickles' 'people show' *Can I Come In?*, a foreign man talking about driving on British roads, *Children's Hour* (reading a slightly sugges-tive story) and *Melody Time*, in which he sang a parody of 'Girl in the Wood'. Effecting Wilfred Pickles' chummy Yorkshire tones, and also the hesitant cheekiness of a young laundry-woman, one extract went:

'Pickles' Luv, I understand that you do the washing for the waxworks
museum. I go there meself quite a lot, and I've often wondered –
those famous statues of actresses and duchesses and suchlike.
They're all wearing beautiful dresses. Tell me, luv, do they wear
anything else underneath?
Girl Well, now you're asking aren't you! Don't know as I should say,
really. Well actually, they don't. But there's only me and a few
American soldiers know about that!

This line brought the house down. (A northern house at that.)

Not in Benny's pre-submitted script, but slotted into his act at short notice was a radio 'announcement':

There's a police message just come in. 'A football pools coupon, I repeat
a football pools coupon, was lost last night in Chelsea. Will the finder
please communicate at once with New Scotland Yard, phone number
WHItehall Home-Away-Home-Away.'

Police appeals were an everyday aspect of broadcasting in this period, and everyone in Britain knew the phone number of New Scotland Yard in London, WHItehall 1212. The joke here is that on a football pools coupon a home win has a value of 1 (point), an away win has a value of 2.

In terms of theatre work, Benny contrived to do only a little in this period. At Christmas 1951 he performed in a stage pantomime for the last time, at Eastbourne, playing Idle Jack in *Dick Whittington*. And in the late spring of 1952, with no TV bookings on the horizon, he reluctantly went back into Variety, joining the cast of a revue, *Folies Bergère*, touring provincial theatres under the promotion of Bernard Delfont . . . and the watchful eye of the Lord Chamberlain. Originating in Paris, the Folies was famous for its nudes. Some of the women were indeed semi-nude but they remained immobile, and, as *The Stage* noted, 'in their proper place, as an eye-catching incidental, not as a main feature'.

While on the Folies tour, Benny wrote a letter to the star comedian of his 1949 summer season at Newquay, Ron Clark, who was seeking permission to use the football sketch Benny had written for them. 'Yes, sport, of course you may use "Football" this summer. There's no charge,' Benny replied, 'just offer up a prayer for me next time I play Sunderland.'

That moment almost arrived a month later, but the week before *Folies Bergère* was due at Sunderland Empire, Benny – to what must have been his huge relief – had to leave the company to rehearse for a summer season at Ramsgate, playing from June to September in a Tom Arnold presentation, *The Big Show*. The prestige of *Hi There!* slipping away, Benny didn't even top the bill, playing second, if not third, fiddle to double-acts Penny Nicholls and Billy Merrin, and Billy Low and Arthur Webster. 'Benny hated that summer show,' says Richard Stone, '*hated* it. He hated the director, and one of the double-acts bullied him a bit. They treated him badly and he was unhappy.'

He was probably not pleased, either, with a review in *The Stage*, which declared:

> Leading the humour is another favourite, Billy [*sic*] Hill, whose broken English is a sure laughter-raiser. One of his most amusing acts is a burlesque of the 'Romeo and Juliet' balcony scene, in which he plays both parts.

Though he was given star billing in two radio programmes in October, and could take pride in their title, *A Date with Benny*, the shows were broadcast only in the BBC's North of England Home Service and in Northern Ireland. Both were beamed live from the Palais-de-Danse in

Ashton-under-Lyme, giving rise to one of the most improbable opening announcements in radio history:

Good evening everybody and welcome to Ashton Palais-de-Danse. And here's that man you've all got a date with, Benny Hill!

And yet even in his own radio show, listeners' opinions canvassed by the BBC placed Benny stone last in the list of acts who had provided 'exceptional enjoyment'.

9. And the Bright New Hope of Lime Grove . . . Wins!

Although unaware at the time of its personal significance, one of the key dates in Benny Hill's life was February 6 1952. Early that morning it was announced that King George VI had passed away – and as the nation launched into a protracted period of mourning it also opened its hearts to a new monarch, a fresh dawn after the misery of the war years. The BBC quickly foresaw the coronation of Queen Elizabeth II, set for May 1953, as the perfect platform on which to mount a major advance in television viewing. Benny Hill would be a prime beneficiary of this expansion.

High-ranking opposition to the BBC's plans to screen the coronation in its entirety, with cameras inside as well as outside Westminster Abbey, was quelled by no less a person than the twenty-six-year-old Princess herself, a decision later saluted for its wisdom. As the BBC had anticipated, the opportunity for British citizens to witness a coronation in their own living room, coupled with the accelerated opening of new transmitters and a loosening of post-war strictures on the supply of necessary parts, led to a surge in sales of television sets. In 1947, the number of joint 'sound and television' licences was fewer than 15,000. With the coronation looming, that figure soared to almost 3,250,000. By 1960, it had exceeded 10 million. These were new viewers to a new medium, a hugely impressionable audience unlike any since, less critical and more welcoming of the new faces popping up in flickering monochrome at the merest turn of a knob. 'Personalities' who made waves in these early years of television, from panel-game participants to genial gardeners, were its first 'celebrities'. And there, in the perfect place at the perfect time, was Benny Hill – soon to be a huge star and hailed as the first comedian 'made' by television.

There was more to it than this, and Benny's rise to fame was erratic rather than dramatic. He had been on television in 1949, 1950, three times in 1951, including his own show, but just once again in 1952, six appearances in all. Late in 1952, however, at an informal audition, he succeeded in making an impression on a BBC TV producer by the name of Kenneth Carter, and from here Benny never looked back.

One of Carter's duties, with a mere £350 budget, was to produce a monthly entertainments programme, *The Centre Show*. It was so named because it was broadcast, live, from the Nuffield Centre, a London club for 'the Forces of the Crown' established under the auspices of a charitable institution, the Nuffield Trust.

Located in Adelaide Street, behind St-Martin-in-the-Fields, just a few strides from de Wolfe & Stone's office, the Nuffield was the only place in central London where, for no admission fee, servicemen and servicewomen could obtain meals at reasonable prices, occupy themselves in the games-room, read and write in the lounge, take a shower, get a shoeshine, visit the barber or tailor, dance to a live band and enjoy twice-weekly Variety shows.

Benny knew the Nuffield well. He had entertained the troops here frequently for some three years from 1948, rubbing shoulders with the likes of Bob Monkhouse, Peter Sellers, Spike Milligan, Harry Secombe, Barry Took, Tony Hancock, Frankie Howerd, Richard Attenborough, Janet Brown, Terry Scott, Bill Maynard and even his old pal Harry Segal. None of the artists appearing at the Nuffield was paid, but there was a free meal, the chance to try out new material on an ever-enthusiastic audience, and the possibility of impressing an impresario.

The Nuffield also had a strong link with television. Mary Cook, its entertainments organizer, was part-time head of the BBC's Television Auditions Unit. (It was she who had considered Benny Hill a suitable TV performer as early as 1948.) Since 1950, the BBC's auditions had been held solely at the Nuffield, even though Cook herself did not possess, and never would possess, a television set. 'Ready when you are, darlings!' she would command to the auditioning artiste, upon which she would strap on a pair of opera glasses to gauge how they might appear on the small screen. Many future stars were given the thumbs-up here, including one of TV's earliest and most unlikely celebrities, the Australian-born zither-playing Shirley Abicair. None could see what Cook was noting down – to maintain privacy she wrote her audition reports in Portuguese. One strongman act took exception to the Nuffield treatment. When, menac-ingly, he demanded payment for his audition, the unflappable Mary Cook coolly handed him a penny. The strongman put the coin between his teeth and bent it at right angles.

From 1950, successful audition artistes were given a chance to make their television debut in *The Centre Show*. But although the performers were newcomers, the show always had an experienced compère – Frank Thornton, Jack Warner, Bob Monkhouse and others. In January 1953, Kenneth Carter asked Benny Hill to compère the next edition. Such was his impact, the job would become his exclusively.

Benny's idea of packaging together his jokes and impressions in the form of a media pastiche (in the manner of his *Variety Fanfare* act, cited in Chapter 8) was about to pay rich dividends. Instead of simply performing his oft-broadcast, Danny Kaye-like 'Chef' song dressed in an apron and tall white hat, he hit upon the idea – classically simple – of performing it in the guise of the first television chef, Philip Harben, adding to the costume a light beard and squinting his eyes, *à la* Harben, to effect a visual imitation. The piece now had a double edge – it was, he hoped, 'funny' (and this skit was) and it was also a lampoon, an impression recognizable most especially to viewers of the very medium in which it was being performed. It was the old 'Ribbing the Hips' ploy all over again – the piece was the same as before yet with the merest dressing it became 'clever'. (And there was a bonus this time, too, in that the real Harben was on screen immediately after this *Centre Show* finished, which improved the joke further.)

> For I'm Fritz the chef, from the Hotel Targinev,
> And I'm as contented as can be.
> But if I had my wish I would only serve one dish,
> It's the only meal that would appeal to me.
>
> It's Obermir Litzen, und noodle von Spitzen,
> Und souveront so Aotzen,
> Mit vermi so chilli, ein stück Piccalilli,
> Und cuffer so hofle, and lustige kartofeln,
> Or in English . . . sausage and mash.

With its blend of nonsense and genuine German, beyond the ken of most British viewers, this was complex stuff. The construction, too, seems illogical, but Bob Monkhouse witnessed Benny performing such material time and again. 'He didn't write good scansion,' Monkhouse comments, 'and if you read it on the page, it looks terrible. But he knew how to make it rhyme. Though he'd have too many syllables in one line, it didn't seem that way when he did it.'

Kenneth Carter, the BBC director, was instrumental in Benny's success in these early days. 'I can't tell you how much I'm indebted to Ken,' wrote Benny in a magazine article.[1] 'We found, almost at first meeting, that we get along well together – and [with] every show we get an example of how we seem to think alike.'

Seven years older than Benny, the London-born Carter had been schooled in the theatre and brought a considerable knowledge of stagecraft to his BBC productions. Richard Stone had recognized Carter's abilities early and signed him to the agency. 'Ken nursed Benny a lot,' says Stone. 'He was a lovely director, a lovely man and marvellous with Benny. They were very close. I think he understood Benny's comedy very much, and he encouraged him and was very creative. Unequivocally, Kenneth Carter was responsible for Benny developing on TV.'

The son, grandson and brother of theatre people, Carter had started in the business as a chorus-boy at the age of fifteen, before working (like Benny) as Assistant Stage Manager, and then graduating into production. When Benny Hill was first in Cliftonville with Reg Varney, Carter was at the nearby Margate Winter Gardens with *Bubbles of 1948*, and they ran into each other again in the same resort in 1950.

Carter brought several qualities to Benny's TV shows, chiefly patience, understanding and sympathy for what the artist was attempting to create, and there seems little doubt that Benny saw Carter as his ticket to stardom and veritably attached himself. Bob Monkhouse observes, 'Ken Carter had class, a beautiful speaking voice, very cultured. It was the first of several times I saw Benny cleave on to somebody whom he could look up to and respect.' Bill Lyon-Shaw, although no longer working directly with Benny, was also aware of what was happening – 'Benny always knew where his TV career was going,' he states. 'From Day One he could see Day Ten ahead of him. And in Kenneth Carter he found a receptive producer, one who would allow him to rule the roost. Benny decided what they were going to do and how they were going to do it, and all Ken had to do was make sure they did it.'

Carter, then, became the first of several TV directors to receive calls at the most unexpected of hours. Eve Lucas, who worked as a PA in BBC TV Light Entertainment, remembers, 'Sometimes poor old Ken would arrive in Lime Grove in the morning and say, "My God, I had Benny on the phone in the middle of the night *for three hours*! He had some idea and wanted to tell me exactly how he thought he would do it." And Ken would just listen to him – I think he might have been afraid to argue.'

'Ken was very meticulous and terribly calm,' says David Croft, another Stone client, later to work with Benny – and not enjoy the experience – and also co-write and produce *Dad's Army*. 'He wasn't dynamic or flamboyant but he made things happen and was very supportive of Benny. He was also homosexual, which was illegal then but totally accepted in show-business. There was no trouble at all if people kept quiet about it.'

Benny compèred *The Centre Show* again in June, August and September and along the way picked up his second TV straightman, Kim Peacock – best known as the voice of the private detective Paul Temple in BBC radio dramatizations of Francis Durbridge's thriller stories. Benny also began to put together a roster of new comedy characters, starting with Miss Primrose Hill, named after the leafy district of north-west London where Richard Stone had just bought a luxury house.

This was the first time – the first of many – that Benny went in front of the TV cameras in drag. For Primrose, he went for the full Diana Dors effect, pitching his voice high and donning a pudding-basin wig and what he called a 'Thungy' dress, a piece of curtain material he would pin at the back of his neck and which would then drop straight down without shape. In her first appearance she was working as a cook at the Nuffield Centre.

Kim Tell me, Miss Hill, do you like the work here?
Primrose Well, it's quite nice, you know, what with the cooking and the soldiers and the games room and everything – and everything. Course, the trouble is we've only got the one gas-ring. They did say something about gettin' me a griller, but I don't want one of them 'airy things chasing me all over the place. I have enough trouble with the manager as it is. He pops in now and again to have a look at me dumplings, bless 'im.

Any viewers familiar with Benny's radio work would have recognized virtually all of Primrose's lines – odds and ends from the Bill 'n' 'Arry two-'anders and a mish-mash of Light Programme comedies. There was little new. But the manner of presentation was, and it caught the public's imagination.

Benny's most popular early character was a strange bod in medieval costume, initially called Percy Lamhead but swiftly renamed Herbert Fudge, who stood on stage with a mandolin and sang madrigals in the exaggerated West Country dialect Benny would come to use so much. Here is part of 'Herbert Fudge's Indian Lament':

> The Rajah fell in love with her, begged her to be his wife.
> When she refused, the Rajah banished her for life.
> He sent this lovely maiden of only twenty-four,
> To live alone on an island not fifty yards from this very shore.
>
> That is why you see me here, why you hear my sighs,
> Standing by the water's edge with tears in my eyes.
> Fifty yards away there's a maiden soft and slim,
> But I must stay on the shore for alas! I cannot swim.

'He took every chestnut joke you could think of – big ones, belters – and he made them into madrigals,' reflects Reg Varney, who was watching the shows at home, open-mouthed at how his former 'feed' was suddenly carving a name for himself. 'I recognized quite a lot of our material coming back at me. He was a brilliant boy, Benny, twisting these things round and round . . .'

Soon, however, it was the Nuffield Centre that was getting things in a twist. During Benny's fourth appearance as compère of *The Centre Show*, on September 15 1953, he dropped into the script his phoney news announcement:

> There's a police message just come in. 'A football pools coupon, I repeat a football pools coupon, was lost last night in Chelsea. Will the finder please communicate at once with New Scotland Yard, phone number WHItehall Home-Away-Home-Away.'

Two days later, the Nuffield's controller, a Wing-Commander D. A. Davies, DFC, late of the Royal Air Force, received a complaint from the

War Office stating that the broadcast 'was in deplorable taste and that there was an atmosphere of, and repeated reference to, homosexuality'. The main issue was Hill's 'police message', which – to the cloth ears at the War Office – had concluded with the words 'homo-way, homo-way'. What was this tomfool comedy-wallah trying to do? Suggest that our brave boys in blue were raving woofters?

All protestations of innocence fell on stony ground, although at issue was not this single joke but whether the Nuffield had right of veto over the content of *The Centre Show*. The BBC does not care to be challenged over its editorial independence, and the altercation went as high as the director-general on the BBC's side, Lieutenant-General Sir E. I. C. Jacob KBE, CB, DL, and, on the other, Lieutenant-Colonel J. S. Freeland, an assistant adjutant-general attached to the War Office, and Lieutenant-General Sir Geoffrey W. Howard, KCB, SMG, DSO, DL, from the Nuffield. A summit meeting took place, but once beyond the introductions – which must have taken some minutes – the BBC stood its ground, refusing the Nuffield any access to scripts in advance of broadcast. Within three weeks of Benny Hill's supposed gaffe the BBC and the Nuffield had ended a hitherto harmonious relationship of five years.[2]

The popular press lapped it up – they love a skirmish between two intractable institutions – and the coverage did no harm at all to Benny's career. The BBC probably leaked the story, since it had the most to gain (including publicity for its *Centre Show* successor), and the item hit the front page of the *Daily Mirror* under the headline 'Big TV Show Taken Off'. (*The Centre Show* was never 'big', but Fleet Street had a point to make.) The article quoted Benny Hill as saying, 'I'm flabbergasted . . . I'm quite sure there was nothing suggestive or improper.' On an inside page was a stern 'leader column' which, in the usual manner of tabloid editorials, leapt off the fence and bawled in bold letters, 'The public does not want its entertainment to be vetted by Colonels.'

Away from the Nuffield, *The Centre Show* was no longer relevant as a title; in its stead came *The Services Show*, still performed before an audience of Her Majesty's Forces but at a new venue. New to the BBC, that is – it was the Shepherd's Bush Empire, one of the many places Benny had worked during the tour of Harry Benet's *Send Him Victorious* away back in 1942. The BBC had bought the building and renamed it the Television

Theatre. TV was now in full march – the cinema was being battered and Variety bludgeoned. Those with serious investments were getting out fast, insurance companies noting that a number of Variety theatres were suddenly burning down in mysterious circumstances.

Benny was the resident compère of *The Services Show*, and in the first programme had to introduce none other than Reg Varney as one of the guest acts. Varney achieved only middling acclaim in the BBC's subsequent audience research, yet his former straightman, still only twenty-nine, was soaring into the stratosphere, a phenomenal 82 per cent of viewers finding him 'very enjoyable'. *TV Mirror* called Benny 'the Bright New Hope of Lime Grove', and the *Daily Mirror* spouted 'Thank goodness the BBC haven't sacked Benny Hill, even if that War Office colonel doesn't approve.' Why, the boy was almost a hero.

This was certainly a momentous period in Benny's life, and after years of struggling the key ingredients for success were coming together very fast. Four days before the end of 1953, with Kenneth Carter now established as his director, Benny met a second long-term player in his future career, the talented yet undiscovered comedy writer Dave Freeman, who would soon be scripting some of the best 'Benny Hill' TV sketches as well as remaining a friend to the end. They met by chance when the six-foot-three-inch former policeman was working as security officer at Winfield House, the American Officers Club in Regents Park, London, built for the Woolworth heiress Barbara Hutton. (It later became the American ambassador's residence.) Freeman's job also entailed booking the cabaret for Saturday-night dances, and after his wife Allie (Alberta) had told him about 'this very funny man on the BBC's Nuffield Centre show, who plays a mandolin and sings madrigals', Freeman offered the minimum fee, £30. Benny accepted. Jimmy Edwards had asked for £80; Benny derived the benefit of his moderate demands.

'Benny was very much an impressionist in those days,' says Freeman. 'He did a little bit of patter and sang the madrigals. He went down very big with the Americans, even then. I always used to take the comedians to the bar for a drink before they left and I got chatting with Benny, just generally. He was very impressed with my job – Winfield House was a glitzy place in its heyday and the fact that I was running it somehow gave me importance in his eyes. Then I told Benny that I had written the odd comedy sketch for the BBC in my spare time, and he said, "I'm always looking for material. Television eats it up. I write most of it myself but I'd be glad for some help." '

And – fantastically – there was yet a *third* vital player in Benny's success coming into view at this time: Jeremy Hawk. He was a Richard Stone client, an accomplished actor whom the savvy agent was keen to see employed. Stone was a past-master at finding work for his clients and shoe-horning as many as possible into the same show. Hawk took over from Kim Peacock as Benny's straightman for the TV series *Showcase*, the BBC's successor to *The Services Show*, which featured Benny as resident host through all of 1954. Born in Johannesburg in 1918 and educated at Harrow, Hawk[3] had been trained for the stage at RADA and gone on to grace dozens of West End productions. As straightman to Benny Hill he brought a deal of class to the comedy and would never steal a laugh. (Most unusually, however, Hawk would sometimes be *given* the punchline. Benny was rarely precious about who got the laugh, so long as someone did.) 'They worked beautifully together,' observes a BBC producer, John Street. 'It was a very good relationship and Jeremy was probably Benny's favourite straightman of them all.' Once again, Benny's friend Bob Monkhouse has an observation. 'Jeremy Hawk was, and is still, a man of enormous charm,' he says. 'To Benny he probably represented the upper echelons of society, the officer class. So, again, here's an example of Benny cleaving on to somebody he could respect.'

Showcase was intended to provide a platform for first-time television performers,[4] but few viewers were taking any notice of the other acts. This was *The Benny Hill Show* in all but name; more, far more, than *The Centre Show*, the *Showcase* series cemented the success of the Southampton comedian, causing him to become a household name in every part of the country that had television – which, by now, was almost everywhere.

To use the key phrase of the day, Hill was 'telegenic'. His mannerisms and facial movements were too small to be effective in the theatre but could have been tailor-made for the television camera, an instrument which then faithfully beamed the face into millions of impressionable living rooms. *That* Benny Hill face. The cheeky cherub. The boyish smirk.

The exaggerated, expressive entreaties. The darting eyes, brimming with suggestion, lingering long enough for any hidden meanings to become clear. The healthy mop of hair, the chin sagging already at thirty.

Most comedians at this time, their craft honed in the mighty Empires, were unable successfully to reduce the exaggerated antics of the Variety stage for the cameras. This was a problem that Benny never had to overcome.

'He has the gift of being able to underplay, which is so important in television – he can be funny with a glance, or the raising of an eyebrow,' Ken Carter commented of his 'discovery' at this time. He perhaps was unaware that Benny had always 'underplayed', and that, until now, it had been his downfall.

In essence, Benny's crippling inability to project himself 'beyond the first few rows of the stalls' was suddenly, for the first time, immaterial. And by sheer happenstance, he had fallen into television at the very moment the Queen was lighting the blue touchpaper.

'Of all the up-and-coming comics, I name Benny Hill as the surest for the big time,' trumpeted the *Sunday Pictorial* newspaper. 'He looks good. He invents funny characters. He has enough of them to ring the changes on his act. And he THINKS television.'

All those silly jokes and the unamusing though oddly appealing gags, suddenly, with the close-up face, amounted to something.

Television viewers genuinely adored Benny Hill. His appeal ran the gamut: male, female, children, grannies, even across the British class system, at least for now. *Everyone* liked him. Everyone except most of the established comedy writers, that is, among whom Benny was never to be popular throughout his career. There was envy that this young man, unimpressive in most endeavours, using corny old nicked material, had tapped into the richest developing gold seam invented. And this was indeed a goldrush. 'In the early days, when I first wrote for Benny, he had a *terrible* reputation for pinching material,' says Dave Freeman. 'People would go to shows at the London Palladium and there'd be Benny with a notebook. The most flagrant thing he did was when an American comic, Dick Shawn, came over to London. Shawn did a Civil War/Confederate sketch, a cod dramatic piece, "Are you there Mammy?" and all that, and Benny pinched the whole thing. Twenty years later, when Shawn came back to the Palladium, he said from the stage, "I'd like now to do my Civil War memoirs, which I gather have been done for many years here by Benny Hill."

'Benny didn't feel guilty about it, though. He had an *odd* attitude about it. So when I started writing for him I felt I had to lean over backwards to do original material, to try and salvage his name.'

To his credit, there was one element of Benny's comedy that was singular to him – those pastiches. More than anything else, it was these that brought him stardom. The buzzword at the time was 'guy' – to make fun of – and there was none better at 'guying' television than Benny Hill. Quickly, he became an accomplished and adventurous parodist, being perhaps the first comedian to realize that anyone watching his show was also likely to be watching other programmes, too. TV was still so new that it mesmerized viewers – from the moment the BBC beamed its opening pictures of the day until the white dot receded into the darkening tube when the set was switched off. Many even followed the 'Interlude' films, those hands on the potter's wheel, shaping a pot from a lump of wet clay. Benny obtained (rented) his first TV in 1953 and when he was at home in Kilburn he was one such viewer – he watched it constantly, absorbing every tiny detail.

The 'guy' that really set the nation talking about Benny Hill – more even than his impressions of Philip Harben, and the famously camp hairdresser 'Mr Teasy-Weasy' Raymond – was first performed in the June 21 1954 edition of *Showcase*. At this time, the most popular programme on television, more modish even than *Showcase*, was the panel-game *What's My Line?*, the British adaptation of an American TV show in which a member of the public mimed his or her 'line', occupation, which the resident panel then had to deduce by assiduous questioning. The chosen 'lines' were invariably tricky – over the years, viewers (who were given the answers on screen, invisible to the panel) witnessed bizarre speechless impressions of such oddities as a jelly-baby varnisher, a weighbridge operator (Benny would have guessed this one – it was his first job), a black pudding stringer and, most notoriously of all, a 'sagger maker's bottom knocker'. Viewers adored it, and the show was literally front-page news most days in the popular press. Overseen by chairman Eamonn

Andrews, the panel comprised the royalty of TV 'celebrities' – the irascible Gilbert Harding; the wisecracking Barbara Kelly; the kindly David Nixon; and the delightful Lady Isobel Barnett.

In his parody, Benny imitated all four of them, and he did so in a *live* show from the Television Theatre, effecting super-fast changes of costume and props – glasses, a moustache and a grumpy manner for Harding; a mostly bald pate for the genial Nixon; a curly blonde wig, top-heavy dress and Canadian accent for Kelly; and a brunette wig, gown and dangly earrings for Barnett. Alfie's dedicated hours in Westrow Gardens, performing impression after impression of film stars and radio heroes, had come a long way. He had, at most, thirty seconds to effect these changes, during camera cutaways to Jeremy Hawk, the actor, who expertly adopted the guise and Irish brogue of chairman Andrews.

It was pioneering stuff, the most sensational comedy sketch British television had witnessed. Bob Monkhouse was awed. 'Some of those send-ups were just superb, done with great energy and speed,' he considers. 'It was Benny's idea, and a brilliant one.' Benny himself later revealed that the *What's My Line?* parody was conceived very much at the last minute, in rehearsal with Kenneth Carter, 'the result of our minds working parallel'. (Though he omitted to mention that Dave Freeman had contributed to the script.)

There was more. Ever the keen observer, Benny's close scrutiny of the *What's My Line?* panel had revealed certain characteristics that would mark out his impressions as splendidly accurate. The way that Nixon fluttered his eyelashes in mock surprise; Harding's open-mouthed grimace when there was a cuss just along the way; Benny even sucked in his cheeks to give the impression of Lady Barnett's aristocratic bone structure.

Seeing this, the *Sunday Dispatch* nailed its colours to the transmitter mast. 'Benny Hill is the most original and refreshing comedian that British TV has discovered.'

Being 'a TV star' changed everything. Though Richard Stone was taken aback at the sudden fame of his client – whom he had all but dismissed just a couple of years earlier – he realized that the artist had to capitalize on what might be short-lived success. He heaved Benny back on to the Variety stage once more. This time with a difference – the young man was a proven star.

In 1953, Benny had played only a little Variety, in keeping with his wish to jettison this part of his life altogether. He worked a few weeks with the singing duo Teddy Johnson and Pearl Carr; he played briefly in a revue, *A Little Bit of Heaven*, with singer Patrick O'Hagan and a quintessential Variety act, Itrebor's 15 Wonder Pigeons; he toured with Vic Oliver, the Viennese comedian whom he had gone to see in 1942, dressed still in dungarees, to celebrate his eighteenth birthday (such was Benny's respect, he felt he could never call him 'Vic', only 'Mr Oliver'); he even played for a week in *Jane Comes to Town*, a revue promoted by the emerging Variety impresario (and future strip-club owner) Paul Raymond. 'Jane' was the *Daily Mirror*'s wartime strip-cartoon, with the emphasis on 'strip' – she removed her clothes in accordance with the Allies' prevailing successes, and it was said that the fewer clothes she wore the better the effect on British forces' morale. On the day that victory was declared Jane finally bared her all. *Jane Comes to Town* played at the Grand, Southampton, for a week in August 1953, the first time Benny had performed in Variety in his hometown. Among the audience were Nelson and Irene Brown, Benny's 'second family' from Eastleigh, with their now fifteen-year-old daughter Pauline. 'We went there to see Alf,' says Pauline, proudly, still using the comedian's 'old' name. 'But it wasn't exactly a family show – Jane stripped behind a curtain and then remained quite still, not allowed to move. But we still went backstage to see Alf.'

Benny's Variety bookings had steadily improved in 1954 – though there was more work with Teddy Johnson and Pearl Carr, and several weeks on a bill with the singer Jimmy Young, Michael Bentine and the new comedy double-act Joe Baker and Jack Douglas. *Showcase* elevated Benny to the top, though. When Richard Stone suggested he make a high-profile return to the Sunderland Empire, Benny resisted. The *Sky High* humiliation had been too great.

Stone persisted, recognizing that his client needed to lay the ghost.

Benny hadn't realized. There was nothing at all to worry about, because television had done the spadework, bridging the previously insurmountable north-south divide for comedians. *Showcase* was avidly watched and enjoyed everywhere, and the 'daunting' Sunderland audience already loved him with a passion.

Benny Hill's top-of-the-bill week at the Sunderland Empire at the beginning of September 1954, in which he was 'fed' by Jeremy Hawk, was received with enormous enthusiasm. He even drew laughter and applause for the one-man *Romeo and Juliet* balcony scene that had died a death there three years previously, and with which he – bravely – opened on this return visit. The local *Echo* newspaper noted this warmth, though it also observed that Benny still had work to do if he wished to become a consummate stage performer:

TV STARS JUST OFF BEAM
by Compère

The man everybody came to see last night (or so it seemed by the applause) was up-and-coming TV idol Benny Hill. But there is obviously a big difference between television and the live stage.

Mr Hill, despite his likeable manner and obvious talent, does not come over with a bang. He get laughs a-plenty (but so many are lost in the process); he works hard, but something is lacking. His television material, undeniably clever, does not always click. At the same time, when he does break through we realize that with more appropriate material he might well repeat his television hit on the stage.

The reception was warm, but underlying it all was the feeling that this audience was determined to show Benny how much they thought of him – as a first-rate television artist.

In October 1954, with Benny Hill's television popularity at a new height, Stone sent a hastily packaged Variety touring revue on the road – cheekily called *The Benny Hill Show*. 'Harry Harbour, the bookings manager for the Stoll circuit, offered £100 a week for Benny and I wanted £150,' recalls Stone. 'So I said, "OK, £100 and 10 per cent of the box-office." Benny came out with about £1,000 a week, really good money in those days. He packed the theatres, absolutely packed them.'

The show's producer – going under the name Ian Stuart; later, as Mark Stuart, the director of some of Benny's 1970s TV shows – recalls, 'There were queues that we hadn't seen the like of. The theatre managers were going out of their minds because there were queues right around the block to get in. They hadn't seen business like that in maybe twenty, twenty-five years.'

The Stage was especially impressed with the box-office. Reviewing a show in the opening week, at the Empire, Wood Green, it blindly enthused:

> The size of the audience here this week gives the lie to those who say that people would sooner sit at home and watch their favourites.

So in Variety's final years – it was dead by 1960 – it suffered the indignity of having to trade heavily on television names, those whom it could also have *cheerfully* murdered.

Aided once more by Jeremy Hawk, and supported by the usual weird and wonderful assortment of Variety artistes, Benny performed five sketches in each *Benny Hill Show*, twice-nightly. (This was actually more generous than strictly necessary.) One was the sketch everyone wanted to see – *What's My Line?*, Benny's 'greatest hit'. Though done less effectively than on TV – Benny was always on stage, so the costume and wig changes were visible – it was still a triumph. *The Stage* noted, much as the Sunderland paper had noted, 'With his TV successes behind him, Benny Hill can do no wrong as far as the audience is concerned.'

After Wood Green *The Benny Hill Show* played in Bristol, Cardiff (the same theatre where, twelve years earlier, the young draft-dodger had been arrested by the military police), Hackney, Chiswick and Manchester. Then it paused until the spring. Benny had other things on his plate. Richard Stone, like all entertainment agents, was cramming it in while his star was 'hot'.

Benny's TV reputation made him a radio star, too. Throughout 1953 he had continued to flog his way around the far-flung regions, appearing in everything from the unglamorous Welsh Home Service *Talent Theatre* ('direct from the Alhambra Cinema in Shotton!') to the 'glamorous' *Workers' Playtime* at Fawley Refinery, Southampton. (Well, at least it was near 'home'.) If anything, Benny's appeal to wireless listeners had been diminishing, rather than improving, with every broadcast – when he appeared on *The Star Show* in January 1953 only a humbling 9 per cent of the listeners polled by the BBC said they had derived 'exceptional enjoyment' from his act. Benny was even moved to grab at a straight part.

Besides character pieces, he had done no 'acting' since the unfortunate *Happy Week-end!* – his wartime Stars in Battledress play. With an adventure serial broadcast in April/May 1953 in the BBC's North of England Home Service, he was George Medhurst in *Danger is Our Business*. Benny played one of two newly 'demobbed' army pals who had formed the Beaufort Detective Agency and investigated a weekly mystery. There was 'The Case of the Stolen Car', 'Murder on Two Wheels', 'The Big Top Mystery' and others, all done with a slightly light-hearted touch. The series was only moderately successful and didn't return. Certainly, no one ever investigated The Case of the Cancelled Radio Drama.

As he was finding with the Variety stage, though, television success was suddenly making all the difference. With every *Showcase*, so bigger and better 'wireless' work came Benny's way. There was no bigger radio show at this time than *Educating Archie*, and suddenly the producer was on the doorstep. And who should it be but Roy Speer, one of Benny's earliest champions at the BBC from seven years earlier.

Educating Archie was a fantastic anachronism of post-war radio. In America, the ventriloquist Edgar Bergen had swept to success as a radio star with his insolent dummy Charlie McCarthy. Aping America, as all spheres of British entertainment have done since the early twentieth century, the ball was picked up in Britain by Peter Brough, whose wooden dummy, a pesky little English knave called Archie Andrews, became a huge star. Brough also ran a family textile business, with an overcoat factory in the East End of London. 'Peter was only interested in the money side – he was a terrible performer,' muses one of the series' key writers, Ronnie Wolfe. 'He did the radio shows with Archie on his knee, but he got very lazy. He used to ask us, "Can you see my lips move?" and we used to reply, "Only when Archie's talking." All the same, Peter was earning £2,000–£3,000 a week, and this was still the early 1950s.' Few seemed to object to the notion of ventriloquism on the radio. When, in 1951, the wooden doll was 'kidnapped', the nation held its breath, and emitted a collective sigh of relief when 'he' turned up in the Lost Property Office at King's Cross station in London.

Moreover, Archie's show proved a fertile ground for up-and-coming young performers. Virtual 'unknowns' transported to fame as the wooden doll's supporting players included Max Bygraves, Tony Hancock, Hattie

Jacques, Harry Secombe, Julie Andrews (Archie's girlfriend!) and Beryl Reid. Eric Sykes, one of the most brilliant comedy writers on radio, and subsequently television, earned his stripes on the show. Now the series took a leap into uncharted territory – it went after an acknowledged star, Benny Hill. 'I was very envious of Benny getting that job,' says Bob Monkhouse, 'because it was a tremendous step forward, one that I was constantly being promised but never given.'

The role was also playing into Benny's hands. Richard Stone had written to BBC radio's Light Entertainment department in March 1954 declaring, 'He [Benny] feels his voice is not distinctive enough in itself for him to make the same success on radio as a compère, as he has on television. On radio he feels his strength is in his characterization.'

By August 1954, Roy Speer was asking to see Benny. It was a Saturday-morning meeting but there was the young comedian, still eager, riding the bus from Kilburn to the BBC's Aeolian Hall office in New Bond Street. Benny told Speer that joining *Educating Archie* had been one of his radio ambitions for years.[5]

It wasn't *Educating Archie* any more, though – when Benny joined, the title changed to *Archie's the Boy!* and the storylines reflected a slightly more mature dummy. The series ran for twenty weeks, from November 1954 to March 1955. Television was beginning to steal its thunder, but the golden era of BBC radio comedy was not yet over – this was one of four shows recorded consecutively at the BBC's 'Paris' studio in London every Sunday afternoon, preceding *Life with the Lyons*, *Ray's a Laugh* and *Take It from Here* (which, by now, included the self-contained recurring situation *The Glums*, a comedy masterpiece by Frank Muir and Denis Norden). 'It was marvellous training for us writers,' says Ronnie Wolfe. 'We'd all go to the pub and discuss which actors hadn't read their lines, or even opened up their envelope.'

Benny always opened the envelope. 'He was very confident and easy to get on with,' says Wolfe. 'There was no sign of nerves and he was completely without "temperament", one of the nicest guys. Many of the other artistes were temperamental, usually worrying over whether they'd get a certain number of lines in the script. Benny didn't really want [to have] very much.' This time, it mattered not that he was performing someone else's material; he even gave the writers tips about certain of his TV characters, who, to maximize his presence, were written into the show.

Millions listened to *Archie's the Boy!* every Thursday evening, and Benny – until now a consistent disappointment in radio – was suddenly, universally, 'tops'. One very satisfied listener, quoted in the BBC's Listener Research Report for the December 23 1954 broadcast, declared, 'He's the best pal Archie's had so far.'

As early as February 1954, after just one edition of *Showcase*, a full own-name TV series for Benny Hill was mooted by the BBC. The clamour escalated throughout the year – by the autumn, there were questions in the newspapers asking why it had not been forthcoming. But in November, when the BBC announced its winter schedule, there it was – Arthur Askey, David Nixon, Eric Barker . . . and Benny Hill were to be given their own series. Benny was given the best slot; according to the *Daily Mail*, he was 'to become the first TV star to have his own regular Saturday-night series'. *The Benny Hill Show* was born.

On the eve of his first full series, the newspaper made a further announcement. In the *Daily Mail*-sponsored National Television Awards 1954–55, Benny Hill had been voted 'The Personality of the Year'.

At the February 1955 ceremony, shown live by the BBC from the Scala Theatre, with a subsequent supper-dance at the swanky Grosvenor House Hotel, Benny performed a sketch and one of his madrigals ('Hill at his droll best,' drooled *The Stage*, the paper that, not two years before, had referred to him as *Billy* Hill). The applause, throughout the British Isles, was deafening. 'Benny Hill proved by far the most popular of the artists appearing,' noted the BBC, with typical restraint.

The night of the awards, Benny was performing a long-booked Sunday concert at the Barking Odeon, east of London. In a precisely executed manoeuvre, the BBC sent a car to collect him, a breathless internal memo meticulously planning to transport the VIP . . .

. . . on the dot of 8.50pm, and the car should be a high powered one to get him over to the Scala as quickly as possible, as Mr Hill is not likely to get away from Barking until 8.55pm and *must* arrive at the Scala Theatre by 9.25pm.

It was thirteen years but just a mile from the old East Ham Palace, soon to be demolished, to the Barking Odeon where the limousine's engine was purring. After all the struggle, Alfie Hill, Benny Hill, *Mr Hill* yet, had reached the top.

3. A Certain Talent

Radio Times Incorporating World-Radio February 21, 1952. Vol. 125. No. 1789.

FEBRUARY 23—MARCH 1

TELEVISION **BBC** AND SOUND

RADIO TIMES

PRICE THREEPENCE

The Benny Hill Show

Meet the many Bennys
in Television on Saturday

★

Donald Wolfit
and Mai Zetterling in
'THE MASTER
BUILDER'

Television: Sunday

SUPPLEMENT: COOKERY

10. The Same Old Benny

So what did television's Personality of the Year do? Dine at the Ritz, shop in Mayfair, buy himself a car or a boat or a pile in the country, or perhaps move into a smart West End apartment?

He did none of these.

Personality of the Year or not, Benny was as Benny was and Benny always would be. 'He was an enigma wrapped in a mystery,' declares Bob Monkhouse, echoing Winston Churchill's considered view of the Soviet Union. 'The glimpses we had of young Benny are only clues to the old Benny.'

The young Benny Hill was the product of parents whose thrift was obsessive, and whose material requirements, such as they were, had long been fulfilled. They no more wanted than expected their suddenly famous and relatively wealthy son to treat them to life's luxuries. Likewise Benny, who was steeped in their ways and never questioned the possibility of changing. He was familiar with, indeed comfortable, living in meagre circumstances. He too had what he needed, though this wasn't very much. More he simply did not want and could not use.

Money poured in all the same, however, presenting Benny with a problem. What would he *do* with it all? 'I can only wear one shirt at a time,' he was fond of saying – a 'line' that would be trotted out as often as his response to questions about being a bachelor – 'Why buy a book when you can join a library?' and 'I have a mental age of seventeen – far too young for marriage.' Benny always had a quip for those who questioned his lifestyle.

Regarding money, his 'solution', such as it was, was the ostrich approach. He stuffed cheques out of view and tried to pretend they weren't there. Only occasionally, when they had not expired, did he pay them into a bank. Very few other entertainers, if any, were not driven by money, and none understood Benny Hill. Their grapevine was always

217

buzzing with rumours about his sexuality and especially his – to them, bewildering – attitude to wealth. Benny kept a plaster ornament of Mephistopheles on his mantelpiece and the rumour was that he routinely 'filed' cheques behind it. He was said to say, 'Only when the devil's about to tumble off the mantelpiece will I pay the cheques in.'

'People always ask me if he was a mean man,' reflects Jeremy Hawk. 'Benny wasn't mean, he just didn't see the point of spending money. He had no use for it. His expenditure for the day, when I was with him, would be a copy of the *Evening Standard* newspaper. That would be the only money that left his pocket, which was about thruppence at the time. He didn't see the need for spending money because he didn't feel that he lacked anything.

'I was once in his flat, going over a script, and he said to me, "Could you get me a pair of socks out of the drawer?" And when I pulled it out, there were the socks and also what must have been seventy-five cheques, which fell out of the drawer and on to the floor. They had never been spent and had no value because they were out of date. He simply had no need to spend the money he was earning. It was, as I say, a lack of *need* of money.'

Benny also had little necessity for creature comforts. At the time of being made Personality of the Year he was still renting a single bedroom in Connie Rhodes' Kilburn boarding-house for £4 a week, along with a performing duck, a yapping Pekinese and two increasingly unemployed Variety artistes, the dashing man and his stacked blonde partner. Benny saw no reason to move, and wouldn't have but for the fact that with his TV, tape recorder (for writing and rehearsing material), scripts, contracts, books and rapidly growing collection of press cuttings (which he stuffed into shoe-boxes), he was running out of space.

'That's why, even though I'm going to miss "Auntie Connie's" wonderful North Country cooking and good humour, I must leave,' Benny wrote in March 1955, in his own column in the weekly film magazine *Picturegoer* – one of several high-profile endeavours that followed in the wake of his prestigious award.

For the first time I'm getting a home of my own ... It's small, unfurnished and in Maida Vale, which is a convenient part of London, not too far out. I look forward to furnishing it, though I don't know much about these things. Just one rule I've decided on: don't clutter up the room too much.

He moved into 16 Cunningham Court, a couple of miles down Benny's oh-so-familiar London bus and pedestrian route – Toto's 'Edgvare Strasse'. A recently modernized apartment block, the red-brick Cunningham Court backed on to the Grand Union Canal at Little Venice, a decent and quiet place in a pleasant area, by far the best he had ever known, family homes included. But he didn't buy the apartment; cautious about how long his fame would last, he took out a short lease, five years. It was entirely within character – Benny hardly ever bought anything. Even his TV was rented. And his self-imposed 'rule' about clutter was to be another hallmark. For 'don't clutter up the room too much' read 'spartan'.

'It was a nice flat,' says Dave Freeman. 'He was on the top floor, with two rooms and a kitchen and a pleasant living room that looked out over the canal and Blomfield Road. But the way Benny furnished it was peculiar. At this time, celebrities were often asked to open shops, cutting the ribbon and that kind of thing, and Benny was often doing it. He didn't get paid but he'd get furniture for free. The trouble was, nothing matched. He had one of those Italian renaissance-style mauve/purple/gold sofas which an old dealer I knew used to call "early Jewish" because it was very popular in Golders Green. The chair didn't match the sofa. The dining-table and chairs were out of another period and he had black sheets on his bed, another gift from a shop. But Benny was happy, and he didn't have to buy.'

In addition to Dave Freeman, Benny had established another important new friendship at this time, with Peter Charlesworth. (Once again, following his father's doctrine, both men were Jewish.) A theatrical agent in later years, at this time Charlesworth was a plugger for a London music publishing firm, and had first approached Benny in the hope that he might include a certain song in his act. They soon became friends. 'When Benny wanted a piece of furniture he'd ring someone, offer to open a new shop and say, "I'll pick myself out a dining-room suite while I'm there,"' Charlesworth recalls. 'He did a lot of Times Furnishings openings, so his flat was full of antique-reproduction teak. But another piece was modern

Swedish, he had a Grundig record player, and a print on the wall – a girl with a tear in her eye and a bare bosom. Benny had no real taste whatsoever, and he simply didn't care about it.'

His eating habits remained unchanged, too. He could now afford the best food, especially as post-war rationing had finally been lifted. The Hills were a family of large people and Benny's appetite had been abundant for longer than he could remember. But his preference remained for a Wimpy burger or a sausage sandwich or a dozen fish-fingers, with the plate veritably wiped clean every meal, and he saw no reason why having a few cheques – deposited in the bank or stuffed inside a drawer – should alter anything. Moreover, Benny drew extraordinary satisfaction from finding cheap food – buying old, bruised fruit from a greengrocery in Tottenham Court Road, for example. One of the most-told tales about his self-imposed frugality was witnessed first-hand by Peter Charlesworth (whom, rather oddly, Benny often addressed only by his surname):

One morning when he was in Maida Vale Benny rang up and said, 'Charlesworth will come and do Hill a favour, and then Hill will cook Charlesworth lunch.' I had a beat-up car and Benny of course never had any transport. He came downstairs from his flat with two or three huge, empty sacks, in which he had received fan mail, and handed me an address in Paddington, a shop called Wally's Surplus, I think. There was a long queue of housewives all around the store and Benny wanted to join the queue. I told him there'd be a riot – he was famous by this time. So I went inside and talked to the manager, we took the car around the back, and eventually Benny and three other guys came out with the sacks bulging. The suspension on my car almost hit the ground but I managed to drive very slowly back to Maida Vale. Even with the aid of the porter it took us half an hour to get the sacks upstairs.

Though aware of Benny's curious dietary habits, Peter Charlesworth was in for a surprise. 'When he opened up the sacks they were full of tins – dented, rusty, all without labels, rescued from a ship that had been sunk in the [Thames] estuary during the war. They were being sold at three pence each. And out of them he made the most fantastic meal.' (How The Captain must have been proud.)

Benny evidently ate this way for some years. In 1959, when he appeared in the movie *Light Up the Sky!*, the director, Lewis Gilbert, collected him from Maida Vale *en route* to the studio. One morning Gilbert asked Benny if he had eaten breakfast and Benny responded that he'd had a tin of soup. 'I said, "That's a funny thing to eat for breakfast! Why?" and Benny replied, "I've got a good situation going. If you go to my local supermarket on Saturdays, just before they close, they give you a huge box of unlabelled tins for practically nothing." I said, "But Ben, you might get a tin of dog food!" and he said, "Well, if that happens I'll throw it away. But most of the time it's soup. Sometimes it's salmon – it's interesting to find out what's there." '

'The range of what gave Benny pleasure was extremely narrow and excluded a great deal – not ignored, excluded,' reflects Bob Monkhouse. 'Good clothing, for example. Generally speaking, he stuck with the same stained old anoraks and plastic things that he'd worn for years and years and years. He seemed to have no notion of wanting to treat himself to something finer.'

Benny had an obsession about people trying to take advantage of him, typified by his reaction when he suspected people were tapping him for money. 'I once asked him for a loan, when I was out of work and on my uppers,' says Peter Charlesworth, 'and he refused. But two weeks later he said, "Charlesworth will come over and drive Hill to Oxford so that Hill can perform in a show," and he gave me way too much to cover the cost of the petrol. That was his way of giving. He had a heart of gold . . . provided that you didn't trespass on him.'

Benny's reaction to being famous was also curious. 'He was certainly the least star-like star I ever worked with,' remarks Dave Freeman. 'He had an ego but it wasn't at all out of control.' So that people wouldn't recognize him in the street, Benny asked his dentist to make him three sets of protruding covers to go over his front teeth. It worked for a while, but then Benny blew it because he told journalists about the disguise; he even wore one on television in a character part. 'He just couldn't resist it,' says Freeman. Benny could accept being recognized, just so long as people didn't intrude. If they accosted him, or wanted to engage in a conversation, he became hot under the collar and hurried away.

When the touring *Benny Hill Show* revue played a Brighton theatre in

1955, one of the devoted fans in the audience was Bella Emberg, later to become an actress and cast – as, in her own words, a 'character-bag' – in his TV shows. Straight away, at the age of just eighteen, she realized that this was a most unusual man. 'We decided to wait at the stage door and see him come out,' she recalls. 'We thought we'd be the only ones but there must have been a couple of hundred people there. And out he came, a very shy man surrounded by a crowd. The crowd parted, he walked off down Middle Street and then turned back and very gently, almost whispering, said, "Good night!" And we all said, "Good night!" back; nobody pressed for an autograph. And he was all alone. I wanted to run after him, put my arms around him and tell him we loved him, he was so alone.'

Alone, yes – but was he, as so many attest, lonely? Loneliness is subjective. Most people who knew Benny Hill assert that he was lonely simply by imagining his lifestyle for themselves. But one must not overlook the abiding influence of Benny's upbringing; he sought solitude and seemed entirely at ease with it.

Weighing up all he saw of Benny, his stage accomplice Jeremy Hawk declares, 'I don't think Benny ever had a happy life, as a child or as an adult. He wasn't a miserable man and he didn't have a miserable life, but he never tested the boundaries to see whether he could have been happy in some other way. He didn't give the impression of being a lonely man, and – not being a complainer – he never admitted to being lonely, but I think he was. If you've never been happy you simply don't know what you're missing.'

Bob Monkhouse offers an alternative viewpoint. 'The notion that Benny was a lonely man is so depressing and wrong,' he says, 'and he certainly wasn't a loner in the sense that he'd pick up a chainsaw and murder someone. He just liked his own company. He was very happy walking alone, living alone, eating alone, taking holidays alone and going to see shows alone. Not, I would say, because he was lonely but because he was actually very contented, he was all of a piece. I often wonder whether he needed anybody else in his life at all . . . except perhaps a cameraman.'

Around the time of his *Showcase* success, Benny entered into his last meaningful relationship, going steady with Doris Deal, a dancer from the Windmill Theatre. (An actual, moving dancer – not a stationary nude.) When they were both free for an evening, which was not often, Benny took Doris out, tripping London's light fantastic. Strictly forty-watt, of course.

Benny had been seeing Doris for three or four months when Peter Charlesworth became his friend, and he observed them together for the next year and a half. 'Doris was the one he really liked,' Charlesworth declares. 'He was with her the longest and was more serious about her than he had been or would be about any of the others. She was a nice, hard-working girl and they got on wonderfully well together.'

It seemed a good match. Unlike most of the women in whom Benny was to invest serious interest – who, typically, did not share his boyish relish for a relationship – 'Dottie' was a sensible, unpretentious young woman, with feet planted firmly on the ground. She cared for Benny as he cared for her, and although they didn't live together theirs (says Peter Charlesworth) was a full and affectionate relationship. When Charlesworth started to date Doris's best friend, a foursome developed, and they would all go out in his wreck of a car, day-tripping down to Margate for a few precious hours away from the pressures of work.

Eventually, inevitably, it became clear that the relationship either had to be cemented by marriage or come to an end. 'I think Doris's mother was pushing Benny to marry her,' says Dave Freeman. Peter Charlesworth concurs. 'The trouble was,' he says, 'Benny just wasn't ready for it. Doris said to him, "You either marry me or I'll go." And as Benny couldn't ever bring himself to commit, she left, which upset him terribly. Responsibility was not Benny's strong point – not for a house, not for a car, not for a wife, not for anything. She was quite right to knock him back because he'd been with her a long time and was procrastinating like mad.'

Although his own inaction had precipitated the breakup, Benny's pain ran deep, and, privately, he spoke of Dottie right up to his death. He did not do so publicly, where his talk of women was confined, principally, to the times when he had been spurned – especially the doomed Margate relationship of 1950. But Charlesworth noted the extra degree of sadness that Benny always felt about Doris Deal, observing, 'He was never the same after they broke up. Doris was the one he really cared for, and after it finished he became more and more withdrawn with women. When the chips were down he hadn't the "bottle" to get married and take the responsibility. So far as I know, and I believe he told me everything, after Doris he never again went "all the way" with women.' (Doris Deal, who eventually married another man, died in January 2000, just as this author had traced her and was requesting an interview.)

Instead, Benny sought sexual satisfaction in relationships where he could maintain complete control – where, as he had told Bob Monkhouse a decade earlier, he could be a 'knight in shining armour' to a not very bright young thing, who would be happy to give to 'Mr Hill' but not expect to take.

During the recording of *Archie's the Boy!*, that strangely popular radio ventriloquism series, Benny befriended the accomplished comic-actor Graham Stark, cast in the show as Nigel Bowser-Smythe. One Sunday afternoon at the BBC's Regent Street recording studio, Benny invited Stark to the cinema – quickly adding, 'I'm not a poof, you know. I'm not trying to pull you,' in case Stark got the wrong impression. Stark understood, and he had nothing better to do, so he and Hill crossed the street and headed for the Plaza. 'We went over there in our broadcasting dark suits,' Stark recalls. 'The BBC always made sure you had to look good. And we were just about to go in when we saw three girls standing there. I'm not being snobby but they were real supermarket check-out types, cooing "Ooh look, Ethel, there's that man on the telly, Benny 'Ill!", sweet but idiotic and, to me, about as attractive as a tram. And Benny went straight into The Chat, offering to sign autographs for the three of them. Then, to my absolute horror, he said, "It's a pity there isn't two of you, 'cos you could come to the pictures wiv us." Thank God there were three, that's all I can say – one of them would have died rather than back out. I was so relieved, but baffled at how Benny could even entertain the idea of being with them. They weren't at all attractive; these days, men would call them "dogs".'

Going out on tour with Benny in 1954–5, Jeremy Hawk, too, witnessed the star's predilection for 'factory girls'. 'He liked them with dirty fingernails,' Hawk says, 'and heaven knows what they got up to. His highlight, as he once expressed to me, was to pick up a girl from

Woolworth's or Marks & Spencer, buy some black underwear and fit it on her. That seemed to be his idea of sex.

'He wanted women who would laugh at him, fans, girls who would go back and tell their friends they'd been with Benny Hill. He felt comfortable in their company. He was ill-at-ease with a witty companion because he didn't feel he could join in.'

Benny was not and never would be a sophisticate. According to Hawk, the main reason Benny opened so many shops and factories was not for the free goods or the occasional 'crisp pound notes in a dirty envelope' but because these jobs enabled him to meet the shop-floor or factory women. 'That was the class he liked,' says Hawk. 'He always flirted and got on well with them. But I never heard him say, "I'm taking a beautiful girl out and I'd like to be on my own with her." That wasn't Benny's style at all.'

Benny's technique, as he told actor Henry McGee years later, was to keep 'handout' photographs of himself in both pockets of his jacket. For the prettier shop-girls he took a photo out of one pocket and signed it, and on the back of the photo was his phone number. For the less pretty girls he would take a photo from the other pocket, and still sign it, but there would be nothing on the back. 'You'd be surprised at the number of phone calls I got,' Benny told McGee.

Benny's friendship with Peter Charlesworth covered an assortment of bases. 'We were both from similar working-class backgrounds, unpretentious and ambitious, with a dislike of authority and the upper classes,' says Charlesworth. 'We were always very frank with each other.' And there was something else. 'We were both terribly naughty boys and liked to go hunting for girls.'

In the words of Richard Stone, Hill and Charlesworth were 'crumpet-chasers'. Like Bob and Terry in the great 1960s British TV sitcom *The Likely Lads*, their conquests were planned in great detail, although the results usually lacked finesse. 'We didn't succeed very well at it,' Charlesworth admits. 'Sometimes it was a bit tacky but we had our moments.' Benny had kept in touch with a kindly Margate landlady from the Reg Varney era and he and Charlesworth, who had the car, would often drive down to pay a visit. While there, they would walk the promenade and hang around the Dreamland amusement arcade 'trying to pull some birds'.

Another favoured haunt was the Hammersmith Palais ballroom in London. Here, Benny would loiter around the bar until he was recognized; then he would pick out one of the admiring girls, chivvy them along to the Chocolate House in Regent Street for a cup of cocoa and get a bus back to Cunningham Court. In return for certain favours, usually fellatio, these 'conquests' would be bestowed with gifts. A chap named Leslie Cohen had sold Benny, at wholesale prices, a job-lot of inexpensive Max Factor 'Primitif' perfume which he kept in a bedroom drawer (probably next to the socks and cheques). In another he kept a stock of see-through nighties, in shades of green, blue and pink. According to Bob Monkhouse, if a woman got all three nighties and a bottle or two of 'Primitif' then she had 'fulfilled the contract'.

Above all else, Benny liked to be *seen* with women. 'He always wanted you to think that his flat had just been vacated by fourteen giggling beautiful girls and as soon as you left another fourteen were coming in,' remarks Monkhouse. 'I really believe that the delusion was one he not only enjoyed but believed in. He really thought it was true. I think there was an enormous amount of self-deception in Benny's life.'

This need led to Benny suggesting dates even to those with whom he did not plan to transact 'Primitif' and nylon nighties. In 1949, during a trip back to Southampton, Benny took lunch to his father at Stanley & Co. – Helen's usual hot meal, sandwiched between two plates and rushed downtown from Westrow Gardens – and, while there, he invited out The Captain's valiant condoms-packer, Doris Lamb, ten years his senior and a mother of seven. 'He said to me, "Would you like to come to the pictures one evening?"' she remembers. '"No, I don't think so," I said. "I'm married and I've got a home with seven kids to keep going, so I can't get out at nights!"'

In the mid-1950s, Benny, the TV star, was no different. According to Graham Stark, one day Benny asked the actress Joan Heal, wife of Jeremy Hawk, out for dinner. Thinking she might be dining in the Café de Paris or the Ritz, Joan kitted out in full evening wear – mink stole and all. Guileless, oblivious, Benny took her into the Lyons self-service cafeteria in Piccadilly where one slid a metal tray along a rail and took food out of little hatches. 'I always come here,' he told her, 'it's very good food, you know. Come on, get your tray!' As they sat there, at a tile-top table, with

Benny tucking into a sponge pudding and custard, Joan felt like 'the local tart, all dressed up' and thought this was the blackest of humour. But it wasn't. Benny simply loved Lyons restaurants – didn't everyone?[1]

During his time at Cunningham Court, Benny engaged a secretary for the first and only time. Doris Jones, twenty years his senior, was the widow of an RAF officer, living alone in the same apartment block. Formalities were observed. He called her Mrs Jones, she called him – as his father had always insisted in his business relationships – Mr Hill.

As he grew busier, and correspondence mounted, Benny came to depend on the frequently exasperated Mrs Jones to help him get through. Without her, it was all a muddle – as it would prove in the years after her tenure ended. Dave Freeman often visited Benny for writing sessions and observed the relationship with interest. 'Although she was employed to type letters, if she came in and saw a sink full of dirty dishes she couldn't stand it and would do the washing-up,' he says. 'She once said to him, "Mr Hill, do you think I could go and buy a pot-scourer?" "Oh, you don't need to buy one," Benny said, "I'll show you how to make one." And he got half a dozen of the old metal milk-bottle tops, strung them through with a piece of string and said "There you are!" He also said to her, "And don't throw away those little bits of soap because if you press them together, put them in a colander and shake it up, you don't need to buy any soap powder." Mrs Jones was not very impressed! She said to me, "He's very *careful*, you know."'

Mrs Jones also became aware of Benny's nocturnal companions, and how he would treat them. Freeman laughs heartily as he recalls her conspiratorial whisper, 'Do you know, he had a girl up here last night. He invites them up for dinner and he gives them poached egg on toast. When I was a young girl I wouldn't go *anywhere* for poached egg on toast.'

Fifteen years after leaving home, Benny also had to contend with his familial relationships, and these were, as ever, far from easy. His two siblings had grown up and scattered: Len along the south coast, to Worthing, where he had married and started a family; and Diana to Australia, where she, too, had married. Both, incredibly, had become communists, an extreme reaction to their father's dominating spirit. 'Diana

227

got it [communism] from Leonard,' observes cousin Hugh Stevens, wryly. 'He used to take her on one side and explain how it all worked. It was their lifetime's duty to overthrow the oppressive regime under which they had suffered!'

Despite the distance, Benny and his sister, nine years his junior, maintained a close relationship. She was an outgoing person and Benny loved her lifestyle and what he called her 'wall to wall people'. Bubbly, free-spirited and compassionate, she was the kind of woman who attracted friends. Having qualified as a nurse at Southampton Eye Hospital, she – like her siblings – had flown the nest at an early age, leaving for Australia at nineteen. There she met the man she would marry, Noel Olive, a trade unionist. 'He too was a communist, a revolutionary,' observes cousin Bill Jaques. 'He used to march with banners and Diana joined him and I think got arrested a couple of times.' Benny regularly wrote and sent money to his sister but apparently didn't care for her husband. 'Benny didn't like him at all,' Jaques observes. 'He thought he was belligerent and drank a lot.'

Benny's relationship with his brother was altogether more trying. Theirs had always been a testy alliance – good times had followed bad, and so it bounced. Yet the association had survived Benny's rise to fame, never an easy matter for a sibling, let alone one prone to jealousy as Len had been since his brother's arrival thirty-odd years earlier. There were new problems on the horizon, too. Len had always endured a fractious relationship with his parents – his father especially; now his wife Marjorie had joined him in the battle. Though Benny attempted to be the peacemaker, when sides were taken he was caught in the crossfire, and this badly affected his sibling relationship. Impaired once more in the late 1950s, the attachment teetered in the 1960s and was then severed altogether. After this the two men did not speak for twenty-something years.

Even at Len and Marjorie's wedding, in April 1954, the problems were an open sore. Big Alf's sister, Violet Stevens, recalls, 'Benny did everything he could for his brother. I think he even bought him his house. All the family was at the wedding and for his speech at the reception, which Benny had also financed, Len got up and said, "If I'd had my way, none of you would be here, it would just be Marjorie and me." That was typical of Len. The two brothers were miles and miles apart.'

Matters continued to take a turn for the worse. Once settled in their new home in Worthing – named Charivari, one of Len's favoured words, meaning dissonant sounds, a cacophony – Len and Marjorie produced a family but kept them away from his parents. 'I think what started the rift between Benny and Len was that Len didn't want his kids to see the grandparents,' says Dave Freeman, to whom Benny disclosed his problem. 'So the parents said to Benny, "We never see Len, we never see the grandchildren, please find out why," and Benny went to ask him. "I can't be bothered going there," Len evidently told him, "dad bores the bloody backside off me."'

As the relationship wavered, the knockout blow came over money, a perennial difficulty within families, especially this one. Len was supporting a young family on a schoolmaster's salary and Benny wanted to provide him with a regular, additional retainer. When Benny's income had grown to the point where he was advised to establish a company (Benny Hill Productions Ltd, incorporated in January 1957), he appointed Len as a director. In return, Len lobbed the odd comedy joke or idea in Benny's direction, free for him to exploit. But trouble soon surfaced. 'The arrangement involved Len in a certain amount of paperwork,' says Hugh Stevens, 'where his signature was required, at fairly regular intervals, to justify the balance sheets. But he was frequently late in sending them back, which got Benny into stew with his auditors. Len had nothing to do other than sign the papers but he couldn't be bothered and Benny lost patience with him, because he was getting well paid for a signature. And that caused a certain amount of resentment in Len, because gratitude has a nasty habit of turning rancid. The resentment dominated for twenty years.'

It is said that the final straw came when Benny paid Len and Marjorie a visit and discovered impardonable profligacy. Dave Freeman heard the full story. 'Benny said to me: "They *waste* money! I cannot tell you how they waste money! I went to put something in the dustbin and there was a bottle of shampoo in there, only half used!" Evidently they then had a row. Benny said, "I'm not giving you good money if you're going to waste bottles of shampoo!" He thought they were extravagant wastrels. He'd have used the shampoo even if it made him come out in spots – he'd have looked like a leopard until he'd finished the bottle.'

Back in Westrow Gardens, Alf and Helen were in their fourth decade of married life. Although Benny's fondness for his Auntie Lulu forged a closer relationship, one that would reach fruition in the 1970s and 80s, he and his mother continued to get along. She still hoped he would 'settle down', suggesting potentially eligible brides from women she saw on television, but she must also have sensed that the day would never come. For a while – until he began using the services of TV producer Ken Carter's PA – Benny had been sending his mother scarcely legible handwritten comedy scripts to type. 'I posted my scribble home with the request "Just one and one, dear" and back it would come, one clean top copy and one clean carbon,' Benny proudly told *TV Mirror* in January 1955.

'He was very fond of his mother,' says Peter Charlesworth. 'I met her on several occasions. He brought her to shows and we went to lunch together. She was an ordinary woman, and completely bewildered by the success, but very proud of him. Benny was incapable of a deep emotional display, though.' Gladys Green, firmly ensconced as the Hills' cleaner – the lady who 'does' – at 22 Westrow Gardens, remarks, 'I could tell that Mrs Hill absolutely worshipped Benny. She did. And he worshipped her. He used to call her lovely names, "my darling", "my precious" and so on. And they'd often have their arms around each other. He wasn't so close with Mr Hill.'

Indeed he was not.

'It's not that Benny and his father weren't "close",' says Peter Charlesworth, 'it was worse than that. There was a definite gap between them. But he never discussed it very much. What he did was suffer inwardly.' Benny had conferred with his brother though. Len later wrote that when he and Benny visited Paris together in 1948, Benny had been uncharacteristically outspoken about The Captain, using 'explicit language'. Swearwords were something that few ever heard Benny utter. On this occasion, as the elder brother, Len had seen fit to reproach Benny about speaking ill of their father, a situation that almost defines the proverb about the black pot and the kettle.

In 1955, having sold condoms and fitted trusses for forty-three years, before and beyond two world wars, Big Alf finally left Stanley's employ. Jack Stanley had latterly died and Alf did not get on with his widow. It was time, finally, to retire. Despite the strained relationship, Benny sought to provide a regular stipend for his father, to supplement the government's basic pension. It was an income that the habitually thrifty Big Alf did not spend – instead, he went into business as an unregistered money lender. 'He had plenty enough to loan out,' says Hugh Stevens, 'and yet whenever we went on holiday he was still very careful. If he could get a stale cake for 3d instead of a fresh one for 6d he would take it every time.'

The financial arrangement between father and son, which went through Benny's accounts for tax relief purposes, was given an official front, leading to this highly unlikely, indeed preposterous, article in Southampton's newspaper, the *Southern Daily Echo*, in January 1955:

> If Benny Hill soon revives the old catchphrase 'I'll have to ask me Dad!' it will be for a good reason.
>
> His father, Mr A. H. Hill, who lives at 22, Westrow-gardens, Southampton, has become his manager.
>
> Said Mr Hill, senior, this week: 'My first job as Benny's manager will be a trip to Australia to explore the possibilities of a tour. I'm going to see theatrical agents out there and find out how show-business is.'

Richard Stone had nothing to fear. He remained Benny's sole agent, and the role of 'manager' was strictly honorary. The trip to Australia was actually nothing more than Alf and Helen's first visit to Diana since her emigration.

All the same, the man who had for so long given Benny cause to revolt, and also spurned and been hugely disparaging of his career aspirations, had performed a sudden and most surprising *volte-face*. 'As soon as Alfie became famous He Loved His Son,' says Florence Jaques. 'He was welcomed everywhere as The Father Of Benny Hill.'

Numerous others who knew the history were also aghast at The Captain's about-turn. 'He always carried a picture of Alfie in his breast-pocket and he'd bring it out in company,' says Bill Jaques. 'He called it his "passport", guaranteed to open any door. "This is My Son," he would announce. "I've always loved him."'

11. The Harvester

For almost forty years, until his death, Benny Hill's most valued possession was his passport. Travelling was the one luxury he consistently permitted himself.

Ever since the war, when he had served in France, he had become a first-degree Francophile. Subsequent trips to Paris had only hardened his resolve to explore the country as frequently as possible. More than this, it was his bolt-hole. As he became famous in Britain so he escaped to his beloved France at every opportunity, eventually discovering the Camargue. He could lose himself in the Rhône delta, and when he first went to Marseilles he felt he had found heaven on earth. The important and historic south-coast port became a second home to the Southamptonian – he enjoyed soaking up the atmosphere of the old quarter and the harbour, and taking a boat across to the Île d'If to peruse its famous castle. 'He absolutely loved Marseilles,' declares Anne Bruzac, a French actress who later worked with Benny on TV. 'He used to commute from Arles to Marseilles practically every day, always using public transport.'

Benny travelled in a uniquely individual fashion. Although he stayed occasionally in grand hotels, he was more at ease in the cheap backstreet pensions, away from the throng and in touch with everyman. And though he might occasionally treat himself to a first-class flight, no airport porter ever had to struggle with Benny Hill's luggage. Not for him a matching set of suitcases. These indicated 'taste', and Benny had little. They also indicated the accoutrements of wealth, and much of Benny's was stuffed into the sock drawer or tucked behind Mephistopheles on his mantelpiece back home.

Working the weekly Variety circuit from the age of seventeen, he was used to travelling light, his bits and pieces packed into no more than a battered case or a couple of carrier-bags, and the one constant in the life of Benny Hill, true in every respect, was that he never altered his habits. Everyone who knew him in these last forty years says the same: when Benny popped overseas, sometimes staying for several months at a time, he took only the clothes he was wearing. Arriving at his destination, he would buy a new shirt and underwear and wash the dirty clothes in a sink. His cousin's wife, Florence Jaques, remembers how Benny explained his technique – '"I dry things on the mirror," he told me. As a new housewife I looked at him and said, "What do you mean 'on the mirror?'" And he replied, "Well, you don't need to iron them." I tried it myself. He was quite serious – that was the way he conducted his laundry.'

Benny took a great shine to French people. Anne Bruzac says that he knew everything about prominent Frenchmen, and that he could converse extensively about French literature. 'His knowledge was astounding,' she says. He also loved French food. Benny's idea of paradise was to sit at a café table, with some pâtisseries to sate the Hill sweet-tooth, and perhaps a glass of wine – though he was no great drinker at this point in his life – and while away the hours, observing the passers-by from behind a pair of sunglasses. Anonymity was irrelevant for him in these early years, though. His fame had yet to extend beyond the United Kingdom.

The ability to exist without recognition was paramount to Benny. Ann Croft, an agent working in Richard Stone's office, knew the score. 'He was so sexually insecure that it was better for him to meet up with women who didn't know who he was,' she says. 'Hence Marseilles. The women there did not know him, not until the 1980s anyway, and he could socialize with people who wouldn't "report back". This was the quiet side of Benny Hill's life, the side that none of us knew.'

Benny spoke French and several other languages – Spanish, German, Dutch and Italian among them – passably well, gaining a reasonable level of understanding of vocabulary, basic grammar and, above all, the cadences. Some skills he acquired from old 78rpm records that he picked up for a few shillings at a London market – Berlitz-like 'Teach Yourself' courses that require the student to listen and repeat phrases. Here was an extraordinarily single-minded individual, a man who also would go to bed in London listening to French radio, a good deal of which he couldn't fully comprehend, as it ebbed and flowed over the long-wave.

In the light of Benny's oft-voiced quip, 'I can get my face slapped in half a dozen languages', it came to be accepted that he spoke these fluently. In reality he did not, though he could certainly 'get by'. Mastering foreign languages was beyond Benny. His cousin Hugh Stevens, who emigrated to Australia, went on to run the language department at Melbourne High School, and they often discussed the subject. 'Really, he just had an ear for accent,' says Stevens. 'He made no bones about it – he told me that he only gave the impression that he could speak them. He said that going through the declensions of nouns, and working out inflexions, was a total mystery to him.'

Stevens notes, too, how quick Benny was to use these skills for his comedy. 'If you're talking in an Irish accent you can say all sorts of things that you wouldn't dream of saying in your own tongue. You can get away with things, because it's not you talking, "it's that Paddy-feller". Benny became excellent at giving the impression of a Chinaman speaking Chinese or a German speaking German – in the same way that a mime artist can give the impression of pushing into the wind. An accent becomes another aspect of the mask.'

There was a further, key element to Benny's overseas jaunts. Though none could deny that he genuinely loved France, and Spain, and Belgium, and Holland, and Germany, and the Far East, and Australia, and numerous points in between, these trips were also gathering missions. In France and Spain especially, he sought out the cabaret clubs and the circuses, and there he witnessed swaying fields of ripened comedy ideas, jokes and sketches completely unknown in Britain.

This was Benny the Harvester. His pen was his scythe and he reaped 'new' ideas by the cartload, scribbling them on to whatever scrap of paper came to hand – serviettes, menus, the cardboard stiffener from that new shirt. It was typical of Benny that, though his cropping mission was conscious, he never thought to buy a notebook. He was happy to scrawl around the margins of a newspaper.

For Benny, a day in Paris would begin with a long, brisk walk, then he might stop for a glass of wine to make the day sparkle, walk a few hours more, stop for lunch and a coffee, tearing out the comic strips from the French newspapers, catch a bus somewhere and at night be at a circus or floor-show, pen at the ready. There were plenty of venues to choose from – the Lido, Moulin Rouge, Olympia, Casino, Crazy Horse, Folies Bergère, the ABC music-hall in Montmartre, the Bobino music-hall in Montparnasse. And he would see not only comics but also the *ooh la la* of naked women who, unlike in Britain, moved on stage. 'What really fascinated Benny was that in one club they had nudes who ate biscuits,' says Dave Freeman. 'Instead of standing there posing, like in England, they'd be moving around the stage *munching*. He thought that was wonderful.'

As previously noted, Benny had no compunction about exploiting the work of other comedians. He saw it as fair game, rarely hid the fact ('I steal all my shows,' he would say) and raised no objection if anyone appropriated his ideas. (Though very few did.) Benny had been using other comics' work since his earliest Eastleigh days. Every newcomer does it to a certain extent before going on to develop his own style. The arrival on British radio of AFN had then widened the scope considerably, enabling him and others to reach across the Atlantic for gags, but he was alone in turning to the European continent for ideas. Bob Monkhouse, for one, was fascinated with his friend's new discovery. 'I thought how smart it was of Benny to seek his inspiration in Europe,' he says. 'The British somehow didn't pay any attention to what was going on there. People were far more conscious of the possibility of ripping off, say, Jack Benny or Bob Hope.'

Already a passionate devotee of the great silent-film and early talkie comedians – Chaplin, Keaton, Lloyd, Langdon, Laurel and Hardy, Fields – Benny Hill now added continental mime to his repertoire: the genius of Marcel Marceau and his many imitators, and the scatological, visual humour of the French dialogue-free movie creator Jacques Tati, whose *Monsieur Hulot* films Benny adored. From this point, a good deal of Hill's comedy would be silent. He little knew it, and he certainly did not seek it, but this, above all else, would provide the key to his eventual global domination.

Of course, there was also a third element to Benny Hill's comedy, the most fundamental ingredient of them all, his obsession with sex. For the quintessential Benny blend, one must take the essence of Chaplin and Hardy, and Marceau and Tati, and add what has been – too easily, perhaps – labelled as British 'seaside-postcard' humour: young parlour-maids with pointy breasts and skimpy knickers, voluptuous older women with bouncing boobs and parachute-size drawers, fat old horrible harridans with rollered-hair and rolling-pins, meek and weedy men quivering under female domination, a double-entendre in every gaze and line.

While much of Hill's comedy does echo saucy 'postcard' humour, and some of his jokes were certainly 'postcard' in origin –

Man Do you like Kipling?

Woman (suggestively) I don't know, you naughty boy, I've never kippled.

– this was more because he was an inveterate lifter of gag material from every source imaginable, postcards included, than any particular influence by the likes of Donald McGill, the courteous Victorian gentleman who, fantastically, challenged establishment prudery with his colourfully crude cards – at the expense, that is, of being considered 'poor taste'. Hill, like McGill, merely disseminated the prevailing domestic humour of recent centuries – that oh-so-British blend of smut, sauce and suggestion.

More than in postcards, Benny Hill's leering comedy was rooted in the Variety stage, where many seemingly mild-mannered comedians, acting as if they were stags, brashly hinted at sex and ogled at women but when faced with the genuine prospect of intimacy would stammer, not stiffen. From the age of twelve, when he had been exposed to the innuendo and simpering 'subtlety' of Variety comics at Southampton Hippodrome, and indeed glimpsed the stockings and suspenders of their 'French maid' accomplices, this was Benny's very own humour.

It also suited his lifestyle to a tee. Benny was fixated on being seen with beautiful women off stage as well as on, implying that he could (and did) take who he liked – when, in reality, riven by insecurity, he shrank at the prospect. No matter what those big blue saucer-eyes lecherously suggested on screen, Benny Hill would have been the last man on earth to rip a woman's clothes off and force himself upon her.

Since childhood, Benny had developed a quite remarkable fund of comedy knowledge. According to Dave Freeman, 'He had a fixation about it. He ate, drank and slept comedy routines and had an encyclopedic knowledge of every performer, old and new – film, music-hall, radio and TV people, mostly ones I'd never heard of. He could tell me their history and who they'd worked with. He wasn't very interested in anything else, to be honest.'

By adding the essentially visual comedy of the Continent, Benny enlarged that reservoir exponentially. When he talked of 'writing comedy sketches at café tables', as he frequently did, he was, in reality, usually noting down an English or anglicized translation of a French or Spanish comedian's act he had seen in a club or circus the night before, or conceiving a new routine based closely upon it. 'Benny wasn't really a writer,' declares Brian Tesler, a senior British TV producer and executive for almost fifty years, director of some Benny Hill shows in the late 1950s and later responsible for his switch from the BBC to Thames Television. 'He was a *compiler*, a collector of bits and pieces, a recycler of jokes – old dirty jokes particularly.' The talent lay in the interpretation, and this was an aptitude Benny had in abundance.

In the 1950s, Benny's expressed penchant for 'writing abroad' caught the imagination of a British public still unfamiliar either with comedians who wrote their own material, or for that matter with people travelling overseas for any peaceable reason. This was still before the era of the package-holiday. 'Benny Hill Goes to Paris – to Write a Script!' declared the headline of a *TV Times* feature in 1957. In this interview, Benny was at pains to maintain the allure of his continental handiwork, drawing a veil over the fact that he was purloining as much as he was creating:

Yes, it's easy to write in Paris, and this lark gives me a double thrill every time I'm booked for TV. I must have a script – so Paree here I come again. I write much better abroad . . . One of the best programmes I've ever done was dreamed up in Paris. There's so much to write about. It makes scripting easy.

Waxing lyrical about his method of working, and perhaps also giving a clue to concern over the cost of such trips, he further explained:

But I have a conscience, and I have to live with it. I call it Charlie. If I write a script in Paris then I've justified my trip, and Charlie is clear.

One way of appeasing Charlie was to disguise the provenance of the material. To conform the work to his own style, Benny rarely lifted a total comedy routine, preferring instead to adopt and adapt. 'He was unhappy just to use an idea unless he could improve it, enlarge it and polish it,' observes Bob Monkhouse. 'I thought it was like taking somebody else's bike and turning it into a motor-bike, or even into a Rolls-Royce. He became a walking warehouse of ideas and tricks and gags that he accumulated. If he had just replicated them exactly, or weakly, we wouldn't be talking about him today.'

Benny's bent for French material was quickly evident. In the second edition of *The Benny Hill Show*, televised in February 1955, he and Beryl Reid (who supported throughout) performed a musical comedy piece, without dialogue, in which they changed into swimsuits in adjacent bathing-boxes, singing snatches of a love song and idealizing one another – until they see each other. Critics piled on the superlatives, *The Stage* considering it 'delightfully witty' and 'straight from the intimate revue school'. The reviewer did not know how right this was – nine months later, in November 1955, the French comic/entertainer Robert Dhéry brought his successful Paris revue *La Plume de Ma Tante* to the Garrick Theatre in London and there was the bathing-huts routine. Benny had seen it in Paris and brought it to England before its originator. Feeling no guilt, Benny praised Dhéry in numerous interviews, perhaps believing that he had smoothed a path for the Frenchman's success across the Channel. 'Benny loved Robert Dhéry,' comments Dave Freeman. 'He made sure to change the bathing-huts routine a little before doing it, and then he did variations of it for ever more.' (Another continental comedian whom Benny much admired, and from whom he stole – again, his own word – was the versatile Dutchman Wim Sonneveld, whom he saw in Amsterdam and in a 1959 BBC TV show.)

Even before he went to France, two of Benny's principal comedy characters had been liberated from a previous existence. Toto, his German pal with the splayed ears and pidgin-English, who had first surfaced in 1946, was similar in several respects to a German who formed part of Jack Warner's canon of characters, Professor Schtopundschtart. Warner was not at all happy about it. Benny once remarked to Dave Freeman, 'I saw Jack Warner the other day, said "Hello" and, do you know, he walked away!' This may, too, be indicative of Warner's personality – Bob Monkhouse observes, 'For such a genial man on screen it was astonishing how mean-spirited he could be about young performers. He once gave me a drubbing for telling a "disgusting" joke about a woman – "Both her sisters were bow-legged and she was knock-kneed. When she stood in the middle it spelled OXO." It took some figuring out but I liked it.' (So did Benny Hill – he too used this gag in radio and TV appearances.)

In 1954, when he rose to fame in the BBC series *Showcase*, Benny unveiled a new comic character, one who would serve him admirably for forty years. Though initially named Ben Bloggs, this was the gormless but cheerfully optimistic Fred Scuttle – an inept northern nitwit in 'granny-glasses', his tongue protruding through lisping lips, a man inexplicably appointed to a position of authority in some business or other, masterminding Britain's space effort, for example, or running the BBC's audience research department. (His first TV appearance was as a wheelbarrow tester, the first sketch written for Benny by Dave Freeman – 'He sent me five quid for it and said if I had any more ideas I should let him know.') Fred had not yet learned to salute – that daft horizontal hand to the temple he enacted when he didn't know what else to do or say – nor did he yet exclaim, 'Good evening, viewers!', but he quickly became an established part of every Hill TV show, baffling *Showcase* straightman Jeremy Hawk with his non-sequiturs, as he would Hawk's successors in future decades. All had their reasons to be thankful for the creation. Says Hawk, 'You knew the Scuttle sketch was going to rescue anything that had gone badly before, and he did it very well.' Nicholas Parsons reflects how Scuttle 'Always talked in terrible music-hall type language but was a fabulous character for allowing Benny to recycle old material'. Henry McGee saw in Scuttle 'An absolute fool who thinks he knows everything, a way of sending up the establishment, or bureaucracy at any rate'.

It is a widely held view that Benny found Scuttle somewhere, that he did not create him, but the precise provenance has remained foggy. The answer could reside in a comedy persona created by the sketch comedian Horace Kenney. Born in 1889, Kenney was a contemporary of Charlie Chaplin and Stan Laurel in Fred Karno's Variety troupe at the start of the twentieth century, and a stalwart of early British broadcasting, recording and the Variety stage. Kenney invented a character who, like Fred Scuttle, was rather gentle and quietly pathetic, a downtrodden soul. (He, too, required a feed and a situation.)

What follows is an excerpt from Kenney's sketch 'Almost a Film Actor', issued on record by EMI[1] in 1930.

> **Producer** What kind of parts have you played?
> **Kenney** I've played all parts, sir.
> **Producer** All kinds?
> **Kenney** Yes sir, all kinds.
> **Producer** Have you ever played leads?
> **Kenney** Leeds, Sheffield, Manchester . . .

With his encyclopedic comedy knowledge, Benny certainly knew of Horace Kenney – he referred to him, in passing, in a couple of press interviews. And the above dialogue is certainly Scuttle-like, with its superfluous obsequiousness, though Benny – the man who took pains to adopt and adapt – delivered the material far more robustly. The leads/Leeds joke was one that came up, verbatim, in several Hill sketches.

In the wake of his *Showcase* success and Personality of the Year award, 1955 and 1956 were ludicrously hectic years for Benny Hill. He starred in his first 'own' television series, which cemented his previous success. He starred for eighteen months, twice nightly, in a successful West End of London stage production – and hated virtually every minute of it. And he also starred in his first movie, an experience that Benny enjoyed but the critics and public patently did not. By the end of this period he was exhausted, and emerged determined that he would never again work at such a pace.

The Benny Hill Show was launched on BBC TV in January 1955, produced by Kenneth Carter, broadcast live from Television Theatre in west London, and with the eye-catching credit 'written by Benny Hill' – a not entirely accurate billing in more ways than one, as Dave Freeman was beginning to make a sizeable but at this point unaccredited contribution. The shows were hour-long, monthly, and Benny committed to no more than three programmes in this first season. Straight away, he had established a pattern of working that would remain more or less unchanged for the next thirty-five years.

The problem with these early editions, especially the première, was that there simply wasn't enough of Benny on screen. Because the shows were live and his comedy was by now entirely character-driven, the bill had to be extensively padded in order to provide time for his costume changes and makeup.

What there was of Benny was impressive, however, especially – in this first edition – one of the staples of his recent stage act, a medieval skit in which he played all seven roles and where everything went intentionally wrong. (The great English Variety comedian Sid Field performed something similar.) Benny arrived on the set as a prisoner, a ball-and-chain around his leg, and then went off to fetch another character. The sound of unintelligible cursing and banging then arose from backstage as he tried to remove the shackle. Unable to do so, he came back as the next character with the great ball 'hidden' inside his costume. Another element of the sketch, which he would recycle time and again, was an elaborate death scene that had to be undone when he realized he had still to come back as one of the other characters, rising from the floor to exclaim, 'I'm . . . not quite dead, but ever so nearly, I'll go now and die in some other place.' Benny's absence from much of the show led to some criticism, but *The Stage* gave its usual wholly positive review and called this sketch 'easily his funniest business'. It also singled out a 'guy' of the BBC's primitive yet oddly compelling children's puppet series *The Flowerpot Men*. In the wake of his *What's My Line?* success, spoofing other programmes had become a prerequisite for *The Benny Hill Show*. His 'research' for these entailed nothing more than constant scrutiny of television itself; when he wasn't out working, he could usually be found plumped in front of his set, making notes.

After the third and final programme for now, Ronald Waldman, still the BBC's Head of Light Entertainment, Television, wrote to the star:

22nd March 1955

My dear Benny
    This is a belated, but none the less very sincere letter of thanks to you for your series.
    As you must know, it was a really first-class job and fully justified everything that we have been dreaming about you for the last two

years! I need hardly tell you how very much we are looking forward to having some more shows from you later in the year[2] and there are many millions of people who are feeling the same.

As *Showcase* had proven, Benny Hill's popularity with the British TV audience at this point was universal – across the classes and generations. Even though he was prone to be 'saucy', he traded on a larky, good-natured, boy-next-door image, epitomized by his cheeky looks and grin, and his comedy remained, at times, pioneering for the small-screen. It was not yet embarrassing for anyone to admit to watching his show – unlike in his final years, when his comedy was anathema to many, and where his typical viewing audience in Britain was male-oriented and, in advertising terms, mostly downmarket and 'tabloid'. The excesses that marked many of those later shows were reined back by director Kenneth Carter and by the restraints of pre-1960s permissibility, leaving scope only for pure comedy. Not everything worked, but much of it did.

Though he was now the centrepiece of BBC light entertainment – his own-name show, primetime Saturday night – Benny was still a relative newcomer to the television medium, with fewer than thirty appearances under his belt. There were still some rough Variety edges to be smoothed, and Carter remained vital to Benny's continued progress. Jeremy Hawk observed the two closely and states, 'Kenneth had so much influence. I was there when he said, "You can't be picking your nose and kissing a girl at the same time, Benny, that's vulgar. It's not funny, it's disgusting." I don't think Benny would have ended up the star he was if he hadn't had Kenny or someone like him to present him at his best, because he wasn't at his best in the end – he was indulged and undisciplined. That's why I didn't like later Benny Hill shows – that vulgarity. I kept saying to myself "Kenny would have cut that." '

Under Carter's watchful eye, and with the tide of public goodwill behind him, Benny had only to come up with the right material for assured, continued success. Using some of his best tried and trusted jokes, including plenty from those old reliable gag books ('Don't let anyone kid you that a book of gags isn't essential,' Benny openly declared in February 1955), performing more 'guys' of TV programmes and some fine new Scuttle sketches written – anonymously still – by Dave Freeman, Benny had the right mix. He impressed critics and audiences alike with his willingness to play the fool and participate in everything going, even classical ballet sequences. An ever-interesting aspect of his shows was the comedy song, where Benny's ability to pen a witty lyric – his talent alone, not borrowed – remained a particularly strong suit. And he added a further dimension to the scripts, too – a deliberate 'dispute' with Bob Monkhouse that attracted considerable press and public comment.

In America, Fred Allen and Jack Benny, and also Bob Hope and Bing Crosby, frequently indulged in good-natured slanging matches. In Britain, Frankie Howerd and Derek Roy were taking pot-shots at one another over the radio airwaves, as were Ben Lyon and Vic Oliver. (In later years, Morecambe and Wise and Des O'Connor would do it, too.) The ground for another war of words seemed occupied, but Hill and Monkhouse pulled it off, to the pronounced benefit of both. 'Benny was very nervous to begin with because insults weren't his style,' says Monkhouse. 'But a lot of people reacted to it. I'd get calls saying, "I saw Benny Hill on TV last night having a go at you," and then he'd get the same thing. We were phoning one another gleefully.'

Benny even turned up in Monkhouse's TV series, *Fast and Loose!*[3] where the two ding-donged face to face:

Bob I have your fee with me at this moment. (Removes sixpence from ear and hands it to Benny.) Don't spend it all at once, Belly.

Benny That's *Benny*.

Bob Not from where I'm standing.

Benny That's ridiculous. I'm so slim and lissom my fans refer to me as Bony Hill. Remember that in future, Blob.

Bob That's *Bob*.

Benny Not from where I'm standing, Boob.

Bob Call me Robert.

Benny All right. You were saying, Rabbit?

Bob I didn't say a thing, Bunny. Let's stop this arguing, Bummy. After all, Christmas is coming and you're not the only goose that's getting fat . . .

The 'feud' furthered the fledgling careers of both men, and it only ended when Benny decided he'd had enough. 'Benny stopped doing it so it seemed ridiculous for me to continue,' Monkhouse says. 'My feeling is that Benny already knew he was destined for greater things than I could achieve, so that remaining at my level in a feud was not going to benefit him. In the nicest way, I mean. I don't think he would ever think as unkindly as I've just expressed it, he just felt "I'm moving into a different area for myself" and I understood that completely, it's entirely practical.'

Except that Benny never did quite leave it be. The recycler in him saw no reason why some of the pot-shots could not be aimed a second time. In two 1980s TV shows he lobbed friendly grenades in Monkhouse's direction. One sketch, in which a schoolmaster read out comical pupil names, included 'Monkhouse, B. F.; Monkhouse, O. L.; Monkhouse, Y.?'[4] In another, a woman thumped her television because the picture had gone fuzzy; when Monkhouse's face appeared on screen she thumped it again to bring back the fuzziness. 'All comedy depends upon choosing your targets correctly,' laughs Monkhouse. 'I'm proud that it was still me.'

The 'different area' that Monkhouse observed Benny moving into was the stage. The theatre had never been kind to Benny Hill, though goodness knows he had tried for long enough to be successful, slogging his way around the decrepit Variety halls of Britain over fifteen years. All the same, confident though his TV success must have left him, it remains surprising that he should have allowed Richard Stone to cut a long-term deal with Bernard Delfont, the leading stage impresario of the period. The contract would see him star in two major West End productions and a couple of extensive summer seasons at seaside resorts over the next four years, effectively tying up the rest of the decade.

The first of these was *Paris by Night*, a Folies Bergère revue that combined French glamour with British stars; it opened in the West End, at the Prince of Wales Theatre, in April 1955. Delfont was a long-term supporter of the famed Folies Bergère, bringing it to England in 1949 – Benny toured the Variety theatres with one such show in 1952 – and then promoting two West End productions: *Paris to Piccadilly*, starring Norman Wisdom, and *Pardon My French*, with Frankie Howerd. Supporting Benny Hill in *Paris by Night* was Tommy Cooper, another rising comedy star of

Top: 'Don't let anyone kid you that a book of gags isn't essential.' The magpie comedian blithely plugs one of the prime sources of his material, 1955.

Above: Surrounded by leggy dancers for the very first *Benny Hill Show*, January 1955. With skimpier costumes, the photo could be from any subsequent decade.

Top left: Benny and his friend, the writer Dave Freeman, whose handiwork anonymously embellished Benny's career long after their professional relationship ended.

Top right: Benny with comic-actress Beryl Reid and his first steady straightman, the actor Jeremy Hawk; *The Benny Hill Show*, January 1955.

Above: 'You could hear the hoof-beats pound as they raced across the ground . . .' Benny relives his Eastleigh milk round, 1956.

Top left: The saucy boy, his end-of-the-pier predilections firmly established.

Top right: Three bathing beauties and one imposter. The opening titles for
The Benny Hill Show, November 1957.

Above: Surveying the medium of his success. This photo, and the previous 'gag book'
shot, were taken inside Benny's new Maida Vale apartment in 1955.

Opposite, top: Benny with the woman he could have married, Doris Deal, seated front, left. He procrastinated so long that she ended the relationship. Benny's close friend Peter Charlesworth is seated front right.

Opposite, bottom: Pushing the boat out: dinner with Annette André at the London Hilton. If Benny proposed to her, she scarcely noticed.

Above: An on-set embrace from actress Elaine Taylor; *The Benny Hill Show*, 1965. Off set, she proved more elusive and Benny's heart broke once more.

Right: Benny's friendship with Phoebe King – and also with another disabled woman, Netta Warner – spanned almost forty years, unbeknown to even his close friends until near the end.

The 1960s. Twenty years a TV performer, Benny Hill attempts to branch out.

Top left: Talking to BBC broadcaster John Ellison and producer Rosemary Hart at Queen's Gate. (Quotes from this radio interview appear in the book.)

Top right: 'I like them big. *BIG!*' Benny gets to grips with the part in *The Italian Job*.

Above: With Dick Van Dyke and Sally Ann Howes in *Chitty Chitty Bang Bang*.

Top left: A rare change of role – as a brutish servant in *The Waiters*, the short film Benny again hoped would enable him to ditch television.

Top right: The defining moment in Benny's autobiographical comedy, the dialogue-free *Eddie in August*. His pursuit of the beautiful nurse ends in rejection as she meets her manly lover.

Above left: The aspiring director, in his carpet slippers.

Above right: The man who knew everyone's job, finally a union-recognized director.

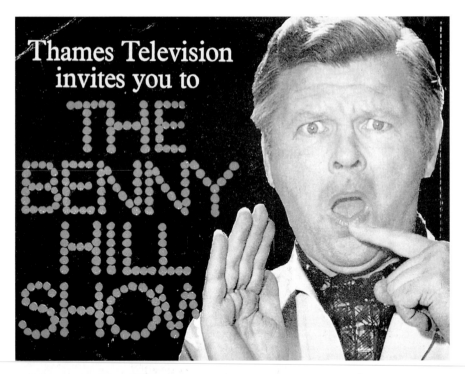

Thames Television invites you to THE BENNY HILL SHOW

After fourteen years on the BBC, *The Benny Hill Show* switches to Thames, where even greater success beckons. New straightman Henry McGee now has to contend with two imbeciles: Chow-Mein, the inscrutable Chinaman, a character stolen outright from the American comic Buddy Hackett, and the twerp Fred Scuttle.

the post-war period whose act, mostly visual, was that of the failed magician, the giant man in the daft fez unable to complete even the simplest of conjuring tricks. (This was a ruse – Cooper was actually a fine magician.)

Benny also enjoyed the support of straightman Jeremy Hawk, and a cast packed with a miscellany of performers typical of the continental cabaret he always enjoyed. These included the chanteuse Claudine Céréda (whom he had previously admired in Paris), a Hawaiian knife-throwing dance act, a rubber-jointed 'gollywog' novelty piece and all the rudiments of a Parisian Folies Bergère revue – strutting showgirls bedecked in plumes, and an array of topless women. These, of course, had to remain motionless, standing stock-still in a number of tableaux, usually set in 'windows' a few feet above the stage, while others, their breasts just about covered, pranced around the dais to brassy music.

For a short while, Benny enjoyed being a West End star. This was Prestige, and with it came maximum publicity and commensurate compensation. Not that he cared for the money; he travelled by bus to the theatre every afternoon. Maurice Chevalier was in the audience on the opening night and he and Benny chatted comfortably about great French entertainers. Benny was also delighted to have the services of a 'dresser', Bertie Lind, a comedian of the 1920s who, in his present capacity, had worked with many a great star. The comedy enthusiast in Benny relished listening to all the stories.

The appeal quickly evaporated, however. Benny still carried virtually no stage presence, and the Prince of Wales – between Piccadilly Circus and Leicester Square – is a large auditorium, seating over 1,100. Worse, Tommy Cooper was going over much better with the audiences, especially when he produced his 'hats' routine so beloved of TV viewers in later years. ('The evening's one first-rate thing,' considered *The Times*.) Peter Charlesworth agonized for his friend. 'Benny hadn't realized how difficult it would be, and every night he used to go on and loathe it. Tommy would paralyse the audience, mostly because he was visual and had marvellous bits of business, but nobody laughed at Benny's sketches, especially the long one at the end. He would sway on stage, almost fainting, with perspiration running down his neck.'

Benny had several pieces in the show, and the best received was his

'Dress Parade' – a sketch he later performed several times on television – in which a number of beautiful women sashayed on to model some new outfits, and then on strode Benny as a camp male model, sporting some odd garb.

Once the show had bedded in, it became part of the London tourist circuit, and the audiences comprised greater numbers of foreigners, men tempted into the theatre by the prospect of seeing topless women on stage. 'Benny only got laughs with the visual stuff,' says Dave Freeman. 'The Japanese couldn't understand the patter at all. But Tommy Cooper still went over terrifically because it was *all* visual. Benny hated it. He used to wake up in the nights with a cold sweat and think that no one would laugh at him.'

Coach parties made up significant sections of the twice-nightly audience. The Sports and Social Club section from Dorset Dairies – ex-James Hann & Son – made a trip to London expressly to see their former milkman colleague, a deputation venturing backstage to glad-hand him. Back-slapping and photo opportunities were part and parcel of starring in a West End show but rarely had a star been as reticent as this one, or so desperate for his show to finish. Quite apart from his pathological dislike of the stage, Benny was never one for doing the same thing night after night. 'I think he enjoyed the girls, but he hated going to the theatre six nights a week for months on end,' says Richard Stone. 'It was the sheer monotony of it. Benny was a creative man but once the script had been approved by the Lord Chamberlain's office, it couldn't be varied.'

With his interest in the psychological aspects of comedy, Bob Monkhouse paid a visit to the Prince of Wales and was immediately questioned by his friend. 'Benny said, "I have great difficulty with gestures. Do you have that, Bob? Do you find it difficult to make a natural gesture when you're on stage?" His own analysis was, "It's not me going out there. I'm in the wings." So one of us came up with the fact that he was not the jester, he was the jester's messenger, or he was the puppet to the puppet master who was in the wings, pulling the strings. But it didn't have much effect.'

'Benny could do good impressions but never be himself,' remarks Peter Charlesworth. 'He could never go out on stage and say "Good evening, ladies and gentlemen. A funny thing happened to me on the way to the theatre tonight . . ." And he was also upset that when Noël Coward and Tyrone Guthrie stopped by the theatre they did so to visit Jeremy Hawk, their fellow actor. He moaned, "They didn't come near me."' Benny knew his limitations, and *Paris by Night* was a step too far, but he was under contract for the duration – possibly as long as two years. There was also the nerve-racking honour of appearing before the Queen and Prince Philip in the Royal Variety Show – this was held on November 7 1955 at the Victoria Palace, London, and Benny performed two extracts from *Paris by Night* and sang a madrigal. (In the same show, Robert Dhéry and his supporting company worked a scene from *La Plume de Ma Tante*, so Benny got to meet his hero.)

As if performing twice-nightly at the Prince of Wales and arriving home after midnight every night was not tiring enough, Benny also spent the summer of 1955 getting up at six o'clock every morning to rush to Ealing Studios, where he was shooting his first movie, *Who Done It?* He'd have been better advised to stay in bed. The British film industry has made some terrible comedies in its time, and this is very much one of them.

Television had caught the British public's imagination in a manner unenvisaged by those in other spheres of entertainment. The American colloquialism 'couch-potato' had yet to be coined but this is what it was: Britons preferred staying in to going out. TV had killed off Variety, put the knife into dancing, decimated crowds at many sporting events – Benny's beloved speedway, which drew huge attendances in the 1930s and 1940s, was on its knees by the late 1950s – and now it was strangling the cinema. Like Variety, the British movie business tried to shake hands with the enemy, hoping to draw people back into the Odeons, Classics and Essoldos by promoting TV stars. Right from when he was compère of the talent-spotting series *Showcase*, Ealing Studios, that fine but ailing west London production house, targeted Benny Hill as its saviour. The company, like the entire British film industry, badly needed one.

Producer and studio head Sir Michael Balcon recruited T. E. B. 'Tibby' Clarke to provide the script for Benny's first film. Clarke had written the acclaimed screenplays for *Hue and Cry*, *Passport to Pimlico*, *The Blue Lamp*, *The Lavender Hill Mob* and *The Titfield Thunderbolt* – droll observational comedies in which downtrodden people quietly rebelled against authority. He came close to blowing his reputation with *Who Done It?* though. Twenty years later, in his autobiography *This is Where I Came In,*[5] Clarke wrote, 'My authorship of *Who Done It?* is something I rarely let out of my skeleton cupboard.'

This was a shockingly bad film. Considering his impressive track record, Tibby Clarke must have dashed off the script in an afternoon. He seemed uncertain about whether or not he was writing a parody, and if irony was his intention he failed. The plot was weak and literally unbelievable; worse, for a comedy it barely raised a laugh. The direction, too, by Basil Dearden, was obvious and predictable. *Who Done It?* carries none of the charm of the great Ealing productions. As the last comedy made at the studio before it was sold to the BBC – ironically, Benny went on to create some of his best TV work here in the ensuing years – it was a sad epitaph.

To be fair, *Who Done It?* was not meant to replicate the subtlety that was the hallmark of Ealing's finest. Balcon, Clarke and Dearden were obviously possessed of a single, quaint idea – to make a throwback to the fast-paced, slapstick films of pre-war, the madcap movies starring George Formby and Will Hay. But this paid no regard to the cause of Benny Hill's television success, those subtle facial movements so accurately picked up and conveyed by the TV camera, nor indeed to his – not inconsiderable – talents as an actor. Bob Monkhouse was aware of Benny's ambition – 'He had in mind Red Skelton and every other good-looking young comedian whom he'd ever seen,' he says – but the script and direction conspired against him. In his autobiography, Tibby Clarke candidly admitted that Benny 'deserved a better break', while Richard Stone, with characteristic honesty, declares, 'It was entirely my fault. We had the greatest Ealing team and it just all went horribly wrong. I thought I'd done the best thing for Benny, but I hadn't.'

The only aspect of *Who Done It?* that in any way played to Benny's strengths was his dressing-up in a number of character guises – including an East European, a Jewish furniture salesman and a 'Primrose Hill'-like woman. All the same, he ended up drowning in his own film. Jeremy Hawk, who had a brief cameo role, speaks for many when he pronounces *Who Done It?* 'In every sense unmemorable, except to say it wasn't very good. What Benny was asked to do in this film didn't bring out the best in him at all. It did not encourage us to think that this was a future Bob Hope or a future Jack Benny.'

The screenplay, loosely based on a novel written by Clarke in 1938, *Two and Two Make Five*, had Benny cast as Hugo Dill, a clumsy ice-rink sweeper obsessed with cheapo thriller-detective novels. Of course, he's soon swept into just such an escapade himself – foiling a plot to ruin the British Empire, no less, by outwitting spies who seek to assassinate Britain's top scientists and control the weather system. The police chased Dill, Dill and his bloodhound chased the criminals. Love interest was provided by bottle-blonde bombshell Belinda Lee, cast as Frankie Mayne, but Tibby Clarke couldn't decide whether to make her a man-eater or a wailing, helpless female.

Rumours suggested that, off the set, Benny fell for the former Rank starlet and proposed marriage within two weeks of starting filming, but no one today can confirm their veracity. 'Benny was wont, in romantic moments, to propose to women out of a sense of guilt or honour,' submits Peter Charlesworth. 'He was engaged several times for half-an-hour.' The film ended with Dill and Mayne locked in a passionate snog, but Benny, if he was indeed romantically interested in Belinda Lee, achieved no such luck off-camera. (She was to die in a car crash in 1961, aged twenty-six.)

Ealing (and the distributors, Rank) must have known *Who Done It?* was a stinker for the film opened quietly, playing only a single week in the West End of London upon its release in March 1956 (and even then at a couple of the less important cinemas, the New Victoria and the Dominion) before heading out into the suburbs and provinces. Rank's advertising blurb – 'Benny Hill joyously granting your every laughter wish in his first uproarious screen comedy!' – was complemented by one or two kind reviews, the *Daily Sketch* enthusing that the film 'Packs more gags into each of its 85 minutes than any offering since Mack Sennett's Keystone Cops', but wiser heads prevailed. Writing in the *Sunday Times* the venerable Dilys Powell pronounced *Who Done It?* 'a sad bundle', while *Variety*, the American trade journal which Benny Hill read avidly, considered 'the situations and stock ingredients corny'. Moreover, a short comedy B-feature written by Benny about the life of a milkman, filmed on his old round in Eastleigh the previous month, was never used; the Hampshire town was proud of its Benny Hill associations, but even here

Who Done It? played at the Picture House ('the cinema at which he was once a regular patron', boasted the local *Weekly News*) for just three days.

Just as *Paris by Night* had served to underline to Benny Hill that he was better off sticking to television, *Who Done It?* was a major personal disappointment. It remains, justifiably, one of the few British post-war comedies not promoted on video or trotted out on television. (On one rare occasion when it was scheduled for TV, Benny quickly announced that he was 'off to Marseilles'.) He would go on to appear in several more films but never as the main attraction. As a movie star, Benny Hill had shot his bolt, and, says Richard Stone, the effect was permanent – 'The total box-office failure didn't do Benny any good in the film industry. Nobody came running [to us] after that.'

All this time – before, during and beyond the film's making, beyond even its release – Benny continued to grind out twice-nightly performances in *Paris by Night*. Another who journeyed to see him at the Prince of Wales was Harry Segal, his *Stars in Battledress* saviour. Benny was helping a number of old Variety pros who had hit bad times, Segal included, suggesting they send him gags on a scrap of paper for which he then paid well over the odds, usually £100 – his way of taking care of friends down on their luck. But Segal was distressed over Benny's *Paris by Night* predicament, later noting, 'It was filling the theatre, packed every night, but Benny was not happy in it. All he wanted to do was to get back into television.'

Eventually, Hill could take no more and begged Bernard Delfont to bring down the curtain. Delfont had not become the show-business mogul he was by letting people off the hook so easily. His brother, Lew Grade, was managing director of Associated TeleVision (ATV), one of the companies that comprised ITV, Britain's new commercial network. Benny was forced to commit to eight hour-long shows for ATV from 1957 to 1960, a decision that greatly angered the BBC. But with this, and a special performance of *Paris by Night* for the ITV cameras, the Prince of Wales show eventually came to an end in September 1956, after seventeen months and 890 performances – almost all of them hated by its star.

12. 'He's good. Who is he?'

January 1957 brought the hugely anticipated return of *The Benny Hill Show* – primetime Saturday-night. The BBC recognized Hill's worth with a fee so large it required special dispensation: 500 guineas a show. It became 610 guineas in the next series.[1] Moreover, Dave Freeman, the giant ex-policeman, was now fully employed (and credited) as co-writer. The programme was about to enter its golden period.

Freeman's involvement brought an added dimension to *The Benny Hill Show*. He was providing entirely new material – and the lion's share, too, receiving 75 per cent of the total script fee. What he delivered, in essence, while not exactly sophistication (something no Benny Hill programme achieved – or especially sought), was simply a quality of writing – a finesse and slightly satirical edge entirely new to Benny's work. The Fred Scuttle sketches were better defined and the spoofs of other TV shows, the 'guys', became more adventurous – although their primary function remained the same, serving as 'wraparound' for sketches and songs that were otherwise unrelated and might equally have stood alone.

There were changes behind the scenes, too. While Benny had been despising *Paris by Night* and drowning in *Who Done It?* Kenneth Carter had (in BBC terms) 'defected' to ITV company Associated-Rediffusion. But Benny knew his replacement well: it was Duncan Wood, who had graduated to television after *Anything Goes* – the 1951–2 series that, it had been hoped, in vain, was going to make Benny Hill a radio star. When Wood himself moved on, to direct Tony Hancock's sensationally good *Hancock's Half-Hour*, Benny was more than happy again with his replacement – John Street, whose background in film direction and editing at MGM he would quickly seize upon. Technically, production of *The Benny Hill Show* was now much improved too, and there was 'tele-recording' – for the first time, a live broadcast could be captured on film (crudely done, by pointing a camera at a monitor) and given a repeat airing, usually a few months after first transmission.

Benny Hill and Dave Freeman were especially close at this time. 'We worked a lot at my house,' says Freeman. 'My kids called him "Uncle Benny". Sometimes he'd sleep on the sofa, when it was too late to go home. Other times it would get to about six in the evening and we'd ask him if he wanted a meal. "Oh no, because I bought some chicken yesterday and I've got to finish that off," he'd say. He'd go home to finish off food so that it wouldn't spoil, even though he could have had a free meal with us. We always found that a bit strange!'

Regarding the writing, Benny and Dave developed a system. 'We used to do one show a month, and spend all month writing it. He had a much wider comedy background and a good "sense" of comedy, so while I'd hold him back and say, "No, don't do that", he'd do the same for me and say, "No, that won't work". It was a very good partnership, and I know I would never have succeeded as a comedy writer without Benny's assistance.'

Freeman still has a clear memory of those early shows. 'For the first,' he says, 'I came up with the idea of a cod *Picture Parade*, lampooning obscure continental producers. Not quite Toulouse-Lautrec but the French new wave of films which were in vogue at the time. Then we got more ambitious and sent up *This is Your Life*, *Tonight* [the BBC's nightly topical news and current-affairs show], Armand and Michaela Denis [who made exotic wildlife programmes], *The Perry Como Show* and *6.5 Special* [the BBC's first toe-in-the-water rock and roll show].'

The writers also harked back to one of Benny's earliest radio appearances, extending a sketch from Frank Muir and Denis Norden's 1948 show, *Listen, My Children*, into a recurring situation they called the Layabouts, featuring two gormless working-class lads, Harry and Albert (or sometimes Lofty). The former, played by Hill, had long sideburns, black shirt and a white bootlace tie, the latter – played by Freeman, who could just about act – wore a tight suit and pork-pie hat. Harry was pushy and dim, Albert just dim; the Layabouts became the first such television double-act, anticipating, among others, Dud and Pete, the two Ronnies and Smith and Jones.[2]

The theme of most Layabouts sketches was Harry and Albert's pursuit of a pair of women, usually played by pert young blonde Liz Fraser and dumpy middle-aged Patricia Hayes (also from *Listen, My Children*). Harry, of course, always went for Fraser's character and ended up with Hayes', it being a truism of every *Benny Hill Show*, as in life, that Benny never 'got the girl'. These sketches were particularly well received.

Harry Hand round your wine gums.

Albert I've only got a quarter.

Harry Hand 'em round!

Albert But they're ninepence a quarter!

Harry Give us 'em 'ere. Would you care for one of his wine gums?

Hayes No thanks. I don't want to be under an obligation.

Harry You won't be under an obligation. Not for a wine gum! It isn't like a bar of chocolate!

To make the Layabouts convincing, Freeman worked hard at encouraging Benny into delivering a good cockney accent – which he was suddenly unsure about, says Freeman – and taught him some appropriate character-acting, such as holding and smoking a cigarette from the back of his hand, something he had seen done by a fitter.

'Guys' remained the backbone of every *Benny Hill Show*. The *Film Night* pastiche included as subtext one of Benny's outstanding pieces, which he reprised several times in later years, a send-up of the 1956 film *Baby Doll*, based on a Tennessee Williams vignette set in the Deep South of America. Freeman and Hill called theirs *Baby Boy* and packed it with the sleazy, sordid jealousy which made the movie so depressing – with Benny held in emotional subjugation by an overpowering older woman and never being allowed to grow up. The *Sunday Dispatch* resisted any possible psychological parallels between the sketch and its artist and merely noted: 'Whether a skit which means little to many people should have been included is another question, but his [Hill's] enormous ability to imitate cannot be disputed.'

Spoofing the BBC's concurrent dramatization *The Diary of Samuel Pepys*, Benny wrote a typically saucy medieval song and delivered it – replete with wide, surprised eyes and suggestive smirks – wearing the very wig that actor Peter Sallis wore in the real series.

A fair young maid has took a room down at the local inn,
Her bedside light is oh-so-bright and the curtain's oh-so-thin.
At nine o' clock she enters her room, at ten o' clock she sleeps,
Lord Clarendon he just walks on but naughty Samuel peeps.

I went to view a lady's house, she handed me the key,
She said, 'It's to be let as it stands, with all that you can see.'
I said, 'Are you to be let with the house?' in a very saucy tone,
She said, 'I'm not to be let with the house, I'm to be let alone.'

Benny liked 'Pepys' Diary' more than virtually anything else he created and returned to it several times in later years, even when the Sallis series was long forgotten.

In another medieval song, 'The Woods and Fields of Wapping', Dave Freeman had the idea for the backing singers to vaguely echo the last few words Benny was singing in the verses, so that after he chirruped (about a bird) 'he flew right off my head', the backing singers chimed in with 'off his head', and 'I wonder what lies around the bend' became 'round the bend, round the bend, yes he is round the bend' – to Benny's affected disdain. Years later, after accepting endless accusations that he was a plagiarist, Benny was amused to hear this same idea used, to similarly good effect, in one of the musical sequences in *The Two Ronnies*.

The first edition of *The Benny Hill Show* to be tele-recorded in its entirety is the one with these two aforementioned songs, April 26 1958 – and the programme still exists in the BBC archive. Because it was a live broadcast and Benny had to make costume changes, he does not feature throughout, the filler items – a glee group, dancers, singer Alma Cogan and a circus double-act – underlining just how Variety-accented this kind of television comedy was in the 1950s. Tele-recording was also a far from perfect method of capturing the moving image (and of course the show's production values – though state-of-the-art at the time – fall well below the standards of television as we know it today). Nonetheless, the recording gives a good example of Benny Hill's comedy at this time, and he turns in an impressive and versatile performance. First, he acts the fool as a gendarme in a Parisian café dance. There is a Layabouts sketch with Dave Freeman which evolves into a spoof of amateur theatre in which Benny makes six costume/character changes inside a minute. 'Pepys' Diary' and 'The Woods and Fields of Wapping' fall within a 'guy' of the BBC show *Music for You*, with Benny impersonating its front-man, Eric Robinson. There is a 'guy' of the BBC show *Sportsview*, with Benny impersonating its presenters Peter Dimmock and Raymond Glendenning, and which also incorporates sub-sketches, one showing Benny in drag as show-jumper 'Emily Biskitt' in a somewhat suggestive interview, and the other a Fred Scuttle interview set in a gymnasium (a piece he later reprised on at least two occasions). After a musical comedy number with Benny and Alma Cogan, the show ends with Benny stepping out of character and, for just fifteen seconds, appearing as 'himself', accepting the applause of the studio audience, waving, winking at the camera and – for the only time in the entire hour – looking a little uncomfortable.

On the occasion when Benny spoofed *6.5 Special* (his was called *8.5 Special*) he played no fewer than ten characters. The female presenter/ producer Jo Douglas, the co-presenter and boxer Freddie Mills, the saxophonist Don Lang and the rock and roll singer Wee Willie Harris ('Wee Willie Hill') were all done live, with lightning-fast costume changes in the cutaways. His portrayal of half a dozen teenage girls hand-jiving in the audience was pre-filmed and deftly inserted, stopwatch in hand in the director's gallery, as the programme went on air.

This was top-drawer television comedy, and the critics drooled. Esteemed reviewer Kenneth Baily declared in the *Sunday People*, 'I doubt if any TV star has ever reached such heights in comedy mimicry.' *The Stage* simply ran out of words – 'At a rough count the morning after I can recall *eleven* different characters he mimicked and they were all so screamingly funny that I couldn't hope to convey how funny in this column.' One of the programmes smashed the BBC's Saturday-night audience record, with almost 12 million tuning in. The *Yorkshire Evening News* reviewer Ronald Stott was particularly on the mark, observing of Hill, 'He's a superb clown, but no fool.'

The BBC's audience research was overwhelmingly positive. After a February 1958 transmission, a report quoted five viewers as representative of the phenomenal 92 per cent who had enjoyed Benny Hill's performance 'very much'; again it can be noted that, at this time, admiration was across the board – in particular, 1950s women took no offence from the comedian's odd suggestive joke or expression:

'The very best programme of its kind for a long time. I nearly had hysterics at the 'skits'. Absolutely wonderful.' (Shopkeeper)

'A wonderful laugh from beginning to end. Benny Hill is just the tops.' (Driver's wife)

'What a brilliant show. Hill was simply terrific.' (Hairdresser)

'A jolly good show, best Saturday show for some time. Benny Hill was quite wonderful in the sketches.' (Clerk's wife)

'Just excellent – never a dull moment from beginning to end.' (Salesman)

With such overwhelming praise, Hill could walk tall down the BBC's corridors of power – if, that is, the bus could deliver him to the offices on time.

After a repeat screening of the April 1958 edition, Kenneth Adam (Controller of Programmes, Television) wrote in an internal memorandum:

Have we got any more tele-recordings of the Benny Hill Show? If so, for goodness' sake let us schedule them. One hadn't laughed, one realized last night, for months. The tragedy of losing him to the other side is underlined. This really is a major blow.

(No more repeats were possible at this stage, and the next *Benny Hill Show* to be tele-recorded was in 1961. 'The other side' meant ITV, the BBC's new and hotly opposed commercial rival. Though Benny's loyalty to the BBC was without parallel, Bernard Delfont had forced him to work on ITV as well, in exchange for releasing him from the stage-show *Paris by Night*.)

Only the prudish Cecil McGivern (Deputy Director of Television Broadcasting) was cautious. He wrote in a memo to Ronald Waldman (Head of Light Entertainment, Television):

This, I thought, was in places brilliant. (At the same time, I am always worried that Hill will say or do something unacceptable!)

John Street, who was allowed sight of this latter memo, took the liberty of relaying its content to Benny Hill, who responded, says Street, by putting on a Jewish accent and saying, 'He should worry!'

Benny's personal commitment to making his series a success was total.

The opening 1957 edition, for example, included four minutes of 'mime effects' that he had conceived, taped and paid for himself privately at a London recording studio. He had also written several new songs, not just spoofs but entirely original pieces like 'Gather in the Mushrooms', later to be released as a single and make the British Top 20 – the first of Benny's four chart hits. He displayed a clever manipulation of lyrics, once again managing to rework ageing rhymes and gags into a new format.

As the 8.5 *Special* sequence had shown, he was eager, too, to push the boundaries of television Variety comedy. Until now the format was resolutely stage-bound but Hill saw greater possibilities. 'He was the first person to cut film into TV Variety shows,' says John Street. 'This was unheard of – film was a preserve of drama in British television. And Benny made it his business to know everything about how television worked – close-ups, lenses, playback sound, the lot. He was well ahead of his time. His aim, he said, was to "fill the picture" as much as possible.'

As this indicates, Benny was rapidly developing an interest in every aspect of television production. Street, for one, was not going to stand in his way. 'He always asked to come up to the gallery during run-throughs,' he says. 'During the musical items I actually used to let him take over, because he knew what he wanted and he knew the lingo. He even sometimes "called the shots" [a technical term for directing the cameras, switching from one to another during a recording or live transmission] and was very good. The cameramen loved it. He quickly had technical knowledge to the fingertips. I even saw him work out the camera trick shots. Though he used my brains for the 8.5 *Special* sketch, he knew what was possible. You couldn't fool him by saying something wasn't possible because he would know when it was. On the studio floor, Benny's way of guiding me was to have someone stand in for him while he looked at a monitor. Then he'd say, "I'm not doing this quite right, it should be this way", when really he was advising me how it would look better. I recognized it and accepted it. He knew everybody's jobs.'

Benny was beginning to run the show. The die was cast. From this point, television directors would find it hard to work with Benny Hill unless they allowed him the high level of input he desired. Those who cast their ego aside and allowed him this involvement would enjoy the good professional relationship that resulted; those who did not would fall foul of a developing, though rarely seen, aspect of Benny's character – pointed taciturnity.

Benny's interest in the technical side of television production, which far exceeded that of most other comedians, was very much in the realm of Chaplin, Keaton and Tati. He was beginning to harbour a new ambition. After only four years as a TV star he was questing for a new direction. He also wanted to work less. He began to see his future as a talent-spotter and producer, with only a little 'regular' work on the side.

Such a development caught everyone by surprise but it was consistent with previous turning-points in Benny's career of which none knew. In 1946 he had hoped to become a writer, something he had then tried again after the Sunderland débâcle in 1951; in 1952 he had eyed an entrepreneurial role, dipping a toe in the water of theatrical promotion. Any one of these aims, if seen through, would have prompted his retirement from performance.

The news broke big. 'Benny Hill's secret plan – to turn TV showman' trumpeted the headline in the London *Evening News* in November 1958. 'The Secret Ambition of Benny Hill is no secret any more,' wrote Kendall McDonald. 'So it's over, then, to Benny Hill, Impresario.' Benny was then quoted. 'I've always wanted to do this,' he said, 'but it's not something you can do straightaway. You've got to know the business.'

He went on to outline his plans:

> For every idea I get for myself, I get twenty others that I can't use. One, for example, might make a good series for a comedienne, but not for me.
>
> So this is how I plan to work. Supposing I had thought up *The Army Game* [one of the most successful British comedies of this period, made by Granada for ITV]. I cast it, write one or two scripts and then offer it around. Then I get another idea and do the same.
>
> There is a lot of basic talent about but it needs coaching. I know where to find it.
>
> So supposing I put a young comedian into a television series I'm doing. I've worked with him, written for him, coached him. Then I give him a spot in the show ... not big enough to let him steal the show, mind, but enough to make people say, 'He's good. Who is he?'
>
> Then I can use him in say four out of a TV series of six and then

gradually let him alternate with me, and perhaps finally take over the next series. All under the Benny Hill banner.

I may quite well soft-pedal my own appearances if this comes off.

The BBC, not surprisingly, was alarmed over the developing situation, and sought urgent meetings. Tom Sloan (Assistant Head of Light Entertainment, Television) flew to meet Benny in Paris, where the star was enjoying another of his regular sojourns. 'It is quite clear from my talks with him that he has aspirations of going into some sort of management of his own,' Sloan noted in an internal memorandum on his return, though he added 'but I think this is a bit premature.' He indicated, too, the loyalty that was a hallmark of all Benny Hill relationships, business and social, concluding, 'I do not think there is anything we can really rely upon except the tremendous amount of goodwill [to the BBC] on the part of Hill himself.'

While the BBC and Richard Stone puzzled over precisely where Benny's ambition lay, the man himself had plenty of work. Bernard Delfont was exercising contract options right, left and centre, propelling the comedian back on to the stage not once but many times, and putting him into ATV *Saturday Spectacular* shows that the star himself earnestly wished were not necessary. So much so, indeed, that he was not prepared to create much new material for these programmes. 'We were tickled pink to have him on ITV,' says Brian Tesler, then a senior producer at ATV, 'but he didn't do anything new for us. He was coasting, recycling the material he'd done on the BBC, the [Dick Shawn] Civil War/Down South sketch and so on. I couldn't stop it because the shows were done in a hurry, and because I didn't want to offend Benny. Lew Grade was always on at Richard Stone to get Benny permanently on ITV, but it just didn't feel right for Benny to be anywhere but the BBC at this time.' A decade later, Tesler would discover that Benny still felt guilty about having given him the small change.

Delfont and Richard Stone jointly promoted long summer seasons for Benny Hill in Great Yarmouth in 1957 and Scarborough in 1958, in shows titled *Light Up the Town*. In both resorts he was greeted as a superstar, playing packed houses, attending charity functions with local mayors, opening shops, signing autographs and judging bathing-beauty contests. Benny's straightman throughout this period was Peter Vernon,[3] who had appeared in the 1958 TV series after Jeremy Hawk left to chair the popular ITV show *Criss Cross Quiz*. 'He was slightly bitter about my going,' says Hawk. 'He didn't want to have to work with another straightman again and instruct him in his ways.' It speaks for Benny's equable personality that, after four tumultuous years together, Hawk says this was the first and only time Benny was unfriendly to him.

Though Benny hated *Paris by Night*, Delfont had coveted the appreciable box-office takings. More than anything else, the impresario wanted the star TV comedian back in the West End. Though distressed at the idea, Benny was strong enough to make it plain that he must have a greater role. He had a single ambition in mind – to emulate Robert Dhéry. Benny's admiration for the French comic entertainer was becoming almost slavish. At this time, citing Dhéry's London stage show *La Plume de Ma Tante*, and a recent 'wonderful, but wonderful week in Marseilles', he chose a Dhéry composition as one of the eight cherished pieces of music he would happily live with as a *Desert Island Discs* castaway.[4]

Quite simply, Benny wanted to make his own *Plume*. 'Dhéry had things like a singing fisherman, wearing oilskins, riding a horse,' says Dave Freeman, who – again – wrote most of the material. 'His comedy was really offbeat and Benny was very keen on doing something similar.'

The new revue was *Fine Fettle*, subtitled 'A Musical Romp in Cloth Cap and Tails'. It opened in London at the huge Palace Theatre on Cambridge Circus in August 1959, after warming up in Manchester and Nottingham. Benny had vetoed a suggestion that the show be titled *Boo to a Goose*. With the spectre of Sunderland still much in evidence, he conjectured that the word 'Boo' might give the audience the wrong idea; 'Goose', he said, wasn't exactly ideal either. But the signs were that Benny would enjoy *Fine Fettle* much more than he had *Paris by Night*. In addition to Dave Freeman's hands-on involvement, the show would be directed by Kenneth Carter, his astute television mentor, and a number of the sketches, including the ball-and-chain act and a *This is Your Life* spoof, had already proven successful on the small screen. (Kenneth Horne had played the subject on TV; on stage it was Robertson Hare.)

Among an array of new pieces, *Fine Fettle* featured a cod-Greek sketch with Benny as a centaur, a mime piece with Benny playing a guileless country kid at a fairground, and 'The Pride of Lower Tidmarsh', in which the Lower Tidmarsh Fire Brigade, a motley crew led by Benny, sang a saucy song about hose-pipes, bells, dongers and choppers.

In another sketch, a dummy elephant's trunk came out between the curtains and, as it gathered Benny around the waist, he was hoisted high by a scarcely visible wire. There was also a Lady Godiva sketch with Benny as a stable-boy, anticipating how best to lift the naked female on to her mount. Also, a number of film items were projected on to a screen – some spoofing the kind of advertisements shown in cinemas ('For exquisite Indian cuisine, visit the Maharajah restaurant at 15 King Street . . . Calcutta'). These had been filmed, in colour, in Dave Freeman's north London back garden.[5]

The highlight for Benny, though, would be a sequence in which he played Paraguayan harp. Melody was looming large in his life at this time, and his tastes, he told a reporter, were 'Yiddisher music, Latin-American music, Arabic music'. The Paraguayan harp was one of his latest acquisitions, bought in Harrods at (to him) great expense; all latter-day visitors to Cunningham Court had been regaled with his keenly primitive plucking. At rehearsals, says Dave Freeman, Benny drove everyone to distraction with his playing. 'There wasn't much comedy in the piece, he just loved the sound of the instrument and the fact that he'd learned to play it. He thought it would be a novelty, but I went to rehearsal every day and every time we looked for Benny he was off in the corner somewhere playing the harp – at the expense of time when we might have been improving the material.' Benny needn't have bothered. The piece was cut. 'We opened with a fortnight in Manchester,' recalls Freeman, 'and after about five minutes of the first night Ken Carter said to me "That bloody Paraguayan harp piece can go."'

Reviews of *Fine Fettle* were (to put it kindly) mixed. *Manchester Evening News* critic Alan Bendle declared, 'Too much of the material is deplorably thin and a lot of it pointless.' When the production reached London the *Daily Mirror* reviewer labelled it 'A seaside show masquerading as a West End one', while the *Daily Telegraph* critic managed to combine faint praise with faint damnation in his opening sentence, calling it 'A cheerful and good-hearted entertainment of no particular distinction or shape.' *The Times* did the same – 'A large, noisy and cheerful revue with a great many cloth-cap jokes and with virtually nothing in the way of ideas.'

Though he didn't care much for the show, doyen critic Milton Shulman, writing in the London *Evening Standard*, had nothing but praise for Hill himself:

> His cherubic face, with its eyes fluttering like some berserk windscreen-wiper, represents on the surface the orthodox little man buffeted and baffled by fate.
> But he brings to this traditional comic characterization a secret, lip-smacking irreverence which gives his humour a boisterous, even bawdy quality.

Fine Fettle closed in January 1960 after just 179 performances and a preview spot in the 1959 Royal Variety Show.[6] Benny would never again appear in the West End. 'He didn't hate it as much as he had hated *Paris by Night*,' says Dave Freeman, 'but it certainly hadn't gone as well as he had hoped. He had wanted to do a real, modern, surreal *La Plume de Ma Tante* and we had failed to achieve it.'

There were obvious differences between the specialist show Benny had hoped to create and what Bernard Delfont had wanted to achieve at the box-office. The size of the theatre didn't help, either – intimate revue is best suited to a smaller venue than the Palace. Irving Davies, who choreographed the show (and also worked on the 1958 series of *The Benny Hill Show*), remarks, 'To be honest, Benny wasn't great in *Fine Fettle*. He wasn't broad enough and the writing was too "small" for him in that place. The show had everything but it was patchy. He wasn't happy.' Before *Fine Fettle* finished, Benny was visited by Ron Clark, the star comedian from his 1949 Newquay summer season. Clark was amused to observe how Benny, though earning £1,000 a week, was still as economical as ever. 'He offered me a cigarette,' says Clark, 'and it was a Woodbine, the cheapest brand on the market. Afterwards, when he was dressed to leave the theatre, he was wearing an old roll-neck jumper and the same blasted grey trousers my wife had stitched up for him in Newquay more than ten years earlier.'

Just as *Fine Fettle* closed, Benny went into the studios to shoot his second movie, *Light Up the Sky!* After the horrors of *Who Done It?* he was not the star, but one of a number of players in a Second World War ensemble piece about an army searchlight battery somewhere in rural England (filming took place in Normandy, Surrey). Pathos and a faint comedic touch sat uncomfortably together. The film was produced and directed by Lewis Gilbert, who had just made *Sink the Bismarck* and would go on to direct three James Bond blockbusters. Shot in eight weeks at a cost of just £80,000, *Light Up the Sky!* was no 007 epic, though, and Benny was no Sean Connery.

He enjoyed the experience. Lewis Gilbert found him '100 per cent professional. There was nothing he wouldn't do. Whatever I asked him to do he'd say "Yes, great. I'd love to do it that way." He gave the impression that he really enjoyed what he was doing.'

In the film, Benny Hill and Tommy Steele – the latter ostensibly Britain's first rock and roll star but already well on the way to becoming a family entertainer – were cast as brothers, Syd and Eric McCaffey, a music-hall song and dance pairing whose act has been curtailed by call-up.[7] The script called for a stage performance, a scene that was meat and drink for Benny. 'We wanted to make it deliberately corny, because the brothers weren't meant to be very good,' says Lewis Gilbert. 'Lionel Bart wrote the song and Benny and Tommy cobbled the thing together. Benny wrote most of it, though. He was never stuck for a line. If you said to him we need a gag here on a particular subject he could reel off about a hundred in no time at all. He had the most wonderful memory for old music-hall jokes.'

A few of them were written into this very scene, battle-scarred veterans of Benny's former stage act and early radio broadcasts. Now they were featured in a movie – albeit accompanied by some entirely appropriate put-downs from bystanders. Two young girls commented sarcastically on the age of a joke that Benny had been trotting out in his stage act just before he became a TV star.

Lewis Gilbert considers Benny to have been a fascinating man. 'He was very, very talented,' remarks the acclaimed director, 'even though when you met him he didn't appear to show *any* kind of a talent, and also didn't have a great personality. I thought he was very good in *Light Up the Sky!* though it didn't extend his repertoire – he did what I knew he could do; he always played the "music-hall" Benny. He could have gone on to become a very good actor, but it would have required someone writing specifically for him.'

One off-screen moment was typical Benny. The youngest actor in the cast was Johnny Briggs, a good-looking lad-about-town later to achieve fame as Mike Baldwin in *Coronation Street*. One day Benny said to Briggs, 'I'll tell you what we'll do, which might be a bit of fun. You bring a girl for me, and I'll bring a girl for you. And we'll have an evening out together.' He was setting-up a double blind-date. The next morning Johnny told Lewis Gilbert, 'I brought a girl for him, but he didn't bring anybody for me!'

Such tactics were used by Benny on a number of occasions. The comic-actor and scriptwriter John Junkin appeared in a couple of *Benny Hill Shows* in the 1960s and the same proposition was put to him – although no such swap subsequently took place. Says Junkin, 'The strange thing is, it was suggested quite genuinely. We never did it, but he was serious – it would simply have been another way for him to meet a bird. And it was said like a seventeen-year-old boy would say it. There was nothing murky in it. It was the kind of thing you'd say when you're a teenager and on holiday. It was *child-like*, as opposed to childish.'

Light Up the Sky! was released in July 1960 and did modest business. It arrived in the cinemas and then vanished, like thousands of other quite ordinary films. All one could say was that in contrast to the excruciating *Who Done It?*, *Light Up the Sky!* was at least watchable and Benny had played his middling role with conviction.

During *Fine Fettle*, the producers of television commercials for the fizzy-drinks company Schweppes persuaded Benny to appear in a series of adverts.[8] Benny insisted on his 'team' – Dave Freeman as writer, Kenneth Carter as director. The fee astonished Benny. For just a few days' work, and no writing, he could earn thousands of pounds – £10,000 in the first year alone. One contract, for four fifteen-second spots, paid £3,000, well in excess of the average man's annual salary at this time. And all he had to do was turn up, get into whatever character Freeman had written for him – a gardener, an astronomer, a burglar, a shopper, a ship's commander – and work for a couple of hours. If earning money was this easy, Benny reasoned, why was he worrying his guts out on the stage?

He went on to appear in more than fifty Schweppes commercials over the coming five years, earning handsomely throughout. Moreover, the commercials were also advertisements for himself – all of them attracted plaudits and one of them won an award: the Grand Prix de la Télévision, won at the Cannes International Festival of Publicity Films in 1961. (It beat over 500 entries from twenty-one countries and was the first such award won by an English TV commercial.)

With money pouring in faster than ever, Benny made a decision that would have been out of character had he not a specific reason in mind. He decided to treat himself to a nicer apartment. His five-year lease at Cunningham Court was about to expire and he felt he deserved somewhere more upmarket. 'He didn't want to buy a house because he didn't want "the worry of it,"' says Dave Freeman, who was chauffeur for the property-hunting exercise. 'But he wanted something a bit more ritzy than his flat in Maida Vale. I drove him around and we looked at one or two places in Hampstead. He ended up in Kensington, buying a lease on a first-floor flat for, I think, £20,000 or £25,000.'

Flat 7 at 2 Queen's Gate would be Benny Hill's London home until 1986. It was a splendid Victorian residence in a fine location, and Queen's Gate was home to consulates and legations, diplomats and the idle rich. It was also a hundred yards from Kensington Gardens, where Peter Pan frolicked, and a stone's throw from the Royal Albert Hall, where Benny, still the boxing fan, would watch many a bout in the ensuing years.

With its impressive high-ceilinged rooms, Benny saw his new home as the ideal place to fulfil the entrepreneurial and talent-spotting role to which he aspired. Here, he imagined, Benny Hill, Manager, would audition future stars of the screen and rehearse the shows destined to appear under his 'Benny Hill Presents . . .' television banner. A journalist from the London *Evening Standard* went to interview him at his new pad and found the star, wearing nothing but a dressing-gown, sitting on his first-floor balcony busily typing scripts. Decorators were inside, sprucing up the place in a manner suitable for the mogul-to-be. 'I won't tell you how much I earn,' teased Benny, 'but I read somewhere that it's supposed to be around £20,000 a year. So why should I work harder? If a fellow can't live on £20,000 a year he must be mad or have more expensive tastes than I have. As long as I have enough money to be able to fly to Paris when I feel like it, and have a bit of a giggle, I'm a happy boy.'

Benny informed the newspaperman that in 1961 he would be appearing in six TV shows 'and present and partly direct six others'. Television comedy had become, he said, 'tired – the same old thing keeps coming on at the same old time. TV needs rejuvenating.'

Benny was looking to start a new chapter. Before that unfolded he would take a long break. Richard Stone had engaged him as guest star in *Let's Make a Night of It*, a summer stage-show in Weymouth, but Benny told his agent he would commit only to fifteen days, not the full season. He was booked to appear on Australian television in October and November and intended to make his way there *slowly*, taking the best part of two months to travel around the world.

By the end of July he had left the stage and was ready to set off on a grand tour.

13. 'A sweet-faced man; a most lovely, gentleman-like man'

Benny Hill made his way Down Under by the proverbial slow boat. Richard Stone had told him he could work the full summer season in Weymouth and fly there in a day, but the star comedian balked at the suggestion. His passion for travelling was outstripping his passion for making people laugh, and the trip to Australia, where he would make four television shows, was not much more than an excuse for a paid-up excursion. It was the first of many such junkets in the years to come. Though capable of financing any trip, Benny would always look to see if someone else might pick up the tab.

Benny's private world tour of 1960, to and from Australia, encompassed Japan, China, Ceylon, Burma, India, Singapore, Hong Kong, Turkey and several west European countries. 'Happy hunting ground for script ideas,' he remarked on his return, from which one can deduce that this publicly perspicacious people-watcher also made sure to catch as many circuses and club cabarets as he could.

The Far East, where he discovered some houses of ill-repute, was a particular eye-opener. Benny was familiar with the delights that Hamburg, Amsterdam and certain other European cities could offer the single male 7traveller – 'As a bachelor I am permitted to do this,' he would say about this particular pursuit – and he was no less thrilled to be able to tell tales of his experiences in the Orient. Bob Monkhouse, already a confidante through fifteen interesting years, found this out to his disgust when his friend related some especially colourful blow-job anecdotes upon his return.

Benny also enjoyed using Japanese bath-houses, about which he spoke with surprising candour in an interview for the BBC's (progressive) radio programme *The Public Ear* in November 1963:

Tokyo is very much a gentleman's city. I wouldn't recommend it to ladies. I think Paris is a ladies' city, but Tokyo is for gentlemen.

It has some very, very nice sociable ladies. I was very friendly with a lady there and did the bath-houses. I'd like to open one over here, but I don't think I'd get away with it. [Laughs.] I'd be my own best customer, I can tell you that. A very pretty girl takes you by the hand into a big steamy room and says 'Please you take your clothes off, no be shy because all day long I have to bathe the gentlemen and it's not much to me.' They're great little flatterers, Japanese girls. They don't say 'old fatty', they say 'I like you, you nice big man.' And they give you a bath and they give a massage and it's always jolly nice. Several times girls said to me, 'Here, you just have bath. What you want another bath for?' because I came out of one place, walked down the road and went in another one.

Since parting company with Doris Deal five years earlier, Benny had dated dozens of young women, but he had grown close to only one – a dancer, Norma Lewis, who appeared in some of his ATV shows. Newspapers reported sighting Benny and Norma in Paris.

'He usually travelled alone,' says Dave Freeman, 'but sometimes he took girls abroad with him. I heard that he once took two of them to Paris, booked them into the room next door and never touched them. He just wanted to be seen with them. Benny really didn't have enough resilience to operate as half of a couple. When he went abroad he'd have his day mapped out in his mind – get up at eight, have breakfast, walk along the Champs Élysées, have coffee, take a trip somewhere. As he always moaned to me, if he had a woman with him "at half-past-eleven she'd still be in the bathroom, fiddling about with makeup". Benny couldn't abide that.'

Introduced by Peter Charlesworth, Norma Lewis and Benny went together on and off for about a year but they didn't live together and the ending was entirely characteristic. 'She left Benny because she wanted marriage and he didn't,' says Dave Freeman. 'She married an Italian restaurateur, which upset Benny because although he didn't want to marry her, he wondered why she had to leave him for someone else. She also told me that she had gone off Benny a bit because he didn't like spending money. His idea of a good meal in those days was still egg on toast. He became more lavish with women in his later years.'

The sexual orientation of Benny Hill was a newspaper issue in the 1960s, and the subject of endless speculation among his fellow performers. Some, who didn't know him, thought he was homosexual; others, aware of his foibles, knew well that he was not. When the decade began, Benny was aged thirty-five; if he had not married by the end, at forty-five, he probably would not.

His ideal, as is plain, was to be seen in the company of beautiful young women, and this he could maintain by employing them in his shows. Outside the TV studio, though, the number of gorgeous twenty-year-olds genuinely seeking to get 'serious' was naturally diminishing with every passing year. When Allie Freeman, Dave's wife, asked Benny point-blank if he was ever going to get married, he blusteringly replied, 'I'm not going to do that! I'd have to buy her dresses. It'd be two of everything. I'd have to buy her food as well!'

Dave Freeman recognized this as the defence it was. Benny certainly proposed enough times – just never to the right kind of woman, while the women who had proven their durability and waited for him to pop the question heard only silence.

It is clear that no woman was interested in maintaining more than a platonic friendship with Benny Hill, and no one appears to have made him a matrimonial target – not even to grab a share of his wealth. Benny's inability to understand the nature of women increased accordingly. He was clearly unable to commit to relationships, to give fully of himself, and there was, too, his foreboding about intercourse, a prospect that had alarmed him unceasingly since puberty. One associate, who prefers to remain anonymous, says that he had become impotent – a state that would be consistent with his apprehensions. It was surely the greatest irony that a man whose father made a career from selling condoms should not himself have cause to use one.

Benny had 'fallen in love' in Australia, too – with a bright and bubbly twenty-one-year-old blonde actress, Annette André, who appeared in his TV shows there (and was later to achieve success in Britain). 'It was absolutely platonic,' she says. 'He liked me and I liked him and we hit it off straight away. In a friendly way, not leaping into bed. I knew I didn't have to worry – Benny wasn't going to jump on me. In all the time I knew him, first in Australia and then later in England, I never felt that he was secure enough to make a pass. Well, he made a pass, but it was a *shy* pass.'

Benny and Annette went out around Sydney several times, down to the beach and the harbour. He even went so far as to cook her a lobster dinner. He was, of course, also very sweet to her mother. 'It was, "Hello, how are you? I'm working with your lovely daughter," that kind of thing,' Annette says. 'He was always so courteous. But you never really got to know Benny or find out what was underneath. Anything personal, anything emotional, was hidden, that's when he'd retreat into this shy, insecure man. He was sweet and sensitive, though. I said I'd like to go to England one day – Australians had to go there or America if they were ambitious – and he replied, "Come to England, and when you do, here is my address and number."'

Benny was in Australia for a month, appearing four times in Sydney Channel 7's primetime Variety show *Curtain Call*. Peter Vernon and Kenneth Carter had flown out to ensure Benny had his straightman and favourite director on hand, though Dave Freeman had not made the trip because he had work and family in England. Benny grew cross in the studio, though – he was dissatisfied with the paucity of the wardrobe, which meant that he had to tweak some of the sketches – and he was unhappy with the accommodation that had been laid on. All the same, the Hill *Curtain Calls* received rave reviews. The local *TV Times* declared, 'We owe him a debt for proving that good comedy does not require a comedian to throw a pie, don female clothes or lose his trousers.'

Benny also appeared in the Lord Mayor's Command Performance at Sydney Town Hall, and was able to spend some time with his cherished sister Diana, whom he had not seen since her emigration. As she grew older, Diana had begun to look more and more like Benny; when he returned to England and showed some photographs of them together he would say, 'There's me, and there's me in drag.'

Throughout 1960, Richard Stone and the BBC had been locked in negotiations over Benny's next TV contract. Until now, he had been engaged on a show-by-show basis; this time, Stone and Hill wanted the security of a long-term (twelve-month) agreement. The BBC is not the speediest organization when it comes to contract negotiations, but its hands were tied anyway because Benny was unable to specify what it was he wanted to 'produce' in his role as impresario – a key element of the new agreement.

In the end it was decided that in 1961 he would appear in six 'A' shows – his standard TV fare – and present or devise/produce six 'B' shows ... whatever form they might take. Richard Stone sums up the difficulties by saying, 'Benny was getting bored. He'd been on TV at the BBC since 1953 and was looking for something else to do. The whole suggestion was fairly impractical, though. Benny didn't really know what he wanted to do, He just wanted *something* else to do.'

By the time the agreement was thrashed out Benny was back from Australia and under pressure to deliver the first of his regular programmes. Having found his 'happy hunting ground for script ideas', he wanted to work without Dave Freeman for the first time in five years. (This was probably also a slight, to repay Freeman for not going to Australia. Benny never liked people saying no to him.) Viewers of the opening show were certainly left in no doubt that the star was a globetrotter – the show was subtitled 'A lighthearted look at the world in Benirama Hillascope and glorious black & white', the linking items were shot in an aeroplane, and sketches were set in a Paris night-club and street, a Colombo hotel (Benny in white housecoat and turban), Tokyo (Benny as a Japanese travel agent), Mexico, Hong Kong (Benny as a peasant and nobleman), Hamburg, Copenhagen and Athens. There was also a raft of spoof TV commercials, something that would remain a cornerstone of Benny's shows for the next twenty years. Oddly, though, while the products being sent-up were recognizably British, Benny performed them in cod-German.

For the first time, viewers were less than wholly enthusiastic. The producer, John Street, saw the problem, writing in an internal BBC report:

This show suffered from Benny's desire to 'go it alone' script-wise.
    There must be a guiding influence of a script-writer. A Producer has so little defence because as charming a person as this artist is, he is one

of the most difficult to guide and be made to see that so much of his own material is out-dated.

The second show, a month later, was only a little better. It included, though, one of the absolute highlights of Benny's entire career, a spoof of *Juke Box Jury*. This was the BBC's popular Saturday-evening show in which a celebrity panel listened to new pop singles and predicted which would be a 'hit' and which a 'miss' – decisions signified, respectively, by the pinging of a bell or the sounding of a klaxon. Benny's spoof was titled *Soap Box Jury*. (Thankfully, it remains preserved on film in the BBC archive.)

Seven years earlier, when he had sent-up *What's My Line?*, Benny had no choice but to perform the entire piece live. Now he wanted to do it on film and had cooked up the idea of not only appearing as the host (his one-time TV straightman David Jacobs) and several members of the audience but also the two male and two female panellists, ending with all four panellists in a single shot.

John Street told Benny it had never been tried on television. Hill replied that it had been done in movies – he had seen them – so surely they could do it too. 'He could,' says Street, 'run circles around a lot of directors.'

The sketch was shot over two painstaking days at Ealing. Benny's wish was accomplished, as he had realized, by using a 35mm Mitchell camera, exposing only a quarter of the film's width and then running it back three more times, each time masking off the other three sections. 'The timing was crucial,' Street remarks, 'but Benny was never less than perfect.' It was a trick that other comedians soon took up, bewildering television viewers for years.

In addition to the technical accomplishment, the sketch also provided ample evidence once again that the greatest weapon in Benny Hill's comedic armoury was not the tired gag-book 'joke' but his perceptive observation of human characteristics – male, female, young, old, and every idiosyncrasy under the sun – combined with his special talent for mime. There were no 'jokes' in this sketch, and certainly no witticisms, but it was funny, and exceptional television.

The spoof was also apposite, for Benny himself was about to become a recording star. He had released a couple of singles in the 1950s, with decidedly ordinary results,[1] and around 1959 Richard Stone had failed in an attempt to persuade George Martin, Beatles producer-to-be, to take on Hill as a client. Stone hoped that Benny might emulate the outstanding success of Peter Sellers, produced by Martin, as a comedy recording star. 'Richard was quite anxious to get Benny on the Sellers bandwagon,' says George Martin. 'So I spent a session with him at Abbey Road, going through various ideas and songs. But it never happened, partly because I wasn't terribly satisfied with the material, and partly because I wasn't sure he was right for what I had in mind. Peter [Sellers] could paint a picture in sound and did great vocal mimicry, whereas Benny's talents seemed to be more visual in origin. Also, Benny was very cautious and wanted control over what he was doing. I thought he might be a problem, so we never proceeded.'

Since that time, though, Benny had continued to flower as a composer of catchy pop-style recordings, developed his singing voice and learned to play a few more instruments. Stone got him signed to the ever-keen Lew Grade's record label, Pye, and here he fell under the wing of house producer Tony Hatch.

The result was a succession of singles, three in 1961 alone, for the modern-day folk singer, starting with the ubiquitous 'Pepys' Diary' and, on the B-side, 'Gather in the Mushrooms'. Benny mimed to 'Pepys' Diary' on the ITV pop show *Thank Your Lucky Stars*; after switching promotion – 'Mushrooms' became the A-side – the record broke into the charts, landing up at number twelve.

Being involved with the young blades of the pop business slightly unnerved Benny, so he set out to make a particularly Benny-ish impression on the hip young producer. 'It was arranged that I'd go to his apartment in Queen's Gate for 5.30 one afternoon,' says Tony Hatch. 'I arrived on time, rang the doorbell and waited a hell of a long time before his "yokel" voice came over the entry-phone system, "Oh, 'ang on, me dear, I'm just a bit busy at the moment. I'll open the door, you pop up and make yourself comfortable in the lounge." I went upstairs and sat down. Quarter to six came and went, six o'clock, quarter past, still no sign of Benny, and then at about half past six I could see, up the hallway, a young lady just leaving. She was hardly his housekeeper! Then Benny appeared saying,

"Sorry, I just had to finish some business." I was meeting him for the first time so I wasn't going to ask any questions, but my assumption is that Benny was being the Benny we came to read about much later on. He clearly had an enormous crush on lovely young ladies, though. This one was about eighteen or nineteen.'

Hatch and Hill forged a good working relationship that spanned five years. But, says the producer, 'I never got inside his character. We were good mates yet the limit and extent of our friendship was being at his home, where we worked on the songs, and in the studio.'

Benny performed his last ever concert tour in May 1961, a Middle East troop shebang for Combined Services Entertainment, arranged by Richard Stone and undertaken by the comedian for a mere £50 a week.[2] British 'tommies' serving in Cyprus, Malta and North Africa were the last to see Benny Hill 'live' in a theatre until he made a one-off charity appearance in 1984. After a deeply uncomfortable twenty years on stage, two decades in which that discomfort had often been all too visible, he exited, stage left . . . and quickly took comfort in another extended holiday. When he returned, he got down to fresh business.

Benny had always fancied himself as a talent-spotter. Way back in 1953, when he was just a fresh-faced unknown appearing in *The Centre Show*, he had generously advised Ken Carter to check out another new young comic, Bruce Forsyth. (This handwritten letter is still on file at the BBC; Carter didn't do anything about it but Forsyth became a star anyway.) Benny also brought a steady stream of continental cabaret artistes whom he had seen in French and Spanish night-clubs to England to appear in his TV shows. None made the splash he was hoping for, but he wasn't going to stop looking. He was especially fond of Los Paraguayos, a singing and guitar act, and Dorita y Pepe, a struggling (British-born) Latin American musical duo. In her crinoline lace dress Dorita would wriggle attractively while Pepe, with 'George Raft' sideburns, played flamenco with a flourish. Benny put the pair into several shows hoping to turn them into major stars; in turn, Pepe – alias Peter Sensier – gave Benny expert guitar tuition and exquisite homemade string instruments (one was a Charango, made from the shell of an armadillo). That was a good Alfie Hill trade.

Los Paraguayos and Dorita y Pepe never made the big time either, but Benny never ceased searching. In 1973 he discovered a British-born singer, Diana Darvey, in a Spanish night-club and brought her back to appear in *The Benny Hill Show*, hoping she would achieve stardom. She became a Richard Stone client but never quite made the big time. Benny sought what he fondly called 'twinkle', an indefinable quality perhaps . . . but he'd know it when he saw it.

Maybe he wasn't looking in the right places, though, for when push came to shove in autumn 1961, nine months into his twelve-month development deal with the BBC, Benny's desire to become The Great Impresario vanished overnight. The BBC had run out of time. Whatever were those 'ideas' he had been nurturing, the Corporation never found out, nor did it learn the identity of the 'basic talent' he had been intending to coach to stardom. Instead of six indeterminate 'Benny Hill Presents . . .' shows in which he would have been, at most, the introducer, the BBC suggested that the 'B' element of his contract become situation comedies in which he – in a variety of roles – would be the fulcrum.

Situation comedy – the sitcom – was emerging rapidly at the start of the 1960s. Humour and British television had been uneasy bedfellows since the service began in 1936, but twenty-five years into the relationship the sitcom had finally evolved into the ideal TV comedy format. The invention of video-tape guaranteed an acceptable and consistent visual quality for studio productions and also permitted viewers to see more of their star. With pre-recording, it became possible for a half-hour show to feature the comedian for fully thirty minutes, not fifteen with the remaining time padded out by dancers, singers and acrobats. Just as Variety in the theatres had died a death, so the best days of Variety on television were suddenly past. *The Benny Hill Show* would soon be one of the few long-term survivors of a dying and anachronistic art. Eventually it would be the last.

The sitcom developed first in America, where *The Honeymooners*, *I Love Lucy* and *The Phil Silvers Show* set the trend for slick, witty, half-hour comedies. But while the structure was similar, the British model developed interesting variations. American television warrants a show's 'season' to run for what was then, in the 1950s, thirty-nine episodes a year, with teams of writers employed to produce the scripts. Shorter runs – typically just six episodes – became the pattern in Britain, usually written throughout by the same writer or writers. Moreover, a pair of talented young men, Ray Galton and Alan Simpson, were introducing a dose of social realism into the developing genre. Their scripts for Tony Hancock, first on radio and then on TV, were miniature masterpieces of hilariously flawed humanity. The same writers then raised the stakes higher with *Steptoe and Son*. This sitcom dealt with an underclass previously seen on television only in urban dramas, and its underlying theme – of the son trying desperately to escape the clutches of his wily father – imbued the episodes with pathos and poignancy. On top of all this, it was also marvellously funny. When, in 1965, writer Johnny Speight chipped in with the controversially racist – but again very funny – *Till Death Us Do Part*, the transformation was complete. The British had taken the American sitcom invention and nudged it on to a higher plane.

It was hoped that Galton and Simpson's work for Hancock, *Steptoe* and the BBC's *Comedy Playhouse* single episodes would form the template for Benny Hill's sitcoms. Benny readily acknowledged that this form of writing was beyond him, so Dave Freeman, who had already been brought back into the fold for the autumn 1961 shows, was asked to prepare some scripts and the first half-dozen episodes soon sped into production. (Benny was given a co-writing credit for these but he made scarcely no contribution; after these six, Freeman was given sole credit.)

For the next two years, then, Benny Hill gave up his usual Variety shows and starred instead in situation comedies, nineteen of them. These in turn stirred a desire to be 'an actor' and work in films, leading to parts in box-office-busting movies *Those Magnificent Men in Their Flying Machines*, *Chitty Chitty Bang Bang* and *The Italian Job*. He even took a starring role in a Shakespeare play.

For Dave Freeman, casting Benny Hill in weekly studio-bound situations provided a stiff challenge. 'People at the BBC had begun saying that Benny had to get away from the sketch-shows, that people were getting sick of them,' he says, 'but the question for me was "Who was Benny Hill?" The public knew that Tommy Cooper was Tommy Cooper, that Sid James was Sid James, that Arthur Askey was Arthur Askey, but who was Benny Hill away from those sketches? He was an impersonator, really, like Peter Sellers, with a range of characters. So all I could do was write a different half-hour each week, like playlets, in which he appeared in various parts. This meant that viewers had to adjust to a different set-up every week. That was the main thing that militated against the series. But people who liked the programmes liked them very much, and we got respectable viewing figures – about 15 million.' (A figure beyond the dreams of British TV comedy producers in today's multi-channel era.)

Several of the half-hours were spoofs. 'The Time Bicycle' was a pastiche of H. G. Wells' *The Time Machine*, set in Hampstead, north London, in 1902. Benny played an inventor who got astride a bicycle, started to pedal and arrived in 1917 in a lady's boudoir just as she and her brigadier husband were entering the room. The inventor cycled on to 1940 to find that the war was still going on, and then once more to 1962, by which point the room had become a toilet. Benny emerged saying, 'My word that was a long pedal, I've been in there since 1902.' Another episode, 'The Taxidermist', anticipated the *Monty Python's Flying Circus* 'Dead Parrot' sketch by six years, Freeman's script calling for Benny to pass off a stuffed duck as a parrot, blaming its different appearance on 'the steaming' and 'the shrinkage'. (John Cleese, who along with Graham Chapman wrote the *Monty Python* 'Dead Parrot' sketch, recently stated that although he used to watch *The Benny Hill Show* in the 1950s he was unfamiliar with this particular piece.)

Dave Freeman had a real talent for writing period pastiches, and Benny could certainly act, so the combination was potent. For Benny, these playlets were akin to the sketches he had witnessed – and in which he had often participated – on the Variety stage in decades past, where gentle overacting was not only permissible but enhanced the comedy. His flair for characterization, and for mime and facial gestures, were also put to effective use. For its part, the BBC – which had recently lost the services of Tony Hancock and doubtless was looking for a successor – injected considerable technical expertise into the production, giving Benny's TV work a resolutely 'modern' appearance for the first time. If the surviving episodes were shown again now, they would present an image of Benny Hill very different from that which the world currently has of him: not a leering sex-obsessive but a smart comedian, sharp of mind and character, cosmopolitan rather than suburban.

Because they were shot on video, Benny was working for the first time in an intimate studio in a purpose-built television facility (the BBC's Television Centre, opened in 1960) rather than a converted Variety theatre. He never went back. Video permitted Benny the close-up flexibility he had long sought. Although location filming would remain a key element of his work, he had now found his ideal working environment. He enjoyed, too, the familiarity of a regular company of supporting players – in this case June Whitfield (also a Hancock alumnus), Graham Stark, Patricia Hayes and David Lodge, all of whom gave him fine service. This again was something he would strive to maintain in his future work.

The sitcoms were generally received with enthusiasm by critics. Kenneth Adam, Director of BBC Television, wrote Benny a personal letter, declaring:

> I would like you to know how much pleasure you have given my family and myself in your recent series, which has been a 'must' for all of us. These programmes, from a purely professional point of view, seem to me to mark a very significant step forward in your television life.

Benny replied promptly and, without Mrs Jones to type for him now, by hand:

> Dear Mr Adam
> You know that was very kind of you to write me that nice letter. I've certainly enjoyed doing the shows & hope to be doing some more before long. I must say those studios are a pleasure to perform in.

By the third series, Freeman and Hill were perhaps 'pushing the envelope' a tad too far, however. In 'Mr Apollo', Benny was cast as the seedy proprietor of a 'health-and-vigour agency' and he played it to the hilt. The BBC's audience research noted the viewers' general reaction – that the part was 'distastefully lecherous, dirty, continually coughing and revoltingly sleazy, too disgusting to be even faintly funny'. The *Daily Sketch* reviewer commented snidely, 'All the best artists grow up and mature. But on this showing the immature Hill of five years ago was nearly five times as funny.' Perhaps the tide was turning. Producer John

Street, who hated the sitcom series from start to finish, told Benny so –
at the expense of not working with him again for nearly twenty years.
'He thought it was a success,' Street says, 'and parts of it were funny.
But some of the ideas were sad. He played poor men, rundown men,
and he was no Royal Academy actor. It was rather like Gene Kelly being
allowed to make *Invitation to the Dance* [his balletic 'pure dance' movie]
– a reward for all the past work he had done.'

The continuing highly paid Schweppes TV commercials and the substantial BBC sitcom work – he received £1,000 for each one, with further
fees for the repeat showings – made Benny Hill a wealthy man by the
mid-1960s. With astute investment of his money he might have managed
to give up work altogether. This appeared to be what he wanted – and
yet the word 'investment' was not in his vocabulary. Back in the late
1950s, when his client first secured a sizeable income, Richard Stone
had urged Benny to seek financial advice. He put him in touch with
Dennis Blake, a very exact chartered accountant with London firm Baker
Todman.

Throughout a twenty-year association, Blake was never less than
bewildered by Benny's lack of interest in his own finances, to the point
where he had difficulty fulfilling a professional requirement to ensure his
client knew what was going on. 'I would tell him something and
sometimes he didn't even bother to react,' Blake says. 'He'd hope I
wouldn't have to go on talking to him because he was bored, bored with
his own affairs. He would virtually sign any bit of paper that I put before
him.'

Blake soon realized that the only thing that concerned Benny was
whether he had enough money to do what he wanted – and as this wasn't
very much, he had ample. 'He was consistent throughout his rise to
prosperity,' Blake comments. 'If he wanted something he hired it – his
television or his transport. He didn't spend money on the acquisition of
property and he had a very simple living style. I used to go to his place in
Maida Vale, and also Queen's Gate, and everything was simple, functional,
inexpensive – rather boring, frankly. He disliked the lavish lifestyle and
wasn't interested in appearing to be wealthy or chucking his money

around. I think he was quite generous to people of whom he was fond, but he was very unobtrusive about that.'

Blake established Benny's limited companies – the first in 1957, a second in 1970, a third in 1979 – and also made some pension arrangements, but still his client expressed no interest. Once a year, when Baker Todman had to prepare tax returns, Benny would come to his office and dump down a plastic bag full of scrappy receipts and airline tickets. Blake's staff would valiantly wade through the pile and extrapolate accounts.

Benny made his first and – as it transpired, controversially, thirty years later – only will in 1961, and he asked Dennis Blake to draft the document and act as executor. His bequest was to be divided into three – one third going jointly to his parents, one third to his brother Leonard and the other to his sister Diana; if the named beneficiaries were deceased then the estate was to be divided among the children born to his brother and sister. It was a simple, straightforward, two-page statement signed 'A. H. Hill'. 'Those were his wishes, and not necessarily what I suggested,' says Blake, cautiously, 'but he had firm ideas of what he wanted to do.' Three years later, a codicil indicated that Benny had loaned Leonard and his wife Marjorie £4,000 to purchase a house – at an annual interest rate of 5 per cent. The codicil stipulated that any outstanding amount was to be cancelled in the event of his (Benny's) death. Not long after this, though, the brothers ceased to speak, and would not resume relations until the end of the 1980s.

Throughout this time, there were friendships that Benny kept strictly private, the 'unobtrusive' associations to which Dennis Blake alluded. (He too didn't know about them until much later.) Dave Freeman was unaware of them, as were Peter Charlesworth and Kenneth Carter and Richard Stone and everyone else. These were the platonic companionships that Benny maintained with at least two disabled women. While a few people knew that he was a quietly generous giver to charities, none was aware how he took care of Jeanette 'Netta' Warner, severely physically handicapped, nor of Phoebe King, handicapped by cerebral palsy at birth.

Both friendships began in the *Showcase* period of the mid-1950s, after the women had him sent fan-letters. He had responded with warm, handwritten replies. Phoebe then sent him a photograph of herself and they subsequently met when he performed on stage in her hometown of Felixstowe, the east coast port; and they met again during his 1957 summer season in nearby Great Yarmouth. When, in the mid-1960s, Benny learned that Phoebe's father had died, he decided to visit her, to comfort her in her grief. These visits became annual – initially for a weekend, then for a few days and eventually for a week. When Phoebe moved into sheltered accommodation, Benny would pack a small suitcase and stay in the guest room. Wrapping up against the bracing North Sea breezes, he would take Phoebe for long walks around Felixstowe, pushing her in the wheelchair, comfortably chatting about the lighter side of life and enjoying some easy silences. 'We had a lot of laughs together but he was a very quiet person as well,' says Phoebe. Along the way, Benny would find a place for lunch, the Indian restaurant or the local hotel, and never let Phoebe pay.

There soon developed a genuine, touching affection between the two, as indeed there was between Benny and Netta Warner in South Wigston, just outside Leicester. When Benny discovered that she had never walked unaided, he began to pay visits to her as well, staying in a tiny spare bedroom in her parents' terraced house. Benny also pushed Netta great distances in the wheelchair, usually stopping for lunch. Netta enjoyed watching horse-racing on television and dreamed of attending a meeting in person. Benny arranged for them both, and Netta's mother, an aunt and a nurse, to go to the races, and funded the trip, including all their betting.

At Conford House in Felixstowe, the nursing home where Phoebe lived, Benny would chat to the inmates who peeped out of their doors as he came along the corridor. One of the most famous men in Britain had come to stay in their drab, sterilized environment and the excitement was palpable. 'The residents were always as pleased as Punch to see him,' enthuses Phoebe, 'it was quite a jolly crowd. He'd take my cleaner out to lunch, and others who looked after me, to thank them for their work. I felt like a princess, waiting for his visits. They were lovely. But it was horrible when he went away. It would take me about two months to get over it, I used to cry so.'

These were friendships that demanded little of Benny but gave him, and his companions, great sustenance. He was in control and could come and go as he pleased, and his appearance would always be hugely appreciated. He would go to great lengths to ensure that Phoebe and Netta – who never met – be given the red-carpet treatment, paying for a chauffeur-driven car to bring them down to London, taking in lunch at the Savoy and an afternoon matinée at the theatre, or the cinema if there was a new James Bond film. He would visit restaurants in advance to check wheelchair access and establish whether the ladies' toilet could be reached without stairs. And for almost thirty years, neither his friends nor the media knew a thing about it.

One of the viewers of the *Benny Hill* sitcoms was Joan Kemp-Welch, an esteemed British television drama producer. It was said that she could trace her family tree back to 1200, numbering several artistes among them. She was decorated by her profession and became the first woman to direct a royal occasion in Westminster Abbey, staging the 1963 wedding of Princess Alexandra and Angus Ogilvy. And now she wanted to direct Benny Hill in a production of *A Midsummer Night's Dream*.

Benny was no special Shakespeare fan, and his reaction to Kemp-Welch's approach was to burst out laughing and ask, 'You're joking, aren't you? You must have got me muddled up with someone else!' But it was no joke. She had seen the qualities necessary for the role of the weaver, Bottom, in Benny's TV performances – a man with a roguish sense of humour, capable of inspiring endearment and laughter in equal measure. She wanted, she said to him, 'someone young and eager', someone suited to Quince's description of Bottom's Pyramus, 'A sweet-faced man; a most lovely, gentleman-like man'. Put like that, Benny couldn't say no.

This was, beyond question, the most challenging part in Benny's career. He had the starring role. To learn the lines he obtained multiple copies of the play and placed one in every room in his Queen's Gate apartment. 'And I mean every room,' he declared in the programme's considerable publicity material. He attended no fewer than eighteen days of rehearsals before the day-long video-taping; when others broke for lunch, Benny –

the eternally unstar-like star – would stay behind with an apple and a sandwich and perfect his stage movements.

The broadcast – on midsummer's night, 1964 – was a dazzling success, perhaps the first great modern Shakespeare production on British television. Benny's contribution, delivered in his broad West Country accent, was hailed as a performance of considerable subtlety and confidence. The Bard did not faze him, it seemed. He said he specially admired the – as he put it – 400-year-old gags.

Critics rose to their feet and applauded. *The Times* praised his 'innate conviction of superiority'. The *Sunday Times* – unable to resist a pun that the comedian himself would surely have employed – remarked upon 'the engaging spectacle of Benny Hill's Bottom'. The *Observer* rhapsodized at length: 'Benny Hill's Bully Bottom, as you might expect from this highly intelligent clown, was a pleasingly original variation. His idiot-boy embroidery was done on a firm background of obstinate megalomania, and his skipping gait, when metamorphosed with a Daliesque ass's head, was delightful.'

A Midsummer Night's Dream sold strongly overseas, and in February 1965 was screened in New York, Washington DC and Los Angeles. *New York Times* critic Jack Gould pronounced it 'the hit of the season' and admired Joan Kemp-Welch's astute showmanship by casting Benny Hill, whom he praised by writing 'in gesture and physical appearance he is the Buddy Hackett of the Thames and a funny man'.

This was not, however, Benny's first *New York Times* notice; it was simply the first to be kind. The future megastar of American television had made several appearances there to date and fallen flat each time. The first attempt to break Benny Hill in America occurred in 1959. Richard Stone had flown to New York in the company of Ronald Waldman, Benny's former champion in BBC TV Light Entertainment who had just been appointed head of BBC Enterprises, the worldwide programme-sales division. Struggling under the weight of outsized film cans, Waldman carried a BBC *Benny Hill Show* and Stone carried an ATV *Benny Hill Show*. Neither was able to rouse any American interest. 'We flew out first-class on BOAC and sat around in the Algonquin Hotel,' says Stone. 'Nobody came to see us, and we went to see nobody. We were very unimpressive. I thought at least that Ronnie would be welcomed, but it seems the BBC was not world-recognized in those days.'[3]

Although a lifelong admirer of American comedy, taking his stage forename from one its top practitioners, Benny was only mildly interested in cracking the US market. Other British comedians were far hungrier for it, though few got the chance and even fewer succeeded. Morecambe and Wise, huge in Britain, tried and failed time and again; at this time, only one English comic attained stardom in America – Richard Hearne, who became a regular performer on *The Ed Sullivan Show*, usually in the guise of 'Mr Pastry', his accident-prone old man character who practised slapstick comedy. The force behind the attempts to crack Benny Hill in America was Richard Stone, who saw great opportunities for his client there. Benny, though, refused to travel across the Atlantic to push for a breakthrough. 'He wasn't very keen at all,' says Stone.

A compromise was reached whereby he agreed to make American TV appearances from England. In 1961, he turned up in an edition of *The Great All-Star Show*, made at ATV studios in Borehamwood – near Elstree, north of London – for the American market, and featuring the US singer Jo Stafford and actor Peter Lawford.[4] Benny was their 'special guest'. This kind of appearance was anathema to him. 'You go on for three minutes,' he moaned in the press, 'you sing a madrigal, say, and it doesn't go down. So they think you're a madrigal singer. You don't have time for mime or impressions or sketches.' America, too, showed no interest in him. Though the *Daily Express* boasted patriotically that 'the programme chief of one of the major US networks' had seen some taped Benny Hill shows and pronounced him 'the greatest comedy talent I've seen in Europe', these big words were not backed up by a big offer.

The prospect of Benny making headway in America flickered briefly once more when he was one of three BBC stars whose work was screened by NBC in its *International Showtime* series in March 1962. It was a bold move for the network to give primetime exposure to British humour since, as Jack Gould noted, this was 'an undertaking that in the past has frequently put something of a strain in Anglo-American amity'. *International Showtime* featured Galton and Simpson's 'Blood Donor' episode from *Hancock* in its marvellous entirety, and some of *Sykes and a Bath*, an admirable episode from Eric Sykes' inspired sitcom. Benny was the final part of the BBC's triumvirate presentation and his section was a ten-minute 'wraparound' sequence, *Television Today*, taken from an April 1961 show. It began with a Fred Scuttle interview about audience research – blending stupidity and sauciness in the usual Scuttle measures – and led into some clever skits about the medium's technical developments since the 1930s. Jack Gould enthused greatly about Hancock and Sykes in the *New York Times* but found Benny Hill sadly lacking and 'trapped in a forbiddingly forlorn presentation'.

Globally, too, Benny was a long way from the huge success he would become. The *Benny Hill* sitcoms had been sold to New Zealand, Australia and Rhodesia, but there was no interest beyond the British Common-wealth, and not much more even when the BBC became aggressive in its marketing, using the 1965 Montreux TV Festival to put *The Benny Hill Show* in its shop window.

By 1964, Benny had begun to pursue a film career once again. Shortly after *A Midsummer Night's Dream*, 20th-Century Fox contracted him to appear in its new madcap adventure movie *Those Magnificent Men in Their Flying Machines*, a wacky epic, co-written by Jack Davies and the film's director Ken Annakin, about the 1910 London to Paris air race, full of wonky bi-planes and dodgy moustaches. Cast as Perkins, a bumbling, north England fire chief, this was still little more than a cameo role, though. His contribution was shot in England over four days and he was paid just £2,000. He did it well enough, mind. Benny had played a fireman before and, as he might have said, knew how to handle his hose.

When he had first moved into Queen's Gate, Benny had the flat painted and decorated according to his grand entrepreneurial ambitions. He even thought to fix acoustic tiles to the ceiling. Later, to maintain privacy and not cause offence to the neighbours, he had also taken out a lease on the adjoining apartment, number 5, and (after applying for permission) had the two knocked into one.

After these ambitions had capsized, however, and for the next twenty years, Benny scarcely spent another penny on the upkeep of his now double-apartment. Despite the splendour reflected in the Kensington address, Benny's residence began to resemble a rundown council-flat. 'It is a room, you feel, still waiting for the kiss of life,' one visiting journalist noted.

'His flat in Queen's Gate had a chair to sit on, a table to eat off, a bed to sleep in and a chest of drawers to keep things in,' says Jeremy Hawk, who worked with Benny again on TV in 1965. There was also a black-and-white TV situated plumb in the middle of the main reception room, perched on top of a packing case. He was still an avid viewer – it provided a continual production line for his 'spoof' wraparounds. Awards and photographs were arranged haphazardly on a mantelpiece; one photo, which Benny occasionally took pains to point out to visitors, was of Jean, his 'girlfriend' from Woolworth's perfume counter in Eastleigh twenty-five years earlier. The kitchen cupboards were mostly empty. Visitors might be offered fish-fingers but he was known to serve food on paper plates and with plastic cutlery, to save on washing-up.

While his great ambition was crumbling, Annette André, Benny's belle from his 1960 visit to Sydney, arrived in England, and, picking up on his earlier invitation, got in touch. A stranger in a foreign country, in need of work, she was certain to contact a friendly and possibly influential star. Benny, inevitably, interpreted the approach as the green-light to a steady relationship. Annette thought otherwise. 'I know he was strongly attracted to me,' she says, 'but I just thought he was a very good friend. He was a lovely guy – he had a special gentleness and thoughtfulness, he was sensitive to people's feelings, especially to women, and he was courteous.'

Benny set out to pursue his dream woman in the only way he knew. While shop-girls and factory girls were suitable for 'pleasing Mr Hill', beautiful, respectable, articulate women like Annette André he treated with the utmost delicacy. He courted them like an Edwardian gentleman, with flowers and chocolates, soirées at the Blue Angel night-club in Mayfair and Casa Pepe in Fulham Road (his favourite Spanish restaurant) and with polite small-talk about show-business, boxing . . . and his mother. 'He had a very strong affinity for her,' Annette remarks. 'It was clear that he loved her.'

Annette noted too how Benny 'was continually making sure that he wouldn't be put into a too emotional situation'. As for his Queen's Gate flat, she comments, 'It was the kind of place where you'd say, "Let's go out for dinner."'

Fifteen years his junior, Annette found Benny's old-fashioned attentiveness charming and flattering, but she denies consciously leading him on. 'We went out quite a few times and I knew that he was very fond of me and hoped things might go forward. He even mentioned it. But I didn't think that way at all and always kept it at friendship level. He'd make little passes and then laugh and throw it off, so I never knew whether to take him seriously or not. And I was young and probably not as sensitive to his feelings as maybe I would have been at another time.'

Benny and Annette didn't go to bed together and scarcely progressed beyond hand-holding, but after an appropriate interval Benny felt compelled to ask her to marry him. Proposing had never been his strong suit. It required a nerve steadier than he could hope to muster; also, because he was convinced that the answer would always be no – and perhaps because he wanted it to be – he had invented a curious method of popping the question. He would toss the proposal into a conversation so obliquely and hurriedly that it could pass unnoticed. In this way, if a woman challenged him – 'Did you just say what I think you just said?' – he could pass off his proposal as a joke remark; if it went unnoticed he had not made an ass of himself; if she said 'yes' . . . then, well, he would have to face up to the situation. But by choosing the wrong women the answer was never going to be 'yes'.

The result of these tortured solicitations is that Annette André can never be sure whether Benny proposed marriage to her or not. 'I *think* he did,' she says, 'but it wasn't said in such a way that I could say, "Oh Benny, I'm sorry, please put the engagement ring away." It wasn't as clear cut as that. He didn't go down on one knee, he intimated, he threw it into a conversation to the extent where I didn't even have to respond.'

Sadly, Benny chose to interpret Annette's 'response' – her silence – as rejection, and, consistent with the other rejections in his life, was crushed. He confided his feelings in Hettie Tack, personal assistant to BBC producer John Street. Benny and producers' secretaries always got on famously. These were 'safe' women who cared for him. Right from the start he had been close to Valerie Willis, Ken Carter's PA; he then formed everlasting friendships with Hettie Tack, Anne Ling in BBC radio and, in later years, René Bloomstein at Thames Television. Again, though, just like his two disabled friends, these women never met one another.

'Benny used to phone me fairly often and cry on my shoulder,' says Hettie Tack, still with affection. 'I was always ready to listen and try to offer advice. On one occasion he was really depressed, saying, "Oh, darling, my love life is such a mess." He explained that there was a woman he really had a thing about and that she had "led him on" for some time. This had prompted him to get the flowers and chocolates and go to see if he could cement something. She then told him there was somebody else and that he, Benny, wasn't in the picture and never would be. Benny was shattered – he thought he'd been really kind and considerate and helped her in this way and that, and that this was the way she repaid him.'

A motherly Jewish matchmaker, Hettie longed for the right woman to take her friend's hand and give him stability. 'This was the period when Peter Sellers had Britt Ekland on his arm,' she says, 'and Benny wanted a little starlet for himself, to be able to say that she was his. But as far as I could see, he got used. He was a star, and going out with him could make women stars, too. He would have done better if he'd found himself a really nice girl and had children. He adored them and told me on several occasions that he wanted more than anything else to have a family.'

A while after the 'relationship' broke, Benny made one final attempt to win Annette André's affections, booking her as a supporting player in a 1967 television show. It was no use – in the interim, she had fallen in love with another man. 'I heard later that Benny was upset by that,' she reflects, 'although I didn't know it at the time.'

Though he did not name her as the source of his gloom, Benny mooned about Annette André for years, in a manner out of all proportion to their true relationship. It was almost as if being hurt was a badge of pride, indicating that he was capable of love if only women would understand him. 'It can be rotten to be really in love,' he generously informed *TVTimes* readers in 1969. 'It is like a physical pain in the chest, literally choking you. I cannot bear it, even now, when she appears on TV. [André had a major role in the ITV crime-adventure series *Randall and Hopkirk (Deceased)* at this time.] I have to go out, anywhere, because when you've had a gutful of unhappiness you can't torture yourself any more. In the end you console yourself with the thought that things wouldn't have worked out anyway. But it's all over now – at least, I like to think it is.'

Had she read this, Annette André could have been forgiven for being astonished that Benny was talking about her. In later years, however, he decided to name the name. 'Not long before he died I read some things that absolutely shattered me,' she says, 'how I'd hurt him and so on. They made me sound like I'd been a terrible woman who had ruined his life. He was in hospital and I phoned and told him how upset I was to have read those things, but that I had been totally unaware of hurting him. I'd never have wanted to upset him like that. I offered to visit him in hospital but he said, "Oh no, no, no, I'm not very well and I get very tired . . ."'

Though his hopes of becoming an entrepreneur had amounted to nothing, Benny pulled off his shrewdest ever piece of business in 1964. He suggested and clinched a quick and simple trade that would both make and save him, quite literally, a fortune in the years to come. In return for a one-off £1,000 payment he secured the full copyright in all of the scripts written for him by Dave Freeman, including Freeman's share in their co-written material. (Freeman preserved ownership of the half-hour sitcoms, however.) Benny would now be at liberty to plunder a library of someone else's sketches and jokes entirely under his ownership. 'It seemed like quite a good deal at the time,' says Freeman. 'I thought, "He's already done everything twice, how much more can he use them?" Also, he seemed to be launching himself more into films at this time – it didn't seem likely then that he'd do much more on TV. Little did I know!'

Freeman says that Benny sweet-talked him into the deal by saying, 'If I use this stuff I can't fiddle about saying, "I wrote this bit, you wrote that bit and I'm not sure which of us wrote the other bit", and I also can't keep paying you a small sum each time I do use something. So if you take £1,000 now, I'll have the lot.'

The deal spotlights a rarely seen, hardened aspect to Benny Hill's character. The global sale of his 1970s and 1980s television shows, in which he time and again recycled Freeman's work, earned him literally millions of pounds, but he made no subsequent comment to his friend nor volunteered any further payment. (Similarly, it says much for Dave Freeman that when Benny became massively rich on the back of his writing, he did not sue, complain or even consider breaking their still strong friendship.) Remarkably, there wasn't even a written agreement – 'He just sent me a thousand quid and that was it,' Freeman laughs.

Only one thing would perturb Freeman. On every subsequent show, Benny removed his name from authorship of the work, a development they had not discussed. 'Written by Benny Hill' the credit would run, always some distance from the truth. This airbrushing did nothing to improve Benny's standing among Britain's comedy writers, a group who for more than a decade had been holding him in contempt over his magpie tendencies. They did not like to see him claiming credit for their fellow craftsman's work, and thought £1,000 a derisory buy-out fee. On the subject of the money at least, Freeman himself was and remains more sanguine. 'In the light of Benny's huge American success I'm sure I could have earned much more,' he says, 'but I'm not that money-orientated. As long as I have enough to live on, that's fine.'

Benny made back his £1,000 before the year was out. Freeman had started contributing to the Benny Hill Bank of Comedy Material in 1954, just as the aspiring star was becoming established as the first great television comedian. He had also written for Benny's stage work, principally the revue *Fine Fettle*. One medium in which this material had scarcely been exposed, however, was radio; it was also the medium in which, hard though he had tried, Benny had failed to make his mark. Now, capitalizing on his stature, he talked the BBC into giving him his own radio show, *Benny Hill Time*. It took to the air in February 1964 for the first of three series; when the last of these ended, in April 1966, twenty-six half-hours had been broadcast; all drew heavily upon Dave Freeman's TV sketches, updated where necessary, yet carried the credit 'Written by Benny Hill'. Only two people would have been aware of the deception in Benny's launch press statement, 'It'll be the first time I've ever written a series by myself. A number of ideas came to me on holiday and I jotted them down.'

A few astute listeners also recognized the material, but not many. Benny was certainly *au fait* with it, though. Anne Ling, who was PA to producer John Browell in BBC radio Light Entertainment, and who immediately struck up a warm friendship and working relationship with him, remembers how he would dictate the entire show in her Aeolian Hall office, as she scribbled furiously in shorthand prior to typing the script. 'He would say, "Are you ready? Ready, steady, GO! Hello everyone and welcome to *Benny Hill Time*," and he would do all the characters, not just his own, sometimes leaping around the office and checking my reaction to see whether an item was funny. At the end he'd say "The End!" That first radio series was entirely in his head.'

Benny Hill Time still did not make Benny a radio star. Try as he might, he simply wasn't suited to the medium. Though there were some good moments, it was obvious by now that to find Benny Hill funny you had to see the saucy twinkle and the smile curling up at the corner of the mouth. Without vision, many of the sketches were ordinary and the cruder material simply crude. He never tried again.

In the final series of *Benny Hill Time*, Richard Stone planted another of his clients in the supporting cast, a beautiful blonde actress, Elaine Taylor, aged twenty-one. (She also appeared on television with Benny in 1965, cast as the temptress in a remake of his emotional subjugation spoof *Baby Boy*.) She could almost have been a double for Annette André. Certainly, what had passed between Benny and Annette was all but repeated between Benny and Elaine. He developed a huge crush on her, they went out a couple of times, she liked him but did not love him, she tried to prevent him from getting carried away, he did anyway, she walked away, later taking up with someone else, and his 'love' was shattered. It was the old, old story. The difference here was that Benny was now forty-two, not thirty-four or twenty-six. It was, he decided, the last time.

'You know when someone fancies you – there was a lot of staring,' Elaine remembers. 'I gathered later that he developed crushes on many of the young women he worked with. He went for dolly birds, young women who really weren't much use to him, when he could have done with someone his own age, someone he could have shared things with.'

Elaine and Benny went out a couple of times, though it was innocence itself. 'I suppose now that going out to dinner might have raised his hopes,' she concedes, 'but he was good company – very attentive, fun to be with and gentle. I sensed he was very lonely. I had no desire to have an affair with him, and I remember nipping it in the bud, showing that I wasn't interested. I would claim to be tired and say that I wanted to keep it to a working relationship, and he backed off. I realize now he was perhaps wounded by this, and I can't say, being so young, that I would have handled it very well. But I think he would have been wounded no matter how I might have said it.'

As PA on *Benny Hill Time*, Anne Ling was well aware of Benny's infatuation with Elaine Taylor. 'He asked me if she had a boyfriend and I said that I didn't know her well enough to know,' she says. 'I found out the answer just a little after he did. He was down for a long while after that.' Elaine was starting to date Christopher Plummer, the dashing star who fuelled the fantasies of millions of women watching *The Sound of Music*, the film in which, as Captain von Trapp, he had captured the heart of Julie Andrews. Benny felt he could not possibly compete with such a manly man. (Taylor and Plummer were married in 1970 and are still together today.)

Perhaps realizing that he had been humiliated – or had humiliated himself – over women once too often, Benny lashed out, and it was Richard Stone who received the brunt of his irrational ire. 'He blamed me for putting Elaine in the show,' says Stone. 'He chased her around London and then had a go at me for it. It was "all my fault". He wrote me dreadful, dreadful letters. I think perhaps he didn't have anybody else to hit out at.'

Benny had never been so idle. His life had settled into a pattern – one TV series a year, those final radio shows, a few TV commercials (although the Schweppes deal had now ended) and the occasional record (and consequent chart success), the latter usually released when he was abroad and needed to maintain a public presence back home. He now reckoned to spend around twenty weeks a year on the Continent, usually in France and Spain. Outside his own series he rarely turned up on television, making no guest appearances and flatly refusing to do chat-shows, a policy that he claimed kept him fresh in the eye of the public. If viewers saw him only three or four times a year, he reasoned, they would not grow bored. There is a shrewd logic here. The London *Evening Standard* writer Maureen Cleave noted in 1966, 'When you reflect that he was Television Personality of the Year in 1954 and that twelve years later we are still pleased to see him, you will appreciate his cleverness in keeping himself to himself.' This was also a policy born of fear, though. Other than singing, there was nothing that Benny could do on another TV show. He was no standup comedian and was hopelessly nervous in anything he could not control.

He had, too, more than enough money, being content to average his £20,000 a year when, with greater effort, he could have doubled or tripled it. Dennis Blake, Benny's accountant, found Benny unresponsive even when he arranged a spectacularly good investment deal on his behalf, a legal yet complicated tax avoidance scheme with a City company named Constellation Investments. It netted Benny in excess of £100,000 but, says Blake, 'It was another occasion when his eyes glazed.'

Richard Stone, who had a reputation for finding work – any work – for his clients, considered Benny the most puzzling person he had ever represented, a performer who did not want to perform. He didn't want the money either. At the end of one financial year, Stone's auditors had difficulty balancing the agency's books, and it was only after a good deal of head-scratching that it was discovered Benny had not been cashing his cheques again. 'I went around to Queen's Gate,' says Ann Croft, one of Stone's agents, 'and he opened the drawer of a small desk just by the front door. It was full of them – some from our office, some from other companies. He had never paid them in. It didn't matter, inasmuch as nobody suffered from his action, but he was *that* uninterested in material goods.'

When Richard Stone's office was contacted by the chairman of a major public company, wanting Benny to deliver a witty after-dinner speech, Ann Croft discovered too just how determined Benny was to earn 'enough and no more' – and, underlying this, how fragile was his self-belief in his abilities. 'Every man has his price,' the businessman declared when he heard that Benny had said no to £500 for the fifteen-minute job. He had never met Benny, who was cranky at even being approached. The chairman kept raising the offer, eventually reaching £2,500, a decent annual income for most people at this time. Ann Croft rang Benny one final time and was given a simple reply – 'He said to me, "You can tell him to stuff it up his jacksie."'

Benny was also, of course, still penny-wise. Having a cup of tea with Ann Croft after a recording session, he asked if she would like a slice of cake. The waitress pointed out that some of the fare on her trolley cost sixpence and some a shilling. 'Benny said to me, "You can have a sixpenny one,"' Ann recalls. 'I didn't really care what I had, but because I thought he was joking I said, "Oh, go on, let me have a couple of shilling ones!" and he replied, "No, I'm being perfectly serious. You can have a sixpenny one" – and I did. Then, when we left the tea-shop, it was pouring with rain. He had an umbrella but I didn't, and I said, "Well, goodbye, see you next week at the show." He said, "Where are you going?" and I said, "I'm getting a cab, of course." And he looked at me and said, "I'll walk you back." He walked me under his umbrella from Regent Street to Charing Cross Road, rather than see me waste my money – *my* money – on a taxi. It was another fascinating insight into his character.'

Without much work, and with time on his hands, those hands turned to food. They had no choice. A propensity for junk-food, marzipan, chocolate, cream-cakes and puddings, the parentally instilled obsession about not throwing away leftovers, and the inherently large Hill frame all combined to ensure that Benny would forever have a weight problem.

The pattern was always the same – when Benny wasn't working he would pile on the flab, especially if he went to France where he indulged in quantities of food and wine. Then, with a TV or film appearance looming, he would embark on a crash weight-loss programme, restricting himself to apples and bowls of lettuce. At such times, he would preach the language of the converted, arriving at the TV studio with a carrier-bag full of fruit and insisting that everyone take a piece – 'There's your vitamin C. Here you are, that's from Mr Hill for you. And you, you're not having an orange today because that would be two oranges in a row, so here's an apple instead.'

'He always had a weight problem, right from when I first got to know him in 1954,' says Dave Freeman. 'Even then, I remember that Ken Carter came up with a high-protein diet, where you ate nothing but lean meat and a certain proportion of fat but no vegetables. It was called the stone-age diet, because some clown had worked out that in stone-age times this is what people ate – the fat would burn away the fat, apparently. I went on this with Benny and we chewed our way through loads of meat until we got bored with it.'

Whatever the diet, and he endured a succession of faddish rations, Benny knew that his greatest enemy was gluttony. If he had six cans of fizzy drink in the fridge he would guzzle them all, so he tried to restrict himself to buying one or two at a time. If he bought a packet of a dozen fish-fingers he'd eat the lot in one sitting, so he bought in packs of six – just one, if he was strong enough to resist temptation. If he opened a bottle of wine he would have to drink it dry, and if anyone at his lunch table left anything in their glass he would drain it off as they got up to leave. He ate in a particular way, too – if he was having fish, chips and peas he would eat all the fish, then all the peas, then all the chips. He especially loved Chinese food because it would be served in perhaps a dozen different dishes, and he could finish them all off one by one. Benny was inextricably wedded to a regime instilled in him by a man who had foraged for food throughout a poverty-stricken childhood at the turn of the century. 'There's no such thing as bad food,' Benny would say to people. The words were right out of The Captain's mouth.

Benny's preferred method of countering his weight problem was walking. Having grown up in a car-less family, where walking long distances saved precious pennies, he remained a lifelong, dedicated pedestrian. Back in Southampton, when he visited his parents, he would trek immense distances – out to the eastern suburbs to visit his cousin Chris, up to Eastleigh to drop in on Ivy Lillywhite, and even as far north as Winchester, twelve miles away, to sit quietly at his beloved St Catherine's Hill and drink-in the green and pleasant land below. In London, though buses and taxis sped by, Benny thought nothing of trotting from Kensington to Ealing to film sketches for his television shows. He also liked to take a bus or train to a point some fifteen or twenty miles from home and then walk back. He'd go at a fair pace, too, one that occasional companions found hard to match. 'He always moved very, very fast,' says René Bloomstein, his PA at Thames Television in later years and a trusted friend. 'I saw him once in the local High Street and he was moving so quickly that I really had to call after him. He was shooting along like a loony.'

Like so many celebrities, Benny also kept his head down, avoiding eye contact with passers-by. If anyone did think they had recognized him, by the time they turned around to take another look, the man in the mac with the omnipresent plastic bag was long past. He told himself that the exercise would promote weight-loss, but usually, after walking to a point far from home, he would congratulate himself on his achievement by buying a handful of Mars bars for the journey back. There were also financial considerations. 'He'd walk across Hyde Park for the exercise,' laughs Peter Charlesworth, 'but on the other side of the park, just off Edgware Road, was a fishmonger's where lobsters were £1 cheaper than they were at Harrods. So it was a deal – he had shed a few calories, got the exercise and "saved some money."'

Benny Hill's nine television shows, from November 1964 to January 1966, numbered among his best ever. Such was his creative muscle – and so great the BBC's determination to keep him sweet, so that he wouldn't switch to the commercial channel – that when he insisted on Kenneth Carter as director, the BBC gulped and took back the former 'defector' on staff. Jeremy Hawk returned, too, and with a mix of reheated Dave Freeman sketches, newly written material, and location filming and studio sketches taped in front of a minimal audience, another winning formula was found.

There was a new Hill song in every show, usually delivered as a send-up of a pop-act – Peter and Gordon, Sonny and Cher, the Rolling Stones, Donovan and others. There were many splendid send-ups of TV commercials – notably of the one for Fairy Liquid, in which Benny played a tiny child enquiring of his mother (Pat Hayes) why her hands were so soft – he received a clip around the ear for asking and then complained that they were not soft at all. And there were several more film spoofs. *The Knack* became *The Knock* and *The Collector*, starring Terence Stamp, became *The Stamp Collector*, starring Benny Hill in another emotional-subjugation piece. For this, Benny utilized a new character, Mervyn Cruddy, a camp soul who spoke through tight lips and in a slightly high pitch. (Dave Freeman recalls that Benny modelled the voice on the former boxer and TV presenter Freddie Mills.) Cruddy's smiling eyes would acknowledge that the things he said in innocence also had another, saucier meaning. He featured in numerous sketches in later years and was always good value; Benny later proclaimed him his favourite character.

There were many other masterpieces. One was a pastiche of a badly edited and poorly projected feature-film, *Passengers of Passion*, set on board a ship, with the sound and vision continually going in and out of sync, dialogue cuts that – naturally, but smartly – led to double-entendres, obvious continuity errors and literally negative images. Even Benny's peers had to doff their cap at such inventive comedy. 'It was,' says Denis Norden, 'a memorable and impressive piece. It's so easy to think of Benny doing the smutty sketches and broad seaside-postcard characterization, but he also did some really first-class stuff. He was very clever as a director because it was not enough for him to be able to do it, he had to get the others to play along with him, and he picked a team that he could rely on.'

Despite his tendency to steal ideas, Benny was always at his best when he made the effort to create fresh material of his own. One of his most inspired pieces – oddly, one that he never rehashed – was a mime, performed in an April 1965 show, in which he and two women[5] made and ate breakfast in the kitchen to the bossa-nova rhythm of 'House-wives' Cha Cha' – slicing bread, making toast, filling a kettle and cracking boiled eggs to the beat of the music from the radio. Nine years later, Morecambe and Wise performed a sketch along precisely the same lines (to the tune of 'The Stripper') that has gone down as one of their most creative pieces. Its creator, Ernest Maxin (who worked with Benny in the 1950s), swears that the idea occurred to him in the rehearsal studio, but it is possible he may have subconsciously recalled Hill's piece from the previous decade.

Another innovative sketch drew on Benny's observations of a new television technique – the live-by-satellite interview. In his parody, the female interviewer in London (Pat Hayes) loses audio contact with her male interviewee in Heidelberg (Hill as a German baron speaking in broken English). Both, it is explained, have pre-written questions and answers. After an early moment of confusion, interviewer and interviewee go out of sync and the Baron responds to the question before the one we have just heard. Although these answers make sense, they are funnier juxtaposed against the wrong question:

Hayes How are you, Baron?
(Still fiddling with his earpiece, the Baron does not hear the question)
Hayes Is it true that you're coming to England soon?

297

Hill I am very well, thank you.

Hayes Is it true that this time you will be marrying your fiancée, Lady Thelma?

Hill Yes, and I hope to see much more this time than I was able to see on my last visit! There are several interesting and out of the way places I would like to visit. I would have visited them on my last trip but I was not given the opportunity.

This was an original and highly amusing idea, worthy of Benny's subsequent repetition. (Again, it was later explored by other comedians, notably in a spoof of the BBC TV quiz show *Mastermind* by Ronnie Barker and Ronnie Corbett in *The Two Ronnies*.)

A quite excellent piece of Benny Hill work was broadcast by the BBC in the 1964 edition of its annual comedy jamboree *Christmas Night with the Stars*. This was *The Lonely One*, a parody of a social television documentary about an eighteen-year-old delinquent, Willie Tredder. Benny played Tredder – thick, aloof, bored and on probation – and also the many commentators who looked at what had gone wrong in the young man's life: his fatuous female teacher, his over-zealous youth-club leader preaching the dangers of marijuana, his dim mother, his uninterested probation officer and his gruff factory foreman. In just seven minutes Benny Hill sent up the whole genre and managed to fit in a couple of inspired mimes.

Fully ten years after being named TV Personality of the Year, Benny was voted BBC Personality of the Year in the 1965 Variety Club awards. He had high-ranking fans, too – *The Benny Hill Show* was named among a handful of television programmes enjoyed by the Queen at this time. (The others were sitcom *Hugh and I*, *The Avengers*, *Danger Man* and, fantastically, *Thunderbirds*.) Playing the game his way, Benny had managed to stay at the top in a business that can create stars in the flicker of a cathode-ray tube and brusquely cast them aside in another instant.

Despite the honour, Benny still insisted that his future lay in films, not television – which he now, rather disparagingly, had taken to calling 'photographed radio'. Instead of capitalizing on his Variety Club award he would make no more BBC shows for two years; he enjoyed instead what he later described as 'A sudden spurt of ambition'.

He went on, 'I realized that I'd been making a very comfortable living on television for fifteen years – fifteen years! – and if I wanted to meet and beat other challenges, it would have to be elsewhere.'[6] On a brisk calorie-shedding walk one day across Kensington Gardens, Benny saw workmen demolishing the block of buildings on Queensway that had been his first post-war London home. Twenty years had passed since then; it was right that he should be seeking fresh horizons.

Benny found a new champion in a London-based American film producer, George 'Bud' Ornstein, an executive with James Bond co-producers Harry Saltzman and Cubby Broccoli's company Eon Productions. Eon was planning an extravagant new motion picture for all the family, *Chitty Chitty Bang Bang*, based on Ian Fleming's book of that name. When the lead actor, American comic Dick Van Dyke, suggested that some of the scenes in Roald Dahl's screenplay needed to be funnier, Benny was asked to script the re-writes. Working closely with director Ken Hughes, he spent five enjoyable weeks sprucing up the script.

Six months later, during principal photography, Benny was cast in the movie, too, in a substantial part – the kindly Toymaker who shelters children from the clutches of Robert Helpmann's evil child-catcher. Seemingly a simpleton, with a wide-eyed, mouth-curling smile, and yet possessed too of cunning, it was a role Benny knew well. With a hobbling, emasculated gait and Germanic accent, he turned in a sincere performance, imbued again with a keen sense of mime. When location shooting took him to the Hansel and Gretel-like south German village of Rothenburg-ob-der-Tauber in September/October 1967, Benny enjoyed an all-expenses-paid holiday, and when there was idle time on the set he and Dick Van Dyke talked at length about their mutual passions – Charlie Chaplin, Buster Keaton and Stan Laurel. 'We both thought that we were born in the wrong era,' Van Dyke said in a 1997 interview for the British TV series *Heroes of Comedy*.

Chitty Chitty Bang Bang renewed Benny's appetite for films, and he was delighted when Ornstein, who had left Eon and been appointed head of international production at Paramount Pictures, put him under contract. Benny prepared two scripts, both of which were accepted. The first was a short silent film, *The Waiters*, about two hired-hands who serve up food and mayhem at a country house dinner-party. The second was a feature-film, *The Only Way to Live*, in which he planned to co-star with a French actress. Acknowledging Benny's ability to play comic characters, film executives were beginning to dub him 'the Peter Sellers we can afford'.

While he set about developing *The Waiters* he accepted a cameo role in *The Italian Job*, one of the all-time-great adventure films: a stunt-filled, comedic gold-bullion-robbery caper starring Michael Caine. Benny took the part because Paramount asked him – though he had previously turned down a chance to appear in the James Bond spoof *Casino Royale*, made by Columbia. (And he had refused, too, an invitation to appear in the gentle northern England comedy *The Family Way*.) Benny's role in *The Italian Job* was the antithesis of his part in *Chitty Chitty Bang Bang*, though – he played a sexual deviant.

He was Professor Simon Peach, Britain's cleverest computer expert, whose function in the robbery is to hack into the mainframe system controlling the traffic in Turin, to create the ultimate gridlock. In the original script, Peach was encouraged to take part in the crime by being given a deluxe model train-set. Benny felt this was an insufficient incentive and suggested instead that Peach have a bent for unattractive plump ladies – 'Big, *BIG!*' – and that his inducement should be a sports car with two of them seated in the rear. After some high-ranking discussion at Paramount he was allowed to go away and write himself the role.

What evolved was an unsavoury creation, that of an irredeemable sex-menace who could also blissfully pick wild flowers. As well as stretching credibility – it was difficult to believe that Britain's foremost computer expert was such a dope – there was a dark side to Peach. He was an unsettling individual, harmless yet harmful, feeble yet intimidating. Though funny in the context of the film, he was the least palatable character Benny had created . . . and was it just coincidence that one of the fat women whom (out of view) Peach has molested without invitation – rape, in other words – he named Annette?

Benny gave Peach a Yorkshire accent. After filming, Paramount got the jitters about this, fearing that American audiences might not be able to follow it. He became angry when he had to dub on a new voice in regulation English, claiming that the comedic nuances of the role were eradicated in the process – a spurious argument considering Peach's sexual menace. In a fit of pique, he vowed never again to work in a film where

300

he could not maintain complete creative control. For a man whose chequered film career was finally beginning to prosper, this was a disastrous move. In television he was big enough to call the shots – literally, if his director was amenable. In films he was no great star and no particular box-office draw; no studio was going to give him such licence.

Consequently, when Bud Ornstein arranged for Benny to audition for the role of Captain Duvalle in the First World War spy movie *Darling Lili*, he had already lost interest. He arrived in director Blake Edwards's suite in the London Hilton in an arrogant mood; when the director asked him to demonstrate a French accent Benny turned smart-aleck and replied, 'Which kind? Parisian? Northern? *L'accent du midi*?' Edwards countered, 'Mr Hill, God hates a smart-ass.'

Soon afterwards, Bud Ornstein and Benny Hill parted company and the Paramount contract was severed. Having ditched the stage, and radio, and turned his back on TV, the aspiring film-maker was cast adrift.

14. The Rejected Director

Fifteen years after finding fame, Benny Hill, forty-five, was trying to find himself. He was throwing his weight around – though burning half-built bridges in the film world would be proven unwise. Newspaper articles about the comedian were suddenly carrying an edge, with headlines like 'Whatever's Happening to Benny Hill?', 'The Lonely World of Benny the Birdman' (not an Alcatrazian interest but a play on the subject's interest in women) and 'The Private Face of Benny Hill'. The malevolent trait he had uncovered for Professor Peach in *The Italian Job* would be continued when he finally got to make his own cinema film, *The Waiters*.

These were the watershed years, and the man who usually revealed nothing of himself was peeling back the veneer just a smidgen. He told *TVTimes* writer Kenneth Passingham how he had spent New Year's Eve, 1968. 'I sat down with a bottle of wine and my diary to discover the nicest thing that had happened to me all year. Do you know what it was? A tree. Something about its shape, the way it was mottled in the sun. It was beautiful. A tree! The best thing in my life. Can you believe it?

'Trouble is,' he went on, 'I don't get excited any more. I'm doing the same thing as I was seventeen or eighteen years ago. Nothing's changed except the money.' And then the repeated assertion. 'What I'd really like to do is direct feature films.'

Having alienated Bud Ornstein at Paramount, this seemed an unlikely prospect. During recent visits to Paris however, staying in L'Hôtel Tuileries Montana, a £5-a-night pension on rue Saint Roch, he had attempted to – as he described it – 'crash into French films'. Quite what this entailed he never made clear, but his ambition was transparent: he wanted to make films like his great hero Jacques Tati, the former French music-hall comedian who had switched to making inspired dialogue-free movies. 'The French go in a lot for funny films of the sort that are badly neglected by the British,' Benny said at this time. He intended to rectify the situation.

He got to meet his idol, too. 'They spent an afternoon together,' says Peter Charlesworth. 'Tati was shooting in the East End of London and Benny went down to there to meet him. Tati didn't quite know who he was to begin with but they spent a good two or three hours together, talking about the business of making comedy films. Benny came back and told me that he'd had a marvellous afternoon – it was a big moment in his life.'

Benny launched into making *The Waiters*. Paramount had kicked the project into action and then into touch; a small London production company, Fanfare Films, owned by the veteran producer George H. Brown, was assigned the contract. Benny believed it might be the start of a fruitful relationship. 'He hoped it would become a cult and that he might win some kind of prize for it,' reflects Pamela Cundell, who was cast in the movie.

Benny was desperate to direct *The Waiters* and yet – officially, at least – was unable to do so. To direct a film in Britain one had to be a member of the Association of Cinematograph Television and Allied Technicians, the trade union ACTT, which was particular about those whom it admitted. It did not want to see comedians or actors becoming directors, taking work away from their members. As virtually all of British film-making and TV business was unionized at this time, and few technicians would have worked under a director who was not a member, the result for Benny Hill was pure frustration.

He evaded the problem by appointing a puppet director, someone malleable to his point of view, someone inexperienced in comedy who would not object when the star wanted to take a long look through the lens and proffer instruction to his cameraman or fellow performers. The chosen man was Jan Darnley-Smith, who was just breaking into films after directing a sixty-five-episode TV series about yoga.

In the canon of Benny Hill's work, *The Waiters* remains a curiosity. Scarcely seen since its release, it was a three-reel (thirty-minute) movie with music but no dialogue – not even much muted or mouthed speech. The storyline depicted two hired hands employed to wait on the guests at a small middle-class dinner-party in a country house somewhere in

England. The event was hosted by Pamela Cundell's somewhat blowsy character (none of the parts was given a name); Benny and David Battley, the lugubrious comic-actor, were the waiters.

Benny's character was a devious man who created and inwardly rejoiced in others' misery, and who chewed, smoked and belched while serving. In his sketch-comedy Benny was the perennial fall-guy. He never got the girl, nor even understood the girl; women rang rings round him, indeed they often found him so irksome that they chased him and he, feckless chap that he was, ran away from them. In *The Waiters*, far from being the soiled cherub, he was a sexual incubus, literally molesting and forcing his attentions on a pretty young woman, bringing her almost to tears. He leered aggressively at another woman's breasts and gripped her leg under the hem of her short skirt, on both occasions looking her square in the eye, defying disapprobation.

Benny (and, to a lesser extent, his cohort) ruined the dinner-party and didn't care. He took their money at a card game, tried to steal from the hosts and, for the denouement, left the gas-tap open in the kitchen. As he cycled away, not a worry in the world, an explosion rocked the house. Firemen rushed past him on their way to the blaze but he didn't even turn around to look.

This really was fresh territory. Evidently, Benny had been doing some deep thinking about the nature of comedy. The seeds of *The Waiters* were still being sown when Benny gave an interview to the British journalist Marcelle Bernstein in 1968:

> To me, comedy is exposed emotion. It's the way people feel and their consciousness of it, and you've got to have a knowledge of certain reactions. I care a lot about what's going on in people's minds, what makes them tick and how they feel about things. You have to dig down, winkle out thoughts buried in their minds and push them in front of people – anger, jealousy, embarrassment, indecision. They're all good comedy.

There was, however, an unreal quality to *The Waiters*. Despite the endless indignities meted out by the waiters, neither hosts nor guests complained. 'To my mind,' comments David Battley, 'none of the people were acting properly. Even in a ridiculous comedy you wouldn't have people who were being treated like that just sitting there quietly. That was the director's fault.' Battley observed other shortcomings, too. 'I was a bit disappointed in the way it was shot,' he says. 'Some of the gags needed more impact. They ended up lost. It could have been much more slick. And even in those days I'm not sure how much audiences were prepared for half an hour without dialogue.'

In such a menacing piece, Benny needed a running visual gag to lighten the load. David Battley became the persistent recipient of a new idea – the patronizing slap. At (or without) the merest provocation, Benny would slap Battley about the head, asserting his authority. Benny slapped everything, including the party hostess's plump rear. The head-slap – something he had seen done in the larkish American musical comedy act Spike Jones and his City Slickers – would soon become one of Benny's comedy perennials, his perpetual victim in *The Benny Hill Show* being a tiny, bald-headed Irishman, Jackie Wright. The curious thing about the slap is that no recipient ever complained or retaliated. It was an unchallenged dominance. Indeed, only once in *The Waiters* did anyone respond to Benny's endless aggression. After forcing the pretty young woman to dance in a tight embrace, against her struggle and her boyfriend's wishes, Cundell broke them apart and pushed Benny back against the fireplace. His lip began to quiver, suggesting that this was the first time anyone had admonished him – but he was soon back to his customary brusquerie.

So much for the theory and execution. There was also the making. The film was produced on a shoestring budget – the orange satin and chiffon gown worn throughout by Pamela Cundell was her own, and it was damaged in a scene at the end. 'He said to me, "We're going to make a film without any words, a silent film, like in the old days,"' says Cundell. '"It'll be a laugh and we'll have a good time." I don't know that we even had a script, though – Benny just told us what he wanted as we went along.' She notes, too, that Benny 'did it all' on the film – including the direction, that is – and that he clearly played a 'harder' character. 'I think he hoped to go somewhere different with the role,' she offers.

A crucial element in *The Waiters* was the incidental music, and for this Benny turned to Cyril Ornadel, a Richard Stone client whom he had known since the early years of post-war struggle. He had also been involved in Benny's first TV series, in 1955. 'Benny was pinning a lot of hope on *The Waiters*,' says Ornadel. 'It was a new territory for him and he masterminded the whole thing. He was very insecure about it, though, asking me "Is it funny?" I thought it was good. Honesty was the basis of our friendship – if I had said that something wasn't good I'm sure he would have looked at it again. He was a big man but not a big-headed man, and completely for his art. That was his life.'

Benny said nothing about *The Waiters* on its eventual release in September 1970, when it was screened (though not by all cinemas) as support to *Catch-22* – as bizarre a coupling as any the British cinema has devised. There weren't many laughs to be had from Joseph Heller's desperately dark war comedy. Then again, there were scarcely any in *The Waiters*, which came across as an unfunny and ultimately disturbing piece, dreary and lacking both atmosphere and comedy invention. It was not in Tati's league.

Benny had, however, spoken about the film after its completion, saying, 'We have high hopes. If it is well received and then goes round the world – because, having no dialogue, there are no language problems – it could make the kind of money that will attract British film-makers into this field.' Working again with Benny in 1972, Pamela Cundell talked with him about *The Waiters* and remembers, 'He was very disappointed that it hadn't worked. His way of handling it was to say, "We're ahead of our time, darling, that's what it is, we're ahead of our time."'

By this point, however, Benny's film aspirations were out of time.

His TV career was in limbo, too. It was 1968 and he hadn't made a show for the BBC since January 1966. The only television he had done at all in 1967 was for Lew Grade's ATV. Always the most commercially minded British TV mogul, Grade liked to make shows in England – ostensibly for his ATV company – that he could also sell on to America, where the really big money could be made. In addition to numerous adventure serials made by his ITC offshoot, Grade was still producing American entertainment 'spectaculars' at the ATV studios in Borehamwood; in 1967 he reached a deal with CBS to make nine such shows, *Spotlight*, as a summer replacement for *The Red Skelton Show*. As intent as ever on prising Benny Hill from the BBC and on to ATV, Grade invited the comedian to appear in two editions of the series. Benny was reluctant – he hated this kind of show, still equating guest spots to the old Variety stage, where artistes were given five minutes to prove their worth – and yet he found it hard to say no to Richard Stone. For his part, Stone – who was also being wooed by Grade, who wanted to take over his agency – was keen for Benny to make these appearances, hoping once more that his client might become a star across the Atlantic.[1]

Spotlight came at the wrong time for Benny. He was more interested in film-making than in television, and he was still loyal to the BBC and didn't want to upset any apple-carts. Richard Stone, who didn't get along with some of the new, younger BBC executives, was less sentimental. He was hoping to persuade Benny to move permanently to ITV, preferably to ATV. 'I was thinking that I was furthering his career,' he says. 'Lew Grade made good programmes. Also, he was bringing over big American stars for the *Spotlight* shows, making them in colour for America. I thought it would be good for Benny to be in them – and he had very little to do.'

Things did not go at all well, of course. With the customary stubbornness that surfaced when he was forced into doing something, Benny made life difficult for everyone in *Spotlight* and complained from first to last; singing a duet with Paul Anka was *not* what he wanted to be doing. 'They were disastrous shows,' says Stone. 'Benny was very angry about it all. As we left Borehamwood for the last time he swore "I'll never come here again."'

As well as killing any chance of a permanent move to ATV, Benny had sabotaged, yet again, the prospect of any American breakthrough. Evidently, this was fine by him.

To prove his loyalty to the BBC, and perhaps defy Richard Stone in the only way he knew, Benny made his first appearance back on his beloved BBC at Easter 1968. 'I don't want to do another TV series,' he said in a promotional interview. 'I really want to develop in films as a writer and performer. But an occasional one-shot TV – that's fine.'

It certainly was. This was a crackerjack show, stuffed to the gills with film send-ups and impressions. In a 'Jean-Paul Satire' spoof, *Mondo Rompo*, full of baffling flashbacks and meaningless dream sequences, Benny got his own back at ATV with a joky screen credit, 'filmed at Borehamstiff

Studios'. Later in the show he performed an impersonation of the singing duet Esther and Abi Ofarim and then, in a marathon eleven-minute sequence, *Hollywood and the Stars*, managed to cram in impressions of Harpo, Chico and Groucho Marx, Elizabeth Taylor and Richard Burton, Oliver Hardy, an especially convincing Sydney Greenstreet and Peter Lorre (exactly as he had performed them in the 1947 London revue *Spotlight*), Nelson Eddy, a bald and bloated Rod Steiger and a hopelessly unintelligible Marlon Brando in *On the Waterfront*, and, quite brilliantly, both W. C. Fields and Mae West, whom he had first impersonated in childhood. It was worth every penny of the £2,000 fee wrested out of the BBC by Richard Stone, a negotiation that again exceeded the BBC's long-established yet confidential 'Fees for Star Artists' code. By now agitating for a move, Stone had told the BBC that if it could not meet his demands then Benny would work elsewhere. The BBC clearly meant to hang on to him.

At the end of 1968, Benny agreed to make three further shows. For these, a new straightman, Henry McGee, was tried out for the Scuttle sketches, an attractive actress, Jenny Lee-Wright, was brought in, as were a bald, moon-faced character-actor named Bob Todd and a tiny ageing Irishman, Jackie Wright. With further additions, this would be Benny's resident support company for a long time to come.

These shows included numerous spoofs – one, *Gavin Blod*, sent up the work of film director (and contemporary pupil of Taunton's School, Southampton) Ken Russell; another was a portrayal of children's fairy tales in the style of modern drama, Bo-Peep as a National Theatre production being one. There were also recycled Dave Freeman sketches and, to show that Benny still retained his magpie tendency, an idea pinched from Bob Newhart's comedy repertoire: a one-sided telephone conversation between a TV producer (Benny) and William Shakespeare:

> Hello, Will, what is it you've got for us? *Romeo and Juliet*? How many do you think you could squeeze out of it? They die in the first episode? We wanted a series! *A Midsummer Night's Dream* – full of fairies and one of them's a queen? Maybe in a couple of years time, Will, but I don't think they're ready for that yet. A comedian who's a weaver? He's called what? Will, I mean, couldn't you change it? Well . . . Behind, or Sit-upon? Bottom is so *blatant*.

No one, including Benny, knew these were to be his last shows for the BBC.

After *The Waiters*, Fanfare Films was not interested in anything else Benny Hill had to offer, and yet he remained desperate to turn his screenplays into reality. He had even written another one, which he said would feature an American pop group, with several roles for himself. Whether he really wrote screenplays is another matter, though. No copies have surfaced and Benny scarcely typed. More likely, they were handwritten 'treatments', outline ideas on a few scrap-pad pages. Richard Stone said as much in a meeting in 1971 when he reported that his client 'has spent hours preparing film treatments'. Films take months or years to write, not hours. (The meeting was to discuss a possible movie for Benny Hill with Hammer Film Productions, the 'horror' studio which was moving into British TV-related comedy features at this time. Benny himself blocked the idea.)

The idea Benny most wanted to explore was another half-hour silent piece, the Tatiesque *Eddie in August*. He was not shy about its premise. It was, he said, 'unrequited love – and those two words are the complete biography of my life'. Replete with all the lovelorn hallmarks of Benny Hill's comedy, this was a rare excursion into autobiography. Gone, for good, interestingly, was the depravity of Professor Peach and the waiter's brutal insolence. This was back to the familiar frame of reference. Benny could never get the girl, nor would Eddie. The roles were interchangeable.

The film would embody Benny's bewilderment with women. He aspired to those he thought refined – the Annettes and Elaines – yet could never land them. Pursuing these dreams, he would always fall in life's cowpat, and the melancholy of his situation would haunt him. Meanwhile, he scorned the shop girls to whom he would always return. He danced courtly attendance on the unattainable but treated those he could attain with something like contempt.

Who, though, would make *Eddie in August*? No British film company was interested, and Benny was still smarting over the fiery end to his Paramount association. Three years later he was telling the *Sunday Mirror* that he would brook no 'American interference' in his work. Adopting an accent to imitate a typical Hollywood producer, he jibed, 'Ya gotta do it like this, buddy, or they won't get it in the Mid-West!' He also declared, 'Most American producers are twenty years out of date. I'm not anti-American. I've been asked many times to work over there, but it's not for me.'

As the rejections mounted, Richard Stone took decisive action and approached Brian Tesler, Director of Programmes at Thames Television. Formed from the ashes of former franchisees ABC and Rediffusion, Thames was a new ITV broadcaster, awarded the weekday monopoly of commercial television in London. It commanded the richest advertising revenues and produced the lion's share of primetime programmes for the national ITV network. Poaching Benny Hill from the BBC on a permanent basis would be a sweet victory indeed for the aggressive new company, and in Richard Stone it found a decisive ally.

'Richard made the approach,' says Tesler. 'He talked about the *Saturday Spectacular* shows I'd done with Benny at ATV ten years earlier, saying that Benny always felt guilty about how poor they had been, and how "he'd like to make amends to you". He then explained how he wanted Benny to leave the BBC because he wanted to get him away from the producer he'd been with all this time [Kenneth Carter], who, by now, inevitably, was running out of ideas. He said Benny was "too soft-hearted to ask the BBC for another producer." So, putting those things together, he said, "I'm ringing you to ask if you'd like Benny to come to Thames, and if you would, who would you put in charge of the show?" I replied, "a) yes, and b) Philip Jones, our Head of Light Entertainment. And, incidentally, c) there's no need for Benny to feel bad about the old shows, it was just one of those things."'

Richard Stone told Benny he had found a maker for *Eddie in August*, with the corollary that he would also have to make some other shows for the ITV company, leaving the BBC. Even though Benny's loyalty to the Corporation was almost fanatical – 'He would have been happy to stay with the BBC for ever,' swears his former producer John Street, 'he wouldn't hear a bad word against it' – his desire to make *Eddie in August* was literally overwhelming.

The BBC – Benny's broadcasting capital since 1947 – was beside itself with rage. What hurt most was that, if money was the cause of his departure, as Stone suggested, the agent had denied the Corporation the chance to mount a counter-offer. Besides, it had always paid or exceeded the going rate for a star of Benny's calibre, and provided him with all the production facilities he sought.

Benny kept his head down to avoid the flak; the BBC *took* his head down – the photograph of a grinning Benny Hill was removed within days from a gallery of stars adorning a wall in Television Centre. Contractually obliged to rerun his last three 1968 shows in 1969, the BBC paid the repeat fees, refused to air them and erased the tapes. (All that exists of these last BBC programmes is a twenty-minute film insert for the final edition. Most of the previous shows going back to 1964 were kept and remain in the archive.)

Thames was ecstatic at its coup, and the timing was excellent. When Benny had 'arrived' on British television, at the time of the Queen's coronation, the medium was on the verge of its great breakthrough, taking a giant step towards overtaking the dominance of radio. Now mainstream British television was about to undergo its great upgrading – to colour. BBC2, the Corporation's second channel, not yet available to all viewers, had been broadcasting in colour since 1967, but Britain's two main channels, BBC1 and ITV, were black-and-white until November 1969. In the week of the great switch-over, much hyped by the broadcasters (although few viewers had colour sets yet), ITV unveiled Benny Hill with the trumpets blaring. He would work wonders for the balance-sheet.

More than anything else, Benny wanted to know what Thames could do for him. Richard Stone and Philip Jones met him at Queen's Gate to discuss important early business, and Jones says, 'The facilities were his prime concern. It started that way, and it remained so. This is not to denigrate any of the Thames producers, but Benny really was his own producer, in the sense that he knew what he wanted. He even drew diagrams about the dimensions of a set. He would ask for a staircase to have six-inch risers – "NB, six, not eight."'

The producer Jones appointed to direct Benny's shows (at this time there was no discernible difference in job-description between 'producer' and 'director' in British TV light entertainment) was John Robins, who had started out as a film cameraman. Benny was very happy with this, and wasted no time in getting down to work with Robins on *Eddie in August*. The script header emphasized the ambition.

BENNY HILL

in

EDDIE IN AUGUST

T.V. Screenplay by

BENNY HILL

Again, Benny wanted to direct; again the ACTT said no. Robins did so – with persistent input from the writer/star ringing in his ear. It was only after the film had been shot, but before its broadcast, that the trade union relented and awarded Benny his prized director's ticket. But he hadn't really bothered to wait. The credit for *Eddie in August* – 'directed by John Robins and Benny Hill' – reveals the degree to which he had already been secretly deployed, and a photograph shows him lying flat on the ground looking through the viewfinder of the Arriflex film camera. 'You have your own ideas,' Benny explained to Shaun Usher in the *Daily Sketch* when news about the granting of his ACTT card broke, 'especially when you've written it yourself.'

Once again, Benny worked hard to make his project a success. He personally composed twenty minutes of French-style incidental music and was a close observer at the recording session. He also took sole responsibility for the casting – and while he enjoyed working with familiar faces in *The Benny Hill Show*, he had chosen a different set of actors for *The Waiters* and did so again for *Eddie in August*. There was no place here for Hayes, McGee, Todd, Wright *et al.*

Because there was no dialogue, the script ran only to a few pages of direction:

Eddie's flat. Eddie has just zipped up a new pair of trousers. A bit tight. He looks at himself in the mirror – yes, he will have to do something about that tummy.

While there was once again a single theme, the subject's pursuit of a nurse (named Kathy in the script, and played by Nicole Shelby) whom he foolishly believes to be the love of his life, *Eddie in August* was more episodic than *The Waiters* – like an extended television spoof, it served as

312

a wraparound for a number of self-contained mimes. Some of these were thoughtfully developed – also unlike *The Waiters*. Sleeping in bed in his basement flat ('a £4 a week one', Benny scrupulously detailed in the script) Eddie is dampened by a passing street-cleaning vehicle, the water splashing through an open window. As he wakes up, he sees a dog by the window, appearing to have relieved itself.[2] In a suburban park, Eddie and no fewer than four other men nonchalantly manoeuvre themselves into ludicrous positions in order to look up the pretty nurse's dress as she lies on the grass, talking to a friend. And in a fantasy sequence, Eddie – who is suddenly an eminently able doctor – sets out to impress his nurse assistant, by now literally the woman of his dreams, by performing an operation on a sick car as if it was a delicate medical procedure.

The recurring statement in the film was that Eddie was frustrated. He pursued a new 'dream woman' every month.

> Church. From steeple, pan down to discover Kathy and Roger
> getting married – Flo and four other guests throw confetti as
> photographer tries to get them into position. Pan to other side of
> street. A sad Eddie stands there. His face is red, but his eyes are
> white. A quite pretty girl passes by. She stops to look at the
> wedding. Then glances at the red-faced Eddie and smiles. Eddie
> mistakes it for a smile of friendship. As she goes off, Eddie follows
> her. In long shot, he begins to catch her up.

Each woman was a little plainer than the last, yet Eddie's chase always ended with the same pathetic result. By February, however, his sights sufficiently lowered, he married Flo, the plain woman who could have been his all along. This was where Benny's life and the 'fictional' script parted company, though – there was no Flo in Benny's life.

After filming entirely on location – in and around Slough, west of London – in August 1969, *Eddie in August* went into post-production (various processes in which Benny was closely involved), then was played to a studio audience for a laughter track. There was no laughter for *The Waiters*, for which no audience had been hired or, for that matter, earned. For *Eddie in August*, which was – in places – good fun, Thames somehow managed to find, as it so often could, a member of the public whom all comedy producers adore, a woman liable to burst into raucous laughter at any moment. Her cackles adorn the soundtrack of *Eddie in August* much as Benny had noted the big women laughing in Southampton's Variety theatres in the 1930s, when he had first looked at a comedian and thought 'That job's for me!'

If the reaction to *Eddie in August* was good, he hoped to return to a film-making career, leaving his regular show behind. In the same month that he recorded Thames' first *Benny Hill Show* he spoke publicly only of his pet project, telling *Reveille* journalist Dennis Holman:

> I have already taken a step in the direction I want to go.
>
> I am playing in and directing my next film, which is being made by Thames Television.
>
> My directing job is the attainment of a very strong ambition.
>
> In fact, if I 'made it' as a director I would be quite happy to bow out as a performer.

But Thames wanted *The Benny Hill Show*. And, to his credit, Benny wanted to make amends for what he regarded as his ITV disappointments of ten years before.

The new era was launched on November 19 1969, and the first item in the first show was 'Ye Olde Wishing Well'. Benny, a middle-aged man in a trilby hat, arrives at a wishing-well with his old-bag wife. He drops a coin into the well and she disappears. Benny cannot believe his luck. He drops in another coin and a beautiful young woman in a bikini takes his arm. She then throws in a coin and a muscle-man materializes, dressed only in bathing trunks. Benny is crestfallen. The muscle-man then pitches in a coin, the bikini girl disappears and he advances to take Benny's arm. Benny drops in another coin, the muscle-man disappears and his old-bag wife returns. Accepting his lot, they move off. It was the quintessential Benny Hill routine, a Chaplinesque mime distilling the essence of his comedy in just fifty dialogue-free seconds.

Accompanying this same sketch was a piece of music Benny was also using for the first time – 'Yakety Sax', a honking tenor-sax piece he felt was ideally suited to silent comedy. It would soon become his trademark, associated especially with the 'run-off', the chase that closed this and every subsequent Thames show. No other piece of music summons up an image of Benny Hill better than 'Yakety Sax'. You hear it, you see him, a chubby man with a peculiarly hamstrung gait, fleeing a posse of people. Loosely based on the Jerry Leiber and Mike Stoller song 'Yakety Yak', a vocal hit for the Coasters in 1958, 'Yakety Sax' was an instrumental tune composed by Randy Randolph and James Rich and issued as a single in 1963 by the former – a noted Nashville session saxophonist – under the name Boots Randolph. It cracked the American Top 40 but was not a success in Britain. Benny chose the music for all of his Thames programmes and, altruistically keen to see the freelance musicians remain solvent, insisted that Thames finance a new recording session for every show. Orchestra leader Ronnie Aldrich especially profited from this, as did sax player Peter Hughes, who cut a new version of 'Yakety Sax' each time.

The 'run-off' was yet another new idea, though this first effort was nowhere near as ambitious as they would become. Wielding an outsized butterfly net, Benny creeps up on a beautiful woman wafting in chiffon through some woods. Having lowered his net, he discovers he has captured an ugly old battleaxe by mistake. Though he is disappointed, she is enthused, and so the chase begins, hotfoot through the undergrowth. In later run-offs a snaking stream of people, mostly women but occasionally men too, would chase Benny for some perceived misdemeanour or other, weaving their way around a field or a park. Though they might shake their fists, they would always run at the same speed as their quarry and so never catch him.

It was like an old silent-comedy chase, as Benny had seen so many scores of times in his childhood at Southampton picture-houses – the inevitable Benny Hill 'twist' being that instead of showing a woman being chased by men, he was being chased by women. Technically, the key to the 'run-off' was 'undercranking', a filming method that dated back to that same silent-film era, when cameras, not yet motorized, were cranked by hand. Shot at a slower speed than the normal setting of twenty-four frames per second, 'undercranked' action is accelerated when played back. Benny loved the process, often specifying 'fps' speed in his scripts:

> Go to 6 fps with police ladies chasing Benny and friends. And later, have all girls joining in the chase.[3]

Despite these innovations, Benny also remained the artful recycler of old material, sifting through veteran ideas and reviving them with a new wrinkle. The 'answering the question before last' sketch that had shone for the BBC in 1964 was given a fresh airing just five years on, with Henry McGee as the interviewer and Benny in the guise of Edith Clackett, a former Thames TV employee who has become a French Viscountess:

McGee Do you still get the *TVTimes*?
(Still fiddling with her earpiece, the Viscountess does not hear the question)
McGee What's it like being married to a seventy-year-old Viscount?
Hill Well I don't get it as often as I used to. I used to look forward to Thursday mornings and the postman's visit. But when I do get it I think of you, Alan.
(later)
McGee They tell me that from your villa there's nothing but vineyards, full of grapes as far as the eye can see. How many acres have you?
(the Viscountess answers the previous question)
McGee Do you hope to have children?
Hill Probably twelve- or fifteen-hundred, mostly white ones but one or two black ones. They say the black ones fill up the barrels quicker.

The entire third section of the first show was given over to a spoof of the Eurovision Song Contest. Again, Benny had done this before on the BBC and it remained 'interminably protracted' (*Sunday Telegraph*), and 'showed quite a bit of self-indulgence' (*Sunday Times*). It was, nonetheless, eye-boggling to see Benny as a butch French chanteuse, Mireille Matante, wearing a pink dress and knee-length white socks. 'Her' opening greeting was vintage, though – Toto's exceedingly well-worn 'Good body every evening'.

Compared to latter editions, which were more bitty and faster-paced, the first Thames show was laboured. But working in colour suited Benny Hill admirably – it freshened up the older material, and those eyes that never stopped twinkling and widening with saucy surprise were most clearly blue. Though forty-five, he looked scarcely older than he had back in the days of *Showcase*: a little podgier, certainly, but with the same fresh complexion and lustrous head of hair. The studio audience audibly loved it – and him – and so did viewers at home, and the Thames era began with *The Benny Hill Show* at number one in the ratings, a position it would stroll into, with ease, for several more years.

This success probably startled Benny Hill. With the exception of his second show, broadcast on Christmas Day 1969 to lesser ratings, he seemed more popular with TV viewers than at any time in a decade. (Thames was careful not to schedule Benny Hill on Christmas Day again – his December shows always went out a few days either side of the 25th and then ceased altogether, his later series usually beginning in January.) The top brass at ITV were enthralled; it was common for artists to be fostered on the commercial channel and then 'promote' themselves to the BBC for even greater success, whereas talent that moved in the other direction tended to do so in the twilight of their careers. Here was an exception.

Though he had not wanted to leave the BBC, Benny quickly settled at Thames. He liked Philip Jones, who professed to being star-struck and whose light entertainment department was always artist-friendly; he was happy, too, with the director John Robins, appreciating his understanding of film technique. He also enjoyed working at Teddington. Custard pies had flown here in the name of comedy when it was a studio in the silent-film era, and a later generation of Benny's Variety heroes – including Max Miller, Harry Champion, Jimmy Nervo and Sid Field – had graced its soundstages. A rabbit warren of workshops, offices and post-production suites, everything Benny needed was here on one site, abutting the River Thames by a cascading weir. And by some miracle of London Transport planning, the 27 bus could take him from the bustle of Kensington out into the leafy south-west suburbs and virtually to the studio gate.

The plaudits that greeted his new era *Benny Hill Show*s contrasted greatly with the decidedly lukewarm reaction that met *Eddie in August* when it was screened in June 1970. This, emphatically, did not please the masses, scraping only into thirteenth place in the ratings and failing to crack the Top 10 in London and all but one of the ITV regions. (The exception, curiously, was Ulster, where it ranked number one.) Worse, the critics were unimpressed. While *The Times* called it 'the bravest of tries ... pleasantly funny but not hilarious', the *Daily Mail* critic Peter Black bemoaned 'the film's lack of any really worked-out central idea' and declared, 'He really must drop this character he has created for himself.

The one thing that a baffled amorist is not is funny; and there was something in Benny's performance of following girls about, ogling at them, crouching on the grass to get a better look up their legs, that was much sadder than he seemed to realize. The character has become a ball and chain to his art.' Hardest of all was the *Daily Telegraph*, which called the film 'feeble and depressing' and suggested 'Benny Hill has none of the talents needed for this type of comedy'.

And that was that. The ambition that had been burning within Benny since 1958 and especially since 1966, at which point – at the expense of television – he had made films the focus of his future career, was now punctured. His longing 'to walk past some provincial Continental cinema showing a big picture of me outside'[4] was ruined. The man who took rejection so deeply and so personally received the collapse of his film aspirations with silent acceptance. He could no longer escape the truth, which was that the only aspect of his work the public wanted (and that he was at least comfortable with) was the hour-long TV Variety show.

After the failure of *Eddie in August* the word 'ambition' disappeared from Benny Hill's vocabulary. There would be no more 'I see my future as a producer' or 'I want to direct' headlines. He would bide his time, make three TV shows a year and spend six months abroad, having fun. Though he would write some fresh material, he would also re-use (and re-re-re-re-use) his past work – until perhaps, one day, someone blew the whistle.

As well as the lisping Fred Scuttle, still an ever-present in *The Benny Hill Show*, Benny introduced another regular character at this time, the belligerent and bespectacled Chinaman, Chow-Mein. He was to become extremely popular. A generation of schoolchildren impersonated him, as did workers in offices and factories, hectoring 'Rye you no risten? You shtoopid iriot!' Viewers loved Chow-Mein, the fat-headed, aggressive Oriental with the slicked-down black hair and inscrutable personality, whose command of English was, to say the least, tenuous, and who had a curious manner of slipping into Yiddish at unexpected moments, crying 'Oy vey, we got a right meshuggenah here!'

Like Scuttle, Chow-Mein was best served in the interview situation, when Henry McGee would be the recipient of some withering Chow-Meinian put-downs. 'Where *else*?' he would rant when McGee, failing to grasp the Chinaman's tortuous tautology, asked what his subject considered a 'shtoopid' question. Chow-Mein was also a vehicle for some childish word-play – a woman 'blessed with two nippers' became a woman 'breast with two nipples', and a 'lovely lady' became a 'rubbery rady'; there were also some standard Chinese jokes from the gag book, including the ubiquitous election/erection confusion and the two-thirty/tooth-hurtee pun that is usually the first English-language Chinese joke learned by children.

Chow-Mein also represented the greatest piece of comic larceny ever staged by Benny Hill. While he never indicated that the character was anything other than original to him, it was in fact stolen outright from the American comedian Buddy Hackett. Benny had bought Hackett's 'The Original Chinese Waiter', one of the best-selling 1950s comedy discs in America, but unknown in Britain. It is all there on Hackett's recording – the same tone of voice, those same misunderstandings, the same belligerence and riotous confusion of l's and r's, even the same 'shtoopid iriot'.

When some of Benny's associates loyally defend his practice of redeploying other comics' material, they tend to refer to some general themes common to all comedy. Chow-Mein, though, was straightforward theft of another man's invention. Dave Freeman was with Benny when he bought the Hackett record – 'We were in Imhof's, a shop behind the Dominion Theatre in Tottenham Court Road,' he says. 'It sold imports and Benny used to buy lots of American records made by comics unknown over here. One day he bought this record, all about a 'shtoopid iriot' and lifted the whole character. He threw in the "oy vey", though – that was his.' (Chow-Mein had been appropriated by Benny some years prior to being unleashed in the Thames era. One early appearance was in a BBC radio show, *Benny's Bandbox*, recorded in January 1964 for the Light Programme. In this, true to his Hackett roots, Chow-Mein was a Chinese waiter, from the London restaurant U Pong.)

Buddy Hackett declined to be interviewed for this book, but Benny's friend Peter Charlesworth, as an agent, got to know him in later years, and says that the American was aware of Benny's act. 'Buddy knew all about it and would have killed Benny with his bare hands if he'd ever have got hold of him. But Benny had no shame about it at all.' Bob Monkhouse thinks that Benny may ultimately have forgotten where the idea came from – 'One of his great knacks was that he was able to completely obliterate something he found distasteful or unpleasant to remember. He *really* forgot it. It was a kind of mental block that he was able to whip up within himself.'

Benny's contracts with Thames required him to guarantee that all the writing was entirely original to him, and to agree to absolve the company from any subsequent claim over copyright infringement. When, in later years, the shows were repackaged for the American market, Benny ran the risk of a legal action from Hackett that, given the huge sums of money claimed in American lawsuits, could have bankrupted him. As Bob Monkhouse indicates, he seemed not to give it a thought, however – and indeed, he got away with it. The only concern at Thames was that Chow-Mein might be labelled racist in America. 'They were very scared for reasons of political correctness,' says Henry McGee, 'but when I went there with Benny we went through customs and a civilian was walking across the airport concourse – she was of Chinese origin and when she saw Benny she said, "Oh, I just love it when you do the Chinaman."'

One area where Benny could be original was music. His last recordings for Pye had been made in 1965 but he had continued to compose witty songs for his TV shows – although nowhere near as many as it seemed because he performed each one several times. Thames Television, not yet a public company, was owned outright by EMI at this time, and through this association Benny was invited to capitalize on his TV popularity by recording an album. In August 1971 he spent two half-days at EMI's Abbey Road studios working with esteemed record producer Walter (Wally) Ridley; the result, above all else, was 'Ernie (the Fastest Milkman in the West)', a swinging comedy single that soared to number one for four weeks over the Christmas period, selling more than 600,000 copies and earning Benny a gold disc and two prestigious Ivor Novello awards, including Best Novelty Song of the Year.

'Ernie' celebrated Benny's few months as a teenage Eastleigh milkman, when, gripping the reins of his excitable mare, he had envisaged himself as a Wild West cowboy:

You could hear the hoof-beats pound as they raced across the ground,
And the clatter of the wheels as they spun round and round,

And he galloped into Market Street, his badge upon his chest,
His name was Ernie, and he drove the fastest milk-cart in the West.

Sung in the broad yokel burr he often employed in character parts, the story related how Ernie loved a widow, Sue, and 'got his cocoa there three times every week'. He had a rival, though, 'Two-Ton Ted from Teddington, who drove the baker's van'. A Western-style shoot-out ensued and Ernie perished after being hit in the eye by a stale pork pie. He exacted revenge from beyond the grave, however, a rattling of 'the ghostly goldtops' interrupting Ted and Sue's wedding night.

One of the most inventive and entertaining musical comedy records of all time, 'Ernie' showcased a fine performance from Benny, brimming with quaint touches and suggestive pauses – and recorded in a single take. 'It was a very, very good piece of songwriting,' comments producer Ridley, 'like the old-time music-hall songwriters used to do. I know songs, and knew straight away that "Ernie" was a hit. The other tracks we recorded, quite frankly, were not worth thruppence, but after we recorded "Ernie" I went down to the studio floor and said, "Benny, you have just made a number one for Christmas." He laughed out loud and thought this was a huge joke, and repeated it to all and sundry afterwards, but I knew I was right – the potential was there for it to be the number one record. And it was.'[5]

'Ernie' was not a new tune – Benny had composed it for the unreleased (and now presumed lost) short film he made in support of *Who Done It?* – when he had returned to Eastleigh in February 1956 and ventured out on his old milk-round with a film crew. Curiously, until his January 1971 TV show, when he sang it as part of a spoof of the BBC's weekly chart programme *Top of the Pops*, he had never been tempted to perform it; as Bob Monkhouse says of his friend's comedy cache, despite his disposition to 'borrowing' others' work, 'He could also keep some original ideas in his noggin for years before he used them.'[6]

When 'Ernie' became a hit Benny was invited to appear on the genuine *Top of the Pops* but emphatically rejected the offer. He was not going to embarrass himself, a paunchy forty-seven-year-old, on a glam and glitter kids' show. It would also mean going back to Television Centre, and after leaving the BBC under a cloud two years earlier he was too embarrassed to set foot in the place. The Thames clip could not be used either because it had been shot in black-and-white;[7] instead, with his ACTT card burning a hole in his breast-pocket, Benny offered to direct a promotional film – like a modern-day pop video.

Casting himself as Ernie, and with Jan Butlin (from *The Waiters*) as Sue and Henry McGee as Two-Ton Ted, a film crew descended on Maidenhead one morning in late November and Benny set to work, hamming it up here and undercranking there, just like the Keystone Cops. Shown by BBC1 to a Boxing Day holiday audience, Benny had finally become the silent-film director he had long wished to be – for all of four minutes.

4. Up and Down

15. As Grateful as Hell

Working with him in the recording studio when they made 'Ernie', Wally Ridley was immediately made aware of Benny Hill's consuming interest in sex. 'He approached it in 50,000 different ways but the core of his whole being seemed to be sex,' suggests Ridley. 'Every song he wrote was about it and he wouldn't stop talking about it. He told me about some lady whose husband was in the navy, and if I took her out to a function she'd be happy to do whatever I wanted. He also boasted that he sometimes let a room in his second apartment to one of his producers, to screw some lady, and seemed to suggest that he could fit me up, too. It was endless. I had to say to him, "Oh for Christ's sake, Benny, we're here to record, stop all that bloody sex business and let's get on with the work." The man was a professional, so he handled the recording session well, but if he'd only stopped talking about sex for five minutes it could have been a lovely afternoon.'

The sexual content of Benny Hill's shows for Thames Television was becoming more marked. A core of suggestiveness had run through his BBC programmes, but no scantily clad women. At Thames, suddenly, it was different – there was a steadily increasing proportion of stockings and suspenders, skimpy dresses and bikinis; why, even Benny himself was starting to strip down to his undies when his writing required it.

To a certain extent, this reflected changes in society. A scan through any popular British magazine of the early 1970s – *TVTimes*, for example – reveals an abundance of editorial and advertising material featuring scarcely dressed women, or women in tight T-shirts with no bra underneath, the kind of material that, within a few years, would be outlawed as 'sexist'. This was the allegedly 'permissive' era, when 'blokes' ogling at 'birds' who wore mini-skirts or hot-pants or bikinis was deemed fair game . . . especially in British TV comedy, a genre that had lost its 1960s radicalism and, with certain honourable exceptions, was going right down the pan. Benny was always aware of where the censor might intervene. His cousin Hugh Stevens makes the astute observation, 'Benny liked to be able to see a chalk line on the ground and get as close to it as possible without overstepping it. He based his whole career on that. He didn't push the bounds, he sort of crept up to within a whisker of them.'

It follows, then, that *The Benny Hill Show* was starting to become more raunchy. Three or four years earlier, the programme, though saucy, had been entirely within the bounds of good taste. Now – even though so much of the material was literally the same, just recycled – it possessed an altogether more ribald tone. By 1972, leering at 'Benny's girls', as Benny himself did in a manner more pronounced than ever before, became a favoured pastime among the show's male viewers, and Mary Whitehouse, the former schoolmistress and founder of the 'Clean-up TV campaign', was publicly complaining of 'degrading moral overtones' in his work.

Benny's insistence that he maintain sole responsibility for casting his show ensured that literally dozens of these modern-day bathing-beauties were trooping along to Queen's Gate to audition. When one of his attractive walk-ons, Yvonne Paul, planned to establish an agency supplying models for photographic and TV work, Benny helped her to fund it; this enterprise, Blondes, then provided many 'girls' for his show.

The auditioning process eminently fulfilled Benny's need to be seen in the company of good-looking women. Sometimes he would keep them waiting on the doorstep in order to gain maximum local 'nudge-nudge' prestige. This kind of thing went on for years – he was still at it even in his sixties. *En route* from her home in south-east London to a *Benny Hill Show* location shoot at Thorpe Park, Surrey, Lorraine Doyle, whose assets always turned a man's fancy, was invited by Benny to take the train to his place and travel the rest of the way with him in his chauffeured car. 'It was only on the third morning that I realized what was going on,' she says. 'He wanted me to come up to the flat so that we'd emerge from the front door together. He'd have a grin from ear to ear because it looked as though I'd spent the night. And he'd drag it out, fiddling around on the doorstep with keys and taking forever to get into the car. And of course it caused raised eyebrows when we arrived on the set. It was a game, and I went along with it, hooking my arm through his. He liked the idea of people thinking, "Oh look, Benny's got that girl." '

While he may have accepted that this was not quite the calibre of acting talent he had once envisaged summoning to Queen's Gate, Benny still endeavoured to make his auditions genuine and was ever keen to encourage whatever skills he detected. If he did find someone with a useful talent he would promote it, enjoying any resultant success. This applied throughout the cast: when character-actress Patricia Hayes was invited to appear in a compelling TV drama about a vagrant, *Edna, the Inebriate Woman*,[1] he allowed her to withdraw from a commitment to *The Benny Hill Show*. It turned out to be her greatest role and a multi-award-winner. During an acceptance speech at one such gathering she announced, 'I could not have won this award if it had not been for Benny Hill, who released me from a contract.'

Although he selected his audition candidates for their looks and figure, Benny still sought that elusive 'twinkle'. 'It can't be cultivated – either you have it or you haven't,' he explained to *TVTimes*, still leaving everyone none the wiser. Sue Bond, a petite, busty twenty-something blonde, had it. Her most memorable work with Benny was his (now much bawdier) remake of the Lower Tidmarsh Volunteer Fire Brigade sketch, in which she first slid up and down a fireman's pole and then climbed a ladder while Benny, holding his hose, leered up her mini-skirt and clocked an eyeful of stockings and knickers. Sue remembers being 'petrified, quite petrified' at having to go for the audition. 'He was a big star and I was very nervous,' she says, 'but this jolly, lovely face opened the door and welcomed me in. He made me laugh straight away. It was "Come in, dear heart!"

'I wasn't there very long. We improvised some sketches and then I left. This kind of auditioning was unheard of, but there was no chat-up line, and I never heard the other girls say any different. All I remember him saying was that tights were forbidden if I was to work with him – he thought stockings were wonderful, and fun, and naughty. I got a booking for his show a few weeks later. When we worked together he tried to encourage my talent as much as possible and taught me a lot about comedy – awareness of the camera, which way one should look, how to count the timing and so on.'

Though this is all admirably generous, Benny clearly resisted the notion of hiring proven performers for these roles – even though it was not his money he was saving. Lorraine Doyle remembers, 'His three favourite words were "practise, practise, practise", as in "If you want to be an opera singer, practise, practise, practise."' The implication of this – that through dedicated application one can manifest one's heart's desire – was something Benny believed he had proven true. When sending friends photographs of himself surrounded by under-dressed women, something he did regularly, he would scrawl 'NOW will you practise?!!!!' across the image.

In the early 1970s, in common with many other TV personalities of the era, Benny was suddenly becoming more theatrical. He had taken to dressing in bright pink shirts and a cravat, and was also, as Sue Bond discovered, starting to call people 'little heart' or 'dear heart', archetypal 'luvvie' terms of endearment. Also, a generation older than these attractive women, he had begun to assume an avuncular air, calling and signing himself 'Uncle Benny' or 'Uncle Ben' and encouraging them to unburden their problems. It was another badge of pride – he would say to journalists 'See that shoulder? Rheumatism! They come around and cry on it. They say, "Benny, what am I going to do? My boyfriend's left me and I'm so unhappy." I say, "Well, George will be back soon, darling." And they say "No, it's not George, it's John now."'[2]

'It was like having an older brother,' says Sue Bond. 'He was kind and caring and willing to listen. You always thought you could ring him up, and he wanted to know what everybody was getting up to. Uncle Ben he was – he loved to have a natter and he cared that we were all right. And if someone had a broken love affair he would always listen. There was a cautiousness, though. He never talked about his past and we knew we couldn't ask. There was a barrier, and we all respected it.'

That wild rumours began to spread about exactly what else Benny got up to with these women was scarcely surprising. He himself was an inveterate hint-dropper, and when people did pick up the wrong end of the proverbial stick Benny was never in any hurry to disarm them. Indeed, he coined a new quip just for these occasions:

'I don't yell, I don't tell, I'm as grateful as hell!'

This pat line was constructed to cause, not quell, speculation, to suggest salaciousness. What was it that he was grateful for, and why could he not yell about it? The answer, of course, was trifling – simply that he possessed an almost pathological need to be considered the Lothario of Queen's Gate. That this was untrue was irrelevant: as with his comedy, he craved mere association with naughtiness – just as he still cherished, with a frisson of delight that never left him, the memory of showgirls billing and cooing around him that third night of *Follow the Fun* at East Ham Palace.

There was only a little genuine action. Two women, one a player in his TV show, the other not, were to spill similar 'tell all' stories to the press in later years, accounts that the vast majority of Benny's girls strenuously – and in virtually all cases genuinely – deny also apply to them. Both these women claimed to have performed oral sex for him, to 'please Uncle Benny'. (It was hardly the greatest sin in the world.)

One of them was Cheryl (Cherry) Gilham, a topless model in the *Sun* newspaper who appeared in four editions of *The Benny Hill Show* from 1972 to 1975. The veracity of her claims and the quality of her character have been called into question by many of the other showgirls whom Benny did not approach, yet her account is consistent with the pattern of his proclivities.

'Nobody on the show knew I was going to see him privately,' she says. 'I'd go to Queen's Gate for lunch and he'd make *salade Niçoise* and strawberries and cream. We'd also have champagne – I'd drink most of the bottle and get a bit drunk. Then we'd talk about the show, and he would point out the bits of my work that he liked, and be very complimentary. After that we'd adjourn to his bedroom. We never used the other part of the flat, where his living quarters were. He had covered himself in cologne and I had to be "nice to him". He wasn't interested in doing anything for me. Once or twice I took a friend around, to share the burden and have a laugh.'

Cherry affirms that Benny would not have considered seeking personal services from any of the 'legitimate' actresses on the show, just the scantily clad glamour, and acknowledges, too, that she could have said no. Having been abused by her father she was particularly susceptible, however. 'I was vulnerable, and when he said to me, "Be nice to Uncle Benny," I thought

I should, because he'd been nice to me, putting me in the show and making me a nice lunch. I continued going there for years. He gave me a lot of money one time. I owed £2,000 on my mortgage and he wrote me a cheque. He could be very generous. In later years I heard that he had paid off the mortgage of a particularly favoured Thames producer to the tune of about £40,000.'

Cherry also perceived a less pleasant side to Benny's personality. 'My feeling about Benny is that the more he got involved the more he started to hate and get jealous,' she says. 'I'd be a bit brash when I was drunk and he would criticize me a lot, saying snide remarks like, "You should be behind the camera, not in front of it," not in an encouraging way but in a nasty way. Then I'd hear from other people how lovely he thought I was. My son was born in 1975, and I was on the show when I was four months' pregnant. I felt he was very spiteful to me on that occasion, making me do difficult and dangerous things. Then, when I gave birth he sent me a £200 cheque "to buy booties for the baby".'

At most, perhaps half a dozen of the bikini beauties on *The Benny Hill Show*, a single-figure percentage, were invited to 'please Uncle Benny'. Consequently, the others viewed him – then and now – as harmless and cuddly and generous and supportive. In later years, as he grew old and unwell, Benny seems to have cut down on the 'pleasing' idea, except perhaps vicariously. A reliable source, who insists on remaining unnamed, says that Benny gave one of the showgirls an expensive camera and instructed her to take topless shots of several of her colleagues. He is said to have disposed of the photos when, late in life, he moved from Queen's Gate.

Despite the increased smuttiness, and the first sniff of a public backlash from Mary Whitehouse and her moral campaigners, *The Benny Hill Show* was named Best Light Entertainment Show at the 1972 British Society of Film and Television Arts Awards; at the same event, Benny won 'Best Script' prize, and he was also named Top ITV Personality at the 1972 Variety Club awards. He was scoring major ratings with every broadcast, too – a *Benny Hill Show* in March 1971 was watched in nearly 10 million homes, ITV's highest-rated programme since the new franchise contracts began in 1968. Yet despite all of this, from the moment Benny joined Thames in 1969 until his exit twenty years later, he committed only to a show-by-show contract, and the company never knew if its prized programme would be back for another season. It was only when Philip Jones, the Head of Light Entertainment, received a phone call from Richard Stone each summer to say that Benny would do another run (usually three shows) that the company could breathe a sigh of relief and start the major resource-planning operation these required. It was indeed a long time since Benny had last stretched himself for his TV work – or, indeed, for anything. Come the spring, production of *The Benny Hill Show* would wind down for six months and Benny would whizz off around the world for at least four of them, out of reach from everyone.

Most editions of the show were structured the same, set out in Benny's handwritten notes and diagrams. They would open with what he called a 'quickie', a simple and corny joke from a gag book or newspaper. Next would come a song, with Benny always backed by a trio of female singers, the Ladybirds, followed by a mixture of film and video items and a few more quickies. After this there might be a few of what he called 'boo-boos' – often these were spoofs of TV commercials that had 'gone wrong' in some way, causing the director, out of vision, to scream, 'Cut! Cut!' Next would be a Scuttle rehash or Chow-Mein barrage, followed by either a musical item or a long sketch that might dovetail into the 'run-off'. Benny would time the shows meticulously, aware of when the two real commercial breaks had to fall, cast them and send in his scripts on scraps of paper for the production secretary to type. This was René Bloomstein, who still laughs as she remembers how the award-winning sketches would arrive. 'He sent in a Chow-Mein script on a shirt cardboard from somewhere in Europe – I had to twist it round and round before I could make out what on earth it meant. Another sketch was written on a paper napkin, and one time he sent in an idea on a piece of toilet paper.'

Although much of Benny's comedy was simple, its delivery was complex – especially in matters of timing, set-design and wardrobe – and the perfectionist star was never less than totally demanding of his cast and crew. He did not suffer fools gladly. All who worked with Benny at Thames can recall the tuneless humming- or whistling-sound he would make and the way he would pick the skin around his fingernails when he was unhappy. Someone would then have to ascertain what he was displeased about – a task that often befell Thames' young 'floor manager', Dennis Kirkland, who was a great admirer of comedians and Benny in particular.

Producers, though, were having a tough time. After nine shows, John Robins took a break (he later returned to work on five more), and others came and went, falling foul of the star if they failed to carry out precisely what he wished. Philip Jones, always the soul of discretion, remarks, 'One would have been aware that it was demanding to work with Benny. Demanding in terms of, "We've got to get it right or he won't be very happy", but you always get this on a big show. Occasionally one would hear Benny say, "If only people would read the script and look at the requirements this wouldn't happen!" But it's fair to say that those who worked with him the longest got on best with him, and the shortest-spell producers liked it the least.'

The producer who had the shortest spell on *The Benny Hill Show* was Peter Frazer-Jones, who directed just one programme. 'It wasn't a particularly happy show for me,' he says, 'because Benny did everything and then told me how to shoot. He used to hand out details of how he wanted things shot and how many frames. As unofficial director he knew what he wanted to achieve and I just pointed the cameras. Directors take pride in being able to contribute something of their own, and I wasn't able to.'

Another less-than-enamoured producer was Mark Stuart – who, in 1954, under the name Ian Stuart, had directed Benny's first touring Variety show as the main star. He and Benny had real difficulties; in letters to René Bloomstein Benny sarcastically called Stuart 'Sir', as in 'he who must be obeyed'. 'Our relationship wasn't that good,' Stuart accepts, 'in the sense that I didn't like him particularly, and I don't think he liked me particularly. It didn't ever come to the surface but we sort of avoided each other. When he started humming, though, it was just a matter of waiting. How long?

'He also wasn't the easiest man to build a relationship with. I knew the part of the Camargue he used to go to, because I kept a boat there, but once we'd exhausted that there was nothing else to talk about. What you wouldn't talk to Benny about was what you *felt* about something. You could join in with him in talking for a little while about pretty girls and "crumpet", but you couldn't say "What about those riots in London the other day, eh?" So you stood there with nothing to say.'

When Benny found himself up against an insoluble problem or an intractable producer his cry would go up at Teddington, 'PHILIP!!' (this was usually how Benny wrote it) and along would hurry the Head of Light Entertainment to pour oil on troubled waters. As he stood talking, Philip Jones had a habit of jangling coins in his trouser-pocket; Benny was soon imitating him.

True to form, Benny rapidly developed a close (yet platonic) friendship with Thames production assistant René Bloomstein. Such was their mutual respect that from 1972 Benny asked her to become a director (and, later, minority shareholder) in his businesses. Company law at this time stipulated that limited companies had to have more than one director; as he was no longer on speaking terms with his brother, Benny asked René. She was paid a salary of £300 for signing on several dotted lines once a year. 'He was a very modest man, a very talented man and a very quiet man,' says René. 'He liked to feel that somebody was a friend to him but I don't think anybody, apart from his parents, really knew him. He didn't reveal himself in any way.'

Benny appreciated René's staunch reliability. At this time, location filming was usually done, with a very early start, at a sports club local to Teddington, or in the grounds of a mental hospital adjacent to the studios. Spurning Thames' offer of a chauffeur-driven vehicle or a refund on taxi fares, he asked René to pick him up in her old green Datsun and drive him out to the location. 'He used to walk from Queen's Gate to the Hammersmith Odeon, near where I lived, and wait for me,' René recalls. 'He'd stand there, looking inconspicuous and carrying a plastic carrier-bag. We'd do the day's shooting and then I'd bring him back to town. Sometimes I'd drop him at Queen's Gate, if it was late, but often it was to the Odeon and he would walk back to Kensington. In all this time, though, he never used to say very much.'

Richard Stone had much the same experience. The main raft of sketches for every show, especially the song numbers, were taped in front of an audience in the large Studio One at Teddington. (Philip Jones says, 'If there could have been an alternative to putting the show together without the studio audience I'm sure Benny would have taken it. "Sweetening" the sound was never considered, except for perhaps some pre-recorded bits. But the monologues needed the audience: his eyes reacted to the laughter, which itself was reacting to the innuendoes.') These nights – Sundays at first, Fridays in later years – were never less than a fear-filled ordeal for the star; Stone considered that he could best support his artist by attending the run-through, offering a few suggestions and then watching the taping via the internal Teddington closed-circuit 'ring-main' in Philip Jones's office. (Benny did not agree but could never bring himself to tell his agent that his presence was not required.) Afterwards, Stone would take Benny home. 'Benny never went up to the bar after a show,' he says. 'He went back to his dressing-room, took off his make-up, put all his props back into plastic bags – make-up, bits of food, and so on – and I'd say "Ready, Ben?" "Yes, squire." We'd walk to the car and I'd drive him home to Queen's Gate. We always talked about the show on the way – what had gone well, what hadn't gone well and what he might take out when he edited it – but not in nearly twenty years did he ever ask me up to his flat. I didn't mind, I went there for the occasional daytime meeting, but it was extraordinary. I'd leave him on the doorstep and drive away. Time after time, as I drove along, I'd be thinking, "Is he going to do it this time?" and he never did.'

Stone should have learned to talk about boxing. This was a topic that Benny and René Bloomstein had in common. Benny had maintained his boyhood interest in pugilism cultivated by The Captain, and he often attended bouts, not just in England but overseas. René's father had also been a fan of the sport, and the constant exposure had commanded her childhood attention. 'One day,' says René, 'I mentioned something about some fighter or other and Benny said, "Oh, great, lovely, let's go to see a fight!" He lived very near the Albert Hall and there were monthly bouts, so I'd go along to Queen's Gate, he'd cook us a Spanish omelette and a salad and then we'd nip along to the boxing for the evening. It was good fun, very simple, and he enjoyed it. He was happy at not being recognized, though when he was he didn't mind signing autographs.'

Spending this amount of time together, René quickly became aware of all the familiar traits in Benny's life, as others before had observed:

He rarely talked about his family – 'just occasionally about his mother and father, and his father's "truss shop".'

He was a singular man – 'he didn't really like people questioning him about his private life'.

He was odd about money – 'I saw a cheque lying around on his sideboard for sales of "Ernie". It was a lot of money and all he said was "Oh yes, I must put that in the bank some day."'

He was especially private about his secret friendships with Netta Warner, Phoebe King and perhaps other disabled women, hinting only, 'I'm going to see my lady next week.' Though tempted to enquire further, René bit her tongue. 'One felt it would be wrong to ask,' she reflects.

In these first years at Thames Benny developed one of the most remarkable supporting casts in the history of television comedy, kept on the payroll for their strong visual value more than their verbal abilities. He had always loved the 'stock company' in vintage Laurel and Hardy films, where the same actors would crop up time and again in different roles – James Finlayson, the squat Scotsman with the bald head, short fuse and biggest 'double take' on celluloid; the rotund and explosive Billy Gilbert; the diminutive, short-tempered Englishman Charlie Hall; and the vampish Mae Busch. Benny decided to employ the stock company principle for his show, although he was wise enough not to have anyone on screen with him who could diminish his comic presence; they were all, in essence, cartoons. Under his wing, quite fantastically, this motley cast of colourful characters would attain world fame and unimagined wealth.

Bob Todd was one. Tall, round-faced and almost bald – his appearance was immortalized by the British band Half Man Half Biscuit, who sang '99% of Gargoyles Look Like Bob Todd' – this Richard Stone client (actually Brian Todd) was a former Second World War flying ace, a survivor of many successful sorties over Germany. He had then turned to cattle-farming and comic-acting, quickly becoming a favoured accomplice in Spike Milligan's work. Todd had a fine facility for playing drunks – which is not surprising because he was generally inebriated anyway. 'Dad was a heavy drinker,' affirms his daughter Anne, 'and it was always party time when he was around. He was also completely hopeless with money.' Bankrupted three times, Todd was renowned for cadging cash from everyone on the show and not repaying it, and in the 1960s he had embarrassed the BBC by failing to pay a personal hotel bill, claiming it was their responsibility; correspondence between the Corporation and the hotelier ran for months until the BBC, irritated by the affair, agreed to settle.

Lee Gibson, a singer who appeared in *The Benny Hill Show* from 1973 to 1981, says of Todd, 'If he wasn't high on grass, which he used to grow himself, he was drunk. You'd turn up for the film sessions at 6.30 in the morning and Bob would be walking around with a triple vodka. The more drunk or high he was, the funnier he became.' With his demand for professionalism, Benny Hill was less than enamoured of Todd's personal habits, and dropped him from the programme after he disappeared from a London Palladium show for five days. He had gone on a tremendous bender and come to in a Dublin hospital – events all widely reported in the newspapers. It was Dennis Kirkland, after graduating to producer/ director, who persuaded Benny to take him back, pointing out that Todd's drinking rarely affected his work and that he gave so much to the show. Bob's finest moment in *The Benny Hill Show* came in a spoof of the husband-and-wife television cooks Fanny and Johnnie Cradock; he played a hilariously drunken Johnnie and got 'inside the role' by getting totally plastered before the recording.

Benny's straightman throughout the Thames era, and in his final BBC shows before this, was Henry McGee, nicknamed 'Super-Stooge' or 'Double-S' by the production team. Born Henry Marris-McGee, he appeared in forty-five of the fifty-eight editions of *The Benny Hill Show* made at Thames. (When McGee was not available Nicholas Parsons was a reliable replacement, appearing in eleven shows.) McGee was at all times every inch 'an actor', an acclaimed and hugely experienced player of theatrical farce and TV sketch comedy; those thin lips and collapsed chin would maintain their composure whatever the verbal idiocy of Messrs Scuttle and Chow-Mein.

The most unlikely member of Benny's stock company was a wizened yet spry Ulsterman, John 'Jackie' Wright, standing only four feet eleven inches, virtually hairless, almost toothless and – like a wasted Duane Doberman from Phil Silvers' *Bilko* show – scarcely able to deliver a line without fluffing it. As soon as Benny first saw him – in 1968, when

Wright was signed to an extras agency for 'walk-on' parts – he knew that this old man was the perfect comedy foil, with a face that would have been grabbed too by the Keystone Cops or Three Stooges; being bald, he was also an ideal recipient for the head-slapping that was now a regular part of Benny's comedy (an action cleverly accentuated by the dubbing, in post-production, of more slap-sounds than there were slaps).

Born in 1905, Wright was already approaching retirement age when he joined *The Benny Hill Show*, but he simply had nothing else to do. Unmarried, he divided his time between a tiny phone-less bedsitter in Walworth, south London, and a home in Belfast shared with a disabled sister – one of eleven siblings. Much about Wright's past was a mystery: he claimed to have tap-danced and played trombone in Chicago speakeasies in the Prohibition era, and then returned to Britain for a life so poverty-stricken he even pawned the trombone. A teetotaller, Wright consumed endless cups of tea, continually crunched apples and biscuits and was rarely without a cigarette. Filming a Roman scene for *The Benny Hill Show*, smoke would rise from the back of his hand, where he had hidden the burning tobacco. Benny would forgive Wright anything, and soon gave lines to his cherished protégé to deliver in his staccato Ulster brogue. Wright's involvement in the show ceased only when the frailty of eighty years insisted.

The phone always rang at ten o'clock on Sunday mornings at 22 Westrow Gardens, Southampton, with Benny dutifully calling his mother from wherever he was in the world. He continued, too, to take the train to Southampton, to visit his parents in the house they had bought for cash in 1931, as indeed he visited Bexleyheath to spend precious times with his Auntie Lulu, who was starting to become particularly important in his life. She, more than anyone else, would provide sanctuary in the mad years ahead.

Benny went 'home' every Christmas, walking with his folks across Southampton Common to the local pub before returning for Helen's grand dinner, a diet-busting spread of roast turkey, roast potatoes and all the trimmings, with desserts and mince pies. Benny's protestations about the calories would fall on deaf ears; he, in turn, would disregard his mother's continued pleas for him to marry – 'I saw you on that programme with such a pretty little girl, and I thought to myself what a nice daughter-in-law she'd make.'[3] Benny would shift uneasily and wait for the cloud to pass.

During one visit, in 1971, The Captain, now seventy-seven, declared that he would like nothing more than for his son to take him – just him – on holiday to Spain, where they could 'get to know one another'. For Benny, the idea came out of the blue. Though he felt unable to say no, relations had been strained for so long that he was full of trepidation. He knew, too, that his father's manner was to order everyone around and have things done his way, and that he was very much the same himself. On a Spanish holiday, with Benny in command of the language and customs, he would have to be the boss. Could he do this with his father after forty-seven years of being interrupted and overruled, and would his father accept it?

Little detail is known, but it went better than Benny expected. 'The Captain wasn't used to being "taken" anywhere,' he told a *TVTimes* journalist a decade later, 'but he loved it. In Madrid we went to a night-club. At two in the morning dad asked, "Isn't there any more?" So we stayed for the next cabaret at 3.15, and then he said, "We don't need a taxi, let's walk."' Touchingly, Benny then added, 'I have this lovely picture in my mind of an old man, pushing eighty, stepping out two miles along the Gran Via through the dawn.'

The trip lasted ten days, at the end of which Benny saw The Captain on to a plane bound for England while he stayed on the Continent and treated himself to a peaceful respite. Just a few months later, however, Big Alf was diagnosed as suffering from advanced lung cancer. When Benny visited him in Southampton General Hospital he noticed that all the other patients had been given handout photographs of 'My son, the great TV star' and that none had dared defy the forceful implication to put the glossy image on display. These visits would turn into veritable perform-ances – 'Go and say hello to that man over there,' and 'Sign an autograph for this nurse's daughter.' Benny did as duty bound, as he always would.

Big Alf was allowed home to die. He slept downstairs and was pushed around in a wheelchair, and just made it along to his bowling club's annual dinner-dance. 'When I saw him for the last time his face was lined with pain,' says Benny's cousin Tony House, 'but he accepted it amazingly well – he bade us farewell as we left, saying, "I won't be seeing you again, it's been lovely knowing you." He faced death calmly, perhaps because he'd seen so much of it during the First World War.' Big Alf, the lesser known Alfred Hawthorn Hill, the remarkable Captain, died in May 1972, aged seventy-eight.

'Helen told me that when my brother Alf died Benny cried and cried – more than she did,' comments Violet Stevens. Benny himself said as much in later years. He was closer to his mother yet shed more tears on his father's death because, he said, they had never been close and had just started to form a real relationship for the first time. Benny also told his brother some years later that, on his deathbed, The Captain had turned to him and said, 'If any man should thank another man for anything, I thank you for that holiday in Spain.'

Benny stayed in Southampton for several weeks, taking care of his mother, registering the death, organizing the funeral and musing nostalgi-cally upon his childhood, taking long walks in and around the town. The *Southern Daily Echo* printed a letter from two housewives who had seen a man they thought looked like Benny Hill, walking along the main road in Marchwood, and then hopping on a Southampton-bound bus. Was it really him? The newspaper contacted Benny, who confirmed that yes, it was – he had been out for a nostalgic walk in the Waterside area. 'I used to go out fishing with my father on Hythe Pier,' he reflected.

From now on, Benny would return ever more frequently to South-ampton. The job of cooking the calorific Christmas feast, now just for two, would be his.

Helen was not only alone, she was suffering from acute arthritis that crippled her hands and feet. The drugs prescribed to counter the pain caused stomach problems, and then her health deteriorated further when she suffered a stroke. It was no longer practical, even with the considerable neighbourly help she received, to live in Westrow Gardens. Benny paid for her to go into a nursing home in Portswood and would travel down from London as often as he could, taking her out for long walks across Southampton Common. Pushing wheelchairs was something Benny Hill was doing more and more frequently in his fifties – when he wasn't wheeling his mother around Southampton he was propelling Netta around

Leicester and Phoebe around Felixstowe. 'He was very worried about his dear mother's arthritis,' Phoebe considers. 'He was still close to her because he was the only child not married. A son is a son until he takes a wife.'

Helen died at Southampton General Hospital in February 1976, at the age of eighty-one. Despite her estrangement from Leonard, he was on hand at the end, and heard his mother say of The Captain, 'I have been loved as no other woman has ever been loved.' Still not on speaking terms with his brother, Len then hurried home, not returning for the funeral. Benny came down from London later in the day and was soon joined by his Auntie Lulu and old army pal Harry Segal, who, without being asked, sped south from Yorkshire to be at his friend's side. The coffin was placed in the drab front room at Westrow Gardens, while, in the back, Benny, Lulu and Harry sat talking through the night. There were few tears but many memories.

In their final conversations together, Helen had told Benny that she was bequeathing the freehold of the house solely to him, requesting his verbal agreement that he would never sell it and would uphold their cautionary attitude about visitors. The Hills had always been a wary lot; before his death Big Alf had taken to saying the house was 'like a limb of my body, we would hate to have strangers here'. A *Southern Daily Echo* journalist, Jasmine Profit, who went to Westrow Gardens in June 1972 to interview Benny – she was, incidentally, a good-looking blonde – wrote in her subsequent article, 'I was the first visitor to the family home for twenty years – the last was Reg Varney.' This information, given to her by Benny or his mother, may have been exaggerated, but Big Alf and Helen certainly treated visitors as curiously as they conducted so many other aspects of their domestic life – their fanatical frugality being uppermost.

Helen's will was proven. Benny was left the house and the rest of her estate was divided between Leonard and Diana. Writing to Leonard from Australia, Diana declared of Benny, 'The poor old bugger's got nobody over there that really cares about him but you.' But still they did not speak for another dozen years.

Though he would continue to live in his London flat (for the time being), the boy who had run away from home at sixteen now took sole possession of the semi-detached house in Southampton – unmodernized and undecorated for decades and packed with a thousand childhood memories. 'Soon after Benny's mother died I rang and asked him what he was up to,' says Peter Charlesworth. 'He said he was down on his knees lighting the paraffin heater. It was the middle of winter, he was freezing cold – and as happy as a sand-boy.'

Benny had been entrusted with the keys to his parents' suffocating kingdom. Aged fifty-two, unmarried, petrified of female relationships, a man with scores of acquaintances but no genuinely close friends, he would loyally accede to his mother's wishes, to the last.

16. Global TV's Top Banana

When Benny Hill turned fifty he told Henry McGee, 'I've had a very good life and I've been very lucky. I wouldn't mind if I died tomorrow.'

Had he done so, he would not have witnessed an astonishing escalation in his popularity. A performer at fifteen, a TV star at thirty, his last remaining ambition blunted at forty-five, Benny Hill could never have predicted global superstardom at sixty.

There was no warning of this extraordinary surge in his popularity; moreover, he did precisely nothing to precipitate it, except to carry on doing what he had been doing for twenty-five years. It just happened, and he just sat there, simultaneously bemused and receiving vast sums of money he neither sought nor spent.

Until the late 1970s, Thames enjoyed steady but unremarkable success selling *The Benny Hill Show* overseas. Around a dozen countries bought it, including the Netherlands, Sweden, New Zealand, Hong Kong, Australia, Canada, West Germany and, behind the Iron Curtain, Poland and Yugoslavia. Where necessary, the voices would be dubbed, but it was clear that mime 'translated' best.

In the summer of 1974, Anglo-EMI Films had released *The Best of Benny Hill* into cinemas. This was a compilation of highlights from the first four years[1] of the Thames show, cobbled together without any new linking material. The movie did reasonably well at the British box-office – and Benny himself was spotted going to see it in Southampton – but it did precious little anywhere else. (Benny himself had suggested the film after reading a news item in *Variety* about Sid Caesar. The great American comic had stitched together a movie using kinescopes of his landmark

1950s TV series *Your Show of Shows*. Benny reasoned that if Caesar could do it, he could too.[2])

At this time, the only other country in which Benny was truly popular was Australia. He had been a TV draw Down Under since his 1960 visit, and Thames did brisk export business with Channel 10. Having lost his father and then his mother, and still not speaking to his brother, Benny made three 1970s visits to his sister Diana, who had now separated from her husband. An early example of the interest Benny's presence could generate beyond Britain occurred in 1974 when he turned up unannounced at Melbourne High School to see his cousin Hugh Stevens, who ran the language department. This flagship of the local state-education system, its mock-gothic architectural style known locally as 'baronial birthday cake', was reduced to a standstill. 'The moment Benny's foot hit the front step the whole place collapsed,' says Stevens. 'The kids surged out and so did every teacher from the headmaster down. It was three o'clock in the afternoon so no more work was done that day.'

As usual, Benny liked to secure free travel by agreeing to do some work. Back in 1973 he made the rarest film of his career on a freebie – *Your Palace in the Sky*, a fifteen-minute comedy about a businessman's journey on board an Air-India flight, was made solely in exchange for a round-the-world ticket. For a visit to Australia in 1976 he obtained a first-class round-trip air-fare and daily expenses, plus a generous fee, for shooting six commercials. Likewise in 1977, when he filmed an entire TV show in Sydney and then treated Diana and her daughter Tessa to a holiday with him in Singapore.

All the old material was trotted out in this Channel 10 show ('Some of the jokes may not be new, but he gives them a new shine,' enthused the Sydney *Sun-Herald*), including the creaking Lady Godiva sketch and a long mime piece about Benny Kelly, son of Ned, that had been done in Britain with different characters. In an example of how Benny always worked to 'the chalk line', this show – on the permissive Aussie channel – included full female nudity (full rear view, topless front view) for the only time in his career. It was a remarkably licentious moment – Benny was beating a rug at the time; as a busty beauty appeared stark naked in front of him he instantly broke into faster beating.

Thames had no success trying to sell *The Benny Hill Show* to American television. Only rarely did the networks – NBC, ABC and CBS – buy imports, and besides, the show was way too sexy for these safe, ultra-conservative channels. The less politically sensitive independent stations that proliferate in the major towns and cities – known as 'markets' – resisted it too. They felt *The Benny Hill Show* was too long and too 'local', with British references beyond American viewers. British comedy had always been regarded in America as of an inferior – and most certainly different – quality than the homegrown variety. Only one show had broken through, *Monty Python's Flying Circus*, which was odd because it was as resolutely British as a British comedy could be. Lightning had thus struck; it wasn't likely to happen again, and *The Benny Hill Show* and *Monty Python* mined different seams anyway. When, ambitiously, Thames bought a week of programming space on WOR-TV, New York, in September 1976 (in which Benny's show was such a low priority it didn't even figure in the advertisements), offence was taken at the way he romped trouserless in a field with a scantily clad girl, and as a hospital patient suffering a fatal heart attack after patting a nurse's bottom; there was little sign yet of his impending American success.

The man charged with the task of selling Thames shows in the USA was Don Taffner – a stocky, energetic New Yorker who had joined the talent agency William Morris in 1951, working in the mailroom, while he studied at university to become a teacher. He enjoyed it, stayed, and was promoted to the television arm of the company. The great comedian Milton Berle was a William Morris client and he took a shine to the new boy. 'He liked the way I laughed,' Taffner recalls. 'He made me sit at the back of the room, to start the laughs going.' Eventually Taffner was put in charge of international deals, selling *I Married Joan* and other Fifties sitcoms to the BBC. After a spell at Paramount, and a period trying to market BBC shows in America, Taffner formed his own independent company, D. L. Taffner Ltd, in 1963 (he used Ltd instead of Inc because it sounded British), enjoying his first success by selling the Australian children's series *Skippy, the Bush Kangaroo*, to American TV. From its founding in 1968 he had been Thames' agent in the USA.

Though Taffner is an accomplished salesman, his task, to begin with, was as difficult as the proverbial 'selling coals to Newcastle'. Apart from Lew Grade's consciously international productions for ATV, the only

British shows evident in America were the classy BBC and ITV dramas screened by the subscription-financed Public Broadcasting Service. In the 1970s, however, Taffner's marketing of Thames programmes enjoyed greater fortunes. The London company produced perhaps the exemplar model of television journalism, *The World at War* – a twenty-six-part series about the 1939–45 conflict, narrated by Laurence Olivier – and this sold around the world, America included. Then Taffner pulled off a masterstroke by adapting the Thames sitcom *Man About the House* into the American *Three's Company*. The show was snapped up by ABC – which wouldn't have gone within a mile of the British original – and it enjoyed roaring success on the network for seven years. Along with the crime series *Charlie's Angels*, *Three's Company* defined a new genre in American television – the 'jiggle show' – so called because it provided plenty of opportunity for well-endowed women to oscillate. Clearly, the climate was coming together for a Benny Hill breakthrough.

The sale of Benny Hill to the USA resulted from one simple question that Taffner put, in 1978, to Philip Jones at Thames – 'What is it that you have enough episodes of that we can do something with?' British TV's disposition to making series of six or thirteen editions was causing Taffner no end of difficulties selling in America, where programmers generally require at least twenty-two episodes to fill a fall-to-spring season. Ideally, Taffner was seeking a show with sixty-five episodes so that it could be 'stripped' on the independent stations, Monday to Friday, for thirteen weeks.

Jones's obvious rejoinder was *The Benny Hill Show* – by the end of 1977 there were thirty-one hour-length programmes in the Thames archive. Taffner hit upon the idea of breaking these down into half-hours. They might be ideal for the American 'syndication' market, freer of network interference and their narrow viewpoint, stations that assembled their own schedules from repeats or less well-known material. Thames went ahead and edited a single, trial show; Taffner grabbed the tape for NATPE, the annual convention of TV programming directors, in Los Angeles. It began with 'Ye Olde Wishing Well' – the opening 'quickie' from Benny's first show for Thames in 1969 – and, though there were no buyers, there were a few encouraging guffaws.

Taffner earnestly believed that *The Benny Hill Show* could break into

American television. 'I laughed at and enjoyed those shows,' he says, 'and it was the enthusiasm of my enjoyment and my laughter that gave me the dedication to get this on. My fight was always, "I couldn't give a damn what you, Mr Program Manager, want, give me a chance to get to the public. They'll love it."' A shrewd operator, Taffner realized that if he could persuade just half a dozen stations to take Benny Hill then there would be enough money in the deal to cover the expense of editing a batch of the hour-long shows into half-hours, and transferring them to the American TV standard. He found four – in Philadelphia, Miami, Seattle and Cleveland – and decided to chance his luck. The ball passed back to Thames.

Here, however, there was one unforeseen drawback. Benny was not bothered about his shows being screened in America.

Don Taffner, though he did not yet know the man, conjectured, accurately, that the comedian didn't want to see his work rejected in America. 'In the context of what we saw on screen this will sound silly,' he says, 'but Benny was clearly a sensitive, shy guy. He had a barrier around him: he didn't want to be hurt. This feeling was greater, I believe, than his desire to be a success.'

What Taffner did not yet know were the other reasons – Benny also had no need for any extra money, did not really seek the fame, and possessed no special desire to go America. He had passed up innumerable chances to break into US television since the end of the 1950s and remained quite unperturbed about it. Richard Stone, who had been smart enough to withhold Benny's overseas rights from Thames in the first place, was instructed to go back and tell them 'No'. But, being an agent, he kept on talking . . .

So began a series of negotiations between Muir Sutherland (the managing director of Thames Television International) and Benny's agent. Stone was in the perfect bargaining position – his client did not care if the deal failed. Thames cared very much, sensing this just might be the start of something big (it could not have guessed *how* big). It kept increasing the offer. Benny kept rejecting the deals, not in the hope of a better one but because he simply didn't want it. Other British comedians, desperate to crack the US market, would have grabbed at any of Thames' offers.

Eventually, Stone suggested a 50/50 split of Thames' net profits. Deductions from the total sum would have to be made first – a share for the TV stations and a commission for Taffner, and then Thames would make residual payments to all the actors, musicians and directors. The net revenue would then be divided equally between Thames and Benny Hill. Stone recalls, 'I said to Muir Sutherland, "Let's split the thing! I don't want any guarantee at all. Nothing. Let's have half of what's left after you've paid all the people – and if it doesn't sell in America, too bad." Muir said "Oh, all right," thinking it was a good deal for Thames. It was a *wonderful* deal for Benny, the best deal I ever did in my career.'

Benny, indeed, was so astonished at the pact that he agreed to set aside his objections and sign. He wasn't likely to be a success in America anyway.

The first American station to screen *The Benny Hill Show* was Channel 29 in Philadelphia, WTAF-TV, at eleven o'clock at night on January 8 1979. Though screened in Britain at eight o'clock, the show was deemed 'late-night' material in the States.

Describing Benny as 'a master of mugging and a maestro of mime', writer Lee Winfrey gave the launch a plug in the *Philadelphia Inquirer*:

> *The Benny Hill Show* is hilarious vulgarity. Benny Hill has been a popular comedian on British TV for almost a decade [*sic*]. Don't miss Benny Hill. He'll make you laugh out loud, not once, but often.

More risqué and adult than anything seen on American television, *The Benny Hill Show* was an immediate success and became a real talking point among Philadelphians. WTAF knew it was on to something and promised its viewers the first forty episodes of *The Benny Hill Show* being touted by Taffner. At this point, however, it had received just three, and had to screen them over and over until more arrived. Back in England, a charmingly old-world production line had been set up, at Benny's insistence. He didn't want just anyone hacking his show about, he wanted someone he could trust, someone who understood his comedy. He suggested that Richard Stone approach John Street – Benny's director at the BBC from 1957 to 1963 – now sixty-five, retired, and living in Bude, Cornwall. Thames equipped Street's bungalow with video equipment –

sufficient to make rough cuts – and he slipped into the routine of taking the train to London, filling a suitcase with U-matic video tapes and returning to his seaside home ready to start assembling the next batch of shows to wow America's late-night TV viewers.

The programmes being edited by Street spanned a decade, and it was only by his deft insertion of costumed 'quickies' and 'boo-boos' in between the sketches that the obvious differences in Benny's age – and paunch – could be blurred. Street was also paring back some of the sketches, ruthlessly at times, in order to keep the comedy punchy. 'Every American comedy is sharp, very sharp, and I told Benny what we needed,' he says. 'The shows ran for twenty-three minutes with two commercial breaks, which we were told they called slugs. Neither Benny nor I knew what "slugs" were until we were told; we laughed and laughed. I never saw Benny laugh so much – his whole face went.

'I told Benny I'd keep back the recent, really sexy sketches until after we'd got established, and he said, "I know what you're saying, John, and that's OK. We'll get to them." The great thing was, he never interfered unless I asked him for advice.'

It was perhaps as well that the 'really sexy' material was held back, because parts of America were already agog at the quota of stockings, suspenders, bras and leering that made up *The Benny Hill Show*. It was like nothing they had ever seen on the small screen; it was like nothing they had seen at all since the distant days of vaudeville and burlesque. And apart from the omnipresent 'jiggle', the silent comedy was of a style so outmoded in America it could bounce back as fresh – Keaton, Chaplin, Lloyd, Laurel and Hardy. Benny was mining the folklore memories of a distant past – the silent Keystone Cops epoch and the vaudevillian era of Neil Simon's *The Sunshine Boys* – but in colour, seemingly new and original. In Britain, these were words that had not been used to describe Benny Hill's work for a long time.

As news spread about the booming ratings in Philadelphia (and Miami, Seattle and Cleveland) so other stations bought into the deal with Taffner – in Boston, Dallas, San Francisco, Washington DC, Los Angeles, New York and elsewhere. The *New York Daily News* was calling Benny's programme 'the most outrageous show on television' and cited how the minnowish WOR-TV was rivalling the big networks in the city. It remarked, 'Channel 9 says it gets more complimentary mail than protests about the overtly sexy material presented on the series. "It's sexy but not offensive," said a station spokesman. "It beats *Monty Python* coming and going." '

When *The Benny Hill Show* first aired in New York, writer James Wolcott produced a scornful review in the hip newspaper *Village Voice*, complaining of its 'pornographic grubbiness'. A year later, he was retracting his attack and heaping praise upon the show:

> Despite all the dips and bumps, *The Benny Hill Show* is an exhilaratingly smutty spree – the funniest gift the British have dropped on our laps since Bea Lillie.[3] It's Benny Hill's pornographic grubbiness that makes him so special, so subversively sane. He's a music-hall lech, with a jovial belly, porky eyes and cheeks so plump and shiny they look like unnippled breasts[4] . . . He remembers that life's a nasty treacherous comedy and sex a glorious joke.

In the *New York Times*, Tom Buckley was likening the interest in Benny Hill to the quaint sport of British-observing, writing 'Like fish and chips and room-temperature ale, he is at least an amusing novelty for New Yorkers.' Buckley's downbeat opinion was overwhelmed by the sheer numbers of viewers, however. Quite quickly, and for a while, watching Benny Hill became something of an American obsession, with the show broadcast twice a night, five nights a week, all over the country. The comedy was so unusually broad that it commanded the attention of all ages, classes and creeds. While his shows never attracted the ratings of the network productions on ABC, NBC and CBS, a state of mild Bennymania took hold.

The secret, once again, was that 'chalk line'. The American one was drawn a few feet behind the British. Making the shows in England, Benny had gone up to the local line – and far past the American. Viewers in Nebraska, Minnesota, Utah, Idaho and elsewhere sat in a state of nervous expectation over what next would appear in the name of comedy. It was the most ribald show they had ever seen, and some even watched it in secret. This appeal of *The Benny Hill Show* was to endure a long time before it became accepted as mainstream. As critic Howard Rosenberg noted in the *Los Angeles Times*, the show was 'A sort of polished drivel, a triumph of trash so revolting that, unbelievably, you tend to like it.'

Once America was broken, the rest of the globe quickly followed. There was a buzz about *The Benny Hill Show* and TV stations worldwide wanted a piece of the action. France fell in love with him, reciprocating the passion Benny had cultivated since 1944. The channel FR3 showed his programmes at peak-time on Sunday – and despite sniffy critical notices the public loved him. Spain also fell, and West Germany, and indeed all of Europe. He became massively popular among Swedes, Finns, Norwegians and Danes. In towns throughout south-east Europe, where outdoor, communal viewing is the norm on warm evenings, crowds gathering to see Benny Hill became commonplace. A friend of the author witnessed 200 men, women and children crowded around a TV in a Venice piazza, watching *The Benny Hill Show* and laughing loudly.

The only downside of such fame was that Benny could no longer travel incognito. Even this had its compensations, though – he cheerfully told people that he was recognized by a stripper in a Hamburg club, who said to him, 'Do I know you from somewhere?' He sent Philip Jones a postcard that said, 'Last week in Nice I couldn't venture out without being stared at, photographed, asked for my autograph, and generally pestered. It really was quite worrying. I've been in Madrid for two days now and not a soul has noticed I'm here. It really is quite worrying.' Libby Roberts, a choreographer who accompanied Benny to the south of France in 1986 on a talent-scouting mission, observed his fame at first-hand. 'He was such a funny sight,' she says, 'walking along in a Hawaiian-type shirt, long shorts, brown shoes and socks up to his knees, carrying a plastic bag. This was in Cannes! And everyone was shouting "Benny 'Eel! Benny 'Eel!" It was quite incredible.'

Countries throughout Africa soon imported the show, too, including South Africa, where television had only recently been introduced. Eventually, after initial objections, state television in the pre-Glasnost Soviet Union decided that Benny Hill was good entertainment for the comrades. Dark, bitterly-cold winter nights in Novosibirsk would be punctuated by the sound of Siberian sniggers as Benny was chased around an English suburban park by scantily clad models and old bags wielding umbrellas.

The undercranked Benny rampaged across India and the Far East, and the entire continent of Central and South America, communist Cuba included. And there were few bigger Benny Hill fans than the Japanese, who were intrigued about this angel-faced, barrel-chested comedian with the wide, cheeky eyes. Even the Chinese joined the fray, sending delegates to an international TV conference in France expressly to buy *The Benny Hill Show* for the delectation of the proletariat. A group of American fans launched the Jackie Wright Fan Club and wrote letters to the scraggy Ulsterman – sent care of 'Thames TV, England' – to which the former pauper, suddenly an international star at seventy-four, would reply in shaky, uncertain handwriting. Benny himself received a phenomenal postbag, letters homing in from dozens of countries, applauding him . . . and asking, gloriously, whether he really was on intimate terms with the bikini beauties.

The number of countries taking *The Benny Hill Show* eventually exceeded 100 – constituting virtually every TV-receiving nation on the planet. Employing its inimitable style of prose, *Variety* famously headlined him 'Global TV's Top Banana'. It was a truly amazing chapter to occur in the final years of a long career.

Of course, such adulation settled uneasily on the shoulders of the quiet and unassuming comedian, the man who liked nothing better than to rip into a packet of fish-fingers in his spartan flat, or spend an innocently wicked time in the company of glamorous but unchallenging young beauties. And though flattered by the attention, he had no desire to go to the places he was popular in order to capitalize on his success or promote himself. His comedy was old-hat, too – in many instances, old tat – yet his remarkable grasp of the mechanics of comedy, his lifelong understanding of how it worked, of what made one thing funny and the next thing not, and his amazingly expressive mime, had propelled him into a realm of international stardom that no comedian had achieved since his own personal hero, Charlie Chaplin. The little Englishman was said to have been the most recognizable man in the world in the mid-1920s; in the mid-1980s this honour was quite possibly Benny Hill's.

While it was preposterous to call him the funniest comedian in the world – he wasn't even the funniest man in Teddington – Benny Hill had become, indubitably, effortlessly, The World's Most Popular Comedian.

Like many people involved in *The Benny Hill Show*, Marian Davies – one of the three women who comprised the Ladybirds, Benny's backing singers throughout his Thames period – experienced at first-hand the sheer scope of Benny Hill's global acclaim. In 1992, a few months after his death, she was working on a cruise ship sailing up the Amazon. 'We got up to Manaus, right up the top of Brazil,' she recalls, 'and the ship's agent said to me, "Do you want to have a trek into the jungle?" Why not? So we sprayed ourselves with mosquito repellent, got in the car, drove to a village and there were loads of Amazon Indians there, living in really basic places. He told the chief that I was a friend of Benny Hill and, honest to God, the whole village came out. I have never seen anything like it, all these pygmy-type Indians wearing hardly any clothes, with absolute hero-worship on their faces at me. Then there was a general murmuring, and the translation was, "We hear he is dead. None of my people believe it because we still see him on television. How can he be dead?" And this was right up in the Amazonian jungle.'

Benny Hill owed worldwide success to a number of factors. Uppermost, undoubtedly, was his comedic obsession with bawdiness (which his success demonstrated to be not the sole preserve of the British). His Variety-steeped stereotypes – pathetic males, faithless females, empty-headed floozies and goggle-eyed lechers – were literally universal, and as old as the Hills. While the material was perhaps 'adult', however, Benny Hill clearly was not – he wasn't going to rape anyone; he saw and 'understood' women as would a naughty schoolboy. As indeed he did.

The girls, too, were a sizeable part of the attraction – especially for male members of the global audience. Glamour has long been a part of TV-Variety entertainment the world over – *The Benny Hill Show* was a vibrant, colourful remnant of a genre that was clearly still in good working order.

Benny also achieved spectacular results through his sheer lack of sophistry. You did not need to be a genius to understand this comedy. The hundreds of millions who watched *The Benny Hill Show*, from the backstreets of Shanghai to the slums of Rio, loved the slap-and-tickle sauce, happily ignorant of the more pioneering aspects of his work. Low taste is universal and so was *The Benny Hill Show*.

Also key was the silent comedy, those dialogue-free sketches that had long been a hallmark of Benny Hill's work. The verbal pieces were translated into local languages and inevitably lost something along the way, but the mime knew no boundaries, much as Chaplin had found before him, and as Rowan Atkinson's Mr Bean would find later.

What, though, would he do with the monetary rewards of his global TV success? Benny was not someone who could change, yet from 1979 the man who cared little about personal wealth was awash with money. Just as the first cheques began to trickle in, his accountants formed a new company, Benny Hill Entertainments Ltd, expressly to handle his overseas income. (René Bloomstein was his co-director and company secretary.) This is where the bulk of his wealth would reside for the rest of his days. The company's turnover was spectacular – £434,202 in 1982, £823,074 in 1983 and £1,457,109 in 1984. It exceeded a million in the next two years, too, the peak being 1985 (£1,552,863). A man like Benny Hill could never spend this amount of money. And these riches accrued as taxation in Britain for top earners was slashed, so Benny retained the larger part of his income.

And he kept it . . . in the bank. On the advice of his accountant, Dennis Blake, Benny did own a few shares but speculative investment was simply not his style. (He had small holdings in BP, Imperial Tobacco, Prudential Insurance, General Electric and one or two other companies, though he knew little about them. When someone asked him how much he had lost on the October 1987 stock-market crash he honestly declared, 'I have no idea.') He still did not buy a house – he already leased the flat in Queen's Gate and had inherited ownership of 22 Westrow Gardens, and that was more than enough responsibility. He did not consider buying villas in any of his favourite continental resorts. The cash simply mounted up. He kept a six-figure sum on deposit with a local Barclays Bank, he lodged a million in an account with a City investment bank, and the lion's share of the money, eventually more than 4 million pounds, was deposited in an account at the Halifax Building Society – the standard form of saving for most British people, accruing modest interest. Few better indications of Benny Hill's unchanging nature exist than this. When he came out of the services in 1947, he deposited his £52 'demob' money in a Post Office savings account and popped the passbook in his pocket. Now he possessed a Halifax passbook – showing a balance in excess of 4 million.

And Benny's Queen's Gate flat continued to resemble a station waiting-room. 'The main area was a big room still with virtually nothing in it,' recalls Henry McGee. 'He was in the kitchen once, preparing us some lunch – fish-fingers with a dollop of peas and a cup of coffee – and I got up to have a look at some things on the mantelpiece. They were all awards – but they weren't arranged in any way. Some of them had fallen over, lying higgledy-piggledy. He came in from the kitchen and I said, "You've got a lot of awards" and he said, "Oh, there's a cupboard over there full of 'em." And he wasn't boasting.'

This room was set to be given an outlandish makeover, however – and, as usual, Benny got it done for free. *TVTimes* had launched a bound-in supplement, *Family Scene*, and in 1980 its editor wanted to splash a feature on Benny Hill's fabulous Kensington apartment. Unfortunately, he didn't have one. The main room was strewn with debris, with discarded papers, magazines and bits of rubbish on the floor; there were two threadbare plants, a couple of giant brown-paper sacks filled with goodness knows what, and six chairs, every one of them a different design from a different period and all freebies from furniture-store openings – from an antique Bentwood upright to a 1960s foam bucket-seat with a rounded chrome base. The place was a tip, and *TVTimes* faced a stiff challenge. The editor offered Benny the chance for a luxuriant designer makeover, with all new furniture and fittings – at no cost to him. The *quid pro quo*, of course, would be a colour splash in the magazine. 'Hill was immensely taken with the idea,' *Family Scene* wrote in the resulting feature; he gave the team 'a pretty free hand' and set them only one specific task – to devise a storage system to replace what the magazine called the 'cardboard boxes scattered all over his flat'.

The outcome was a vulgar confection: a crimson Dralon velvet sofa, another in midnight blue, and a chaise-longue in champagne beige; a soft-green deep-pile carpet; blue suede-effect wall covering; blue, pink, red and green curtains; rows of ornaments in a floor-to-ceiling cabinet; a remote-control hi-fi; and, the *pièce de résistance*, a false ceiling with an off-white carpet glued to the underside with no fewer than forty lights recessed into it. (This was in place of the peeling acoustic tiles he had put up in 1960 ... Benny clearly felt that soundproofing was still necessary.) As for his storage problem, the designer's solution was upholstered coffee-tables with lids.

The net result of the magazine's handiwork was akin to what Benny's friend Peter Charlesworth calls 'a Victorian brothel'. And only the one room was treated, so the rest of the apartment remained 'unimproved'.

'Benny thought it was great that someone had come in and done this for him,' says Mike Phillips of Thames Television International, a frequent visitor at this time. 'But the rest of the flat was like it had never been decorated. It all looked brown – and what he called his office was full of brown boxes.'

TVTimes printed numerous colour shots of the new design.[5] And here is Benny in his freebie room, a pink-cheeked, greying, fifty-six-year-old loner in his curious *family scene*, redundantly draped with seven likely lasses, all holding a glass of champagne. Each left Queen's Gate that day with an ornament of their choice. He certainly had no need for such trinkets.

17. The Political Football

Reaction in Britain to Benny Hill's global fame was one of incredulity. His comedy was so utterly British, how could he be The *World's* Most Popular Comedian? And why Benny Hill anyway and not, say, Morecambe and Wise, much more admired homegrown comics?

'Apparently, smut is as popular in Athens and Abilene as it is in Ashford these days,' explained a bemused London *Evening News*.

Yet as Benny became a success around the globe, his long-enduring appeal to British viewers haemorrhaged. There was one overwhelming reason for this – a sudden, pronounced leap in the bawdiness of his shows. Not only did this alienate a good percentage of his natural audience, it happened to coincide with rising feminism and a new generation of comedians mounting a humour revolution in Britain, sweeping away the old and ushering in a new 'politically correct' comedy.

Just three years earlier, energetic young punks had blown away what they saw as the 'dinosaurs' dominating British rock music; now a new wave of young, brash, savvy comedians was bursting out of the clubs, with a newly elected right-wing government to decry, and a mission to sweep away what they saw as 'the old school' of comics and their endless mother-in-law gags and dreary double-entendres. These 'alternative comedians' offered a more worldly, less idealized view of sexual relationships, rendering *passé* the hint-hint style redolent of previous generations. Virtually to a man, and woman, they viewed Benny Hill's comedy with distaste.

And yet, at this very time, when Benny's usually sharp antennae should have detected the impending revolution, not to mention the hardening of feminist attitudes, the smut-ometer in *The Benny Hill Show* went off the scale.

An increase in ribald material had been gradual. In 1976, Benny introduced a new, recurring dance act in his show, Love Machine. They were not especially sensational, simply a more arresting variation of Pan's People, the mildly arousing yet ultimately angelic dancers from *Top of the Pops*. When Love Machine performed a piece entitled 'Dancing in the Nude' the outfits were skimpy but still covered the essentials and the camerawork was conservative. Benny's first show of 1979 set a different tone, however. In this, he parodied the dance act from the Thames Television pop/comedy programme *The Kenny Everett Video Show*. They were Hot Gossip, a mixed-sex, mixed-race troupe dressed usually in leather, and laced with irony, who would – as Everett called it – provocatively 'bump and grind' their 'naughty bits' in a manner choreographed to be the antithesis of Pan's People.

Benny's spoof was Hot Gossamer (a title his dad would have appreciated). He and Jackie Wright blacked up to play the guys, Henry McGee was Everett and there were several sexy girl dancers. Benny's script for the piece specified the customary fare –

Table gag, balloon gag, legs gag, feet gag, lollipop gag, chair gag [Benny puts foot on chair, girl slaps his knee, his foot goes through the chair], steam gag, handbag gag, dirty marks gag [a girl in white goes behind a kiosk with Benny and returns with black hand-prints on her bum], legs over chairs gag, lamp-post gag, dragging on floor gag, finale

– but there was something gratuitously sexual in the way that it was shot. Even beyond the fact that Benny liked doing spoofs, there was an unsettling, lingering emphasis on the women. 'It ended up looking trashy,' says Libby Roberts, who had been one of the Love Machine quartet and would later choreograph much of the dancing on *The Benny Hill Show*. 'Hot Gossip were very, very good dancers, technically outstanding, Arlene Phillips was a wonderful choreographer and David Mallet was an amazing director. So to try and copy that with girls who were not so good, grinding and rolling around phallic poles, was dreadful. I really thought it was awful.'

There was a chink in the curtain, and two shows later, in February 1980, Hill's Angels were unveiled. A play on the title of 'jiggle show' *Charlie's Angels*, and the motor-bike gang Hell's Angels, this was a group of dancers – the personnel fluctuated, although it only comprised girls who had passed a Queen's Gate audition – who were prepared to writhe in the approximate name of the comedy . . . inasmuch as their appearances were usually, like the Hot Gossamer piece, within a comedy framework. They made their debut in a long, virtually dialogue-free sketch with disco music, ostensibly set at Chez Ben, a beach/disco in France. Ten nubile women in skimpy bikinis coiled themselves around poles, held their legs open while suggestively applying sun-cream, and peeled off their bikini tops (seen only from behind) like striptease dancers. The comedy, a rehash of an old idea Benny had used before (and would use again), had him trying to imitate a muscle-man by lying on the ground and holding various Angels in the air above him. But – oh ho! – Benny is no biceps-rippling hero. The first girl he lowers ends up sitting on his face, the second is manoeuvred in cunnilingal proximity. It looked for all the world like a dirty old man's voyeuristic fantasy, with Benny ogling bosoms and leering up skirts. It was comedy, of a sort, but devoid of taste or wit.

Hill's Angels became a permanent fixture in *The Benny Hill Show* for the next nine years, and for the first six of these sullied the show with an element of degradation that had hitherto scarcely featured in his work; it invited a tremendous amount of criticism, from which – to this day – the reputation of Benny Hill in his home country has not recovered. Certainly he had been lecherous for years, and of course he had over-egged the sexual content more times than it was possible to count. But he had never been as *dirty* as this, and nor, just as crucially, had his camerawork been so licentious.

More and more, *The Benny Hill Show* came to resemble a grubby, tin-pot theatrical Variety show groping around for a lifeline in the final years before that genre had become extinct. This was a slippery slope, and it is again hard to understand why Benny Hill, the man who understood comedy inside and out, and who had witnessed at first hand Variety's descent into smut, and then its demise, did not see the warning signs.

The show also had a new director, Dennis Kirkland. He had been 'floor manager' on the programme from 1969 to 1973, and though he did not return to the production team until becoming director in March 1979, he had served for five years as 'warm-up man' on the nights the show was taped before an audience in the cavernous Studio One at Teddington. Kirkland was not only a skilled director, he was also a lively performer – a Geordie with a bubbly sense of humour, dominating personality and a drive to be the life and soul of the party.

Dennis and Benny struck up a good working relationship from the start, and they had soon knocked up some amusing double-acts for those warm-ups, which the ever-nervous Benny greatly appreciated. Though his shows were watched by millions, he was always frantic about stepping in front of the 300 appreciative folk at Teddington, an audience described by Philip Jones as 'middle-of-the-road, not too young, not too old'. If he had to face them alone he could only do so carrying a heavy book, to weigh down his trembling hands.

Through the late 1970s Benny had worked with several directors at Thames and was annoyed and unsettled by the changes, yet Philip Jones says that Benny had been rejecting the possibility of using Kirkland for some years. 'Dennis was a very good comedian's floor manager,' Jones remarks. 'He was a very good understander of comedy, comedians and their ways, and he always laughed at the jokes – whether they were funny or not. But much as Benny liked Dennis, respected him and wanted him on the show, he was hesitant for a long while before allowing him to become director. Then one day he said, "OK, let's give it a whirl."' (Dennis Kirkland remembers all this differently, saying, 'Benny had been asking me to be his producer for some years but I kept turning it down. He was hard work – he never lost his temper but was very nervous about everything, especially props and costumes. He used to pick his nails and hum "If It Takes Forever". But Thames finally persuaded me by forcing some money into my hand.')

Dennis Kirkland directed every remaining edition of *The Benny Hill Show* during the comedian's tenure at Thames, twenty-five shows from 1979 to 1989 – a number bettered only by Kenneth Carter, who had counselled Benny for fifteen years at the start of his TV career and who, incidentally, passed away just before this new development occurred in his former protégé's life.[1] Carter had served Benny best by curbing some of his baser instincts. Kirkland felt that his duty was to give the star everything he needed to keep him happy. This spelled trouble. More than ever before, Benny was being given free rein to do whatever he pleased – and, in the heady atmosphere of Thames' global sales phenomenon, Kirkland found him ever-bigger budgets with which to achieve it.

Benny and Dennis fast became close buddies on the set and drinking companions off it. They were Ben and Den, almost inseparable – 'joined at the hip', as several observers have remarked. Benny seemed to need Dennis, coming to use him as a protector, publicist/spokesman, 'feed' and, virtually, manager. Dennis, who seemed to crave the company of comedians ('I adore comics; why we adore these maniacs I don't know, but to me it's a drug,' he told the author), allowed the producer-artist relationship to get too chummy for the good of the show, with objectivity the first casualty.

Everyone involved in the final years of Benny's life has an opinion on his relationship with Dennis Kirkland. 'He seemed to think that anything to do with Benny was his property,' says John Street, who was editing the shows for America. 'I can understand it, and I can understand why he didn't approve of me. He produced good shows for Benny, but he did *possess* him – and Benny, in turn, was completely over the top with Dennis.'

'With Dennis the atmosphere was bubbling the whole time,' says Hill's Angel Lorraine Doyle. 'It was great fun, a good working environment.'

'All comics need a sounding-board, a confidant, a father-confessor figure,' remarks Dave Freeman. 'I had been that for Benny in earlier times, now it was Dennis. Fair enough. But it became Dennis's *raison d'être*. It was like a badge for him – I Am Benny's Best Friend.'

'Benny ran from confrontation, and hoped that someone would look after it for him,' says Jon Jon Keefe, one of the regular players on the show. 'In that respect, Den knew how to handle him, and how to create the atmosphere that was going to make it all work. He had to give Ben what Ben wanted.'

'Benny and Kirkland used to be an act, twenty-four hours a day,' says Don Taffner.

'They were bantering the whole time,' recalls Marian Davies of the Ladybirds singing trio. 'They were always doing a Laurel and Hardy routine, "After you, Ben. No, after you, Den."'

'Dennis didn't change for anybody. He was rude, crude and didn't care who was present. But he made us laugh, I have to say,' says Ladybirds singer/leader Maggie Stredder.

Anxious not to slay the goose that lays the golden eggs – being, in this case, the 'residual' cheques that continue to flow in from worldwide sales – those associated with the last decade of *The Benny Hill Show* formed a curious brotherhood, active then as now, attesting that these were the best years – and showcased the best comedy – of Benny's life. This is a tragic misconception. These were his worst programmes, embarrassingly *schlocky*, ludicrously oversexed shows that were difficult to watch then and are doubly so today.

They led, sadly yet inevitably, to a hostile public reaction, especially among women, and to diminishing audiences. In the last five years of its life, the show that had always so effortlessly topped the ratings made the Top 10 only twice, and the average audience halved, from around 18 million to 9 million. Of those who did watch, there was also a radical shift in profile, toward the blue-collar male. Benny's appeal originally was across the board.

All of this led, ultimately, to the severance of Benny's (and also Dennis Kirkland's) relationship with Thames.

Benny Hill had been a target for would-be television censors since soon after his arrival at Thames. In 1963, a former schoolmistress, Mary Whitehouse, had launched her 'Clean-up TV campaign', the public face of a pressure-group calling itself the Viewers and Listeners Association (VALA) – whose members were, in their very British way, religious fundamentalists. (One VALA supporter signed off her letters 'In His Service, Always'.) Whitehouse then became VALA's secretary, and bombarded broadcasters, newspapers, advertisers, regulatory bodies and the government about a variety of moral issues facing society. Television provided VALA with much to complain about. The permissiveness of the 1960s was shaking awake a dour post-war Britain and there was a sudden increase in swearing, nudity and radicalism on screen – in drama and comedy programmes especially. With its satirical slant on overt racism and bigotry, the BBC's Alf Garnett sitcom *Till Death Us Do Part* was a particular bone of contention.

Whitehouse is not known to have complained about any of Benny Hill's BBC programmes, but his third show for Thames, in February 1970, prompted her to open what became a sustained salvo. It started with a sketch in which Benny interviewed a vicar who was unaware that his fly was undone. Whitehouse wrote to Lord Shawcross, chairman of Thames Television, claiming that one of VALA's members found it 'in very poor taste'. Shawcross – who had been the chief British prosecutor in the Nuremberg war-crimes trials – replied that the item passed scrutiny 'on the grounds that the situation happens at least once in the lifetime of almost everyone who wears trousers'.

Another organization which took exception to *The Benny Hill Show* was the Festival of Light, an evangelical Christian movement espousing 'traditional family values', counting Whitehouse, Cliff Richard and Malcolm Muggeridge among its supporters. It complained bitterly to the Independent Broadcasting Authority (IBA), the governing body of the ITV companies:

> Cheap laughs from obscene puns, suggestive double-entendre, perversion or promiscuity have usually been the province of the schoolboy lavatory-wall humour. We see no reason why Mr Hill, for all his wit, should be allowed to project this kind of nauseating stuff into the nation's living rooms. Many viewers switch off, agreed. But why should they be denied entertainment when the Authority is committed to avoid what is offensive? And for those millions who do not switch off, the coarsening, de-sensitising process goes on by slow degrees sapping the will, eroding the sense of shame, eating away at the protective walls of reticence and the vision of high ideals.

The IBA did not handle this particular complaint very well. It likened Hill's comedy to music-hall and end-of-the-pier shows, then conceded that living rooms, where people watched his shows, were not music-halls or located on piers.

With few exceptions, the general attitude among broadcasters to VALA and the Festival of Light was one of disdain. They believed there was sufficient self-regulation to prevent the dissemination of obscene or inflammatory material, and that Whitehouse was a meddling old busybody. When she complained in 1974 about Hill being 'preoccupied with breasts and bottoms', Brian Tesler, Thames' Director of Programmes, merely thanked her for her interest and replied, disingenuously, 'Mr Hill's humour has of course as ancient and honourable a pedigree as his jokes.'

But all this was a trifle compared to the ammunition that *The Benny Hill Show* gave its detractors from 1979. Whitehouse had already complained bitterly about Hot Gossip (which was a badge of honour for the ever controversial Kenny Everett – he mentioned it on air, much to her disgust), so when Benny staged the Hot Gossamer spoof she was incensed, citing in particular a sequence in which a girl 'licked a lollipop in a way which has obscene connotations'. One VALA member likened the tone of the piece to 'the front cover of *Penthouse* magazine', while another complained about the malign influence it would have on her children. (Benny's reaction to this is not known, but John Street recalls receiving a letter from a mother in San Francisco around this time, which stated, 'My little boy stayed up to watch *The Benny Hill Show* last night. When he went to school in the morning, walking down the sidewalk, he touched up every little girl who went by. I would like to say to British TV, "Thank God for Benny Hill" because now I know my little boy's not going to be gay.' 'The letter was forwarded to me and I showed it to Benny,' says Street. 'He loved it.')

Whitehouse was soon complaining about Hill's Angels. In a letter dated April 22 1980, she wrote to Lady Plowden, chairman of the IBA:

> ... as a number of critics have pointed out, the dancing in the matter of dress – stockings and suspenders for example – and gesture can fairly be described as 'soft porn'. Since this programme is transmitted during Family Viewing Time one is bound to ask what effect this will have on the vast number of children known to be watching at this time and wonder whether, in fact, a generation raised on 'soft porn' will not find it fairly simple to graduate to 'hard porn'.

Lady Plowden's response, though the usual stonewall, revealed that the IBA had latterly started to keep a closer watch on *The Benny Hill Show*.

Such pressures filtered through to Thames. In an internal memorandum in 1979 Philip Jones wrote to a colleague:

> I attended the recording on Friday night and it is a funny show and will be excellent when edited together. I honestly do not think it is naughtier than usual – there are a couple of 'near' lines but these aspects are subjective and naturally we would value your thoughts if you feel there could be problems.

In the wake of Hill's Angels and associated controversies, a Thames staff member whose job was routinely to check over scripts and, where necessary, review tapes before transmission, advising on any potential problems, began to pay special attention to *The Benny Hill Show*. One resulting memo objected to a line in Benny's script – 'Greta sits up, topless'; another queried 'the swift despatch of a courgette and two Brussels sprouts down the trouser leg'. Dennis Kirkland dismissed this latter complaint by scribbling underneath the typed message 'We've done it before.' (The fact that it might not bear repeating seems to have eluded everyone.)

Hill's Angels also ensured that *The Benny Hill Show* caused offence beyond Mary Whitehouse and her godly flock. In 1981, newspapers reported that thirty women office-workers in Sheffield had sent a petition to Thames slamming the 'lewd, rude and downright disgusting' dancing and the way it had been shot with 'cameras zooming up for saucy close-ups'. One of the protesters was quoted as saying 'We are not prudes, we are not even women's libbers, we are just girls who think that Benny's dancers are going too far.' Another suggested that the Angels were being used merely as sex objects, saying, 'We think there is a limit to how far the show should degrade women.'

This article appeared in the *Sun*, Britain's archetype tabloid, next to the daily photo of a 'Page 3 Stunna' – a topless model. The *Sun* enjoys a rumpus, and loved being associated with a man who promoted good old British slap and tickle. Controversy over Benny Hill was right up its Wapping alley. More and more, *The Benny Hill Show* was being watched by male tabloid-readers, so the paper was on safe ground. And this was an extraordinarily political period in the newspaper's history – the time when, under the union-busting stewardship of owner Rupert Murdoch and editor Kelvin MacKenzie, it staunchly supported Margaret Thatcher, her governing Conservative party and all the right-wing views they espoused. Benny, the *Sun* said, was nothing more than 'a saucy comedian', a veritable hero, and any 'loony lefties' – be they feminists or 'alternative comedians' – who attacked him or his work would be fair game for a *Sun* kicking. Benny, who had always been apolitical, had become a political football.[2]

With tabloid journalists and photographers ligging around on location and on set more than ever before, Benny's (unchallenged) defences against the public criticism of his shows would run in these newspapers.

About the sexist allegations, he told the *Sunday People* in 1982, 'It's always the men who come off worst. Terrible things happen to me and the other men in the show, but the girls retain their dignity. It's the men who are the idiots. Nothing nasty ever happens to the girls. They show their knickers but it's never nasty.' And, 'You'll never see anything offensive or dirty on my shows, and you'll never hear any bad language. I don't swear and I don't use four-letter words. It's all suggestion, all harmless fun.'

He also said, to the *Daily Mirror*, 'There was a time when you couldn't say ruddy or damn, vicar or knickers in a comedy show. I go a bit further now, but I'm not a trailblazer. I've got no messages to get across. I don't apologize for the girls – every show needs all the plusses it can get.'

Benny was bemused at why his show was being singled out for trouble when swearing and nudity on television was on the increase generally. '[My show is] nothing like the nude scenes and the things I hear said in television plays. These really upset me. I find so much of today's television quite shocking, I really do. Do you know what my sister Diana says about me? She says I'm a prude.'

Notwithstanding their evolution from Love Machine, Benny's general – and probably honest – explanation about the inception of Hill's Angels was simple, yet it puzzled him: Hot Gossip had helped deliver good ratings to Kenny Everett's show, and a similar troupe could do the same for his show. So why, he now asked, were people up in arms about him and not Everett, whose show was broadcast an hour earlier? He could not see the answer. Everett's was a pop music/comedy show, with predominantly teen and young-adult viewers not at all fazed by a bit of raunch. *The Benny Hill Show* had always, since 1955, been family viewing, likely to attract pensioners as well as younger generations. A great many of these people found the sexy dancing objectionable, especially the way it was staged and shot. The tabloids were right – there was nothing really wrong with Hill's Angels. They were simply unsuitable for this audience.

The hyped-up arguments over sexism plagued *The Benny Hill Show* from this point and obscured the real issue. To this day, virtually the entire cast and crew stick to the original defence. As Dennis Kirkland says, 'The word "sexist" must mean being "anti" a particular gender, either men or women. So why is it always meant as anti-women? Yes, *The Benny Hill Show* was undoubtedly sexist . . . because it was totally anti-*men*. Anybody who has missed the point is an idiot. The show was not anti-women: the men always lost and the women always won. Look at the men: Benny, Jackie, Toddy, Henry . . . the boys are back in town?! They try and chat up the birds, they fuck it up. The girls always win and Benny always loses. Now *that* is sexist.'

That is correct . . . and also poppycock. While Benny did always lose out with women – this had been the hallmark of his work, and life, since Day One – the girls simply did not need to be so provocatively dressed, nor pout so much, nor hold their legs open. If they were not ornamental, they could have worn other clothing, as women in Benny's TV shows had done for the preceding twenty-five years; and if it was not exploiting women's sexuality for the express gratification of men, why did the camera-scripts now include such directions as 'crutch shot' and 'downline bums' for a Hill's Angels 'strip sequence'? (Script for February 10 1982 show.)

One particular Hill's Angels routine typifies the regrettable sexploitation in these latter-day *Benny Hill Show*s – a sequence set in a gymnasium, with the dancers vaulting over the horse, skipping and exercising in various sexy ways. Not only did they cavort, pout, writhe and give come-ons to the camera, but as the lens zoomed in on the crotch of one of the dancers the action went into slow-motion. (And what had this to do with comedy anyway?)

'Sure there was a little bit of jiggling in there, I wouldn't deny it,' Kirkland retorts. 'But Benny had been very difficult that day. Much as I adored him, I can tell you that he behaved like an arsehole that day. We'd done all his gags and I'd been left only forty-five minutes to do this whole routine. So I ran it and shot it and took away the tapes for editing. And the timing was under, so I slow-mo'd a couple of shots, including one of a girl doing a cartwheel and landing in the splits. I didn't do it because it was dirty but because it was pretty. Well, you'd think I'd shot the bloody Pope! People accused me of "slowing down on a crotch shot".'

Though Benny continued to defend Hill's Angels, proudly acknowledging now that his show represented the last bastion of the old stage Variety shows, he began to mount a counter-attack to the criticism – a charm offensive – highlighting other aspects of his life.

He played his strongest hand right away. In the *Sun*, on March 12 1983, the man who always looked down on those who paraded virtue gave away his near-thirty-year secret about Phoebe King and Netta Warner.

'BENNY'S OFF-SCREEN ANGELS' ran the headline; 'His wheel-chair pals come first':

> Bachelor Benny, 58, is rarely seen in public without one of his beautiful Hill's Angels on his arm.
>
> But the two women he is closest to are far removed from the glamorous world of television and its scantily-clad showgirls.
>
> Both are in their forties and both are spastics.
>
> The man whose sexy antics have been denounced by parents, teachers and spoil-sports on both sides of the Atlantic actually blushed when I asked him about the two ladies in his life and his kindness to them.

Benny went on to explain how he had met Phoebe and Netta, how he spent a week with each of them every year, and also brought them down to London to dine at the Savoy. And he revealed that three other 'ladies in similar circumstances', whom he had also befriended, had died. (Their identities are not known but two of them may have lived in Blackheath, south-east London.)

But another aspect of Benny's character revealed itself, too – the wounded boy who liked to bite back. In a 1985 show (and not for the first time) he attacked the TV critic Clive James, who had said some unkind things about him. In Benny's sketch, a woman was watching television when the announcer remarked, 'It's after midnight and time to watch Clive James.' The woman says, 'Oh no!', gets up from her chair and pulls a toilet-chain, which fills up the screen – still depicting James's face – with water. 'He always hit back,' says Benny's old friend Dave Freeman. 'The writer Celia Brayfield once had a go at Benny and he did a thing about her, siting a sketch at a place called Braynfeeble Farm. He'd have been better forgetting it.'

When, in typically unrestrained style, the catty columnist Nina Myskow attacked Benny Hill in the *News of the World* in 1986, his reply was sharp and over-the-top. She called his latest show 'Worse than any nightmare . . . the same tacky, tedious trash except WORSE and OLDER', and added, 'You can only get away with it if you don't look like the sort of rancid creep who terrorizes women in trains.' Benny let rip in his next-recorded show (which was two years later) by imagining Myskow as an item on a restaurant menu – 'Jaw-bone of an ass, with a double helping of tongue, on a plate of tripe, with a side order of ugli fruit.' Anne Diamond, a TV presenter and journalist, must also have passed comment upon Benny's leering comedy, for she came in for similar treatment, being described as 'a sheep's head, with the brains taken out'. A year later, Benny still hadn't got over attacking Myskow, calling her 'Nina Cowpat' and, in a double-insult, exclaiming, 'A lot of people think she's as thick as two planks. There are others who think she's quite stupid.'

Perhaps the most stinging attack on Benny Hill was delivered by Ben Elton in an interview he gave to the rock magazine *Q* in January 1987. A writer and standup 'alternative comedian', Elton was renowned for his rapid-paced ('motormouth') rants about Margaret Thatcher and the Conservative Party, targets that made him Public Enemy No. 1 for the *Sun*, which mounted mercilessly scabrous attacks upon his character.

Elton told *Q*:

I believe that the non-use of stereotypes – Irish people are stupid, women's tits are funny – is noticeable in my act. I mean, you have Benny Hill in the late '80s chasing half-naked women around a park when we know in Britain women can't even walk safe in a park any more. That for me is worrying. And while Benny Hill is chasing naked women about the park I could say 'fuck' a thousand times on telly and I wouldn't be nearly as offensive as that.

The general tenor of Elton's opinion was worthy of debate, reflecting the thinking of virtually the entire rising generation of comedians, but there was a crucial flaw in his argument that Hill-defenders could seize upon and so deflect the issue. Benny did not chase women, they said, the women chased him.

'Benny *never* chased the girls at the end of the show,' proclaims Dennis Kirkland. 'So what made people think that he did?

'Ben Elton was not our favourite person after this. We always felt that there were enough people out there having a go at us without a fellow artist pitching in. Even if Benny thought someone was shite he would never have said it. Why should a young comic knock a master? But the laugh for us was that Benny was a megastar and who was Ben Elton? I told Benny, "They know you in Hollywood. They wouldn't know Ben Elton in Cricklewood."'

Benny was deflated that another comedian should have knocked him. As Kirkland has said, in his code of practice, written after the war, this was simply not done. Richard Stone felt his client's wrath – 'I remember him saying to me, "I've watched television and I counted forty 'mother-fuckers' in one of these 'alternative comedy' shows. *Why are people picking on me?*"'

The *Sun*, of course, needed little excuse to lace up the bovver-boots and exact revenge on Elton for his attack on their beloved feature-filler. 'He's a prattling prig who could live to be 100 and still never be one tenth as funny or as loved as Benny Hill,' it declared. 'The only place he's big is between the ears.' Such was the lingering contempt that five years on, when Benny died, columnist Richard Littlejohn was still simmering, writing an ode to the well-known tune of 'Ernie' that began:

You can hear the Lefties howl,
And the right-on comics scowl,
And the chatter of the feminists
As the thought policemen prowl,

and continued:

Now Benny had a rival, a sneering little prig,
In shiny suit from public school, who liked to have a dig
At all the jokes which made us laugh
About knickers, bums and tits,
Couldn't understand why Benny Hill had millions in fits.
His name was Elton,
And he had the biggest ego on the Left.

Two decades later, in 2000, Ben Elton (who remains a successful comedy writer and performer, known now in both Hollywood and Cricklewood)

369

clarified his comments in a BBC Radio 2 programme, *There'll Never be Another Benny Hill*:

> I was actually known for a while as somebody who was supposed to despise Benny Hill. Not at all. I certainly was not moved by the titillating obsessions of the later shows. Half the jokes were about girls in bikinis – [and] apart from the fact that I felt that some of the stereotyping was unhelpful and unuseful, one of the reasons I hated it most was because it took some of the emphasis off the great comic. I don't know if you've seen any of Benny Hill's '50s work, the work he did at the BBC? Astonishing stuff, really subtle, interesting stuff . . .

Such was its downfall that *The Benny Hill Show* was voted the most disliked TV show in Britain by readers of *Woman's Own* in 1986, and it was criticized by female delegates during a Trades Union Congress conference. The feminist movement especially hated it. Speaking on the BBC World Service in 1991, Harriet Wistrick of the London Women's Centre laid out the reasons, interestingly repeating Ben Elton's primary misconception:

> I think Benny Hill is one of the archetypal examples of a sexist comedian – a leering, leching man chasing after scantily clad women, wanting them for sexual gratification. They're running away from him. The reality of many women's lives is that they actually live in fear of sexual violence and rape from men, and it's not a laughing matter.

This was materially wrong in several respects, and one can only wonder how familiar such complainants actually were with Benny Hill's comedy. While it is just about conceivable to broaden the word 'chase' – he may not have literally run after women but he did leer at them and edge menacingly along suburban park-benches towards them to such an extent that this was a form of pursuit – 'running away' from him did not enter into it. And it is only by the word's broadest interpretation that 'rape' could be associated with Benny Hill. In its literal definition, the act was well beyond him.

Benny, who was still innocence personified, was so flummoxed by all these attacks that he took the unusual step of speaking directly to the camera at the end of two TV shows. Typically unaccustomed at examining the real causes of his problems, however, the tone was one of humorous, direct rebuttal.

In the first[3] he responded to a recent critical notice in the *Daily Telegraph* ('or was it the *Melody Maker*? I get them muddled up'):

> It said 'Some of the girls' dresses were cut low enough to make a baby cry.' I don't design the dresses! It's nothing to do with me! It's him up there [nods towards Dennis Kirkland in the gallery]. Director? Couldn't direct traffic! I said to him, 'Do we have to have girls running around half-naked in all the shows?' He said, 'Well I look at it like this . . .' [affects stare].

Two years on,[4] Benny was back for a second stab:

> I was at the last Montreux television festival and while I was there a Swedish journalist came up to me . . . eventually he got around to what he really wanted to say (and you won't believe this): that there were some women in Sweden who thought that I was sexist! Can you believe that? Me, sexist! I don't know the meaning of the word. I had to look it up in my Boy's Own dictionary. Nowadays I'm almost afraid to say dictionary, because 'dic' is masculine, you see. It should say Bettytionary.
>
> And I looked up sexist and it wasn't there. So I looked up feminist, it said 'see sexist'. Because you hear a lot about feminists nowadays, don't you, eh? You never hear of masculinists. Perhaps there's no such word. Perhaps the masculine equivalent of a feminist is a male chauvinist pig. It's a bit unfair – you never hear about female chauvinist sows, do you? Not outside this studio!
>
> But I will admit some shows are sexist, obviously they are. There's *Woman's Hour* – there's no Man's Hour, *Listen with Mother* – there's no Listen with Father, *Watch the Woman* – there's no Watch the Man. And look at the sexist magazines they've got – there's *Woman*, there's *Woman's Mirror*, *Woman's Own*, *Woman's Realm*, *Woman's Weekly*. Us fellas have only got one – *Men Only*. And what's that full of? Pictures of women!

To say the least, this was not a good period for Benny Hill – despite his worldwide successes. Constantly overweight and nudging sixty, his health was beginning to fail, too. He had quietly had a kidney removed in the late 1970s, after his doctor diagnosed a tumour. It turned out to be benign but the organ was removed anyway, and a prostate problem was sorted out at the same time. Ironically, Henry McGee had one of his most pleasant times with Benny when he went to visit him at King Edward VII's Hospital for Officers. ('Are you sure it's all right?' Benny enquired upon admission, 'I was only a private . . .') Says McGee, 'I went to see him a few days later, intent on staying only a short while; I didn't want to tire him out. I was in there for about an hour and hardly said a word because he had me in stitches. He wasn't telling jokes, he was relating anecdotes. I came out totally exhausted. The truth of the matter is, a shy man goes out of his way to put you at ease.'

Benny had been with the same Harley Street doctor, Ernest Page, since the early 1950s. Distinguished by a crater in his forehead, Page was some fifteen years older than his patient but they socialized together, going out on double dates; the doctor loved the company of women and was a pathological bottom-pincher. He was in the right job for it, too, for Page was a gynaecologist, not a general practitioner. 'Benny was the only man who consulted a gynaecologist when he had a cold,' laughs Dave Freeman. 'He didn't trust people, so once he found "Old Doc Page" that was it. He said to me once, "I've had these pains in my chest and I saw Old Doc Page and he said it was rheumatism around the heart." I said, "Page doesn't know about anything above the hips, Benny! You've got indigestion – get some charcoal tablets." From then on, Benny consumed charcoal like a stove. And I was right, it was heartburn. But Benny consulted Old Doc Page right to the end. He was his medical guru.' (Benny also consulted a Wimpole Street laryngologist, Norman Punt, on audience nights at Teddington. 'He often lost his voice before these recordings,' says Henry McGee. 'It was purely a nerve thing about going out on stage. I'd hear this legendary man Punt walking past my dressing-room door, going into Benny's and then coming out again. He probably gave him a squirt of something, possibly even a placebo, just to give him confidence.')

Benny's health problems in 1983 involved something that would nag away at him for the rest of his life, a stomach ulcer. He was admitted to Cromwell Hospital in Kensington (one thing Benny always treated himself to was private healthcare) but doctors decided not to operate. 'They gave him a medicine which seemed to cure it,' says Henry McGee. 'This was a Friday and they said, "You can go home now, Mr Hill." But he was quite happy, sitting there writing scripts, so he asked if he could stay the weekend, and did.' On his release Benny gave an exclusive interview to the *Sun*, declaring that he was fit again and raring to get on with the show.

Shortly after leaving hospital, Benny received word that his sister Diana was suffering from leukaemia. He had last been out to Australia in February 1982 (flights paid for by Walton Stores, for whom he made half a dozen TV commercials), though he had found the visit a little difficult. As he explained it to Henry McGee, Diana didn't like him to go out, not even to any local shops, as she didn't want people to know who she was. Still a communist, Diana was taken ill while on a comrades' holiday in Cuba. The doctor diagnosed leukaemia and she returned to Sydney, phoning Benny with the news. 'He got into a terrible flap and was offering to pay for the finest surgeons,' says Dave Freeman, 'but he told me she'd never take any money off him. His money was tainted by capitalism, apparently. She wouldn't come to England or go to America for medical help, and said to Benny, "I've got two years, I'm going to enjoy myself." She was dead in three weeks. Benny didn't even go out for the funeral because it was all so quick.' (This has been contradicted by others, who say that Benny often sent Diana money, and that in her final months she was driving a car he had bought for her.)

More than ever, Benny sought refuge in a private world well beyond the reach of his professional associates and acquaintances, beyond even Dennis Kirkland. There was one, key focal point – his relationship with his mother's younger sister, Auntie Lulu (Alice Louise Jaques, also known as Louie). Theirs had always been a special bond – he had mentioned her during his 1959 *Desert Island Discs* appearance and in a couple of other radio shows – and he often visited her house in Bexleyheath, Kent, southeast of London. Louie's husband George, who did not care for Benny, disliking his fidgeting, died in 1964, and the visits then became more regular, as did his sending of brief yet loving postcards. (As many of his friends and acquaintances can readily prove, Benny was a dedicated sender of postcards.)

By the 1980s, with Louie four years older than the century, the relationship had grown particularly close. 'Alfie answered all her needs,' says Louie's son, Bill. (Being family, Bill Jaques and his wife Florence continue to call Benny by his real name.) 'My mother had lost her husband, and my brothers and I had moved away, and in Alfie she found a man who wasn't married and was quite content to stay at home with her, watching TV. When she turned sixty-five [in 1961] my mother had said, "I'm not going out again"; apart from when I took her to hospital, she rarely did so for the last thirty years of her life.'

'Alfie would usually travel down by train to Blackheath, where he would visit a couple of old ladies, and then he'd get on a Green Line bus to my mother's house,' Bill recalls. 'He'd have a small suitcase and a big bag of Mars bars with him. He always had the front bedroom – that was the best room – and mum would switch to the spare room. I would know when he was visiting because he wore cheap Old Spice after-shave and as I opened the front-door I could smell it.

'To be honest, I was always pleased to see him there, because they were always so happy together. Mum would say "Alfie's upstairs" and there he'd be, singing away. I'd say, "That's OK, then, bye-bye," and leave them to it. They loved it together, and it eased my conscience that she wasn't alone. He'd stay a few days, then mother would wash and iron his clothes and pyjamas and put them back in the drawer for his next visit.'

While people in more than 100 countries were hooting over *The Benny Hill Show*, the great comedian was removing himself into this very particular paradise – a small suburban house on a busy main road at 119 Watling Street, Bexleyheath. Auntie Lulu's company gave him enormous, easy satisfaction, and the nearest he ever got to domestic bliss.

'My mother would be singing in the kitchen and Alfie would be singing upstairs,' says Bill, 'and the frying pan would be on. Mother didn't do "slimming cooking" and they both loved their food. Alfie especially loved fried breakfast – sausages, fried bread with jam spread on top, and everything else – and they'd pour the fat from the pan over the plate. She also used to make him condensed-milk sandwiches with a sprinkling of sugar.'

Inevitably, Benny would pile on the pounds during these visits. 'My mother had a cane-backed sofa,' says Bill, 'and one time I went there it had a big hole in the seat. Mother said, "Alfie sat down a bit heavy last time he was here." Most people would have arranged a repair but Alfie didn't think like that. Another time, one of the local kids fired an air-gun into his bedroom window, making a hole in the glass. Alfie got some Sellotape and sealed it up – he never thought of phoning for a glazier, and neither did my mother.'

Florence Jaques observed what she calls a 'peculiar affinity' between Alfie and Louie. 'The generation gap didn't exist,' she says. 'They were like an old married couple, happily together for years and years. In fact, it was even better than that – it was so comfortable that they didn't need words. They both loved old movies, especially the silents, and they'd sit and watch together the whole afternoon, Alfie with his old carpet slippers on, both of them with a Mars bar or a raspberry truffle or whatever it was. Sometimes Louie would say to Alfie, "Who was the drummer in such and such a band?" – Harry James, Henry Hall, all the way back – and he would know and they would reminisce together. If the neighbours came by, Louie wouldn't let them past the front door. She was very protective. She'd simply say, "Alfie's here, I'm busy," and they would be excluded.

'The affinity between Alfie and Louie was one that he didn't have with his own mother or anybody else,' Florence concludes. 'Nellie [Benny's mother, Helen] had never seemed too bothered about wanting her sons around, but Louie wanted hers, and when they weren't she turned to Alfie. And I always felt that he got from Louie what his own mother couldn't give him. They definitely found one another when they needed to. Watched from the sidelines, it was a beautiful thing to see between two people who weren't married, something that you don't come across very often.'

Two other personal relationships were particularly important to Benny in this period when, professionally, he was coming under increasing personal attack. They were members of Hill's Angels and, in his own unique way, he loved them both.

Sue Upton was a petite blonde who passed a Queen's Gate audition in 1976 and first appeared in *The Benny Hill Show* soon afterwards. A bit-part actress, she giggled her way through the inexorably bawdy British film-comedy *Confessions from a Holiday Camp*, and appeared as a common, gum-chewing youth in a BBC comedy pilot with Thora Hird. But she was never going to make the big time, and was no great dancer either, even though she writhed with the other Hill's Angels for a while. What she did have, Benny said, was 'twinkle'.

Benny took a particular shine to Sue. When she became too obviously old for dancing with the younger girls he gave her character parts, like 'Wondergran', a Superman-like granny with an exploding bra, and as Stan Laurel to his Oliver Hardy in an affectionate imitation of his comedy heroes (which he had done twice before). In fact, everyone liked Sue. Prone to making incomprehensible comments, which the cast and crew called 'Uptonisms', and speaking in Estuarial tones, Benny wrote to her strengths and ensured that she had a part in every show.

They also formed a friendship that gave Benny great succour in the remaining years of his life. At first, Sue did not reveal to him that she was married, fearing that it might interfere with their working relationship, but Benny was not troubled by it, and when she tentatively invited him to visit her home in Hornchurch, he turned up. It soon became a regular stopping place, and he would visit for a week every year just as he stayed in Felixstowe (with Phoebe King), Leicester (Netta Warner) and Bexleyheath (Auntie Lulu). The tabloid papers, of course, lapped it up. 'Cor blimey! Costa del Hornchurch has really got the lot,' headlined the *Sun*, rapidly becoming a repository for all Benny Hill 'news'.

Benny took Sue Upton's children to see the Moscow State Circus when it was in London, and they day-tripped to Southend and strolled along the promenade eating fish and chips. In Hornchurch, he turned up at the local playgroup to meet her infant son, and at the local hospital when she was giving birth to a baby girl. (He then became the godfather.) At the house, Benny watched football with Sue's husband Roger – a decorator by profession – and played endlessly with the children, whom he called 'our little kiddies'. 'You should see Benny when he is staying here,' Sue enthused to the *Sun*. 'The children stamp on his toes and shove him about and he'll be down on all-fours giving them piggy-back rides.'

'He used to call me Mummy,' Sue told the *Daily Mirror* in 1992. 'He would say "Come on Mummy, let's take the littlies out for the day" . . . He would come round the supermarket with me . . . We always walked arm in arm or held hands – he had big, warm, chubby hands . . . Roger never interfered, bless him. He understood what Benny wanted. But I

don't think Benny would have liked it if he had come on our outings . . .
I think he would have wanted to marry me if I had been free. I know he
really loved me, and I loved him.'

Benny's other new friendship was rather different. This young woman
was Louise English, a rarity among Hill's Angels in that she had a definite
stage ability in addition to her cute, pouting looks and slender figure. Also,
she was the daughter of a soubrette, Elizabeth Reid, whom he had warmly
befriended during his portentous Margate summer season in 1950. When
Louise was a teenager, Elizabeth wrote to Benny asking for advice about
how she could enter the profession. Benny replied, 'Work at her accents,
work at everything, and I'll keep my eye out for her.' When, some time
later, they met for the first time, Benny said to Louise, 'You could have
been mine!' From this moment, she held a unique place in his affections.

Still the frustrated impresario and talent-spotter, Benny was always
trying to encourage his Angels to realize that they would not be young
and beautiful for ever, and that they had to add some other dimension to
their talent if they wished to sustain a career in show-business. But he was
usually wasting his breath – asking them if they planned to work in
summer seasons or pantomimes the usual response was, 'Nah, my boyfriend don't want me to do that.' Louise English was different. She
possessed talent and acumen to match her dark beauty; Benny sensed that
she alone among his 'discoveries' might make a mark beyond the show.
The teacher set out to broaden the pupil's talent.

'I had to audition for him, to read, to do accents, to sing, to dance, to
do comedy,' she says. 'It was difficult and he was very strict. He told me
I had to learn *every* accent, and when he learned that I couldn't do Welsh
very well he gave me everything in a Welsh accent until I mastered it.'

Louise quickly realized too that Benny was not only her employer.
'I was like a daughter to him and he was like a father to me,' she affirms.
'I didn't have a father, so he instantly filled that role. He didn't let me
smoke and he wanted to meet my boyfriends. When an important
relationship finished, and I was heartbroken, Benny wrote me a beautiful
letter saying that he'd had his heart broken too and that it's a terrible
thing to accept, and that one has to take life one day at a time. "But I still
believe you're going to be a big star," he wrote, "so it might be best that

it has happened now, because imagine how the boyfriend would feel in a few years' time being Mr Louise English – he wouldn't like that very much." It was *so* sweet.'

To his delight, Benny's faith and investment in Louise English would pay off – but there was another Angel whose much greater success after leaving *The Benny Hill Show* he did not foresee. One of the girls he auditioned at Queen's Gate in 1982 was Jane Leeves, a slim young dancer/ actress from East Grinstead, Sussex. She passed his various tests and donned the stockings and suspenders for some studio recordings inserted into shows in 1982–3, after which she departed, heading for America. Benny made no subsequent comment about her – there was a rapid turnover of showgirls and she was one of many whose association with the show was as brief as the costumes they were made to wear. And he did not live long enough to see Leeves, alone among his Angels, graduate to the top, claiming a major role as the English immigrant Daphne Moon in the hugely successful American sitcom *Frasier*. Considering how much time and energy he invested in trying to groom his girls for the big time, it is ironic that she should have passed through unnoticed.

Throughout this period, the over-emphasis on sex in *The Benny Hill Show* was in full flow. Benny was still handing his critics all the brickbats they could throw. Also, since this man was The World's Most Popular Comedian, one can but wonder what on earth he was playing at. So many of the items in these 1980s shows were undeveloped, or bankrupt of invention. Indeed they were not always Benny's ideas. Just as he had done with his old pal Harry Segal and others since the 1950s, he remained partial to paying modest amounts of cash for a comedy suggestion . . . and claiming authorship and copyright.

'His idea was "everyone can contribute,"' says Lorraine Doyle. 'He was always saying, "If you get an idea, write it down and I'll look at it." Once we were walking in Hyde Park on a lovely sunny day and I said, "Wouldn't it be funny if that man over there, the one in shorts, stubbed out that cigarette . . ." And he was saying "Yes, what then, what then?" because he was grilling me for more. And I carried on, ". . . and he was looking at a woman and stubbed out the cigarette with his bare foot. Ow-ow, his feet are burning, he grabs an ice-lolly and puts it on his feet to cool them down." And this idea turned up in the very next show –

without any payment for me. And he turned to me and said, "*That's* for not writing it down. If you'd have written it down I would have had to pay you. So have we learned our lesson?"'

Examples of how primitive and lazy the comedy could be were now occurring in every show. Here is a 'quickie' from Benny's script for a 1983 edition:[5]

Knickers
Man sneezes, and girl, standing nearby, sees her knickers fall down.

And that was it.

In another piece, a pretty woman, shackled high up a dungeon wall, is shown to be heavily pregnant. Standing a few feet away, Benny's exaggerated look to the audience makes it clear that he has sown his seed from the most enormous of appendages.

And – in a straight steal from a Laurel and Hardy film, *Their First Mistake* – Benny needs to feed a baby and unbuttons his shirt; as bystanders watch, appalled, he pulls out a bottle of milk.

There was, blessedly, some good work, too. Benny's best piece in his last decade was 'The Clown Striptease', shown in 1982. 'This is a rather complex routine. It requires very careful costuming. The diagram should help,' Benny wrote to Dennis Kirkland when submitting the script, adding 'It's a bit time consuming but I think worth it.'

Benny is dressed as a clown, standing before a black background. After a little trickery he begins to shed his clothes, item by item, until he is down to skin. Then he peels off his skin, to reveal his skeleton. Then the skeleton is dismembered, until finally only one hand remains.

It was a piece of high invention, which Benny would have seen performed by one of his favourite continental comedy outfits, the Black Theatre of Prague – a troupe of skilled puppeteers dressed in black against a black backdrop and thus virtually invisible, who manipulated lifesize figures. All the same, his mime execution was highly skilled.

Bella Emberg, cast in *The Benny Hill Show* as an old bag, happened to witness Benny recording the entire sketch; it made an indelible impression, and she saw too the benefit of Dennis Kirkland's affinity with his hero. 'After lunch one day I went back to the studio to see what our calls were for the next day – and there was Ben dressed up as a clown,' she says.

'I thought I'd wait five minutes and see what he was doing, and it was the most brilliant thing I'd ever seen. I was still there two-and-a-half hours later because it took all afternoon to shoot. It was painstaking, stop-start the whole time, and Benny was nervous. Dennis was saying, "Come on, Ben, come on BH, you're going to do it." I was transfixed – it was one of the most magical afternoons of my life. To me, that was the pinnacle of Benny Hill's greatness. That's what he could do. There are some very good new comics around today but they don't come up to that standard.'

All this time, Benny was receiving countless offers to appear in the USA – and rejecting every one of them. Movie comedies, TV comedies, appearances on the Johnny Carson and David Letterman chat-shows – they were all dangled before him, and all were firmly declined. In particular, Benny refused several invitations to play floor-shows in Las Vegas and Atlantic City. Peter Charlesworth was present at a dinner in Queen's Gate when Benny had been misled into hosting two Vegas promoters who were quite desperate to have him star in their casinos. They offered $100,000 a week. 'It was a strong pitch,' Charlesworth recalls. 'They said, "We'll get Jackie Wright over! We'll get Bob Todd over! We'll get Henry McGee over!" and Benny replied, "Yes, but what am *I* going to do?" They said, "Well, you'll . . . do your show!" And Benny replied, "Yes, but what do I *do*? I don't tell jokes, I don't do stage shows, I do *television* shows."'

The Vegas men were struck dumb – this guy was putting obstacles in the way of serious amounts of dough. But Benny knew his limitations all too well. If the Sunderland Empire had been too much when he was unknown, how could he possibly endure Caesar's Palace and all the 'star trip' that goes with such an engagement? 'I'd disappoint them,' he told Louise English. 'They're going to want me to be funny and I'm not funny.'

Though he had no intention of working in America, however, Benny did like to say that if the right offer came along he might just do so. And he blamed the lack of this 'right offer' on Richard Stone.

Benny and Richard had been together for nearly forty years by this time, but the relationship – which had never been close – was coming under increasing strain. Stone was entering semi-retirement, delegating

Benny's business to Lynda Ronan, an agent within the newly formed Richard Stone Partnership. Several of Benny's associates were aware that he could have left to sign with another agent – perhaps with his friend Peter Charlesworth, or with another acquaintance, Iain Burton, whose agency provided several Hill's Angels. Such was Benny's unswerving loyalty, he could never do so.

Such admirable fealty did not stop him carping, however. Stone received several more 'dreadful letters' from his client during this period. 'He wrote saying, "In all the years I've been with you you've never introduced me to anybody interesting except Hal Roach."⁶ He also accused me of not looking after him properly; the worst was when my son opened an office in Hollywood. Naturally, I asked him to look after Benny's interests in America. Benny didn't really want to go to America but he kept goading me that I wasn't getting him the right offers, and that it was Tim who was buggering it up for him. But I just don't think he wanted to go. We got him all the offers we could – for his own show, his own series – but he turned them down and then blamed me. He was a huge star in America at this time – he could have done anything.'

Benny was still a devoted friend to the various PAs he had encountered over the years. Though she no longer worked on his show, René Bloomstein at Thames remained a director of his companies, and Anne Ling in BBC radio had started to type all his Thames scripts (previously René's job) in her spare time. Benny wrote this in a 1987 letter to Hettie Tack (PA to John Street at the BBC in the late 1950s), who had subsequently gone to live in America:

> I do not have a representative in the US. I'm sure Tim Stone is OK but his father dotes on him; I felt like I was his Xmas present. His father wanted me to work in the US so that his son would have a name client. He was trying so hard to get me to go [that] he was advising me to take on totally unsuitable work. Of course, now he tries to talk me out of working there, as neither of them represent me there.

Not only would Benny not work in America, but for several years after his US breakthrough he had still to meet Don Taffner, the man who – to quote Henry McGee – 'had been responsible for the miracle'. When, finally, the tenacious impresario announced that he was coming to England,

Thames accorded him special guest status at a recording of the show and threw a party on its boat (moored on the Thames, hard by the studio lot), a venue reserved for VIP entertaining and executive lunches. Thames forgot, however, that such occasions were anathema to Benny Hill. 'He couldn't stand this kind of thing at all,' says McGee, 'so he gravitated to the prow of the boat. It was winter and the rest of us were inside. Don boarded at the back. We were all thinking, "They're never going to meet! They haven't even said hello!" Eventually someone did get them introduced, but I was standing a few yards away, watching, knowing that Benny never liked meeting strangers. He would put on a show of affability but you knew he wanted to get away. Sure enough, I don't think they spoke for more than three or four minutes before Benny had got away and gone.'

Taking Dennis Kirkland as his companion-protector, Benny finally made his first visit to America in October 1984, to have what he called 'a looksee'. It was to be a private trip, to quietly check for himself if all the wild stories about his fame there were true. They were. (One particular anecdote that tickled Benny, one he liked to repeat, was that night-duty policemen in a town in Alabama would greet each other with the Fred Scuttle salute.)

Thames and Don Taffner were miffed when Benny insisted that the visit receive no publicity, but just a day after arriving in San Francisco every star's perennial paradox reared its head. 'We had been down the docks, around Chinatown and gone shopping and nobody had particularly noticed us,' says Dennis Kirkland. 'Benny phoned me in my room and said, "Er, have you . . . had any messages from the press, little heart?" "No, nothing." "Well perhaps we should, er, arrange a photocall or something?" Next day it all happened – girls in bikinis, the Scuttle salute on Golden Gate Bridge and pictures in all the papers. Later, we were at a Spanish restaurant with some outdoor tables and the waiters spotted Benny and came out and sang to him, beautifully, "*Cuando calienta el sol* . . . ". He *loved* it. The whole place stopped – people were applauding and cheering.'

After a week in San Francisco, Ben and Den left for Los Angeles. Writing to Hettie Tack, Benny described what happened:

After a celibate week in Frisco, Den & I arrived Sunday evening at the Westwood Marquee [*sic*] Hotel in LA. I noticed the pool outside. I said,

'Tomorrow morning, you & me, by the pool. An actress, a couple of models, some dancers must pass by sometime. They'll say Hey, don't I know you? & then we'll be away.' So – next morning at 10 we are on our sun loungers looking hopeful. We even had lunch out there. At 3pm the 1st person passed by. Who was it?! Bruce Forsyth!!![7]

The Englishmen had a good week in Los Angeles, being invited out to *Playboy* founder Hugh Hefner's mansion (they were disappointed to find no women there either), and dining at Chasen's restaurant with a party including Jack Lemmon and veteran comedian Steve Allen. Both were big Benny Hill fans (as was Phil Silvers, who wrote several letters of admiration) – they recognized what, to them, were the burlesque and silent-film roots of his comedy, and were thrilled that someone was still doing it in the 1980s. 'It was an odd evening,' Steve Allen recalled later.[8] 'All of us Americans were impressed to be in Benny Hill's presence . . . I remember being impressed at how shy he seemed and how softly he spoke, and he didn't try to amuse anyone.' The next day, Benny and Dennis went out to Burt Reynolds' house, where Dom DeLuise turned up, and then they all went on to a TV recording where Benny met Vic Damone, and stood up in the audience to take a prolonged ovation.

New York went well, too. 'Donald Trump invited us along to Trump Tower,' says Kirkland. 'He was thrilled to meet Ben, and I was cracking jokes. I suggested a photo outside, not realizing that Trump doesn't do that, but he came out and he was doing the Scuttle salute! His security men nearly died with fright. He also offered us free use of his jet and helicopter, though we never used them.' Benny asked Don Taffner, to whom he was beginning to warm, to get them tickets to see Marvin Hagler defend his World Middleweight crown at Madison Square Garden, which – to the boxing-mad boy from Southampton – must have been heavenly. Then they went to see Twiggy on Broadway in *My One and Only* and dined with the cast.

Despite the revelry, Benny had one lingering regret about this first American visit: the lack of female company. He wrote to Hettie Tack:

The main drawback was that for the 3 weeks we were in the company of men. And of course we'd hoped to meet some pretty actresses and dancers. But 'twas not to be.

'Benny often used to say "What's in it for me?"' recalls his dance choreographer Libby Roberts. 'So he was particularly cheesed off when he went around Hugh Hefner's Playboy mansion and spent the entire evening talking to men. He told me that people in America were constantly asking him over for dinner to meet their parents, and he said, "What was in it for me? If they'd have suggested meeting a young daughter or her young friends I might have said yes. I certainly didn't want to be stuck with a granny at a party."'

Benny was back in America in March 1987, not merely to attend but – shock, horror – to perform in a stage gala mounted in honour of Thames Television at Lincoln Center.[9] Moreover, considering how many times Benny had turned down sky-high fees for American appearances, he did it for nothing – as a gesture of gratitude to Philip Jones.

'I asked him to do it, quite certain that he'd say no,' says Jones. 'I said it would be terrifically helpful for the company, and rather nice for me, and, amazingly, he agreed. We rehearsed it pretty well in London before we left and I had to promise him there'd be no television at all, not even news coverage.'

This was Benny's one and only American stage appearance. It comprised a short Fred Scuttle interview with Henry McGee, and a Diary sketch (a stream of simple gags) that enabled him to hold his usual heavy book, both to prevent his hands from trembling and in case he 'dried'. As it happened, he sweated profusely the entire evening, watching while various other Thames personalities were on stage, panic-stricken that he would mess it all up. He didn't; basking in the glow of an ecstatic reception from the New York glitterati, he boasted to Dennis Kirkland at the post-show Hotel Plaza dinner, 'I felt so much in command, I got bored halfway through.'

Benny's many postcard confrères received the good news, modestly reported, a few days later. His card to Ivy Lillywhite, his mentor from wartime Eastleigh with whom he always remained in contact, read:

> Did my first live US show yesterday. The audience was very responsive. I'm staying on for a few days holiday to catch a couple of Broadway shows and see the sights.
> Hope all is well with you and yours.
> Take care, Little Alf

Having been nicknamed Little Alf at birth, Benny always liked to sign himself 'Wee' or 'Little' – or, when writing from France, 'Petit' – but now, given his ballooning size, there was a concomitant sense of irony.

Apart from wanting to make the gesture of thanks to Philip Jones, Benny had found the courage to face a live audience again because of another career landmark – his first stage appearance anywhere in almost twenty-five years. This took place in November 1984 at the London Palladium, with Benny among a star-packed cast paying tribute to the late Eric Morecambe – a comedian as loved by his fellow professionals as he was by his adoring British public. The great man had died from a heart attack six months earlier; the tribute show *Bring Me Sunshine* was held in aid of the British Heart Foundation and performed in front of a packed house, with Prince Philip as guest of honour.

It is curious that Benny should have chosen to re-enter the live arena after so long, albeit briefly. His decision may have rested on two factors – one, quite likely, it would provide another sliver of good publicity to counter the constant barrage of criticism. Secondly, he had always loved Eric Morecambe; as *Bring Me Sunshine* director Mark Stuart says, 'He probably could not, in conscience, have refused to do the show. It was such a big shock for everyone when Eric died.'

Since 1978, Morecambe and Wise had been fellow Thames artistes, too, the double-act having ended a gloriously successful run on the BBC to return to ITV for their final years. Dennis Kirkland observed Eric and Benny together in the Thames restaurant and says, 'Eric would always come and have one little drink with Ben and he used to say, every time, "It's all based on fear, Benny." They were both nervous as hell about every word of every line of every gag they performed. And Benny would say, "Fingernails and aspirins, Eric, fingernails and aspirins." '

Benny almost bit his fingers off for *Bring Me Sunshine*. He insisted that not only would he hold the obligatory heavy book to hide his shaking hands but that he must stand behind a lectern (to hide shaking legs) and play a black-gowned schoolmaster (to hide drenched armpits). The material was easy too: quips straight from a gag book:

What is the hottest part of the sun? – Page 3.
What is a Hebrew? – A male tea-bag.
You could tell Moses was sick by the size of the tablets.

Benny also gave the schoolmaster a Scottish accent, and Scuttle's granny-glasses, to give him a character to hide behind. Inside seven minutes he performed two pieces and a few gags; the sketches were the school-register skit and an item he had performed numerous times on radio and TV, *Fatricia and Feter*, a poem typed on a typewriter where the F and P keys were transposed, the laughs arising from some consequent double-entendres.

Lee Gibson, a singer in *The Benny Hill Show* and *Bring Me Sunshine*, was delighted to see Benny backstage on the night, but she detected, in an instant, his state of agitation. 'You could almost smell the fear,' she says. 'He was absolutely terrified. And as soon as it was all over he was gone. Gone! We didn't see him again that night.' The show was screened by ITV on Christmas Day 1984 and Benny must have watched from behind the proverbial cushion. Judging from the fact that he insisted the Lincoln Center appearance three years later was not televised, one can surmise he was unhappy with what he saw. And after these two unlikely stage appearances, he never again put himself through the agony.

18. The End

After twenty-six years at Queen's Gate, Benny Hill moved out in June 1986. For the preceding two years the building of a penthouse apartment had imposed scaffolding outside his beautiful tall windows, blocking his balcony and letting the workmen peer into his apartment. Strangely, though, having put up with it all this time, he left just as the work was completed. 'He stayed there all through the terrible noise,' says Richard Stone, 'and as soon as the scaffolding came down and his lease ran out he told them, "No, I'm annoyed with you, I'm going."'

Peter Charlesworth remembers his friend's departure from London in detail. 'When he was in Cromwell Hospital [in 1983] he said to me, "The lease is up soon, they want me to buy a new one and it's £175,000 per flat. I won't pay that!" And with that, he literally mopped his brow with a Richard Stone cheque that he'd just been given, for £350,000, at the same time saying, "It's more than I earn in a month!" A couple of years later, with six months to go on his lease, he wrote to the agents and said, "I've decided I'll buy it," but they wrote back and said, "There's only one problem, Mr Hill, it's now £500,000 for each of the flats." And that's why he moved out. He couldn't face the prospect of writing a cheque for a million pounds. Not that he would have missed it – he was worth five million by then.'

In 1960, Benny had house-hunted around London with Dave Freeman, who drove the car. Now he turned to Mary Kirkland, Dennis's attractive wife, to provide advice and transport. 'He wanted a flat in this area [Hampton/Teddington] and told us he was prepared to spend "a million or two",' Dennis recalls. 'Well, the two of them had a ball going out to look at flats, the days always including lunch somewhere. Nothing was ever right with them for Benny, though – there was always something "not quite good enough". Then Mary realized: all he really wanted was the lunches. He was enjoying the days out.'

So there was only one place for Benny to go – *home*. Home meaning 22 Westrow Gardens, Southampton, the humble suburban 'semi' where Alfie had lived from seven to sixteen, and which he had inherited on his mother's death in 1976. In the last ten years he had popped down about one week in every six; now he returned, permanently. His Queen's Gate possessions, such as they were, found new homes – some stored in a warehouse, others stacked in the garage-like 'outbuilding' on which his father had claimed a rates reduction all those decades ago. Echoes of the past crowded around this simple, complicated man, The World's Most Popular Comedian, as he slipped his key into the lock, entered the tiny, darkened hallway and shut the door behind him.

Incredulous neighbours soon became familiar with the pattern. A mini-cab from the station would deposit the famous Benny Hill in Westrow Gardens. Five minutes later, wearing a jacket, open-neck shirt and – vaguely to obscure his identity – fake spectacles, he would be back outside again, on foot, destined for the Co-op supermarket on nearby Bedford Place, walking past the eye hospital where his late sister had trained to become a nurse, almost down to Southampton's main *Titanic* memorial that could so easily have honoured his father. Clutching a couple of plastic carrier-bags laden with fish-fingers, baked beans and diet drinks, he would then trot back by way of the fruiterer and a newsagent.

Benny continued to retain the services of Gladys Green, the Hills' long-time cleaner. They got on well. When his mother died, Benny gave Gladys £100 to take a holiday, and he continued to bestow the occasional gift. 'He gave me a bottle of whisky once and, gratefully, I kissed him on the cheek,' she recalls, giggling. 'He was a true gentleman, in the old-fashioned sense of the word – he said, "I'm not going to wash this face any more, Gladys!" '

Benny slept in the tiny back bedroom, the one that had been his until his baby sister came along in 1933. He piled the bed with blankets to keep out the cold. Writing to Hettie Tack from Westrow Gardens in January 1987, he reported, quite straightforwardly:

> The above address is where I spent my childhood. I go to London once
> a month, & look at houses in the Richmond area. So far I've not found
> quite what I'm looking for. In the mean time, it's no hardship living

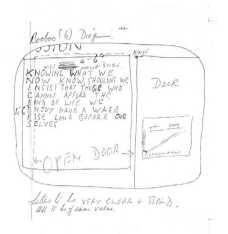

The Benny Hill Show, suddenly – unexpectedly, bizarrely – loved the world over.

Opening photo in section: Benny and his 'stock company' – moon-faced Bob Todd, wizened Jackie Wright and the unflappable Henry McGee.

Facing, top: Happy among the Hill's Angels, including Sue Upton (back row, third left) and Louise English (kneeling, front left). **Facing, bottom left**: The child-like comic with a stripped-down Jane Leeves, the future *Frasier* star. **Facing, three images, clockwise**: Little Jackie Wright's bald pate receives the inevitable slap. The conga drummer, unsurprisingly diverted by a dancing Diana Darvey. The peeping postman.

This page, top: Benny's scribbled script, *left*, for the sketch that developed, *right*. This was an old joke from the Variety era. **Above**: Another 'run-off'. Benny's 1980s over-emphasis on scantily clad women delighted audiences from Albania to Zambia but repelled the British in droves.

Left: Collecting a SFTA (BAFTA) award, 1972, with Thames executives (left to right) Jeremy Isaacs, Brian Tesler, David Bell (producer) and Philip Jones.

Above: Benny's sixtieth birthday party, with (left to right) Dennis Kirkland, Richard Stone and Philip Jones. Benny's fear of change was such that Stone remained his agent – and, in essence, manager – for forty-three years, yet there was scant warmth between the two. There are perhaps four photographs of them together.

Left: A rare photo of Britain's post-war comic greats together. Eric Morecambe, Benny Hill, Frankie Howerd and Ernie Wise at a Thames party, 1984.

Top, left and right: Having spent carefully at the Co-Op, The World's Most Popular Comedian trots back to 22 Westrow Gardens, Southampton, his home in the cash-strapped 1930s and the bank-bulging 1980s.

Above left: The shy star with Jack Lemmon, Hollywood, 1984. 'Benny didn't try to amuse anyone,' observed fellow diner Steve Allen.

Above right: Posing self-consciously with his sister Diana during a holiday in Singapore, 1977. 'There's me, and there's me in drag,' Benny would say.

Cast adrift – Benny in the declining years after Thames let him go.

Top left: Auntie Lulu outside her house in Bexleyheath, where Benny indulged in fat-soaked fried breakfasts and endless Mars bars. She would pop his pyjamas back in the drawer for his next visit.

Top right: Benny and Monica Albon at her Southampton guest house.

Above: Benny and Dennis Kirkland. 'They used to be an act, twenty-four hours a day.'

Top: Look at me! Benny in silicon valley, happily engulfed at the Miss Hawaiian Tropic beauty competition.

Above: 'Oh I'll be all right, little heart!' After his heart attack, and having declined potentially life-saving bypass surgery, Benny – overweight and drinking heavily – knows his death is imminent. The brave face is for Libby Roberts and her children, February 1992. He was dead seven weeks later.

Left: Suddenly looking his sixty-eight years, Benny Hill leaves Royal Brompton hospital after the heart attack, February 1992.

Below: The new flat but the same old cardboard boxes, absence of wealth and switched-on television; Teddington, April 1991. Benny died a year later in these very circumstances, slumped on the sofa, watching TV, but his death was undiscovered for two days.

here. At the moment, Britain is having its coldest spell for 2 decades. I've got my pyjama trousers on under my normal trousers.

Shortly after he wrote this the house flooded, when a frozen pipe burst in the bathroom. 'I got there to find water running out of the front door and down into the garden,' says Gladys Green. Eventually, Benny realized that the place simply had to be modernized – it still had its outside loo (although there was also one upstairs) and a 1930s kitchen. He asked Sue Upton's husband, Roger Whatling, to refit the kitchen and bathroom. But at Christmas-time, neighbours would continue to feel sorry for the great star, who was alone in his cold house. 'My sister took him a little bottle of Chartreuse, mince pies and a piece of Christmas pudding,' Alice Moore, an original Westrow Gardens resident, told the press, 'but he told us not to worry about him. He said he had his TV for company and was quite content.'

Benny more or less maintained his mother's wish that he not allow visitors inside the house. Dave Freeman was one of the few to get beyond the front door – his daughter had moved to Southampton and whenever he visited he looked in on his old chum and writing partner. 'It was a tiny little house, 22 Westrow Gardens – I mean *tiny*,' he says. 'When you went in the hall you only had to take half a step and you were going up the stairs. And the stairs were steep. There was a little room to the right which was still cluttered with his late mum's and dad's stuff. And the people next door had some kind of domestic problem – Benny told me, "It's grim, I try and go to sleep at night and I can hear them shouting." But because he grew up there it was Home. Personally, I always thought there was something funny about it, like Citizen Kane and his sled.'

Benny lived here for the next two years, and it was hardly a secret – A. H. Hill was listed in the local telephone directory. During this time the house was twice burgled. There wasn't much for the thieves to take. 'They smashed the glass in the back door and took the stereo and a few other things,' says Gladys Green. 'We laughed later because the police told Benny the thieves had created a hell of a mess, when actually that's how he always left it.'

With nowhere to stay in London until he found a place there (he clearly wasn't going to pay for a hotel), Benny made no new TV shows for almost two years, skipping 1987 entirely. What he seemed to miss more than anything were his lovely auditions. He mentioned this to his choreographer, Libby Roberts, and she offered to do some preliminary work for him, finding the right girls and suggesting them to Benny. He then took the train to her house in Wimbledon, south London, to meet them. 'I knew he liked quite young-looking girls with quite boyish figures, not big boobs like everybody thinks,' says Libby. 'He preferred blondes but with a fresh face, not too heavily made up. A woman with back-combed hair, red lipstick and big breasts would not have been his choice. There was one change that I made, though – which was that I didn't want models who could move, I wanted real dancers. Until this point the pretty face had come before the enquiry as to whether they could dance.'

Although she had gone through the Queen's Gate auditioning process herself a dozen years earlier, Libby Roberts was agog at how Benny went about the business of casting for his shows – which, these days, were aired worldwide. 'The auditions were *a day out* for Benny,' she says. 'I know that he looked forward to them for weeks. We could have done them in half an hour in an office in London. But no: it was *lunch* – I'd prepare chicken or salmon salad, and wine, and lots of champagne – and it was all very relaxed. We had a good laugh, chit-chatting about nothing. He'd pay for taxis to tootle the girls backwards and forwards from the station, but when they arrived he never asked them to do anything like read a script, or dance – he just chatted. One question he always asked was, "Have you got anything that you do that most people wouldn't ask about? For example, can you do twenty handstands in a row, or play the flute – something extra I could use?" One girl, trained as a gymnast, could perform with sticks and ribbons, so he used that in a sketch.'

Benny's overseas image as something of a womanizer – all those enquiries about his personal relationship with the Hill's Angels – were more wide of the mark than ever these days. 'It was all pure,' says Libby Roberts. 'He never made advances at the girls, nor they him. And if any of them had come on at him that would have been a turn-off. Benny always liked the girls he could never have. Always. He did express interest in one or two of them but they weren't interested in him at all – they saw him as an uncle, not a sexy, fanciable man. A lot of young women do fancy older men, but none of them ever fancied Benny. And if he was trying to attract women he didn't present himself very well – his clothes were never very nice, quite old-fashioned, and he always wore old brown shoes.'

Dear Philip!!
The other night I had to choose between a gala dinner with a lingerie fashion show & a boxing match. I chose the boxing. I think it's called old age.
[postcard from Benny to Philip Jones; Marseilles, August 1987]

Sitting around the south of France and Southampton, the star had plenty of time to mull over the state of his career and his paradox – loved abroad, vilified at home. By the time he returned to the studios he had made a crucial decision – the jiggle-count had to be slashed. He instructed Libby Roberts to 'clean up the dances'. Though he may not have understood public objection to the sexual content of his show, he saw the need to check its escalation.

After all these years, though, change was not easy. Carla De Wansey, a dancer who was also handed acting parts (this was typical), recalls a rare moment of disagreement between Benny and Dennis Kirkland on location in 1988. 'In one sketch Benny was playing an old butler and I played the young maid,' she says. 'Dennis had suggested I wear a flimsy outfit, with a little lacy petticoat – you can imagine – but when I arrived on the set Benny went ballistic. "That's NOT what I want! I want the proper image for an old-fashioned maid. I DON'T want that!" I was quite shocked, and went back to wardrobe where they made me a skirt that went down to my knees.'

Along with the more sanitized sequences, Benny also introduced a recurring element in these new shows, Hill's Little Angels. These were beautifully innocent sketches with Benny and a gaggle of tiny children, blatantly in the style of Chaplin's *The Kid*. If this didn't introduce an aah factor, nothing would.

As ever, Benny sought less than the best talent. Instead of going to one of the established child-actor agencies in London he used the kids of friends on the show – Joanna Kirkland, Richard and Louise Whatling (Sue Upton's children), Adam Johnstone (Libby Roberts' son) and Jade Westbrook (daughter of Jenny Westbrook, a dancer in the show). Thames staff had to write to the children's schools asking permission for them to have a day out; they also had to be chaperoned. And there was Uncle Benny with bucket-loads of sweets to tempt even the most camera-shy kiddie into action. 'He always thought that if you gave a kid a bar of chocolate he'd do anything,' says Dennis Kirkland, 'because that was him – if you gave Benny a bar of chocolate he'd do anything.'

All the participants considered Hill's Little Angels a real hoot, and there is no doubt they aided the family appeal that Benny was deliberately seeking to promote, both on the set and in the show. It was a particular thrill for the parents, and for the children in later years, to watch the videos – and yet it did little for the comedy, which is what *The Benny Hill Show* was supposed to be about. Apart from the odd cute moment, these sketches were trite for a man of Benny's global reputation. Henry McGee, one of the very few genuine actors in the show, may have been only half-joking when he turned to Libby Roberts and said, 'I don't know – people come on to *The Benny Hill Show* and by the time they're five they're doing lines.'

Heedless of the Bowdlerization, the camerawork remained garish, however; considering the ever-rising budget, these last twenty-five shows always looked strangely 'cheap'. This was certainly not for lack of rehearsal: ten years earlier, each show had a week of rehearsals in a church hall; now there were four weeks' in a new venue – a room at the Cardinal Wolsey pub at Hampton Court, close by Henry VIII's palace and just a few minutes' drive from the studio. It is perhaps no coincidence that the cast and crew were beginning to notice Benny becoming 'a drinker' at this time (and as his birthday usually fell during these rehearsals 'Ben's birthday bash' became a fixture). Mike Mulloy, employed as his stand-in, recalls, 'When we rehearsed at the Cardinal Wolsey, Dennis would say to me, "Go and get [yourself] a pint, I'll have a glass of wine and Benny will have his usual Carlsberg Special Brew."' Alcohol defeated Benny's habitual crash-dieting before every series – and at sixty-four years of age, in declining health and with only one kidney, it was inadvisable.

The Cardinal Wolsey also served good food. 'There was a very gracious host there,' says Henry McGee, 'and Benny liked roast-beef salad for lunch – with great thick slices of beef.' In previous years Benny had confined himself to apples and lettuce during show production. There was no hiding it from the viewers: he had never looked so fat.

Any suggestion that the reduction in jiggle might improve his image was forlorn. The harm caused by those previous shows was proving hard to redeem. 'We did a fantastic *Carmen* sequence, quite brilliant I thought,' says Libby Roberts, 'but, as an example of how the press were out to get Benny, the reviews went on about bikini-clad girls bumping and grinding when in fact they were in full costume.'

There was an obvious reason why these new shows were failing to burnish Benny's reputation. Though he never explained why, he had suddenly given consent for Thames to screen some compilations on British TV. Since 1955, he had carefully restricted his small-screen appearances in any one year to a handful of shows, or fewer, to keep himself in demand. Yet in the 1980s he allowed Thames to saturate the market with more than fifty half-hour compilations. In the nearly two years he was away from Teddington, grappling with the plumbing in Westrow Gardens, *The Benny Hill Show* aired nineteen times on ITV, and in the same year that he was attempting to introduce a toned-down variation of his show, there were eight primetime repeats of bawdier precursors. Before repeating any shows, Thames was required to obtain permission from the artistes who had appeared in them, and to pay them an additional fee. Underlining just how besmirched Benny's standing had become in his home country, two successful comic-actors who had been happy to appear with him in the 1970s – Paula Wilcox (1972) and Paul Eddington (1976) – refused permission for their sketches to be shown again in the 1980s.

Benny finally moved back to the capital during 1988 – or, more precisely, south-west of London. He rented a flat in a newish apartment block in Teddington – by the river, opposite a bus-stop, close to the shops and to his and Dennis's favourite King's Head pub, and, most handily of all, just five minutes' walk from the Thames studios.

Flat 7, Fairwater House, at 34 Twickenham Road, would be Benny's home from now on, and he resumed his routine of popping down to Southampton only one week in every six, when he had to push open the front-door against a mountain of letters. Though he would claim that Fairwater House was only as a stopgap ('while looking for the right house,' he wrote to Hettie Tack) Benny quickly settled, almost ceasing to pretend looking for anywhere else. When the residents' association held Guy Fawkes' Night firework parties, there would be Benny – for a few minutes at least – with some bottles of champagne and an Angel or two on his arm.

The second-floor flat was just what he needed: a single double-aspect reception room, a tiny balcony, two small bedrooms, a kitchen and a bathroom. It was the kind of apartment in which someone of moderate wealth might stow away an ageing parent. It was furnished – just – and Benny didn't bother to bring much back from Westrow Gardens. The main room remained empty but for a sofa, an armchair, a few cardboard boxes and his two rented televisions and two VCRs (one a multi-standard machine enabling him to play American tapes). Flat 7, Fairwater House, was soon just as barren – yet messy – as Flat 7, Queen's Gate.

Ironically, at this same time, just when Benny was hoping that the decreased bawdiness in his show might give him an easier ride, he became the subject of another newspaper witch-hunt. By courting the tabloids throughout the 1980s he had been playing with fire, for now – in their predictable, populist fashion – they turned on him, splashing page after page on his 'meanness'. The charges of sexism were arguable, even if self-inflicted, but Benny had every right to be flummoxed by this new assault. Yet, like a rabid dog with a juicy victim in its teeth, the tabloids would not let go.

'FILTHY RICH. Saucy Benny Hill is now a millionaire 10 times over,' screamed the *Sun*'s first missile – its main front-page headline on February 25 1988. The figure was from *Money* magazine, one of those tables of celebrity fortunes which always fascinates and is usually several millions wide of the mark. (It certainly was in this instance – Benny's wealth never totalled much more than £7,000,000.) It seemed at first glance like a bit of fun, but the tenor of the *Sun*'s piece was ominously aggressive and the next day came the inevitable follow-up, the opening sentence of which read:

> Comic Benny Hill is so mean he has hardly touched his £10 million fortune – but now he hopes it could bring him a BRIDE . . . Benny, so tight with cash that a slap-up treat is oven chips and cheesecake from the Co-op, wants a woman to share his wealth.

This was nonsense. That same day, the *Sun*'s editor, anxious to somehow maintain the good relationship with Benny carefully cultivated over several years, sent him a personal letter apologizing for the 'insensitive and half-witted' treatment of the feature. And yet the *Sun* (and its Sunday sister *News of the World*) would soon be meting out much more in the same vogue. And the rival *Daily Mirror* was waiting to pounce, too. Its banner headline read:

WORTH £10 MILLION – but he uses a Tesco's plastic bag to carry his scripts. He lives in his mum's crumbling semi and spends £12 a week on food.

This was all too much for Benny's old army pal Harry Segal. He had recently suffered a heart attack, and Benny – who affectionately called his Jewish friend 'Bubeleh' – had sent a cheque for £1,000 as 'a cheer up pressie'. Then, when Segal was out of hospital, Benny had arrived in Leeds to look after him for a few days. 'It was better than any medicine a doctor could have prescribed,' Segal later remarked. 'Everybody liked his sincerity – and, as usual, we came up with some new comedy ideas and gags!' Segal was incensed that his friend should be receiving such appalling press and hurried to the *Daily Mirror* office in London, demanding to be seen. Two days of big, positive stories resulted.

Benny himself also tried to redress the balance, granting an interview to one of his few favoured journalists, Margaret Forwood, for the *Sunday People*. 'I used to be called sexist,' she quoted him as saying, 'now I'm tagged a tightwad.'

He might have thought this would be the end of the matter, but no. Back came the *Daily Mirror* with a picture story – 'Mister money bags!' – accompanied by a paparazzi photo of Benny walking along the street with a Tesco's bag. And so it went on, tacky headlines on top of sensationalized (and often inaccurate or made-up) stories:

THE SECRET OF BENNY'S BAGS – They're stuffed with thousands of pounds (*Sunday People*)
SKINFLINT BENNY GOES BONKERS AT BEACH CLUB
(*News of the World*)
SCROOGE BENNY SPLASHES £20,000 ON PLUMBING
(*News of the World*)

The *Sun*, as ever, outmired all its rivals. It sent a hack to Southampton to trail Benny as he left Westrow Gardens and headed for the shops.

('Canny Benny checked prices before shelling-out £2.80 on apples, bananas, celery and three pounds of spuds.') It followed him to the Co-op, the newsagent, the bakery and then back home, snapping a surreptitious photo as he carried his Co-op bags. Piling the bizarre on top of the ludicrous, it illustrated an itemized shopping list showing how much he had spent on his various groceries, and declared:

> Filthy rich comic Benny Hill, who has a fortune of at least £10 MILLION, slipped out on a shopping spree . . . and spent a mere £13.07. Down-to-earth Benny preferred to buy apples, a loaf of uncut bread and a copy of his favourite newspaper – the *Sun*.

*

In 1986, Thames Television marked the silver jubilee of Philip Jones's employment[1] with a surprise lunch party at which tribute was paid to the esteemed Head of Light Entertainment by many of ITV's foremost executives and an impressive array of British comedy stars. Benny had always impressed upon Thames, which produced *This is Your Life*, that he would never countenance being a subject of that show (as, indeed, he had told the BBC when both his show and *This is Your Life* were screened by the Corporation in the 1950s),[2] but he gladly turned out for Jones's *This is Your Lunch* – hosted, like the TV show, by Eamonn Andrews, and video-taped for private circulation. There could have been no more convincing endorsement of Jones's qualities. Benny was the closing guest, and the ultimate surprise since it was well known, in this knowledgeable gathering especially, that he so rarely appeared as 'himself'. Looking smart, though a little edgy, Benny recalled a quick anecdote and remarked, 'May I just say, we've had seventeen very happy years together, and I hope I shall be saying "PHILIP!!" for another seventeen years.'

It was not to be. Jones retired less than two years later, in March 1988, and Benny lost his most devoted ally in the upper echelons at Thames.

His replacement was a man of proven comedy pedigree, John Howard Davies, whose track record at the BBC – as producer of *Monty Python's Flying Circus*, *The Goodies*, *The Good Life*, *Steptoe and Son* and *Fawlty Towers*, and head of the department commissioning *Not the Nine O'Clock News* and *Only Fools and Horses* – was second almost to none. Davies knew of a life in front of the cameras, too: he had been a child actor, claiming notable starring roles in the movies *Oliver Twist* (1948) and *Tom Brown's Schooldays* (1951). His father, Jack Davies, had also been in the business – among many film comedy credits, he co-wrote *Those Magnificent Men in Their Flying Machines*, in which Benny Hill had a cameo role, back in the distant days when he saw his future in films.

Davies, inevitably, arrived with a new broom, and used it to make a sweeping review of his department's output. Philip Jones had earned devotion from staff and stars alike as a benevolent paternalist with a fine ability to smooth ruffled feathers. Davies started by coolly auditing Thames' comedies, measuring audience figures against budgets. He didn't only look at *The Benny Hill Show* – but careful consideration was important. This was a high-profile programme, and it ate a considerable chunk of the department's spending.

The cost of making *The Benny Hill Show* had been rising exponentially in recent years, principally because, in the wake of his global success, a no-expense-spared attitude had formed at production level. Benny's first show for Thames, in 1969, cost £11,375. This increased by a few thousand each year until the end of the 1970s, at which point it began to multiply – from £47,000 in 1978 to £69,850 in 1979, £115,550 in 1980 and £163,120 in 1981. A change in the method of calculating the budgets then skews the picture somewhat, but by the end of the decade *The Benny Hill Show* was costing Thames £1,357,340 for a batch of three shows, or £452,446 per show, and the other ITV companies were themselves making an additional contribution. Thames was spending £70,000 per show on design, £55,000 on artists' fees, £16,000 on wardrobe and an extravagant £10,000 on 'production staff expenses'. 'It was incredibly expensive,' says Thames' Director of Programmes David Elstein. 'This was because of the way Benny worked. He would take over a complete studio, or an outside-broadcast unit, for the whole day, with a complete company of actors and crew, and whatever he shot, he shot. And if he shot nothing, he shot nothing. The show was a one-ring-circus and it was very much down to what he and Dennis could conjure during the course of a shooting day that made it work.'

Not much of the budget was devoted to Benny's fee, either – this had risen from £2,800 (plus £1,000 for the script) in 1971, to £3,900 (plus

£1,250) in 1978, to £10,000 (plus £7,500) in 1989. For a star of Benny's calibre, these were trifling sums, and he both knew and happily accepted it. 'We never quibbled over money,' says Philip Jones. 'Richard Stone would ask for modest rises each year, but Benny was much more interested in the facilities we had, asking me for assurances about studio time. He would tell me to take what could have been his increase and invest the money into the show.'[3]

'The trouble was,' says David Elstein, 'Benny had been indulged. He had been allowed to work in a particular kind of way. Whether that was the only kind of way he could work was never, in the end, put to the test, because we also ran into a second issue, which was the nature of the Thames/network supply of programmes. To cut a long story short, we realized that if we carried on making *The Benny Hill Show* we couldn't introduce a show which we had been waiting to bring in for a while, which was [Rowan Atkinson's] *Mr Bean*. Obviously, to some extent, *Mr Bean* was a gamble, but it was a much easier show in terms of the network schedule because it was half an hour. And it was all done on film – you didn't need to allocate expensive studios.'

Elstein says that, in an ideal world, there would have been enough room and enough money for more *Benny Hill Show*s, and he insists Thames had no problems with its bawdiness. 'There was certainly no sense at all of it bring too rude for us to make,' he comments. 'We had no problems with that. In my view, the various attacks on Benny Hill made no difference at all, and it is a complete myth that Thames ended his contract because of "political correctness". I even heard a rumour that we ended it because my wife objected to the show. My wife hadn't the slightest interest one way or the other.'

The reality is, for as long as *The Benny Hill Show* was attracting good ratings at home, the steady increase in its cost could be swallowed. It was when the domestic audience began to slide that the trouble began. 'His audience profile was mostly male,' says John Howard Davies, 'and by quite a substantial majority. Then he became so worried about women not liking him that he started to tone down the bawdy aspect of the show – and, in so doing, lost a lot of the male viewers. It was rather sad, because having first alienated half of his old audience he was now depleting the other half. And if you don't get bums on seats on ITV, if you don't deliver the audience to the advertiser, you're not doing your job. It's very dangerous to have a show on ITV that doesn't appeal to women because they hold the purse strings, in a sense. You have to get the right demographic profile to satisfy the advertisers, the right "cost per unit". It sounds all rather hard but ITV is about that, and you join knowing that. One thought differently at the BBC, but at ITV that's the system under which you work.'

Benny, who was essentially unaware of the rumblings and grumblings in the Thames executive dining room, might have thought that, whatever else was wrong, his future would be secure because of the huge wealth the company accrued selling his show overseas. But this was not exactly the case. While global sales of *The Benny Hill Show* reaped a good deal of money for Thames, it was never as much as people imagined. 'It was a huge windfall for Don Taffner,' says David Elstein. 'And it was a huge windfall for Benny. Least of all – although it was still pretty welcome – was it a windfall for Thames.'

The financial accounts filed in the company's annual reports are spectacular, yet tell only half the story. The contribution made by overseas sales had grown exponentially, from £116,000 in 1970 to £19,253,000 in 1985 – so much, indeed, that Thames was given the Queen's Award for Export Achievement in 1984. Yet *The Benny Hill Show* was not the sole contributor to this. Thames was still selling *The World at War* and drama series like *Edward and Mrs Simpson* and *Rumpole of the Bailey*; and tidy sums were flowing in from sitcom format sales. (Not only had Don Taffner adapted Thames' *Man About the House* into *Three's Company*, but its sequels *George and Mildred* and *Robin's Nest* had turned into *The Ropers* and *Three's a Crowd*. Also, the London-based sitcom *Keep It in the Family* – nine episodes of which were written by Dave Freeman with his son Greg – had been transmogrified into the San Francisco-based *Too Close for Comfort*, a long-running ABC network show starring Ted Knight from *The Mary Tyler Moore Show*.)

During his review of Thames' comedy output, John Howard Davies sought the opinion of Mike Phillips, the new managing director of Thames Television International (TTI). 'Mike took the view that he had enough [shows] in the kitty and that, like Deep Purple, he could just remix the tracks *ad nauseam*,' says Davies. 'Benny was a popular figure in America, but let's not get this out of proportion. While his show was the only way on American TV that you could see pretty girls with very few clothes on, the amount of people who actually watched Benny Hill there on those independent stations, in comparison with a network show, was infinitesimally small.' Phillips confirms Davies' query, commenting, 'John's question to me was, "If we were to stop making *The Benny Hill Show* is that going to have a big financial impact on TTI?" And my answer to that was "No", because we had over a hundred half-hour shows to sell by then. The marginal extra value of each new half-hour was not huge. Besides, Benny's success had peaked in America by this point. It didn't last forever.'

Davies also had other problems with the show, including what he saw as Dennis Kirkland's particularly strong influence over Benny. 'I tried at one stage to separate the show from the producer,' he says, 'but unfortunately I couldn't – this was during the last days of the Philip Jones era and he quite properly said to me, "No, no, you're talking nonsense." It's a cruel thing to say, but the trouble is, when producers become identified with artists it is almost impossible to separate the two. And Benny, I think, wouldn't have been separated from Dennis anyway, because he loved him, and they loved each other, and were very, very loyal to one another. Benny was quite insecure about some things and Dennis was always there when he wanted him. If he wanted to have a drink at night, Dennis was there.'

These were difficult days for Thames Television. Launched in 1968, it had safely secured an extension to its franchise in 1981, but was now steeling itself to jump through the hoops once more, to beat off competitors in another franchise renewal tussle in 1991. This time, it knew it had problems. Prime Minister Margaret Thatcher had announced that, once bidders had passed a quality threshold, franchises would be awarded by straightforward auction – the highest acceptable bid wins – rather than by even-handed adjudication of finance, programming and responsible public service. She was also known to be close friends with Michael Green, who was mounting a rival bid with Carlton Communications. And she was livid beyond description with Thames over 'Death on the Rock', an edition of the company's flagship current-affairs series *This Week*, which had questioned the government's verdict on the shooting dead of three IRA terrorists by the British secret service; it led to an official enquiry, and though this found for Thames, Thatcher contested the findings. All this was much on the minds of the company's staff, who faced the prospect of unemployment if the franchise was not renewed. There was certainly no desire to court any more controversy.

As an experienced comedy producer himself, Davies looked hard at the style of *The Benny Hill Show* and did not care for what he saw. 'I thought it had become repetitive,' he says, 'repetitive in *style*. The truth of the matter is that Benny, over the years, had been one of the most inventive, forward-thinking ideas-men that we'd seen. He wrote all his own material and he was very clever. When he was smutty he was very smutty, and very funny, and vulgar in the proper sense of the word. Rabelaisian, almost. But as the show went on he became just slightly too repetitive in context and texture. The format hadn't changed for years. And it seemed to me that it wasn't going to go anywhere unless he had a period of rethinking the whole way the show was structured.

'This, in a nutshell, was the problem with *The Benny Hill Show*,' Davies continues. 'We could have lived with diminishing audiences for a little while longer, we could have lived with the increasing costs, particularly if they could have been capped, but what I couldn't live with, if I'm really and truly honest, was the diminishing standard of the show. I was very fond of Benny – he was a very likeable man – and I didn't want him to suffer the indignity of having his show taken off the air because it wasn't reaching a proper audience. I felt it was better to have a gap, maybe two or three years, and see what happened. Philip Jones would never have done this, but then he's a much nicer man than I am.'

Davies made one final check. He contacted the five other major ITV companies – Central, Granada, LWT, Yorkshire and TVS. 'I asked them if they might want to continue making *The Benny Hill Show*, and they all said no. I'm not saying the other ITV chiefs were in agreement with my course of action, but they certainly didn't want to take him on. And that was it. I knew we had to stop it. Rather that, than let him diminish into obscurity. I told Thames' managing director [Richard Dunn] what I was about to do and he said, "Ah, that's rather sad." That was his only comment. It wasn't his decision.'

While all these machinations were going on, Benny was making what would turn out to be his final series of three shows: back at the Cardinal Wolsey pub for rehearsals, down at Thorpe Park for the location work and safely inside Teddington Studios for the taping. Apart from the odd moment, these were woeful programmes, though. In purging the overt sexual content from his work Benny had thrown the baby out with the bathwater. Now *The Benny Hill Show* was a children's comic with the best pages torn out . . . and the gags were just about as ambitious:

Henry McGee Think of her [your wife] as a delicate, fragile flower, waiting to blossom!

Benny You mean I gotta put manure on her?

Benny also looked bigger than ever. He turned sixty-five in January, celebrating his birthday with the now-customary party during rehearsals at the Cardinal Wolsey. He was a pensioner, and – overweight, and in uncertain health – suddenly looked it; the glamour girls, now tastefully covered, could have been his grandchildren.

With ironic symmetry, the final show opened with yet another recycling of 'Pepys' Diary', a sketch now more than thirty years old, and it finished, appropriately, with Benny and the five Hill's Little Angels – six children – dancing off down the road. A cloud had hung over the production, too. Little Jackie Wright, he of the slapped bald head, died while the shows were being made, aged eighty-three ('I am saddened beyond words,' Benny said in a Thames press statement), and the newly formed Broadcasting Standards Council (BSC), which had already pronounced *The Benny Hill Show* as 'increasingly offensive', was laying into it once more, director Colin Shaw remarking:

It's not as funny as it was to have half-naked girls chased across the screen by a dirty old man. Attitudes have changed. The kind of behaviour that gets a stream of men sent to magistrates' courts each year isn't at all amusing.

This was the usual inaccurate piffle and Benny bit back straight away; during a spoof of ITV's hard-hitting consumer programme *The Cook Report* he managed to work in a couple of superfluous insults, calling IBA officials 'them plonkers' and BSC chairman William Rees-Mogg 'a pillock'. The words were queried before transmission but allowed to air.

In April 1989, Benny went to Cannes, to smile politely at the annual MIP-TV trade festival. Thames was marking its twenty-first anniversary, and TTI was delighted to have the star on hand, to cement a few more international deals. In a press release it called him 'a world legend in his own lifetime' and 'a genius'.

John Howard Davies was in Cannes, too, speaking of imminent changes to Thames' comedy programmes.

The last edition of *The Benny Hill Show* was screened by Thames on May Day, 1989. Four weeks later, John Howard Davies summoned Benny to a morning meeting at Teddington. Dennis Kirkland went along too. Waiting outside the first-floor office, with its pleasant view of River Thames, the pair assumed that Davies wanted to discuss the next series.

Benny was invited in, and Dennis got up, too. They went into their Laurel and Hardy act – 'After you, Ben. No, after you, Den', bumping and fumbling in the doorway – while Davies sat and watched them from behind his desk.

'I said, "I'd like to see Benny privately,"' Davies remembers. 'Dennis then tried to insist on staying in the room, saying, "Anything you can say to him you can say to me." Like a married couple might. And I said, "No, I want to see Benny *privately*." So Dennis, with some reluctance, left the office.'

'In what seemed to me like a minute later I was called in,' Dennis recalls. 'Benny was just sitting there. John made pleasantries towards me and then Benny said, "You can tell him, you know. He's a big grown-up lad . . ."'

After a fantastic fifty year run, Benny Hill's career was over – bar the shouting.

19. The After Life

'In my view,' says Richard Stone, his agent for forty-three years, 'Benny was happy until he got the sack from Thames. Then he was miserable. In those last three years he was really shattered. He couldn't believe it. He might have said, "It's only business", but he didn't feel that inside. He started drinking too much and eating too much and his weight increased. It was an awful time. I think the Thames decision brought on his death.'

Although, technically, Benny wasn't sacked, this assessment of his demise seems on-the-mark. They may not have been personally close but Stone could see well enough that his client was in steep decline.

Throughout his life, Benny Hill had handled rejection quietly, but terribly badly. Moreover, writing for and performing on television – and being seen with his glamorous Angels – were the essentials of his existence. He fell into a tailspin. 'His well-organized life was gone,' observes Dennis Kirkland. 'I'd catch him staring blankly into space.'

The news of Benny's departure from Thames made the British press on May 31 1989. 'BENNY HILL IN "I QUIT" SHOCK; Fed-up star pulls out of TV,' tooted the *Daily Mirror*'s front-page headline, the editor having meekly accepted some regrettable Thames spin-doctoring which indicated that Benny had decided his own retirement. It supported this with a direct quote: 'I'm just having a little rest, that's all. I'm just going to be a bit later than planned with my next show.'

Four days later, though, the *Sunday Mirror* chose a new tack, splashing the front page with 'BENNY HILL'S SACKING ANGUISH; TV moguls dumped "too dirty" star who made them millions.' Clearly based on a 'leak' from Benny's camp, this, too, was a kind of spin. But it made a much better press, the subtext being 'Our British Hero has been

unceremoniously dumped by liberals with scant regard for the wishes of
the public or the star himself.'

A pitiful aspect of the ending of Benny Hill's twenty-year relationship
with Thames, then, is that it turned on the same ideological arguments
that had dogged him for the last decade.

As Richard Stone noted, though, Benny himself was typically restrained,
uttering this mild, gently spoken rebuke:

> Business is business, and I don't mind them saying, 'We've had enough'
> or 'We can't afford it' or whatever, but I would have liked a small pat
> on the back.
> (*from* Clown Imperial, *an* Omnibus *programme shown by BBC1 on
> December 20 1991*)

Benny was not allowed to disappear quietly because there were vested
interests who wanted their say on the subject. The tabloids, for one, chose
to see Thames' 'sacking' of Benny Hill as proof that the forces of political
correctness were now holding sway:

> Po-faced left-wingers forced Benny Hill off the box, aided and abetted
> by gutless Thames TV bosses who didn't have the bottle to stand by
> their man.
> (*Sun*)

There were others, quieter yet no less emphatic, who subscribed to the
view that Benny was simply the last guttering flame of an extinct genre:

> Are we really to believe that a commercial television company like
> Thames would willingly lose the revenue to be gained by a truly popular
> programme and bow to the wishes of a few feminists, mysteriously
> swept into all-powerful positions in the TV hierarchy?
> (*Guardian*)

Virtually all Benny's friends and associates stuck loyally to the line that
he had been 'sacked' out-of-hand, in what was fast becoming crystallized
as 'a two-minute meeting', disbelieving the possibility that Thames might
have had legitimate reasons for letting him go.

John Howard Davies ('The Axe Man' – *Daily Express*) merely says, 'I'm
not sure that people really want to hear the real reasons for Benny's

association with Thames coming to an end. They'd much prefer that it was some vitriolic politically correct reason.'

There is, however, little dispute that Benny's departure from the company was poorly handled. 'The sacking was *disgraceful*,' thunders Richard Stone. 'They sent for him like a naughty schoolboy. Only a month before they'd been saying in Cannes, "Benny Hill is the jewel in Thames's crown" and then, pssssshht, he's out. John Howard Davies should have taken me to lunch and said, "The shows are getting rather expensive," or "There are too many of them," or whatever, and asked, "How can we sort this out?" And I'm sure we could have sorted them out.'[1]

Now largely absent from the agency that bore his name, Stone was working on his retirement allotment on the Isle of Wight when John Howard Davies called him. 'He said, "We're not going to do any more *Benny Hill Show*s,"' says Stone. 'I said, "Good God! Have you told Benny?" And he said, "Oh yes, I've had him up here this morning and I've told him." He told him, and then he phoned me – it was appalling handling after a twenty-year relationship. The most touching thing for me, though, was that Benny got on to me in a flash, and I belted up to London and we went out for lunch.'

Philip Jones, Davies' predecessor, was most upset over this turn of events, coming not much more than a year after his retirement. 'I was surprised, and greatly disappointed on Benny's behalf at the apparent way it was done,' he affirms. 'It's the easiest thing in the world to cancel a programme – you pick up the phone. It's the hardest thing to create a programme, especially a successful one. At the very least, in my opinion, they could have said to Benny, "It's been great. We're not too sure of the future. Why don't we make just one show next year? And do something a bit different if you want." If I had been given the job of letting him go I would have done this, and it would have been much kinder. He'd been a loyal friend to the company. But, of course, no one owes anybody anything in this business.'

Don Taffner, who was still selling *The Benny Hill Show* in North America, is also blunt. 'I'm still so pissed off at Thames,' he says. 'My nastiness doesn't come from *what* they did but the *way* they did it. My argument to them was, "You can have any kind of a judgement you want, but why do this to someone who has been so successful to you for twenty years?" It was around the same time that NBC was slowing down Bob Hope, who was as successful for them as Benny was for Thames; and the way NBC approached it was to say to Hope, "Instead of doing four specials a year, do two, or one." They gradually brought it to an end.' (This is true, but does not take into account the poor quality of Benny's last few shows. Perhaps they could have been scaled down from, say, 1985, but by 1989 they were so bad they almost had to be stopped.)

Dennis Kirkland remains impassioned about the impact of these events on his buddy. 'Benny was totally and utterly stupefied,' he says. 'These shows were his babies, so when John Howard Davies sacked him it was like losing his family; his whole life; his reason for getting up in the morning.'

Sue Upton and Louise English, Benny's two favourite Angels, saw him a few days after the press announcement. It had come as a great shock to them (as it had to all the cast and crew). The pair had a long-standing arrangement to take Benny out to Berkshire for the day – for lunch and afternoon shopping in Marlow and then, in the evening, to see Louise perform in an Ivor Novello tribute musical in nearby Sonning. Louise recalls, 'I phoned Benny and said, "It's OK if you don't want to come along." And he said, "Oh, I'm coming along. I want to talk to you, to tell you what's happened."

'We went for lunch at the Compleat Angler, but he was very quiet. He kept saying, "Yes, I understand why they had to do it." He was certainly upset about the *way* it had been done. He showed me a letter from Thames that read something like, "Thank you for your twenty years of service . . . goodbye." I read it and cried my eyes out, but he never once raised his voice in anger. I even said, "I hope they lose their franchise!" and he replied, "Oh, little heart, you mustn't say that. There are lots of people working there. All the make-up girls, the cameramen, what would they all do?" I know he had terrible pains in his chest that night, too, and was taking lots of indigestion pills. And he was almost doubled-up with pain from his ulcer.'

As Benny would later tell Louise English, this was a day that he would always cherish: to be so emotionally troubled, yet out in the summer sunshine, and in a charming riverside town, with his two dearest girl friends, and with the added thrill of seeing his pretty protégée perform in a 'legit' stage show in an important theatre – it was almost too much to handle.

In the absence of work, socializing became the big thing in Benny's life. With it, however, came a further pronounced increase in his drinking. Gladys Green, the cleaner at 22 Westrow Gardens, observed him drinking sherry straight from the bottle (although, being Benny, this could have been to save dirtying a glass); in London he'd take friends out for hefty, boozy lunches at the Royal Garden Hotel in Kensington; and he told Dave Freeman that he had 'discovered the joys of pub crawling'.

Benny's closest companion in these last three years, Dennis Kirkland, witnessed the way Benny drank. 'If I was going to his flat for a meeting he'd buy a bottle of champagne or two so that we could drink while chatting,' he recalls. 'And he'd finish them – not because he was an alcoholic but because he was a glutton. I don't believe that Benny developed an alcohol problem – he'd have been as happy with a glass of ice-cream as a glass of anything else – but when he drank he downed everything in one hit. He didn't sip wine, he emptied the glass in one go, and then had another. He'd pour a bottle of beer into a glass, leave it awhile and talk, then pick it up and down it in one go.'

Carla De Wansey, recruited as a Hill's Angel just before the Thames shows ended, invited Benny (but not Dennis, with whom she didn't get along) to a Sunday-afternoon party at her house near Putney, south-west London. 'He arrived by cab with a bag of booze,' she says, 'vodka, brandy and champagne, and some soft drinks. I said to him, "Do you want me to introduce you to anybody?" "No, little heart, I'm fine, I'm just going to go into the conservatory to sit down there next to that table." And on the table he put a bottle of vodka and a big bottle of Diet Pepsi, and he sat there, all afternoon, and drank them. People were milling around chatting to him, and he spent an hour chatting idly to some kids – feeling totally at ease with them because they were no threat. Then, come six-thirty, seven, he said, "Little heart, I'm going to go now, thank you very much." I offered to call him a cab or drive him home but he said, "No, no, I'm going to walk." And off he went. I watched him trot off down the road. I rang him later to make sure he had got home, and he told me he'd walked all the way back to Teddington, five miles, stopping off at pubs *en route*. By the time he got there he must have been pickled. But he was quite happy.'

Just before he parted company with Thames, Benny was greatly surprised to receive a phone call from his brother, breaking more than twenty years' silence. Still living in Worthing, Leonard had separated from his wife and found a new partner, but he was in poor health. And the Hill family curse had struck him as it had struck Benny and, in her final years, Diana: Leonard was now considerably overweight, tipping the scales in excess of twenty stone. The *Sun* – which reported the reunion, although neither brother would speak to the paper about it – quoted a neighbour as saying, 'He has always been such a jolly, big-hearted man. But we never guessed he was Benny Hill's brother. How on earth did he keep it a secret all these years?'

Now the secret was out, and Benny and Leonard worked at putting past differences behind them. They had lost their parents and their sister; they were the only two left. Aged sixty-seven, retired and in need of cash, Leonard asked Benny for permission to write his biography. It is a measure of Benny's generosity that he assented, and then spent many days with his brother, talking him through wide-ranging, though expurgated, aspects of his life. Benny insisted on right of editorial veto and removed several passages from the manuscript, especially those which pilloried The Captain. Benny felt that no purpose would be served by his brother venting his spleen quite so vehemently. All the same, he allowed Leonard to report on many matters which, though run-of-the-mill, he had kept private. He also personally paved the way for Leonard to interview more than a dozen key friends and former associates. An accomplished English master, his brother employed a wry style, and the resulting manuscript – *Saucy Boy* – was an affectionate and amusing account that wanted only for objectivity.

In June 1990, however, just as Leonard completed his project, he died from heart disease. The book was published posthumously – with a new photo of the Hill brothers that indicated mutual good humour and, just possibly, a lingering discontent: Benny is holding Leonard in a neck-lock. Having eschewed religion, Leonard's funeral was a celebration of his life, with jazz music and speeches. Benny sat quietly and made no contribution. His brother had made it to just sixty-eight years of age; and now there was one.

Benny suffered another huge loss just three months later, when his beloved Auntie Lulu died, aged ninety-four, after suffering an aneurysm. 'I phoned him at his flat in Teddington,' says her son Bill Jaques. 'He said simply, "Oh dear, she was a very special lady." She wanted an old-fashioned funeral, with a big oak coffin, but there were only a few people there, and I felt that Alfie was strangely calm, as if he was thinking, "I've enjoyed it, but now it's over."' Bill's wife Florence observes, 'Not even at Louie's funeral did Alfie give his feelings away. He never showed emotions. I think he *felt* emotion, but his childhood experiences still prevented him from showing it.'

Soon afterwards, Benny embarked upon a nostalgic trip that touched upon numerous aspects of his early life. In Southampton, he had taken to walking the same route around the Common that his mother had taken him in his infancy.

He maintained his lifelong link with Mimi Levy, the by now very elderly Westrow Gardens resident. She had been sending her cholesterol-packed Jewish cooking across to the Hills since Benny was in short trousers, and was still making him plates of meringues with fresh cream. Through Mimi, Benny also established an important new friendship, with Monica Albon, a jolly woman who ran a boarding-house for show-people playing in Southampton. Recently widowed, Monica drove an old Comet Roadrunner camper-van with a red stripe down the side, and the two would take off for day trips around the local area. Benny asked Monica to drive him out to Hythe Pier, pointing out where his father had taken him fishing; they also shopped together in Marks & Spencer and British Home Stores, popped into the Red Lion pub in Below Bar, formerly a court-house, and spent a day with Mimi Levy in the pretty port town of Lymington. 'It was so nice to have someone to go around with,' Monica says. 'There were no complications, no pressure – we were just good friends.'

Benny also popped over to the Isle of Wight on a regular basis, socializing with an agent, Sylvia Thorley, who had supplied *The Benny Hill Show* with several Hill's Angels. While on the island, he liked, too, to relive old times with an old Variety double-act, the husband-and-wife comedians Billy Whittaker and Mimi Law, whom he had first befriended in the 1940s. During his 1957 summer season in Great Yarmouth, Benny had been rushed into a local hospital for an appendectomy; he missed two weeks of the show and Whittaker & Law had been among the acts who deputized. Now they were running pensioners' tea-dances at Ryde Pavilion. Benny turned up to see them at one such function and was invited to preside over the raffle, drawing the tickets and presenting a fluffy toy to the lucky winner. What he *didn't* do on the Isle of Wight was visit Richard Stone at his house in Seaview. 'He never came to see me,' says Stone, still pained. 'He knew I was here and he never came.'

Back in Southampton, Benny visited the combined grave of his parents, in Hollybrook Cemetery. As he arranged flowers on the tablet – which he'd had inscribed 'fell asleep' and 're-united' – he would hear them talking to him:

Helen You spent £12 on flowers, Alfie? You've got more money than sense, you have!

Big Alf Give us it here, you bloody idiot! I'll do it – you've got no idea. *That's* what you've got to do![2]

After a long period without contact, Benny wrote to, and then visited, the man he still described as 'a second father', Nelson Brown – with whom he had lodged at the start of the Second World War. Nelson's daughter Pauline recalls, 'He said he would like to do something for my dad, to make up for all the things he had done for him. But my dad was widowed and old, and there wasn't really anything he wanted. Benny's final words were, "Well sort yourself out a nice holiday, Nelson, and have it on me." Dad didn't live long enough to do that, but he died knowing of Benny's kindness.'

Another important person from his Eastleigh past was Ivy Lillywhite, who had accepted the young Alfie Hill's breezy enthusiasm for the stage back in 1940, welcoming him as part of her amateur troupe. She was his mother figure and he had always kept in touch, visiting when possible and sending postcards; now he was a more regular caller, taking her out to lunch at a Winchester hotel, and then quietly chatting the afternoon away in the Cloisters. He would call her 'My Ivy', and himself 'Your little Alfie'.

Ivy's daughter-in-law, Doreen Lillywhite, witnessed them together, and her words echo those of Florence Jaques, who felt privileged to have observed Benny's great relationship with his Auntie Lulu. 'Benny adored

Ivy,' says Doreen. 'When he spoke to her it was *with love*. Not for show, but genuinely. He loved taking her out, and he'd confide in her, and she would tell him off if she didn't agree with something. It was a real mother-son arrangement. And she never boasted about their friendship, she kept it private. They were two of a kind in that way.'

Benny was not someone who could indulge in a life of pleasant, sociable retirement for ever, though. His need to work was overpowering. He had elected to rest on one or two occasions (notably in 1986 – when he moved back to Southampton) but he had never – not even after his 1951 crisis on the Sunderland stage – been denied the opportunity to work.

Encouragingly, there seemed to be plenty of ideas in the air. The British newspapers frequently ran stories announcing that Benny was 'bouncing back' with this or that TV project – a series for America, some shows for London Weekend Television, and a French series that would, according to one typically over-the-top tabloid report, feature 'a new band of French Angels in designer underwear, nearer-the-knuckle scripts, thigh-high mini-skirts and French starlets with big boobs.'

In most cases, however, especially this French one, the reports lacked real substance. Only one man, Don Taffner, was putting together a serious proposal. He flew to London and set up a meeting of friendly faces – Benny, Richard Stone, Dennis Kirkland and Philip Jones – and they kicked around some ideas. They settled on *Benny Hill's World* (also known as *Benny Hill's World Tour*). This would be six hour-long shows filmed in as many cities – Benny in New York, Benny in Paris, Benny in Madrid, and so on – chosen to illustrate his global popularity (and perhaps, too, give the star some more expenses-paid travel). The deal hinged on whether Taffner could pre-sell the show to stations in different countries; as Benny was The World's Most Popular Comedian this surely would not be a problem.

To the team's surprise, it was. The shows were competing in the marketplace against Benny's old programmes. If TV companies could buy a ready-made show from Thames for £50,000, say, there was little reason why they would shell out £400,000 for a new one.

It is also true to say that, for all the passionate declarations that the great man had been unfairly 'dumped', TV companies were not exactly rushing to sign him up.

Dennis Kirkland – whose contract with Thames was paid off by the company soon after it allowed Benny's to lapse – took on the role of his unofficial agent, trying to find work for them both. A miscellany of activities came and went over the next thirty months, none as artistically satisfying as a full TV show but all taken to earn them some money, get them out of Teddington and get Benny back in the proximity of gorgeous gals.

Such employment had actually started before Benny's parting from Thames. There was the 1986 unveiling of the waxwork Fred Scuttle at Madame Tussaud's museum in London (cue photo opportunities with two Bennys, a head-scratching Dennis and a gaggle of Angels in bikinis). And there was Scuttle's cameo appearance in a 1987 video, 'Anything She Does', for the rock band Genesis (drummer Phil Collins was a big Benny fan). Now suddenly there were a number of foreign TV commercials, which gave Ben and Den expenses-paid trips to Athens, Madrid and Paris, where they encountered varying degrees of public adulation and *The Benny Hill Show* on their hotel-room TV. (It was only in Britain that the programme was off the air.) 'We were drunk together in most countries of the world,' Dennis remarks. 'He [Benny] was a great drunk, and we'd get the giggles. He wasn't particularly funny, though – I used to make him laugh more than he made me laugh.'

On a trip to Paris, Benny did a photo session with girls from the Crazy Horse revue. 'I couldn't believe it was me saying, "You'll have to put more clothes on,"' he wrote to his friend Hettie Tack a few days later, in November 1989. 'I am in enough trouble in England with the Feminists. I can't afford to have pictures of me with topless girls going around the world.'

Amsterdam was a favoured haunt. 'We often went there for a week,' Dennis says. 'We loved it – we'd do one day's work and the rest of the time go on the piss, eat everywhere, walk everywhere . . .' In March 1990 this 'one day's work' was a booking Benny had accepted to appear on a Dutch TV chat-show, for which there was a single fee but expenses for two.

Benny had never appeared on a chat-show so his assent was uncharacteristic, but he said yes knowing that he could use Dennis, on stage, as his buttress. The programme affords an insight into the mechanics of the friendship. They were now, literally, a real-life double-act. Dennis was on stage with Benny the whole time, laughing loudly and encouragingly at his rather lame witticisms as if hearing them for the first time; feeding him lines; and doing little 'bits of business'. They even performed a short skit together, with Benny as a woman standing on a tube train, and Dennis as a man standing tight up behind her:

> *Man indecently grabs the woman's right breast.*
> 'Young man, would you mind moving your hand?'
> *Man rotates hand, massaging the breast.*
> 'Ooh that's lovely, thank you.'

For almost a full minute Dennis held centre-stage. Responding to host Ivo Niehe's question about directing Tommy Cooper (Dennis directed a 1978 TV show for the comic-magician), he started by pretending that his microphone was faulty, then he stood up and faced the studio audience, then he sat down again, and then affected an impression of Cooper's gravelly voice, at no time actually answering the question. As one Thames executive cynically commented after viewing a tape, this was almost *The Dennis Kirkland Show*.

Dennis refutes any suggestion that he was stealing Benny's limelight, however. 'Ben asked me to do that show,' he asserts. 'He was shitting himself with nerves, and I was cool. Afterwards, in the dressing-room, he said, "Den, can I come on your show again another time?" and we collapsed with laughter. That's where I was really, really handy for him. We did it in Spain as well [in October 1990]. The only thing was, when we got back to England he'd say to everybody, "Do you know what Dennis did? He stole my show." When what he was really saying was, "What a ball me and Den had."'

Benny's conventional straightman, Henry McGee, confirms this attitude. 'He told me, "I got Dennis to go on this chat-show with me and it was marvellous – I hardly said a word and he did it all!" And I knew Benny well enough to recognize that he was being honest.'

Further fun times for the unlikely lads arrived when Benny agreed to make commercials for Hawaiian Tropic suntan lotion, and accepted a judging role in the Miss Hawaiian Tropic beauty competition, held in Daytona Beach (Florida) and the Bahamas. 'It's a tough job but somebody's got to do it,' Benny told Dennis as they packed their passports for another good time, with food, drink and trimmings laid on. On these trips, and others, a third party was in tow, a photographer named Barry Breckon. His shots of Benny draped with upwards of ten American babes – grinning like a portly teddy-bear amid a forest of peroxide hair, sunbed tans and silicon twin-peaks – were splashed in the British tabloids. Benny had extra prints made and sent them to friends, such as his former PAs Hettie Tack and Anne Ling. This may seem inappropriate, but Benny had always needed an audience when frolicking with scantily clad women. Instead of it being millions of TV viewers it was a couple of very nice middle-aged ladies.[3]

There were numerous other 'interesting' projects. In May 1990, at a Variety Club luncheon which he attended with a pneumatic blonde on his arm, Benny bumped into Wally Ridley, the producer of his number one single 'Ernie' twenty years earlier. He asked Ridley if he would be interested in making a new EMI album, featuring some songs composed for the 1980s Thames shows. Ridley listened to a cassette and declined, considering the material substandard. A few months later, however, through the office of a local friend and businessman, Dennis Kirkland brokered a deal with a minor – indeed unknown – American company, Continuum Records.

As he had hoped, Benny went into Abbey Road Studios with some musicians led by his old Thames arranger, Ronnie Aldrich, but not for EMI. And by including a new recording of 'Ernie', contrary to the terms of his 1971 EMI contract (and also 'Pepys' Diary', against the terms of his 1961 Pye deal) the resulting album, laughably titled *Benny Hill . . . The Best Of*, could not be issued in Britain. When a company tried importing it, EMI instructed its lawyers. The album circulated (to quote a letter on file at EMI) 'among the "schlock" merchants'. It was not a project from which any participant could emerge with glory, and plans in 1991 to shoot an accompanying video fell flat when Benny – heavily overweight, wearing a silly pink bathing-cap and enveloped by a score of Hawaiian Tropic Barbie-dolls – lost his cool while Kirkland's cameras rolled on Daytona Beach. It was too tacky for words. After Benny's death,

Continuum loudly marketed this and some other material as 'the last video footage ever shot of Benny'. (This was also not strictly true.)

It was possibly with relief, then, that Benny finally returned to some real TV work. Don Taffner had managed to raise finance for the first in their planned series *Benny Hill's World*, the New York edition. Though there was enough money for some location filming on Manhattan, the studio material would be taped in England, disguised as the Big Apple. (Hence Benny wearing an 'I♥NY' T-shirt and baseball cap.) 'It was lovely to be back in harness again,' enthuses Dennis Kirkland, who, inevitably, was director. 'It was the first time we'd made a show purposely for the Americans. We never pandered to the Americans in the Thames shows. I made sure that New York was recognizable in every scene, otherwise it could have been anywhere.'

So here is a fat Fred Scuttle in the back of a yellow cab, here is an ageing Benny cavorting in Central Park with some nurses and a tramp, the latter played by the veteran burlesque comedian Joey Faye, and here is an unfunny Benny standing outside Rockefeller Center, the gag being that he steps aside and 'unwittingly' reveals a sign reading 'Made In Japan'. (In his 1978 Australian TV special he had done the same with Sydney Opera House.)

For Benny, the highlight of this final visit to New York occurred when Taffner took him to lunch at the Friars club, where all the old comedians socialize. Many of them had been Benny's personal heroes. It is an intimidating place for the meek – there are few better at razor-sharp one-liners, witty wisecracks and devastating one-upmanship than veteran New York Jewish comics, shouting across the tables and finishing one another's jokes. But, says Taffner, they loved Benny. 'He met with all of them and they treated him as if he was a God,' Taffner says. 'They idolized the son-of-a-gun. Television had moved out to California and these guys had all been left behind. Benny's humour brought it back to the New York centre of old, and they could reminisce.'

When it came to shooting in a studio back in England, there was one obvious place to work – Teddington. This was where Benny could reminisce. Marking a period of immense upheaval in British TV, Thames was now contracting out its studios to non-company work. Benny knew everyone there, and lived just five minutes' walk away.

416

The sense of *déjà-vu* was extraordinary as, after a seismic break in their lives, the cast – the short and the tall, the fat and the thin, the old and the young, the battleaxes and the Angels – trooped back for what would turn out to be the last time, to work with the familiar wardrobe, makeup and designers, and Philip Jones out of retirement as executive producer. Rehearsals, too, were back in the Cardinal Wolsey pub in Hampton Court. It was almost like old times. Almost. (Some of the material certainly was.) But even Benny's closest companions admit that the sparkle of the Thames era – such as there was in those last few shows – had disappeared in the intervening period, drowned in a surfeit of alcohol, over-eating and melancholia.

It took until 1994, two years after Benny's death, for the show to be screened in Britain (and it was divided into two half-hours). Everyone could see that it was bereft, especially the merciless critics. Don Taffner also observed the problem. 'There wasn't the energy and the happiness I used to see in the Thames shows,' he remarks. 'It had been a case of Benny saying, "I just want to keep on working."'

'He was a fat old man,' reflects Richard Stone. 'The scenes in which he'd once been so charming became sort of sad.' 'There's no doubt that he had gone, creatively,' says Peter Charlesworth, 'and I think he knew it. He was drinking very, very heavily, had taken to smoking little cigars, and he was huge.' Even Philip Jones concedes, 'Perhaps the moment had gone.'

While so many observers attribute Benny's decline to his being ditched by Thames, for those who had done the deed the Taffner show seemed a validation of their decision. 'We had access to all the Teddington studio output on the ring-main monitors in the office,' says John Fisher, who worked for John Howard Davies. 'John called me in and said, "Have a look at this." We took no pleasure in what we saw, but John knew he'd made the right decision. The show looked so tacky and nasty.'

A year and more after making his last Thames shows, Benny was quite unexpectedly on the receiving end of a positive, intellectual backlash to the accusations of his being sexist. The tide was turning for political correctness. However well-found its origins, the process was held to have gone too far. Even some of the 'alternative comedians' agreed with this; Jennifer Saunders, who had been in the vanguard of the new wave at the Comic Strip in Soho, was in the throes of writing and recording *Absolutely Fabulous*, a rollicking, rude, crude BBC sitcom that waged war on PC. It took the public by storm in 1992. The man perceived as the ultimate British victim of PC, Benny Hill, was given a better press in this light, finding himself the unlikely receiver of laudatory articles in broadsheet newspapers. These presented better arguments on his behalf than anything he had ever mounted.

John Mortimer – the barrister, playwright and author – interviewed Benny for the *Sunday Telegraph* and was much taken with his intelligence and charm, going out of his way to give him an easy ride; Chris Dunkley attacked the excesses of PC when praising Benny in his TV column in the *Financial Times*. Most interestingly of all, the novelist, critic and man of letters Anthony Burgess used a *Guardian* review of Leonard Hill's *Saucy Boy* to reopen the case for Benny Hill as 'a comic genius steeped in the British music-hall tradition.' He was, said Burgess, 'one of the great artists of our age'.

This re-examination of Benny's status reached its apogee in 1991 when BBC1 commissioned a TV documentary about him for its *Omnibus* arts strand. *Clown Imperial* was an independently produced hour-long summary of his public life and work, the first of its kind. Benny was closely involved in the production, committing to eleven days of filming; he received in return a £10,000 fee plus a share of profits from overseas sales. (It was sold abroad as *Benny Hill – The World's Favourite Clown*.) This was, then, an authorized, almost entirely uncritical appraisal – a celebration rather than an objective view.

The programme included tributes from admirers Michael Caine, Mickey Rooney, Burt Reynolds and the great American newscaster Walter Cronkite, and from various important British players in Benny's career. The cameras filmed him in Southampton, reflecting on the past with his cousin Chris; standing in front of Woolworth's in Eastleigh; out and about down Teddington High Street; and attending an unlikely reception thrown in his honour by the British ambassador to France, Sir Ewen Fergusson, with his wife Lady Sara, at the Paris embassy. This event was held to 'celebrate Benny's fifty years in show-business' but was almost too perfectly timed for the *Omnibus* filming to be coincidental.

Throughout the documentary Benny spoke with his usual amiable elegance, gently outlining aspects of his life and career, but there seemed to be a quiet sadness about him; he was lacking his usual verve. And the programme also hit a small but telling hitch when the director tried to film Benny revisiting Western District School in Shirley, from which he had graduated at the age of ten. The headmaster was quoted in the local paper as saying, huffily, 'We run an equal opportunities school and I wouldn't want it to be used for sexist sketches.'

The cameras were also on hand to film Benny being honoured as the latest recipient of the Charlie Chaplin Award for Contributions to Comedy, at an annual festival in Vevey, Switzerland, the last home of Britain's original world-conquering comic. The prize was the idea of Chaplin's son Eugene, and he spoke of Benny following in his father's tradition. As Benny accepted the award – a golden image of Charlie in his famous tramp guise – he declared, in fluent French, 'Charlie Chaplin est toujours mon idole. C'est un très grand honneur pour moi.'

The award was of real significance in the last months of Benny's life. His love for Chaplin was boundless. Libby Roberts recalls a visit she made to Queen's Gate a few years earlier, when Chaplin had figured prominently. 'After lunch Benny made us sit and watch Chaplin videos all afternoon,' she says, 'and he was in tears. Really crying – they weren't tears of laughter. He was very moved by it. I didn't know what to say, though nothing could be said because we had to watch in silence.' So one can only imagine the ecstasy Benny must have felt when, during this trip to Vevey, Eugene invited him to sit at his late father's desk. While he did so, Dennis Kirkland spotted a row of Benny Hill videos among Charlie's possessions.

'Eugene said to Benny, "He was your biggest fan", and Benny had tears in his eyes,' says Kirkland. 'He said later that he would loved to have died right there.' It is another indication of the extraordinary friendship and mutual admiration between the two that Benny handed over the award to his director as soon as he stepped off the stage, saying, 'There you are, Den, you deserve this as much as I do.' Kirkland remains its proud owner to this day. (However, the statuette was visible behind Benny while he was being interviewed for the *Omnibus* documentary.)

All this time, Don Taffner was having great difficulty trying to raise finance for further editions of *Benny Hill's World*. While waiting, Benny tried to re-ignite his career by getting Philip Jones to talk to Channel 4, Britain's newest commercial channel, launched in 1982. As the home of many an 'alternative comedian', and with its specific remit to cater for minorities, Channel 4 seemed an unlikely place to find a new Benny Hill show, but there was sufficient interest for Benny to scribble some ideas and send them to Jones, who still has them. The most eye-catching aspect of the outline is that Benny was clearly facing up to the idea of a more modern approach, ditching at last the Variety format he had employed stolidly since his first starring TV show in 1951. The opening item in his planned running-order read:

> *Live.* Benny (as himself) casual/smart, chats to aud[ience]. Possibly on stool. Removing jacket & rolling up sleeves, he strolls to small set for 'Inept D.J.' with his own request phone-in radio show.

The thought of Benny Hill not in character but as himself, cracking jokes while sitting alone on a stool, without Angels or a straightman to lean on, is not easy to envisage – and it seems fantastic that Benny could.

The proposal also included its usual share of recycling, with another raid on Bob Newhart's 'phone conversation with Shakespeare' idea. But there were some novel spins – a spoof of the Three Tenors with Benny as José Carreras, Placido Domingo and Luciano Pavarotti; and a send-up of Alan Bennett's television monologues *Talking Heads*, which he planned to call *Talking Faces*.

These were interesting ideas, but they did not progress. Channel 4 withdrew.

In October 1991, after twenty-three years, Thames was given notice that its ITV franchise was to end. It was a dark day at the office and at Teddington studios, 'a day when everything stood still,' as one executive remembers. Though the hand-over, to Carlton, would not take place until New Year's Eve 1992–3, Thames looked to an uncertain future as nothing more than an independent production company, trying to flog its ideas to TV channels like any other producer. It was in this vein that Thames performed an about-turn late in 1991, approaching Benny about making some new shows. Although those close to the comedian saw this as vindication that they were right – and that Thames had realized the error of its ghastly ways – John Howard Davies' line all along was that the company had not sacked Benny but wished merely for his show to take a break. The question was, would Benny feed from the hand that had bit? The answer – unsurprisingly – was yes.

'We were aware that Benny was out there, filming in New York, being fêted with the Charlie Chaplin award in Switzerland, and being chaperoned by Dennis Kirkland to judge beauty contests in Florida,' says John Fisher. 'And considering he was a multi-millionaire, you'd have thought this was all he needed. But of course Thames had taken away from him the one thing he'd have traded millions for. So we had a discussion – me, John Howard Davies and David Elstein – to see if there was a way of bringing Benny back. It wasn't that we wanted the *old* show back, though – there was no way we were going to allow the show to return in its old form.'

Fisher met Benny soon afterwards. 'Benny said to me, "The thing I most want is to be on screen again – quickly." He even reminded me that Thames had repeat-rights to his last shows but had not yet put them out; he suggested we show them, and we did. I then told him that I had an idea for a new show based on novelty acts – like *Benny Hill's Comedy Circus*, though a bit more sophisticated than the title suggests – with Benny doing the odd monologue, comic song and sketch, and introducing the acts. He liked the idea because not only would he have had a show but it would have re-invented him. We didn't get around to talking about what the show *wouldn't* have – that would have been inappropriate at the first meeting. This was not the moment to say, "The new show will have a new producer." But we at Thames knew that if he didn't agree to this, the option would have gone away.'

Thames' dislike of Dennis Kirkland had been clear for some time – to them, at least. And it was reinforced when Benny returned to Teddington for another meeting and brought Dennis with him. This was to discuss Benny's Thames comeback – an appearance on *Des O'Connor Tonight*, a light-entertainment show in the guise of a chat-show. No chat-show is kinder to its guests than this: they get to perform, and the 'interview' with Des is rehearsed, with re-takes if anything goes awry. 'We had one incredible meeting,' recalls John Fisher, 'with everyone present from our team – including Des – plus Benny and Dennis Kirkland. We were saying to Benny, "It would be a good idea if you did something here," and, "You could perhaps do the Chinaman there," whatever, but instead of replying to me, Benny kept turning to Dennis, saying, "Little heart . . ." and whatever his response was. Dennis then relayed Benny's answers to us. It was a bizarre triangle of communication. There was no malice intended – he liked our ideas and was enthusiastic – but he was not prepared to speak for himself and looked to Dennis to tell us his thoughts for him.'

For all of Benny's public claims to be constantly writing new material, there had been little of it in the New York edition of *Benny Hill's World*, and there was none of it on *Des O'Connor Tonight*, shown on October 30 1991. The reality is that he was scarcely writing at all now. Benny's friend Marian Davies recalls an occasion at this time when they spoke on the phone: 'He was very depressed one day when he rang me. He was talking for an hour. And I said, "Aren't you doing any writing, Ben?" and he said, "What's the point?"'

One item recorded for *Des O'Connor Tonight* was dropped – this was yet another remake of the 'answering the question before last' sketch, jointly performed with O'Connor; sweat gathered on the Hill top lip when it kept going wrong – but a Fred Scuttle sketch made it through to transmission, as did a song duet with the host and a Chow-Mein 'interview':

Des This is your first time in England?
Chow-Mein No, I was here in 1992.
Des You can't have been, it's only 1991 now.
Chow-Mein I was here in 1990, too.
Des And what were you looking for?
Chow-Mein Knowledge.
Des You were looking for knowledge? And did you find it?
Chow-Mein Oh yes.
Des Where?
Chow-Mein In Norfolk.

Des Why in Norfolk?
Chow-Mein [getting riled] 'cause that where it is!
Des Oh, Norwich! The city of Norwich!
Chow-Mein Yes! [Aside] Oy vey, we got a right meshuggenah here.

The centrepiece was Benny's chat, as himself, with O'Connor. Wearing his customary sports jacket and luminous pink shirt, his mop of hair now snow-white, Benny seemed at ease in this unlikely scenario but the conversation was lifeless, comprising merely a tapestry of pensionable gags. Asked why he had never married, he trotted out the age-old response, 'Why buy a book when you can join a lending library?', and 'questioned' about the accusations of being sexist, he reeled off a list of inane jokes that, as usual, entirely skirted the issue. The answer was, in fact, substantially the same as his comic monologue at the end of a 1986 show, going on about his Boy's Own dictionary, listing all the women's magazines on the market and uttering the daft statement, 'The masculine equivalent of a feminist is a male chauvinist pig.' His masters at Taunton's School would have been appalled at such poor debating skill.

Unbeknown to Thames, Benny had also begun a dialogue with Central Television, the ITV company for the Midlands. Or rather, Dennis Kirkland had. 'Dennis came to see me, asking whether we'd like to do something with Benny,' says Richard Holloway, then Central's Head of Light Entertainment. 'I spoke to my Director of Programmes and he said we could proceed – the Thames shows were still selling well abroad and we were interested in doing similar business.' Central planned two one-hour specials, to be recorded in its Nottingham studios and networked at primetime. 'I don't doubt there would have been more in the end,' Holloway says, 'but we were going to dip our toe in the water; another reason for committing only to two was that we wondered if Benny was still up to the task, health-wise.'

Central was somewhat bemused about having to deal directly with Kirkland rather than through Richard Stone's office, but, as Holloway notes, 'The situation was: if you're going to have Ben you've got to have Dennis. Anyway, we wanted to have Dennis. Nobody worked better with Benny.'

Speaking only with the director, not the star, Holloway laid down some ground rules for these new shows. 'Times had changed,' he says. 'The scantily clad girls in bikinis would have gone. And some of the leering. There would have been a toning-down, and we would have said "Try and be a bit more clever." '

Marian Davies saw Benny at this time, and he told her how he had to choose between Thames and Central. 'I asked him which one he would take,' she says, 'and he replied, "Well, I haven't decided yet, dear heart, but probably Thames." I said, "What? After what they did to you?" And he said, "Yes, it'll mean I can walk to work . . ." '

But it wasn't Thames that Benny said yes to, it was Central. Dennis Kirkland was the deciding factor. 'I thought that Central was best, and that we would make the shows in Nottingham,' he says. Contractual discussions began but were never completed because Benny died. 'I've since read that our contract was "in the post to him" or even "on the doormat, waiting to be signed" but this is melodramatic,' says Richard Holloway. 'Negotiations were well advanced, though, and a contract was certainly in preparation.' (Central had, however, pre-sold the two programmes to the ITV network and been given transmission slots. Even though Benny was dead they still had to be filled, so Dennis Kirkland directed a couple of specials, followed by a full series, with Freddie Starr. 'They could have been *The Benny Hill Show* with Freddie in his place,' says a Hill's Angel, by no means the only former associate of Benny's to be angered by the programmes. 'They had a similar cast, the same gags, same tricks, same effects, same silent sketches. And it did Freddie's career no favours either.')

Death was suddenly all around Benny. Having lost his brother and Auntie Lulu in quick succession, he was now reeling as several friends passed away in a short space of time: his much respected Auntie Lena (mother of cousins Chris and Tilly), Nelson Brown from Eastleigh, and Mimi Levy from Westrow Gardens. 'We went to Mimi's funeral together,' says Monica Albon. 'While we were at the cemetery Benny showed me his parents' grave and told me he had already decided he wanted to be buried with them, and share the stone. He was particularly generous that day – he wrote out a £1,000 cheque towards the cost of a new roof at the Red Cross HQ around the corner from Westrow Gardens.'

Soon after this, two more good friends died – the veteran Thames TV photographer Jack Breckon (father of Benny and Dennis's photographer friend Barry), and the musical associate from the Thames shows, Ted Taylor. Benny attended both funerals, and also Breckon's subsequent memorial service. (This took place at St Bride's church, just off Fleet Street, where Benny's much loved grandparents Henry and Sophia had married 102 years earlier.) For Dennis and Benny these were social occasions, too. 'For Ted's we all met up in the pub first, had a couple of pints, went to the funeral and then back for more drinks,' says Kirkland. 'At Jack's, Benny had loads to eat and we stopped off at a pub on the way home. To me, he seemed OK, health-wise. He wasn't complaining about anything.' Lee Gibson, a singer from *The Benny Hill Show*, strongly disagrees, saying, 'I thought Benny looked absolutely dreadful at Ted Taylor's funeral: bloated, very overweight and grey. But he was still lovely – I hadn't seen him for twelve years and it was "Hello, dear heart!", the old, old Ben underneath everything else.' To Maggie Stredder, though, Benny was uncommonly reflective. 'In the pub before Ted Taylor's funeral Benny said, 'It makes you think, Mag – Ted has died and he was younger than me. We're not invincible; we're all vulnerable and we've all got to die.'

On February 10 1992, his weight in the region of seventeen stone, his heaviest yet, Benny suffered a heart attack – while sitting in his Fairwater House flat. He didn't realize it at first, as he seemed to be experiencing nothing more than breathlessness. Old Doc Page advised he check into hospital; Benny went straight to the Cromwell, in South Kensington. Spokesman Dennis Kirkland, fearing that news of a heart attack might jeopardize the impending deal with Central, told the press that Benny was merely having a routine check-up, for insurance purposes. But the truth was soon out, and Benny himself was open about his problem, writing to Monica Albon on February 15:

> I have been in the horse-piddle for about a week now. I seem to have had a mild heart-attack. I should be out in a few days. I'll give you a ring then.
> Love, Wee Benny

Though he had dozens of visitors at the Cromwell, and tried to put a brave face on things, it was obvious to all that Benny was a sick man. Several of these friends were seeing him for the last time. Harry Segal, not a well man himself, came down from Leeds and spent four hours with his fellow Variety trouper. When he was leaving Benny walked with him to the lift, and Harry got down on one knee and sang, 'Powder your face with sunshine, put on a great big smile!' It was a magical moment between the two old stagers, then they hugged and said goodbye. As the lift doors closed, Benny called out, 'Look after yourself, Bubeleh!'[4]

Even here in hospital, though, Benny was not safe from bad news. While Segal was with him, he learned that Netta Warner, one of his two disabled companions, had died at her home in Leicester. She was just fifty-eight and Benny had known her most of her life. He was doubly distraught when he realized he would be unable to attend the funeral; all he could do was ask his agent Lynda Ronan to send a wreath.

Benny was at the Cromwell for eight nights, and the press made a big deal of his departure. Dennis Kirkland had arrived with the Fred Scuttle beret and glasses, and Benny saluted for the massed ranks of photographers as he stood alongside a matron every bit as prim as can be seen in British comedy films of the 1950s. This larking around distracted attention from a key factor in his release – to save his own life, Benny had been ordered to shed at least two stone. The *Sun* did its best to help, however, listing '10 ways Benny can laugh himself lean', the tenth of which was 'Get the Hill's Angels to chase you around the park!'

Within four hours of leaving the Cromwell, Benny was back in hospital. After returning to Fairwater House he again suffered breathing difficulties and was rushed into the Royal Brompton National Heart & Lung Hospital in Chelsea. The problem this time was not with his heart, weak though it was, but with an accumulation of water on his chest. He stayed six more nights. Among the visitors here was Michael Jackson, who happened to be in England and professed to being a big Benny Hill fan. 'Michael never stopped talking about the show,' says Dennis Kirkland, who took a couple of photos of this most unlikely twosome which flashed around the world. 'Michael knew every gag and kept saying to Benny, "Remember that bit when . . .?" It was obvious that Benny was one of his heroes.' After chatting for about forty minutes, and discovering a mutual enthusiasm for Charlie Chaplin, Jackson left, but not before discussing plans for Benny to appear in one of his future music videos.

When Benny checked out of the Royal Brompton on February 24 he did so with a secret – one that he did not share for several days, and only with very few. The specialists had told him that without urgent heart-bypass surgery he could die at any time, but there was strong evidence of heart disease, so the organ might not withstand the operation. Benny weighed up the choice and decided against the surgery. He now knew that, at any time, he would suffer a serious and possibly fatal heart attack.

When he finally revealed this to Dennis Kirkland, his friend was furious. 'He didn't tell me until he was out of hospital, the bastard,' Kirkland exclaims. 'He might be here today if he'd said yes. They'd have cut out all the fatty tissue and given him a zip up the front. So we wouldn't have done Tarzan sketches any more – big deal.'

Benny's long-time producer and friend John Street tried to talk him into having the operation, but Benny refused. 'He was terrified of it,' says Street. Every time Street had seen him in recent times he had felt that Benny looked worse; and he detected too the increasing sense of nostalgia. During a preview screening of the *Omnibus* documentary, Benny had touched Street on the arm and remarked, 'John, I remember so many good times, those wonderful years of sunshine, and my lovely Hettie [Tack].' Street is of the opinion that the documentary marked 'the end of the line' for Benny. 'I could sense he was poorly,' he declares. 'His face was bloated and he was very quiet. I think we all felt something was wrong.'

Knowing his heart was diseased, and that death was only a matter of time, Benny made no real effort to lose the weight that the doctors had previously said was essential for his longevity. Although, at home, he kept to a routine of diet drinks and low-fat foods, it was quantity that remained his undoing. The tabloid papers were not slow in telling readers just what a gluttonous appetite this man possessed; the *Sun* reported how, after leaving hospital (the second time, presumably), he feasted on a multi-course Chinese meal with desserts, and beer, wine and brandies. Even before his heart attack, he had been pushing his luck. Benny's final New Year's Eve, 1991 into 1992, was spent at the home of his friend Iain Burton, an entertainment agent who lived in Midhurst, Sussex. 'He was not his usual self that night,' says Burton. 'He looked very tired and drank very heavily. He drank wine followed by brandies, and sweated. He didn't look at all well and had put on a lot of weight.'

Mindful of the Central TV contract, however, Benny still hoped to maintain an illusion of good health, and when he learned that Libby Roberts was releasing a fitness video he offered to drum up some publicity for them both. 'He phoned me saying, "I'm coming out of hospital tomorrow, let's do a press photocall,"' she says. 'He asked if I could arrange for a couple of models to pose with him, which I did. But he looked very ill that day. I once did a show with Billy Fury when he had a greyness about him, and he died the next day. Benny had that same colour – he looked really awful. I said to him at lunchtime, "Should you be drinking wine?" – he was knocking back whole glasses – and he replied, "Oh I'll be all right, little heart!" He wasn't being at all careful. But he still asked if he could stay and see the children when they got home from school, and made a fuss of them. He was always the same in that respect – never less than marvellous with the children. Every year towards the end he took all of us to the circus, and to the pantomime at Wimbledon Theatre.'

This was a period when Benny could have been ensuring that his affairs were in order, yet he did nothing. Of crucial importance – though, clearly, not to him – was his will. He had more than 7 million pounds washing around in various accounts, and its fate was bound to be keenly anticipated. Benny kept everyone guessing.

Although all his intended beneficiaries had predeceased him, the will he had sworn in 1961 – in which he planned to divide his assets equally between his brother, sister and, jointly, parents – had not been superseded and so remained in force. Even before the last of these kin had died, Benny was aware of the need to draw up a new document. He said as much to the *Sun*, in a feature published in January 1990. And he said it again during a phone conversation with Marian Davies after he came out of hospital.

For years, Benny had been telling people that they would be 'well looked after' when he died, indicating that he was leaving them a (presumably considerable) financial legacy. It is the sort of thing a rich person might say, especially a rich comedian, and was usually taken in the light-hearted spirit it was intended to carry. Latterly, however, Benny had taken to telling friends that they were indeed named in his will. Too many people were told this with the same sincere emphasis for it to have been a joke.

Libby Roberts recounts one such incident. 'We [she and her husband] had a slight financial crisis at one point in the late 1980s and were looking at downsizing,' she says. 'One day, when Benny and I were discussing the recession, I briefly filled him in about our troubles and he offered me the money, there and then, to pay off our mortgage. He didn't ask how much, he simply offered to pay it off. He said, "Look, you're in my will anyway, do you want some of it now, to get you out of this predicament?" I was so dazed that I said, "Oh no, no, Benny, don't be stupid, I couldn't possibly." I was embarrassed but thrilled at the same moment. He said there were five people named in his will and that I was one of them. He was very short and sharp when he spoke like this. Short sentences, matter of fact. "It's there. You're welcome to it" kind of thing. I asked him if he would be leaving anything to his family and he said, "I've got nieces and nephews but I don't see them any more." We left it at that. In the end, we dug ourselves out of trouble and Benny didn't have to write us the cheque.'

Benny was clearly very fond of Libby and her young family, but he also spoke in the same way to people of his age – or older. Before her death in 1990, Benny repeatedly told his adored Auntie Lulu, twenty-eight years his senior, that she would be a beneficiary on his death. 'I heard him say it many a time,' says Florence Jaques, 'and I was sure it was no lie. "You have no need to worry, you are well looked after," he told her. And Louie would reply, "What would I want your money for?" '

This paints a picture of a man assiduously buying friendship, a man perhaps so fearful of being left without any friends that he was prepared to promise them a legacy he had no real intention of leaving. It wasn't 'you'll be in my will' he was saying but 'you are in my will' – fact. On at least three occasions Benny took Iain Burton aside and whispered, 'I want you to know that you're in my will.' Burton, naturally, was uncertain how to respond, but finds it hard to believe that Benny would have played with people's sensitivities, especially those of Sue Upton and Louise English, both of whom were given the same assurance. Though Burton remains surprised that the promise turned out to be untrue, he also recalls

Benny saying to him, 'Iain, life is an unspoken bargain', while another of his favourite remarks was 'I'll scratch your back, you scratch mine.' Burton concludes, 'There was an unspoken bargain in many of Benny's relationships.'

The pity is that such statements would come to wound those whom Benny cherished the most. One can only imagine how Netta Warner and Phoebe King felt when, in December 1991, Benny was quoted in the *News of the World* saying, 'Sadly, all my family have gone before me, so I must make a new will. And I can safely say that these two ladies will be Numbers One and Two in that will.' Netta died two months later anyway, but for Phoebe, her legacy was not what the press was assuming on the basis of Benny's words – guessing it was as much as 10 million pounds. It was a posse of paparazzi and news crews, gathered on the steps of her Felixstowe nursing home, clamouring for a word with the 'heiress'. (The absence of a new will owed to no lack of effort on the part of Benny's advisers, either. Dennis Blake, his now-retired accountant, the executor of the 1961 will, is certain that his successor made repeated efforts to have Benny draft a new document.)

Dennis Kirkland makes perhaps the most perceptive comment on the subject when he declares, 'Benny told me many, many times that he didn't have a will. I was always urging him to set up a trust – his money could have funded a Benny Hill Home for Under-Privileged Children, perhaps in Southampton. But trust was one thing Benny didn't have.'

Benny was hospitalized again on March 7, returning to the Royal Brompton. The cause was a panic attack brought on by more breathlessness and probably imagined chest pains. It was his third spell in hospital inside a month, and newspapers quoted a 'TV insider', probably Dennis Kirkland, saying, 'Those who love him are more than a little uneasy.' The pair were photographed strolling in the hospital grounds, both putting on a brave face.

To deflect the gloom, it was announced that Benny was busy choosing his eight favourite pieces of music for a second appearance on the BBC radio programme *Desert Island Discs*. (The programme was never made because of his ill-health.) Louise English visited him in hospital and recalls, 'He could hardly breathe – he said it was like drowning in his own body – but in between the breaths he asked if I had made a recording of

"Glamorous Night", a tune I had sung in the show at Sonning. Unfortunately, there wasn't one. Benny told me he had two very happy memories of that song – the first was when he heard it during the war, and the second was "the happiest time of my life, the day I took you and Sue out for lunch". And he'd just been sacked that week! God love him.'

Another visitor was Lynda Ronan. At the end of April, Richard Stone and his wife Sara would be celebrating their golden wedding anniversary, and one of their sons was compiling a video of goodwill messages from close friends and some of Richard's clients. Ronan came to the hospital with a camcorder and, in so doing, captured the last moving images of Benny Hill. And moving it certainly was – wearing a green bed-jacket, with a drip plumbed into his neck, looking old, obese and blotchy, he staggered to raise himself from his slumber, and, with intense melodrama, and a voice that suggested he'd be knocking on death's door at any moment, declared:

> Hello Richard and Sara. I'm speaking to you from my bed of pain here at the Royal Brompton ... here at the Royal Brompton chest and H-H-H-H-H-Heart Hospital. Many congratulations on your fiftieth wedding anniversary. I wish you both long life and happiness.

It was a heart-rending sequence that ended with a pronounced coughing fit. It was also a great Benny Hill joke. Betraying that his performance had been a pretence, he suddenly brightened, turned to Lynda Ronan and said:

> Are we off? Good. Thank God for that. Let's have some champagne! Do you want some champagne? There's plenty of it there. Listen eh, poor Sara. Fifty years! Poor woman!

There wasn't much the hospital could do for Benny this time around – he had declined the bypass operation and wasn't really bothering to diet or reduce his alcohol intake. He was sent home with some pills after five days. Within forty more, he would be dead.

Benny spent his final weeks quietly, frustrated that his breathlessness prevented him from taking long walks, unable to get to Southampton, and with little prospect of being fit to return to any work. He watched television from morning until night and, as he so often did, recorded late-night shows to view the next day. Dennis Kirkland popped by most days and did any little bits of shopping that Benny needed, and Benny politely refused the countless offers of help from other concerned friends. He turned down, too, opportunities to spend Easter away from home, with Libby Roberts and family at their new house in Esher, and also Marian Davies and husband at their holiday home in Weymouth. Marian recalls, 'I said to Ben, "It's nice and quiet and nobody will know you're there. You can sit outside, look at the sea and take in the fresh air, and we'll drive you down and drive you back again."' Both offers seemed too good to refuse, but Benny refused.

The week leading up to Easter was his last. On Tuesday April 14 he watched himself on television. Thames was screening the six half-hour compilations he had alerted them to during his recent meetings. They were pulling in fair audience figures, too, about 11 million, hovering around twentieth place in the weekly ratings. That said, the comedy still looked weak and lazy, a far cry from some of the old BBC clips included in the recent *Omnibus* special, when he had been really trying. Only one item stood tall in the last edition of *The Benny Hill Show* to be seen by the man himself – a short musical piece in which he appeared as Otto Schtuk, a flamboyant tambourine-waver, working with a gaggle of Hill's Angels dressed in lederhosen as 'die Bavarian Schtompers'. This was a simple skit with a filmic twist: the Angels' actions were choreographed eight times slower than usual while Benny worked at the standard pace. When the video tape was replayed at eight times normal speed the Angels seemed fine while he appeared to be going berserk.

Also on Tuesday April 14, Benny sent Monica Albon £100 worth of flowers, with the message, 'To Moniker, kos yor a nyce ladie. Happy Easter from your Seecrit admyer,' and he sent a similar bouquet to Phoebe King, who had fallen and broken her femur. In recent times, Benny had given Phoebe a ring, which she wore on her engagement finger. They had also taken to using pet names – he called her Kitten, she called him Teddy Bear ('because he was so big and cuddly'). When they spoke on the phone at this time Benny said to Phoebe, 'Darling, you've broken your femur bone and I've got a bad heart – we're a right pair, aren't we?' Benny's death would hit Phoebe particularly hard.

This same week, Benny spoke to Dave Freeman for the last time. Like so many of their conversations, it bordered on farce. Freeman is a pragmatist and Benny could be both obtuse and obdurate.

Freeman was mystified from the first minute, when Benny explained how he was having to watch his diet carefully, eating heart-friendly food, and then in the next breath said that Dennis was out at the shops buying them lobster. 'I said to him, "Surely that's hard to digest,"' says Freeman, 'and he said, "Oh no! It's protein."

'I asked him how he was feeling,' Freeman continues. '"Not too good," Benny said, "it's like being half drowned – my lungs are full of fluid." And for the first time since he was ill he said he ought to think about making a will. I said, "Haven't you made one yet?" and he said, "Well, I made one about twenty years ago and left everything to my family, but now they've all gone."

'Benny was very naïve in many ways. He said he didn't know how to make a will . . .'

Freeman Well, you go to see a solicitor. If you're not well they'll come to you, if you pay them enough.
Hill But can you trust them?
Freeman More or less! Or you can make one out yourself.
Hill How?
Freeman You go to the stationers – send Dennis if you have to – get a will form, make it out, and all you need are two witnesses to your signature. It's perfectly legal.
Hill But I've got all these little girls I've been friendly with over the years, and the woman in Felixstowe, I'd like to leave them a bit.
Freeman So you write 'I leave Sue Upton £100,000 . . .'
Hill *£100,000?!!*
Freeman Well £3.50 then, whatever you like!

'Then he asked me to explain death duties,' Freeman says. 'I said that whoever he left his money to would have to pay forty per cent duty on it. "The only thing you can do to avoid it is draw money out in cash and give it to people. And when the solicitors settle your estate they won't be able to trace any of it. You could have spent it on toffee, or backing horses. It won't exist."

'It didn't happen,' Freeman concludes. 'Even if he was interested he could scarcely have got out of bed, he was in such a bad way.'

Benny did nothing about his will, but he managed to get out for one very special appointment. On April 15 he took Sue Upton and Samantha Spencer-Lane (another former Hill's Angel) to lunch at the Savoy Hotel, and then went to a matinée performance of the musical *My and My Girl* at the nearby Adelphi Theatre. He was desperate to see his protégée Louise English, who was cast in one of the major roles: as cockney girl Sally Smith. For more than thirty years Benny had aspired to groom someone for the big time, now at last his work had borne fruit – Louise had 'made it' in the West End. 'He was sitting in Row G,' says Louise. 'Some rows are hard to see from the stage but I could see him. He had a look of great pride and there were tears. He told me later he had been planning to stand up in the audience at the end and say, "*That's* how it should be done!"'

There were increasing signs that Benny sensed his imminent demise. Though usually camera-shy in public, he asked Louise to arrange for a photographer to take pictures of them together. Then he went back to her dressing-room to chat while she relaxed prior to preparing for the evening performance. Louise found him in a sentimental mood, less joky than he had been before his illness. She recalls, 'I sat on the floor and Benny sat on the couch, and I noticed his neck looked very dark, almost blue, even though he was wearing a cravat. He said to me, "I've been really hard on you in the past – but I can't tell you how I admire what you've done."

'We talked about everything. He said how hard he had found it to get work after being sacked by Thames – though he also rebuked me for being pleased that Thames had lost its franchise. He spoke about his new series for Central, his health, and Michael Jackson's visit. He wasn't at all impressed by that, though – he liked Jackson but had nothing to say to show-business people; the only people he really wanted to meet were boxers.' Visitors had to leave the theatre by five o'clock but Benny wouldn't go. Alfred Marks popped in to see him and they reminisced, and so did another member of the cast, Les Dennis. 'I could sense he still didn't want to go,' Louise says.

At twenty-past-seven Benny realized that Louise had to get back on stage and so finally, reluctantly, he took his leave. 'I suppose I'd better be

going, little heart,' he said, as he wished her goodbye. Louise sensed something was very wrong, and cried as he walked slowly away.

Easter 1992 was a bad weekend for British comedy. Frankie Howerd
died from a heart attack on April 19, aged seventy-five. Benny was quoted
as being very upset at the news – but actually he said nothing about it,
because he was already dead himself. A journalist had phoned Dennis
Kirkland for Benny's response and Dennis, the unofficial press agent, had
invented Benny's quote.

Dennis had been unable to reach Benny by phone for a couple of days
and was starting to worry. During the evening of Monday April 20,
Benny's Fairwater House neighbour Bill Greenham began to notice an
unpleasant odour coming from Flat 7, and realized too that the television
had been on for a long time. Kirkland was summoned; though he has no
head for heights he climbed a ladder to the second-floor balcony and
looked in through the window. Amid the messy piles of papers, the
unwashed plates, the dirty glasses and the scattered video tapes, his best
friend was slumped on the settee opposite the TV – distended, blue, blood
seeping from his ears.

Benny Hill had died at sixty-eight, the same age as his brother; the
official cause, given after a post-mortem without inquest, was 'coronary
thrombosis' – that is, a heart attack caused by a blocked artery. Although
the official certificate gives the date of death as 'On or about Twentieth
April 1992', it was estimated that he had already been dead for up to
forty-eight hours.

It was a solitary, sad death, especially poignant for a man loved by
people all around the world. And yet, considering how he had conducted
his life, it was also an entirely typical manner for Benny Hill to have
shuffled off.

Postscript: The Forgotten Man

It poured with rain at Benny Hill's funeral, drenching the eighty or so mourners, a figure so few it surprised many yet ought to have surprised none. As the cloudburst splattered her cigarette, an eighty-nine-year-old Southampton woman watched the cortège pass and said to a journalist from the *Southern Daily Echo*, 'He used to make me laugh, and you don't get many laughs when you live on your own.' It was an appropriate epitaph for the world's most popular loner.

As he had wished, Benny was buried in the same grave as his parents. His former showgirls wore stockings and suspenders in a silent tribute, and Benny would have been most amused to see Old Doc Page, his octogenarian gynaecologist doctor, going around pinching their bottoms. Five months later there was a memorial service at St Martin-in-the-Fields, in London, yards from the former site of the Nuffield Centre from where Benny had risen to fame fully forty years earlier. As people filed out of the eighteenth-century church, musicians struck up 'Yakety Sax' and everyone tripped into that oh-so-familiar double-speed run-off.

The world grieved the death of its favourite funnyman. It was reported on news bulletins on every continent, and French TV ran an immediate two-hour tribute. In Britain, however, there was almost a sense of 'good riddance' to the man whose first quarter-century as an acclaimed TV comedian was cast into shadow by a shabby final decade. The day the news broke, Thames replaced its scheduled screening of a *Benny Hill Show* compilation to run a half-hour tribute – but it was imbued with not only a sense of melancholia but also a defensive air. (In an ironic twist that Benny's close friends would certainly not have appreciated, the programme was produced by the never-to-be-forgiven 'axe man' John Howard Davies.)

After a day of tributes and obituaries, British newspapers switched to speculation about the will. Reaching back into the files, journalists quickly found Benny's recent quote about disabled friends Phoebe King and Netta Warner – 'I must make a new will. And I can safely say that these two ladies will be Numbers One and Two in that will.' Netta had subsequently died, but Phoebe, his 'Kitten', was tracked down to Felixstowe; owing to her broken femur she could not attend the funeral but sent a wreath in the shape of a cat, with the wording 'To Teddy Bear. I love you very, very much. Kitten (Phoebe).' It was quite a story for the press.

If this was Benny's intention, though, where was the will to prove it? Dennis Kirkland found a note close to the body that listed around ten first-names (of intended beneficiaries, perhaps) with a figure (an amount of money, perhaps) alongside each one. But this was just a scribble, not a witnessed legal document. Kirkland has never disclosed the names and figures.

It was Benny's final, disappointing act. There was no new will. As an unseemly but understandable scrabble followed, Dennis Blake, executor of the 1961 document, was forced to emerge from retirement and oversee the procedures. The will was clear: if the named beneficiaries were deceased then Benny's estate was to be divided among the children born to his brother and sister. Leonard had two sons and two daughters, and Diana two sons and one daughter; these seven nieces and nephews inherited a net estate of £7,526,777.

Opinions are sharply divided about the justice of this, but Benny's own slothfulness and indifferent attitude to money make the debate academic – he could have changed the will, and he didn't. For the numerous friends and relatives who were expecting their grief to be assuaged by a promised inheritance, what hurt most was that Benny wasn't even close to his siblings' children (though he had at least enjoyed spending time with Diana's). It was a bitter pill to swallow, and a residue of sourness lingers.

The nieces and nephews continue to reap the reward of their uncle's endeavours – the royalties that flow in from around the world. Funds are paid into the A. H. Hill Trust of Residuals and then shared out. Though the Trust's returns are not made public, it is likely that each of them receives a generous five-figure sum every year. Benny probably would have been delighted to see that Caroline, Leonard's eldest child, invested some of her money in a British comedy film – *Caught in the Act*, released in 1996 – which she also co-wrote. (And, unrelated to the will business, he would also be thrilled to watch any modern episode of the Australian TV soap-opera *Neighbours*. Holly Valance, the pretty teenager who plays Felicity Scully, is his cousin Hugh Stevens' granddaughter – that is, she is the great-great-granddaughter of Henry Hawthorn Hill.)

Considering his fame – one might even say infamy – Benny Hill became a forgotten man very quickly in his home country.

Those of his possessions not disposed of immediately sold for very modest sums at auction. Monica Albon, one of his dearest friends in the final years, bought several items of Benny Hill's furniture. Still tucked deep at the back of a drawer in an old bureau from Westrow Gardens is an apt reminder of this magpie comedian – a two-line 'funny' clipped out from a tabloid newspaper, doubtless bound for some future TV script.

There are Dead Comics Society/Comic Heritage plaques to Benny Hill outside 2 Queen's Gate and Teddington Studios. There is also a plaque in Eastleigh, on the approximate site of the long-demolished dairy where he worked as a milkman in the early days of the Second World War. Yet there is nothing in Southampton to indicate it was the home of The World's Most Popular Comedian. The city fathers seem embarrassed by the association. A handful of local residents have lobbied for a Benny Hill memorial but nothing has been done; and no one seems to be aware of his birthplace, which, despite all the Luftwaffe bombs dropped in the vicinity, and also widespread council demolition in the 1950s, stands at 111 Bernard Street, near the Town Quay. (In 1925, a year after his birth, Bridge Road was subsumed into neighbouring Bernard Street to make one long thoroughfare. 30 Bridge Road, Benny's birthplace, became 111 Bernard Street.)

After sixty-one years in the Hill family, the house in Westrow Gardens was sold late in 1992, at 'normal' value, and has since changed hands again.

With condoms widely available over the counter and from vending machines, Stanley & Co. finally went out of business in 1978. Canal Walk is now little more than a car-park, yielding no hint of its excitingly murky past.

Taunton's School has relocated across the Common, where there is a small garden in Benny's honour, founded and tended by Monica Albon. The former Taunton's, the establishment that scarcely noticed A. H. Hill as he passed through, is now a university faculty of arts.

Just occasionally, a group of Japanese tourists will arrive at quiet Hollybrook Cemetery and pay homage to their comic hero. Monica Albon, and also Shaun Connolly, a mini-cab driver who gave Benny lifts around the city, lay fresh flowers on the Hill tablet, which bears the apt inscription 'Eternal Boy'. Six months after the funeral, vandals tried to rob the grave, believing Benny had been buried wearing a valuable ring. Although they dug down to the coffin it was not breached, and there is now a foot-thick concrete slab to prevent another attempt.

The Benny Hill Show can be seen every Sunday night on French television, and every evening on Dutch and other European channels, and Don Taffner recently completed an extensive new deal with an American cable channel. Elsewhere around the globe, though a little less evident than he was twenty years ago, Benny is still shown, still talked about, still loved.

In Britain, though, Benny Hill is a dead comedian. The prevailing attitude – among women especially – remains the one that dogged his last dozen years: that his work degraded women. No one performs his style of humour any more, and though some comics admire his work there is no obvious influence on the rising generations. This may also be because it is a decade since his show last appeared on mainstream, terrestrial television.

It is forgotten that Benny Hill once had a much happier career, that twenty-five years before being tainted as 'sexist' he was Television Personality of the Year, renowned for his groundbreaking comedy, a man who delivered an original brand of humour – cheeky but harmless – to a new medium.

His pre-Hill's Angels work deserves reappraisal . . . and there is an increasingly strong sense that his time will come again, that we may not have seen the last of that inimitably saucy, wide-eyed smirk.

Notes

1. Before Benny: The Alfie Years

1. A Remarkable Ancestry

1 Stopes advocated the use of the cervical cap as the ideal method of contraception.
2 Named after the eighteenth-century English demographer Thomas Malthus, who recognized a need for birth control.
3 The Mandrells were of Spanish ancestry, the original name being Mandrello.

2. Alfie

1 Throughout his life 'Benny' Hill frequently witnessed the misspelling of his middle name, as Hawthorne. Even his mother gave it as such when registering his birth, and then had to make a return trip to the registrar to have the certificate amended. He signed his own Last Will and Testament knowing that the typist had misspelled his middle name, not bothering to point out the error, and even the certificate of his death perpetuated the mistake.
2 *Desert Island Discs*, BBC Home Service, November 16 1959.

3. 'That's for me!'

1 Radios Luxembourg and Normandy were run on commercial grounds, with sponsored programmes and advertising breaks just like American radio. Often brighter and more upbeat than the BBC, their comedy and dance-band programmes ensured that Alfie Hill was often tuned in, to Luxembourg especially.
2 Decades later, in his seventies, Arnold Ridley achieved the role for which he died famous, Private Godfrey, the weak-bladdered Home Guard soldier in the hit BBC sitcom *Dad's Army*.
3 These lines have been distilled from two separate 'takes' recorded by Benny Hill for *Desert Island Discs*, one being broadcast and the other unused (but still transcribed by the BBC). The episode was related slightly differently in each, both including unique details.
4 From the 'Southampton Notes' column by 'Aitch Aitch', *The World's Fair*, October 24 1936.

4. Milk-O!

1 Nana – Sophia Hill – outlived her husband by fifteen years; she died in May 1958, aged eighty-five. They are buried together in an Eastleigh cemetery. In his will, Henry left his entire estate to Sophia; she in turn left everything to Benny Hill's parents Alf and Helen.

5. The Dogsbody's Dogsbody – with Small Parts

1 Written by David Nathan (Peter Owen, London).
2 Still operative at this time was an organization called the Music Hall Artistes' Railway Association, established in late Victorian times to negotiate reduced fares and a greater charge-free luggage-allowance for travelling performers.
3 A postscript to this story is that Waring, who had convinced everybody he was Peter Roderick-Mainwaring DSO RN, invalided out of the Navy after his arm was injured in a sea battle, was nothing of the sort. He was a con man who had been dismissed from a pre-war clerk's job at the BBC after absconding with a cash box; his arm had been injured leaning against a hot pipe on a ferry boat. Waring's fraudulent lifestyle eventually caught with him, and he was imprisoned. Tragically, he then hanged himself in his cell. 'I only met him a couple of times and I was heart-broken when he died,' Benny Hill later reflected.
4 Written by Dion Titheradge, *Happy Week-end!* originally opened in London in May 1934. Alfie Hill's role, that of Richard (Ricky) Brant, was played then by the Hungarian-born actor and frequent BBC broadcaster Steve Geray, whose wife, Magda Kun, was also in the cast.

2. Benny Hill: Comedy Specialist

6. The Sunshine Personality

1 A dazzling Technicolor fantasy, *Wonder Man* starred Danny Kaye as both a mild-mannered academic and an effervescent night-club performer embroiled with gangsters. Added glamour came in the shape of Virginia Mayo. Her 'diaphanous nightie' also caught Benny Hill's eye.
2 The Light Programme was one of three national radio stations established post-war by the BBC; as the name suggests, its programming was essentially easy on the ear – comedy, Variety, popular music and light classics, talks, quizzes and panel-games.
3 The marching music of American bandleader John Philip Sousa (1854–1932) obviously lends itself well to the comedy theme tune. *Monty Python's Flying Circus* adopted his 'Liberty Bell', which is now impossible to hear without mental insertion of a raspberry.

4 Eric Spear went on to become a writer of television theme tunes, including those for soap-operas *The Grove Family* (British TV's first concerted attempt at the genre) and, most notably, *Coronation Street*.

5 It was known among comedians that BBC producers tended not to listen to programmes they hadn't made, and that some didn't speak to one another. So one or two went ahead and used Benny Hill, despite the failed audition. His next appearance was on *Beginners, Please!*, broadcast live to the nation from Aeolian Hall on October 25; this show's producer, Roy Speer, was to become a useful ally in the ensuing years. The producers' unfamiliarity with other shows also encouraged Benny to recycle his material, which he did ruthlessly in this period, and beyond. He was to turn recycling into an art form.

6 Palary (or Palare) is Romany talk, words of gypsy or fairground origin seized upon by some members of the theatrical profession – especially, though not exclusively, by homosexuals – as a secret slang language.

7 The BBC continued to calculate artists' fees in guineas, although increasingly archaic, until the 1960s. A guinea was £1 1s, equivalent to £1.05 in post-1971 decimal currency.

7. Doubled Up

1 It has never been definitively established whether Benny Hill actually signed a contract with Richard Stone – some friends and associates indicate that he did, others that he didn't. During an interview for this book the author asked Stone, who replied, 'I would think [he did sign], although I couldn't swear to it. I signed up almost everybody at the beginning, and then forgot about it. Nowadays nobody signs anybody in the entertainments business. Chances are I might have signed Benny for [the first] two or three years.'

2 Another agent, Philip Brown, had represented Benny Hill for a short period in 1947–8 but the arrangement was never formalized. Benny's *Show World* advertisements in this period always stated 'no sole agent'.

3 Sir George Lynskey was a British High Court judge who chaired a tribunal in 1948 inquiring into 'irregularities' in government departments. A number of resignations resulted. It seems improbable that Benny Hill, who (despite his parents' socialist leanings) scarcely followed politics and had no interest in the subject, would have been lampooning such a situation. More likely, the reviewer in question made an incorrect connection, reading complexities into a simple naughty schoolboy skit where none existed.

4 Benny Hill never forgot and never ceased to be impressed by Johnny Hutch. Forty years on, in 1988, when the acrobat was seventy-four, he joined the regular cast of Benny's TV show.

5 Much of Norman Evans' work was subsequently imitated by Les Dawson.

6 The BBC's gradual expansion of transmissions also brought TV to the Midlands in

1949, the north in 1951, Scotland, Wales and the west of England in 1952 and Northern Ireland in 1953.

7 Once again, the BBC's confidential Listener Research Report would have given Benny cold comfort. For the show aired on March 27 1949, only 22 per cent derived 'exceptional enjoyment' from his contribution. But another comic fared worse: last, with a mere 15 per cent, was Tony Hancock.

8 Recorded for broadcast every Wednesday evening, with a Friday repeat, *Petticoat Lane* was a Pat Dixon production. In addition to another up-and-coming young talent, Max Wall, Benny Hill appeared throughout the series, sixteen programmes in all. The show's content was driven by the title – Petticoat Lane, located in the East End of London, is famed for its street market. The various artists barked their wares, be it a song or a comedy sketch. Benny's pitch was selling books and sheet music, yet another frame on which to hang a succession of elementary gags, many of them previously broadcast. One gag was censored, when Benny attempted to sell a book about a part-time lawyer – 'he took his girlfriend out one night and tried to make her change her will.' Rather more exactingly, resident stars Elsie and Doris Waters were performing dialogue in the guise of their gossipy cockney characters Gert and Daisy. Benny was impressed and set about writing some cockney dialogue sketches of his own. These would be broadcast in 1950–1.

9 Benny Hill's technique of evading landladies while pursuing intimacy was something he explained to Monica Albon, a close friend in the period shortly before his death, herself a landlady for visiting theatricals in Southampton. She says: 'Benny told me the trick of how to fool a theatrical-digs landlady, which he devised when he was a touring Variety artist: he'd go the loo, whistling, make a lot of noise, pull the chain, whistle all the way back but go to the door he wanted to go to rather than to his own. Even if the landlady was listening for creaking doors she wouldn't know which room he had gone in.'

10 This may have been the touring Variety revue *Nudes are News*, in which Segal appeared at this time. As Variety managers struggled to fill the theatres such unsubtle titles were becoming more and more prevalent. Local authorities began to look closely at shows with the word 'nude' or French allusions in the title, not because they were suggestive but because they were 'catchpenny and misleading'.

11 *Richmond and Twickenham Times*, December 31 1949.

12 There is a puzzling postscript to all this. Louise English, a dancer and aspiring actress who worked with Benny Hill on television towards the end of his life, says that her mother went out with him in Margate in 1950, after his rejected marriage proposal. ('She and Benny went out a couple of times for egg and chips, and she cheered him up. They got on well together.') Her mother's name is Elizabeth – then Elizabeth (Betty) Reid – and she was working as a soubrette in a Margate show, *Evening Stars*. Louise is adamant that her mother was not the Elizabeth whom Benny asked to marry, although another source says that Louise's mother has claimed that he did propose to her. Louise also says that the first thing Benny remarked to her when, as a

teenager, she auditioned for him in 1976, was, 'You could have been mine!' Requests by the author to speak with her mother during the course of writing this book, to clarify the situation, were rebuffed. Most likely, however, there were two Elizabeths: Benny later spoke of how the woman to whom he proposed went on to marry a dentist, and Elizabeth Reid did not do so.

13 Another agent to journey down to see Varney was Bernard Delfont. He wrote in his autobiography (*East End, West End*, Macmillan, 1990): 'Reg was as good as ever but I could not take my eyes off Benny Hill who had the gift of all great comedians of attracting laughs just by standing there on stage.'

8. After Sunderland, Anything Goes

1 George and Alfred Black, especially the latter, who was the producer, were uncertain about the worth of such a piece and had insisted on a pre-tour try-out. After some rehearsal in his William IV Street office, Richard Stone laid on a one-night-only performance in London, at the Queen's theatre in Poplar, with Reg Varney, Benny Hill and three of his other clients as extras: the actor/director Ian Carmichael, opera singer Ian Wallace and actor (and future TV director) Philip Dale. Stone paid them £10 each and the Blacks loved it.

2 Benny was filmed by Pathé newsreel cameras at Battersea funfair on two occasions in later years, indulging in larks and banter with fellow celebrities and participating in autograph-signing sessions during charity functions.

3 Interview with John Ellison for the BBC Home Service programme *Turning Points*, broadcast March 14 1966.

4 In publicity, interviews and CVs Benny Hill had started to give his year of birth as 1925 instead of 1924 – a fabrication he would maintain until his last ten years. Such misrepresentations are common in show-business – Reg Varney always claimed to have been born in 1922 instead of 1916 and Frankie Howerd in 1922 instead of 1917. Benny's decision to shave off just a single year is puzzling in that it was of no material benefit.

5 A services acronym – a 'Wren' was a member of the WRNS, the Women's Royal Navy Service.

6 This is the second-earliest audio recording of Benny Hill in the BBC archive. The earliest is a dialogue sketch with Johnny Morris from *Anything Goes*, March 6 1952.

9. And the Bright New Hope of Lime Grove . . . Wins!

1 *Picturegoer*, February 26 1955.

2 It was later patched up, but the link was never as strong again, and after stumbling on until 1956 relations between the BBC and the Nuffield Centre ended altogether.

3 Jeremy Hawk's real surname is Lange. With his first wife, the actress/singer Joan Heal, they had a daughter who has achieved success as an actress – Belinda Lang.

4 Charlie Drake, Terry Scott, Warren Mitchell, Norman Vaughan and Rolf Harris were among those given their TV 'break' in these Benny Hill-hosted editions of *Showcase*.

5 Stated in a letter from Roy Speer to BBC executive Pat Hillyard, August 16 1954, on file at the BBC.

3. A Certain Talent

10. The Same Old Benny

1 This particular branch of Lyons was much used by West Indians at this time, the immigrants welcoming the fact that it was open all night and would serve them – racism was openly rampant in Britain in the late 1950s and black people were turned away from many establishments.

11. The Harvester

1 Columbia DX 216.

2 These late-1955 shows never happened – other commitments kept Benny Hill away from TV until 1957.

3 November 24 1954 edition. Written by Bob Monkhouse and Denis Goodwin, produced by Kenneth Carter.

4 The format and delivery of the schoolmaster sketch was identical to a standup piece by Rowan Atkinson, written by Richard Sparks, first performed in 1978. Benny did not acknowledge this.

5 Michael Joseph, London, 1974.

12. 'He's good. Who is he?'

1 These figures were equal to £525 and £640 10s [£640.50] respectively.

2 Respectively, Peter Cook and Dudley Moore 'scruffy herbert' characters from their 1960s series *Not Only . . . But Also*; a pair of pub-dwellers performed by Ronnie Barker and Ronnie Corbett in the 1970s in *The Two Ronnies*; and the gormless numbskulls performed in 'head to head' dialogues by Mel Smith and Griff Rhys Jones in their 1980s TV series *Alas Smith and Jones* and 1990s successor *Smith and Jones*.

3 The fresh-faced Peter Vernon had trained as a baritone singer before turning to acting. Born Peter Vernon Thomas in London in 1921, he too was represented by Richard Stone. His tenure as Benny's straightman ran from 1958 to 1961 on television, and to 1966 on radio.

4 This edition of the BBC radio series was broadcast by the Home Service on November 16 1959. Benny's eight choices were:

i. 'Viens Danser' by Gilbert Bécaud ('music to get up to, first thing in the morning').

ii. 'Sur la Plage' (co-written by Robert Dhéry) by Gérard Calvi and his Orchestra ('to remind me of Marseilles').

iii. 'Aurora' by the Andrews Sisters, chosen because it would remind Benny of his days as ASM with Harry Benet's company, especially of his stage debut at East Ham Palace.

iv. 'With Every Breath I Take' by Bing Crosby, described by Benny as 'our tune' when speaking of his pubescent 'relationship' with the girl at Eastleigh Carnival ('I don't think I could ever love anybody the way I loved this girl').

v. 'Le Gamin d'Paris' by Yves Montand ('because the happiest moments of my life have been spent in that wonderful city of Paris').

vi. 'Lullaby of the Leaves' by the BBC Dance Orchestra directed by Henry Hall, a reminder of childhood nights with his family on Southampton Pier.

vii. 'Would You' by Frank Chacksfield and his Orchestra, often sung by his Auntie Louie.

viii. Vaughan Williams' 'Fantasia on Greensleeves' by the Philharmonic Promenade Orchestra conducted by Sir Adrian Boult ('I think this is so English – to me, it's the New Forest and St Catherine's Hill [Winchester] and green fields – it's just England').

Asked to nominate one of the eight as his ultimate choice he plumped for 'Greensleeves'. His chosen book was an imaginary one: 'An international language course, all the languages, so I could sit and learn them', and his one luxury item was 'A cine-camera . . . to make some interesting films on the island' to which he could then add commentary in all the languages he had learned.

5 This was not the first colour footage of Benny Hill. In the summer of 1956 he was among a number of film/television/stage personalities engaged to model genuine historical costumes for a BBC TV series, *Men, Women and Clothes*. The six fifteen-minute programmes were devised and introduced by the plummy-voiced Doris Langley Moore from the Museum of Costume, in Eridge Castle, near Tunbridge Wells. This was the BBC's first ever stab at colour production, an event of such significance that the Queen Mother, personally known to Langley Moore, attended a preview screening. Along with Jeremy Hawk, Benny appeared in the third programme (subtitled 'Fashions in Faces and Figures'), wearing – among other things – an elaborate handlebar moustache. Although shown at the time in black-and-white (the edition with Benny went out on May 5 1957), the primary intention was to preserve the series for screening when colour television was introduced; it was never seen again, however, although it remains in the BBC archive.

6 This was held on June 23 1959 at the Palace Theatre, Manchester, in the presence of the Queen Mother. It was Benny's second Royal Command performance, the first being in 1955 (see Chapter 11). He also appeared in the 1960 event (May 16, at the Victoria Palace, London), which was the first to be televised.

7 The film was based on the Robert Storey play *Touch it Light* which had opened in London in February 1958; the roles were played then by Peter Jones and Robert Desmond respectively.

8 Though Schweppes was his first television commercial, Benny had previously appeared

in a number of print-media campaigns, beginning with advertisements for Stork margarine in early 1955.

13. 'A sweet-faced man; a most lovely, gentleman-like man'

1 Benny's most recent record, his second, was 'Who Done It?', recorded at Abbey Road and issued by Columbia (EMI) to tie in with the film. Like that movie's box-office takings, sales of the disc were pitiful – Benny's royalty cheques over two years amounted to just over £1.

2 While in Tripoli, Libya, on May 28 1961, Benny jointly presented an edition of the BBC Light Programme radio show *Three-Way Family Favourites*, reading out forces' record requests. This earned him an additional twenty-five guineas.

3 Correspondence in BBC files alludes to an American 'showing' of one of these two Benny Hill programmes at this time, but offers no further details. Whether this was a private screening for executives or a television broadcast has not been possible to prove, and Richard Stone was unable to remember.

4 In Britain, this particular programme was held 'in the can' for almost a year owing to Benny's exclusive arrangement with the BBC. It was shown by ITV under the banner *Bernard Delfont's Sunday Show* on July 15 1962.

5 His screen wife, played by Sylvia Tysick, and her mother, played by Doris Hare.

6 *Daily Sketch*, October 7 1967.

14. The Rejected Director

1 The two editions of *Spotlight* in which Benny Hill appeared were headlined, respectively, by the singers Abbe Lane and Paul Anka. In his brief sketches Benny was supported in the first show by Patricia Hayes and Julian Orchard and in the second by Hayes, Jeremy Hawk, Ronnie Brody (often in Benny's 1950s TV shows) and – in the hope of resurrecting their 'affair' – Annette André. One of the pieces was a reprise of the Lady Godiva sketch from *Fine Fettle*. ('He liked perfection and was tough to work for – there were no favours,' André remembers.) The shows were screened in Britain by the still monochrome ITV on October 8 1967 and April 14 (Easter Day) 1968. In between these, as part of Lew Grade's shrewd contract negotiation, Benny also had to appear in his own hour-long ATV special, *The Benny Hill Show*, screened by ITV on Boxing Day 1967. Dorita y Pepe provided some music and Nicholas Parsons, Rita Webb, the splendidly thick Arthur Mullard and Dave Freeman supported in the sketches. 'He asked me if I'd do a Layabouts sketch for old times' sake,' says Freeman. 'I was a grandfather by this time but played a teenager hanging about outside a dance-hall!'

2 Benny had used this idea in *The Lonely One*, his excellent contribution to the BBC's 1964 *Christmas Night with the Stars*. On that occasion the heavy-handed crew had accidentally caused water damage to the flat rented for the filming.

3 From his script for *The Benny Hill Show*, February 6 1980.

4 *Sunday Mirror*, February 20 1972.

5 Following the success of 'Ernie', Benny appeared in TV commercials for the dairy company Unigate, advertising its Farmer's Wife bread. This entailed, once more, donning a milkman's uniform and clambering aboard a (now mechanized) float. Just like old times.

6 It has been suggested that 'Ernie' is a crib of an American comedy single by Frank Gallop, 'The Ballad of Irving (the 142nd Fastest Gun in the West)', a US hit in 1966. The songs are dissimilar in numerous respects, however, and Benny Hill's was composed, at least substantially, in or before 1956. As Gallop's record was itself a pastiche of a 1964 American number one – 'Ringo' by the actor Lorne Greene – at most Benny could be said to have been spoofing the entire genre.

7 This was during a technicians' dispute over payments for working colour cameras. Three *Benny Hill Show*s were affected by this dispute; although they remain in the archive they have never formed part of Thames' sales or repeat packages.

4. Up and Down

15. As Grateful as Hell

1 A BBC1 *Play for Today* in October 1971.

2 *Daily Mail*, November 23 1970.

3 Quote from *TVTimes Extra – Christmas with the Stars*, published 1969.

16. Global TV's Top Banana

1 Actually fourteen of the first seventeen shows – the three black-and-white programmes were excluded from consideration, which disappointed Benny as he felt they contained good material.

2 When Caesar had made a BBC series in 1958 his straightman was also Benny Hill's – Jeremy Hawk.

3 Beatrice Lillie was a Canadian-born British singer and revue comedienne who became a huge success on Broadway in the 1920s.

4 Wolcott was not the only writer to make this comparison. A French journalist once described Benny's cheeks as 'deux seins sans points' – two bosoms without nipples.

5 Issue dated May 31–June 6 1980.

17. The Political Football

1 Carter died in Birmingham in May 1977, aged sixty, having latterly descended the scale, from directing West End shows to becoming director of the low-budget ATV soap-opera *Crossroads*. 'Benny and I were about the only two show-business people who went to the funeral,' recalls Richard Stone. 'It was really rather sad.'

2 Benny never spoke publicly about politics, and had no particular allegiances. His attitude, according to Henry McGee, was 'A pox on both your houses.' He was, incidentally, taken on a tour of the House of Commons in the company of Dave Freeman and the Labour MP Bessie Braddock, just prior to the 1964 General Election. 'Before she showed us around we had lunch in the dining-room,' says Freeman, 'and Sir Winston Churchill, who recognized Benny, came over to say hello and have a few words.'

3 *The Benny Hill Show*, April 25 1984.

4 *The Benny Hill Show*, March 12 1986.

5 *The Benny Hill Show*, March 16 1983.

6 Laurel and Hardy's well-known producer had visited England with a view to remaking some of their films with British comedians. Stone took Hal Roach around England in his car, and introduced him to Benny. The project never reached fruition. Years later, Roach was asked during a campus lecture in America if any modern comic measured up to the greats of the past, and he replied, 'I guess there's only one – Benny Hill. But I sure wish he'd clean up his act.'

7 While Benny Hill had become a huge success in America without lifting a finger, Bruce Forsyth – always desperate to be a star there – never quite succeeded, despite mounting his one-man stage show on Broadway and in Hollywood, and hosting a TV game-show.

8 Interviewed for the Channel 4 series *Heroes of Comedy*.

9 This event was organized by the National Academy of Television Arts and Sciences. A previous New York event, not attended by Benny, was *A Tribute to Thames Television*, which ran at the Museum of Broadcasting for three months over 1984–5. A compilation of *The Benny Hill Show* was among the programmes shown, as was – almost certainly at Benny's suggestion – *Eddie in August*, the one and only screening in America of his pet project.

18. The End

1 Thames launched in 1968 – the twenty-five-year figure included Jones's tenure at ABC.

2 Benny Hill made just one appearance on *This is Your Life* – for Bob Todd, screened in February 1984.

3 The close friendship of Richard Stone and Philip Jones – they went fishing together every Friday for twenty years – was another of Benny's problems with his agent. 'He implied that I was too friendly with Philip,' says Stone, 'and that therefore I was looking after Thames' interests and not his. It wasn't true. The truth is, it was a wonderful trio, all three of us working towards the same goal.'

19. The After Life

1 There had been little affection between Richard Stone and John Howard Davies for some years before this. Davies had been at public school with Stone's sons and there may have been a hangover from that period; Davies acknowledges that when he was at the BBC he found it difficult to have a good working relationship with the agent, and when he took over at Thames he says that Stone was expecting to continue certain customs he had enjoyed with Philip Jones, like watching the show being recorded from the comfort of his Teddington office. Davies says that he 'withdrew that privilege'. But he emphatically rules out any possibility that any of this played a part in his decision to let Benny Hill go.

2 From *Clown Imperial*, an *Omnibus* programme shown by BBC1 on December 20 1991.

3 Through Anne Ling, Benny made his first appearances on BBC radio for twenty-five years in 1991, when he was twice a gently spoken panellist in the Radio 2 light-hearted nostalgia quiz *On the Air*. Ling was PA to the producer. He also turned up at this time on the pop station Radio 1, in a vacuous interview with DJ Steve Wright.

4 This account is from an amateur video recording made by Harry Segal shortly before his own death, in which he related incidents from his friendship with Benny.

Benny Hill on Stage

Benny Hill worked on stage solidly for more than a decade from 1947 and this list details only a small fraction of his extensive itineraries, reflecting the most noteworthy engagements. No precise information is available for his working-men's club, concert, cabaret and private bookings.

1940
October 27: Town Hall, Eastleigh
December 1: Southern Railway Institute, Eastleigh

1941
August 11–December 6: *Follow the Fun* touring Variety revue (a Harry Benet production)
December 26–January 31 1942: *Robinson Crusoe* pantomime, Pavilion, Bournemouth (Harry Benet)

1942
March 16–November 20: *Send Him Victorious* touring Variety revue (Harry Benet)

1946–7
Stars in Battledress performances in Europe, including a play (*Happy Week-end!*) and Variety (*It's All in Fun*)

1947
September 1–6: week in Variety at Camberwell Palace, London
September 29–October 4: week in Variety at Playhouse, Weston-super-Mare
November 14/15: *Spotlight* revue, Twentieth Century Theatre, London
November 24–29: week in Variety at Collins' Music Hall, London

1948

Touring in weekly Variety

April 12–17: week in Variety at Playhouse, Weston-super-Mare

May 24–29: week in Variety at Kilburn Empire, London

June 11–October 2: *Gaytime*, Lido Theatre, Cliftonville

December 21–February 13 1949: *The Boltons Revue 1948–49*, Boltons Theatre, London

1949

February 14–19: *The Boltons Revue 1948–49*, Theatre Royal, Brighton

Touring in weekly Variety

May 28–October 1: *Gaytime*, Cosy Nook Theatre, Newquay

October 10–December 10: *Montmartre* touring Variety revue

December 26–January 14 1950: *Aladdin* pantomime, Richmond Theatre, Richmond, Surrey

1950

Touring in weekly Variety

May 26–October 7: *Gaytime*, Lido Theatre, Cliftonville

Touring in weekly Variety

1951

February 26–April 21: *Sky High* touring Variety revue

Christmas–January 1952: *Dick Whittington* pantomime, Devonshire Park Theatre, Eastbourne

1952

March: *Anything Goes* touring Variety revue (West Country venues)

May–June: *Folies Bergère* touring Variety revue

June 26–September 20: *The Big Show*, Granville Theatre, Ramsgate

Touring in weekly Variety

1953

Touring in weekly Variety, including revues *A Little Bit of Heaven* and *Jane Comes to Town*

1954

Touring in weekly Variety

October 4–November 13: *The Benny Hill Show* touring Variety revue

1955

March 14–April 2: *The Benny Hill Show* touring Variety revue

April 9 onwards: *Paris by Night*, Prince of Wales Theatre, London [until September 1956]

November 7: Royal Variety Show, Victoria Palace, London

1956

Until September 8: *Paris by Night*, Prince of Wales Theatre, London

November 19–December 8: *The Dave King Show*, Hippodrome Theatre, London (deputizing for Dave King)

1957

May 13–25: *Light Up the Town*, Empire Theatre, Nottingham

June 7–September 28: *Light Up the Town*, Wellington Pier Pavilion, Great Yarmouth

1958

June 9–14: *Light Up the Town*, Globe Theatre, Stockton-on-Tees

June 16–September 20: *Light Up the Town*, Floral Hall, Scarborough

1959

June 23: Royal Variety Show, Palace Theatre, Manchester

July 14–25: *Fine Fettle*, Palace Theatre, Manchester

July 28–August 1: *Fine Fettle*, Theatre Royal, Nottingham

August 6 onwards: *Fine Fettle*, Palace Theatre, London [until January 1960]

1960

Until January 9: *Fine Fettle*, Palace Theatre, London

May 16: Royal Variety Show, Victoria Palace, London

July 14–30: *Let's Make a Night of It*, Pavilion Theatre, Weymouth

October 30: Lord Mayor's Command Performance, Town Hall, Sydney, Australia

1961
May: Middle East troop tour of Cyprus, Malta, North Africa (including Libya)

1984
November 9: *Bring Me Sunshine*, London Palladium

1987
March 26: *Salute to Thames*, The Alice Tully Hall, Lincoln Center, New York City, USA

Benny Hill's Appearances on British Radio

	b'cast	station	programme title	rec/live	from	producer	miscellaneous
1	3/9/1947	Light	Variety Roundabout	live	Camberwell Palace	Eric Spear	
2	5/10/1947	Light	Variety Bandbox	live	People's Palace	Joy Russell-Smith	
3	25/10/1947	Light	Beginners, Please!	live	Aeolian	Roy Speer	
–	n/a	n/a	Get Going	19/12/1947	Paris	Pat Dixon	trial rec, not broadcast
4	14/11/1948	Home	Works Wonders	live	Aspro factory, Slough	Brian Johnston	
–	n/a	n/a	Listen, My Children	24/3/1948	Camden	Pat Dixon	trial rec, not broadcast
5	1/6/1948	Home	Listen, My Children	8/5/1948	Camden	Pat Dixon	*
6	8/6/1948	Home	Listen, My Children	8/5/1948	Camden	Pat Dixon	*
7	15/6/1948	Home	Listen, My Children	15/5/1948	Camden	Pat Dixon	*
8	22/6/1948	Home	Listen, My Children	22/5/1948	Camden	Pat Dixon	*
9	29/6/1948	Home	Listen, My Children	29/5/1948	Camden	Pat Dixon	*
10	6/7/1948	Home	Listen, My Children	30/5/1948	Camden	Pat Dixon	*
11	13/7/1948	Home	Listen, My Children	5/6/1948	Camden	Pat Dixon	*
12	20/7/1948	Home	Listen, My Children	5/6/1948	Camden	Pat Dixon	*
13	11/10/1948	Home	Starlight Hour	live	Aeolian	Roy Speer	*
14	18/10/1948	Home	Starlight Hour	live	Aeolian	Roy Speer	*
15	25/10/1948	Home	Starlight Hour	live	Aeolian	Roy Speer	*
16	1/11/1948	Home	Starlight Hour	live	Aeolian	Roy Speer	*
17	8/11/1948	Home	Starlight Hour	live	Aeolian	Roy Speer	*
18	15/11/1948	Home	Starlight Hour	live	Aeolian	Roy Speer	*
19	22/11/1948	Home	Starlight Hour	live	Aeolian	Roy Speer	*
20	29/11/1948	Home	Starlight Hour	live	Aeolian	Roy Speer	*
21	6/12/1948	Home	Starlight Hour	live	Paris	Roy Speer	*
22	13/12/1948	Home	Starlight Hour	live	Paris	Roy Speer	*
23	20/12/1948	Home	Starlight Hour	19/12/1948	Kilburn Empire	Roy Speer	*
24	26/1/1949	Third	Third Division	6/12/1948	Camden	Pat Dixon	*

No.	Date	Network	Title	Date	Venue	Broadcast	Producer	
25	2/2/1949	Third	Third Division	8/12/1948	Camden		Pat Dixon	*
26	9/2/1949	Third	Third Division	11/12/1948	Camden		Pat Dixon	*
27	16/2/1949	Third	Third Division	16/12/1948	Camden		Pat Dixon	*
28	23/2/1949	Third	Third Division	18/12/1948	Camden		Pat Dixon	*
29	2/3/1949	Third	Third Division	29/12/1948	Camden		Pat Dixon	*
30	27/3/1949	Light	Variety Bandbox		Kilburn Empire	live	Bryan Sears	@
31	19/4/1949	Home	The April Revue		Aeolian	14/4/1949	Pat Dixon	
32	17/5/1949	Home	The May Revue		Paris	13/5/1949	Pat Dixon	*
33	5/6/1949	Light	Variety Bandbox		Kilburn Empire	live	Bryan Sears	*
34	29/7/1949	Home	Petticoat Lane		Paris	24/7/1949	Pat Dixon	
35	5/8/1949	Home	Petticoat Lane		Kings Theatre	31/7/1949	Charles Chilton	
36	12/8/1949	Home	Petticoat Lane		Kings Theatre	7/8/1949	Charles Chilton	
37	19/8/1949	Home	Petticoat Lane		Kings Theatre	14/8/1949	Charles Chilton	
38	26/8/1949	Home	Petticoat Lane		Kings Theatre	21/8/1949	Charles Chilton	
39	2/9/1949	Home	Petticoat Lane		Kings Theatre	28/8/1949	Charles Chilton	
40	9/9/1949	Home	Petticoat Lane		Kings Theatre	4/9/1949	Charles Chilton	
41	16/9/1949	Home	Petticoat Lane		Kings Theatre	11/9/1949	Pat Dixon	
42	21/9/1949	Home	Petticoat Lane		Aeolian	18/9/1949	Pat Dixon	
43	28/9/1949	Home	Petticoat Lane		Aeolian	25/9/1949	Pat Dixon	
44	5/10/1949	Home	Petticoat Lane		Aeolian	2/10/1949	Pat Dixon	
45	12/10/1949	Home	Petticoat Lane		Aeolian	9/10/1949	Pat Dixon	
46	19/10/1949	Home	Petticoat Lane		People's Palace	16/10/1949	Pat Dixon	
47	26/10/1949	Home	Petticoat Lane		People's Palace	23/10/1949	Pat Dixon	
48	2/11/1949	Home	Petticoat Lane		People's Palace	30/10/1949	Pat Dixon	
49	9/11/1949	Home	Petticoat Lane		People's Palace	6/11/1949	Pat Dixon	
50	24/1/1950	Home	First House – Look Who's Here!		Piccadilly	live	John Hooper	
51	29/1/1950	Light	Variety Bandbox		Camberwell Palace	live	Bryan Sears	
52	24/2/1950	Home	Up – and Coming!		Aeolian	live	Dennis Main Wilson	
53	4/4/1950	Home	First House – Look Who's Here!		Piccadilly	live	John Hooper	
54	21/4/1950	Home	First House Presents		Aeolian	live	Dennis Main Wilson	

	b'cast	station	programme title	rec/live	from	producer	miscellaneous
55	30/4/1950	Light	Variety Bandbox	live	Camberwell Palace	Bryan Sears	double-act with Reg Varney
56	21/7/1950	Light	Summer Showtime	16/7/1950	Winter Gardens, Margate	John Ellison	
57	8/10/1950	Light	Variety Bandbox	live	Kings Theatre	Bryan Sears	double-act with Reg Varney
58	6/11/1950	Home	Henry Hall's Guest Night	live	Paris	Alastair Scott-Johnston	
59	14/11/1950	Home	Workers' Playtime	live	Harding, Tilton & Hartley Ltd, Taunton	Duncan Wood	
60	15/12/1950	Home (West)	Western Music-Hall	10/12/1950	CWS Hall, Bristol	Duncan Wood	double-act with Reg Varney
61	14/2/1951	Home	Henry Hall's Guest Night	live	Playhouse	Alastair Scott-Johnston	
62	10/3/1951	Home	Music-Hall	4/3/1951	Aeolian	Bill Worsley	double-act with Reg Varney
63	22/3/1951	Home (West)	Western Music-Hall	11/3/1951	CWS Hall, Bristol	Duncan Wood	
64	6/6/1951	Home (West)	Western Music-Hall	27/5/1951	Victoria Rooms, Bristol	Duncan Wood	
65	17/7/1951	Home	Workers' Playtime	live	Forum Cinema, Jersey	Duncan Wood	
66	19/7/1951	Home	Workers' Playtime	live	Odeon Cinema, Guernsey	Duncan Wood	
67	2/8/1951	Light	Happy-Go-Lucky	28/7/1951	Paris	Roy Speer	*
68	15/8/1951	Home & Light	Variety Ahoy!	15/7/1951	HMS Heron, Yeovilton	Duncan Wood	
69	22/9/1951	Home	Calling All Forces	15/9/1951	Playhouse	Leslie Bridgmont/ Frank Hooper	*
70	26/9/1951	Home	Henry Hall's Guest Night	live	Playhouse	Alastair Scott-Johnston	
71	31/10/1951	Home	Henry Hall's Guest Night	live	Playhouse	Alastair Scott-Johnston	

No.	Rec date	Station	Programme	Bc date	Location	Producer	trial rec, not broadcast
–	n/a	n/a	Anything Goes	24/10/1951	HMS Heron, Yeovilton	Duncan Wood	
72	12/11/1951	Light	Happy-Go-Lucky	11/11/1951	Paris	Roy Speer / John Hooper	*
73	17/11/1951	Light	Golden Slipper Club	live	Paris	Leslie Bridgmont/ Frank Hooper	*
74	2/12/1951	Light	Calling All Forces	1/12/1951	Playhouse	Duncan Wood	
75	3/12/1951	Home (West)	Anything Goes	25/11/1951	RN Hospital, Haslar, nr Gosport	Duncan Wood	
76	4/12/1951	Home (London/West)	Variety Ahoy!	21/10/1951	RN Barracks, Devonport	Duncan Wood	
77	10/12/1951	Home (West)	Anything Goes	2/12/1951	Waller Barracks, Devizes	Duncan Wood	
78	17/12/1951	Home (West)	Anything Goes	9/12/1951	RAF Station, Hullavington	Duncan Wood	
79	20/12/1951	Home	Workers' Playtime	live	Martin Webb Ltd, Darlaston	Philip Garston-Jones	
80	24/12/1951	Home (West)	Anything Goes	10/12/1951	Blandford Camp	Duncan Wood	
81	31/12/1951	Home (West)	Anything Goes	16/12/1951	Royal Naval Barracks, Devonport	Duncan Wood	
82	7/1/1952	Home (West)	Anything Goes	30/12/1951	RAF Yatesbury	Duncan Wood	
83	14/1/1952	Home (West)	Anything Goes	6/1/1952	Houndstone Army Camp, nr Yeovil	Duncan Wood	
84	22/1/1952	Home (West)	Anything Goes	13/1/1952	HMS Collingwood, nr Fareham	Duncan Wood	
85	29/1/1952	Home (West)	Anything Goes	20/1/1952	RN Barracks, Portsmouth	Duncan Wood	
86	5/2/1952	Home (West)	Anything Goes	27/1/1952	RAF Lyneham	Duncan Wood	
87	12/2/1952	Home (West)	Anything Goes	10/2/1952	RAF Watchet	Duncan Wood	
88	18/2/1952	Home	Up – and Coming!	live	Paris	Alastair Scott-Johnston	
89	21/2/1952	Light	Anything Goes	17/2/1952	Bristol studio	Duncan Wood	

	b'cast	station	programme title	rec/live	from	producer	miscellaneous
90	22/2/1952	Home	Workers' Playtime	live	Ultra Electric Ltd, Acton, London	John Ellison	
91	28/2/1952	Light	Anything Goes	25/2/1952	Bristol studio	Duncan Wood	
92	6/3/1952	Light	Anything Goes	2/3/1952	Bristol studio	Duncan Wood	
93	20/3/1952	Light	Anything Goes	9/3/1952	Bristol studio	Duncan Wood	
94	27/3/1952	Light	Anything Goes	16/3/1952	Bristol studio	Duncan Wood	
95	2/4/1952	Home	Henry Hall's Guest Night	live	Playhouse	Alastair Scott-Johnston	
96	3/4/1952	Light	Anything Goes	23/3/1952	Bristol studio	Duncan Wood	
97	15/4/1952	Home	Workers' Playtime	live	N J Esthoven & Sons Ltd, Rotherhithe, London	John Ellison	
98	1/5/1952	Light	Variety Fanfare	28/4/1952	Radio Industries Exhibition, City Hall, Manchester	Ronnie Taylor	
99	10/5/1952	Home	Music-Hall	4/5/1952	Collins' Music Hall	Bill Worsley	
100	25/5/1952	Light	Variety Bandbox	live	Kings Theatre	John Foreman	@
101	11/6/1952	Home	Henry Hall's Guest Night	live	Playhouse	Alastair Scott-Johnston	
102	19/6/1952	Light	Variety Fanfare	15/6/1952	Hulme Hippodrome, Manchester	Ronnie Taylor	
103	8/7/1952	Light	Variety Fanfare	6/7/1952	Hulme Hippodrome, Manchester	Ronnie Taylor	
104	22/7/1952	Home	Variety Road Show	20/7/1952	RAF Watchet	Duncan Wood	
105	29/7/1952	Light	Variety Fanfare	27/7/1952	Hulme Hippodrome, Manchester	Ronnie Taylor	
106	3/8/1952	Light	Summer Showtime	live	Ramsgate	John Ellison	
107	13/8/1952	Home	Henry Hall's Guest Night	13/8/1952	Paris	Alastair Scott-Johnston	

No.	Date	Network	Programme	Broadcast	Venue	Producer	
108	19/8/1952	Light	Variety Fanfare	17/8/1952	Hulme Hippodrome, Manchester	Ronnie Taylor	
109	23/9/1952	Light	Variety Fanfare	21/9/1952	Hulme Hippodrome, Manchester	Ronnie Taylor	@
110	29/9/1952	Home	The Spice of Life	26/9/1952	RAF Wilmslow	Ronnie Taylor	
111	8/10/1952	Home	Henry Hall's Guest Night	8/10/1952	Playhouse	Alastair Scott-Johnston	
112	9/10/1952	Home (North/Northern Ireland)	A Date with Benny	live	Palais-de-Danse, Ashton-under-Lyme	Alick Hayes	
113	16/10/1952	Home (North/Northern Ireland)	A Date with Benny	live	Palais-de-Danse, Ashton-under-Lyme	Alick Hayes	
114	24/10/1952	Light	Variety Fanfare	19/10/1952	Hulme Hippodrome, Manchester	Ronnie Taylor	
115	4/11/1952	Home	Workers' Playtime	live	British Sailors Society, Commercial Road, London	Bill Gates	
116	14/11/1952	Light	Variety Fanfare	9/11/1952	Hulme Hippodrome, Manchester	Ronnie Taylor	@
117	2/12/1952	Home	Workers' Playtime	live	W D & H O Wills' factory, Swindon	Duncan Wood	
118	9/12/1952	Light	The Forces Show	6/12/1952	Paris	Leslie Bridgmont/Frank Hooper	
119	26/12/1952	Light	Variety Fanfare	7/12/1952	Hulme Hippodrome, Manchester	Ronnie Taylor	
120	3/1/1953	Home	The Star Show	28/12/1952	Playhouse	Tom Ronald/Michael North	
121	9/1/1953	Home (West)	Debut	1/1/1953	CWS Hall, Bristol	Duncan Wood	
122	16/1/1953	Home (West)	Debut	8/1/1953	CWS Hall, Bristol	Duncan Wood	
123	23/1/1953	Home (West)	Debut	16/1/1953	CWS Hall, Bristol	Duncan Wood	
124	23/1/1953	Light	Variety Fanfare	18/1/1953	Hulme Hippodrome, Manchester	Ronnie Taylor	
125	30/1/1953	Home (West)	Debut	22/1/1953	CWS Hall, Bristol	Duncan Wood	

b'cast	station	programme title	rec/live	from	producer	miscellaneous
126 3/2/1953	Home (Wales)	Talent Theatre	27/1/1953	Alhambra Cinema, Shotton	Mai Jones	
127 6/2/1953	Home (West)	Debut	29/1/1953	CWS Hall, Bristol	Duncan Wood	
128 13/2/1953	Home (West)	Debut	5/2/1953	CWS Hall, Bristol	Duncan Wood	
129 20/2/1953	Home (West)	Debut	13/2/1953	CWS Hall, Bristol	Duncan Wood	
130 20/2/1953	Light	Variety Fanfare	15/2/1953	Hulme Hippodrome, Manchester	Ronnie Taylor	
131 27/2/1953	Home (West)	Debut	19/2/1953	CWS Hall, Bristol	Duncan Wood	
132 6/3/1953	Light	Variety Fanfare	22/2/1953	Hulme Hippodrome, Manchester	Ronnie Taylor	
133 13/3/1953	Home	Midday Music-Hall	live	Playhouse	Trafford Whitelock	
134 n/a	n/a	Variety Ahoy!	23/3/1953	RN Barracks, Portsmouth	John Foreman	@
135 n/a	n/a	Variety Ahoy!	23/3/1953	RN Barracks, Portsmouth	John Foreman	@
136 7/4/1953	Home	Workers' Playtime	2/4/1953	Fawley Refinery, Southampton	Duncan Wood	
137 10/4/1953	Home (North)	Danger is Our Business	27/3/1953	Manchester studio	Alick Hayes	The Case of the Stolen Car
138 17/4/1953	Home (North)	Danger is Our Business	10/4/1953	Manchester studio	Alick Hayes	A Case of Kidnapping
139 21/4/1953	Home	Top Flight	15/4/1953	RAF White Waltham, nr Maidenhead	Bill Gates	
140 24/4/1953	Home (North)	Danger is Our Business	17/4/1953	Manchester studio	Alick Hayes	The Missing Landscape
141 1/5/1953	Home (North)	Danger is Our Business	24/4/1953	Manchester studio	Alick Hayes	The Case of the Missing Bridesmaid
142 2/5/1953	Home	Variety Playhouse	26/4/1953	Playhouse	Tom Ronald	
143 8/5/1953	Home (North)	Danger is Our Business	30/4/1953	Manchester studio	Alick Hayes	Murder on Two Wheels
144 15/5/1953	Home (North)	Danger is Our Business	10/5/1953	Manchester studio	Alick Hayes	The Painted Lady
145 20/5/1953	Home	Midday Music-Hall	live	Paris	Trafford Whitelock	

146	22/5/1953	Home (North)	Danger is Our Business	17/5/1953	Manchester studio	Alick Hayes	The Seeing Eye
147	29/5/1953	Home (North)	Danger is Our Business	24/5/1953	Manchester studio	Alick Hayes	The Big Top Mystery
148	30/5/1953	Home (West)	Variety Cavalcade	19/4/1953	CWS Hall, Bristol	Duncan Wood	
149	2/7/1953	Light	Show Band Show	live	Paris	Johnnie Stewart	
150	9/7/1953	Home	Workers' Playtime	8/7/1953	YMCA marquee, Royal Show Ground, Blackpool	Philip Robinson	
151	22/7/1953	Home	Midday Music-Hall	live	Playhouse	Trafford Whitelock	
152	13/10/1953	Home	Workers' Playtime	live	Betteshanger Colliery, nr Deal	Bill Gates	
153	26/10/1953	Home	Midday Music-Hall	live	Playhouse	Trafford Whitelock	
154	6/11/1953	Light	Variety Fanfare	1/11/1953	Hulme Hippodrome, Manchester	Ronnie Taylor	
155	19/11/1953	Home	Workers' Playtime	live	Saxon Cotton Mill, Droylesden, Manchester	Philip Robinson	
156	23/11/1953	Light	Show Band Show	live	Paris	Johnnie Stewart	
157	27/11/1953	Light	Variety Fanfare	22/11/1953	Hulme Hippodrome, Manchester	Ronnie Taylor	
158	17/12/1953	Home	Workers' Playtime	live	Newton Bank Printworks, Hyde	Alan Clarke	
159	11/1/1954	Home	Midday Music-Hall	live	Playhouse	Trafford Whitelock	
160	2/2/1954	Home (North)	Variety Fanfare	10/1/1954	Hulme Hippodrome, Manchester	Ronnie Taylor	
161	8/2/1954	Home	Midday Music-Hall	live	Playhouse	Trafford Whitelock	
162	27/2/1954	Light	Golden Slipper Club	live	Paris	John Hooper	
163	13/3/1954	Home	Variety Playhouse	26/2/1954	Playhouse	Tom Ronald	
164	18/3/1954	Home	Workers' Playtime	live	RAF Finningley, Doncaster	Alan Clarke	
165	22/3/1954	Light	Show Band Show	live	Paris	Johnnie Stewart	
166	2/4/1954	Home	Henry Hall's Guest Night	2/4/1954	Playhouse	David Miller	

	b'cast	station	programme title	rec/live	from	producer	miscellaneous
167	24/4/1954	Home	Saturday Show	live	Paris	Johnnie Stewart	
168	1/5/1954	Home	Saturday Show	live	Paris	Johnnie Stewart	
169	4/5/1954	Home	Workers' Playtime	live	Martin Rubeck Ltd, Redhill	Bill Gates	
170	8/5/1954	Home	Saturday Show	live	Paris	Johnnie Stewart	
171	15/5/1954	Home	Saturday Show	live	Paris	Johnnie Stewart	
172	17/5/1954	Home	Midday Music-Hall	live	Playhouse	Trafford Whitelock	
173	22/5/1954	Home	Saturday Show	live	Paris	Johnnie Stewart	
174	29/5/1954	Home	Saturday Show	live	Paris	Johnnie Stewart	
175	10/6/1954	Light	Variety Fanfare	6/6/1954	Hulme Hippodrome, Manchester	Eric Miller	
176	24/6/1954	Home	Top Flight	17/6/1954	RAF Cardington, Bedford	Bill Gates	
177	26/6/1954	Home	Variety Playhouse	20/6/1954	Camden	Alastair Scott-Johnston	
178	27/7/1954	Home	Workers' Playtime	20/7/1954	Crystalate Ltd, Tonbridge	Bill Gates	
179	30/7/1954	Home	Henry Hall's Guest Night	30/7/1954	Playhouse	David Miller	
180	14/8/1954	Home	Variety Playhouse	8/8/1954	Camden	Bill Gates	
181	18/8/1954	Light	Blackpool Night	17/8/1954	Jubilee Theatre, Blackpool	Ronnie Taylor	
182	22/8/1954	Light	The Forces Show	live	Scala Theatre	Trafford Whitelock	*
183	23/8/1954	Home	I Hear Music!	21/8/1954	Aeolian	John Simmonds	
184	2/9/1954	Home	Workers' Playtime	live	Alfred Morris Furs Ltd, Shildon, County Durham	Geoffrey Wheeler	
–	n/a	n/a	Archie's the Boy!	26/9/1954	Paris	Roy Speer	trial rec, not broadcast
185	31/10/1954	Light	Top of the Town	live	Garrick Theatre	Bill Gates	

186	11/11/1954	Light	Archie's the Boy!	24/10/1954	Paris	Roy Speer	*
187	16/11/1954	Home	Workers' Playtime	live	British Legion Poppy Factory, Richmond, Surrey	Bill Gates	
188	18/11/1954	Light	Archie's the Boy!	7/11/1954	Paris	Roy Speer	*
189	18/11/1954	Home (West)	Star Turns	13/10/1954	Bristol studio	Duncan Wood	i/v by Cliff Michelmore
190	25/11/1954	Light	Archie's the Boy!	14/11/1954	Paris	Roy Speer	*
191	28/11/1954	GOS	On Stage – London	15/11/1954	Aeolian	John Hooper	
192	2/12/1954	Light	Archie's the Boy!	10/10/1954	Paris	Roy Speer	*
193	9/12/1954	Light	Archie's the Boy!	21/11/1954	Paris	Roy Speer	*
194	16/12/1954	Light	Archie's the Boy!	28/11/1954	Paris	Roy Speer	*
195	23/12/1954	Light	Archie's the Boy!	5/12/1954	Paris	Roy Speer	*
196	30/12/1954	Light	Archie's the Boy!	12/12/1954	Paris	Roy Speer	*@
197	6/1/1955	Light	Archie's the Boy!	19/12/1954	Paris	Roy Speer	*
198	13/1/1955	Light	Archie's the Boy!	2/1/1955	Paris	Roy Speer	*@
199	20/1/1955	Light	Archie's the Boy!	9/1/1955	Paris	Roy Speer	*@
200	25/1/1955	Home	Workers' Playtime	live	Woods Ltd, Brainwick, Colchester	Bill Gates	
201	27/1/1955	Light	Archie's the Boy!	16/1/1955	Paris	Roy Speer	*
202	3/2/1955	Light	Archie's the Boy!	23/1/1955	Paris	Roy Speer	*
203	10/2/1955	Light	Archie's the Boy!	30/1/1955	Paris	Roy Speer	*
204	17/2/1955	Light	Archie's the Boy!	6/2/1955	Paris	Roy Speer	*
205	19/2/1955	Light	Your Pied Piper	18/2/1955	Broadcasting House	Michael Bell	i/v by Eamonn Andrews deputizing for George Formby
206	20/2/1955	Light	Top of the Town	live	Garrick Theatre	Bill Gates	
207	24/2/1955	Light	Archie's the Boy!	13/2/1955	Paris	Roy Speer	*
208	3/3/1955	Light	Archie's the Boy!	20/2/1955	Paris	Roy Speer	*
209	10/3/1955	Light	Archie's the Boy!	27/2/1955	Paris	Roy Speer	*
210	17/3/1955	Light	Archie's the Boy!	6/3/1955	Paris	Roy Speer	*
211	24/3/1955	Light	Archie's the Boy!	13/3/1955	Paris	Roy Speer	*
212	26/3/1955	Home	Variety Playhouse	6/3/1955	Kings Theatre	Tom Ronald	
213	14/6/1955	Home	Starstruck	29/5/1955	Paris	Pat Dixon	*

b'cast	station	programme title	rec/live	from	producer	miscellaneous
214 25/6/1955	Home	Variety Playhouse	12/6/1955	Playhouse	Tom Ronald	i/v by Rex Palmer
215 10/7/1955	Light	These Radio Times	24/1/1955	Broadcasting House	Alfred Dunning	
216 13/11/1955	Light	Royal Variety Show	7/11/1955	Victoria Palace	Brian Johnston	
217 28/12/1955	Light	Woman's Hour	live	Broadcasting House	Antony Derville	i/v by Jean Metcalfe
218 4/2/1956	Light	Your Pied Piper	3/2/1956	Broadcasting House	Michael Bell	i/v by Eamonn Andrews
219 24/2/1956	Home	Henry Hall's Guest Night	24/2/1956	Paris	John Simmonds	
220 24/4/1956	Home	Workers' Playtime	live	R S Murray & Co, Millwall, London	Bill Gates	
221 10/6/1956	Light	Calling the Stars	live	Camden	Alastair Scott-Johnston	
222 13/7/1956	Home	Henry Hall's Guest Night	13/7/1956	Paris	John Simmonds	
223 25/8/1956	Home	Henry Hall's Guest Night	23/8/1956	Radio Exhibition, Earls Court, London	John Simmonds	
224 12/10/1956	Home	Henry Hall's Guest Night	12/10/1956	Paris	John Simmonds	
225 17/11/1956	Home	Variety Playhouse	29/10/1956	Playhouse	Tom Ronald	
226 3/12/1956	Home	Midday Music-Hall	live	Playhouse	Bill Worsley	
227 16/4/1957	Home	Workers' Playtime	live	Sperry Gyroscope Ltd, Brentford	Bill Gates	
228 14/7/1957	Light	Yes! It's Great Yarmouth	20/6/1957	Windmill Theatre, Great Yarmouth	Charles Chilton	
229 9/2/1958	Light	Follow the Stars	9/2/1958	Paris	John Simmonds	
230 4/6/1958	Light	Variety Ahoy!	7/5/1958	HMS Victorious, Portsmouth	Bill Gates	
231 27/7/1958	Light	On Stage – Scarborough	23/7/1958	Spa Theatre, Scarborough	Eric Miller	

No.	Date	Station	Programme	Date	Venue	Personnel	Notes
232	21/1/1959	Light	Roundabout	20/1/1959	Cecil Sharpe House	Vernon Harris/Trafford Whitelock	i/v by Roy Bradford
233	28/6/1959	Light	Royal Variety Show	23/6/1959	Palace Theatre, Manchester	Roy Speer	
234	16/11/1959	Home	Desert Island Discs	30/10/1959	Broadcasting House	Monica Chapman	i/v by Roy Plomley
235	15/12/1959	Light	Workers' Playtime	9/12/1959	Mount Pleasant Post Office, London	Bill Gates	
236	18/5/1960	Light	Royal Variety Show	16/5/1960	Victoria Palace	Arthur Phillips	
237	31/12/1960	Home	Variety Playhouse	18/12/1960	Playhouse	Alastair Scott-Johnston	
238	4/2/1961	Home	In Town Today	2/2/1961	Four Feathers Club, London	Peter Duncan	i/v by Tony Bilbow
239	n/a	Transcription (Pacific Unit)	Report from London	17/2/1961	Queen's Gate	John Laird	@ i/v by John Laird
240	28/5/1961	Light	Three-Way Family Favourites	live	Tripoli, Libya	Douglas Lawrence	reading record-requests
241	3/6/1961	Light	Saturday Club	live	Broadcasting House	Jimmy Grant	i/v by Brian Matthew
242	10/6/1961	Home	Holiday Music-Hall	4/6/1961	Playhouse	Bill Worsley	
243	22/7/1961	Home	Holiday Music-Hall	4/6/1961	Playhouse	Bill Worsley	
244	4/11/1961	Home	Variety Playhouse	29/10/1961	Playhouse	Alastair Scott-Johnston	
245	11/11/1961	Home	Variety Playhouse	5/11/1961	Playhouse	Alastair Scott-Johnston	
246	18/11/1961	Home	Variety Playhouse	12/11/1961	Playhouse	Alastair Scott-Johnston	
247	25/11/1961	Home	Variety Playhouse	19/11/1961	Playhouse	Alastair Scott-Johnston	
248	9/12/1961	Light	Saturday Club	live	Broadcasting House	Jimmy Grant	i/v by Brian Matthew
249	28/5/1962	Light	Music-Hall	live	Playhouse	Bill Gates	
250	28/3/1963	Light	Star Parade – The Benny Hill Show	11/2/1963	Playhouse	Eric Miller	
251	7/5/1963	Light	Pop Inn	live	Paris	Derek Chinnery	i/v by Keith Fordyce

b'cast	station	programme title	rec/live	from	producer	miscellaneous
252 30/5/1963	Light	Star Parade – The Benny Hill Show	11/3/1963	Playhouse	John Browell	
253 22/6/1963	Light	Saturday Club	live	Broadcasting House	Jimmy Grant/ Bernie Andrews	i/v by Brian Matthew
254 14/7/1963	Light	The Billy Cotton Band Show	25/6/1963	Aeolian	John Browell	
255 25/8/1963	Light	Star Parade – The Benny Hill Show	6/7/1963	Paris	John Browell	
256 n/a	Light	The Public Ear	27/11/1963	Queen's Gate	John Fawcett Wilson	i/v by John Fawcett Wilson, not broadcast
257 19/1/1964	Light	Benny Steps In	14/1/1964	Playhouse	John Browell	deputizing for Tommy Steele
258 23/2/1964	Light	Benny Hill Time	4/11/1963	Paris	John Browell	@
259 1/3/1964	Light	Benny Hill Time	11/11/1963	Paris	John Browell	@
260 8/3/1964	Light	Benny Hill Time	18/11/1963	Paris	John Browell	@
261 15/3/1964	Light	Benny Hill Time	25/11/1963	Paris	John Browell	@
262 22/3/1964	Light	Benny Hill Time	2/12/1963	Paris	John Browell	@
263 29/3/1964	Light	Benny Hill Time	9/12/1963	Paris	John Browell	@
264 5/4/1964	Light	Benny Hill Time	16/12/1963	Paris	John Browell	@
265 12/4/1964	Light	Benny Hill Time	23/12/1963	Paris	John Browell	@
266 19/4/1964	Light	Benny Hill Time	30/12/1963	Paris	John Browell	@
267 26/4/1964	Light	Benny Hill Time	6/1/1964	Paris	John Browell	@
268 3/5/1964	Light	Benny Hill Time	13/1/1964	Paris	John Browell	@
269 10/5/1964	Light	Benny Hill Time	20/1/1964	Paris	John Browell	@
270 17/5/1964	Light	Benny Hill Time	27/1/1964	Paris	John Browell	@
271 1/1/1965	Light	Benny's Bandbox	21/1/1964	Playhouse	John Browell	
272 21/2/1965	Light	Benny Hill Time	20/12/1964	Paris	John Browell	@
273 28/2/1965	Light	Benny Hill Time	3/1/1965	Paris	John Browell	@
274 7/3/1965	Light	Benny Hill Time	10/1/1965	Paris	John Browell	@

No.	Date	Station	Programme	Broadcast	Location	Producer	Notes
275	14/3/1965	Light	Benny Hill Time	17/1/1965	Paris	John Browell	@
276	21/3/1965	Light	Benny Hill Time	24/1/1965	Paris	John Browell	@
277	28/3/1965	Light	Benny Hill Time	31/1/1965	Paris	John Browell	@
278	9/5/1965	Home	On Films	23/4/1965	Broadcasting House	George Angell	i/v by Philip Oakes
279	6/11/1965	Light	Late Night Saturday	live	Broadcasting House	Derek Chinnery	i/v by Pete Murray
280	9/11/1965	Light	Pop Inn	live	Paris	Derek Chinnery	i/v by Keith Fordyce
281	26/11/1965	Light	Late Night Extra	live	Broadcasting House	John Simmonds	i/v by Peter Haigh
282	11/12/1965	Light	Late Night Saturday	live	Broadcasting House	Derek Chinnery	i/v by Pete Murray
283	21/12/1965	Light	Pop Inn	live	Paris	Derek Chinnery	i/v by Keith Fordyce
284	29/1/1966	Light	A Look on the Lighter Side	28/1/1966	Broadcasting House	Steve Allen	i/v by George Martin
285	4/2/1966	Light	Late Night Extra	live	Broadcasting House	David Carter/ David Hatch	i/v by Peter Haigh
286	16/2/1966	Light	Woman's Hour	live	Broadcasting House	Teresa McGonagle	i/v by Marjorie Anderson
287	27/2/1966	Light	Benny Hill Time	30/1/1966	Paris	John Browell	@
288	6/3/1966	Light	Benny Hill Time	6/2/1966	Paris	John Browell	@
289	13/3/1966	Light	Benny Hill Time	13/2/1966	Paris	John Browell	@
290	14/3/1966	Home	Home This Afternoon: Turning Points	3/2/1966	Queen's Gate	Rosemary Hart	i/v by John Ellison
291	20/3/1966	Light	Benny Hill Time	20/2/1966	Paris	John Browell	@
292	27/3/1966	Light	Benny Hill Time	27/2/1966	Paris	John Browell	@
293	3/4/1966	Light	Benny Hill Time	6/3/1966	Paris	John Browell	@
294	10/4/1966	Light	Benny Hill Time	13/3/1966	Paris	John Browell	@
295	27/6/1967	Home	A Matter of Fact	15/6/1967	not known	George Angell	i/v by Gordon Watts
296	15/11/1968	Radio 1 & 2	Late Night Extra	live	Broadcasting House	David Carter	i/v by Terry Wogan
297	30/11/1968	Radio 1 & 2	Pete's Saturday People	live	Broadcasting House	John Billingham	i/v by Pete Murray
298	21/11/1971	Radio 4	The Best of British Laughs	14/9/1971	Broadcasting House	John Browell	i/v by Barry Took
299	11/12/1971	Radio 1	Scene and Heard	not known	not known	John Walters	i/v by Johnny Moran
300	9/1/1972	Radio Solent (local)	At Your Leisure	?/12/1971	Queen's Gate	Graham Freer	i/v by Graham Freer

b'cast	station	programme title	rec/live	from	producer	miscellaneous
301 11/7/1991	Radio 1	Steve Wright in the Afternoon	10/7/1991	Broadcasting House	Mike Wilkojc	i/v by Steve Wright and others
302 7/8/1991	Radio 2	On The Air	30/6/1991	Paris	Richard Edis	quiz-show panellist
303 4/9/1991	Radio 2	On The Air	30/6/1991	Paris	Richard Edis	quiz-show panellist

KEY

*	not written by Benny Hill
@	known to have been distributed on disc to subscribing overseas radio stations by the BBC Transcription Service
i/v	interviewed
n/a	not applicable

All recording venues/places of broadcast are in London except where stated

Locations of key London studios: Aeolian – New Bond Street; Paris – Regent Street; Camden – Camden High Street; Kings Theatre – Hammersmith Road; Piccadilly – 201 Piccadilly; Playhouse – Northumberland Avenue; Scala Theatre – Charlotte Street; Broadcasting House – Portland Place

Repeats are excluded; some of the programmes were also broadcast worldwide by the BBC General Overseas Service (GOS)

WHAT STILL EXISTS?

The BBC Sound Archive holds six of the above programmes – #92 (*Anything Goes*, March 6 1952, short extract only); #116 (*Variety Fanfare*, November 14 1952), #186 (*Archie's the Boy!*, November 11 1954), #234 (*Desert Island Discs*, November 16 1959), #263 (*Benny Hill Time*, March 29 1964) and #277 (*Benny Hill Time*, March 28 1965).

A separate archive, BBC Radio International (formerly Transcription Service), holds all 26 editions of *Benny Hill Time* as well as some episodes of *Archie's the Boy!* and several of the programmes marked '@', above.

A few other programmes are believed to exist. Bob Monkhouse recorded many BBC radio shows off-air on good quality equipment and his private archive includes at least one early Benny Hill appearance, from an edition of *Calling All Forces* (#69 or #74).

Benny Hill's Appearances on British Television

	b'cast	channel	programme title	rec/live	from	producer/director	miscellaneous
1	23/3/1949	BBC	Music-Hall	live	Alexandra Palace	Walton Anderson	compère
2	21/10/1950	BBC	Mud in Your Eye	live	Alexandra Palace	Michael Mills	revue with Reg Varney
3	20/8/1951	BBC	Hi There!	live	Lime Grove	Bill Lyon-Shaw	first own-show
4	5/9/1951	BBC	Starlight Symphony	live	Radio Show, Earls Court	Bill Lyon-Shaw	compère
5	12/12/1951	BBC	In the Mood	live	Lime Grove	Bill Ward	guest
6	29/2/1952	BBC	Kaleidoscope	live	Lime Grove	Bryan Sears	guest
7	20/1/1953	BBC	The Centre Show	live	Nuffield Centre	Kenneth Carter	compère
8	9/6/1953	BBC	The Centre Show	live	Nuffield Centre	Kenneth Carter	compère
9	25/8/1953	BBC	The Centre Show	live	Nuffield Centre	Kenneth Carter	compère
10	15/9/1953	BBC	The Centre Show	live	Nuffield Centre	Kenneth Carter	compère
11	20/10/1953	BBC	The Services Show	live	Television Theatre	Kenneth Carter	compère
12	24/11/1953	BBC	The Services Show	live	Television Theatre	Kenneth Carter	compère
13	4/12/1953	BBC	Three Little Girls in View	live	Alexandra Palace	Kenneth Carter	guest in Beverley Sisters' show
14	21/12/1953	BBC	The Services Show	live	Television Theatre	Kenneth Carter	compère
15	19/1/1954	BBC	Showcase	live	Television Theatre	Kenneth Carter	compère
16	27/2/1954	BBC	Well – You Asked for It!	live	Television Theatre	Michael Mills	guest in viewers' request show
17	15/3/1954	BBC	Showcase	live	Television Theatre	Kenneth Carter	compère
18	29/3/1954	BBC	Showcase	live	Television Theatre	Kenneth Carter	compère
19	26/4/1954	BBC	Showcase	live	Television Theatre	Kenneth Carter	compère
20	24/5/1954	BBC	Showcase	live	Television Theatre	Kenneth Carter	compère
21	21/6/1954	BBC	Showcase	live	Television Theatre	Kenneth Carter	compère
22	19/7/1954	BBC	Showcase	live	Television Theatre	Ernest Maxin	compère
23	16/8/1954	BBC	Showcase	live	Television Theatre	Kenneth Carter	compère
24	13/9/1954	BBC	Showcase	live	Television Theatre	Kenneth Carter	compère

	b'cast	channel	programme title	rec/live	from	producer/director	miscellaneous
25	26/9/1954	BBC	What's My Line?	live	Television Theatre	Dicky Leeman	guest celebrity
26	24/11/1954	BBC	Fast and Loose!	live	Television Theatre	Kenneth Carter	with Bob Monkhouse
27	15/1/1955	BBC	The Benny Hill Show	live	Television Theatre	Kenneth Carter	
28	6/2/1955	BBC	This is Television: Daily Mail Awards Show	live	Scala Theatre	Bill Ward	receiving award and performing two short sketches
29	12/2/1955	BBC	The Benny Hill Show	live	Television Theatre	Kenneth Carter	
30	15/2/1955	BBC	Find the Link	live	Television Theatre	Ernest Maxin	guest celebrity
31	12/3/1955	BBC	The Benny Hill Show	live	Television Theatre	Kenneth Carter	
32	17/4/1955	BBC	Guess My Story	live	Television Theatre	T Leslie Jackson	guest celebrity; show also known as *Something to Shout About*
33	13/2/1956	BBC	Off the Record	live	Prince of Wales Theatre	Francis Essex	promoting 'Who Done It?' single
34	11/3/1956	BBC	Talk Of Many Things	live	Lime Grove	Bryan Sears	with Basil Dearden, promoting *Who Done It?* film; i/v by Richard Attenborough
35	18/3/1956	ITV (ATV)	Val Parnell's Sunday Night at the London Palladium	live	London Palladium	Bill Ward	guest
36	3/5/1956	ITV (Granada)	Tribute to the BBC	23/4/1956	Kay-Carlton Hill Studios	Andrew Miller-Jones/ Gilchrist Calder	i/v by Aidan Crawley
37	9/9/1956	ITV (ITP for ATV/ABC)	Paris by Night	Sept 1956	Prince of Wales Theatre	Quentin Lawrence	stage show excerpts
38	5/1/1957	BBC	The Benny Hill Show	live	Kings Theatre	Duncan Wood	
39	2/2/1957	BBC	The Benny Hill Show	live	Kings Theatre	Duncan Wood	
40	4/2/1957	BBC	Twenty-Five Years Non-Stop	live	Trocadero restaurant	Alan Chivers/ Ernest Maxin	with Bob Monkhouse; marking Windmill Theatre anniversary
41	2/3/1957	BBC	The Benny Hill Show	live	Kings Theatre	Duncan Wood	
42	30/3/1957	BBC	The Benny Hill Show	live	Kings Theatre	John Street	

No.	Date	Network	Programme	Broadcast	Venue	Producer/Director	Notes
43	27/4/1957	BBC	The Benny Hill Show	live	Kings Theatre	John Street	cameo; filmed in colour
44	5/5/1957	BBC	Men, Women and Clothes	22/8/1956	Ealing Studios	Charles R Rogers	
45	1/6/1957	BBC	The Benny Hill Show	live	Kings Theatre	John Street	stage show excerpts
46	26/6/1957	BBC	Now: A Breath of the Briny	live	Wellington Pier Pavilion, Great Yarmouth	Philip Lewis/ David Martin	
47	9/11/1957	ITV (ATV)	The Benny Hill Show	live	Wood Green Empire	Brian Tesler	
48	14/12/1957	ITV (ATV)	The Benny Hill Show	live	Wood Green Empire	Albert Locke	
49	25/12/1957	BBC	Pantomania – The Babes in the Wood	17/12/1957	Television Theatre	Graeme Muir	playing the role of the Minstrel
50	1/2/1958	BBC	The Benny Hill Show	live	Television Theatre	John Street	
51	1/3/1958	BBC	The Benny Hill Show	live	Television Theatre	John Street	
52	8/3/1958	BBC	6.5 Special	live	Riverside Studios	Duncan Wood	sketch (with Dave Freeman) and i/v by Josephine Douglas
53	29/3/1958	BBC	The Benny Hill Show	live	Television Theatre	John Street	
54	26/4/1958	BBC	The Benny Hill Show	live	Television Theatre	John Street	
55	29/11/1958	ITV (ATV)	The Benny Hill Show	live	Wood Green Empire	Kenneth Carter	
56	27/12/1958	ITV (ATV)	The Benny Hill Show	live	Wood Green Empire	Kenneth Carter	
57	24/1/1959	ITV (ATV)	The Benny Hill Show	live	Wood Green Empire	Kenneth Carter	
58	13/8/1959	ITV (Associated-Rediffusion)	Late Extra	live	Television House	Peter Croft	guest
59	22/11/1959	ITV (ATV)	Val Parnell's Sunday Night at the London Palladium	live	London Palladium	Alan Tarrant	excerpt from *Fine Fettle*
60	2/4/1960	ITV (ATV)	The Benny Hill Show	live	Wood Green Empire	Kenneth Carter	
61	30/4/1960	ITV (ATV)	The Benny Hill Show	live	Wood Green Empire	Kenneth Carter	
62	22/5/1960	ITV (ATV)	Royal Variety Show	16/5/1960	Victoria Palace	Bill Ward	participant
63	28/5/1960	ITV (ATV)	The Benny Hill Show	live	Wood Green Empire	Kenneth Carter	
64	1/8/1960	BBC	Let's Make a Night of It	21/7/1960	Pavilion Theatre, Weymouth	Albert Stevenson/ Duncan Wood	stage show excerpts
65	4/2/1961	BBC	The Benny Hill Show	live	Television Theatre	John Street	

	b'cast	channel	programme title	rec/live	from	producer/director	miscellaneous
66	4/3/1961	BBC	The Benny Hill Show	live	Television Theatre	John Street	
67	1/4/1961	BBC	The Benny Hill Show	live	Television Theatre	John Street	
68	8/4/1961	ITV (ABC)	Thank Your Lucky Stars	2/4/1961	Teddington	Philip Jones	performed 'Pepys' Diary'
69	11/6/1961	BBC	Ask Anne	live	Television Theatre	Bryan Sears	guest in Anne Shelton singing show
70	4/9/1961	BBC	Blue Peter	live	Television Centre	Valerie Willis	judging children's competition
71	4/11/1961	BBC	The Benny Hill Show	live	Television Theatre	David Croft	
72	25/11/1961	BBC	The Benny Hill Show	live	Television Theatre	David Croft	
73	16/12/1961	BBC	The Benny Hill Show	live	Television Theatre	David Croft	
74	23/2/1962	BBC	Benny Hill	14/2/1962	Television Centre	Duncan Wood	Portrait of a Bridegroom
75	2/3/1962	BBC	Benny Hill	22/2/1962	Television Centre	Duncan Wood	A Pair of Socks
76	9/3/1962	BBC	Benny Hill	1/3/1962	Television Centre	Duncan Wood	The Constant Viewer
77	12/3/1962	BBC	Come Dancing	live	Lyceum Ballroom	Barrie Edgar	judging contest
78	16/3/1962	BBC	Benny Hill	8/3/1962	Television Centre	Duncan Wood	The Changeling
79	23/3/1962	BBC	Benny Hill	15/3/1962	Television Centre	Duncan Wood	The Before Man
80	30/3/1962	BBC	Benny Hill	22/3/1962	Television Centre	Duncan Wood	Aunt Mirabelle
81	15/7/1962	ITV (ATV)	Bernard Delfont's Sunday Show: The Great All-Star Show	24/7/1961	Borehamwood studio	Bill Ward	guest in made-for-America show starring Jo Stafford
82	30/11/1962	BBC	Benny Hill	18/10/1962	Television Centre	Duncan Wood	The Mystery of Black Bog Manor
83	7/12/1962	BBC	Benny Hill	8/11/1962	Television Centre	Duncan Wood	Cry of Innocence
84	14/12/1962	BBC	Benny Hill	11/10/1962	Television Centre	Duncan Wood	The Time Bicycle
85	21/12/1962	BBC	Benny Hill	7/12/1962	Television Centre	John Street	Mervyn's Christmas Pudding
86	26/12/1962	BBC	Benny Hill	22/11/1962	Television Centre	John Street	The Secret of Planet Seven
87	4/1/1963	BBC	Benny Hill	15/11/1962	Television Centre	Duncan Wood	The Shooting of Willie the Kid
88	11/1/1963	BBC	Benny Hill	29/11/1962	Television Centre	John Street	The Vanishing Man
89	3/9/1963	BBC	Benny Hill	5/8/1963	Television Centre	John Street	Mr Apollo
90	10/9/1963	BBC	Benny Hill	12/8/1963	Television Centre	John Street	The Visitor

No.	Date	Channel	Show	Recording date	Location	Director	Notes
91	17/9/1963	BBC	Benny Hill	26/8/1963	Television Centre	John Street	Mr Jolly
92	24/9/1963	BBC	Benny Hill	19/8/1963	Television Centre	John Street	The Trouble Maker
93	1/10/1963	BBC	Benny Hill	22/7/1963	Television Centre	John Street	The Dresser
94	8/10/1963	BBC	Benny Hill	2/9/1963	Television Centre	John Street	The Taxidermist
95	24/6/1964	ITV (Rediffusion)	A Midsummer Night's Dream	18/3/1964	Wembley studio	Joan Kemp-Welch	playing the role of Bottom
96	6/11/1964	BBC1	The Benny Hill Show	23/10/1964	Television Centre	Kenneth Carter	
97	25/12/1964	BBC1	Christmas Night with the Stars	6/10/1964	location	Kenneth Carter	film insert 'The Lonely One'
98	10/4/1965	BBC1	The Benny Hill Show	20/3/1965	Television Centre	Kenneth Carter	
99	24/4/1965	BBC1	The Benny Hill Show	16/4/1965	Television Centre	Kenneth Carter	
100	1/5/1965	BBC1	The Roy Castle Show	live	Television Theatre	Bill Lyon-Shaw	brief cameo
101	8/5/1965	BBC1	The Benny Hill Show	30/4/1965	Television Centre	Kenneth Carter	
102	22/5/1965	BBC1	The Benny Hill Show	14/5/1965	Television Centre	Kenneth Carter	
103	6/11/1965	BBC1	The Benny Hill Show	29/10/1965	Television Centre	Kenneth Carter	
104	27/11/1965	BBC1	The Benny Hill Show	19/11/1965	Television Centre	Kenneth Carter	
105	18/12/1965	BBC1	The Benny Hill Show	10/12/1965	Television Centre	Kenneth Carter	
106	8/1/1966	BBC1	The Benny Hill Show	2/1/1966	Television Centre	Kenneth Carter	
107	8/3/1966	BBC1	Variety Club of Great Britain Awards	8/3/1966	Savoy Hotel	Ray Colley	receiving award
108	8/10/1967	ITV (ATV)	Spotlight	spring 1967	Borehamwood studio	Jon Scoffield	guest in made-for-America show starring Abbe Lane; shown in USA on 22/8/1967; colour
109	26/12/1967	ITV (ATV)	The Benny Hill Show	autumn 1967	Borehamwood studio	Philip Casson/ Jon Scoffield	
110	14/4/1968	ITV (ATV)	Spotlight	spring 1967	Borehamwood studio	Jon Scoffield	guest in made-for-America show starring Paul Anka; shown in USA on 25/7/1967; colour
111	20/4/1968	BBC1	The Benny Hill Show	16/4/1968	Television Centre	Kenneth Carter	
112	20/11/1968	BBC1	The Benny Hill Show	10/11/1968	Television Centre	Kenneth Carter	
113	11/12/1968	BBC1	The Benny Hill Show	24/11/1968	Television Centre	Kenneth Carter	
114	26/12/1968	BBC1	The Benny Hill Show	15/12/1968	Television Centre	Kenneth Carter	

b'cast	channel	programme title	rec/live	from	producer/director	miscellaneous
115 19/11/1969	ITV (Thames)	The Benny Hill Show	12/10/1969	Teddington	John Robins	colour from now on, unless otherwise stated
116 25/12/1969	ITV (Thames)	The Benny Hill Show	30/11/1969	Teddington	John Robins	
117 4/2/1970	ITV (Thames)	The Benny Hill Show	9/11/1969	Teddington	John Robins	
118 11/3/1970	ITV (Thames)	The Benny Hill Show	15/2/1970	Teddington	John Robins	
119 3/6/1970	ITV (Thames)	Eddie in August	18/8/1969	location	John Robins/ Benny Hill	half-hour dialogue-free film
120 28/10/1970	ITV (Thames)	The Benny Hill Show	22/10/1970	Teddington	John Robins	
121 23/12/1970	ITV (Thames)	The Benny Hill Show	19/11/1970	Teddington	John Robins	made in black-and-white
122 27/1/1971	ITV (Thames)	The Benny Hill Show	17/12/1970	Teddington	John Robins	made in black-and-white
123 24/2/1971	ITV (Thames)	The Benny Hill Show	28/1/1971	Teddington	John Robins	made in black-and-white
124 24/3/1971	ITV (Thames)	The Benny Hill Show	4/3/1971	Teddington	John Robins	
125 24/11/1971	ITV (Thames)	The Benny Hill Show	14/10/1971	Teddington	David Bell	
126 22/12/1971	ITV (Thames)	The Benny Hill Show	4/11/1971	Teddington	David Bell	
127 23/2/1972	ITV (Thames)	The Benny Hill Show	27/1/1972	Teddington	John Robins	
128 23/2/1972	ITV (network)	The British Screen Awards	live	Royal Albert Hall	Steve Minchin	receiving award
129 22/3/1972	ITV (Thames)	The Benny Hill Show	24/2/1972	Teddington	John Robins	
130 25/10/1972	ITV (Thames)	The Benny Hill Show	13/10/1972	Teddington	Keith Beckett	
131 27/12/1972	ITV (Thames)	The Benny Hill Show	1/12/1972	Teddington	Keith Beckett	
132 22/2/1973	ITV (Thames)	The Benny Hill Show	2/2/1973	Teddington	Keith Beckett	
133 29/3/1973	ITV (Thames)	The Benny Hill Show	16/3/1973	Teddington	Peter Frazer-Jones	
134 5/12/1973	ITV (Thames)	The Benny Hill Show	2/11/1973	Teddington	John Robins	
135 27/12/1973	ITV (Thames)	The Benny Hill Show	30/11/1973	Teddington	John Robins	
136 7/2/1974	ITV (Thames)	The Benny Hill Show	21/12/1973	Teddington	John Robins	
137 13/3/1974	ITV (Thames)	The Benny Hill Show	22/2/1974	Teddington	Mark Stuart	
138 8/1/1975	ITV (Thames)	The Benny Hill Show	15/11/1974	Teddington	Mark Stuart	
139 12/3/1975	ITV (Thames)	The Benny Hill Show	18/10/1974	Teddington	Mark Stuart	
140 24/9/1975	ITV (Thames)	The Benny Hill Show	7/3/1975	Teddington	Ronald Fouracre	

141	17/12/1975	ITV (Thames)	The Benny Hill Show	24/10/1975	Teddington	Mark Stuart	
142	18/2/1976	ITV (Thames)	The Benny Hill Show	21/11/1975	Teddington	Mark Stuart	
143	24/3/1976	ITV (Thames)	The Benny Hill Show	19/12/1975	Teddington	Mark Stuart	
144	21/4/1976	ITV (Thames)	The Benny Hill Show	19/3/1976	Teddington	Mark Stuart	
145	26/1/1977	ITV (Thames)	The Benny Hill Show	22/1/1977	Teddington	Mark Stuart	
146	23/2/1977	ITV (Thames)	The Benny Hill Show	17/2/1977	Teddington	Mark Stuart	
147	23/3/1977	ITV (Thames)	The Benny Hill Show	18/3/1977	Teddington	Mark Stuart	
148	12/4/1978	Channel 10, Sydney	The Benny Hill Show	August 1977	Sydney (location)	Richard McCarthy/ Rod Kinnear	shown in Australia on 3/11/1977; networked on ITV by Thames as *Benny Hill Down Under*
149	30/5/1978	ITV (Thames)	The Benny Hill Show	3/3/1978	Teddington	Keith Beckett	
150	26/12/1978	ITV (Thames)	The Benny Hill Show	24/11/1978	Teddington	Ronald Fouracre	
151	14/3/1979	ITV (Thames)	The Benny Hill Show	2/2/1979	Teddington	Dennis Kirkland	
152	25/4/1979	ITV (Thames)	The Benny Hill Show	16/3/1979	Teddington	Dennis Kirkland	
153	9/5/1979	ITV (Thames)	TVTimes Top Ten Awards	29/4/1979	Royalty Theatre	Steve Minchin	receiving award
154	6/2/1980	ITV (Thames)	The Benny Hill Show	18/1/1980	Teddington	Dennis Kirkland	
155	5/3/1980	ITV (Thames)	The Benny Hill Show	15/2/1980	Teddington	Dennis Kirkland	
156	16/4/1980	ITV (Thames)	The Benny Hill Show	14/3/1980	Teddington	Dennis Kirkland	
157	7/1/1981	ITV (Thames)	The Benny Hill Show	21/11/1980	Teddington	Dennis Kirkland	
158	11/2/1981	ITV (Thames)	The Benny Hill Show	30/1/1981	Teddington	Dennis Kirkland	
159	25/3/1981	ITV (Thames)	The Benny Hill Show	13/3/1981	Teddington	Dennis Kirkland	
160	6/1/1982	ITV (Thames)	The Benny Hill Show	20/11/1981	Teddington	Dennis Kirkland	
161	10/2/1982	ITV (Thames)	The Benny Hill Show	29/1/1982	Teddington	Dennis Kirkland	
162	28/4/1982	ITV (Thames)	TVTimes Top Ten Awards	21/4/1982	Royalty Theatre	Malcolm Morris	receiving award
163	5/1/1983	ITV (Thames)	The Benny Hill Show	26/11/1982	Teddington	Dennis Kirkland	
164	16/3/1983	ITV (Thames)	The Benny Hill Show	28/1/1983	Teddington	Dennis Kirkland	
165	16/1/1984	ITV (Thames)	The Benny Hill Show	11/11/1983	Teddington	Dennis Kirkland	
166	31/1/1984	ITV (Thames)	TVTimes Top Ten Awards	live	Royalty Theatre	Malcolm Morris	receiving award

477

b'cast	channel	programme title	rec/live	from	producer/director	miscellaneous
167 15/2/1984	ITV (Thames)	This is Your Life	7/2/1984	Royalty Theatre	Malcolm Morris/ Michael D Kent/ Terry Yarwood	subject: Bob Todd
168 25/4/1984	ITV (Thames)	The Benny Hill Show	3/2/1984	Teddington	Dennis Kirkland	
169 25/12/1984	ITV (Thames)	Bring Me Sunshine (A Tribute to Eric Morecambe)	9/11/1984	London Palladium	Mark Stuart	participant
170 2/1/1985	ITV (Thames)	The Benny Hill Show	7/12/1984	Teddington	Dennis Kirkland	
171 8/4/1985	ITV (Thames)	The Benny Hill Show	1/2/1985	Teddington	Dennis Kirkland	
172 27/5/1985	ITV (Thames)	The Benny Hill Show	1/3/1985	Teddington	Dennis Kirkland	
173 12/3/1986	ITV (Thames)	The Benny Hill Show	6/12/1985	Teddington	Dennis Kirkland	
174 31/3/1986	ITV (Thames)	The Benny Hill Show	28/2/1986	Teddington	Dennis Kirkland	
175 16/4/1986	ITV (Thames)	The Benny Hill Show	24/1/1986	Teddington	Dennis Kirkland	
176 13/1/1988	ITV (Thames)	The Benny Hill Show	4/12/1987	Teddington	Dennis Kirkland	
177 27/4/1988	ITV (Thames)	The Benny Hill Show	19/2/1988	Teddington	Dennis Kirkland	
178 8/2/1989	ITV (Thames)	The Benny Hill Show	16/12/1988	Teddington	Dennis Kirkland	
179 5/4/1989	ITV (Thames)	The Benny Hill Show	3/2/1989	Teddington	Dennis Kirkland	
180 1/5/1989	ITV (Thames)	The Benny Hill Show	10/3/1989	Teddington	Dennis Kirkland	
181 30/10/1991	ITV (Thames)	Des O'Connor Tonight	22/10/1991	Teddington	Brian Penders	guest
182 20/12/1991	BBC1 (Saffron Productions)	Benny Hill: Clown Imperial	27/8– 2/10/1991	location	Victor Pemberton/ David Spenser	life documentary, screened within *Omnibus* strand
183 12/4/1994	ITV (D. L. Taffner)	Benny Hill – Unseen	spring 1990	New York locations & Teddington	Dennis Kirkland	first half-hour version of hour-long *Benny Hill's World Tour*
184 16/5/1994	ITV (D. L. Taffner)	Benny Hill – Unseen	spring 1990	New York locations & Teddington	Dennis Kirkland	second half-hour, ditto

KEY

i/v interviewed

All venues/places of broadcast London except where stated

Locations of key London venues whose names are not self-explanatory: Nuffield Centre – Adelaide Street; Television Theatre – Shepherd's Bush Green; Kay-Carlton Hill Studios – St John's Wood; Kings Theatre – Hammersmith; Riverside Studios – Hammersmith; Television House – Aldwych; Television Centre – White City; Royalty Theatre – Aldwych

From the 5/1/1957 edition of *The Benny Hill Show*, pre-filmed elements were also incorporated

From the 6/11/1964 transmission of *The Benny Hill Show*, the recording date shown reflects the 'audience night'; in all instances there was also pre-taping and pre-filmed location shooting

Repeats and compilations are excluded

WHAT STILL EXISTS?

All the above shows made by Thames Television still exist, now owned by FremantleMedia. The same company also owns 148.

The BBC Film & Video Archive has programmes 44, 53 (part only), 54, 65, 66, 67, 96, 97, 98, 99, 101, 102, 104, 105, 106, 111, 114 (part only) and 182. (Much of this material was recompiled for home-video release in Australia and the USA in 1999–2000.) Additionally, programmes 74 and 82 were given to the BBC by a private collector in 2000–01, the only editions of the nineteen *Benny Hill* sitcoms to have surfaced.

Carlton Communications is the current owner of shows made by ATV and ITC. Programmes 37, 62, 81, 108 and 110 are known to exist; programmes 47, 48, 55, 56, 57, 60, 61, 63 and 109 are believed to exist.

Programme 36 is owned by Granada Television. Programme 95 is held by the National Film & Television Archive, London. Programmes 183 and 184 are owned by D. L. Taffner Ltd.

The Movies of Benny Hill

Who Done It?
character Hugo Dill
director Basil Dearden
producers Michael Balcon/Michael Relph
writer T. E. B. Clarke
shot 1955
released March 1956
production company Ealing

Light Up the Sky!
character Syd McCaffey
director/producer Lewis Gilbert
writer Robert Storey; **screenplay** Vernon Harris
shot 1959
released July 1960
production company British Lion/Bryanston

**Those Magnificent Men in Their Flying Machines
(or How I Flew from London to Paris in 25 Hours 11 Minutes)**
character Fire Chief Perkins
director Ken Annakin
producer Stan Margulies
writers Jack Davies/Ken Annakin
shot 1965
released June 1965
production company 20th-Century Fox

Chitty Chitty Bang Bang
character Toymaker
director Ken Hughes

producer Albert R. Broccoli
writer Ian Fleming; **screenplay** Roald Dahl, Ken Hughes
shot 1967
released December 1968
production company United Artists/Warfield Productions/Dramatic Features
misc. additional (but not credited) writing by Benny Hill

The Italian Job
character Professor Simon Peach
director Peter Collinson
producer Michael Deeley
writer Troy Kennedy Martin
shot 1969
released June 1969
production company Paramount Pictures/Oakhurst Productions
misc. additional (but not credited) writing by Benny Hill

The Waiters
character waiter
director Jan Darnley-Smith
producer George H. Brown
writer Benny Hill
shot 1969
released September 1970
production company Fanfare Films

From One to Another
director Michael Crosfield
producer Peter Griffiths
writer Benny Hill
shot 1970
released not made for general release
production company Viewpoint Productions
misc. short film made for Oxfam charity, includes sequence by Benny Hill with
    Jackie Wright and Jan Butlin

Your Palace in the Sky
character passenger
shot 1973

released not made for general release
production company Air-India
misc. 15-minute film about a businessman's journey aboard an Air-India flight

The Best of Benny Hill
character various
director John Robins
producers John Robins/Roy Skeggs
writer Benny Hill
shot 1969–73
released May 1974
production company Anglo-EMI/Euston Films
misc. compilation of Thames TV material

Benny Hill on Record

All releases are British except for the album *Benny Hill . . . The Best Of* (issued only in USA).

The last item was issued only on double-cassette.

There have been reissues and reconfigurations of much of this material.

All songs composed by Benny Hill except:

[1] Not composed by Benny Hill

[2] Co-composed by Benny Hill

[3] Instrumental; not performed or composed by Benny Hill

Singles

February 1955	Teach Me Tonight[1]/I Can't Tell a Waltz from a Tango[1]
February 1956	Who Done It?[1]/Memories are Made of This[1]
February 1961	Pepys' Diary/Gather in the Mushrooms [*sides later reversed*]
June 1961	Transistor Radio[2]/Gypsy Rock[2]
December 1961	The Piccolo Song[2]/Lonely Boy
April 1963	The Harvest of Love[2]/BAMba 3688
November 1965	What a World/I'll Never Know
January 1966	My Garden of Love/The Andalucian Gypsies
October 1971	Ernie (the Fastest Milkman in the West)/Ting-a-Ling-a-Loo
October 1972	Fad Eyed Fal/The Dustbins of Your Mind

EPs

April 1963   *Hit Parade – Volume 1*
Gather in the Mushrooms/Pepys' Diary; Gypsy Rock[2]/Transistor Radio[2]

November 1963   *The harvest of Love*
The Piccolo Song[2] /Lonely Boy; BAMba 3688/The Harvest of Love[2]

Albums

October 1965   *Benny at the B.B.C.* (from second series of *Benny Hill Time*)
Interviews; Layabouts Picnic; Film Director-Producer: J Arthur Scuttle . . .
"From Moscow with Love"; The Sunday Ben; Down Your Way Visits Dalton
Abbott; Warlords of East Grinstead; The Holiday King – Mr Fred Scuttle; The
Jolly Robbers

December 1965   *Benny Hill Sings(?)*
Moving On Again; The Andalucian Gypsies; In the Papers; Golden Days; Flying
South; My Garden of Love; I'll Never Know; Wild Women; Jose's Cantina;
Rose; The Egg Marketing Board Tango; Those Days *(with Maggie Stredder)*; The
Old Fiddler[2]; What a World

November 1971   *This is Benny Hill*
Ernie (the Fastest Milkman in the West); Anna Marie; Broken-Hearted Lovers'
Stew; Colleen; Rachel; The Beach at San Tropez; Suzy; Ting-a-Ling-a-Loo; Ted;
Tour Guide; Interview *(with Lesley Goldie)*; Making a Commercial; The Birds
and the Bees

summer 1992   *Benny Hill . . . The Best Of*
Yakety Sax (intro)[3]; Ernie (the Fastest Milkman in the West) *(new recording)*;
Bianca; Gypsy Dance; New York Rap; Star Names; Just Wanna be in Your
Band; Down on the Farm; Unlucky Luke; Pepys' Diary *(new recording)*; Older
Woman; Cafe Ole; Graffiti; Lifeguards; Go Round Again; Yakety Sax[3]

spring 1995   *Benny Hill Time*
Double-cassette featuring four (edited) editions of the BBC radio series, first
broadcast on February 23 1964, March 8 1964, March 15 1964 and April 5
1964

The Addresses of Benny Hill

January 21 1924 born 30 Bridge Road, Southampton (now 111 Bernard Street)

Spring 1924 moved to St Helen's, Wilton Road, Southampton (now 162 Wilton Road)

Spring 1931 moved to 22 Westrow Gardens, Southampton

September 2 1939 evacuated to Bournemouth

Early 1940 returned to Southampton area (the Hills evacuated to Halderford, The Retreat, Hounsdown)

July 1940–August 6 1941 8 The Nook, Eastleigh

Then on the road.

February–March 1942 T Robinson Studios, 36–38 Penrose Street, London SE17 (sleeping in warehouse)

Then on the road until November 20 1942; taken into military detention and served in armed forces

May 1947–June 1948 14a Queensway, London W2

Autumn 1948 moved to digs in Cricklewood area, London NW2 (addresses not known)

October 1948 moved to 62 Ambler Road, London N4

October 1949 moved back to 14a Queensway, London W2

Early 1950 moved to 62 Brondesbury Villas, London NW6

Spring 1950 moved to 6 Thorverton Road, London NW2

September 1951 moved to 40 Mapesbury Road, London NW2

March 1955 moved to 16 Cunningham Court, Maida Vale, London W9

June 1960 moved to Flat 7 (later Flats 5 & 7), 2 Queen's Gate, London SW7

June 1986 moved back to 22 Westrow Gardens, Southampton (after moving to Teddington, below, still stayed here regularly until his death)

Summer 1988 moved to Flat 7, Fairwater House, 34 Twickenham Road, Teddington (found dead here on April 20 1992)

Further Reading

The Benny Hill Story, by John Smith (W. H. Allen, London, 1988; St Martin's Press, New York, 1988).
Informed, if light, biography, by an established Fleet Street journalist.

The Illustrated Benny Hill, by Gary Morecambe (Elm Tree, London, 1989).
Casual, illustrated look at the subject's life and career, written by Eric Morecambe's son with the subject's approval.

Saucy Boy – The Life Story of Benny Hill, by Leonard Hill (Grafton, London, 1990).
The only authorized biography (though not stated as such), written by the subject's brother. Strong on family detail, stylish, recommended.

The Real Benny Hill, by Margaret Forwood (Robson, London, 1992).
Light but lively biography by one of the subject's few favoured Fleet Street journalists, published soon after his death.

Benny – The True Story, by (His Best Friend) Dennis Kirkland, with Hilary Bonner (Smith Gryphon, London, 1992).
Breathless as-told-to memoir of a fascinating friendship, published soon after the subject's death.

Star Turns: The Life and Times of Benny Hill & Frankie Howerd, by Barry Took (Weidenfeld & Nicolson, London, 1992).
Illustrated comparison of two of Britain's greatest post-war comics, who died on the same weekend; by one of the country's foremost comedy writers.

Benny Hill – Merry Master of Mirth, the Complete Companion, by Robert Ross (B. T. Batsford, London, 1999).
Enthusiastic, illustrated guide to the subject's professional activities.

Further Reading

Benny Hill – King Leer, by Jeremy Novick (Carlton, London, 2000).
Frothy, illustrated hardback.

Also of interest

You Should Have Been in Last *Night – An Unusual Agent Remembers*, by Richard
Stone (The Book Guild, Lewes, 2000).
Memoir of the agent who represented some of Britain's greatest comedy talent;
includes Benny Hill anecdotes.

Twice Brightly, by Harry Secombe (Robson, London, 1974).
Humorous novel about a novice comedian working his first week in Variety after
his 1947 'demob', written by one who was there. Recommended for anyone
seeking further colour about Benny Hill's lifestyle in this same period.

Kindly Leave the Stage! – The Story of Variety 1919–1960, by Roger Wilmut
(Methuen, London, 1985).
Entertaining account of a fascinating strand of British entertainment, written
with typical diligence by a respected authority.

Acknowledgements

Although Benny Hill never consented to a *This is Your Life* feature, this *was* his life, and I would like to thank the major supporting players and essential extras who generously offered me their time and in some cases hospitality and told me all they knew about him. That I began my research knowing only the man's basic public image and ended in a position where I could confidently set down his life and work on paper owes largely to these people, and I thank them all warmly. (And though delineated here in different categories, many were able to relate accounts of Benny's life across several or all aspects.)

For details on Alfie's family history and early life: Violet Stevens, Hugh Stevens, Tony House, Bill Jaques, Florence Jaques, Tilly Underwood, Sara Underwood and Victoria Underwood. Also Kenneth C. Ball, Judy Brent, N. J. Crisp, John Harrod, Doris Lamb, Andrew Roberts, Pasquale Spacagna, Jean Watson and Peter White.

For help with the Eastleigh years: Pauline Gill, Win Godwin, Doreen Jannaway, Jack Jones, Hilda Kite, John Lillywhite, Doreen Lillywhite and Hazel Wigg.

For accounts of Benny's formative years on stage and radio: Max Bygraves, Ron Clark, Bill Clout, Cherry Lind, Bob Monkhouse, Denis Norden, Maureen Riscoe, Joy St Edmund, Donald Scott, Graham Stark, Reg Varney, Jan Waters and Ronnie Wolfe.

For help with Benny's 'London years': Annette André, Tito Burns, Peter Charlesworth, Irving Davies, Dave Freeman, Graham Freer, Tony Hatch, Phoebe King, George Martin, Wally Ridley, Marcel Stellman, Elaine Taylor, Barry Took and Michael Winner.

For guidance on Benny on BBC television: Felix Bowness, Mary Cook, David Croft, Josephine Demarne, Jeremy Hawk, David Jacobs, John Junkin, Eve Lucas, Bill Lyon-Shaw, Ernest Maxin, Harry Rabinowitz, Steve Race, Elizabeth Seal, Harold Snoad, John Street and Hettie Tack.

Acknowledgements

Covering his business and financial affairs: Dennis Blake, Ann Croft, Felix de Wolfe and Richard Stone.

The following spoke to me of Benny's endeavours on the big screen: David Battley, Pamela Cundell, Lewis Gilbert, Troy Kennedy Martin and Cyril Ornadel.

Benny's hugely successful twenty years at Thames Television were uncovered for me by René Bloomstein, Sue Bond, Anne Bruzac, John Howard Davies, Marian Davies, Carla De Wansey, Lorraine Doyle, David Elstein, Bella Emberg, Louise English, John Fisher, Peter Frazer-Jones, Lee Gibson, Jimmy Gilbert, Cherry Gilham, Philip Jones, Jon Jon Keefe, Dennis Kirkland, Henry McGee, Mike Mulloy, Nicholas Parsons, Mike Phillips, Libby Roberts, Maggie Stredder, Mark Stuart, Don Taffner, Brian Tesler and Anne Todd.

For background on Benny's final years: Monica Albon, Geoff Baker, Kevin Bellchambers, Iain Burton, Lorraine Clark, Danny Gilbert, Norman Gilmont, Gladys Green, Bill Greenham, Mary Gubb, Alan Hebdige, Richard Holloway, Mary Kirkland, Anne Ling, Emma Smith, June Thomas, Sylvia Thorley and Victoria Wood.

I am grateful, too, for assistance from a considerable body of people during my archival research. The staff of the BBC Written Archives Centre were as knowledgeable and friendly as ever, especially Jeff Walden and also Neil Sommerville and Gwyniver Jones. I extend warm thanks, too, to Tim Ritchie in the BBC Sound Archive, Bill Parker and Julie Richardson at FreemantleMedia, Barrie MacDonald in the ITC Library, Sylvia Cowling at Granada Television, Allan Rouse at Abbey Road Studios, Ruth Edge in the EMI Archive, Joanna Smith and Susan Hill in Southampton Archives, Gordon Cox and Malcolm Dale at the Eastleigh Local History Society, Paul Seaton at Woolworth's, Brian Hornsey at the REME museum, P. E. Thomson at Margate Library, Richard Mangan at the Mander & Mitchenson Theatre Collection, Rachel Lamb at the *Southern Daily Echo*, Katy Hemming at the General Dental Council, Ted Webb at Unigate Dairies, Carrie Starren at the Royal Borough of Kensington & Chelsea Library, Ian Johnston at the London Borough of Brent Community History Library & Archive, and to the staff of the British Library Newspaper Library, London Borough of Barnet local history library, London Borough of Islington local history collection, City of Westminster Archives Centre, British Telecom Archive,

Acknowledgements

Companies House, Family Records Centre, the Principal Registry of the Family Division at First Avenue House, and the Aarkamint archives.

For a range of assistance I am grateful to Trevor Aston, Steffi Colbert, Pete Frame, David Graham, Mike Heatley, Florence Keefe, Thomas Kennedy, Raymond Kingsbury, Allan Kozinn, Pavol Kuchták, Spencer Leigh, Andy Neill, Susanne Ritt Nichol at D. L. Taffner, Piet Schreuders, Peter Sensier, Don Smith, Peter Tatchell, Kate Threlfall, Dave Tossell and Paul Huggett, Irene Von Dorrer and Major Bob Harris.

My agent Bill Hamilton offered support and encouragement at just the right times, and I am especially indebted to Annie Lee and to my astute editor, Gordon Wise.

Richard ('*Tat?*') Buskin and Barry Took rendered timely motivation, and I am grateful, too, to Nod, Mark and Mary Jane, to Peter Lawson for the various language translations, and to Mark Cousins for allowing me to plunder his unrivalled collection of comedy books and records, and (with Carol) for the B&B. For their friendship and astute critique of the draft manuscript, I award honorary gold milk-tops to Dick Fiddy and Adam Smith.

This book has not been authorized by the Benny Hill Estate and the late comedian's nieces and nephews who constitute that body declined co-operation. However, I am grateful for their kind permission to quote from Benny Hill's comedy scripts, and to Lynda Ronan at the Richard Stone Partnership for being an honest broker.

I am also grateful to Nigel Cochrane in the Albert Sloman Library at the University of Essex for allowing me to use copies of correspondence from Mary Whitehouse/VALA relating to Benny Hill, to the BBC for permitting me to quote from staff correspondence, to Bob Monkhouse for permission to quote from *Fast and Loose!* and to Sandra and Ingrid Williamson for allowing me to quote from a private video made by their late uncle, Benny's dear friend Harry Segal.

Last, but most certainly not least, my love to Oliver and Tom, and to Anita who has lived this project from inception to publication, provided astute insight and believed in me when I had mislaid belief in myself.

List of Illustrations

Every attempt has been made to acknowledge the source and/or copyright holder of the images in this book. Unintentional errors or omissions will be corrected in any future editions.

First section:

p1   Helen Cave (Bill Jaques).
Alf Hill (Tilly Underwood).
Sophia Hill (Tilly Underwood).
The Hill family (Tilly Underwood).
Uncle Leonard (Tilly Underwood).

p2   The babe in arms (Tilly Underwood).
Benny Hill's birthplace (Southampton Archives Services).
Canal Walk (Southampton Archives Services).
The Hill family, circa 1937 (Tilly Underwood).

p3   The grammar school boy 1 (Southampton Archives Services).
The grammar school boy 2 (Southampton Archives Services).
Craftsman Hill and his compatriots (REME Museum of Technology, Arborfield).
The unwilling soldier (Bill Jaques).
With Harry Segal (Sandra and Ingrid Williamson).

p4   Publicity photo 1 (Tilly Underwood).
Publicity photo 2 (Ron Clark).
Publicity photo 3 (Monica Albon).
With Reg Varney (Reg Varney).

p5   Relaxing on beach (Donald Scott).

p6   With his parents (*Southern Daily Echo*).
With Ron Clark (Donald Scott).
Leeds Empire (Popperfoto).

Index